A History
of
Kentucky

A History of Kentucky

By
Thomas D. Clark

The Jesse Stuart Foundation

A History of Kentucky
Copyright © 1988 by Thomas D. Clark

Library of Congress Cataloging – in – Publication Data

Clark, Thomas Dionysius, 1903-
   A history of Kentucky / by Thomas D. Clark.
      p.   cm.
   Originally published: New York : Prentice-Hall, 1937.
   Includes bibliographical references and index.
   ISBN 0-945084-30-7 : $24.95
   1. Kentucky – History.   I. Title.
F451.C63   1992
976.9 – dc20   92-1403
                                                                    CIP

Published By:
The Jesse Stuart Foundation
P.O. Box 391
Ashland, KY 41114
1992

To My Wife
ELIZABETH TURNER CLARK

Preface

T HIS is a revised and sixth edition of *A History of Kentucky,* first published in 1937. This text was prepared originally as a brief history of the Commonwealth in as clear narrative form as possible. Hardly a topic discussed in it cannot be covered in an extensive and detailed monograph. It is still the hope, as in 1937, that the book will serve the dual purpose of being a general reader's text as well as one for use by students. I have combed this revision for textural errors, and have tried to up-date the materials.

There still remain fallow areas in the writings on Kentucky, nevertheless a considerable volume of writing about the state has occurred since 1937. Fresh points of view have been developed, there has been uncovered and exploited much original source materials, and there have been marked improvements in writing and publishing. All of this has resulted in a fresher and more exciting presentation of the Commonwealth's history. Every reasonable effort has been made in limited space to present as much revealing statistical material as possible without over-burdening the text with tedious detail. These factual data give both a clear and comparative sense of how present-day Kentucky relates to the past, and to the process of national change and progress.

A central struggle of twentieth century Kentucky has been that of functioning effectively in the mainstream of modern America, of accepting changes within its own borders, and of maintaining a reassuring continuity with its past. The preponderating balance is being tipped each decade toward urbanization of state society. Old rural Kentucky has all but disappeared. The rise of industry, and the shifting of population internally has created a social and economic revolution. So has the construction of modern highways, the rise of the motor freight industry, and an increased use of the rivers as arteries of transportation. Kentuckians' economic and social tastes have changed, and so has their way of life. There have been vast improvements in the quality of Kentucky life as measured in terms of availability of electrical power, home conveniences, and in the nature of the home itself. At the same time the family has departed significantly from most of the old social mores and disciplines.

Politics fundamentally have undergone the least fundamental changes of any aspect of Kentucky history. Even so the impact of the times has forced some revisions in old approaches to solving public problems. The "ancient" 1891 Constitution basically binds the Commonwealth almost inescapably to the past. Only by ingenious expediency does the modern state government function in many areas where, by the strict letter of the law, it is constitutionally handicapped. The modern Kentucky politician functions little differently from the way his nineteenth century forbears operated. There remains the fixed process of frequent elections, and the fickle will of the people.

In this new edition two chapters have been substituted for original ones, and a good many emendations have been made in others. In a concluding chapter I have attempted to present as clearly as possible in brief space a sense of Kentucky in the twentieth century. I have tried to define most of the important areas in which major actions have occurred, and to label some of the forces which have been at work in an era troubled by four international wars, a great depression, and a constantly evolving national history in a highly technological age. Standing figuratively atop a 200 year pinnacle in 1976 there was visible the vast gulf which separated pioneer beginnings in the raw western woods from the age of four-lane interstate highways, of automobiles and motor trucks, airlines, and mushrooming urban centers with their satelite shopping Malls.

In the modern era a constant reappraisal of the relationships of industry, agriculture, social and political organization, and Kentucky's central purposes becomes a necessity. Most important of all education is the central fact of modern Kentucky history. At no time in the state's past has this been a more pronounced fact. Success of the educational process in modern society spells the difference between the great mass of Kentuckians living productive lives or existing miserably in a welfare state depending upon public aid and food stamps.

In brevity this history undertakes to delineate the various periods through which Kentucky has passed in the last two centuries. It attempts to define the continuing forces which have given individuality and personality to a precise piece of American political geography. I have spent much time in the preparation of the bibliography which appears in this book. This list by no means includes all the books published about Kentucky, but it does contain most of the major titles. I have attempted to bring the bibliography down to date. Finally the term "Kentuckian" is interpreted to mean all the people without heed to race or creed, to sectional location, place of origin, or to social and economic position. Collectively Kentuckians have formed a tenacious human element which has accepted the inevitablity of history with certain grace, and have revered the past with the affections of a pioneering people who overcame many of the exigencies of time and the forces of everlasting changes.

THOMAS D. CLARK
Lexington, Kentucky
February 14, 1977

Contents

CHAPTER I

Kentucky: the Land

I n submitting the report of the Second Kentucky Geological Survey in 1857, David Dale Owen made the more or less obvious observation that already Kentucky civilization was three quarters of a century old. In these decades it had established a distinct social and economic pattern. He wrote, "The citizens of Kentucky are pre-eminently an agricultural people. In the Eastern and Northern states the wealth, influence and intelligence of the population are in great measure, concentrated in cities, towns, and villages. Not so in Kentucky; the substantial patriarchial farmer forms by far the larger and most influential part of the Commonwealth. All, therefore, that relates to the cultivation of the soil is of general interest." The geologist recognized the fact that there was a great variety of soils, and even of sections in Kentucky.

These specific and sectional variations exercise both bold and subtle influences on the nature and degrees of maturity of life in Kentucky. From them has stemmed many of the currents of Kentucky history. Pioneers who ventured west of the Appalachian Highland in the last quarter of the eighteenth century were drawn by the magnetism of the land and its basic resources. Land with its heavy timber cover, well-watered surface, and areas of fertility was much sought after. It is doubtful that even one land claimant among the thousands had more than elemental primitive knowledge of the chemically fertile elements of the soil. They judged it by color, friability, tree, weed, and shrub growth, its general topography, and its relationship to a supply of fresh water. Backwoods farmers exerting great human energy to bring a fertile virgin soil under cultivation had no immediate reason to concern themselves with chemical analyses.

If a talented demographer had undertaken to create a state inside an irregular set of boundaries which would include a wide diversity of physical conditions it is doubtful that he could have

1

improved on Kentucky. Within the borders of the Commonwealth there are several sub-states, and each of these comprises more or less a cultural and economically cohesive areas in which divisions in the population exhibit a sense of community. Historically this condition has been reflected in areas of agriculture, commerce, education, politics, social intercourse, the arts, urbanization, and folk mores. Objectively a variety of local statistical categories develope a profile of the responses Kentuckians have made to natural influences. In more general and definitely unscientific terms, the designations "mountaineer," "highlander," "backwoodsman," "bluegrass denizen," "Pennyroyal native," "northern Kentuckian," and "Purchase dweller" at least denotes popular awareness of the impacts of sectionalism. Still dealing in historical and demographic generalities Kentucky novelists have reflected this fact in their books. This was especially true of the writings of James Lane Allen, and John Fox, Jr.

Kentucky is not unique in its geographical sectionalism, the existence of a fairly generous number of natural resources, or the wide diversity of its scenic geographical features. The latter range from the precipitous 4,145 foot pinnacle of Black Mountain in Harlan County to the low elevation of 251 feet in Fulton County on the Mississippi River. Locked inside two natural river boundaries, a sprawling eastern mountain range, and a negotiated surveyor's line is the modern area of Kentucky of 39,650 square miles of land surface, and 754 of watered area. The complicated boundaries of Kentucky represent an involved political history beginning with Virginia's cession of its lands in the Old Northwest in 1784. In this action it retained control of the Ohio for commercial and social reasons. Five years later, December 18, 1789, when Virginia entered into its compact with Kentucky it again reserved territorial rights to the Ohio for its western daughter. It wished to guard free navigational rights, and to prevent interference with the movement of slaves on the stream.

Along the eastern border the Big Sandy-Tug Fork boundary follows a natural division, and so does the eastern-southeastern mountain dividing line between Virginia and eastern Tennessee. To the south the border is a negotiated one with a fairly extensive and complicated history of politics, engineering, and folk lore. Both the United States and Virginia observed the terms of the Hopewell Treaty of January 10, 1786, which reserved the lands west of the Tennessee to the Chickasaw Indians. Actually the small Chickasaw Nation made little or no use of the territory, not even as an occasional hunting ground. In a series of colorful conferences with the Chickasaws in the late summer and fall of 1818, Andrew Jackson and Isaac Shelby were able to negotiate a cession of these western lands. The Chickasaw Purchase Treaty was signed October 19, 1818, and it was ratified by the United States Senate the following January 7, 1819. Eight counties were created from the Jackson Purchase area north of the parallel 36° 30'; Hickman was first in 1821 and Carlisle was last in 1886. The boundary of Kentucky has never been free of controversy, especially that along the low water mark of the Ohio which has been in a constant process of change.

As indicated above geography has been an active influence upon the lives of Kentuckians. The most elementary fact has been the impact of the Appalachian Highlands and the westward flowing rivers. Both have helped to landlock people in the Ohio and Mississippi valleys. The fact that the rivers flowed westward and away from the eastern seaboard served to cut economic, social, and political ties with that area. Kentuckians became westerners with distinctive views regarding commerce and politics. Before 1850 Kentuckians were solely dependent upon the western river system as an artery of heavy transportation.

The People and the Land

The topography and the nature of the land created sharp delineations in agrarian economy. Soils in the Bluegrass, the river valleys, in the Pennyroyal, the Purchase delta, and on the Ohio Flood Plain were conducive to the development of a profitable field crop and livestock economy. It was from the productive farms in these areas that Kentuckians developed a rich river trade to the south. From the outset this southward flowing trade involved Kentucky farmers in both national and international politics in the last two decades of the eighteenth, and the first three of the nineteenth centuries.

Inside Kentucky there came into existence two if not three distinctive cultural and economic layers of human history. Locked behind the eastern rim of mountains thousands of early Kentuckians drifted into the sharply disected valley and coves of the Appalachians. There eddied in these places was an arrested pioneer colonial society which became dependent upon its own human and economic resources. Once the first thrusts of the westward movement had occurred a large segment of eastern Kentucky was by-passed by subsequent American migrations. For more than a century there was too little social intercourse with the outside to bring enrichment to the lives of people entrapped on a static plane of a harsh natural geographical environment.

In the eastern third of Kentucky people lived amidst three of the richest natural resources in North America. These were water, timber, and minerals. Yet Appalachian Kentuckians for generations relied largely upon a bare subsistence type of hillside agriculture. Until well after mid-nineteenth century there were few quanitative statistics which gave an accurate economic profile of the Kentucky localities in general.

By contrast with the highlands of eastern Kentucky the concentric regions of the Bluegrass were productive of large surpluses of field crops and livestock. In this region Kentuckians developed a prosperous agrarian economy, flourishing county towns, a semi-English way of life, political leaders, and they fostered organization of the more sophisticated institutions. These central counties sustained the institution of slavery, cultivated at least three important commercial crops, hemp, tobacco, and grain, laid the foundations for at least two importatnt chapters in American livestock history. As the central and western areas were settled by a new surge of emigrants the more fertile lands added materially to Kentucky's economic growth. In these areas agriculture was of both a subsistence surplus type. Some parts of central and western Kentucky were almost as severely landlocked as were the eastern highlands. There was a lack of roads, and the navigable rivers flowed away from the older central settlements and the middle Ohio Valley.

All sections of Kentucky shared a common resource in the virgin forests. At mid-eighteenth century Kentucky was truly a primeval land heavily covered by a virgin stand of ancient trees. The highland plateaus, river and creek valleys, east and west, produced a magnificent grade of potentially valuable commercial timber. This wooded Eden was penetrated by game and Indian trails, and these were followed by early long hunters and land scouts. The first journals of travel noted the existence of the towering woods, with some travelers taking the time to measure circumference and diameters of ancient patriarchs.

The Forest Resource

Kentucky's rich woodland resource was at once a blessing and a handicap to easy settlement. Near at hand in almost any site a settler chose was an abundance of building materials for homes, barns, and public buildings. The forest, however, blocked the land, and enormous human energy was required to clear it away. Too, the woods harbored Indians which in the early years made surprise attacks from tree cover. Repeatedly the question is asked about the virginal appearance of Kentucky. The Appalachian highlands and the river valleys everywhere grew heavy stands of a remarkable variety of conifers and deciduous trees. This was true in the Bluegrass and in the Purchase. There appeared in places barrens, the largest of which was in the central southern area of Allen, Barren, and Simpson counties. Elsewhere these treeless phenomena occurred, created perhaps by constant burning of the woods, and heavy grazing. Historically there is a certain vagueness about the barrens; on numerous occasions visitors to the areas commented on them in terms of wonderment.

Kentucky forests produced an unusually wide variety of trees, one of the most varied in North America. There were oaks of many varieties, hard and soft maples, black and white walnuts, three or four kinds of pine, the stately tulip poplar, beach, ash, lynwood, red cedar, hemlock, hickories, chestnut, buckeye, black cherry, and sassafras. All of these produced logs for lumber, building timbers, crossties, and firewood. To a dwarfed settler standing beneath the wooded canopy in 1780 it must have seemed that man could never plunder the forest resource. With the advent of the sawmill after 1810 lumbering in time became one of Kentucky's most persistent heavy industries. In the post Civil War decades, 1870-1920, the rivers and creeks in spring and fall floodtide ran full of logs being rafted downstream to sawmills. The hey-day of Kentucky log raftsmen on the rivers was as colorful an interlude in the state's history as lumbering was in the great north woods. In 1880 Kentucky produced 305,684,000 board feet of lumber, and in 1918, and at the end of World War I, it made the heavy cut of 340,000,000 feet.

The *Annual Reports* of the Kentucky Commissioner of Agriculture and Labor for the decades, 1870-1920, constantly emphasize the importance of the forest industries. It is a sad irony of history that Kentucky produced some extraordinarily fine furniture woods, but it never organized an extensive manufacturing and finishing industry, or produced a community of skilled cabinet-makers like that about High Point, North Carolina. Raw materials were shipped out of the state to be processed and used, many of them going abroad to England and Western Europe. Saw mill owners cut-out and got-out with complete disregard to the future of the woods, or the observation of even elementary rules of conservation or replenishment. These were the profligate decades of shameful waste and unforgivable rape of the virgin forest. Kentucky countrymen themselves added further to this shame by pillaging their woods time after time before trees were mature, and by setting wild fires. Literally millions of acres of timber lands were seared at sometime during the span of growth of a single crop of trees. The *Tenth Report* of the Bureau of the Census in 1880 all but screamed condemnation at Kentuckians and Tennesseans for the wanton destruction of their precious forest resource by setting fires. It is not at all uncommon to hear elderly Kentuckians bemoan the fact Indian summers are not what they used to be. They are not! Happily the woods are no longer ravished by fire, and public forest management of state and private woods, and the administration of two large federal forest preserves (2,100 square miles within the periphery of the forests, and actually 635,000 square miles directly under supervision) has contributed materially to the conservation of Kentucky timber resources. There still prevails in the state, however, a wasteful process of harvesting forest resources. In 1970 the annual net growth was 1,198,000,000 cubic feet and the annual removal was 728,000,000, or approximately half the annual growth. In the past quarter of a century more effective scientific attention by the state foresters and the newly organized School of Forestry in the University of Kentucky has resulted in improved timber management. Whether or not the reforestation and management of strip mine areas will add materially to Kentucky timber resources is as yet a thoroughly unproven fact. There are no extensive growth or harvest statistics as yet to document the success of this fairly extensive undertaking.

Water

Intimately inter-related to timber growth and conservation is Kentucky's extensive water resource. Perhaps no other resource in the state has entered so thoroughly into the lore of human welfare and history as water. Whether it be the lonely mountaineer living in semi-isolation behind a highland barrier or urban dweller in the metropolitan centers, water is of the utmost importance. This has been so since April 13, 1750, when Dr. Thomas Walker's exploring party reached the site of the big spring in the east face of the great rock wall in the saddle of Cumberland Gap, and when it descended the west face of the mountain to the creek at the foot of the slope. From that point on the Walker Journal makes frequent references to creeks and rivers. As land scouts the party realized sources of fresh water were almost as important as land itself.

In the decades following 1750 Kentucky settlers were even more conscious of the importance of the location of springs and other readily accessible sources of fresh water. The social and economic patterns of Kentucky history were shaped largely by the location and inter-relationships of eight major drainage systems and their valleys. Two of the most important streams are the Ohio and Mississippi rivers, each with intricate systems of lateral streams. These central drainage channels empty an almost unbelievable network of coves, hollows, and sprawling valleys covering an area of approximately 26,000,000 acres. The ancient boast that Kentucky has within its boundaries the most mileage of navigable channels in the nation may lack factual formulation. This boast obviously rests upon the somewhat shaky foundation of minimum potential navigability. The importance of Kentucky waterways, historically at least lies in other areas.

From the making of initial settlement farms in the more fertile central area of Kentucky began to produce a surplus of agricultural commodities. This produce could be sold with any success only on the gulf coastal market down stream in New Orleans. From 1787 to 1870 the Ohio-Mississippi river navigational system floated millions of tons of commodities gathered along the Kentucky lateral streams to outside purchasers.

The surface of Kentucky is disected by an almost endless pattern of ridges and valleys. In some of the more elevated and rugged areas this pattern is more visible and impressive than in others. This fact has shaped the patterns of settlement, and subsequently the characteristics of isolated Kentucky provincial society. Stream courses formed inlets for emigrants, and the coves and valleys became entrapments for these invaders. No historian can assess with confidence or accuracy the full social impact of the land-stream mass on Kentucky's history. This still remains both a central problem and a central fact. No area of human life in Kentucky has gone untouched by this rugged geographical influence. Since 1920 the watered area of Kentucky has been increased by 328 square miles. This is explained by the creation of three major hydro-electrical-navigational dams, and of several smaller ones, including thousands of farm ponds. The larger dams are on the Tennessee and Cumberland rivers, and there are three high level navigational locks on the Ohio River.

Water for human and livestock consumption, and for navigational purposes has been an essential part of human history in Kentucky. In the minds of thousands of older rural Kentuckians there is no more romantic landmark than that of an ever-flowing fresh water spring nearby a dwelling gushing from beneath a rock ledge at the base of an ancient tree. As appealing as this nostalgic picture may be there is also the negative fact of devastating floods and drouths. Periodically since the beginning of time Kentucky valleys have been swept by flood waters. Kentucky's topography has documented this fact. As the forest cover has been thinned or removed the land has become less absorbant and rain water run-off has become a more destructive force. Everywhere there are elevated hills and narrow valleys where flash floods have threatened human life and property. In strip-mined areas this threat has been heightened by extensive bare land surfaces and debris-ladened streambeds. Historically intensive drouths, in the era before railroads were built, practically closed all the Kentucky rivers to navigational use. Louisville was severely limited in its growth before 1850 because of the recurring drouths which closed the Ohio to steamboat navigation, and thus denied the city both outside communication and an adequate fuel supply.

Mineral Resources

The history of the development of Kentucky's vital coal industry is also associated with some of the headstreams of its intricate drainage systems. Strangely there seems to be no historical association of Indians with the great coal veins of eastern and western Kentucky. There have been found a few artifacts carved from cannel coal by Indians, but beyond this they seemed not to have paid any attention to the mineral. It was not until April 13, 1750, when Dr. Thomas Walker's party descended the western shoulder of Pine Mountain that any documentary record of the presence of coal in the western country was made. For a quarter of a century following this date Kentucky coal resources were notable only for the fact they were ignored. The Second Kentucky Geological Survey in 1859 prepared an extensive chemical analysis of the various Kentucky coal veins. Dr. Robert Peter of Lexington reported on samples from both the eastern and western fields, and it was significant that he published at such an early date not only a chemical analysis, he also noted the petroleum content of the various coal samples and explained the elementary process of extracting it.

There are two major coalfields in Kentucky, the one set inside the Pennyroyal of the Mississippian Plateau or embayment, and the broader one on the eastern Cumberland Plateau. The Western Coalfield was the first opened and for that reason has a more extended history. Counties in the Western Field are Hopkins, Muhlenberg, Ohio, Union, and Webster. The Eastern Field covers thirty-seven counties and approximately 10,400 square miles, with Harlan, Pike, Letcher, Perry, Floyd, and Bell counties being the major producers.

In 1828 the production of coal in Kentucky was recorded in the Western Coalfield, and it was not until the latter three decades of that century, and the extension of railroads in the Appalachian Highlands, that the Eastern Field came into production. In fact it was not until the outbreak of World War I in 1914, and the subsequent discovery that the eastern Kentucky coal could be successfully coked that mines in the area were expanded, and in time greatly over-expanded.

In January 1939, it was estimated that Kentucky had a residual tonnage of coal still in the ground of 123,327,000,000 tons, and to date only 1,248,514,000 tons had been removed. The Eastern Field contained more than half the unmined tonnage. By 1973 the extractors had mined about 3,900,000,000 tons, and it was estimated that there remained in the ground 25,000,000,000 tons of high grade and readily available coal. Altogether in the two fields there was estimated to be 65,000,000,000 tons still in the ground, a revised estimated which reflects the greater accuracy of making mineral resource estimates. In 1975 Kentucky underground or shaft mines extracted 66,000,000 tons, and in all the state produced 107,000,000 tons, the largest amount of any coal mining area east of the Mississippi River. Two years before 30,561 miners produced 127,507,320 tons of coal, the largest amount in Kentucky history.

The full history and impact of the presence of an abundant coal resource in Kentucky is only partially that of the existence of the raw mineral itself. The full history is to be gauged in the broader terms of cash returns, human employment, labor conflicts, outbreaks of violence, depression and boom, human tragedies and resulting grief from mine accidents, and the impact on the national economy. In a final and, perhaps more meaningful analysis, the existence of the vital coal resource has shaped the quality or lack of quality of the lives of hundreds of thousands of Kentuckians. The tentacles of the mining industry and the mineral run deep into the human resource, Kentucky politics, and even into the physical topography of the land itself. No single economic and social aspect of Kentucky history has become so complicated by so many contradictions, complexities, depth of human emotions, and lack of dependable information as that of coal mining and life in the two major coal fields of the state. To date there is no thoroughly extensive and reliable history of the coal mining industry on which anybody, operators, miners, state officials, or general public, can base an intelligent understanding of this important segment of Kentucky development.

The list of Kentucky's mineral and chemical resources is rather extensive, but many of them exist in only limited quantities or as traces. Others exist in a fairly ample supply but as conglomerates which make it difficult to extract and refine them. Several minerals assumed an importance in the making of elementary settlements which historically was out of proportion to the commercial importance of the minerals. One of the most precious elementary resources was salt. Existence of this mineral was dramatized by the famous landmark salt licks in several parts of the state. Among these were Big Bone, Blue, Mann's, Bullitt's, and Salt licks. At these sites chemical-ladened brine seeped upward through fissures in the calcarous sandstone from the underlying ordivician strata and permeated considerable surface areas. Both Big Bone and the Upper and Lower Blue Licks were well known at an early date because of the presence of the mammoth skeletal remains of prehistoric animals lying about them.

Kentucky pioneers using small open kettles to evaporate the salt lick brine produced approximately one bushel of salt for each 400 gallons of water. In January 1778 Daniel Boone and a salt making party from Boonesboro went to the Lower Blue Licks to replenish the Fort's salt supply. On February 7 they were captured by Shawnee Indians, an incident which began an interesting chain of events. Later General James Wilkinson came from Pennsylvania in 1784 to engage in the mercantile and salt trade. After 1787 the Kentucky *Gazette* published numerous brief news accounts and advertisements pertaining to salt making and trade. This was true of the *Acts* of the Kentucky General Assembly after 1792. Salt Licks and springs were valuable pieces of property and it took a considerable amount of legislation to protect them for both public and private access. In all cases salt-makers were encouraged to increase Kentucky's salt output after 1800.

Some of Kentucky's most productive salt works were along Goose Creek in Clay County near the present village of Garrard, at Bullitt's Lick, and the Lower Blue Licks. During the Civil War the Goose Creek works became an important objective of Confederate forces raiding in Kentucky. The South suffered a severe shortage of salt, and the Goose Creek works promised to help supply part of the region's desperate needs. In 1858 the salt-makers in Kentucky were producing more than a quarter of a million bushels a year, a figure which was never again equalled.

Down to 1870 at least salt was a necessity not only for human consumption but for the growing of livestock as well. As the livestock and cured meat trade increased after 1800 salt consumption went up in proportion as a preservative for meats being shipped out of the state. The famous Kentucky livestock industry in the first half of the nineteenth century depended in large measure upon a fairly abundant supply of domestic salt.

Closely allied with the salt industry was that of making gunpowder from the nitrogenous deposits found in the numerous Kentucky caves. This chemical was of two origins, the drippings of water through nitrate bearing soils, and the bacterial actions of certain "nitrifying organisms." Although never a significant commercial industry, the making of gunpowder from potassium nitrate (salt peter) was not without importance. Nitrate deposits were scraped from cave walls and floors and were evaporated in open kettles in the same manner as salt brine. Native sulphur and charcoal were added to the powdery residue to become an explosive. The most dramatic manufacture and use of Kentucky nitrates was during the War of 1812, and some gun powder was manufactured during the Civil War.

Just as early Kentuckians tapped salt and nitrate resources, they early exploited the state's iron ores. The earliest furnace placed in operation was Thomas D. Owings' Slate Creek operation in Bath County. Owings, a native of Baltimore, moved to Kentucky for the specific purpose of becoming an iron-master. In 1790 he built the Slate Creek Furnace, and the famous Owings House in Owingsville. His furnace was able to supply Kentuckians with many products including nails for house construction. In 1814 four-pound cannon balls were cast and shipped by way of the Licking and Ohio rivers and down the Mississippi to General Andrew Jackson's forces in New Orleans. In time other furnaces were placed in operation at Rose Run and Brassfield. Later the Red River and Estill County ores were worked at Furnace, Fitchburg, and Clay City. Like coal, iron ores are widely distributed in Kentucky. Workings were located in Boyd, Carter, and Greenup counties in the east, and in Green, Lyon, Livingston, Crittenden, Trigg, and Muhlenberg in the west. It was at the Suwanee Furnace in Lyon County in 1851 that William Kelley introduced the process of blowing cold air into molten iron to remove the carbon in the making of steel.

An important furnace was built by Aylette H. Buckner at the junction of Pond and Salt creeks in 1837 in Muhlenberg County. Twenty years later Scotch interests built the famous Airdrie Furnace on Green River near Paradise. The Buckner company also built the Stack which, perhaps, became an even more famous furnace in the Muhlenberg area. Following the Civil War General Don Carlos Buell moved onto the Airdrie property for the purpose of exploring for oil, but he found coal in such abundance that he devoted his attention to its exploitation. Nathaniel Southgate Shaler in 1876 reported for the Kentucky Geological Survey that the Cumberland River iron ore region was the best developed in western Kentucky. Kentucky iron ores, however, could not compete with the richer Lake Superior and Alabama fields.

Two interesting facts associated with the processing Kentucky's iron ores could have had a major impact upon Kentucky if the industry had survived. In the Red River and Estill County area an enormous amount of hardwood had to be converted to charcoal in order to flux the ore, and in a short time the region would have been denuded of its rich timber stand. It was discovered that Kentucky coals could be converted into coke, and this industry in time promised to be of major significance.

Geologists and chemists associated with the three early Kentucky Geological Surveys recognized the fact that the bituminous resources of the state contained a fairly rich petroleum base. It was believed oil could either be produced as a by-product of the coal industry or independently. Vaguely the presence of oil in Kentucky was known almost from the beginning of state history. Creeks and springs in places were sometimes covered with an oily scum and they were called "greasy" or "stinking." It was said pioneer women fussed because their geese soiled their feathers with the scum, making their feathers unfit for use in beds and pillows. Martin Beatty bored a salt well on the South Fork of the Cumberland River in present McCreary County in 1819 and struck oil. An even more dramatic oil strike was made at 175 feet in a salt well on Renox Creek near Burkesville in 1829. This gusher was given the name "American", and its flaming overflow blazed up for ten miles along the Cumberland River. Later "American" oil from this well was bottled and sold medicinally.

At the end of the Civil War prospectors and promoters searched Kentucky for oil and gas. Fields were located along the Cumberland River in Wayne, Russell, Cumberland, and Clinton counties. Wells were drilled in Allen, Barren, Meade, Warren, Henderson, and Breckinridge counties. In eastern Kentucky fields were developed in Estill, Lee, Knott, Lawrence, Menifee, Powell, and Wolfe counties. These areas in the late 1920's and 1930's experienced an oil and gas boom. Kentucky wells, 1883-1945, produced 203,415,800 barrels of crude oil. In the years 1959 and 1960 the state produced its largest single returns of 27,279,950 and 21,146,950 barrels of crude oil. After 1960 the annual production of oil went into a decline.

Kentucky's natural and mineral resources are highly varied. They, however, exist in varying quantities. One of the more interesting is rock asphalt which was formed at an early age in defunct oil pools. Geologists estimated that at least a billion gallons of oil went into the formation of the Kentucky asphalt beds. This material appears in Edmondson, Grayson, Hardin, Breckinridge, Logan, and Warren counties. It has contributed materially to the progress of Kentucky as a basic road building substance. Kentucky asphalt has the quality of being easily spread over a road base and of enduring hard usage and temperature changes.

There are numerous vein minerals which have contributed more of less to Kentucky's economic welfare. Possibly the most important of these has been fluorspar, a mineral which has varied uses ranging from the making of paints and varnishes to steel smelting processes. Although fluorspar appears in various sections of the state, the major mining operations have been concentrated in Crittenden, Caldwell, Livingston, Trigg, and Lyon counties. Veins of fluorspar have been mined in Henry, Owen, and Mercer counties. Along with fluorspar there are veins of barite, galena, zinc, and sphalerite. None of these, however, has been of commercial importance.

Two of Kentucky's most abundant and common natural materials are highly diversified and widely distributed. These are various types of clays and stones. The major use of the clays has been the making of bricks and pottery. Since the 1780's Kentuckians have been fond of boasting that bricks and timbers used in the construction of ancestral homes were burned and cut on the premises. There is a wide variety of brick type clays to be found across Kentucky, each one has particular qualities of density, texture, and color. A drive through any town or city street in the Commonwealth reveals the generous samplings of the state's brick clays. More specialized fire bricks and tiles are manufactured from localized clay deposits. One of the most significant of these is the operation at Olive Hill in Carter County. Tile clays in commercial quantities are found in Grayson, Meade, and Warren counties. The white clays found in Hart, Edmondson, and Taylor counties, and the ball, sagger, and wad clays of Graves, Ballard and Marshall counties are adaptable to specialized uses. Pottery clays are to be found in various localities, and historically these have been turned and molded into vessels of all sorts, particularly jugs, churns, and bowls. The most famous of the older potteries is the Corneilson family plant at Bybee in Madison County.

Kentucky's varied stone resource is possibly inexhaustible. It has been historically important in both positive and negative ways. One of the earliest uses was in the elementary construction of foundations and walls for houses, churches, and public buildings. Two major examples of the use of native limestone as structural material are the Old State Capitol in Frankfort, and the massive foundation blocks under the Shaker buildings at Pleasant Hill in Mercer County.

Millions of tons of lime and sandstone have been used in all sorts of construction. More millions have been utilized as crushed "metal" for the surfacing of highways. From the opening of the famous Shelby Wagon Road in 1796 to date the Kentucky highway system has depended upon the state's stone resource for ballast and cement. Introduction of the modern age of hydroelectricity and navigation, and flood control created an almost insatiable demand for stone and concrete.

The existence of a boundless stone resource has also had a deterrent influence. In the building of canals, the improvement of stream channels, railroads, and highways it has been necessary to make heavy cuts through massive stone barriers. Even the excavation of building foundations has frequently required expensive removal of stone deposits. The presence of deep stone formations has been a blessing and a hindrance in mining procedures in both major coal fields. On a more positive note the outcroppings of limestone and that which lies near the surface in the fertile central area has renewed the vitality of the land in a continuing process of decay.

Collectively the presence of numerous natural resources has borne impressively upon the quality of human life in Kentucky. These have ranged from the generation of private fortunes for those fortunately located geographically to the holding of people in a state of social and economic serfdom in the more sterile areas. The clearest examples of the broad impact of resources on people are to be found in areas of the most fertile lands like the Inner Bluegrass and in the coal mining fields. In the latter an industry had a human impact which all but defies an adequate socio-historical analysis. In terms of returned values from mineral resources the Bureau of the United States Census in 1973 listed coal, stone, petroleum, and natural gas in this order.

No scientific source discusses scenery as a Kentucky natural asset, yet it is potentially one of the state's most attractive and valuable features. Measured in the simple terms of viewing it is inexhaustible and varied. Both topography and scenery have the attractive qualities of seasonal changes and varying perspectives. The surface of Kentucky, however, is constantly undergoing modification. Creeping sprawls of urban and industrial communities are absorbing vast areas of farm and rural lands. The rapid expansion of Kentucky industry has produced a real economic return to Kentucky, but at a cost to various aspects of its environment. Four lane highways have gashed Kentucky into a concrete grid of modernity and feverish speed. These have rended lands and mountains alike with fills, cuts, and ribbons of concrete. Amazingly steep mountain ridges have been laid open with cuts which defy the impact of the ages. Even one city, Pikeville, has assaulted mountain and river to modify its topographical situation. Airports have absorbed large areas in three locations, and these continue to spread as modifications of airplanes occur. None of the above changes, however, have begun to have the topographical and long-range geographical influence as the coal strip-mining industry. Only time and a great deal of intensive physiological and sociological study can finally determine the pros and cons of the arguments which have raged about this land mauling industry.

Kentucky Resources and History

Kentucky history has been deeply colored by the presence and exploitation of its natural resources. None, however, has been more important than the land—the mineral earth. It was the lodestone which drew thousands of impoverished emigrants from the leached soils of the east to settle the western country. This mother resource cast a magic spell of semi-paridiscal euphoria over the people, whether they settled thin dry highland soils or those of the rich inner bluegrass and the river valleys. From the coming of the first hunters and scouts people viewed the new country as a haven of economic promise. The specific impact of the land on human beings was to be measured in terms of the kind of livelihood it produced for its exploiters. For those westward-moving emigrants who persevered until they reached the fertile areas of the central and western sections there was rich reward in time in the form of bountiful field crops and fine livestock. Those who settled on less productive soils in isolated areas depended for a century upon a domestic subsistence economy which seldom if ever produced a surplus of either crops or livestock. Remarkably the sectional lines of Kentucky economy have been sharply delineated, and the contrasting ways of life clearly defined.

In a more dramatic sense the sectional divisions of Kentucky have left individual impress upon the Kentucky personality. This fact has been reflected in politics, cultural institutions, and even in the shaping of the state's popular image. Many of the persistently negative reflections in Kentucky history have stemmed from sharp sectional variations. There has never been such a thing as a Kentucky human prototype. The goateed colonel on the one hand and the black-hatted hill billy on the other are humorous regional carricatures. The clearest definition of the character of Kentucky humanity can be made in terms of rural and urban dwellers. Gradually since 1860 the separative statistics between these two elements of the population have been drawn into balance. In 1970 the statistics were tipped in favor of the urban classification. Out of a population of 3,219,000 in 1970, 1,535,000, or 52.3 per cent were urban dwellers. Perhaps of greater importance is that an overwhelming proportion of the urban population lives within the periphery of one of the five standard metropolitan areas. These elementary statistics fail to reflect fully that many rural dwellers are in fact non-farm industrial workers. Hundreds of current Kentucky rural communities feed workers into factories and industrial plants. The location of the new type industrial plants, and the metropolitan centers themselves, reflect a distinctive geographical influence.

Socially and culturally Kentucky has been populated by a provincial people who have cherished their locality. They have resisted major institutional and political reforms. Illustrative of this fact is the deep attachment to 120 counties which are costly and duplicative of the processes of government. To large numbers of Kentuckians the courthouse and its cluster of officials actually comprise the grass roots sources of democracy itself. Kentucky is by no means unique in this respect. Every state in some manner reflects the peculiar local characteristics and influences of geography and environmental conditions. In Kentucky these facts have been a genuine asset because they have heightened local pride and stimulated an acute awareness of general human conditions and relationships to the land. There are contrasts, of course. Where the land is fertile and productive local pride is pronounced, and there prevails a sense of economic security. Where soils are thin and unproductive, or have historically been denied ready access to the "outside," the population has dwindled, prejudices may be revealed, and feelings of both pride and security are limited.

Geographical determinism is not necessarily a hard and fast fact in the history of Kentucky and its people. There are many exceptions to any general statements which might be made in this area. A region which has historically been agriculturally unpromising may be productive of vast sources in the forms of water, coal, and electricity. Thus when properly assessed some areas of Kentucky which give such distinctive surface evidence of prosperity and well-being may in fact be one of high economic potential in the form of unseen resources.

The facts of geography, environmental influences, resource exploitation, and social challenges have been indelible parts of Kentucky history. Kentuckians take enormous pride in having been born within the Commonwealth's political boundaries. Sometimes this pride blinds them to the realities of their history and the everyday conditions of their lives. Again, Kentuckians can lay no monopolistic claim to this kind of reaction to their native land. This is a prevalent condition all across the American continent. The land of Kentucky has produced social and economic variables which at once give color to its history, and the human occupation has created problems and challenges which have ever demanded prodigious human stamina and endurance to effect solutions.

CHAPTER II

England Moves West

The Beginning of the Movement

THE first English people to touch American soil were curious about the land "upstream" but were slow to explore it. In 1642 Walter Austin, Rice Hoe, Joseph Johnson, and Walter Chiles petitioned the Virginia Assembly for "leave and encouragement to explore westward." Somewhere these gentlemen had learned of the New River, and they were anxious to explore its reaches in search of new and fertile lands.

Had these early explorers proved more diligent under the provisions of their grant, they would have discovered an interesting feature of the piedmont river system. The headwaters of the New, Staunton, James, Clinch, Holston, Potomac, and even of the Yadkin and Catawba Rivers are all connected, directly or indirectly, by easily passable gaps. In western Virginia and North Carolina they share the flood waters of the Appalachian Ranges. The Indian warriors were familiar with these head streams, as evidenced by numerous trails through these valleys. But it was not until six years after the first petition was presented to the Virginia Assembly that the forest traders and rangers possessed definite knowledge of the upstream country's topography.

In 1669 the Virginia Assembly again considered the possibility of exploring the western country. A "blanket" charter was granted, enabling any party with proper equipment to explore westward. Governor Berkeley gave his friend John Lederer, the German surgeon-adventurer, a special grant of authority. Lederer found the snowstorms of the Blue Ridge too violent and returned home; subsequently to make two more trips in that direction. On the first of these he reached the present site of Lynchburg, and, on the second, he penetrated the Blue Ridge. During the latter expedition Lederer was supported by the frontier post, Fort Henry (now Petersburg). In 1646 Fort Henry was placed in charge of Colonel Abraham Woods. In 1671 Colonel Woods sent an exploring party into the western ranges for the purpose of locating the "ebbing and flowing of the rivers on the other side of the mountains in order to reach the South Seas." This expedition under the leadership of Thomas Batts and Robert Fallam reached the Ohio River, but their sponsors were little impressed with their important discovery until the French, in 1673, began claiming the western territory by virtue of Marquette's and Joliet's expedition down the Mississippi from the Wisconsin country. The French even went so far as to claim the western territory on the basis of La Salle's expedition. La Salle accepted the Senecas' assurance that *la belle rivière* flowed to the east, and, because of ill health, he returned to the Northwest. Nevertheless the French claims stirred Colonel Woods out of his lethargy, and in 1673 he sent James Needham and Gabriel Arthur into the West on what became an unsuccessful adventure.

Such fruitless expeditions, fraught with hardships and despair, cooled English curiosity about the transmontane country. It was not until 1742 that the English ventured so far westward again. In this year John (?) Peter Salling, John Howard, his son Josiah, Charles Sinclair, and two other men set out to visit the banks of the western rivers. This party reached the Ohio, but not without bloodshed. Salling was captured and taken off to Natchez, New Orleans, and France; three years later he returned to Charleston.

Celeron de Blainville moved southward from the French-Canadian posts in 1749 to re-assert French claims to the West, and, doubtless, to plan a cordon of French forts from Canada to New Orleans. The British, as early as 1730, had foreseen such a move and had attempted to forestall it by coming to terms with the Indians. Sir Alexander Cumming was dispatched to the western woods to hold council with Cherokees, who, it had been erroneously supposed, could at once put 6,000 warriors in the field. The British carried through a long series of negotiations, selecting portions of the northern trans-Allegheny region which were to be controlled by the Virginians, but the Indians violated their agreements almost before the King's representatives left the woods.

By the early thirties of the eighteenth century, the English had become fairly well informed about the extent and topography of the Blue

Ridge and Allegheny areas. Like the *couriers de bois* of the Canadian woods, hunters, traders, and trappers of frontier Virginia and Pennsylvania were ready sources of information for adventurer-settlers.

Woodsmen of the Blue Ridge and Allegheny ranges became quite familiar with trails and streams of these regions. They were the first to view the Appalachian trough formed by the parallel Blue Ridges and Alleghenies, a trough which extends from western Pennsylvania to northern Alabama, and is crossed and recrossed by numerous streams and fertile valleys. This basin forms, virtually, an unbroken gorge from the Potomac pass at Harper's Ferry to the Cumberland Gap. At the southern end of this great valley the Tennessee River gorge leads off to the southwest into the plains of northern Alabama and thence through central and western Tennessee into Kentucky. It was through this great natural Appalachian trough that the stream of westward immigration was to flow. It was a direct route for immigrants coming from the Carolinas, Virginia, Maryland, and Pennsylvania by way of Cumberland Gap to Kentucky. Other immigrants followed the Tennessee River to its mouth on the Ohio and thence up the Cumberland River to the neighborhood of the present city of Nashville, Tennessee.

With all their curiosity and determination, the English moved westward slowly, for they were still in the lower reaches of the eastern piedmont one hundred and eighteen years after their landing at the mouth of the James in 1607. It was even considered a bold achievement in 1716, when Governor Spottswood stood with his "Knights of the Golden Horseshoe" and peered into the bowl beyond the Blue Ridge.

The savages of the forest were numerous and often warlike in temperament. Whether they were Cherokee, Creek, Catawba, or Chickasaw from the south, or Iroquois, Wyandotte, or Shawnee from the north, the Indians were always ready to preserve their western hunting grounds from white settlement. The great valley was an ideal passage between the southern and northern tribes. For centuries warriors had journeyed back and forth through this region on hunting and warring expeditions. As the Virginians crowded westward, however, intermittent Indian raids became so fierce that it was necessary, in 1722, for the Virginia Governor to exact what proved to be a short-lived treaty from the Iroquois. This treaty guaranteed that the Indians would not come east of the mountains without the Governor's consent, and then in numbers of not more than ten.

Both the English and French knew that there was to the west of the Appalachian ranges a long, rolling stretch of fertile territory, open to settlement and exploitation by any group of settlers bold enough to face hardships. Since it was known that this beautiful land was the home of no one, danger threatened those who attempted to claim it. Rival Indian tribes hunted and fought in it, crossed and recrossed it, but seldom, if ever, lingered. It had numerous streams, the delight of every savage heart; it had springs, salt licks, and game in abundance. But always the Indian homes were north of the Ohio or south of the Cumberland. Cherokees, Choctaws, Creeks, from the south; Iroquois, Shawnees, Illinois, Wyandottes, Delawares, and other tribes from the north, made frequent visits to this land, but they always hurried back into the safety zones.

The East Reawakens

By the middle of the eighteenth century, land-hungry Englishmen were beginning to realize that the land supply east of the mountains was limited. Colonel Thomas Lee of Virginia petitioned the colonial Governor for a grant of 500,000 acres of western land for his Ohio Land Company. Before the Governor could comply, however, he had to secure a royal title from the King. The Virginia and Pennsylvania Governors jointly petitioned King George II for a western grant. The King in answering this petition commanded that a council, including the Governor of Maryland, be held with the Cherokees and the Iroquois. When the Cherokees were informed that they would be expected to parley with their ancient rivals, the Iroquois, they refused to be represented. Undaunted, Colonel Lee, chief councilor for the English, proceeded with negotiations on the English assumption that an Indian treaty was an Indian treaty regardless of whether both parties agreed thereto or not. So long as the English colonials were able to secure the semblance of a treaty, they were pleased with the council's work, for it opened the way for western land speculation.

The Ohio Land Company secured, in 1748, a grant somewhere between the Monongahela and the Yadkin Rivers. Thus it was that the

King cleared up any doubts which may have existed as to Virginia's claims to the western lands. The following year Colonel James Patton, of Albemarle County, Virginia, expressed a desire to attempt a western settlement. Using the Ohio Company's plan as a precedent, he petitioned the Virginia Governor for 120,000 acres of land near Staunton Falls and obtained it. Pleased with this grant, Colonel Patton led an exploring party down the valley to the southwest, where he hoped to discover fertile territory subject to claim. In Colonel Patton's party was Dr. Thomas Walker, who, by this expedition, added to his reputation as a surveyor and adventurer.

While Patton was exploring the lower end of the great Virginia valley, some of his Albemarle County neighbors also were framing a scheme to secure western lands. In order to carry out their plans, they organized and secured a charter for the Loyal Land Company, and upon Patton's return, Walker was employed as a company surveyor. On March 6, 1750, Walker's party set out for the western country. Traveling down the valley for some distance, they came, on April 13, to the great depression in the Allegheny wall. Walker, perhaps, had heard this passageway called "Cave Gap," for so it appears in his journal. This party was by no means the first, however, to visit this spot, as was evidenced by the presence of numerous crosses and other marks carved on near-by trees by the white man. After traveling inland beyond the gap to the neighborhood of the present town of Barbourville, Walker divided his party and set off into the wilderness with one group, leaving the other to construct a log cabin and establish a post of supply. When he returned on April 28, he found that his companions had constructed the cabin and salted down several bears and other game as a meat supply. Restless and ambitious to be off again, the exploring party entered the woods on May 1, this time following the "Warrior's Trail" inland to a river which they named for Ambrose Powell. From this point, the party came to another stream about seventy yards wide, which perhaps was Gardener's branch of the Licking River, in the present county of Magoffin. In a bend of this river, Walker found a moss-grown "elk stand," and here he pitched his camp: now the site of the courthouse at Salyersville. On June 6 the explorers pushed on to the Big Sandy Valley, where they explored the Levisa Fork, naming it for the sister of the "Bloody" Duke of Cumberland. On June 20 the party, on its return to Virginia, passed through "Cave Gap," renamed Cumberland Gap. In their rambles through eastern Kentucky, these explorers had missed the Blue Grass by one or two days' journey. The mission was a failure as a land-hunting expedition, but Walker had at least named Cumberland Gap, Cumberland River, the Levisa Fork of the Big Sandy, and Cumberland Mountain. Numerous historians denied that he accomplished much. It is certainly true that had it not been for subsequent expeditions, this one would have been insignificant.

Soon after Thomas Walker returned from his scouting venture, Christopher Gist, representing the Ohio Land Company, visited the Ohio Valley. During the early months of 1751, Gist made an extended visit to the Shawnee towns along the Ohio. Here he made the acquaintance of the Indian agent and trader, Colonel George Croghan. Croghan, one of the best informed Indian agents in the whole western country, was obliging enough to furnish Gist with much useful information about the country which he was to visit within a few weeks. About the middle of March, Gist crossed over the Ohio at the mouth of the Scioto, and at the Twigtwee town he met Robert Smith, a general trader, who gave him an order on his agent for two mastodon teeth from the Big Bone Lick. Gist, on hearing of these remains, had expressed a desire for these trophies, for he wished to present one to his employers and keep the other as a memento of his visit to the West. On March 18, while traveling in the direction of the Ohio Falls, he met four Shawnee Indians coming up the Ohio in a canoe. They informed him that they had found sixty hostile French Indians encamped near the falls. This information led Gist to give up his intended visit to the falls, and he returned overland to his home on the Yadkin. In returning eastward through the Allegheny ridges, Gist crossed and recrossed Thomas Walker's route.

English and French Rivalries

Both England and France claimed the western territory which was later to become Kentucky. Each asserted that its agents had made prior claims to the region. France, through the activities of her agent, de Blainville, in the middle of the eighteenth century, had perhaps more effectively established her claims. Preparatory to asserting claims, the French had established forts from Canada to the "Isle d'Orleans." Even though these frontier posts were sparsely populated by frontier officials, Jesuit missionaries, and fur traders, their establishment constituted an act of possession.

The English, on the other hand, by neglecting to establish permanent settlements in the West, had utterly failed to support their Batts and Fallam Claim (1671). English trading shanties were built, but no settlements were actually established. The Virginians had made several unsuccessful thrusts in this direction, but these convinced them that before permanent settlement could be made, the French dispute had to be settled.

With both France and England contemplating expansion in the West, conflict in this region was inevitable. To the English on the Atlantic slope, French control of the western country constituted a real menace. They realized that the French were friendly with the Indians so that they could, on the slightest provocation, hurl an Indian attack against the settlers of frontier Virginia. English settlers in western Pennsylvania, Maryland, and Virginia would remain exposed to Indian attacks so long as the Foreign Offices of France and England quarreled over the possession of the Ohio Valley. The Treaty of Aix-la-Chapelle, in 1748, instead of compromising American colonial disputes between England and France, had acted only as a lull in the storm. It enabled Virginia land-grabbers to prepare for more land seizures.

Back in London, the British Secretary of State, in charge of Foreign Affairs, expressed himself as being anxious to bring the French and English difficulties to a settlement. He instructed Governor Dinwiddie of Virginia to send a commissioner into the West to treat with the French and Indians. Governor Dinwiddie complied immediately by sending the adventurous, twenty-one-year-old, patrician-bred George Washington in 1753 to the western French forts as agent for Virginia. Washington selected Christopher Gist as his guide and frontier adviser. In the West, the youthful Washington was politely and hospitably received by the French officials, who, however, insisted that English claims in the Ohio Valley were unfounded. Washington returned home with the information that the French were determined to hold their western claims.

The heated rivalry between the French and English in the West brought on a furious frontier struggle of nine years' duration. In the beginning of the struggle inexperience with frontier methods of fighting and lack of regard for advice from American scouts cost the British dearly in men and territory. The first stormy years, beginning with 1754, saw Washington's frontier forces back at Fort Necessity from the neighborhood of Fort Duquesne, and later they retreated to their own native Virginia soil. During the following year the headstrong Braddock was defeated in his ill-guided and ill-fated march upon Fort Duquesne. Thus, as a consequence of these two failures at the very beginning of the struggle, 400 miles of western Virginia, Maryland, and Pennsylvania frontiers were exposed to ruthless attack and pillage by the French and Indians. Settlers in western Virginia were in serious difficulty, for they could muster only 1,500 raw and undisciplined militiamen to repel the attacks of the invaders. Occupants of lone cabins far out in the wilderness were subjected to inhuman treatment, and, in many cases, men and boys were killed and women carried off to the Indian villages, there to be subjected to savage cruelties or to be absorbed into the tribes.

In subsequent years fate smiled more kindly on the English; the French and Indians were defeated on every hand. During these latter years the French forts fell like ninepins. The English captured Oswego, William Henry, Louisburg, Lake Ontario, Duquesne, Niagara, Ticonderoga, Crown Point, Quebec, and Montreal. These seizures opened the way for English control of the western country. France found the western war too costly to continue, even though she did receive assistance from Spain. On February 10, 1763, the Treaty of Paris was drawn up between the two powers. By this treaty France ceded to England, among other things, the territory east of the Mississippi, south of the Ohio, and west of the Appalachian range, excepting the Isle d'Orleans. Thus England found herself in complete possession, on paper at least, of the western territory.

The Treaty of Paris brought England much territory, but just how this newly acquired territory was to be governed was a subject for much reflection on the part of the Crown and the Board of Trade. The two Floridas were divided into eastern and western districts, and the Province of Quebec was created, and each one of these divisions was placed under the control of a colonial governor. The country immediately south of the Ohio remained for royal disposition. To settle this problem George III, lately come to the throne, issued his royal proclamation of 1763, restraining his "dutiful" subjects from encroaching upon that part of the newly acquired territory lying immediately west of the Appalachian watershed. This country the English Sovereign wished, benevolently, to be reserved for his recently acquired Indian subjects—and the royal fur trade. To this arrangement the prospective western settlers made immediate protest. The Virginians, having already sent out Walker and Gist to explore these new lands, felt that their claims were justified. The speculators, having gathered information about the West, were preparing to send out land-engrossers and settlers. But thwarted, both settler and speculator took special pleasure in venting their wrath upon the Board of Trade.

Unfortunately for the colonials, George III was too late with his restraining proclamation to salve the Indians' antagonism. The Ottawa chief, Pontiac, had organized a powerful western confederacy and had placed detailed plans for annihilating the whites in the hands of every allied chieftain. The savages were not only enraged of their own accord, but they were incited against the migrating English by disgruntled French traders and trappers, acting with the connivance of the French authorities. Profiting by their knowledge of the English activities along the Atlantic seaboard, the Indians were thoroughly aware of the fate in store for their hunting grounds should the whites be allowed to migrate westward. As a result, they were ready to listen to any scheme which would remove this imminent danger.

Entering the English forts under the pretense of friendship, the allies of Pontiac captured every fort and post except Forts Pitt and Detroit. These fortifications doubtless would have fallen victims to the savage conspiracy had it not been for the timely warning received by their commanders. The atrocities committed in this savage *coup* were many. Women and children were not spared. The whole frontier from the Monongahela River to the southernmost settler's cabin in the Appalachian foothills was thrown into a state of terror. However, during the latter months of 1764, the English frontiersmen had sufficiently recovered from the shock of Pontiac's attempted capture of their forts to reassert their intention to occupy the West. Marching under the command of General Bouquet, they defeated the Indians at Bushy Run and then entered unmolested into the very heart of the Indian country.

Once Pontiac's conspiracy was stamped out, the British undertook to open the interior to white settlement. Two treaties (1768) were negotiated; one at Fort Stanwix, with the Iroquois; the other at Hard Labor, with the Cherokees. The treaty drawn up at Stanwix transferred to the English all the rights and privileges claimed by the Iroquois in the much-disputed Ohio country (and here it may be noted that the transfer was of most doubtful validity). The Hard Labor Treaty transferred to the English all the Cherokee claims to the same territory. In his anxiety to secure generous grants from the various Indian tribes, the English agent, Sir William Johnson, distributed among them £10,-000 worth of baubles. While Johnson was bribing the Indians, he refused at any time to inform Dr. Thomas Walker, the lone Virginia delegate, of the true circumstances surrounding the treaty negotiations. Had Johnson been more confiding, he might not have exceeded his grant of authority from the King by negotiating agreements which involved the major portion of the territory between the Ohio and Cherokee (Tennessee) Rivers in favor of the Vandalia Company. This ill-advised act led to plots and counterplots in the British Government, and even to the resignation from the cabinet of Lord Hillsborough, Secretary for the Colonies. This maneuver on the part of William Johnson also caused considerable confusion on the frontier. Temple Bodley claims, in his *History of Kentucky,* that the West almost failed to bear its share in the fight for independence in its efforts to win back the revolutionary West itself. Nevertheless, with all of their shortcomings, the newly acquired titles to the western lands formed the basis for building a vast northwestern domain. Once these treaties were signed, numerous land-grabbing schemes, promoted by such prominent easterners as Benjamin Franklin and Sir William Johnson, were set afoot.

When the Indian and French raids were quelled, prospective settlers again took heart. By this time the frontier line was drawn tight by restless settlers anxious to be over the western ridges to the fertile lands of Kentucky. Hardly had the last wisp of smoke at the council of Hard Labor disappeared into the air, before the southern pioneers appeared in the lower extremity of the great Appalachian trough. They were satisfied that all restrictions imposed by the proclamation of 1763 had been removed by the Hard Labor agreement, and that henceforth free settlement in hitherto restricted territory was permissible. In 1769 several white settlers from Virginia appeared in the valley of the Watauga, and this served as a beginning for the long dramatic journey to the new western homes. Adventurous men came westward walking at the head and rear of processions, driving cattle, sheep, and hogs. Women and children formed the center, driving pack horses loaded with household necessities, and, perhaps, bits of eastern finery with which feminine hearts were loath to part.

Hardly had these first Virginia settlers finished the task of felling trees with which to construct their rude log cabins, when, in 1771, they were joined by seventeen families from North Carolina, under the leadership of James Robertson. In the following year a third company, under the leadership of John Sevier, joined the swelling ranks of Watauga settlers. The stage was set. The westward-bound settlers were restless, and the Ohio country lay just over the ridges beyond the Watauga. With the establishment of the Watauga settlement, the western adventurers had a near-by post which was later to become an excellent base for western operations.

Scouts, Surveyors, and Settlers

The paid scouts of the middle of the eighteenth century were not the only whites to visit the West in this early period. As early as 1729, and perhaps earlier, the Big Bone Lick had been explored and described by white travelers. Mrs. Mary Ingles, her two sons, and Mrs. Mary Draper were taken prisoners, in 1756, from their homes in Augusta County, Virginia. Later Mrs. Ingles was taken by her captors to the Big Bone Lick. While here she met an old Dutch woman with whom she conspired to escape. Successfully eluding their captors, these two women wandered in a general northeasterly direction to the Kanawha and thence across country in the direction of the Ingles home. But catastrophe befell these lone wanderers, when the Dutch woman, worn and starved by the grueling struggle through the forest, became a raving maniac. Mrs. Ingles' life being threatened by her mad companion, she was forced to continue her homeward journey alone, deserting her friend, who wandered aimlessly in the forest. Through rare good fortune Mrs. Ingles reached her friends and sent a searching party to rescue her afflicted companion. This adventure, filled with hardship and privation, was not without its good returns, for these captive women acquired a vast amount of information, which was later to be useful to immigrants moving westward.

James McBride made a vague claim of being the first man to see the territory around the mouth of the Kentucky River. Whatever claims are to be made for this adventurer, however, rest upon a set of uncertain initials carved upon a tree in the neighborhood of the river's mouth. A second traveler passed through the Kentucky country in 1765. This gentleman, Colonel George Croghan, left the Shawnee town (now Portsmouth, Ohio) on May 28 and arrived at the mouth of the Wabash on June 6. It is doubtful, however, whether this was Croghan's first journey into Kentucky. He had given Gist much useful information, but whether he was repeating first-hand information or what others had told him, is not clear. While traveling from the Shawnee town to the Wabash, Croghan kept a journal in which he noted the Big Bone Lick, the mouth of the Kentucky River, and the Ohio Falls. A third traveler, Captain Harry Gordon, engineer for the Western Department of North America, visited that part of the Ohio country from Pittsburgh to the Illinois country bordering on the Ohio River. This was an interesting journey, and one useful to British colonial officials, since Captain Gordon compiled a table of distances from Fort Pitt to the mouth of the Ohio.

Legend, coupled with some fact, has handed down the romantic story of John Swift, the Blue Jackets, and Swift's notorious silver mine. For nine years, 1760–1769, John Swift is supposed to have carried on intermittent mining activities in eastern Kentucky. Unfortunately, Swift was not to leave the western country with the fruits of his industry. The presence of marauding Indians forced Swift to cache his silver ore and to depart light-handed. Scenes of these activities were along the Red River bed. Hence "old silver" legends have become so widely spread that even at this late date the Red River localities are occasionally excited over reputed finds of the Swift cache. In all of his wanderings Swift kept a journal, but its tattered remnants have been copied and recopied so many times that it has become a disconnected bit of jargon. Remaining fragments of the journal record that Swift brought his western adventures to a close in 1769, at Alexandria, Virginia, "praising God that they were successful."

At an early date John Findley and Henry Scaggs had traveled far into the western country, and Findley's careful observations equipped him for the position of chief scout to General Braddock in that officer's abortive march upon Fort Duquesne in 1755. Uriah Stone, in company with Gasper Mansker, John Raines, and several others, crossed the Cumberland Plateau one year ahead of the "Long Hunters" [1] to escape boring domestic duties at home and to explore western lands. This was not Stone's first trip, however, for he had visited the West in 1766, in company with Captain James Smith and Joshua Horton. These hunters came to Kentucky simply for love of roving in new territory. At the same time that these voluntary scouts were wandering in and out of the wilderness, however, there were numerous other whites in the same territory as captives of the Indians.

Back in the Yadkin Valley, Daniel Boone was yearning for new adventures. He had led a life of constant migration, having moved one step ahead of permanent settlement all the way from Berks County, Pennsylvania, to the Yadkin. Boone felt at once that he would not be happy until he could see this wonderful country for himself. Besides the glamorous tales he heard in the Yadkin settlements, Boone recalled similar tales which Findley had told around Braddock's camp fires. All this determined him to search for the level lands described by the visitors west of the mountains. But, unfortunately, Daniel Boone, like the misguided Dr. Thomas Walker, moped through the winter of 1767-1768 on the mesa of eastern Kentucky and in the Big Sandy Valley. In the spring he returned home disgusted, but to his surprise Findley had also spent the winter in the West.

In May, 1769, Boone, Findley, and four companions, imbued more with wanderlust than love for agricultural labors and domestic tranquillity, set out for the Kentucky wilderness to hunt with abandon. Findley, to make good a promise, led this party of hunters directly to the Red River and thence to the Dick's and Kentucky River Valleys. The hunters realized time had passed quickly. Moreover, delighted

---

[1] A party of forty hunters from the Yadkin Valley in North Carolina who were called "Long Hunters" because of their long stay in the Kentucky wilderness.

with their good luck at hunting, they forgot to be cautious. The Shaw-nees caught the party unawares; Boone and Stewart were taken prison-ers, warned that the wasps and yellow jackets were jealous, and ordered to leave the country. Unwilling to see their horses led off, Boone and his companions pursued the Indians and recovered five of their mounts. The hunters profited not at all from the recovery of some of their horses, for they were again taken captive by the savages and detained seven precious days. Meanwhile others of their companions were pre-paring to leave the Kentucky country. Escaping their captors at an opportune moment, Boone and Stewart overtook their departing com-panions, whom no amount of persuasion, however, could induce to turn back.

In the meantime, Squire Boone, tired of laboring for the necessities of life, had, with a man named Neely, ventured west. It was by acci-dent that this pair met the retreating hunters. Since the two new re-cruits had brought with them a fresh supply of ammunition, Daniel and Squire Boone, Stewart, and Neely elected to remain in the West rather than to return to the Yadkin settlement. These four continued to hunt, but not without fatal mishaps. Stewart was killed by the Indians, and Neely died, perhaps of injuries inflicted by the savages, for his bleached skeleton, found later in the hollow of a tree, bore grim testimony of it.

Thus the Boone brothers were left in the wilderness alone, to hunt at random for profit and pleasure. Twice the younger brother went back to the Yadkin for fresh supplies of ammunition and horses. Each time Squire returned to the "settlements," Daniel was left to hunt alone. Upon Squire's second return, he found that Daniel, in an amusing man-ner, had been found by the Long Hunters. Thinking they were the only whites in Kentucky, the Long Hunters were startled one day to hear a white man singing at the top of his voice. Stealing up near the place from whence the sounds came, they were surprised to see Daniel Boone lying flat on his back singing with as much abandon as if he were in his cornfield in North Carolina. For a short time the Boones joined forces with the Long Hunters and went exploring with them to the "big bend" of the Cumberland River.

In 1771, after Daniel Boone had been away from the Yadkin for the space of two years, he and Squire packed up the remainder of their second cache of furs and attempted to journey home with them. Near Cumberland Gap they were beset by robbing Cherokees and were forced to go home with nothing to show for their labors.

The Long Hunters fared no better than the Boones. Their first semipermanent camp was established in the neighborhood of Monticello, in Wayne County. Here the party split into small groups to hunt throughout the surrounding territory. Some of the members soon went to Natchez to sell their furs and returned home by way of the Atlantic coast. Others went home overland, but several members of the party were killed by Indians. Ultimately there were only nine remaining members, who banded together under the leadership of James Knox. While hunting one day, they encountered a band of Cherokees led by a crippled chieftain to whom the whites gave the name "Captain Dick." Pleased with his new name, "Captain Dick" led the whites to his (Dick's) River and bade them hunt at will.

The subsequent capture of two members of the party, which in the meantime had been enlarged by twelve recruits, persuaded the Long Hunters to abandon their chase and return home. When they reached their central camp, they were disgusted to find their dogs had become wild, their horses strayed, and their fur pens broken into and robbed. Disgruntled by such ill luck, Jesse Bledsoe gave vent to his feelings by carving on a near-by tree, "2300 dear skins lost, ruination, by God." Despite ill fortune, this band of hunters returned home to spread far and wide tall tales of the West. Doubtless these Long Hunter tales stirred anew the spirit of adventure in the Yadkin and Virginia Valley settlements.

Surveyors

Ink had hardly dried on the Treaty of Paris before Virginia's veterans of the French and Indian War were asking that their claims against the state be paid in western bounty grants. To be sure, George III had issued his proclamation stopping white immigration into the West, but the Virginians believed this only a conciliatory gesture toward the Indians. The King's white American subjects proceeded to interpret his western decree to suit themselves. Surveyors were sent to the West. Even Sir William Johnson, the King's commissioner, was guilty of imposing on generous Iroquois imagination in that he persuaded these

Indians to claim the territory as far south as the Cumberland Bend so that they in turn could cede it to the English.

The West was well advertised by returning hunters and adventurers. Daniel Boone, the Amerigo Vespucci of western America, repeated his tales of adventure throughout the eastern settlements. Boone not only described his adventures, but he fired the imagination of land-hungry settlers by describing the wonders of unclaimed forest and prairies beyond the mountains. Adventurers before Daniel Boone had sung praises of the Ohio country to the settlers at Duquesne (Fort Pitt) and in northern Virginia. These tales, with those of the returning hunters in the Yadkin Valley, stirred many hearts to seek adventure in the West. Little did the boasting Long Hunters realize that their Kentucky hunting ground would soon disappear. Soon there was a rush of surveyors and land claimants to the West. In 1770 George Washington set the land rush in motion in the Big Sandy Valley; here the first claim stake driven bore his initials. This Washington plot was patented in 1772 from George III, in the name of John Fry.

With the opening of the western land survey, there came to Kentucky, in 1771, an interesting figure, Simon Kenton, born of Scotch-Irish parents in Fauquier County, Virginia. Kenton had been disappointed in love and in a fit of jealousy had engaged his rival, William Leachman, in a rough and tumble fight. Entangling Leachman's unshorn locks in a near-by bush, Kenton took his revenge. Enraged as he was, he pummeled Leachman almost to death. In an effort to arise, Leachman fell back unconscious, and Kenton, thinking his victim dead, disappeared into the woods as a fugitive from justice. He reappeared at Ise's Ford, on the Cheat River, as "Simon Butler." Here Kenton, unarmed and hungry, fell in with a party of hunters who gave him an opportunity to earn a rifle. Later he accompanied his new companions to Fort Pitt, there to act as hunter and scout for the fort's garrison. It was while acting in this capacity that he met Simon Girty (the white Indian) and heard glowing stories of the territory south of the Ohio from George Yeager and John Strader. Yeager, Indian reared, described in typically exaggerated western terms a cane land which the Indians called "Kaintuckee." Tempted by Yeager's descriptions of the Kentucky country, Kenton, accompanied by Yeager and Strader, set forth into the wilderness. This trio of explorers visited most of the northern Kentucky territory. They became familiar with many Kentucky streams and salt licks but were unable to find Yeager's land of promise. Giving up their search toward the close of 1772, they built a rude, open-faced camp and settled down for the rest of the winter season. They were raided by the Indians early in the spring of 1773, and Yeager was killed. Kenton and Strader put off into the woods barefooted and naked, except for their shirts, and it was by rare good fortune that they secured aid from friendly whites. In the summer Kenton joined a party going in search of Captain Bullitt, who was then descending the Ohio River. Passing him in the night, the party gave up in disappointment, destroyed their canoes, and returned to Virginia.

In June, 1773, Captain Thomas Bullitt landed with his party on the banks of the Ohio to survey lands for Governor Dunmore. A second group, which included James Harrod, had put forth from Fort Pitt in canoes, with the Ohio Falls as their destination. At the mouth of the Kanawha River they came upon the McAfee brothers, who had come overland from Botetourt County, Virginia, to join Hancock Taylor and a party of surveyors.

At the mouth of the Kanawha, Bullitt left the party to go inland for a visit at the Miami village of Chillicothe. Here he made a friendly gesture to the Indians, whom he knew to be dissatisfied with the unfair treatment they had received at Fort Stanwix. Wishing partially to rectify Sir William Johnson's mistake at Stanwix and to establish peaceful relations with these Indians, Captain Bullitt, in an eloquent speech, emphasized the fact that there was land enough for both whites and Indians. When his Indian hearers asked why he had come among them alone and unannounced, Bullitt replied that he had come as the ablest of the white messengers. The savages, however, were as shrewd as Bullitt. Equally willing to make gestures, they sent him back to his party satisfied and positive that he had successfully accomplished his mission. Robert McAfee left the party at Limestone Creek and privately explored the country as far inland as the north fork of the Licking River. From this point he turned back northward through the present county of Bracken to the Ohio. Arriving there after Bullitt's party had passed on, he shaped a bark canoe with his hunting knife and tomahawk and overtook the surveyors in a short time.

The surveyors visited the Big Bone Lick on July 4 and 6, after having passed it in the night of July 3. Here they marveled at the huge bones, skulls, and teeth of mastodon and Arctic elephants. A more pleasing sight than the bones of prehistoric animals, however, were the thousands of live animals which gathered about the salt licks.

On July 7 the McAfee and Bullitt parties separated. The McAfees descended the Ohio to the mouth of the Kentucky, then followed this stream to the mouth of what later was named Drennon's Creek. Very much to their disappointment, they found James Drennon, a former member of the combined Bullitt and McAfee parties, already at the salt lick. Drennon had proceeded one day in advance of the McAfees. While the surveyors were at Big Bone, Drennon had bribed a Delaware Indian into describing and directing him to a salt lick to the south. From Drennon's Lick, the McAfee party moved up to the bend of the Kentucky River where it plotted six hundred acres of land, much of which lies today in the City of Frankfort. In August this party separated, Drennon, Bracken, and Taylor going to join Bullitt at the Ohio Falls. The McAfee brothers and Samuel Adams set out through the wilderness to return home.

At the falls, Bullitt's party pitched camp near the mouth of Bear Grass Creek and the shoals of Corn Island. They proceeded to survey the area around the falls, charting the lands now included within the corporate limits of Louisville. The members of this party were enthusiastic over the climate and the fertility of the soil. Seeing possibilities for future wealth, they quit their surveying and hastened home to bring their families to Kentucky. Fate decreed otherwise, however, for the impending struggle with the Indians made immediate settlement impossible.

Other surveyors visited Kentucky during the year 1773. James Douglas, James Harrod (who had come out with Bullitt), Isaac Hite, and James Sandusky did some surveying along the Ohio. A General Thompson of Pennsylvania made a fruitless trip into the West on a surveying mission.

After having missed Bullitt's party in the spring, Simon Kenton returned to Pennsylvania to live, but unable to resist the lure of the West, he returned in the fall of 1773 to Kentucky, with a group of hunters and surveyors from the Monongahela country. This party hoped to combine surveying and hunting. Its activities were centered in the Big

Sandy Valley. Colonel William Preston, Surveyor for Fincastle County, sent three deputies to the West: Hancock Taylor, who had accompanied the McAfees, James Douglas, and John Floyd. The latter entered the Kentucky country in May, 1774, to survey land for several Virginians, one of whom was the "Scion of Liberty," Patrick Henry. Floyd made subsequent surveys extending in a triangle from opposite the mouth of the Scioto to two miles below the falls and thence to the Elkhorn plains (in the present counties of Scott, Fayette, and Woodford).

All of these surveyors were diligent in staking out large claims, laying out town sites, and noting physical characteristics, but not one of the surveys resulted in a settlement, until the time of Dunmore's War. The reappearance on the Ohio of James Harrod with Isaac Hite, James Sandusky, and twenty-nine other men was the most business-like attempt at settlement made during the early period. Harrod led his company up the Kentucky River to within the neighborhood of the present town of Harrodsburg (first called Harrodstown). After a short march overland, he selected a plot of ground and began building a permanent settlement. Lots were drawn to decide where the prospective settlements should be started. John Crow and James Brown drew the lot near the present town of Danville, James Harrod drew the Boiling Spring lot three miles east of his later settlement of Harrod's Fort, and James Wiley drew a lot three miles east of Harrodstown. At Boiling Springs, Harrod proceeded to build a number of rude log cabins. The land was laid off in one-half-acre "in lots" and ten-acre "out lots," and each member of the party was entitled to one of each.

Working with complete freedom, the Harrodstown settlers were not properly conscious of danger from the Indians. On July 20, 1774, while resting near a neighboring spring, a party of four men was surprised and fired upon. At the first firing, Jared Cowan was killed; two of the men, Jacob Sandusky and a companion, fled through the woods to the Ohio River and went to New Orleans, from whence they took ship to Philadelphia. The fourth member of the surprised party fled to the settlement to inform his companions of the attack.

This attack was to interrupt permanent western settlement for more than a year. Undoubtedly Harrod would have eventually succeeded with his undertaking, however, had it not been for the war provoked by Governor Dunmore and his agents. The defeat of the Indians in the French and Indian War and in Pontiac's Conspiracy, together with the white man's terms of peace at Stanwix and Hard Labor, had only increased ill feeling on the part of the Indians frequenting the Kentucky country. White settlers themselves were likewise at fault. It is true that many settlers along the exposed Virginia and Pennsylvania frontier experienced atrocities committed by Indians. But many were the fantastic stories of gruesome crimes committed by the savages, repeated around frontier firesides for the purpose of stirring white sentiment against the Indians. This propaganda resulted in a determination to rid the country of the Indian menace, regardless of moral considerations. Not only were the whites stirred by propaganda, but likewise the Indians. A story that a backwoodsman had murdered an Indian and his squaw because he believed they had killed his favorite dog, and a tale of the complete annihilation of men, women, and children in the whites' attack upon the savages caused the Indians to become more hostile than ever.

The Indian settlement faced both the western Virginia and Pennsylvania settlements. However, the Pennsylvanians were more adroit in getting along with their savage neighbors. The Indian was confident of fair treatment from the Pennsylvania Quakers, but he justly doubted the Virginians' sincerity. The Quakers felt that their relations with the Indian should be guided by no less moral considerations than similar relations with whites. Using the Quakers' unwillingness to regard the Indian wholly as an uncivilized savage as an excuse, the Virginians, in the spring of 1768, seized Fort Pitt and placed Dr. John Connolly in charge. Connolly and Governor Dunmore had a mutual interest in western lands; it was to the interest of both of these gentlemen to rid the country of the savages as expeditiously as possible. Provoking trouble was Connolly's outstanding skill. In April he sent a letter to the backwoodsmen warning them that the Shawnees were wholly unreliable. The letter caused the reaction which Connolly desired. Both the whites and the Indians regarded Connolly's letter as an open declaration of war. Soon after Connolly took charge of Fort Pitt, there occurred the "Greathouse atrocity." A group of peaceful Indians was ambushed and slain, among them members of the family of Logan, a Mingo chieftain. To avenge this atrocity, the venerable Logan took the war path and did not return until he had collected thirteen white scalps. By this time, the Indians of the whole northwestern region, under the leadership of Chief Cornstalk, were aroused and ready for war.

While Connolly was provoking an Indian war, Governor Dunmore sent three surveying parties into the western country under Hancock Taylor, John Taylor, and James Douglas. These surveyors, with the exception of Douglas, who remained close to the banks of the Kentucky River, were making surveys in the rich Elkhorn area in central Kentucky. Like Harrod they were unconscious of impending danger, and it was not until Hancock Taylor had been fatally wounded that they became alarmed.

Back at Williamsburg, the Governor made arrangements to warn his surveyors. In June he employed Daniel Boone and Michael (Holsteiner) Stoner to go to central Kentucky to order the surveyors to return home until the West was free from Indian troubles. Boone and Stoner made the trip, and on their way to the Ohio Falls they went by Harrodstown. Here Boone became so interested in the process of building a settlement that he forgot for a time the impending Indian war. In the face of danger he accepted a lot and co-operated with Evan Hinton in building a double log house. Trouble, however, was brewing too fast, and Boone was forced to leave Harrodstown, go to the falls, warn surveyors, and lead them home overland. Despite their willful delay, Boone and Stoner made the 800-mile round trip in sixty-two days.

The Virginia Governor, anxious to rid his frontier of the intermittent Indian raids, and, perhaps, to divert attention from the approaching American revolutionary struggle, led a campaign against the western savages. He led one wing of his army by Fort Pitt while General Andrew Lewis marched across country to the mouth of the Kanawha with the other. Having arrived at Fort Pitt, the Governor, taking counsel from a subordinate, changed his plans and marched to Pickaway Plains. A messenger was dispatched to inform the impatient Lewis of this change of plans, but Lewis in the meantime was faced with an oversubscribed and unequipped muster of rough and untrained backwoods militia. All the frontier from the upper Blue Ridges to the Watauga settlements was represented. This force was ideally fitted for individual fighting but was hard to handle as a group. When Dunmore's messenger arrived, Lewis made ready to join him, but Cornstalk was too well informed of the whites' predicament to permit such a thing to happen. When Lewis was ready to move his troops, he found that the promontory between the Kanawha and Ohio Rivers on which he was stationed was surrounded by at least 1,000 Shawnee, Wyandotte, and Mingo warriors. To take advantage of the divided white forces, Cornstalk decided to attack at once. During the night of October 9, 1774, the Indians crossed the river, and hard fighting began early the next morning. The Virginians suffered heavy losses in wounded and killed. Luckily for Lewis, the savages were discouraged because they failed to take the ridge as easily as they expected, and they left the scene of battle during the night of October 10. Although the Battle of Point Pleasant was in itself a defeat for the whites, they, nevertheless, dictated terms of peace. Governor Dunmore, hearing of Lewis' victory, returned his division to Virginia without its having engaged in a single battle with the Indians.

CHAPTER III

Storm Clouds of Revolution

B Y THE latter part of 1774 active efforts at settlement in Kentucky had ceased. Surveyors and prospective settlers had either returned to their homes east of the mountains, or they had gone to join Governor Dunmore's forces in the upper Ohio Valley. Only a few decaying land stakes and a number of unfinished log cabins at Harrodstown remained to tell the grim story of the white man's efforts to settle the West.

Boone, as was typical of all the early western visitors, dreamed of a western empire. When sent in 1774 to warn the surveyors of impending danger, he lingered at Harrodsburg, seeing perhaps in Harrod's activity a fulfillment of his own dreams. He, too, had planned such a settlement. On September 25, 1773, with winter just ahead, Boone, accompanied by his own and five other families, had set out for Kentucky. In the Powell River Valley they were joined by another party with sufficient men to bring their fighting strength up to "forty guns." Boone's superior knowledge of woodcraft made him the unanimous choice as leader. They traveled in pioneer style with drovers and guardsmen marching front and rear to drive the cattle, sheep, and hogs, and with the women and children marching in the center of the cavalcade with pack horses. Near Cumberland Gap the drovers in the rear were attacked by a roving band of savages, and six whites, including Boone's eldest son, were fatally wounded. This attack cooled the ardor of the immigrants, and, despite their leader's protest, they returned forty miles to the Clinch River Valley, where they settled for the winter. Thus one of the first efforts at permanent settlement was blighted in its infancy.

After the Battle of Point Pleasant, October 10, 1774, the American colonist again pushed toward the western country. This time, however, land companies, anxious to make money, promoted the western settlement. Land trading and speculation were considered laudable enter-

41

prises for those of ability. By the terms of the treaties of Fort Stanwix
and Hard Labor, land speculation gained new impetus. The Virginia
General Assembly was besieged by numerous petitioners, and each
petition found the assembly in a receptive mood.

On March 15, 1775, James Harrod and several members of his original company returned to their station and renewed activities of settling
the area south of the Kentucky River. A fort was constructed, and
immediately it became a focal point of activity for settlers coming over
the Wilderness Road from Virginia. There is no question but what
Harrodsburg was the first permanent settlement in Kentucky, but
because of the interruption caused by Dunmore's War and the activities
of Daniel Boone and Richard Henderson at Boonesborough during
the spring of 1775 this point has been disputed at times.

One of the best known of the western land speculators, Richard
Henderson, was, perhaps, representative of the general type. He was
born in Hanover County, Virginia, but moved in early life, in 1745, to
North Carolina, where he prepared himself for the practice of law.
He worked himself into royal favor, and, in 1769, when a change was
made in the English governing policy, Governor Tryon appointed
Henderson associate judge of the western district of North Carolina.
During the next year Henderson found the judicial bed full of thorns.
The tidewater officials were notorious in their discrimination against
and maltreatment of the settlers in the western district. So open was
the dissatisfaction that the Governor maintained armed troops in this
area. In September, 1770, the "Regulators" defied Governor Tryon's
forces, mobbed the Superior Court at Hillsboro, over which Judge
Henderson was presiding, and proceeded to write their own decisions
in a most bizarre manner. Henderson, unharmed by the "Regulators,"
was invited by them to remain on the bench. However, his better
judgment prompted him to take "French leave" during the night
following the raid.

Having no desire further to expose himself to the rage of the up-
country citizens, Judge Henderson deserted the bar and interested
himself in western land speculation; his first company bore his name.
The officials of this organization became eager listeners to stories of
hunters and scouts who had returned from the West. There is, in fact,
a confusing claim made by some of Judge Henderson's descendants

that Daniel Boone's early adventures into Kentucky were subsidized by Henderson. This is improbable. It is highly supposititious that Boone had any connections with the Henderson Company before 1773.

After Dunmore's War had made western settlement fairly safe, the Richard Henderson Company became more ambitious. Definite plans were made, surveys were sketched, and claims made ready. The company subsequently became known as the Transylvania Company. Boone's report of the West fired these promoters with new enthusiasm. Although a proclamation had been issued in the fall of 1774, announcing the organization of the new company and inviting prospective settlers to list their intentions at the company's office, this company had not as yet secured a land grant. On March 17, 1775, Judge Henderson, Colonel Nathaniel Hart, and other representatives of the Transylvania Company met with the Cherokees at the Sycamore Shoals in the Watauga River and concluded a treaty of purchase for that part of the western territory enclosed in the triangle of the Cumberland, Kentucky, and Ohio Rivers—the eastern boundary to extend as far east as the Cumberland ranges. For this huge stretch of territory the Transylvania officials paid 10,000 pounds. (Thus the Transylvania Company purchased land which had been bargained for several times.) With the Sycamore Shoals Treaty completed, Henderson purchased a trail-right to his company's grant and dispatched Daniel Boone with thirty companions to blaze the way from Cumberland Gap to the Kentucky River. Henderson followed in the wake of the trail blazers with a pack train. The hopes of the expedition were soon clouded. Boone reported the death of two of his men. William Calk, a member of the pack train party, recorded in his journal that they met a number of families returning to Virginia because the Indian hostilities in Kentucky threatened their lives.

Despite the deaths of two men, Boone's party reached the Kentucky River and there began the construction of a fort to protect themselves from the intermittent Indian raids. The pack train, after many difficulties, finally reached the Kentucky River camp. But with the Transylvania Company in Kentucky, Judge Henderson was not relieved of his troubles. Governor Martin of North Carolina denounced the project as one of "land pyrates." Governor Dunmore denied that Henderson had any rights under the Virginia laws of settlement. The

Virginia Assembly declared that Henderson's claims overlapped those of Virginia, and frontier officials were instructed to thwart Henderson in every possible way.

Loaded with cares and faced at every turn with obstacles, Judge Henderson insisted upon getting what he considered was his right. Officious soul that he was, he made plans to allot the territory which he acquired by the Sycamore Shoals agreement. On May 23, 1775, he issued a call to the other forts for delegates to meet in a general assembly at Boonesborough. The call stated that Boonesborough would be represented by six delegates, and Harrodsburg, St. Asaph, and Boiling Springs by four each. At the opening of the assembly Judge Henderson delivered the principal address. He drew a picture of a huge western state, the central figure of which was to be Henderson himself. He not only predicted a brilliant future, but dealt with realities by defending his company against scurrilous rumors. The assembly drafted nine legislative acts as follows, with provision for: the establishment of a judicature; punishment of criminals; outlawing profane swearing and Sabbath breaking; issuing writs of attachment; ascertaining sheriff and clerk fees; preserving the range; encouraging the improvement of horse-breeding; regulation of the militia; and provision for the preservation of wild game. This was an ambitious and forward looking program for any western settlement, but in the hands of the Transylvania Company it was a failure. The company disregarded the environmental influences as well as the character of the settlers themselves when they framed their dictatorial scheme of government. Nearly every settler in the western country was there because either he or his father before him had become disgruntled with the semiproprietary form of government and the quitrents of the eastern Atlantic colonies. These settlers had been on the move for a long time and had faced hardships and privations to reach this land of promise. Hand to hand fighting with the Indians would be necessary before the land west of the mountains might be theirs. Because of these conditions, the westerners were reluctant to take orders from a land company, especially when one man's trigger finger was worth just about as much as another's to the settlement.

The Transylvania Company made a valiant effort to gain a legal right to the western lands independently of Virginia. James Hogg was appointed by the proprietors at their session in Oxford, North Carolina, to represent the West in the Continental Congress. Henderson hoped that Hogg might get the ear of Dr. Benjamin Franklin and others who were known to be interested in western lands, so that through their influence Kentucky might become an independent colony. Franklin was interested as were the other eastern speculators, but it was necessary to consult Governor Patrick Henry of Virginia before the Continental legislature could take action. When the Virginia Governor was approached on the question, he promply refused to consider Henderson's proposal, as Judge Henderson, doubtlessly, feared he would.

Throughout the western country prospective settlers were out of sympathy with Henderson's high-handed acts. This displeasure prompted George Rogers Clark to call a meeting at Harrodsburg on June 6, 1776, to discuss the western situation. Unfortunately, Clark was delayed on the appointed date, and the settlers proceeded to act upon what they believed to be his plans. Clark and Gabriel Jones were elected representatives to the Virginia Assembly to request an extension of Virginia's protection to the West. This action displeased the youthful Clark, for he had intended proposing either the recognition of the western country by Virginia or the organization of an independent western colony. However, the people had acted, and Clark could only abide by their decision. Thus, the struggling young western settlement first appealed to the mother state for protection. The two representatives set forth over the Wilderness Trail to Williamsburg, but near Martin's Fort in the Cumberland foothills, they both contracted an acute case of "scald feet" and were delayed for several days while they treated their malady with tannic acid extracted from red oak bark. This delay was unfortunate, for it kept the delegates from arriving in Williamsburg before the adjournment of the assembly. Upon learning this, Jones proceeded to visit the Holston settlements, while Clark went on to Hanover County. Here Clark presented the westerners' case to Governor Henry, who supplied him with a letter of approval to the Council of State. This body was not too enthusiastic, because Kentucky had never been formally recognized as a part of Virginia. They did agree to lend Clark 500 pounds of powder, if he personally would assume all the responsibility. Clark, in his letter of refusal, informed the august council that the West would have to look elsewhere for protection, for a country not worth claiming was not worth protecting. This final argument was effective. The Governor's advisers issued an order on the Commandant at Pittsburgh to supply the Kentuckians with 500 pounds of powder for the protection of their settlement.

While the negotiations for the protection of the western country were being pushed by Clark, Henderson and Campbell of the Transylvania Company were in Virginia adroitly maneuvering a plan to have their company recognized by the general assembly. Possessed of this knowledge, the Harrodsburg delegates delayed their return trip until the meeting of the legislature in the autumn. When the assembly met, Clark and Jones were denied seats but were successful in having Kentucky County created out of the original western Virginia County of Fincastle, on December 31, 1776. This act sounded the death knell of the Transylvania Company, re-enforcing as it did the act of the preceding July which instructed the western settlers to hold their lands without paying quitrents. Henderson was later (November 4, 1778) given 200,000 acres of land between the Ohio and Green Rivers, and the land which the Transylvania Company claimed under the Sycamore Shoals Treaty was opened up to general settlement.

After adjustment of the western problem in the general assembly, the delegates planned to return home over the same route which they had taken into Virginia, but, to their chagrin, they learned that the Commandant at Pittsburgh had not forwarded the 500 pounds of powder to Kentucky. This necessitated a change in plans, and Clark and Jones returned home by way of Pittsburgh. In Pittsburgh they found crowds of Indians, supposedly there to assist in treaty making but in reality there to spy upon the immigrating whites. Clark resolved to leave for Kentucky with his powder at once. At Limestone Creek (near Maysville) the delegates buried their cargo in several places, set their raft afloat, and departed for Harrodsburg. At Hinkston's cabin on the south fork of the Licking they learned from two visiting surveyors that Colonel Todd was in the neighborhood with a company of militia. Clark waited two days for Todd's arrival; then, growing impatient, he resumed his journey alone to Harrodsburg. When the militia company arrived at Hinkston's and learned what had taken place, they immediately left for Limestone Creek with Jones as a Guide. As they approached the Upper Blue Licks, the party was attacked by a marauding band of Indians; Jones and one of his companions were slain, while two others were captured. The Indians drove the whole white party to flight, but not until they had sustained the loss of the Mingo Chief, Pluggy.

The attack at the Upper Blue Licks was the signal for scalping savages, said to be under the influence of the British Commander at Detroit, to overrun the country. After this encounter, the Kentucky forts were sorely tried. Every post in the western country was raided. McClelland's fort on the Elkhorn was the first to be attacked; then followed raids on Harrod's, Logan's, Boonesborough, and other forts. Indian raiders were in the territory and were running from one fort to another, hoping to catch their occupants off guard. By the fall of 1777 all of the settlers in the western country were driven into four forts: Harrod's, Logan's, Boone's, and McGary's. The westerners were suffering from their eastern brothers' struggle. The American Revolution was not confined to the eastern Atlantic coast alone.

When Washington took command of the American Army on July 3, 1775, the British prepared to make a strategic move on the West. Realizing that Washington relied upon hardy frontiersmen for fighting strength, Sir Guy Carlton encouraged British officials in the West to send their Indian allies against the whites. The English anticipated that once word reached Washington's army that frontier homes were being attacked, there would be a wholesale desertion from the American army. The guiding spirit behind the British movement in the West was Lieutenant Governor Hamilton who was stationed at Detroit. Hamilton had acquired a malodorous reputation as a "ha'r buyer." It was said in Kentucky that Governor Hamilton called in thousands of Indians and distributed among them scalping knives, tomahawks, and bloody belts to encourage them to wipe out the Kentucky settlements. That this state of affairs existed is doubtful, but at least the rumor stimulated action in Kentucky.

In Kentucky, George Rogers Clark, fully aware of the impending danger, assumed the leadership of the settlers. This was his chance to put his earlier training in frontier diplomacy and his intimate knowledge of frontier conditions into practice. One trip back to Williamsburg in behalf of the West had seasoned this youthful westerner for a second visit. Hardly had the gunpowder which he had secured on his first mission reached Harrodsburg before he knew that bolder efforts were necessary in order to save Kentucky. Each time a new warring party visited the settlements, the list of fatalities increased.

Conditions on the frontier were desperate. The Kentuckians had to act at once if they were to save their settlements. At Harrodsburg, Clark was planning a campaign against the British in the Northwest. This was daring, to say the least, but salvation was certain if the plan succeeded. Two spies, Samuel More and Benjamin Linn, were sent to the British posts on the Illinois and Wabash Rivers to reconnoiter. During their absence, the Indian attacks upon the settlements grew more regular. Boonesborough was twice attacked, two men were killed, and several wounded. At Kaskaskia, the Kentucky spies learned that the British maintained a drilled and vigilant garrison; that the French would unquestionably favor American occupation; and that the woods were full of savages spurred on to hostilities against the Americans by the English.

With this necessary information and definite plans for a campaign, Clark left for the Virginia capital on October 1, 1777, to solicit aid from Governor Patrick Henry. In Virginia, he first unfolded his plans to the Governor's intimate friends, Thomas Jefferson and George Wythe. They admired his daring but were dubious of the outcome of an attack on the Northwest forts. Clark asked for seven companies of fifty men to assist in the undertaking. This was an ambitious request at a time when Virginia was straining every effort to support Washington and to protect her immediate frontier.

On December 10, Governor Henry granted Clark an audience. The Governor was already familiar with Clark's intrepidity and expressed much interest in his plan. Although he sensibly considered the hazards of such an undertaking, he again signified his intention to support Clark. The Governor and his council agreed that the assembly should appropriate £1,200 in Virginia paper money and issue orders on the Commandant at Pittsburgh for boats and ammunition. Clark was to be commissioned Lieutenant Colonel, and he was to offer each volunteer 300 acres of land in the conquered territory. Because Governor Henry could not send Virginia troops west of the Ohio River without exceeding his authority, he and his council evaded this technicality by providing that all troops so assigned should be for the protection of Kentucky. They made no reference to the specific territory in which the troops were to fight.

Governor Henry issued Clark his instructions in two sets, one secret, and one public. The secret orders instructed Clark to make haste to capture all such artillery as was available in the enemy's camps and to treat all British captives humanely. The public orders instructed Colonel Clark to raise 350 troops for the protection of Kentucky. The secret orders were issued January 2, 1778. On January 15, Governor Henry issued a set of secondary instructions permitting the Kentuckian to extend his attack to any fort he deemed advisable.

Clark began to enlist men in the Redstone settlements on the Monongahela River in Pennsylvania. Since this country had been combed repeatedly for volunteers, Clark was unable to raise the necessary number of fighters. He was encouraged, however, by the promise of a good force from the Holston settlements, in spite of the fact that, by volunteering, the militiamen left their homes exposed to the attack of the enemy. In May, Colonel Clark left the Redstone settlements with 150 fighting men and as many prospective settlers. The destination of this expedition was to be either the mouth of the Kentucky River or the Ohio Falls. When the party reached the Kentucky, it was decided that the Falls were more suitable for a military base. When Clark landed his company at the Falls, he was chagrined to find only one company of Holston men awaiting his arrival, and not more than a dozen of these willing to adventure west of the Ohio. When the Kentucky settlements were solicited for assistance, only twenty men, one of whom was Simon Kenton, were willing to leave their families, since there was constant danger from Indian attacks.

Undaunted, the Northwest Expeditionary Forces set to work to establish a post on Corn Island and to drill the raw militiamen. On June 23, 1778, the Ohio had risen sufficiently to permit the company's light boats to float over the Falls. The war party, after a day and night of celebration, climbed into their pirogues on the morning of the twenty-fourth and pulled upstream a mile or so in order to gain the main channel. Thus began the long trek into the Northwest to conquer an empire. In outward appearances this ragtag party resembled bedraggled Indian traders rather than empire builders. At high noon the little fleet of pirogues drifted into the foaming rapids of the Ohio Falls, and at that very moment, as though a foreboding omen, the sun went into a total eclipse. To the superstitious minds of the backwoodsmen this omen foretold disaster.

From the Ohio Falls, Clark directed his flotilla to Barateria Island at the mouth of the Ohio, and here he prepared his troops for the 120-mile march through the forest and meadows from Fort Massac to Kaskaskia. A few hours after landing, the militiamen spied a party of traders going by in a boat. Clark ordered these men brought into camp, and he learned from them that they were eight days out of Kaskaskia. They reported the fort under the command of Monsieur Rocheblave, and the woods full of spies watching for the appearance of rebel bands. John Saunders, the leader of the party, was singled out as a guide, and the little frontier army set forth on foot for Kaskaskia. Only one mishap occurred during the trip: Saunders lost the trail. This was so extraordinary for a seasoned woodsman that Clark swore he would have Saunders killed if he didn't locate the trail immediately. The poor wretch was granted the privilege of wandering about for one hour under the careful supervision of armed guards; if at the end of this time he had not located the trail, he was to be executed. Fortune smiled upon the miserable Saunders, for he found his way. The party resumed its march and arrived a few miles above the town at a point on the Kaskaskia River on July 4. Clark concealed his men until nightfall. They then crossed the river and moved cautiously down to a farmhouse within a half mile of the fort. Here they learned that the garrison had relaxed its guard and that British soldiers and townspeople were spending a gay evening dancing. Near the farmhouse the little American army was put across the river, and Clark divided his company into two groups. One company was sent around the town while the other rushed into the fort and bound the startled commandant, Monsieur Rocheblave. Runners were sent through the streets to warn the people to stay indoors or suffer a severe penalty. Surprise could not have been more complete, for the Kentuckians had caught the little town of Kaskaskia completely off guard.

The French were frightened, for they had been led to believe by the

English that the "Long Knives" were more ferocious than the Indians. This belief was soon dispelled, however, when Clark allowed the French Catholics to convene unmolested in their church the day after the capture of the fort. At this meeting commissioners were appointed to request that the prisoners might remain with their families, a request speedily granted. The "Long Knives" were even more generous, however. They permitted the French complete civil and religious liberty and informed them that France had joined forces with the American colonies in their struggle for freedom. Accordingly, the French, under the leadership of Father Gibault, joyfully accepted the Americans as friends.

The capture of Kaskaskia was only a beginning. A small force of American and French troops, under the leadership of Joseph Bowman, captured Cahokia, where the French inhabitants greeted them with loud shouts of welcome.

Clark now held Kaskaskia and Cahokia, but the important post at Vincennes still remained in the enemy's hands. It was the central post of the southern division of British influence and lay almost midway between the Mississippi River country and Kentucky. Clark was anxious to capture this post, for he believed it would stifle British control of the territory and prove a useful stepping-stone to successful attempts on Detroit. At Kaskaskia and Cahokia, the Americans utilized their advantages. Representatives of western Indian tribes were called in, and, by subtle diplomacy, were converted from enemies to friends. Clark also courted the favor of his Spanish neighbors at St. Louis. There is a story to the effect that his relations with the Spanish led to a romance between him and the coy Terese de Leyba, the Governor General's sister.

Father Gibault was an able aid to the American cause; when consulted with regard to the possibility of the Americans taking Vincennes, he proved a most valuable source of information regarding Vincennes and its locality. He aided further by volunteering his services as an American agent to Vincennes. Simon Kenton had previously visited this post and reported its French inhabitants friendly to the Americans. Clark dispatched an embassy to the eastern fort on July 14. There were five members in this good-will party: Father Gibault, Dr. Lamont, Leonard Helm, and two American troopers. When the Vincennes natives were assured by Father Gibault that the Americans were friendly to the French, they pulled down the British flag and ran up the American colors. Several British officials and such of their Indian allies as were hanging around the fort were frightened into leaving. With Vincennes in American hands, Clark found that he had considerably expanded his responsibility. He was subsequently faced with three grave problems: protection of the captured forts, securing supplies, and maintaining his fighting force. The three months' term of enlistment for his men was at an end, and only individual choice of his soldiers assured him an army. By wise maneuvering, Clark was able to retain 100 of his men for an additional period of eight months' service. Those who insisted on withdrawing were sent back to the Ohio Falls under the leadership of Captain William Linn, with instructions to establish a fort.

While the Americans were struggling to make the necessary adjustments in order better to protect themselves, the "ha'r buyer" at Detroit was rapidly maturing plans for the recapture of the western forts. In October, 1778, Governor Hamilton personally led out of Detroit a detachment of the King's eighth regiment, a company of Detroit volunteers, a detachment of artillery, two militia companies, and a band of Indians. This army moved by water through the Great Lakes, down the Maumee and Wabash Rivers to Vincennes. Upon Hamilton's arrival at Vincennes, the French repudiated their American allegiance as readily as they had once claimed it.

Here at Vincennes, Hamilton, running true to British form, allowed the policy of procrastination to prevail. As he had four or five times the fighting strength of his American adversary, a move on Kaskaskia would have meant certain defeat for Clark's little force. With winter approaching and the flood waters in the numerous river basins rising, Governor Hamilton preferred to await the coming of spring. He dismissed his savage cohorts and permitted many of his regular troops to leave Vincennes, with instructions to report early in the spring. When this was done, the Governor settled down to spend a comfortable winter of waiting within the fort. At Kaskaskia, Clark realized that he would have to act at once or never. With the return of spring weather, Hamilton would inevitably crush him at Kaskaskia, thereby opening the road for a direct attack upon the Kentucky settlements.

The Americans had two alternatives: to retreat to Kentucky, or to attack Vincennes. To retreat to Kentucky would have, perhaps, resulted in ultimate defeat. To attack Vincennes was taking a long chance. Clark had an able informant and adviser in the trader, Francis Vigo. This obliging friend had just returned from Fort Vincennes, where he had been held a prisoner by the British commandant. While a prisoner, Vigo learned much of what was going on at the post.

Clark resolved to retake Vincennes immediately. On February 4, 1779, he dispatched a galley with a crew of forty-six men. This party was armed with rifles, two "four-pounders" and four "swivels," and carried instructions to meet the overland party on the Wabash River near Fort Vincennes. On the next day Clark and 130 men, 60 of whom were French volunteers, began the 240-mile advance across the flooded plains to surprise the British stronghold on the Wabash. This struggling journey from Kaskaskia to Vincennes is one of the epochal marches in American history. Clark's hardy troops walked and swam for miles through flooded bottom lands, and often they were unable to find an elevation on which to camp. They crossed the two branches of the Little Wabash and their lateral streams, the Embarrass and the Wabash Rivers, and, on February 23, came in sight of Vincennes. Upon nearing the post, Colonel Clark halted his men and sent out scouts to capture several hunters who were shooting ducks on a neighboring lagoon. These captives were dispatched into the town to warn the people to remain indoors. The Americans then watched with anxiety their messengers march into the village but were disappointed to note no immediate excitement. Shortly thereafter, many of the inhabitants appeared on the opposite side of the lake and looked intently in what Clark thought was his direction. He believed they were attempting to ascertain his fighting strength; therefore with youthful enthusiasm he prepared to create an impressive spectacle. He ordered the soldiers from Cahokia who had brought individual colors with them to unfurl these and mount them on staffs. Clark then marched his men around in a continuous formation over a small knoll in order to give the appearance of many hundreds of men marching. The Americans learned, however, that the spectators were watching ducks and geese swimming in the lake.

The rebel forces maneuvered around to the rear of the town; then

Clark dispatched Lieutenant Bailey to open fire on the fort. Even after the first shots were discharged, the British officers obstinately refused to believe that it was Clark and his American "rabble." Suffice it to say that when one of the British soldiers was shot down, the occupants of the fort were finally convinced that the commotion was not caused by drunken Indians as they had originally supposed. An intermittent firing was kept up throughout the night of February 23. The keen-eyed backwoodsmen concealed themselves behind rocks, trees, and walls, and when the British gunners attempted to touch off their cannon, the sharpshooters plucked off the fusiliers through the portholes.

On the following morning Governor Hamilton invited Colonel Clark to parley with him at a place of Clark's selection. They met in the Catholic church. Hamilton refused the terms suggested by Colonel Clark and expressed his determination to stand a siege rather than submit to the American's terms. However, on the second morning, February 25, 1779, Governor Hamilton reconsidered and accepted the honors of war for himself and his men. He and twenty-four of his troops were marched out, shackled, and sent through Kentucky to Williamsburg as prisoners of war.

This last move of the Americans broke British control in the West for the time being. As a direct result, many of the Indian tribes were wholly disaffected. In territorial gains the expedition was of great importance. The territory captured comprised the principal land exchanges embodied in the Treaty of Paris in 1783, although the effect of Clark's expedition on the peace negotiations is still a matter of dispute. Hamilton's surrender was timely in so far as the volunteer American forces were concerned. Had he proved obstinate, the Americans would have found themselves in a sorry plight. Captain Rogers failed to arrive in Vincennes on scheduled time with his galley and its arms, and, even with this assistance, Clark was ill fitted to confront a very powerful foe. If Hamilton had received any help at all from the outside, Clark's Northwest expedition would have had an entirely different end.

While Colonel Clark was busily engaged in planning his Northwest campaign at Harrodsburg, the neighboring fort of Boonesborough was experiencing extreme difficulty. On January 8, 1778, thirty inhabitants of the Kentucky fort went to the Lower Blue Licks to make salt. In order to sustain this party, Daniel Boone furnished its members with fresh supplies of venison. This plan succeeded until early in February, when Boone had the misfortune to be taken captive by hostile savages who marched him into the salt camp and captured twenty-eight of his salt-making companions. The whites were taken to Chillicothe, where they were disposed of in various ways. The Indians were overjoyed. The capture of twenty-nine whites at one blow was so exciting that they completely forgot to raid the fort at Boonesborough. Had they turned southward and stormed this post, it would have inevitably fallen into their hands.

On the march from the salt licks to Chillicothe and Detroit, Boone made himself such an amiable companion that Chief Blackfish refused to accept the large British reward for him. He kept Boone for an adopted son. In this role the Kentuckian was highly successful. His knowledge of Indian habits equipped him for coming events. As a contestant in shooting matches, Boone was always careful to be the poorer shot. In tests of physical strength he was always careful to be the weaker of the contestants, thereby incurring no jealousy on the part of his captors. In fact, Boone made such a good Indian that he was initiated into the tribe and given all the rights thereto, including a squaw and a dog.

Perhaps Daniel Boone would have enjoyed living with the Indians for a longer time had he not overheard their plans to attack Boonesborough. On June 16, while out hunting with his adopted tribesmen, he slipped away and covered the 160 miles to the Kentucky River settlement to warn his white companions of their impending danger. Boone made this journey without food except for a small bit which he was able to smuggle away in his blanket. In returning to Kentucky he did not dare fire his gun during the whole trip for fear he would attract the attention of his pursuers.

At Boonesborough the returned commander received a cool welcome, for some of the occupants of the fort were doubtful of his loyalty. With his plucked head and other Indian appearances, Boone was doubtless suspected of being the forerunner of a savage attack. Later, members of the party within the fort agitated the question of Boone's guilt to such an extent that he was placed on trial, charged with conspiracy and treason. Despite the quibbling over Boone's possible guilt, the Boonesborough inhabitants prepared the fort for an attack as promptly as possible. In due time (September 7, 1778) four hundred Indians and ten white companions, under the leadership of the French-Canadian officer, De Quindre, appeared before the fort. De Quindre demanded that Boone surrender his post. The Kentuckians begged for time to consider this demand. This granted, the besieged proceeded to place the fort and its seventy-five fighting men in further readiness to stand siege. At the end of two days the Americans heartily thanked their enemies for allowing additional time to prepare for an attack and refused to consent to any further terms.

Exasperated, De Quindre resorted to trickery. He invited a number of the settlers to come out of the fort to assist him in drawing up a treaty. The Americans refused to go further than the shadows of the stockade to such a meeting. When a treaty was finally made, the Indians insisted upon shaking hands with the whites, saying that two Indians equaled one white. The whites made a break for the protecting walls of their fort and prepared to fight. De Quindre next attempted to set fire to the fort by shooting fireballs onto the roofs of the cabins, but this plan failed, for there was much rain, and the occupants of the post were able to throw the balls off as fast as they were hurled. The enemy's leaders next attempted to take the fort by surprise. To do this they attempted to burrow underneath the foundations of the walls and then cut through into the yard of the stockade. The whites soon thwarted this scheme, and the Indians retreated, after a thirteen-day siege, in complete disgust. This Boonesborough triumph is of considerable significance in Kentucky history. If Boonesborough had fallen, the other forts would have been captured, and the whites would have been driven out of the West.

The Boonesborough attack was, by no means, the end of the Indian raids. Kentucky settlements were harassed so continually by these marauders that finally the phlegmatic County Lieutenant, John Bowman, was forced to enlist a body of militia, and, in 1779, proceeded against the Indian village of Chillicothe. Here Bowman mismanaged his expedition. His men destroyed the village of Chillicothe, but the Indians recovered this settlement and defeated the whites. Nevertheless this drive helped in quieting Indian attacks on the frontier for some time.

In the Northwest the partially victorious Clark was straining every nerve to make an attack on Sandusky, Mackinac, and Detroit. But he lacked the man power, and in November, 1779, he returned to Kentucky to complete the construction of the fort at the Ohio Falls. Clark encountered difficulties in Kentucky similar to those which had faced him in the Northwest. The hard winter of 1779–1780 caused numerous problems. Settlers, during the summer of 1779, had failed to produce sufficient food crops for even a mild winter. Small wonder then that, with a winter so severe that domestic animals froze and wild game starved to death in the woods, the lack of food almost destroyed this Kentucky settlement. To make the situation more acute, early spring brought 300 migrating families down the river to the impoverished Falls settlement.

Clark had realized for some time that the fort at the Falls might eventually become the key to the Northwest and also to the southern river system. In the spring of 1780, therefore, he set to work to complete Fort Jefferson at the mouth of the Ohio, in anticipation of a British attack which he believed to be imminent.

In the Northwest, British pride was smoldering under the defeat of English forces at Kaskaskia, Cahokia, and Vincennes. Preparations were under way to avenge these defeats. A triple western attack was planned: one force was to advance on St. Louis; a second to march on New Orleans from near Pensacola; and a third was to attack Clark at Fort Jefferson. These drives, however, were all thwarted. Clark sent assistance to his Spanish friends at St. Louis and scattered the British forces in that region. On the Ohio, the plans of the attacking party were likewise disrupted. Clark then hastened to take command of the combined Kentucky troops, but too late to make an offensive attack, for the British Commander, Captain Henry Bird, had recrossed the Ohio River from central Kentucky with his Canadian and Indian troops before the Kentuckians could organize.

Bird's first attacks were upon Ruddles' and Martin's forts. The successful attack on these two forts was perhaps his undoing, for his Indian troops satisfied themselves with the plunder and had no desire to go farther into Kentucky. Clark proceeded across the Ohio against Chillicothe and Piqua. At Piqua he put Simon Girty's Indian troops to rout; so that for some time to come there were few Indian attacks from this quarter.

As has been said, the English planned to attack Clark either at the Falls or at the settlements around Wheeling in western Virginia. This campaign was prefaced by the atrocities inflicted upon the Moravian Indians at the Ohio villiage of Gnadenhutten by David Williamson of Pennsylvania in March, 1782. In June, Williamson was defeated at Sandusky, and later the county seat of Westmoreland County, Pennsylvania, fell into savage hands. From this time on until after the Battle of Blue Licks in Kentucky, the Wyandottes and Delawares were at war with Pennsylvania, western Virginia, and Kentucky. They defeated Estill at Little Mountain (Mt. Sterling) and marched victoriously against Holder's Fort. In August they moved, under the leadership of British officers, farther into central Kentucky and laid siege to Bryan's Station. The invaders reached Bryan's Station on August 15, 1782, but they did not attack the fort until sunrise of the sixteenth. The British kept up an intermittent fire until 10 o'clock in the morning of the seventeenth. Captain Caldwell, despairing of reducing the fort, retreated, but not until he had destroyed several houses and all the livestock in sight. Four Kentuckians were killed and three wounded, but the Indians sustained a loss of five killed and two wounded.

News went out to all the other Kentucky stations that Bryan's was under fire, and by Sunday morning, August 18, a force of 182 men had gathered to pursue the enemy. Of the 182 men, 130 came from Lincoln County and the remainder from Fayette. The Lincoln militia was under the command of Lieutenant Colonel Stephen Trigg, and the Fayette levy was commanded by Colonel John Todd. From Bryan's Station the militia proceeded over the old buffalo trace which may have corresponded roughly with the present road from Lexington to the Blue Licks. On the morning of the nineteenth the Kentuckians reached the promontory overlooking the horseshoe bend of the Licking River, and from this vantage point they spied a party of the enemy silhouetted against the sky, comfortably retreating over the crest of the opposite ridge.

Here, in the bend of the Licking, the Kentuckians were opposed not only by savage foes, but by Mother Nature. This was an unfortunate place to clash with the enemy, because the Blue Licks were located in the Eden Shale belt, which meant that the soil was of poor quality, producing only a sparse growth of scrub oak, cedar, hickory, and maple. The buffalo had browsed down the shrubbery for some considerable area about the salt licks. Daniel Boone's son-in-law, Joseph Scholl, explained the barrenness of this area by saying that the buffalo came to drink at the saline springs, and their appetites were sharpened to eat every green thing in sight.

At the ford in the river the pursuers held their controversial conference. Accounts of the eye witnesses of what took place in this council show a great variation and only partly explain the long debate which preceded the crossing of the river. Undoubtedly, Trigg and his men were puzzled by the unconcern of their retreating enemy. This raised the question of whether they should attack at once or wait for Logan's forces. The Kentucky leaders were thoroughly conscious of the fact that further delay would only give Caldwell time to cross the Ohio River and make his escape, besides making further pursuit ridiculous. Hugh McGary, without question, showed impatience over the delay, as did many of his companions. Regardless of what happened in the council, the expedition finally plunged across the river and was led in fairly good order beyond the crest of the opposite hill behind which the enemy lay concealed. Crawford's forces took advantage of their natural surroundings. They were hidden in the narrow, overgrown ravine which led down to the river on the opposite side of the horseshoe bend, a position which enabled them to pour a devastating fire into the front ranks of the approaching Kentuckians. The enemy, in turn, was protected from receiving a heavy volley into its ranks. Boone led the Kentuckians' frontal attack. Their right wing was soon surrounded and broken; the center and left wing were then disrupted, so that the Kentucky troops were forced to retreat pell mell. The enemy had outguessed, out-maneuvered, and out-manned their rivals. After crossing the river, Benjamin Netherlands, a man who for some reason had an unenviable reputation as a coward and a "lagger," halted a number of his retreating companions long enough to fire a volley into the pursuing enemy's ranks and thus enable many of those floundering in the river to cross in safety.

The results of the Battle of the Blue Licks were most disheartening.

The Kentuckians suffered at least sixty fatalities and eight captures. Hugh McGary was made the scapegoat of the fiasco in that he was accused of spurring his fellow soldiers into the attack against the better judgment of his superior officers. Daniel Boone lost a son in the attack, Stephen Trigg was killed, and with him fell Majors Silas Harlan, John Todd, and Simon Bulger. The enemy's losses remain unknown. The battle marks virtually the end of organized Indian attacks upon Kentucky. Clark and Logan (in November, 1782) led a successful raid 130 miles up the course of the Miami River to destroy several Indian towns and storehouses.

CHAPTER IV

The Foundations of Kentucky Society

THE early pioneers who settled Kentucky were looking primarily for fertile lands. Since medieval times, Englishmen had measured wealth largely in terms of real property. Their descendants whc colonized North America retained this pronounced association between wealth (both economic and social) and land. When the English arrived at the Jamestown settlement, they spent much of their time searching for the choice tracts upon which to grow field crops. As population on the Atlantic seaboard increased, the English settlers, motivated, at least partly, by their inherited desire to possess broad acres, commenced to move westward. In the New World this old English conception of wealth gained new emphasis, especially in the southern colonies where by force of climatic and geographic conditions, agriculture was the chief means of livelihood.

Not only did favorable climatic and geographic conditions make agriculture a basis of livelihood, but the colonial system of cultivation made large plantations indispensable. In the tidewater region tillable lands were rapidly exhausted by the system of planting. Here fields were planted year after year to tobacco and corn, with no rotation with leguminous crops and no use of artificial fertilizers. In order to continue agricultural production, new soils had to be cleared for cultivation at least every seven years.

So definite was the idea that landholding should govern society that nearly all of the colonial legislation reflected its influence, and, in most cases, agriculturists felt that legislators should consider only agricultural and land laws. In every southern colony property qualifications were essential to the franchise. To be eligible for a seat in the colonial legislature, a person had to hold, in his own name, an estate in fee simple. These influences inevitably motivated a westward movement across the Alleghenies into the Kentucky country.

The western settlers were principally immigrants either of the first or second generation from England, Scotland, Ireland, France (Huguenots), and Germany. They had left their homes in order to assert their individual religious and political ideas and to seek fortunes in the West. When they landed in the North American ports of Savannah, Charleston, Norfolk, Baltimore, and Philadelphia, they found the land along the seaboard in the possession of earlier settlers. Therefore, they were forced to migrate farther westward. From Savannah and Charleston they moved up the rivers, principally along the Cape Fear River; or, from Norfolk, Baltimore, and Philadelphia into the Shenandoah Valley. Within these regions a new generation was born and educated to the ways of the western country.

When this general westward movement broke through the Appalachian barrier to enter Kentucky, Virginia, the mother colony, found herself too deeply involved in the Revolutionary struggle to regulate the distribution of her western lands. Several Virginia surveys had been made before the general immigration to Kentucky had begun, but the Virginia Assembly had not foreseen the immediate need of making definite provision for distribution of the western homesteads. None of the surveys, in fact, had provided for land distribution. Indeed, it was unfortunate that Kentucky was settled at a time when Virginia's government, because of the Revolutionary War conditions, was unable to enact orderly land laws.

It is little wonder that Kentucky's land system was in a serious tangle at an early date. Disregarding the King's proclamation of 1763, land speculators attempted to locate choice tracts of land. It is a well-known fact that no act on paper would have proved an effective restraint to restless adventurers and settlers. Even in 1768 the English agreed to keep their settlers east of a line drawn from a point on the North Carolina line, thirty-six miles east of Long Island in the Holston River, to Chiswell's lead mines on the Kanawha River in the present State of West Virginia. This agreement was soon violated, and, in 1770, a third line was proposed, in the Lochaber Treaty, to extend from six miles east of Long Island to the mouth of the Kanawha. Such limits of the grant included a part of eastern Kentucky.

This continual surging against the established line of limitation set up by Virginia resulted in much confusion. Settlers disregarded imaginary lines and were governed wholly by a desire to claim fertile land. Virginia's state government technically was not at fault during the early years; as a part of the English colonial system, it could make no laws abrogating royal proclamations or treaty agreements. It was not until after July 4, 1776, that Virginia could act with authority upon the land question. By this time it had to recognize the claims of squatters, French and Indian War veterans, and the grant of the Transylvania Company. Settlers moving to Kentucky soon discovered that their land claims were involved, in many instances, in a hopeless state of confusion with little chance of adjustment.

Settlers moved into Kentucky to select such tracts as they chose. Surveys were made to suit the individual. If a particular settler's choice had the shape of a crazy quilt, he was none the less satisfied. In this haphazard system of surveying, Kentuckians were hopelessly confused by overlapping claims. To add to this confusion, more than 900 claims, embracing 560,000 acres, had been registered by January, 1776, under the terms of the Transylvania grant.

The number of claimants continued to increase. Original patentees had received their grants at 20 shillings per hundred for 500 acres. Later, however, land prices jumped from 20 to 50 shillings per hundred, and each signer was allowed to claim 640 acres and an option on 340 additional acres for each taxable settler brought into the country. This increase in claimants and these increasing land prices continued to complicate the Kentucky land system.

By late summer of 1776 Kentucky's land system was in a rueful state of confusion. It was not until late in that year, however, that Virginia made an official move to rectify this situation. In 1777 the general assembly passed a law stipulating that all persons claiming land in Kentucky prior to June 24, 1776, were entitled to a grant of 400 acres and preemption rights to an additional 1,000 acres, provided the land were occupied before January of that year. In 1779 the Virginia Assembly passed a general land law which followed the outline of the one passed in 1777. This new statute permitted individual claimants 400 acres at $40.00 per hundred, provided they had built a cabin and grown a crop of corn on the claim prior to January 1, 1778.

This law of 1779 was not nearly so effective as it might have been had the Virginia Assembly followed the principle later instituted by the

Congress of the Confederation in the Northwest Ordinance of providing for surveys on the township and district basis. Most of the subsequent Kentucky land disputes could have been averted by an orderly system of original surveys. This new land law made only one innovation, that all claimants were required to register their surveys with the land court through the purchase of land warrants. This requirement, however, was only partially successful since many of the earlier settlers, who had rightful claims to their lands, were either occupied with making a living or were too ignorant and indifferent to register their claims. Both delinquent and rightful claimants became the victims of scheming rascals, who stood ready to claim all unregistered plots.

Virginia's western land laws were weak, because they did not provide for the supervision of private surveys. Each claimant prided himself upon his ability to recognize good land, disregarded previous surveys, and proceeded to the business of laying out his claim by personal choice. Under the haphazard system of surveying, numerous small plots of ground remained unregistered, and land speculators immediately issued blanket claims in order to secure possession of these neglected plots. Grants of the eighteenth century were not unlike present-day claims, for many of the abstracts rested upon the knowledge of some individual who professed to remember the boundaries of the original claims. In many Kentucky counties today, title lawyers have to walk over the entire area of a tract in order to get a definite notion of its shape, size, and location. Markers for land lines have always consisted of such unstable guides as trees, rocks, streams, and oftentimes houses. Accordingly, the only reliable and scientific guide the land owner has is the surveyor's chain.

The land court which Virginia established in the West in 1779 was composed of four members: William Fleming, Edmund Lynne, James Barbour, and Stephen Trigg. This body sat first at Harrodstown and then moved from community to community to adjudicate claims. The court passed upon claims and issued land warrants by the hundreds, with the result that it failed utterly to prevent duplication of surveys and registry of warrants. Its inefficiency led to innumerable disputes and much litigation. As the general confusion among landholders created a demand for legal talent, a large number of young lawyers found Kentucky a fertile field in which to practice. Perhaps the most outstanding of these young lawyers were John Cabell Breckinridge and Henry Clay. François Michaux, in writing of his experiences while traveling through Kentucky in 1802, noted that the "incertitude of property is an inexhaustible source of tedious and expensive lawsuits which serve to enrich the professional gentlemen of the country."

Great immigration movements to the West brought many human types over the mountains. First of all, as was typical of the American frontier from Jamestown to San Francisco, came the adventurous trappers and hunters who for lack of a stable interest in settlement laid few claims to land. They were followed by Indian fighters and surveyors, who first opened the country to settlement and who in turn were followed by indifferent land squatters. The latter class, by deadening the trees and burning off the underbrush, cleared small cornfields, from which, with a minimum amount of energy, they eked out a mere existence. They were soon supplanted almost entirely by planters who sent agents into the new settlements to buy small farms which they combined into plantations. This forced the squatters to move westward to new fields and leave the ever-expanding Kentucky settlements to newcomers who wished to establish permanent homes. Daniel Boone, the chief representative of the frontier, was typical of this restless and ever-moving pioneer class.

Many of the large estates of central Kentucky were created from numerous smaller claims, for the purchasers of the larger plantations, in most instances, were unwilling to brave the rigors of the frontier. They waited until the plantation home was completed before moving their families into the West. Overseers and slaves were sent ahead to clear land, build houses, and transport the family property from east of the mountains to the new home. Kentucky became almost as noted as colonial North Carolina in furnishing a haven for Virginia's younger sons. Under the primogeniture laws of Virginia, older sons inherited their father's estates, and younger sons were forced to seek their fortunes elsewhere. George Rogers Clark was a second son, who sought a new home in the West.

In a political sense, the institutional growth of Kentucky dates from the formation of Fincastle County in 1772. This county was created by Virginia as soon as it was apparent that the western country was to be settled. With a rapid increase in the western immigration, it was soon found that the authority of Fincastle County, which included all of Kentucky, was quite inadequate. Kentucky County was created in 1776, and Virginia transferred her system of local government to the western country. The Kentuckians were permitted to send two representatives to the assembly and to elect these officers: a sheriff, a county clerk, a coroner, a surveyor, a county lieutenant, and a county court clerk. The sheriff performed the functions of peace officer and tax-collector, and the county lieutenant had charge of local militia units. He had authority to act upon his own judgment in case of invasion within his own county, but at other times he was subject to the Governor's orders. Jurisdiction over minor civil and criminal cases belonged to the county court, or the court of quarter sessions, but major cases were transferred to the State Court at Richmond.

Much confusion arose in Kentucky because of the great distance to Richmond and the hardships of travel overland, factors which necessarily complicated the governing of Kentucky County. Partly to offset the inconvenience of legal jurisdiction, the Superior Court of Kentucky (1783) with George Muter, John Floyd, and Samuel McDowell, justices, and Walker Daniel, attorney general, was created. This court was granted limited appellate jurisdiction over the local courts.

Founding Local Units of Government

Kentucky County was divided into three local units by the creation of Fayette, Lincoln, and Jefferson Counties on November 1, 1780. Fayette County was located to the north and east of the Kentucky River; Lincoln County was located to the south and east of the Salt and Kentucky Rivers; and Jefferson County was located to the south of the Kentucky River and north and west of the Salt and Green Rivers. Each of these new counties was given partial local autonomy. Clerks of the counties were elected by popular choice, but other officials were appointed by the Governor of Virginia.

Along with the creation of three new counties, the western towns were taking form. This was perhaps a result of the interest of the early surveyors in locating town sites. Perhaps the site of Louisville, from the standpoint of original location, is the oldest in the state. Captain Bullitt, with much foresight, selected the territory surrounding the Ohio Falls as an ideal location for a future commercial metropolis

Boonesborough was incorporated in 1779 as the first organized Kentucky town and was followed in 1780 by the establishment of Louisville, Washington, and Limestone (Maysville). Lexington (named, according to Timothy Flint, for the battle of Lexington) was organized in 1781, after Robert Patterson and twenty-five companions had made the initial settlement in 1779. Geographically, the location of Lexington was fortunate in that the town became the transportation hub of the state. Nearly all the early Kentucky trails and roads passed through or near this village. Commerce going to and from the surrounding settlements, except that which went by river, passed through Lexington. Not only was Lexington the highway focus of the state, but it likewise became commercially the "queen city" of the West, a position it maintained until 1818 when Louisville as a river town began effectively to drain it of its commercial resources.

Frontier Society

Early Kentuckians were a simple-living, conscientious people, among whom crimes received immediate punishment. Men away on campaigns were scrupulous in moral conduct. Thievery was an abomination to the frontiersman's soul and reputation. On one particular occasion a poor wretch was caught stealing bread and so given the opprobrious name of "Bread Rounds" by his companions. In the settlements thievery was dealt with in a manner equally as effective. Often thieves were chastised with the "Law of Moses," or forty lashes, and petty criminals were disciplined by application of the "United States Flag," or thirteen stripes. Individuals guilty of horse thievery were punished with death. This crime was a capital offense because it deprived a man of his livelihood and sometimes his means of escape from danger. Gossipy women were permitted to practice their art unmolested but with a distinct understanding that recognized gossips were not to be taken seriously. If a man doubted the veracity of another and called him a liar, a fight was a certainty if the abused man were to save his reputation. Pioneer affairs of honor were settled in various ways. Occasionally the challenged and the challenger settled their disagreements with rifles according to the code duello. Most often, however, they fought it out hand to hand, resorting to the Virginia practice of gouging. In this practice opponents took every possible advantage of each other; ears were bitten off and eyes gouged out.

The pioneer was, generally, an easily satisfied individual. Making a living was a simple process, for the pioneer and his family were perfectly satisfied with what the seasons and the rifle brought them. In matters of clothing, the men were contented if they acquired an outfit consisting of a deer skin or linsey woolsey hunting shirt, a pair of heavy cotton drawers, leather breeches, a pair of woodsman's moccasins, and a coonskin cap.

Perhaps no article of frontier clothing was more important or more interesting than the moccasins the hunters wore, for little effort and few instruments were necessary to manufacture such simple footwear. Shoemakers required only pegging awls and rolls of "whang" leather with which to bind the seams. In many respects, the moccasin was ideal for footwear, since the hunter could walk all day without cramping his feet between stiff soles and uppers. Uppers of the ordinary moccasin were long enough to be tied about the wearer's legs to keep out sticks, pebbles, and snow. Moccasins intended for winter were made with the hair side of the leather turned in to keep the feet warm, and summer moccasins, when worn in winter, were stuffed with hair or wool. In spite of the comfort of this type of boot, the pioneer's feet were the source of nine tenths of his suffering, for the disease of "scald feet" was prevalent, and often its victims were disabled for several days by tender, aching feet. It will be recalled that this malady delayed George Rogers Clark and Gabriel Jones on their important journey to Williamsburg to request assistance for the West. Nearly every pioneer was a victim sooner or later of rheumatic troubles, which came as the result of tramping day after day with his feet encased in soggy, wet moccasins. Leather used in making moccasins was porous, and, of course, not waterproof; hence the wearer's feet were wet continually. The pioneers baked their feet before open fires at night as their only relief from rheumatism. It is interesting to note that Simon Girty, an inveterate woodsman, was an early victim of rheumatism. He was unable to take part in many of his frontier raids without suffering excruciating pains.

Contrary to belief, the pioneers did not live in the stockades for any great length of time, but they lived in separate cabins near the forts. When an Indian raid threatened, they loaded packhorses with household goods, herded together their cattle, hogs, sheep, and chickens, and rushed into the fortification.

Western fortresses were interesting from the standpoint of structure; they doubtless constitute the frontier's architectural contribution. Usually there were several cabins enclosed in strong puncheon walls. These walls were constructed of heavy timbers, twelve or fourteen feet in length, standing on end and placed as close together as possible. These timbers were pegged to railings which, in turn, were fastened to posts planted within the enclosure. In this way the wall presented a solid front, exposing no openings through which attackers could insert pry poles or torches. The upright pieces were pegged with self-expanding pins which made them virtually impervious to external efforts at destruction.

Every fort had from one to four blockhouses, well constructed of carefully notched heavy timbers. Cracks were chinked with clay to prevent an enemy from inserting torches or shooting arrows into the rooms of the house. Blockhouses were taller than the stockade walls, and their upper stories extended from two to four feet over the wall of the fortress. This extension enabled riflemen within the house to protect the walls of the fort against a surprise rush from its attackers. Guards from these upper stories were able to watch for fires which might be started against the walls. Log sides of these guardhouses were pierced with portholes which closely resembled those of a medieval English castle. From these coigns of vantage in the taller structures, frontier riflemen broke up the sieges of Indian invaders and prevented further outrages against their homes.

Life inside the walls of the frontier forts was drab, to say the least; for people, cows, horses, hogs, dogs, sheep, and chickens were crowded into a small space. Human occupants were often not any too congenial, for though there were many families in the forts who were genteel in manner, there were as many others of the rough and tumble, uncouth frontier type. No provisions were made for separation of the sexes, and this led to difficulties. Sewage disposal was impossible, and fortress commons became veritable breeding places for disease. As filth and litter of the courts drained into the springs, it was not uncommon for large puddles of filthy water to collect in the depression of the yards. It was by rare good fortune that the pioneers escaped smallpox epidemics or other contagious diseases during their confinement within the fortresses. Perhaps the only redeeming feature of fort life was an abundance of fresh air and frequent sunny days. No medicines, except simple home remedies concocted from native herbs, were available. There were no physicians to administer to the frontier ailments, and lack of sanitation in the forts caused a great number of families to move out into the open country, since they preferred to stand their ground with treacherous Indian foes rather than endure the exposure and congestion of fort life.

With all the trials and tribulations characteristic of settling a new country, where both animal and human kingdoms conspired against them, the Kentucky pioneers were not without their lighter and happier moments. Distinction in social rank was the exception rather than the rule, for one man's rifle was as effective as another's, if both were good shots.

It is a matter of history that on the American frontier there were fewer women that men and that this condition naturally led to whirlwind courtships and hurried marriages. A single woman was a highly coveted prize by every bachelor, and no woman, regardless of her homeliness of appearance or state of decrepitude, was forced to remain single for any length of time. Widows hardly donned their weeds before being "spoken for."

When courtships resulted in marriage, the whole community prepared to celebrate, for frontier weddings were generally accompanied by as much ritual, pomp, and ceremony as a royal nuptial. The bridegroom's friends gathered at his father's house, and from there they proceeded to the home of the bride. The party timed itself to arrive at the scene of the wedding shortly before noon, for the wedding was allowed to interfere in no way with the customary infare following the ceremony.

The wedding party constituted in reality a frontier dress parade. Guests were clothed in garments ranging from the typical deer skin and linsey woolsey, worn by the hunters as everyday clothing, to that of frayed and faded silks, of another day and another land, worn by some of the ladies. Most of the women, however, dressed in homespuns, and, in some cases, coarse linsey woolsey "Sunday" dresses, trimmed with ruffles taken from former-day finery. A miscellaneous collection of buttons and buckles "from over the mountains" served as ornaments.

After the wedding ceremony, the bridal party went from the home of the bride to that of the groom, where the infare was served. A cavalcade set forth, the young males of which performed numerous antics to the amusement of their lady escorts. Often a young gallant would purposely frighten the horse of his partner to hear her scream and to give him opportunity to rush to her rescue. Occasionally, the wedding party was a victim of practical jokers who preceded it and threw obstacles in the way by cutting down trees or tying grapevines across the path. When the merrymakers neared their destination, two of the more daring boys were singled out to "run for the bottle." This feat (which was really a horse race in the woods) required expert horsemanship, for the run was through the forest, over fallen trees and under low-hanging branches.

At the bridegroom's home, the infare consisted of nearly every kind of food known to the frontier. There were venison, beef, pork, and fowl. Vegetables, such as cabbage and potatoes, were present in abundance. There were biscuit and hoecakes, treacle (molasses), honey, sweetened corn meal mush, and milk. The "bottle" was passed freely, for the feast was a merry affair. Individuals traded witticisms; toasts were drunk to the newlyweds; jokes were told at the expense of the bridegroom; and, inevitably, prophecies of large families were made—prophecies which were soon fulfilled.

When the wedding banqueters had finished their revels at the festal board, the musicians, led always by the fiddler, struck up a merry tune for the dance, which lasted for hours. A unique dance was developed on the frontier in the well-known "square dance," and the Virginia reel was a favorite in some communities. Fiddlers confined their selections to favorite frontier "breakdown" tunes such as *Billy in the Low Ground, Fisher's Horn Pipe,* and *Barbara Allen,* tunes which still enliven dance parties of many Kentucky communities. In the midst of the evening's gaiety (about nine o'clock), a deputation of young ladies stole the bride away and put her to bed in the bridal chamber. This room was most often in the loft, which was reached by climbing a peg ladder to the hatch in the ceiling of the "big" room. When the ladies had finished their task, a group of young men stole the bridegroom away and saw that he was placed snugly beside his bride. Then the party continued until later in the evening, when the merrymakers returned to the kitchen for sustenance. In this lull the bride and bridegroom were not forgotten. A party climbed aloft with food and "Black Betty," the bottle, to minister to the hunger and thirst of the newlyweds.

Weddings were not always free of unfortunate consequences, for often there were those in the community who had been overlooked when the invitations were made. They felt that this snubbing justified revenge, and the favorite trick of the jealous ones was the shearing of tails, foretops, and manes of the wedding attendants' horses. Many were the revelers who returned home in an evil mood because some sneaking neighbor had disfigured their saddle horses.

Honeymoons were short, and bridal trips were unknown. The young couple proceeded to the business of making a home, if neither of the couple had been married before. Land was selected by the husband, often a part of his father's estate, and a site was cleared of trees and underbrush for the house which the neighbors assisted in building. Building a house of the ordinary log or rude frame type was a matter of only a few days' work; many times a log house was built in two days. When the house was finished, the young bride moved in, bringing with her, if she came of a thrifty family, a hope chest, containing some homespun clothing. She brought also a flax wheel, a cow and calf, and sometimes a brood mare. The young man supplied the land, the house, horses, hogs, chickens, and cows. Life was simple, expenses were few, and the young couple could, and seldom failed to, rear a large family. To the pioneer a large family was the symbol of domestic virtue; also, a family of several members could "roll logs," grow large crops, and better provide for themselves.

As there were no organized sports on the frontier, the chief diversions required individual prowess rather than concerted effort. Most of the sports were of the rough-and-tumble type, and athletic games were rugged. Frontiersmen enjoyed foot racing, wrestling (no holds barred), leap frog, kicking the hat (similar to modern soccer), fighting free-for-all, gambling, bragging, and markmanship. Early Kentuckians were proud of their ability to shoot, and able marksmen were numerous. Frequent notices, appearing in the *Kentucky Gazette,* mentioned "squirrel shoots" in which individual riflemen killed hundreds. This sport was interesting, for good marksmen seldom shot this small game anywhere except in the head. To "bark" a squirrel required shooting into the bark of the tree just under its stomach, to stun the animal and knock it to the ground.

Sports along the river were cruder than those of the inland communities. River landings, like the one at Louisville, gave rise to a rip-roaring, notorious people, who called themselves "half horse, half alligators, tipped with snapping turtles." A man's prowess in individual contests was boasted of freely and as freely demonstrated. Mike Fink was typical of the rough, rugged river braggarts. Mike delighted in boasting of his strength and power. His challenge to the whole Louisville river front ran thus: "Whoo-oop! bow your neck and spread for the kingdom of sorrow's a-coming! Hold me down to the earth, for I feel my powers a-working! Whoo-oop! I'm a child of sin; don't let me get a start! Smoked glass, here, for all! Don't attempt to look at me with the naked eye, gentlemen! When I'm playful I use the meridians of longitude and parallels of latitude for a seine, and drag the Atlantic Ocean for whales! I scratch my head with lightning and purr myself to sleep with thunder. . . ." These were extravagant boasts, but these were extravagant times. Men worked hard, played hard, and fought hard. Justice was, to the average frontiersman, an individual matter to be speedily meted out to one's enemies.

There was in the Blue Grass, however, the beginning of a more complex type of society. Society here rapidly absorbed elements of eastern culture. The flow of immigrants to this section brought with it the Englishman's fondness for horses, which naturally led to an early introduction of horse racing. It is impossible to determine the date when horse racing began in Kentucky. Undoubtedly, the first hunters were fond of horses and horse racing; hence the beginning of the institution dates back to the first visits of the whites to the state. In 1789 the first race course was established at Lexington, and from this beginning, organized racing has become one of the three state symbols, and proud boasts—whiskey, pretty women, and fast horses.

Lexington, in the Blue Grass, was not without its gayer moments, for it was visited as early as 1797 by traveling entertainers and wax galleries. Later, a place of amusement and exhibition adjoining Coleman's Tavern was built by George Saunders. Performances began at dark, and spectators paid three shillings and nine pence for seats in the pit, while less desirable seats in the gallery brought only two shillings and three pence. There is an account of a theatrical performance held in the Fayette County courthouse as early as 1798, and in 1807 John Melish, a western traveler, spoke highly of the numerous forms of amusements in the West.

Not only did traveling theatrical companies venture into the unsettled country west of the mountains, but there came carnivals to display waxen figures portraying interesting scenes and incidents in literature and history. Washington at Valley Forge, as President, and in other scenes were favorites. Years later a wax favorite was the duel between Aaron Burr and Alexander Hamilton.

Forerunners of the circus were passing through the West as early as 1805. An entry in the Trustees' Book of Lexington records an ordinance prohibiting citizens of the town from keeping pet panthers. In the same entry the town fathers gave Thomas Arden permission to "shew his lyon" upon payment of $5.00.

No historian can estimate the amount of satisfaction and amusement afforded by the fiddle and the dulcimer in the pioneer settlements. Among Scotch, Irish, English, and, to some extent, German immigrants, this form of entertainment was most popular. These backwoodsmen amused themselves for long hours with dances and music of their own creation (based upon English and Scotch folk tunes). Lovers of folk music are deeply indebted to the frontiersmen of Kentucky for creating and preserving American folk tunes and customs. As central Kentucky became more densely settled, and as planters from the East moved into fine houses in the Blue Grass, the more polite music of the harpsichord in the drawing room forced the "breakdown" fiddlers, dulcimer players, and their folk music and songs back into the highland districts. Frontier Kentuckians found boisterous music and dancing an expression of their contacts with a hardy environment. Indian raids and other hardships would have been unbearable without this familiar form of relaxation.

With the transfer of other social institutions from Virginia, the church found its way across the mountains. It is interesting to note, however, that the denominations were slow in making their appearance in the Kentucky country. The Presbyterians were first to appear. This denomination, under the leadership of Father David Rice and two assistants, under very trying circumstances, organized Presbyterian assemblies. Following the example of the Presbyterians, the Methodist Society (so called until 1820), the Baptists, and the German Lutherans made their appearance. In 1781 the Baptist "Traveling Church" came to Kentucky from Virginia. This congregation moved bodily from Virginia under the leadership of the Reverend Lewis Craig and Captain William Ellis. These denominations were influential in shaping the doctrinal beliefs of the frontier. It is significant that the Episcopal Church was among the last to appear in the West as an organized church. This tells its own story; westerners, for the most part, detested the English social and political systems which the Episcopal Church represented. It was partly this system of society which drove the Kentucky settlers out of the eastern seaboard colonies into the West.

Catholic missionaries exerted an early influence in the settlement of Kentucky. It is believed that Doctor Hart was (with the exception of Doctor Thomas Walker) the first physician to practice in the state. He and William Coomes, an Irishman, came out to the West to found a Catholic colony. Following these pioneers, a Catholic colony moved from Maryland to Kentucky in 1785. Almost the entire Catholic population of Kentucky immigrated from Saint Marys, Charles, and Prince George Counties, Maryland. This colony, which came in 1785, settled on Pottinger's Creek near the present city of Bardstown.

Protestant denominations were in the majority, and their ministers preached at large in an attempt to convert the masses to their particular faiths. By the time the state was admitted into the Union, the various Protestant ministers had become powerful community and political figures.

In recording that the church was tardy in moving westward, it is not to be inferred that the pioneers were without a type of religious faith. Sons of the frontier were believers who applied a practical religious belief of foreordination to their daily lives. Nearly everyone believed that his fate was a sealed book and very philosophically accepted his hardships as God-sent. This belief is typical of people who live close to nature. Religion on the frontier was as rugged and hard as the virgin oak. A dying hunter believed that he could invoke Divine mercy as promptly with oaths as he could with pious supplications.

From 1783 to 1784 the population of Kentucky expanded from approximately 12,000 to 24,000. From October 1786 to May 1787 the Adjutant at Fort Harmar, opposite Marietta, Ohio, counted 177 flatboats with 2,700 persons aboard. In 1788 it was estimated that 10,000 persons had floated down the Ohio River. In 1790, according to the first United States Census, there were over 70,000 persons in the District of Kentucky.

A majority of the immigrants had come into the district principally from North Carolina, Virginia, Maryland, and Pennsylvania. Immigrants from North Carolina and southwestern Virginia came over the Wilderness Road, but those from Maryland and Pennsylvania came down the Ohio River. One traveler has left an account of a visit to Kentucky during the great immigration period, in which he tells of seeing the roads lined with families moving westward. He found many of the immigrants stranded by the roadside for the want of food and clothing, and in one case a family attempted to travel barefooted through the snow.

This wholesale immigration was not without due cause, for a popularization of the frontier, coupled with a scarcity of good land available to immigrants along the east coast, proved influential. In Virginia and North Carolina, Tories had been maltreated, and in most cases they were deprived of their lands and forced to move themselves and families elsewhere. Revolutionary soldiers of Virginia were unpaid, and the state used her western lands to settle these debts; this accounts for the great number of soldiers of the Revolution buried in Kentucky. Richard Henry Lee's explanation of the increase of immigrants was based on the argument that the rate of taxation in Virginia was so rigid that the average family found it difficult to live after paying its taxes. Perhaps Colonel Lee was partly right, but, after all, the basic reason for the general emigration from Virginia to the West was the decreasing fertility of Virginia's soil.

Unlike incoming settlers, eastbound travelers were unable to take advantage of the currents of the streams to transport them to their destination. Parties went overland from Kentucky to Virginia. However, many families never returned to Virginia to visit, once they moved westward. The principal travelers between the West and the East were members of the Virginia Assembly and itinerant preachers and a few private individuals who were willing to undergo the hardships of the trip. Usually, before a journey began, the *Kentucky Gazette* carried a notice to the effect that a party was being formed at Crab Orchard for a trip back to Virginia. Crab Orchard was selected for the meeting place because it was at the forks of the Louisville and Lexington branches of the Wilderness Road. When these eastbound travelers met at Crab Orchard and started towards Virginia, they traveled in the same manner as Chaucer's Canterbury Pilgrims of the fourteenth century. Kentuckians wrote letters to friends in Virginia to be delivered by such travelers. Sometimes members of a family would not hear from one another for two or three years.

With an increase in population and an expansion of settled area, a division of the three counties of Kentucky became necessary. The first of the original trio to be divided was Jefferson County. In 1784 the eastern portion of this county formed Nelson County, and the next year Bourbon County was made from the northern portion of Fayette. In the same year (1785) Mercer and Madison Counties emerged from the northwestern portion of Lincoln.

CHAPTER V

A Struggle for Independence

THE struggle for Kentucky's autonomy was long drawn out, and political leaders were often disheartened over the results of their many conventions. The early Kentuckians were dissatisfied with their existing system of government for many practical reasons. As a large percentage of the population came from states other than Virginia, these immigrants were naturally prejudiced against submitting to the jurisdiction of the "Old Dominion." The distance from Kentucky to the seat of government at Williamsburg, and later at Richmond, was great, even greater than the number of statute miles indicated. Laws passed east of the mountains seldom satisfied the westerner's need for legislation. In many instances, when cases in litigation were subject to appeal from the ditrict courts to the Virginia Court of Appeals, the Kentuckians had to forgo the privilege of appeal because of the high cost involved. Appeals to the state's high court at Williamsburg were possible only in cases in which the parties concerned were wealthy enough to afford the transfer.

So imperative did the need for reform become that the western population resorted to the democratic right of petitioning. Numerous petitions were sent by the Kentuckians to the Virginia Assembly and to the Congress of the Confederation. These instruments were symptomatic of the citizens' chronic grievances. Some of the petitions were a combination of supplications for relief and threats of forcible separation in case the body petitioned did not make a favorable response. The Virginia Assembly was almost always liberal with its western district, and legislation requested by its citizens was given due consideration. These acts, prefaced with preambles summarizing the particular grievances which the acts proposed to remedy, remain a matter of record today.

The matter of public lands was the most frequent source of complaint. Virginia and the Congress of the Confederation were far from being in accord regarding the status of the claims of Virginia to the West. Coupled with this public dispute were the individual misunderstandings of the terms of land tenure. So vigorous were many of the disputes that the more radical leaders encouraged Tom Paine to aid them in their cause. Paine, a liberal philosopher, bearing the public stamp of infidel, proceeded to the task at hand. In his pamphlet, *The Public Good,* he challenged the authority of Virginia, by the limitations imposed upon her by the Proclamation of 1763, to govern the District of Kentucky. This pamphlet had a far-reaching effect. If Paine's contentions had been well founded, the Virginia laws would have been declared void, since all the public property not included within the boundaries of the Thirteen States reverted to the control of the Confederation. In this case, the individual landholder would have been left without a valid title to his property.

Following immediately upon the heels of Paine's stormy exposition were rumors set afloat by two scoundrels who had come into Kentucky for the purpose of land swindling. These swindlers, Pomeroy and Galloway, appeared in Louisville and Lexington respectively. They spread the disturbing rumor that the Congress of the Confederation was going to redistribute the western lands. This frightened the landholders out of their wits. The conspirators, however, were brought to trial and charged, under the provisions of an old Virginia statute, with spreading false news. In both cases, the defendants were convicted and sentenced, but each of them agreed to leave the state if pardoned. Public officials deemed the departure of these vagrants such good riddance that they let them go.

Obviously, with an increase in population there was also an increase in wealth, necessitating expansion of the local governing units. Kentucky, upon reaching this stage of her development, began to chafe under the limitations imposed by the laws of Virginia. Perhaps the most serious bone of contention between the Kentuckians and the Virginians was the question of defending the western settlements against the Indians. The local militia, under the direct supervision of the Governor of the state, could act with authority only after the consent of this official had been secured. Marauding bands of Indians were ever a menace to the communities. The Chickasaws and Chickamaugas from the South and the savage bands from the North played havoc with rural peace. So frequent did these raids become, that, in 1784, Colonel Benjamin Logan set out to remedy the situation. He called for a convention to meet in Danville on December 27, 1784, to discuss Kentucky's predicament and to provide for local protection. This first convention was the beginning of a long, uphill struggle for autonomy. Mann Butler has aptly said: "Nor can there in the whole history of American Government be found a career of such multiplied disappointments and abortive assemblies, as in the labors of Kentucky to be admitted into the Union." The first convention got no further than making immediate plans to check the invasion of the skulking Indian bands which continually laid waste to the countryside. Logan was careful to show that Kentucky was being invaded at will and that there was no central agent west of the mountains with authority to order the militia to make an offensive attack. The militia could fight within the boundaries of the state in cases of rebellion and invasion, but the district line limited its activities. Under such limitations county military officials were unable to attack the enemy's strongholds.

Delegates to the first convention came instructed to petition the mother state for permission to join the Confederation of States. Perhaps at no time in Kentucky's colorful history have the people been more anxious and willing to act. For the seaboard states the surrender of Cornwallis at Yorktown brought to an end many of the problems of the colonial system, but this was not true for Kentucky. Therefore, it was with the greatest enthusiasm that the Kentucky communities answered Logan's summons to send delegates to the Danville convention. At this meeting, Samuel McDowell and Thomas Todd were elected president and secretary. They served in this capacity throughout the ten conventions. The delegates expressed a profound regard for the established law. Until Virginia could reply to their recent petition, they wished to go no further than to voice their sentiments in general debate upon urgent questions confronting the community. The will of the assembly was to proceed along strict, ethical lines that would not antagonize Virginia.

The first convention adjourned, after making provisions for a second assembly. In the following May (1785) this convention met as instructed and proceeded with unfinished business. A second petition asking for relief in the protection of Kentucky's frontier was framed and submitted to the mother state. A set of five resolutions was adopted, providing: that permission for Kentucky's separation from Virginia be requested; that instructions be issued for a third convention to meet in Danville to consider the condition of the district; that delegates to future conventions be elected on the basis of population; and that all matters further concerning the district be referred to the next convention. This second convention, violating its instructions, asked for complete separation from Virginia without promising to affiliate with the Confederation. Doubtless most of the delegates were greatly influenced by the tottering condition of the Confederation, which certainly offered no immediate solution of the problems of protecting the western communities against Indian attacks. Many of the delegates deemed it wiser to await a turn in national affairs before taking further action. The British along the Great Lakes were undesirable neighbors. No American power had proved strong enough to drive them out of the Northwest or to enforce the terms of the Treaty of Paris.

Kentucky leaders were confronted with the problem of advocating immediate separation from Virginia, but, to many, it seemed that separation would be a "jump from the frying pan into the fire." As a western territory of Virginia, Kentucky's right of self-protection was limited. As a member of the Confederation, Kentucky would have to respect all existing trade agreements. These restrictions gave birth to the idea that Kentucky would become an independent state. Two addresses were drawn up and adopted by the second Convention. One of these was distributed as a broadside written in longhand, among the communities in Kentucky; the other was sent to Virginia. These addresses made known the westerner's grievances: a lack of authority to send troops into the enemy's territory; no executive power; laws made in Richmond were not adaptable to the prevailing social and economic system of the west; and, furthermore, these laws were slow in reaching the western country after their enactment; appeal of cases to the high court of Virginia was too expensive, because of the distance and the necessary transfer of witnesses, which tended to deprive Kentuckians of their cash resources; proximity to the seat of government of the citizens living east of the mountains, which caused discriminations against citizens of the West; and Kentucky and Virginia were without a common economic interest, which, of necessity, caused complications in the passage of certain economic laws.

James Wilkinson, who had distinguished himself as a Revolutionary soldier at Saratoga, New York, criticized Virginia's system of taxation as embodied in its new revenue act. This act proposed to tax, equally, all the districts under Virginia's supervision. With feeling running at fever heat, the second convention adopted two addresses, which, in all probability, were the handiwork of James Wilkinson, and before the second convention adjourned, it was suggested that there should be some advertising medium created. This resulted in the establishment, two years later, of the *Kentucky Gazette* at Lexington. The convention planned that this organ should act as a mold for public opinion relating to the district's struggle for separation from Virginia.

Before the adjournment of the second convention, citizens of several communities were electing delegates to a third. This convention, which assembled at Danville on August 8, 1785, considered unfinished business of the second convention and further discussed the question of separation. Perhaps the most notable member of the third convention was General James Wilkinson. He was a man of fine address, sound talent, exceedingly industrious, and wholly unscrupulous. It has been said "he made intrigue a trade and treason a profession." His uncanny ability to express himself in writing explains much of his success. To this bold adventurer the troubled waters of Kentucky proved a perfect setting for the advancement of his nefarious schemes of self-promotion. Wilkinson, through his shrewdness and ability to judge human nature, was able to divine the attitudes of his slower-witted fellow delegates at Danville and design his political maneuvers accordingly. He declared in the third convention that there was no difference between the obnoxious domestic tax of Virginia and the offensive British colonial taxes.

Results of Wilkinson's first address were so flattering that he wrote more. In a second appeal, one address, dispatched to the Virginia Assembly, was a militant threat of separation, while another, distributed in Kentucky, exposed the evils of Virginia's western policy and claimed unreasonable taxation and lack of protection against the Indians.

The third convention was definite in expressing Kentucky's desire for immediate relief. An address was dispatched to the Virginia Assembly by two trusted messengers, George Muter, justice of the Kentucky district court, and Harry Innes, attorney general. So optimistic were the delegates that this appeal would succeed that they adjourned the convention without providing for a fourth, thinking that the call for the next assembly would be for the purpose of framing a constitution. Instead of promoting further schemes of separation, various political leaders concerned themselves with plans for a state constitution. The arch-conservative, Judge Caleb Wallace, became so enthusiastic over Kentucky's prospects that he invited James Madison to move to the West. Madison was polite in his refusal, confessing that he disliked "your wilderness," and in a meaningless reply favored distribution of political powers to executive, legislative, and judicial branches.

Madison and other Virginia politicians were aware of the inevitable separation of Kentucky from Virginia. For proof of this assertion, one has only to study the Virginia Constitution of 1776. This constitution provided that if one or more territories were created west of the Alleghenies, the western line of Virginia was to follow the watershed of the Appalachian ranges. Contemporary politicians were divided in their opinions regarding the immediate need for separation of Kentucky from Virginia. James Monroe believed that Kentucky did not need a separate government, until he visited the West in 1785. He then condescended to say that Kentucky might be a desirable place to live. Jefferson, on the other hand, was loyal to his native Virginia. He opposed separation of Kentucky on the grounds that such a move tended to diminish Virginia's prestige among other states of the Confederation. He perhaps thought that Virginia had been liberal with Kentucky when, in 1776, it was granted representation in the assembly. In this same year the Virginia Assembly authorized the opening of a road from western Virginia into Kentucky over the Appalachian ranges.

On January 10, 1786, the Virginia Assembly responded to Kentucky's petitions and addresses by passing an "Enabling Act" which contained terms for Kentucky's separation. The Virginians were cautious, however, and stated clearly that Kentucky's separation would not be permitted until definite arrangements were made for its admission into the Confederation of States. Virginia was not unaware of what would happen if her western daughter became an independent and separate power. It was no secret that certain Kentuckians were diligently promoting selfish schemes for separation. The great republicans, Jefferson and Madison, expressed uneasiness for Kentucky's future as an independent state.

Sentiment in Kentucky favored the first enabling act, but, doubtless, Kentuckians were shocked when Virginia, instead of calling a constitutional convention, called for a fourth convention to consider further the question of separation. It was evident that Virginia was not going to let the area become a state without every possible safeguard, and, realizing that ambitious and selfish promoters would cause trouble, the Virginia Assembly did not intend to permit her western district to be given over to Spain.

The first enabling act provided that boundaries of the State of Kentucky were to remain the same as those of the Territory of Kentucky; private land claims based upon Virginia land laws were to remain unchanged; residents and nonresidents were to be treated alike; Kentucky was to assume a proportionate share of Virginia's Revolutionary War debt; land which Virginia had claimed to pay her Revolutionary soldiers was to be reserved for her until 1788; the Ohio River was to be free for the use of all citizens of the Union of States; and all disputes over the foregoing matters were to be settled by arbitration. The enabling act further stipulated that the fourth convention should meet in September, 1786, for the purpose of making arrangements to separate from Virginia not later than September 1, 1787, provided the Congress of the Confederation should relieve Virginia of her financial responsibilities to this district prior to June 1 of that year. In this connection, it is well worth noting that the addresses from the people of Kentucky to the Virginia Assembly made no mention of Kentucky's desire to enter the Union. This fact clearly portrays the ulterior motives of their promulgator, General Wilkinson. In Fayette County General Wilkinson's ingenuity was put to a severe test when he became a candidate for election to the fourth convention. He argued for complete independence of the western district. His policies were so bitterly assailed by his opponents that he was nearly defeated.

The Fourth Convention (September, 1786) got off to a slow start. George Rogers Clark and Benjamin Logan were called upon to enlist men to make a raid on the Wabash and Shawnee tribes who were harassing northern Kentucky. Many of the delegates joined the militia forces, thus leaving but a remnant of the original delegation to continue. In January, 1787, the remaining members of the convention selected John Marshall of Virginia to present Kentucky's problems to the Virginia Assembly, one of which was a need for additional time in which to consider the question of separation. Marshall was able to secure the desired extension of time. The Virginia Assembly passed a second enabling act, which made January 1, 1789, the date on which Kentucky might enter the Union, provided the Congress of the Confederation would approve the admission of the state prior to July 4, 1788.

Without further notice, the fourth convention adjourned *sine die*. Citizens of the western district were thoroughly discouraged. As additional fuel to the fires of discontent, Clark and Logan were censured by Governor Randolph for overstepping their authority when they raided the enemy's territory. This whole expedition was little short of an unhappy farce. Clark was not the successful soldier who had won distinction in the Northwest campaign. The "Hero of Vincennes" made a poor showing on his second visit to the banks of the Wabash. Where able courageous leadership had won him fame on his first expedition into the Northwest, failure to secure support of his men brought down censure upon his head on his second campaign.

An effective damper was placed upon the spirit of the West when the Spanish Governor at New Orleans unceremoniously withdrew the Americans' "right of deposit." He not only closed the port of New Orleans to Kentuckians and Americans in general, but he also questioned the free use of the lower Mississippi River. Simultaneously with Spanish withdrawal of the "right of deposit" and free use of the river, the rumor reached the western country (set afloat by a group of Pittsburgh agitators styling themselves a "Committee of Correspondence") that John Jay, Secretary of Foreign Affairs to the Congress of the Confederation, was attempting to trade the westerners' right to free passage over the river in order to gain commercial advantages for the East. John Jay, an easterner, had suggested to Don Gardoqui, the Spanish negotiator, that the Confederation, in exchange for certain trade rights, would cede the privilege of navigating the Mississippi, for a period of twenty-five or thirty years, to Spain. These suggestions violated the Treaties of Paris of 1763 and 1783. Spain had been generous in granting the Kentuckians use of the western rivers during the American

Revolution, but now she desired to strike a forceful blow at Great Britain.

After the Revolutionary struggle, Kentucky's population had increased rapidly, so that utilization of the central river systems was imperative as an outlet to market. Kentucky's tobacco, grain, and hemp fields yielded large quantities of produce which had to be sold if westerners were to prosper. In order to insure profit from their labor it was necessary for the Kentuckians to find a market which they could reach by cheap and easy transportation. The location of New Orleans in respect to Kentucky was ideal. Produce loaded on flatboats at Frankfort was landed at New Orleans without expenditure of any considerable amount of money or energy. Once the Kentucky farmer reached the New Orleans market, he could easily form connections with the eastern Atlantic seaboard, or with Europe by sea-going vessels.

Sectionalism early appeared in the Confederation. The East was diligent in its efforts to secure certain gains by sponsoring favorable legislation at the expense of other sections. The dispute which arose over John Jay's proposed trade agreement with Spain aligned the North against the South. It mattered little to the westerners that Jay's proposal failed of passage in Congress. The rumor had already shaped public opinion. Southerners and westerners were disgruntled. The group of individuals in Pittsburgh, acting as a self-appointed bureau of information, aroused public sentiment by generously flooding Kentucky with handbills condemning Jay's proposal.

A second handbill, dated March 29, 1788, was sent out by Messrs. Innes, Muter, Brown, and Sebastian. It advertised a convention to meet in Danville, in May, to issue a public protest against the Jay "outrage." Before the convention met, however, more definite information was available, and the refusal of the Congress of the Confederation to act favorably upon Jay's proposal was reassuring.

The westerners' feelings were now most sensitive to their situation. The slightest unfavorable move on the part of Virginia or Congress set the pot of discontent boiling. Kentucky was up in arms against Virginia for publicly censuring Clark and Logan for assuming authority to conduct their Indian raids. The mother state was accused of paralyzing the West by refusing free use of the militia. Columns of the *Kentucky Gazette* were filled with acrimonious discussions of the question of immediate separation. There were varying opinions regarding Kentucky's future. Conservatives wishing it to remain a district of Virginia justified their stand by saying that separation would be too expensive. Those who wished to separate from Virginia were also able to produce effective arguments.

On September 17, 1787, the fifth convention met in Danville to consider again the important question of separation. The delegates assembled, but the notorious Wilkinson was absent. He was shrewd enough to foresee the effects which tangible proof of the importance of the Mississippi River would have upon the fifth convention. Consequently, he took a cargo of produce to New Orleans where he disposed of it for a good price. Wilkinson transacted other business on this trip. He was suave enough in manner and glib enough of tongue to hoodwink even the ambitious Spanish Governor-General Miro. Miro agreed to accept Wilkinson's future shipments of produce in trade, if Wilkinson would represent Spain's interest in Kentucky. Sufficient plans were made by them to ruin the future reputations of many Kentucky leaders. Several months elapsed between the strange disappearance of General Wilkinson and his return to Lexington. It was said that when he returned to his home in Fayette County, it was in a "coach and four." After disposing of his produce in New Orleans at a fabulous price, he had gone by sea to Philadelphia. While in the East, he had bought a coach, horses, a store of merchandise, and a coffle of Negro slaves. These were impressively displayed in Lexington. Most important of his new possessions, however, was an agreement with General Miro guaranteeing Wilkinson the privilege of engaging, duty free, in the trade between Kentucky and New Orleans. Wilkinson stated that he had received $9.50 per hundred pounds for his tobacco in New Orleans, which was far above the price of $2.50 per hundred paid by Kentucky merchants.

Wilkinson, for reasons best known to himself, had acted as a self-appointed agent between Kentucky and its Spanish neighbors. Because of this action, Wilkinson was at first considered a friend of the West. He used his friendship to good advantage in both Kentucky and New Orleans.

In Kentucky he and his agent Peyton Short were able to drive a thriving trade. They circularized farmers, imploring them to deliver their produce to the banks of the Kentucky River so that it could be sold in New Orleans through the influence of Wilkinson and Company. These buyers argued effectively that they were in a position to get the best prices for their customers. The circular insisted that "Our J. Wilkinson alone will sell the produce to good advantage." This activity of "J. Wilkinson" definitely catalogued him as a shrewd, selfish promoter. His purpose was to get a strangle hold upon Kentucky's political and economic structure. He became ringleader of the Court Party, so named because it had as its ranking members judges of the court: John Brown, Benjamin Sebastian, and Harry Innes. These men were eager for Kentucky's declaration of independence. They believed that Kentucky as an independent state could open the Mississippi River to free navigation, thus placing it in a position to treat with the American Confederation upon most favorable terms.

In opposition to the Court Party was the Country Party. This latter group was led by such enthusiastic Federalists as Rice Bullock, Humphrey Marshall, and Robert Breckinridge. They opposed almost every principle advocated by the Court Party. They favored immediate separation, followed by immediate admission into the Union.

When the fifth convention met in September, 1787, it renewed the discussion of separation from Virginia. The Virginia Assembly was petitioned to authorize the election of John Brown to Congress. The Assembly complied with this request. Brown departed for Philadelphia in low spirits to begin the thankless task of representing the struggling District of Kentucky in an equally struggling national legislature. When the Kentucky "congressman" reached Philadelphia, he found the National Assembly in its death throes. He waited until the spring of 1788 before a quorum could be assembled to call the legislative session to order. He presented Kentucky's petition on July 3, one day before the expiration of the second enabling act. As the Congressional body was too near dissolution to consider legislation, the Kentucky petition was referred to the Congress of the United States for a decision.

John Brown was impressed with the indifference of the Congress of the Confederation. He construed its failure to act upon the admission of Kentucky into the Union as the handiwork of easterners who objected to the admission of additional western states. He was convinced that the District of Kentucky could drive a much better bargain with the Spanish at New Orleans than with the Americans at Philadelphia. Brown wrote George Muter a letter suggesting that Kentucky might at least consult Spain on the subject.

In Kentucky, arrangements were completed for the calling of a sixth convention. Between the adjournment of the fifth and the calling of the sixth convention (July 28, 1788), the Danville Political Club was organized. This club was a political debating society which met each Saturday night to debate the leading questions confronting the District of Kentucky and the Nation.

The hope of the sixth convention to frame a constitution for Kentucky was shattered by the indifference of Congress. Kentucky was in chaos. James Wilkinson was framing what he hoped would prove a perfect piece of intrigue. He was ready to introduce his plans, with the assistance of several able lieutenants, when the sixth convention adjourned *sine die.*

In spite of Kentucky's opposition, Virginia ratified the new National Constitution. After the report that Virginia had ratified the National Constitution, the District of Kentucky called for the election of delegates to the seventh convention. Wilkinson was again a candidate from Fayette County. He had no chance of winning without trickery. To escape defeat, he allied himself with four unscrupulous Court Party partisans and supported himself through their influence. When the smoke of the tempestuous election had cleared, Wilkinson had been elected by a slight and questionable majority.

When the seventh convention met, Governor Miro reminded Wilkinsion of his sworn allegiance to Spain. The astute Wilkinson answered the impatient notes of the Spanish Governor by beseeching him to be more patient. Wilkinson was certain that his opportunity would rise at the meeting of the seventh convention. He assured Miro that he would have two able lieutenants in Alexander Bullitt and Harry Innes. He further advised Miro that he thought it judicious to expose no more of their scheme to the convention than was necessary.

On November 4, 1788, the seventh convention assembled at Danville. The Court and Country Parties were about equally represented. "Corn Planter" and "Poplicola," in their articles in the *Kentucky Gazette,* brought up the question of separation before the convention met. One poetic contributor to the *Gazette* submitted a poem of eleven stanzas, which contained these ideas: the efforts at securing independence were beset on every hand by evil geniuses; the plots which were influencing the conventions were "forged in Hades under the supervision of His Satanic Majesty."

In the convention Wilkinson was first to speak. In his address he approached the problem in hand by stressing the importance of the Mississippi River to Kentucky. He drew a vivid picture of Kentucky's pitiful plight without the use of this great western river system, and, in closing, advocated an immediate declaration of independence. As Wilkinson finished his speech, he nodded to John Brown who rose to speak before Wilkinson was seated. The plan, as Wilkinson understood it, was for Brown to introduce the Spanish plot to annex Kentucky. However, Brown had experienced a change of heart. He informed the convention that he was going to expose the whole Spanish conspiracy, excepting some private correspondence between himself and Governor Miro. He said that Kentucky was in a favorable position to secure whatever she might desire from Congress, provided the members of the convention acted in "unison." He failed to explain on what points, other than opposing the Spanish conspiracy, the convention should act in unison. When Brown took his seat, he had completely killed Wilkinson's scheme. The Spanish plot was now definitely defeated. The ambitious Wilkinson refused to admit his downfall without putting up a fight. He secured permission to address the convention a second time. On this occasion he asked the privilege to read an essay of twenty or more pages on the navigation of the Mississippi River. This essay was a harmless, practical discourse upon the economic importance of the western rivers to the industrial and commercial development of Kentucky. The only mystery connected with this performance was the disappearance of the essay. Wilkinson was ably supported in this final struggle by Benjamin Sebastian, who was later proved to be a pensioner of Spain. It was learned that Wilkinson handed the essay, page by page as it was read, to Sebastian, who destroyed it. The assembly voted its perfunctory thanks to General Wilkinson and adjourned. The moment for a declaration of Kentucky's independence had passed. The promoters of the Spanish conspiracy were left buried in the wreckage of their grandiose and impossible scheme of annexing Kentucky to Spain.

In the meantime Virginia learned that the Congress of the Confederation had failed to act upon the admission of Kentucky and generously passed (December 27, 1788) a third enabling act. This expressed Virginia's willingness for Kentucky to separate, provided such a separation took place in regular procedure. Two new restrictions were imposed upon Kentucky in the third act. First, Kentucky was asked to assume a proportionate share of Virginia's public debt, and second, the western district was to remain dependent until Virginia could complete the surveys of land which she had begun for the purpose of paying off her Revolutionary officers and soldiers.

The third enabling act created a general state of confusion. In the meantime, the old Confederation gave way to the new Congress, which was inaugurated in April, 1789. In July the eighth convention met in Danville. Stormy debates on the two new provisions imposed by the third enabling act marked the opening of this convention. A memorial was sent to the Virginia Assembly requesting an amendment of the third act to grant Kentucky the same liberal terms as those embodied in the first two acts. Without further action the eighth convention declared a recess to await Virginia's reply. This reply was delayed until December when the recessed convention adjourned *sine die*. The Virginia Assembly on December 18 passed a fourth enabling act, reiterating the terms of the first two acts.

The disappointment of the seventh convention was not sufficient to dampen the spirits of the indomitable Wilkinson. In the months between the meeting of the seventh and ninth conventions he busied himself with plans for reconstructing the Spanish plot. He wrote Miro a reassuring note in which he urged patience. In the same letter he listed what he believed to be the purchase price of prominent Kentucky leaders. The list of prices was as follows: George Nicholas, $2,000; Harry Innes, Benjamin Sebastian, John Brown, Caleb Wallace, Joshua Fowler, General Lawson, Thomas Marshall, and Alexander Bullitt, $1,000; Benjamin Logan, Isaac Shelby, and James Garrard, $800; William Woods, Henry Lee, Robert Johnson, Richard Taylor, Green Clay, Samuel Taylor, and Robert Caldwell, $500; but "Humphrey Marshall, a villain without principles, unscrupulous and may cause us much harm" should have only $600.

When the new National Government under the Constitution came into existence in April, 1789, the matter of Kentucky's protection was one of the first considered. In Kentucky, arrangements were under way for calling the ninth convention. As usual, this convention was expected to pave the way for Kentucky's admission into the Union. On July 26, 1790, the ninth convention met in Danville and accepted the terms set forth in Virginia's fourth enabling act. This provided that Kentucky should be admitted into the Union by June 1, 1792. Definite plans were made to draft a constitution by that time. Virginia's aid was solicited. James W. Marshall was dispatched to Philadelphia to confer with President Washington on the question of admitting Kentucky into the Union. Washington was favorably disposed toward the proposal and recommended to Congress the state's admission. On February 4, 1791, both houses of the national legislature authorized the admission of Kentucky. The westerners, however, were slow in preparing their constitution. The tenth convention met early in April of 1792, but it was not until June 1, that Kentucky became the fifteenth member of the Union. (Vermont was admitted as the fourteenth state.) Perhaps no state in the Union today, unless it be Kansas, duplicated Kentucky's unreasonably long struggle for admission.

An analysis of the first constitution of Kentucky reveals some interesting features of early American democracy. During the interval between the ninth and tenth conventions the public was free to express its views on the approaching constitutional convention. Columns of the *Kentucky Gazette* were flooded with essays setting forth reasonable and unreasonable constitutional theories. Perhaps the arch defender of the common democracy was "A.B.C.," who declared for representation for every class, caste, and denomination. The Danville Political Club found the subject of constitution making of inexhaustible interest. Members of the club spoke at length on the theory and principles of constitutional governments from Plato to Tom Paine. Some of the communities declared for a single-house legislature, while others were as positive that they wanted a bicameral system. The mother state of Virginia had set the example of choosing representatives by counties, disregarding the density of population. Most of the Kentucky communities disliked the district system of representation but favored the apportionment system. The Danville Political Club was vehemently in favor of the latter principle.

So thoroughly were the people aroused over the question of constitution making that many individuals produced sample constitutions. In a county convention held at Sinking Springs in November, 1791, citizens of Bourbon outlined what to them was an ideal constitution. The counties attempted to dictate to their delegates, but fortunately these local instructions were soon forgotten when the delegates assembled.

When the constitution of Kentucky was submitted to the United States Congress for approval, it was found to be a unique document. It was the handiwork of constitutionalists who were devoted to the cause of plain democracy. If the document was not structurally the most democratic instrument of its kind in existence, it was so in intent. The first constitution of Kentucky was the fruit of seven trying years of bickering with the (then defunct) Confederation and the State of Virginia. Many of the principles set forth in the document were based upon experience rather than upon constitutional precedent. The western environment was effective in shaping a new political mind. Both religious and property qualifications were abolished as prerequisites for the franchise. The constitution was emphatic on the point that all free, white males twenty-one years of age or more, and residents of the state, should be permitted to vote.

Following the example of the Federal Constitution, the Kentucky document provided for three departments: executive, legislative, and judicial. The Governor and senators were to be elected for a period of four years by an electoral college. This body in turn was to be elected by the vote of the people in the same manner as in the election of the members of the lower house of the legislature. The members of the lower house were elected annually. Members of the court were elected for life, or during good behavior. The court was charged with the duties of protecting the state's constitution. It was also given both original and appellate jurisdiction.

When the state legislature met for the first time, there were eight senators. This number was increased later to one senator for every four additional members elected to the house, until each county was represented in the upper house. After every county was represented in the senate, additional senators were elected on the basis of population. The senators had to be twenty-four years of age and two years a citizen of the state. The senate was instructed to elect a speaker, who would preside over the senate and act in the capacity of Governor in the absence of that official from the state. (The first constitution made no provision for a Lieutenant Governor.) One fourth of the senators, elected for a term of four years, retired each year. During the first four years the constitution was in effect, the senators were divided into four groups. One fourth of the body retired annually until the four-year plan of rotation could be put into force.

Members of the lower house had to meet the same requirements as those in the senate. The house had forty original members, but this number was increased with the growth of population.

The first constitution granted the legislature power to regulate its own membership; to organize both houses; to punish or expel recalcitrant members, provided two thirds of the membership of each house voted in the affirmative; to keep and publish a journal; one house not to recess for more than three days without adjournment of the other; members of each house to be compensated at the rate of six shillings per day. Except for treason, felony, and breach of peace, members were free from arrest; no member could be appointed to public office during the period of his tenure of office nor for one year thereafter, except to such offices as the people should elect him; all bills of revenue were to originate in the house; every member of the house and senate was to be required to take an oath that he had not accepted or given a bribe or "treat" to any interested person, before he could act upon revenue matters. Every bill passed by both houses was to be sent to the Governor for his signature. Failure of the Governor to sign the bill required a two thirds vote of each house to pass the bill over the executive veto. Every order, resolution, or vote had to be concurred in by both houses and the Governor, or passed over the Governor's veto by the necessary two thirds majority.

The supreme executive power of the government was vested in the Governor. As the chief executive, the Governor was empowered to make official appointments; to act as chief of militia; to fill official vacancies; to remit fines, grant reprieves and pardons; to receive reports from departments of state; to recommend measures to the legislature;

to call special sessions of the general assembly; to execute laws; to issue a statement to the assembly on the state of the Commonwealth; and to sign or veto acts of the assembly.

Affixed to the first constitution under article XII were twenty-eight sections constituting the bill of rights. This article guaranteed: political equality for all men; democracy of government; freedom of religious creed; free elections; free press; the right of the press to publish the true state of public affairs without threat of libel suit; the people to be secure in their persons, houses, and papers from unreasonable search and seizure; jury trial for all criminals, and only persons in public office or militia service to be proceeded against criminally by information; all criminals to be tried and convicted only once for each misdemeanor; courts to be open to all persons; no *ex post facto* laws; no person to be attainted of treason by the legislature; no attainder to work corruption of blood; no forfeiture of suicides' estates; the free right of peaceable assembly, and the right of citizens to bear arms in defense of themselves or the state; soldiers not to be quartered in private homes in peace times; no titles of nobility; free emigration from the state; and a statement that these articles should forever remain inviolate.

Article IX of the constitution, assuring slavery constitutional protection, created a furor. The Baptists and Presbyterians were bitterly opposed to the institution of slavery. Father David Rice, the chief exponent of the Presbyterian view, led the fight against the slavery article. His fight, however, proved detrimental to the clergy's cause, for the legislature made no provisions for a chaplain. Harry Innes was the only member of the constitutional convention, other than the eleven clergymen, who opposed slavery. When the final vote was taken on the question of slavery, the article was adopted by a vote of twenty-six to sixteen. This article prohibited the passage of legislation which tended to abolish slavery in the state.

Another function of the convention was to provide for the seat of government. Article X stipulated that the house of representatives, at its first session, should select twenty-one names. The representatives of Fayette and Mercer Counties were then to strike out alternately all except five of the names. This remaining committee of five was authorized to select the capital site and to lay out a town, unless an established town was chosen.

The first constitutional convention overlooked one factor of importance which prevented its work from being thoroughly democratic. In all its careful procedure to insure the people a maximum amount of democratic control, the first constitution was silent on the subject of public education. No provision was made for the establishment of a public educational commission which would guarantee the common man, upon whom the constitutional convention was so anxious to bestow the right of franchise, equal opportunity in securing an education. The public school idea was not without precedent at this time, since the states of Georgia and North Carolina had already provided for schools at public expense.

The convention which framed the first constitution had no idea that its work would be permanent. Provisions were made in article XI for a vote upon the constitution in 1797. If at that time the people were dissatisfied, they could call a second constitutional convention for the purpose of correcting any blunders made in 1792.

When the Congressional committee presented the Kentucky constitution to President Washington, it called attention to the unique features of the document. This committee suggested to the President that the document was an outstanding monument to the law-making ability of an enlightened people. This democratic document, however, was an incongruous mixture of fear, doubt, faith, and hope. It was the fruit of many years of struggle during which Kentucky feared the loss of the free use of the western river system would destroy its economic and social systems. There is no yardstick by which the influence of local environment can be measured in the framing of this first constitution, but it is a certainty that this influence was great.

Kentucky's admission into the Union in 1792 presented an interesting situation. The state had a population of 73,000 people (13,000 more than the number required for admission by the second Northwest Ordinance), with not one native-born individual old enough to cast a vote under the laws of the constitution.

CHAPTER VI

Statehood and Its Problems

Harmar, St. Clair, Wayne

K ENTUCKY'S Indian troubles were not to end with the close of the Revolutionary War. In 1786 Clark made a brave stand against the Indians, but the National Government failed to treat with them for peace. While the Kentuckians were making an attempt to ·separate from Virginia to enter the Confederation, they were having to fight for the protection of their homes. Before the seventh Kentucky constitutional convention met, Governor Randolph of Virginia expressed the belief that the central government would assume the problem of frontier protection. He implored the Kentuckians to withhold their raids into Indian country and to await further developments, but Kentucky could ill afford to do this, for her exposed frontier along the Ohio was over 500 miles in length. Furthermore, there were indications that a few scattered military posts would be all the protection the National Government could supply, and that these in no sense would be sufficient protection for the Kentucky communities. Almost every day some group of travelers or frontier homes was rifled by skulking bands of Indians, who came from north of the Ohio to kill and to pillage. National military officials of the Northwest post added more worries when they dismissed their paid scouts and left the frontier with no system of alarm, so that Indian attacks came without forewarning.

United States military officials further retarded immediate action in emergencies by requiring settlers to notify county lieutenants of Indian raids, and the lieutenants, in turn, to notify the national officials. This indicated clearly that the Government at Philadelphia regarded Kentucky's numerous complaints merely as those of dissatisfied frontiersmen. However, it is true that the central government itself was really in no position to act.

General Harmar, an official Indian agent, after making a raid up the

Scioto River and into the Indian country, negotiated a treaty with some of the warring tribes, but the savages continued their attacks on Kentucky. Early in 1790 Generals Harmar and St. Clair held a conference at which they agreed that the Indians should be attacked in their villages in the Northwest. This created new difficulties; regular army forces were too weak to conduct such a campaign, and it became necessary to enlist volunteers from Kentucky and Pennsylvania. Kentucky militiamen were independent and scoffed at the idea of serving under men of the regular army, officers whom they believed to be unfamiliar with frontier methods of warfare. Nevertheless, by September 30, 1790, 1,453 men had gathered at Fort Washington. On this date the expedition got under way, after much petty bickering as to whether Colonel Trotter or Colonel John Hardin should command the volunteers. Colonel Hardin was given the major command of the Kentucky militia under General Harmar, while Trotter was appeased with a lesser position. Neither of these officers, however, was truly worthy of his command, for on reaching the enemy's territory they became demoralized and allowed their men to become hopelessly scattered. The appearance of stray Indians caused the Kentucky officers to desert their men to give chase, and, unfortunately, Hardin himself gave too little attention to the exigencies of future battle. On October 28 Hardin's men were led into a trap, and all but nine of them turned and fled, leaving General Harmar's men out of position and ineffective. When Hardin's disgraceful retreat became known, the army "about faced" for Fort Washington (Cincinnati). Hardin, however, in this moment of disgrace, persuaded Harmar to give him an opportunity to regain his honor by making another attack; he was allowed to return to the enemy's villages with 340 militiamen and 60 regulars. Hardin's ill-advised and unsuccessful attack on the Indians from the rear made his second retreat more disastrous than the first.

Hardin and Harmar were court-martialed for lack of caution, but because of the good arguments presented in their behalf, they were acquitted, and Harmar soon thereafter resigned from the service.

St. Clair

Conditions along the Kentucky frontier following Harmar's defeat became insufferable. Parties of immigrants floating down the Ohio

River were attacked constantly by Indians. So flagrant did these attacks become that Judge Harry Innes, in a letter to Secretary of War Knox, estimated that 1,500 persons had been killed or captured between 1783 and 1790. He estimated further that 20,000 horses and property worth over 15,000 pounds had been stolen or destroyed. In response to the West's plea for help, the Federal Government established a weak cordon of posts along the frontier, but few of these, because of the distance from Kentucky, were effective.

President Washington called upon Senator John Brown for advice on the western situation. An interview resulted in the appointment of a military board in Kentucky composed of John Brown, Isaac Shelby, Benjamin Logan, Charles Scott, and Harry Innes. These men were instructed to investigate the necessity for armed troops along the frontier and to report their findings. After considerable wrangling, the board favored war against the Indians in their own territory and a consolidation of regular army troops with a large force of recruits and volunteers. The command of this army was a much debated question; Wilkinson supported General St. Clair for leadership, but St. Clair was already unpopular in Kentucky. However, he was finally appointed, over Kentucky's protest, to command the western troops. The Kentucky militia was placed under Generals Charles Scott and James Wilkinson.

On May 13, 1791, the mixed army of militia and regulars started its long march into the Northwest, and by May 31, it had advanced 150 miles and was encamped temporarily on the upper reaches of the White River. Later two small Indian villages were discovered on the banks of the Wabash. The troops were divided into two parties, which in their initial attacks were successful. In a surprise attack the whites put the Indians to flight and destroyed their houses and cornfields. With a determination to avenge the disgraceful defeat under General Harmar, the militiamen disobeyed their officers to commit many unnecessary atrocities upon fleeing Indians.

For the most part this expedition was commanded by aged Revolutionary officers who were no longer sound of mind or body. St. Clair was a victim of gout and could neither walk nor mount a horse alone. When he made personal inspections or directed an attack, he did so in a litter. Inevitably, disheartening delays and reverses followed. Militiamen who were enlisted for six months began withdrawing, and the constant stream of Kentuckians wandering back home soon thinned St. Clair's ranks. Desertion without reasonable excuse also played havoc with his fighting force, but stubborn as he was, he still felt compelled to advance. On November 3, the "Old" General camped on a small tributary of the Wabash, mistaking it for St. Mary's River, and there he expected to throw up a light line of fortification the next day, but delay was fatal. Before sunrise the Indians had driven the volunteers' front ranks back into the midst of the regular troops, so that a running fight resulted in a day of general carnage, with sundown finding St. Clair's bedraggled men retreating twenty-nine miles to the newly constructed Fort Jefferson. From this point they made their way, disgraced and defeated, back to Fort Washington, after losing approximately six hundred men either killed or captured, a loss which was little short of wholesale butchery. St. Clair, like Harmar, knew nothing of Indian fighting, but he stubbornly refused to carry out President Washington's emphatic instruction to avail himself of sufficient spies and scouts to guard against surprise and treacherous attacks. Again the Kentuckians were disappointed, for the Union had failed in its efforts to protect the frontier.

Fallen Timbers

After the defeat of General St. Clair, President Washington was hard tried in selecting his successor. Washington finally selected General "Mad" Anthony Wayne as commander of the western branch of the army, but with considerable reluctance, for Washington had misgivings concerning Wayne's ability to take charge of a western armed force and successfully to command it. Doubtless General Wayne was aware of his chief's attitude, for he proceeded very cautiously in planning his campaign and used more foresight and time in his preparations than had either of his predecessors. Unlike the leaders of the two preceding futile campaigns, General Wayne made free use of trained scouts and spies, keeping himself well informed as to what was happening in the enemy's territory.

In Kentucky, volunteers were dubious of "foreign" military leaders. They felt that local officers were far superior to those who were not familiar with western methods of fighting. Regulars were looked upon as cowards, and volunteers showed little willingness to serve with the Federal Army. The western commander had to solve all of these problems, which slowed up recruiting. It was not until late in 1792 that there were enough troops to make camp at Legionville, twenty-two miles south of Pittsburgh, where drilling of troops was conducted until the following April, when the encampment was moved to "Hobson's Choice," near Fort Washington. There were encamped 2,600 regulars, 360 mounted volunteers, and 36 spies and guides. The forces were drilled daily while awaiting the outcome of negotiations for peace with the Indians, who, anticipating another white defeat, refused to concede to the United States' terms of peace. On October 24 Wayne's army was joined by 1,000 Kentucky volunteers, but the campaign was again delayed until spring and the Kentuckians dismissed and ordered home, but not before they were convinced that General Wayne was serious in his intentions.

Troops remaining in camp were kept in readiness, and when fair weather came, General Charles Scott of Kentucky marched to Fort Washington with 1,600 mounted volunteers to join the regular troops. On July 26, 1794, these forces were consolidated with the regular army, and, on August 30, the Americans put their savage enemy to rout in the decisive Battle of Fallen Timbers, fought on the left bank of the Maumee. This battle was a typical piece of western military maneuvering and was so successful that only 33 Americans were killed and 100 wounded. General Wayne won the West, thus freeing Kentucky forever from Indian raids from the north.

The French Conspiracy

To the disappointment of the people of Kentucky, June 1, 1792, did not revolutionize Kentucky's precarious position in the West. Men, women, and children suffered at the hands of the Indians of the Northwest, while federal troops were lolling in Northwest forts under the command of the inefficient generals, Harmar and St. Clair. Their failure to correct the troubles of the Kentuckians caused the Federal Government to lose prestige in this frontier state, since Kentuckians looked upon the bungling of its protection as an evil omen, boding future destruction.

Not only did the Federal Government fail to spread its protecting arms about the shoulders of its new-born western state, but it imposed a heavy burden of taxation. Taxation of distilled liquors created an unfriendly feeling throughout the West, but in western Pennsylvania there was an actual show of hostilities. Kentuckians, however, delayed their protest until they could learn of the Pennsylvanians' fate. Although Washington's decisive handling of the situation in Pennsylvania caused Kentuckians to withhold their attack on the tax, it did not mean that they were convinced of its merit.

While western America was in a turmoil over her economic system, Europe was in worse confusion over the French Revolution. In France, the *Ancien Régime* was overthrown, and the government was placed in the hands of unseasoned statesmen and liberal political philosophers. Since the greatest need of this new French republic was, perhaps, international friendship and assistance, it seemed, by every method of reasoning, that the United States would be the most likely source of friendship, especially since a treaty of commercial amity had been entered into with France in 1778.

In order to solicit more effectively the aid and friendship of her trans-atlantic sister, France sent her representative *Citoyen* Edmond Charles Genêt to America. When this "stormy petrel" arrived at Charleston, April 8, 1793, he disclosed plans of a campaign against the Floridas and Louisiana, a campaign which vitally concerned the West.

In Philadelphia, however, Monsieur Genêt was disappointed and shocked at the reception which the great American Revolutionary hero, George Washington, accorded him. Doubtless this French agent expected the President of the United States to volunteer the assistance of the country. Instead, Washington informed Genêt that the United States expected to maintain a strict neutrality in her relations with France. Disappointed in this turn of affairs, the French diplomat turned to those whom he knew favored the French enterprise. Both Jefferson and Madison had already expressed friendliness. Not only did these Republican leaders befriend Genêt, but in the West, a Republican stronghold, political leaders vied with each other in expressing their desires to co-operate.

Before Genêt's arrival in America, extreme Antifederalists in Philadelphia reared striped poles and organized "Democratic Clubs" to promote the principles of republicanism and to sympathize with the French Revolutionists. In August, 1793, a Democratic Club was organized in Lexington, Kentucky, for the avowed purpose of asserting the rights of the western people to navigate the Mississippi River. Following Lexington's example, Georgetown, Paris, and other neighboring towns organized clubs and erected candy-striped "Liberty Poles." Thus, with Kentucky already in line and in an enraged state of mind, Genêt found it an easy task to set his plans in motion. Since a French agent, Monsieur Michaux, traveling under the disguise of "scientist," was already in Kentucky, Genêt dispatched four other "scientists" to the West: Messieurs Delpeau, La Chaise, Mathurin, and Gignoux. When they arrived in Kentucky as scientists, it was an open secret that these agents had been sent west to enlist troops and to secure supplies for an attack upon New Orleans; for not only did they proceed to the task in hand with the blessing of their chief, but also, apparently, with the best wishes of the Secretary of State, Thomas Jefferson. Genêt prevailed upon Jefferson, "through his kindred interest in botany," to write letters of introduction to Governor Shelby for his agents. Even Senator John Brown, showing an absorbed interest in the work of these "scientists," wrote letters of introduction to his fellow Kentuckians.

In Kentucky the French found Governor Shelby's attitude a stubborn obstacle in the immediate development of their plans, but George Rogers Clark professed friendliness to the French cause and a willingness to co-operate. Clark, broken physically, morally, and financially, had never overcome the hardships of his Northwest campaigns. He suffered almost continuous pain from rheumatism, and his spirits were dampened by his disappointing love affair with Terese de Leyba. Furthermore, he was under an almost continuous fire of criticism from many Kentuckians for his actions in the campaigns along the Ohio after the capture of Kaskaskia and Vincennes. So desperate did the "Hero of Vincennes" become, that in 1788 he offered to expatriate himself in favor of an independent colony, and, in 1791, he unceremoniously smashed the sword which Virginia had given him as a token of appreciation for his services. In General Clark, France found an able American lieutenant.

In February, 1793, George Rogers Clark wrote Genêt that despite the fact that "My country has proved notoriously ungrateful for my services," he still had much influence in the West. In this letter he reasserted his willingness to be of service to France and offered to raise a large force of both whites and Indians to attack New Orleans— firmly believing that he could take the Spanish province of Orleans with 1,500 Kentucky and Tennessee troops. This proposal pleased Monsieur Genêt, and he appointed General Clark "Major General in the Armies of France and Commander-in-Chief of the French Revolutionary Legion on the Mississippi."

During the winter and spring of 1793 and 1794, Clark, Michaux, George Nicholas, Charles Delpeau, and Samuel Fulton were busy completing arrangements for capturing Spanish Louisiana. Clark was able to secure from sympathetic Kentuckians large quantities of foodstuffs and ammunition. The list of subscribers to his ammunition fund virtually constituted a roster of Kentucky's leaders: John Bradford, John Breckinridge, Levi and Thomas Todd, Robert Patterson, and others. So sure was General Clark of representing the popular will of the West that he openly proclaimed his purpose and solicited volunteers through the columns of the *Sentinel of the Northwest Territory* and the *Kentucky Gazette*. These same issues of the papers contained proclamations of General Anthony Wayne warning the western populace against taking part in the movement.

President Washington was forced to act. He warned Governor Shelby by letter that such an undertaking must be prevented. He also informed the Governor that the United States was then negotiating a treaty with Spain to open the Mississippi River to free trade, and that these negotiations would be seriously complicated by an adverse move on the part of Kentucky. Shelby pleaded an innocent ignorance of the French plot, assuring President Washington that he would investigate the matter, and if the President's statements were true, he would put an end to the conspiracy. Doubtless Washington's note left Governor Shelby in a dilemma, for he had received letters favorable to the French cause from Secretary Jefferson. On the face of things, it seems that Shelby's hesitancy in taking action was caused by his desire to communicate further with the Republican leader, Jefferson. This he was unable to do, however, for Anthony Wayne, possessing full knowledge of what was happening, had grown impatient and forced the Kentucky Governor to declare his position.

Shelby, writing Wayne one week later, stated his belief that citizens of Kentucky could not be constitutionally prevented from leaving the state individually or in groups. With this statement from Governor Shelby in hand, President Washington instructed Wayne, in order to prevent the success of the French plan, to prepare Fort Massac on the southern Ohio for action. In the meantime, Genêt was recalled, and Washington's vigorous actions brought French efforts in Kentucky to an inglorious conclusion.

The Kentucky Resolutions

Except for disturbances already mentioned, Washington, during his two administrations, succeeded in keeping an outward appearance of national harmony. Even the independent West had bowed its obstinate head in respect for the "Hero of Valley Forge." When Washington left office in 1797, the executive reins were placed in the hands of John Adams, a New Englander, serious of purpose and diligent, but lacking the reputation of Washington. In the West, citizens were dubious of the New Englander, for they remembered only too well the years when their trade rights were threatened by Jay's proposed treaty, which, if passed, would have discriminated against the West in favor of the Northeast. Also, Adams had defeated the people's choice, Thomas Jefferson, by three paltry votes in the electoral college.

Westerners felt that they were at a distinct disadvantage, for they had been a party to provoking the Whiskey Rebellion, to organizing Jacobin Clubs, to attacking the Jay Treaty. In national politics they were pro-French, opposed to pro-British Easterners. Hence those favoring the French cause in America were prompt in accusing the pro-British element of desiring an aristocratic form of government which would sooner or later result in the formation of a monarchy. Even Jefferson, in a letter to Silas F. Mason, hinted that this might be true. He predicted that John Adams would promote this scheme to become king and to pass the American crown on to his heirs.

On the other hand, the Republicans were still carrying on *sub rosa* negotiations with the French. James Monroe, a Virginia Republican, was sent to Paris in 1794. On his arrival in the French city, he found that since he was the first minister from a major power to the new Republic, no arrangement had been made for his reception. Undaunted, he went before the French Assembly, where he was warmly received, and where he was allowed the unprecedented privilege of speaking from the floor. This indeed was an unusual and untimely irregularity which brought loud protests from London, where John Jay was negotiating his famous treaty. This unfortunate incident placed the United States Government in an extremely embarrassing situation. Of course, censuring of Monroe was a natural consequence but a doubtful solution, for immediately France became suspicious of the United States' relations with Great Britain. Henceforth, the French feared that any agreement which the Americans made with England would naturally weaken their preferential trade agreement of 1778.

Monroe, humiliated and stubborn, allowed the American position to be severely criticized in France without attempting to defend it. He was further accused of promising the French a Republican victory and a complete readjustment of Franco-American relations. This latter offense prompted his recall. Charles C. Pinckney, in 1797, was sent as minister to Paris, but, on presenting his credentials, was refused a reception. Not only were Pinckney's credentials ignored, but he was threatened with arrest on the charge of being an alien spy. This treatment of the new minister was in marked contrast with the attention showed Monroe at a farewell dinner. Chagrined at the unceremonious reception of his minister in Paris, Adams promptly appointed a delegation to represent the United States. This commission of three members: Charles Pinckney, Elbridge B. Gerry, and John Marshall, arrived in Paris in October, 1797, but, like Pinckney, they were delayed in presenting their credentials and in being received. This delay became so serious that the Federalists, Marshall and Pinckney, began to protest, but Talleyrand, Secretary of Foreign Affairs, and other French officials of state assured the commission that everything possible was being done. Talleyrand, however, intimated that matters could be greatly facilitated by a gift of $250,000. The commission considered this proposition as insulting and, with the exception of the Republican Elbridge Gerry, returned home. The French, however, intimated to Adams' state department that they would treat with Republicans. Nevertheless Adams recalled Gerry, and the United States became involved in a year of intermittent naval warfare with France.

President Adams, biased by narrow Federalist politics and bitter towards France, acceded to a series of legislative acts between June 18 and July 14, 1798, which created a storm of protest. The naturalization act of 1795 was amended to require fourteen years' residence instead of five for immigrants, and intentions to be declared five years prior to the date of naturalization. The second, or so-called "Alien Act," permitted the President to deport such aliens as he considered dangerous to the country's welfare and peace. A third act expanded the President's power over aliens during time of war, and the chief executive under this act was permitted discretionary powers in deporting certain classes of aliens. A fourth act concerned the Americans who condemned the administration while praising France. Numerous French editors, driven out of France during the revolution, had taken up their profession anew in the United States without essentially changing their editorial policies. They hurled invectives at the government, and more particularly at the pro-British Federalists. Effectively to bridle the arrogant Republican press, the Sedition Law was proposed and passed. Persons guilty of violating this law were subjected to the humiliation of public trial and to a fine and imprisonment not exceeding $5,000 and five years.

Passage of these "Citizen Acts" was a godsend to the Republican fathers, Jefferson and Madison, for never were more effective stumblingblocks placed in the path of an administration. No political leaders were ever more thoroughly equipped with campaign propaganda than were the Republicans at this time; not only was their main plank, the freedom of the press, a noble one, but they were able to enlist the support of the newspaper editors. It became a matter of sport for exiled French editors to hurl invectives and editorials at the Adams administration, of which they naturally opposed all of the administrative policies. It was an unmitigated pleasure for Republican editors to inform their reading public that the Federalists had overlooked the freedom of the press and right of petition.

Jefferson, as Vice President, made good his golden opportunity, and, as has been said, in a letter to Silas T. Mason, October 11, 1798, he accused Adams of wishing to establish a hereditary monarchy. It is doubtful whether Jefferson had fooled himself into believing this, but it was excellent propaganda, and its effects were electrical. Immediately he set forth to discover a suitable field in which to sow this good seed. Because of its reputation as a state of protests, the Republican headmaster selected North Carolina as a starting point, but before he could complete his plans, citizens of Clark County, Kentucky, adopted resolutions expressive of the Jeffersonian ideas. Likewise, since the Kentucky press was waging an effective war against the Sedition Laws, Jefferson turned to Kentucky as an ideal territory in which to fight the cause of constitutional freedom.

In August, 1798, a delegation of citizens of Fayette County, Kentucky, gathered at Maxwell Spring in Lexington to hear a discussion of the new laws of Congress. The Republican cause rested in the hands of the venerable George Nicholas, professor of law at Transylvania University, and general counselor. Nicholas denounced the Federalist laws as an encroachment upon American freedom, and he proclaimed the cause of Republicanism. When he finished his address, and the cheering had subsided, someone in the crowd called the name of Henry Clay, who, at that time, was a much interested spectator but an unknown and untried speaker. Clay, a youth of twenty-one, had been in Kentucky hardly a year, for he had come to the state in.November, 1797, from Richmond, Virginia, to begin the practice of law. So unpromising had this sallow Virginia lad appeared on his arrival in Kentucky that he was forced to sign his own petition to the Fayette County Bar, and by his own assertion expected to satisfy his material desires on a yearly income of 100 pounds. When his name was mentioned in the Cheapside gathering, the crowd took up the cry, and Clay was boosted into the back of a near-by wagon to speak. Fortunately, luck was with him when he continued the theme of Nicholas' address; for an hour his audience was held spellbound by his attack upon the Federalist administration. So effective was Clay's maiden speech that the audience remained silent until William Murray, a Federalist, crawled upon the wagon to defend his party's actions. When the Republican audience realized what was happening, both the Federalist speakers, Murray and McLean, were denied a hearing; if they did not leave the grounds, even violence was threatened, but Clay and Nicholas were borne through Main Street on the shoulders of the Republican mob.

John Breckinridge, a prominent local antifederalist leader, absented himself from Kentucky for a time on a visit to his old Augusta County home in Virginia. From Virginia he wrote Caleb Wallace, asking him to secure the passage of a bill in the Kentucky legislature censuring the acts of the National Government. However, this letter was delayed, and Wallace proved too timid to undertake the task on his own initiative. In the meantime, Breckinridge found it convenient to cross the Alleghenies to visit with the Vice President at Monticello. Here the Kentuckian found Jefferson planning a scheme similar to his, except for a difference in the general aim in view. Breckinridge conscientiously wished to prevent federal encroachment upon states' rights, while Jefferson wanted to expose the shortcomings of the Federalist Party. Numerous conferences were necessary to iron out the differences of these two political leaders. Jefferson, beyond all doubt, was the author of the Kentucky Resolutions, but his draft was toned down in many places, and three resolutions were added by Breckinridge. Breckinridge returned to Kentucky early in November, 1798. On the seventh of November Governor Garrard delivered his message to the general assembly. It was this address which paved the way for the resolutions. In fact, the Garrard message had every earmark of having been dictated at the Monticello conference, for the Governor said that as a member of the Union, sharing in its prosperity and adversity, Kentucky had the right of censuring the acts of the Federal Government. On November 8 Breckinridge was appointed chairman of a committee of three to draft resolutions. On November 9 the committee reported. On November 10 the resolutions were introduced and passed virtually without amendment. The resolutions as adopted were the work of Jefferson's pen, with the exception of the changes already noted.

The only opposition which the Kentucky Resolutions met in their speedy passage through the legislature was that of William Murray. Murray defended the Federal Government in an able attack upon the resolutionists. He pointed out the fact that the people and not the states had entered into the federal compact. His fight, however, was lost before he took the floor. Breckinridge refuted his argument in a perfunctory manner and tone, realizing that his cause was won in spite of anything Murray might say.

In its resolutions, Kentucky early proclaimed the interesting theory "that the several states who formed that instrument (the Constitution) being sovereign and independent, have the unquestionable right to judge of its infractions; and that a nullification, by those sovereignties, of all unauthorized acts done under colour of that instrument is the rightful remedy." These resolutions formed the orthodox principles by which the Republican Party was to defeat the Federalists the next year, and they remained a constitutional guide post for some time. When these resolutions were submitted to the other states, however, they failed of serious consideration. Many of the New England States replied by protesting the resolutions, while the Southern States maintained a discreet silence. Even North Carolina, South Carolina, Maryland, and Tennessee failed to respond.

By the beginning of 1800, Jefferson and his Republican cohorts were jubilant over the apparent defeat of the Federalists. The Republicans, having exposed the weaknesses of the Federalists to public view, were now satisfied to drop the matter, for with the election of Jefferson and Burr to the presidency and vice-presidency, they found no further need of protesting against Federalist statutes.

The Second Constitution

The makers of the first Kentucky constitution realized the difficulty of making a lasting and practical document. A provision was inserted in the first constitution indicating that since it was an experiment, the voters in 1797 and 1798 were to express their views on the success of the instrument. If at this time the constitution were deemed a failure, the voters might favor a constitutional convention. During its first decade as a state, Kentucky underwent a number of very salutary changes, for long before 1797 the first constitution was found to be defective. It was clearly evident that the first convention had wasted time enacting certain measures which were the prerogatives of the legislative body created by the constitution.

By 1794 the cry of "Aristocracy" was heard on every side. Since Governor and senators were chosen by the electoral colleges, they were accused of discriminating against the common people. On one particular occasion, this "Aristocratic" senate almost cheated the Green River settlers out of their lands by proposing to sell them for $500,000 to land speculators. For six years criticism against the existing political system grew steadily more and more violent. Localities battled bravely but ineffectively for a new constitution, but the columns of the papers, pamphlets, and handbills were indicative of the intensity of the struggle. Large landholders lined up in opposition to small property owners, for the planter class feared small holders would carry the day, and with it the system of slavery. Thus, long before the first constitution had come into existence, the rumbling of the voice of emancipation was heard. Religious denominations were emancipationists in sentiment, and every preacher was considered a potential enemy of slavery.

John Breckinridge, a large land and slave owner, took the field in behalf of the other landed gentry and became eloquent in his defense of the old constitution. He claimed that the Presbyterian preachers and the emancipationists had a hand in the agitation for a new constitution. Even the budding young attorney, Henry Clay, had tried his oratorical powers on the subject of emancipation. But Clay's pleas were harmless because of his youth, his short residence in Kentucky, and his too close association with bad "Republican" company. As a result, Clay had to fold his tent and avoid the field of battle, because this was one time when silence on his part was highly desirable.

In May, 1797, the first vote was cast for a new constitution. This vote was somewhat indecisive, however, for five of twenty-one counties failed to report on the question. Those reporting cast a vote of 5,456 "for" and 440 "against" calling a convention. Although this number was short of the constitutional two thirds majority of state voters, it was indicative of public opinion. Determined to succeed, those favoring the call for a convention mustered every possible resource for creating an active public opinion. The press was vigorous in agitating this question, filling the columns of its papers with arguments pro and con on the subject of a new constitution. By 1798, the term "Aristocrat" became derogatory. Large landowners shuddered in their boots, fearing what the commoners would do. On the other hand, commoners shuddered at what the Aristocrats would do. General conversation on the constitution was highly flavored with emancipation, and this was distressing to the slaveholders. In April, 1798, "Gracchus" addressed the question, "Shall there be a Convention?" to the public through the columns of the *Kentucky Gazette*. He declared the time was ripe because the lower house of the legislature was so disposed, and public opinion favored constitutional reform. He argued effectively that the public will was blocked by the will of seven or eight state senators. To cap his convincing exposition, the writer asked the significant questions: "But whence is it that your Great Men are thus jealous of the power of the people? Does it not," he said, "indicate something rotten in the situation of your country? Are you sure your liberties are not in danger?"

In heading off the work of the "Common People," the "Aristocrats" declared for a convention, and, at a meeting held at Bryan's Station, January 21, 1798, the opponents of the constitutional convention drafted a well-outlined policy which they hoped to have adopted in the inevitable convention. They declared for the election of delegates on the basis of population; against interference with private property; for a legislature of two houses; for the independence of the courts and judges; for the continuation of the compact with Virginia, which reserved certain western Kentucky lands to Virginia to be granted Revolutionary soldiers; and against the right of the legislature to emancipate the slaves. Not only did this assembly shape these policies, but it also planned to influence the delegates elected to the convention. It was proposed that candidates should be selected from each religious denomination and two representatives from each militia district elected by a majority vote of all males over twenty-one years of age.

But the general public had its own ideas about the method of electing delegates. The *Frankfort Palladium* suggested that captains of the militia companies should select a committee of five to hold county meetings. While the Aristocrats were in their convention at Bryan's Station, less "Aristocratic" friends of reform at Lexington held a meeting to discuss emancipation and the election of delegates to the constitutional convention. More progressive elements feared the conservatism of the militia companies; especially did they fear the plot of conservatives to dictate the policies of the convention.

Outsiders were consulted on the question of framing a new constitution. John Taylor of Caroline, in a lengthy reply to Harry Innes' inquiry, favored the popular election of the Governor and senators and the complete independence of the courts. On July 22, 1799, the constitutional convention met in Frankfort, with the same number of delegates as there were representatives in the lower house, and elected in the same way, to serve for a period of four months. Andrew S. Bullitt was nominated chairman, while the veteran clerk of the preceding conventions, Thomas Todd, was re-elected to his office. No formal notes of the convention were kept or published; no official records exist of the points of dissension or debate in the convention; the only information preserved is in the scanty newspaper reports. On August 17, 1799, twenty-seven days after the convention met, the second constitution was completed.

The second constitution corrected many of the obvious mistakes of the first one. First, and most important, it provided that the senators and Governor should be elected by popular vote. The electoral college was discarded; provision was made for a Lieutenant Governor whose official duties in the state government were to parallel those of the Vice President in the National Government. The Court of Appeals was established as the supreme court of the state with appellate jurisdiction only, and the legislature was instructed to establish necessary subordinate courts. The section of the constitution concerning slavery was brought over bodily from the first document, with the addition of a clause concerning the trial of slaves in the courts.

The only change made in the constitutional attitude toward slavery from the first constitution was in article IX; this section, entitled, "Mode of Revising the Constitution," made amendment virtually impracticable. When cause for amendment arose, the legislature was instructed to prepare an amendment to be voted on the next year by the people. If the people voted in favor of the amendment, the legislature was then authorized to call a convention for the purpose of amending the constitution. This section of the new constitution clearly indicates the hold which the reactionaries had upon the constitutional convention, for it was impossible to amend the new document under three years.

On June 1, 1800, the second constitution was put into force, eight years after the first had become effective. In the main, the second constitution was a conservative document. Although a reorganization of the state government was the main issue, conservatives wished above all to guard against any attempt by the masses to free the slaves. The amending clause was sufficient check to discourage attempts at change. One reactionary delegate even proposed a property qualification of 500 acres of land for voting, or of the payment of sufficient taxes to cover this acreage. This proposal was a radical departure from Kentucky's much flaunted democratic constitution of 1792, but its adoption would have insured the control of legislation concerning slavery to the slaveholders. Had this qualification been accepted, the second constitution of Kentucky would have shut the door of equality in the face of the "Common People."

The Louisiana Purchase

Kentucky's most outstanding fear between 1780 and 1803 was of losing its free right to navigate the Mississippi River. Rumors of John Jay's negotiations during the later eighties and early nineties brought storms of protest from the westerners. In 1795, however, Charles Pinckney made a treaty with Spain guaranteeing the Americans the right to navigate the river and to deposit goods at New Orleans. During the next few years Kentucky was transformed into a flourishing industrial and commercial commonwealth, with the population of the state increasing from 73,000 in 1790 to over 200,000 in 1800. Towns sprang up to be developed overnight, and western society became well established.

With the increase of its economic importance, Kentucky rapidly became a part of the world about it. Foreign markets were necessary to the prosperity of Kentucky farmers and manufacturers, and it was a matter of public knowledge that this advantage could endure only so long as the treaty of 1795 remained effective. During the first years of its prosperity, Kentucky little appreciated the effect foreign entanglements would have on its commerce, and those Kentuckians who enthusiastically supported Citizen Genêt in the early nineties were unconscious of the trouble which the French would bring their state in less than a decade. The ambitious Napoleon was unwilling to confine his activities to the continent of Europe but cast a longing eye at the prizes of the Western Hemisphere. His first move in this direction was made October 1, 1800, when he effected the secret Treaty of San Ildefonso which transferred ownership of Louisiana from Spain to France. Louisiana Territory was too large and cumbersome for a decadent Spanish throne to control, and, with this in mind, Napoleon frightened Spanish agents by indicating the dangers involved in the westward movement of restless American pioneers. His argument was effective, for Spain did not wish to continue with this burdensome responsibility.

On the other hand, Napoleon disregarded the fact that Louisiana served as a powerful check upon the westward advance of a determined race, for every pioneer on the American frontier was anxious to see Louisiana wrested from foreign hands. France, through its minister, Talleyrand, expressed the belief that Spain could no longer govern its New World possessions nor check American expansion. He believed that the French could, with the possession of Louisiana, confine the Americans to the natural boundaries formed by the Atlantic Ocean and Mississippi River. In negotiating the treaty of San Ildefonso between Spain and France, French officials ordered strict observation of secrecy. However, the Americans were suspicious, for unusual friendliness between Spain and France was not regarded as natural. John Adams, in Berlin, suspected that a plot was brewing.

In 1801 the French made their first open move toward America, for in that year Napoleon sent an expedition west under the direction of General LeClerc, which was eventually to establish the French in Louisiana. General LeClerc, however, stopped at the island of Santo Domingo to subdue its Negro inhabitants and to establish a French naval post in the Caribbean. Unfortunately for the French he was not successful. Toussaint L'Ouverture's forces, with the co-operation of the elements and tropical pestilences, destroyed 17,000 French troops, to force the French leader to abandon the field. Instead of the Santo Domingo episode providing a way station where Napoleonic forces might stretch their limbs and "whet their teeth" before encountering their more determined American opponents, it proved the end of their western dreams.

While Americans were carefully observing French activities in Santo Domingo, they were startled by news which came from New Orleans. Intendant Morales threw a veritable bombshell in the midst of western American tranquillity when, in October, 1802, he revoked the right of deposit at New Orleans. Why this proclamation was issued has never been definitely known. Whether it was instigated by the French authorities or not is a matter of controversy. There is some indication that this order was issued for reasons of personal spite on the part of the Spanish Intendant. Nevertheless, the order was widely published, for enough handbills of the notice were struck to flood the State of Kentucky.

Morales' act came as a great shock to the West. At this season fields were ripe with harvest, and Kentucky warehouses were bursting with wheat and tobacco intended for the foreign trade. Enforcement of this proclamation meant certain doom to Kentucky commerce, for only seagoing vessels were permitted to pass New Orleans free of Spanish duty. Fortunately, the blow came just in time to find the Kentucky legislature in session, and Governor Garrard immediately presented the question to that body. By December a petition had been framed and presented to the United States Congress begging prompt action on the question. In Washington the petition found ready friends, for already President Jefferson was concentrating on the matter of removing all interference in navigating the Mississippi River. He considered this question of the utmost importance, for it affected his western, and stanchest, constituency. He kept in contact with Governor Garrard, assuring this official of his constant and faithful efforts to remedy Kentucky's plight.

The President did not wish to engage in war for settlement of the western disturbance. He wished first to try peaceful procedure, but in the pinch of necessity his strict construction of the Constitution was ignored. He proposed to purchase the Isle d'Orleans and the Floridas from France, and James Monroe was sent posthaste to Paris to open negotiations to this effect. Already Jefferson had instructed his ministers to offer France $9,250,000 for Orleans and the Floridas. But before Monroe reached Paris, Livingston, the American Ambassador, approached the French Minister, Marbois, on the subject and was surprised to learn, after considerable dickering, that France would take $15,000,000 for all of Louisiana.

After further negotiations and delays, in which Talleyrand complicated matters by his interference, the Americans accepted France's offer. On April 30, 1803, the Louisiana Territory became the property of the United States, and the West was technically freed of its nightmare of fear regarding the navigation of the Mississippi River.

News of the purchase of Louisiana was slow in reaching Kentucky. Since the first report was doubted, the *Kentucky Gazette* published the news with reservations, for the results of America's negotiations seemed too good to be true. When the report was affirmed, John Breckinridge hailed the act as the removal of a powerful stumblingblock from the path of western America; westward expansion was now possible without further difficulty or foreign interference.

The West's happy attitude was immediately changed, however, for Spain refused to vacate Louisiana, because she disapproved of the French agreement. So audacious was this act that Jefferson forgot his peace-loving principles and ordered the West to recruit troops and make a forced entry into New Orleans. This summons found Kentuckians ready to fight. Governor Garrard was asked to furnish 4,000 men to coerce the Spanish at New Orleans, and, if several contemporary reports can be accepted, almost every male in Kentucky volunteered. Streets of the Kentucky towns and villages echoed with the shouts of militiamen drilling in preparation for the taking of New Orleans. This show of force was convincing, for the Spanish peacefully handed Louisiana over to the representatives of the United States, C. C. Claiborne and James Wilkinson.

The past ten years had wrought a miraculous change in Kentucky. Days of intrigue with foreign powers were completely forgotten, and leaders who had been such vigorous conspirators in early days became now ultra-patriotic. So strictly American had the Kentuckians become that Francis Flournoy was hailed into court because of a revolutionary article which he published in the *Guardian of Freedom*. Unfortunately Flournoy saw fit to criticize American policies in the recent Louisiana trouble and addressed his remarks indirectly to the Government of France. In court, Flournoy was tried before Judge Harry Innes, who may have recalled with a guilty feeling that only a few years before he had intrigued with foreign powers over the disposal of Kentucky.

The purchase of Louisiana opened the doors for westward expansion, for Kentucky was to grow into commercial and industrial prominence during the following decades.

CHAPTER VII

Kentucky in the Struggles of the West, 1800-1815

Aaron Burr Visits Kentucky

UNFORTUNATELY, Kentucky did not see an end of strife with the framing of a new constitution and the purchase of Louisiana. On May 5, 1805, there appeared before John Brown's door in Frankfort a distinguished visitor who brought Kentucky trouble anew. This visitor was Aaron Burr, duelist, fugitive from justice, and late Vice President of the United States. His appearance in the Kentucky capital was indeed reason for speculation. Many a wise head wagged knowingly that he was on his way either to political banishment or to the governorship of the Louisiana Territory. In both of these speculations they were mistaken.

Colonel Burr's visit to the West resulted in numerous investigations involving many prominent citizens and ended with his reputation as a traitor in the public mind. He prefaced his arrival in Kentucky by conferring several times with the British agent, Anthony Merry, and the arch-trickster of the West, James Wilkinson. These associations hardly supported the unhappy New York politician as a devoted patriot. Despite Wilkinson's honorable position as commander-in-chief of the western division of the United States Army, and despite his governorship of the Louisiana Territory, he could scarcely be classed as a loyal patriot. Numerous private conversations with Wilkinson had increased Burr's longing to visit the frontier; then, too, the West was a happier place for the ex-Vice President. He had written his son-in-law, Governor Allston of South Carolina, "In New York I am to be disenfranchised, in New Jersey hanged. Having substantial objections to both I shall not . . . hazard either, but shall seek another country."

While en route from Philadelphia to Kentucky, Burr met Matthew Lyon in Pittsburgh, and the latter, a distinguished victim of the Fed-

118

eralists' Alien and Sedition Laws, was willing to assist his friend by giving him much information about the West. Lyon told Burr that the state of Tennessee would not necessarily object to the charge of murder lodged against him by a New York coroner's jury and advised Colonel Burr to settle there and run for Congress. If Burr considered this plan seriously, he soon forgot it. From Frankfort, Burr went by river to Nashville, and once in that city, accepting the hospitality of that frontier "hickory withe," Andrew Jackson, he became more ambitious than ever to be great. Louisiana was near, and he, perhaps, fondly dreamed of capturing this rich prize to become a prince of wealth and influence. With many letters of introduction, and with the blessings of Wilkinson, Burr left Nashville to visit New Orleans, where he hoped to determine the possibility of uniting dissatisfied French and Spanish with the western English-speaking Americans to found an independent republic. Burr was wholly unfamiliar with this locality and its manners. Hence some of his moves appeared awkward to Daniel Clark of New Orleans, who said, in a letter to a friend, that many unfavorable rumors concerning Burr were being circulated. However, he intimated that Burr was to become the Moses of the Southwest and was to create for the unhappy westerners a republic of individual freedom and opportunity.[1]

After spending several weeks in New Orleans, Burr retraced his steps northward over the Natchez Trace to Nashville and thence by boat to Maysville, and, on August 19, 1805, he rode down the streets of Lexington. Here he spent several days sounding public opinion and talking with men of influence. Nine days later he returned to John Brown's home in Frankfort. This second visit to Frankfort, however, was injurious to his cause, for the editor of the *Palladium* became suspicious and proposed a series of searching queries which were embarrassing to Colonel Burr. Following the example of this paper, the *Kentucky Gazette* began a careful observation of the "Eastern Culprit's" activities. Perhaps a less engaging personality would have found so much public scrutiny disconcerting and would have shrunk from such criticism, but Aaron Burr knew the secret of winning public sympathy, especially from the ladies. Since he had the uncanny ability of

[1] This is an assumption, however, for Burr never committed himself concerning his plans.

making treason appear an often misunderstood virtue, within a short time he was again basking in the warming rays of public approval.

From Frankfort this indomitable conspirator went to Louisville for a short visit and thence to St. Louis, where he recited his recent observations to an unenthusiastic listener, General Wilkinson. Wilkinson, a coward at heart, had, in Burr's absence, sounded his associates on the question of a western revolution but had found every one of them loyal to the United States. Thus, finding himself the only coward in the western army, his enthusiasm for Burr's scheme cooled considerably. In order to get rid of his fellow-conspirator, Wilkinson requested Governor Harrison of the Indiana Territory to appoint Burr a delegate to Congress. Burr did not tarry longer in Indiana, however, for in a remarkably short time he was back in Philadelphia where he spent several months trying to enlist the services of naval men. He desired especially to secure the assistance of William Eaton, who was disgruntled because he had been maltreated in the Tripolitan War, and Congress had failed to make satisfactory amends. Through him Burr hoped to alienate the affections of Stephen Decatur and Commodores Truxton and Preble. With a naval force to assist him, Burr felt his scheme could not fail.

In the West, Burr's allies were making slow headway. On the Ohio, Harman Blennerhassett, a scatter-brained Irishman, was ready to take part in any venture which would replenish his pocket book. Burr leaned heavily upon his Irish friend for financial assistance, but Blennerhassett, unknown to Burr, was staring frantically at the bottom of his purse. Nevertheless, preparations for a triumphant entry into New Orleans were continued, and Blennerhassett, as an agent of public opinion, and over the pseudonym of "Querist," published several provocative articles in the *Ohio Gazette*. This was an unfortunate move, for John Wood, in the columns of the *Kentucky Western World,* was just completing a thoroughly successful roasting of Judge Sebastian for treason. The editor of the *Western World,* in looking for new fields to conquer, found a worthy subject in the condemnation of Burr's conspiracy. When Wood sounded his warning blast, October 15, 1806, it was a veteran treason hunter who entered the field.

There were others in Kentucky who were carefully watching the activities of Colonel Burr. Joseph Hamilton Daviess, federal district attorney, wrote President Jefferson as early as January 10, 1806, of his fears regarding a western conspiracy. Jefferson requested Daviess to supply further information on the subject, but before he could comply, Burr was boldly pursuing his plans. He had negotiated a loan with the Kentucky Insurance Company for $25,000 worth of its notes of exchange, an act which convinced Daviess that his fears were well founded. On November 8, Daviess appeared before Judge Harry Innes' court and explained that he wanted to make an important motion. He read a brief deposition in which Burr was charged with conspiracy and then proceeded to argue his point, basing his charge directly upon the federal statutes. Judge Innes appeared somewhat surprised, for he delayed his opinion, to the disgust of Daviess. Doubtless Innes wished to consult some of his former fellow conspirators and to determine the procedure of this investigation. Since Burr could be called to court only for an investigation, Innes was afraid to proceed. From numerous letters which passed between Innes and the district attorney on points of law, it also seems that Innes was hazy on the legal ramifications of Daviess' charges. Daviess became insistent in his demands for a court investigation, but still Innes remained hesitant, spending several days in organizing his opinion, only to deny the motion.

Hearing of this proposed investigation, Burr rushed to Frankfort, accompanied by one of his counselors, Henry Clay. Here he met his other counselors, Thomas Posey, Acting Lieutenant Governor, and General Samuel Hopkins, a member of the legislature. With these gentlemen he majestically entered the court room to find Daviess' motion denied. Burr, however, took this opportunity to assume the offensive and in a short, well-planned speech soon won the public's sympathy. Daviess, not to be outdone, said that Burr had voluntarily come into the court and the time was ripe to summons a jury and witnesses to proceed with an investigation. This suggestion was denied, but November 11 was set as the date for the trial, and officers were dispatched to summons both witnesses and jurors. When court convened on the eleventh, Daviess was extremely embarrassed by the absence of his star witness, Davis Floyd of Jeffersonville, who was attending the Indiana legislature. In the face of certain public ridicule, he was forced to ask for a delay of the trial, and again Burr addressed the assembled crowd to good advantage.

When the court adjourned, Daviess worked desperately to get his witnesses in line, nor was all the activity on the side of the prosecution, because Henry Clay was conducting a personal investigation of his client. Clay was uncertain as to Burr's guilt as charged, and, since he had been nominated to fill an unexpired term in the United States Senate, he had become sensitive to charges of treason. Burr assured Clay that he was innocent and that the charges were wholly false. Thus convinced of his client's innocence, Clay was ready to proceed with the trial when the court convened on December 2. Daviess was unable to get John Adair, a major witness, into court and was again forced to ask for delay, but Clay insisted on immediate action. Colonel Allen, a fourth attorney, and Clay undertook to force Daviess into a hasty trial in order to have the matter finished. These lawyers falsely charged Daviess with trying to prevent them from enjoying their free right of speech, and further, of restraining the constitutional rights of a citizen. Perhaps Judge Innes' procedure was most at fault, for he refused to permit Daviess to have an attachment served on Adair, holding that Adair's summons had failed to stipulate the hour he was to appear. Privately, Innes had promised Daviess that he might appear before the grand jury, but when he reached the courtroom, the judge changed his mind.

In the face of all the evidence which Wood and Street of the *Western World* were able to present, combined with the depositions of Daviess, the jury of twenty-two men returned the verdict, December 5, "Not a True Bill."

Burr was not to go free, however, for in Washington, Jefferson had at last awakened from his lethargy. Evil rumors of Burr had come to the President's ears, and he sent a special agent into the West to investigate. Upon the agent's arrival at Marietta, Ohio, he appealed to the Governor of the state to seize Burr's fleet. In the meantime James Wilkinson, having grown tired of the whole venture, betrayed Burr in a thinly veiled exposition to President Jefferson.

Burr and several of his lieutenants succeeded in running the blockade with a remnant of his fleet, consisting of 10 boats and less than 100 men. This move availed the conspirator nothing, for Wilkinson's treachery was his doom. Near Natchez, Burr surrendered to officials of the Mississippi Territory, but again a sympathetic grand jury acquitted him.

His release from court was not a happy affair, however, for he knew that Wilkinson and a company of men were in hot pursuit. He left Natchez and went across the wilds of Mississippi in an effort to reach the Florida coast and friendly British ships. Burr was arrested by Edmund Pendleton Gaines near Fort Stoddart, now in the present State of Alabama. He was sent by boat from Fort Stoddart to appear in the United States Circuit Court at Richmond, Virginia, on May 22, 1807. At Richmond Burr was acquitted for lack of evidence. The failure of this adventure ended the numerous attempts to separate Kentucky from the Union.

The War of 1812

Renewal of the war between England and France in May, 1803, led rapidly to strained relations among the United States, England, and the rest of Europe. In 1805 the British Admiralty Court, in the case of the *Essex,* ordered the capture of all goods shipped directly from the French Caribbean colonies and recommended impressment of English sailors shipping aboard foreign vessels. This ruling was a slap in the face of American shipping, since American merchantmen were paying higher wages for seamen than was the English Navy. Likewise living conditions on board American vessels were far more satisfactory. Much of the shipping on the high seas involved the French colonies, America, and Europe; hence seizure of American produce and American sailors soon became irksome to American shipping interests. This situation created a loud clamor for protection of American interests along the Atlantic seaboard, and between 1804 and 1809 President Jefferson found himself in a quandary over the future policy of the United States. He was not willing to prepare for aggressive war, but how to prepare for coastal defense without giving alarming external evidence of doing so, was a delicate problem. As well as these troubles, President Jefferson was faced with the difficulty of convincing his conservative and frugal Secretary of the Treasury, Albert Gallatin, that the United States could finance adequate coastal defense. When approached on the subject, Gallatin declared himself unwilling to part with his hard-earned surplus but put the responsibility of raising additional revenue upon Congress. Thus Jefferson was convinced that if a war proved imminent, it would be an inexpensive one. He set about preparing for protection of the American coast by ordering the Navy Department to construct a fleet of cheap, flat-bottomed gunboats for coastal defense. This plan resulted in complete failure, as the fate of gunboat *Number One* proved eloquently in 1804, when during a hurricane near Savannah, Georgia, it was washed eight miles upon the shore and left stranded in a cornfield. Because of this misfortune, Jefferson was ridiculed in the toast: "Gunboat *Number One*. If our gunboats are of no use upon the water, may they be the best on earth."

Jefferson now appealed to Congress for legislation regulating American shipping. Such an act was passed on April 18, 1806, restricting commercial intercourse. On June 22, 1807, the British demonstrated the extent to which they disregarded American efforts to remain neutral when in a search for deserting sailors, the British frigate, *Leopard*, fired upon the American frigate, the *Chesapeake*, outside the Capes at Norfolk, Virginia. This attack came so suddenly that Captain Barron of the *Chesapeake* was forced to strike his colors after having fired but a single shot. When the *Chesapeake* struck her colors, four sailors were remanded from her decks by the English, of whom three were Americans and one an Englishman. After the occurrence of this insulting incident the American press clamored for a declaration of war.

Until 1807 the West, an agrarian section, had looked upon the international struggle with little or no definite interest, but after the *Chesapeake-Leopard* affair this attitude underwent a sudden change. In these latter years while the East was losing its commerce, the West was being prodded in an already festered side by British-Indian alliances in the Northwest. When Kentucky newspapers carried news of the *Chesapeake-Leopard* engagement, the westerners were prompt in denouncing England's shameful disregard of the neutral rights of the new republic. In the Kentucky legislature Henry Clay introduced resolutions approving President Jefferson's policies of handling American affairs, while Humphrey Marshall, a contentious Federalist, offered a set of uncomplimentary resolutions which were unanimously rejected. Clay's resolutions were adopted over a single dissenting vote, a vote which brought about a heated argument between Clay and Marshall over the virtues of federalism and republicanism and finally resulted in a duel.

On March 4, 1809, President Jefferson was succeeded in the presidency by his fellow Republican, James Madison. Madison, like Jefferson, was a pronounced lover of peace. He conscientiously believed that he could maneuver the country around a war with England. Kentuckians, although they had approved Jefferson's policy, were now up in arms to drive the British out of the Northwest where they were considered a direct threat to the state. With war sentiment running high, Madison's views were wholly disregarded in the election of 1810. The so-called "Young War Hawks" were elected to the twelfth Congress. Kentucky's contribution to this Congress was two favorite sons, Henry Clay and Richard M. Johnson. In Clay was centered the West's hope for war with England, and he soon justified the confidence of his supporters. He was elected Speaker of the House of Representatives, in which position he was able to assist materially in maneuvering the war decision through that body. Clay's colleagues were, for the most part, youthful. In the total membership of one hundred and forty-two, seventy were young men serving their first term.

The new members of Congress clamored for war, disregarding Madison's diligent efforts to maintain peace. In the midst of this argument, Madison and his cabinet allowed themselves to be completely hoodwinked by Napoleon when the terms of Macon's Bill "Number Two" were accepted. Napoleon had promised to favor American shipping, a thing which he utterly failed to do, provided the United States reimposed nonintercourse with Great Britain. This act cut the Gordian knot! War was certain! Clay and his youthful colleagues would stand foreign insults no longer.

If any Kentuckians seriously opposed impressments, embargoes, and other maritime hindrances, it was in a spirit of injured pride, for Kentucky's welfare was little affected. During the early months of 1810, however, there was a sudden change of local sentiment, a change which was wrought largely in the United States Congress. Senator William Branch Giles of Virginia, in an effort to cultivate a war sentiment, was, perhaps, the first to promote the idea of protecting the frontier from Indian attacks by seizing British territory. A month later Henry Clay of Kentucky was advocating the capture of Canada, saying, "the conquest of Canada is in your power." Clay believed that the militia of Kentucky alone could effect the capture of Canada and by this act protect the white population of the West. Richard M. Johnson of Kentucky supported the conquest idea. Like Clay he desired that an army and navy of sufficient strength should be created to guard Canada and to free the high seas of smuggling. Johnson even stated the belief that the Divine Providence intended that the waters of the St. Lawrence and the Mississippi should form interlocking systems. Debating the Florida bill in the eleventh Congress Henry Clay stated: "I am not, sir, in favor of cherishing the passion of conquest. But I must be permitted to conclude by declaring my hope to see, ere long, the *new* United States (if you will allow me the expression) embracing not only the old thirteen states, but the entire country east of the Mississippi, including East Florida, and some of the territories to the north of us." On December 31, 1811, while debating a bill which proposed to increase the army, Clay declared, "Canada is the avowed object. Suppose you conquer Upper Canada, you must leave men behind to hold it, when you march to Quebec. Your rear must be protected; it would be a new mode of warfare to leave it unprotected! Gentlemen will be deceived, if they calculate upon the treason of the Canadian people. Well, sir, you lay siege to Quebec, garrisoned, I am informed, by seven or eight thousand British forces; you must have at least double that number to take possession of the place. . . . With an army of twenty-five thousand men, the territorial war would probably terminate in one year. . . ."

While Clay and Johnson were advocating the capture of Canada, Kentuckians were becoming more excited over the impending war. Taverns, public squares, and other public meeting places were crowded to overflowing by anxious Kentuckians engaged in "war talk." These Kentuckians had an hereditary hatred of the western Indians, and the "War Hawks" had played upon this hatred and fear to good advantage. After 1810 the *Lexington Reporter,* the *Kentucky Gazette,* and the *American Republic* carried weekly editorial discussions of the approaching war with the British and Indians. Kentucky was by 1811 definitely anti-British. Conversation centered around opposition to Great Britain. Toasts were drunk encouraging war, long-winded orators denounced English trickery, and, at Frankfort, the general assembly passed a bill forbidding the citation of cases adjudged in England since July 4, 1776. Even Clay, a "War Hawk," was forbidden the privilege of reading from one of the prohibited English decisions. In a remarkably short time Kentuckians had regained the hatred of their forefathers against their savage foes. Many of the older men, recalling the days of fighting Indians under the commands of St. Clair, Harmar, and "Mad" Anthony Wayne, were ready to fight again. The time had come to drive the Indians forever beyond possible striking distance and wrest from them a vast area of fertile land. This was sufficient reason, in 1812 at least, for the war. On November 7, 1811, William Henry Harrison fought the Battle of Tippecanoe, which opened the struggle for the West.

In the West the war had become a reality, and it was believed that the British, as in the days of Hamilton, the "ha'r buyer," were again inciting the Indians to action. William Henry Harrison defeating Tecumseh's half-brother, the Shawnee Prophet, in the Battle of Tippecanoe (1811) discovered that his braves were equipped with a good grade of glazed powder, and with British rifles so new that they were still wrapped in their "list." This victory added momentum to the "War Hawks'" struggle, and so strong did sentiment become that even eccentric and amusing John Randolph of Roanoke was unable to gain listeners in his fiery arguments against the war. On June 1, 1812, Madison sacrificed his sacred pacifist views on the altar of Mars and instructed Congress and the Nation to prepare for war. Congress, an anxious listener, was prompt in carrying out this executive order, and preparation was made to push the war bill through at once. The bill, however, was delayed twelve days in the Senate, where the war party was not so well organized. Even Senator John Pope of Kentucky was an opponent of the bill and was largely responsible for the delay. On June 18, 1812, President Madison signed the bill, and the United States declared war on Great Britain.

In Kentucky, news that war had been declared was welcomed, and Senator Pope's actions were regarded as treasonable. Mobs thronging the streets of Nicholasville and Mount Sterling burned him in effigy, and other Kentucky towns were equally vehement in their denunciation of the wayward Senator.

Immediate preparations were made to supply Kentucky's quota of men. Of the 100,000 men asked for in Madison's proclamation, Kentucky's proportion was ten regiments totaling 5,500 troops. In the meantime, General William Hull advanced toward the Northwest and the Canadian border, where he disgracefully surrendered his forces al-

most immediately and without making a single fight for the protection
of the frontier at Detroit. The Kentucky troops had advanced no farther than Georgetown when this disheartening news reached the state.
Everybody denounced Hull's act as one of unmitigated cowardice and
criticized Madison for keeping such inefficient men in the army. The
war, to the West, was a life and death struggle. Before the President
could act, the Kentuckians made William Henry Harrison Major General of Kentucky militia. Harrison was given immediate command
of the Kentuckians then on the march to Detroit. Harrison was highly
regarded by his men, for he had proved his courage at Tippecanoe.
Governor Charles Scott, a soldier of the frontier, cheerfully accepted
Harrison's appointment, but this selection was not altogether pleasing
to President Madison, who had chosen General Winchester of Tennessee as Hull's successor. Winchester, however, was wise enough, when
he assumed command on September 19, 1812, to yield to the westerners' choice of General Harrison.

Kentucky had 7,000 troops in the field, and volunteering was equally
heavy in Indiana. On September 3, 1812, Kentucky troops arrived at
Piqua, from which a detachment under the command of Lieutenant
Colonel Lewis was sent to rescue Fort Wayne. At Piqua, Winchester
made the mistake of marching his men in a disorganized formation
over a large area of territory without having in mind any definite goal.
This aimless maneuvering did nothing but disgust the militiamen, and
since many of the Kentuckians were "six-months" soldiers and their
terms of service were rapidly approaching the date of expiration, they
were anxious to engage their enemies in a fight. These Kentucky
troops did not wish to go home without participating in at least one
skirmish. However, this lack of leadership was soon to react against
General Winchester, who, acting upon the faulty information that
Frenchtown was the abode of a large number of hostile French and
Indians, advanced on that village. On January 18, 1813, a company of
Kentuckians under the leadership of John Allen and William Lewis
had captured Frenchtown, and on January 20, the main forces under
General Winchester joined the victorious troops. At this place the
Americans were left facing the British encampment at Malden, which
was only eighteen miles away.

Fortunately for the British troops the Raisin River was partially frozen over, making of it an open path to Frenchtown. Upon his arrival at Frenchtown, Winchester committed another blunder which cost him most of his meager reputation as a military officer. Following an antiquated military custom, he placed the regulars in the position of honor on the right of his headquarters, and, unfortunately, the right-wing position faced an exposed stretch of level, wind-swept ground. A second blunder was the fact that he established his headquarters at a farmhouse nearly a mile away. To complete his blundering, Winchester, being unable to provide a stockade for all of his troops, allowed Colonel Wells to withdraw his command and to move it to the rapids of the Maumee.

Even when a French scout, friendly to the American cause, warned Winchester that British and Indian troops were advancing from Malden, he failed to make the necessary preparations to repel their attack. On February 22, British troops under General Proctor assaulted the exposed American front lines. The troops inside the small fortress found themselves securely protected against the attack, but the seasoned and valuable regulars were exposed to open fire from which they suffered unnecessarily heavy losses. After a large number of American troops were wounded and killed, General Proctor, unwilling to keep up the assault, offered the Americans liberal terms of surrender. His chief promise to the American officers was that he would protect them against an Indian massacre. These terms were accepted by the Americans in good faith, but General Proctor did not keep his promise! He left the wounded American troops in the unguarded Frenchtown fortress, and on the following morning more than two hundred blackened Indian warriors, mad with victory, invaded the stockade and brutally slaughtered every prisoner. After this inhuman act Proctor deserved and received the severest criticism for his lack of caution.

In Kentucky the alarming report of the "Raisin" slaughter acted as an immediate call to arms. Messengers who carried the news to Frankfort called Governor Shelby from the theater to inform him of the British atrocity. Public opinion reached fever heat, and Governor Shelby, a grizzled, sixty-six-year-old veteran of many hard-fought frontier campaigns, was appealed to for active leadership in the field, an appeal which he heeded before the war ended. Volunteer militia companies were organized at once, and the streets of many Kentucky towns became scenes of military activity. Individuals unfit for military service subscribed generously to campaign funds for equipment. At Georgetown, Congressman Richard M. Johnson and his brother, Lieutenant Colonel James Johnson, busied themselves raising and drilling a mounted troop. Even the women of Kentucky were busily engaged with spinning wheels and looms in order to supply the militia with clothing.

In the midst of all this enthusiastic preparation, Kentucky military officials were confronted with two trying problems; first, the terms of enlistment under the Kentucky laws were for only six months; second, there was a serious lack of training of many soldiers sent to the Canadian front and little opportunity for remedying this situation before they went into battle. Most of these troops engaged in battle with only a hunting knowledge of their guns. In many cases raw militiamen were taken from between the plow handles to the field of battle with only a half dozen indifferent lessons in group fighting.

Notwithstanding many handicaps, the Kentucky militia was soon on the march. The new regiments were placed under the efficient command of General Green Clay whose discipline took the form of appealing lectures on their duty. He placed responsibility of success or failure directly upon the shoulders of his men.

At the rapids of the Maumee, near Lake Erie, William Henry Harrison halted his troops and constructed a fort which he called Fort Meigs. When General Clay and his Kentucky volunteers reached this fort, they found it surrounded by the enemy, but by a careful maneuver most of the men succeeded in getting inside the fortification. In fact, the only part of Clay's forces which failed to enter the fortification was a detachment of unseasoned volunteers whose victorious skirmish with the Indians gave them the conceited notion that they could overcome the opposition of the whole British Army.

General Proctor soon wearied of his indifferent attack on Fort Meigs and withdrew his army to the area eastward, where he came on Fort Stephenson under the command of Major George Croghan. During the early months of fighting in this area Harrison ordered this fort destroyed, but he was persuaded by the twenty-two-year-old Croghan to maintain the fortress as an outpost. Croghan held the fortress with 150 militiamen, and when Proctor appeared with 1,500 men, both officers thought that surrender of the fort would be only a matter of minutes. However a benignant fate smiled on Croghan, for within a short time several officers and one fifth of the assaulting column had been brought down by the sharp-eyed Kentucky and Ohio militiamen. This surprise stand was shocking to the British, and General Proctor, not wishing to risk a further undue loss of British regulars, withdrew to Malden.

The war in the Northwest had lasted almost twelve months, with the Americans showing no definite advance. In Kentucky sentiment was strongly tinctured with anxiety, and more militia companies were raised. In the summer of 1813 Governor Shelby ordered additional Kentucky volunteers to join him at Newport, from whence they would proceed under his leadership to Canada. He stated in his call that he was complying with the legislature's request that he personally assume leadership.

On September 10 Perry defeated the British naval forces on Lake Erie and sent his famous dispatch to General Harrison, "We have met the enemy and they are ours." Thus the way to victory was paved for the land forces. Harrison and Shelby consolidated forces, creating an American fighting strength of 6,500 men. Richard M. Johnson was detailed to Detroit with 1,000 men. Johnson's command, composed mostly of cavalrymen, was rushed to Sandwich and then across the Detroit River. Frightened by information of this move by the Americans, Proctor began retreating, but not until he and Chief Tecumseh had decided to burn the public buildings at Detroit. On September 27 General Harrison issued the order: "The General entreats his brave troops to remember that they are to fight for the rights of their insulted country, while their opponents combat for the unjust pretensions of a master." A second order was more effective: "Kentuckians: Remember the River Raisin; but remember it only whilst the victory is suspended. The revenge of a soldier cannot be gratified by a fallen enemy."

At Sandwich the combined pursuing forces of Johnson, Shelby, and Harrison outnumbered those of Proctor and Tecumseh. On the upper Thames Proctor halted to give fight to his pursuers, but the Kentuckians attacked with too much vigor. British regulars were surrounded by Kentucky cavalry and infantrymen yelling at the top of their voices "Remember the Raisin!" Within a few moments the Americans forced the British to surrender.

In the swamp on the right side of the field of battle the fighting was more intense. Colonel Richard M. Johnson had crossed the swamp and stood face to face with Tecumseh's braves, who were hidden in the woods. Unable to determine their exact location, Johnson asked for nineteen of his best men to volunteer to assist him in drawing the fire of the enemy. As this brave group moved toward certain death, each man was conscious that somewhere in the bushes ahead 1,500 Indian guns were accurately trained upon them. The "Forlorn Hope," as this group was called, moved to the edge of the sheltering thicket before the Indian commander ordered "fire!" When the smoke cleared away, fifteen of these twenty daring men were dying, but the leader, in some miraculous manner, still sat erect, despite the fact that he was painfully injured by a dozen wounds. At the edge of the forest the advancing Americans dismounted, with the exception of Colonel Johnson, who, although seriously wounded, remained seated on his white horse. The conflict between Tecumseh's braves and the Kentuckians raged for a quarter of an hour with no victory. Then Colonel Johnson came face to face with Tecumseh, whom, it is said, he shot fatally with his pistol, thus setting the Indian warriors to flight. They had believed Tecumseh immortal, but when they saw him dying, their courage left them. The victory of the Thames, October 5, 1813, broke the hold of the British and Indians in the Northwest. General Harrison and his colleagues gained this stronghold largely through the use of a determined Kentucky militia which fought to relieve their state forever from the British and Indian menace in the Northwest.

New Orleans

In 1814 the scene of military activity shifted from the old Northwest to the old Southwest. At New Orleans in the latter part of 1814 General Andrew Jackson of Tennessee was busily preparing his defense against British attack. Kentucky's quota for the Southwest division amounted to 5,500 troops, and 2,200 of these were dispatched promptly to New Orleans under the command of Major General John Thomas and Brigadier General John Adair. When they reached New Orleans on January 4, 1815, just four days before the attack on that city, the two armies were already drawn up face to face for the approaching battle. The Kentuckians reported to Edward Livingston, prominent lawyer and adviser to General Jackson, to whom they conveyed the startling information that they were unarmed. When Livingston informed

General Jackson of the Kentuckians' plight, Jackson said: "I don't believe it. I have never seen a Kentuckian without a gun and a pack of cards and a bottle of whiskey in my life."

On January 6, General Jackson was informed that the British were preparing for the attack, and on the seventh he discovered, by the use of field glasses, that they were making sugar cane fascines and ladders. This activity convinced him that the main attack would be made against Morgan, on his left. Jackson reinforced Morgan's forces with 500 Kentuckians, only 170 of whom were armed, but the main body of these troops were bivouacked in the rear as reserves. Four hundred rusty *escopetas* were secured from the veteran police in New Orleans, so that every second man from Kentucky was, at the last moment, provided with arms. Unhappily the guns supplied the Kentucky volunteers were strange to them, and on the morning of January 8, when Brigadier General Adair was instructed to bring up his Kentucky reserves and distribute them behind Carroll's and Coffee's units, they were poorly equipped to fight.

When General Jackson took his stand on the parapet of his Rodriguez Canal fortification to observe the British advance, he gave orders not to fire under four hundred yards, and to aim at the cross plates formed by the white belts over the crimson jackets of the British troops. How well the Americans aimed is best told in a young British officer's account of the skill of E. M. Brank of Greenville, Kentucky. This story has been preserved in manuscript form and is a part of the Durrett Collection.

We marched in solid column in a direct line, upon the American defenses. I belonged to the staff; and as we advanced, we watched through our glasses, the position of the enemy, with that intensity an officer only feels when marching into the jaws of death. It was a strange sight, that breastwork, with the crowds of beings behind, their heads only visible above the line of defense. We could distinctly see their long rifles lying on the works, and the batteries in our front, with their great mouths gapping toward us.

We could also see the position of General Jackson, with his staff around him. But what attracted our attention most, was the figure of a tall man standing on the breastworks, dressed in linsey-woolsey, with buckskin leggins, and a broad brimmed felt hat that fell round the face, almost concealing the features. He was standing in one of those picturesque graceful attitudes peculiar to those natural men dwelling in forests. The body rested on the left leg, and swayed with a curved line upward. The right arm was extended, the hand grasping the rifle near the muzzle, the butt of which rested near the toe of his right foot. With the left hand he raised the rim of the hat from his eyes, and seemed gazing intently on our advancing column. The cannon of the enemy had opened on us, and tore through our works with dreadful slaughter; but we continued to advance, unwavering and cool, as if nothing threatened our progress.

The roar of the cannon had no effect upon the figure before us; he seemed fixed motionless as a statue. At last he moved, threw back his hat-rim over the crown with his left hand, raised the rifle to the shoulder, and took aim at our group.

Our eyes were riveted upon him; at whom had he leveled his piece? But the distance was so great, that we looked at each other and smiled. We saw the rifles flash, and very rightly conjectured that his aim was in the direction of our party. My right hand companion, as noble a fellow as ever rode at the head of a regiment, fell from his saddle.

The hunter paused a few moments, without moving his gun from his shoulder. Then he reloaded and assumed his former attitude. Throwing the hat rim over his eyes, and again holding it up with the left hand, he fixed his piercing gaze upon us, as if hunting out another victim. Once more the hat brim was thrown back, and the gun raised to his shoulder. This time we did not smile, but cast glances at each other, to see which of us must die.

When again the rifle flashed, another one of our party dropped to the earth. There was something most awful in this marching on to certain death. The cannon and thousands of musket balls playing upon our ranks, we cared not for; for there was a chance of escaping them. Most of us had walked as coolly upon batteries more destructive, without quailing; but to know that every time that rifle was leveled toward us, and its bullet sprang from the barrel, one of us must surely fall; to see it rest motionless as if poised on a rack, and know, when the hammer came down, that the messenger of death drove unerringly to its goal, to know this, and still march on, was awful. I could see nothing but the tall figure standing on the breastworks; he seemed to grow, phantomlike, higher and higher, assuming, through the smoke the supernatural appearance of some great spirit of death. Again did he reload and discharge, and reload and discharge his rifle, with the same unfailing aim, and the same unfailing result; and it was with indescribable pleasure that I beheld, as we neared the American lines, the sulphurous clouds gathering around us, and shutting that spectral hunter from our gaze. We lost the battle; and to my mind, the Kentucky rifleman contributed more to our defeat, than anything else; for while he remained in our sight, our attention was drawn from our duties; and when, at last, he became enshrouded in the smoke, the work was complete; we were in utter confusion, and unable, in the extremity, to restore order sufficiently to make any successful attack.—The battle was lost.

During the Battle of New Orleans, an incident occurred which resulted in many heated arguments. When Pakenham, Keane, Gibbs, and other British officers had fallen, and the frost-covered plains of Chalmette were stained red with the life blood of picked British troops, General Jackson was chagrined to learn of Thornton's flanking attack. Jackson again climbed to the top of his scarred parapet and peered through his glasses in the direction of Morgan's division on his right.

He shouted to his men to "take off your hats and give them three cheers!" This burst of enthusiasm was premature, however, for Morgan was falling back, Patterson was spiking his guns, and Jackson's rear was threatened. General Jackson sent General Jean Humbolt on the run with 400 militiamen, but the frontier militia, refusing to serve under a foreigner, made this assistance ineffective. Thus the night of January 8 found the right wing of the American army still in difficulty. This situation, however, was relieved by the retreat of all the British forces during the night.

In an impetuous outburst of temper General Jackson wrote Monroe that the complete destruction of the British Army, an ambition of his since childhood, had rested squarely upon the shoulders of "A strong detachment of Kentucky troops [which had] ingloriously fled." General Jackson was convinced that this was true, and the court of inquiry presided over by William Carroll could not persuade him to believe otherwise. Carroll decided that the Kentucky troops were "not reprehensible," and that their failure on the western bank was due to General Jackson's having placed the incompetent Morgan in command, and then refused to supply him with sufficient reserves. The War Department was also at fault, for it failed to arm the Kentucky volunteers as it had promised.

Treaty of Ghent

The beginning of peace negotiations and the outbreak of the War of 1812 were almost simultaneous. Russia offered its services as mediator in the early period of the struggle. In the summer of 1813 England offered to negotiate for peace, and this plan met with the immediate approval of President Madison. Accordingly, an American delegation was sent to Göttingen and then to Ghent to negotiate with the British commissioners. The American delegation was composed of some of the ablest men in the service of the Government. Before the work was completed, its most outstanding members were Henry Clay, James Bayard, Jonathan Russell, Albert Gallatin, and John Quincy Adams.

The American commissioners were thoroughly familiar with the problem before them, for Henry Clay of Kentucky had been a moving spirit in the whole war and had been in close contact with the foreign relations of the United States since 1810. John Quincy Adams, ambassador to Russia, was reared in an atmosphere of diplomacy, for his father had often represented the United States on foreign missions. Albert Gallatin, although not a diplomat, was a financier of note and was likewise familiar with foreign financial and diplomatic relations. He turned out to be the most useful member of the delegation.

Clay displayed little or no excitement for the task at hand; in fact, he regarded this journey to Europe as combining pleasure and business. Adams was often disgusted with his colleagues, and he recorded in his diary that frequently dining at one o'clock in the afternoon, his profligate companions would not appear until four. It seemed incredible to him that the other members, entrusted with such a mission, could sit for hours about the dining table smoking bad cigars and drinking poor wine.

Nevertheless, the thirty-seven-year-old "War Hawk," Henry Clay from Kentucky, was alert to all that happened around him. He was not given to pious meditation and repentance except when he lost at poker; and, unlike Adams, he took life as it came and with few or no misgivings. It is said that he complained of "long sittings" at the dining table, of bad cigars, and of poor wine only when there were not enough to go around. While Adams was enjoying a full night's sleep, his colleague indulged in an all-night card game. Adams often noted in his diary that he got up at four o'clock in the morning only to find his companions retiring.

In the British commission there were less able representatives, for doubtless the British Government believed it unnecessary to send their best men to confer with the Americans. The more able English diplomats were busily engaged in remaking the map of Europe after the victorious army under Wellington had paved the way at Waterloo for such negotiations. At Ghent the English delegation was composed of Lord Gambier, Henry Goulburn, and William Adams.

When negotiations opened, the Americans found themselves at a disadvantage, for the American Navy was blockaded, and the American Army had failed to penetrate Canada. At this date (1813) the Americans were forced to take what the British offered, and the disaffection of New England cast long shadows over American hopes.[2] At Washing-

---

[2] New England had opposed the war and had gone so far as to give assistance to the enemy. The West was definitely interested in the expansionist movement, while New England was concerned with a sea-going commerce.

ton the capitol was burned, August 24, 1814, and to all outward appearances a British victory along the Atlantic coast was certain.

Thus, with all the advantages in their favor, the British delegates demanded an Indian reserve to be created from the Northwest territory, the northern part of Maine to be ceded to Canada, the United States to forego the privilege of keeping warships on the Great Lakes, and England to enjoy joint rights of navigation on the Mississippi. On the other hand, the Americans were anxious to secure a commitment from England regarding her theories of maritime laws and to determine whether England would surrender Canada.

The Americans flatly refused to accept the British demands, and at this point in the proceedings Clay took the American cause in hand. Although not a trained diplomat, he was an excellent student of human nature and capable of divining the reactions of his adversaries. He soon discovered that British demands were nothing more than smoke screens to conceal their anxiety for peace. He then informed the British that the American delegation was preparing to leave the conference, since they were unable to reach an agreement, for rightly he felt that the British commissioners lacked courage to call his bluff. They inadvertently showed their hands and allowed Clay to see to what extent the American threats had disturbed them. Subsequently the British delegation received new instructions from home, making them less insistent concerning their original terms.

On December 24, 1814, (fourteen days before the Battle of New Orleans) the Treaty of Ghent was signed. This document was a compromise, providing for cessation of hostilities, for release of prisoners, for restoration of conquest by both sides, for a cessation of Indian hostilities, and for settlement of the boundary dispute by a commission. The subject of maritime violations was not mentioned. The Marquis of Wellesley, brother of the Duke of Wellington, said that the Americans, in his opinion, had showed an astonishing superiority over the British commissioners during the whole period of negotiation. This treaty did not mention the rights of navigation of the Mississippi River. This point had caused considerable friction between Clay and Adams. By its silence on this point the Treaty of Ghent secured for the Kentuckians free use once and for all of the Mississippi River.

CHAPTER VIII

An Episode in Finance and Politics

DEPENDENT upon its own resources, Kentucky early became an independent commercial empire, since trade with the South was made possible by use of the river system. One difficulty, however, proved virtually insurmountable, and that was the need for a medium of exchange. Hence banking history practically begins with that of the state's commercial system. Obviously the early banks were not formal institutions, but, like Kentucky's early commerce, were primitive in organization; they served as rude clearing houses where notes were issued on goods deposited.

In 1780, John Sanders came to Louisville by way of the Ohio River, tied his shanty boat at the river front, and went into the banking business. He issued bills of credit on goods left in his charge, and when these goods were sold in New Orleans, his notes were redeemed in Kentucky with foreign coins. Since there was no uniform American currency in the West, the money used by the early traders was representative of the coinage of every country trading with the United States. Nevertheless it satisfied, in a limited way, the need for money in Kentucky. The following note, preserved in the Durrett Collection of Manuscripts, throws an interesting light on this system of banking:

Know all men by these presents that Daniel Boone hath deposited 6 beaver skins in my Keep in good order and of the worth of six shillings each skin, and I have took from them 6 shillings for the keep of them, and when they be sold I will pay the balance of 30 shillings for the whole lot to any person who presents this certificate and delivers it up to me at my Keep. Louisville, Falls of Ohio, May 20, 1784.

"John Sanders."

The scarcity of a medium of exchange often delayed early commercial transactions in Kentucky. Because of the lack of banks and currency, a system of barter grew up. Merchants advertised that they would accept bear, fox, otter, beaver, and raccoon skins, or country

138

sugar and linen in exchange for merchandise. John Bradford, editor of the *Kentucky Gazette,* advertised that he would accept produce in exchange for subscriptions. This situation was not to exist for long, however, because in 1802 the Kentucky Insurance Company was chartered and given banking privileges.

The Kentucky Insurance Company's monopoly on the banking business of the state was short-lived. On December 27, 1806, the Bank of Kentucky was chartered and capitalized at $1,000,000, one half of this amount to be held by the state. Its board of directors was composed of twelve men, six of whom were appointed by the state government. Thus the outbreak of the War of 1812 found Kentucky relying on these two banking institutions.

Kentucky commerce and industry became well established during the years in which British goods were kept off the American market. American products found a lucrative market at home and abroad with high prices for a limited supply of goods. Many new manufacturing enterprises were established, and by the end of the war an investment and speculative fever had gained a strangle hold upon the whole West.

Kentucky powder factories in 1812 produced 301,937 pounds of powder, and her iron furnaces produced large quantities of refined products. Textile mills sprang up to sell their products at fancy prices. Hemp and tobacco advanced to new high levels, and a marked demand for other farm produce developed. With the advance in agricultural and industrial commodity prices, land values were boosted also. In the neighborhood of Lexington, land was selling from $100 to $200 per acre, one large farm having sold at the latter price. John Bradbury, a western traveler, noted that a single acre in Louisville sold for $30,000. Artisans were few, and their charges outrageous. Common laborers demanded prices unheard of elsewhere for unskilled labor.

Coupled with this speculative mania were the blighting effects of an unstable currency. The state had developed so rapidly that the meager supply of foreign coins and the primitive system of barter were no longer satisfactory. The only source for currency was the Bank of Kentucky which was issuing a limited number of notes, but the bank would not redeem its paper in gold and silver, since it was claimed that such procedure would be ruinous to the institution. In the face of this situation, the Federal Government established branches of the first

United States Bank at Lexington and at Louisville. These institutions damaged the local bank's business, for they demanded specie payment of notes issued by the local state banks. This created confusion and brought forth bitter criticism. It was claimed that the United States Bank stifled the Kentucky banks and that it attempted to convey all of the gold and silver out of the state.

Since most of Kentucky's local banking business was conducted by the Bank of Kentucky and independent "wildcat" banks, there was a demand for an extension of the local banking system. This caused further expansion of the Bank of Kentucky and a more rapid development of private institutions. Many of these private ventures were combined with manufacturing or other commercial interests, one such company being capitalized at $1,000,000. There was also a strong sectional plea for more banks, since representatives of both northern and southern Kentucky asked that their respective sections be supplied with a sufficient number of branch banks to facilitate a growing business.

In general, a charter and a printing press constituted sufficient equipment for establishing a successful bank. During the session of the legislature in 1818, the public's requests were granted in the passage of an act, over strong opposition, chartering forty-six semi-independent branch banks with an aggregate capital stock of $8,700,000. These new banks were located in the various towns of the state and ranged in capital strength from $1,000,000 in Lexington and Louisville to $100,000 in smaller towns. Now that the banking system was established, the legislature solved the currency problem by authorizing forty-six institutions to issue $26,000,000 in paper money, an amount which equaled one third of the state's property evaluation in 1815.

The creation of the new banks and the wholesale issuance of paper money excited more criticism. Whereas the state had lacked enough banking institutions to carry on its business in 1812, it was now beset with too many banks. With the two national branches, the private, and state branch banks, there were fifty-nine banking institutions in the state in 1818.

Crisp new notes, fresh from the printing presses, had a demoralizing effect. Persons who were not in debt used their credit to borrow money, and speculators readily encouraged individual indebtedness. Within six months private citizens felt that they were in disrepute unless they were financially involved in at least one speculative venture. In the rapid distribution of the new currency much confusion resulted, for no one had worked out a basis of exchange. This encouraged "shavers" and brokers to practice nefarious trades. At first, individuals were able to exchange their branch bank notes at a ten per cent discount, but soon the rate rose to ninety-five per cent. By midsummer of 1819, the Kentuckians were thoroughly involved in a most unhappy financial predicament. Business houses refused to accept the Kentucky bank currency in payment for goods and services; branch banks of the United States would not accept the Kentucky currency; and the "wildcat" banks, or the so called "Forty Thieves," refused notes from one another. Farmers living in rural sections were almost ruined because their business was transacted without definite information on the status of a rapidly changing market.

So furious did the struggle become that Kentucky, in 1819, found herself the victim of a stringent money panic. Commodity prices sank to ridiculously low levels, and real estate was worth hardly one sixth of its boom market price. So rapid was Kentucky's descent from the peak of prosperity following the war that the state was seemingly bankrupt almost overnight. Homesteads were heavily mortgaged, and business generally was stagnant. The only institutions on a sound financial footing were the state treasury, the Bank of Kentucky, and the two branches of the United States Bank. To relieve the pitiable plight of his fellow Kentuckians, Governor John Adair recommended state support of internal improvements.

As manufacturing interests were driven out of business, labor was compelled to leave the state, and immigrants from the eastern part of the country avoided Kentucky. Many planters and large slaveholders moved from Kentucky to the newly opened cotton states of Alabama, Mississippi, and Louisiana. The institution of slavery was jeopardized in Kentucky by the prevailing panic, because frightened masters sold many slaves to the planters of the Lower South.

One by one the banks felt the pinch of the times and closed their doors. When this wholesale spree of borrowing had finally ended, the Kentucky property holders were indebted locally to the extent of $10,-000,000. In addition to this local debt, merchants in Kentucky owed $4,000,000 to merchants in the East. This plight prompted the calling of "relief" meetings in which efforts were made to save the depressed debtors from complete ruin. Plans ranging from wholesale issuance of additional paper currency to the repudiation of private debts were proposed. The legislature was plied with numerous petitions begging relief. On December 16, 1819, the legislature passed a law granting a stay of sixty days on all judgment executions, provided the defendants would give bonds to release the goods levied upon at the end of this period. A second step was taken on February 11, 1820, the day after the "wildcat" banks ceased to exist, when the replevin law was enacted. By this latter act the plaintiff could stay action on his bill by writing on the back of the note: "Note on the Bank of Kentucky or its branches, (will be) accepted in discharge of this judgment or decree." Otherwise the defendant could delay payment for a period of two years.

The legislature took a third step by revoking all banking charters, except that of the Bank of Kentucky. Thus the Bank of Kentucky, its thirteen solvent branches, and the two branches of the National Bank were the only ones left. But the National Banks made the people feel oppressed, for they did not hesitate to foreclose on mortgages and to execute their rights. An attempt was made to tax these banks out of existence, but the legislature was restrained from taking such a radical step by the McCullough *vs.* Maryland decision of the United States Supreme Court. Not to be thwarted, the legislature extended the time of replevy on judgments of this bank from three to twelve months, and, under certain conditions, to two years.

This latter step on the part of the legislature aroused the people. If it was thought that the legislature could extend the period of replevy, it could also legislate relief. Thus a majority of members chosen for the general assembly in 1820 were elected because of a pledge to support such a program. Governor Adair, in his message in October, 1820, expressed the opinion that some action on the state's financial predicament would have to be taken. On November 29, 1820, the legislature chartered the Bank of the Commonwealth to tide Kentucky over the depression. It was capitalized at $2,000,000, the entire stock to be owned by the state. On the strength of its capital stock the bank was authorized to issue $3,000,000 worth of notes for circulation. These notes were in turn secured by money paid into the treasury by the purchasers of vacant public lands west of the Tennessee River, by unexpected balances left in the state treasury, and by stock of the Bank of Kentucky held by the state. Twelve branches, located according to judical districts, were established, to make a new and complete state financial institution.

The Bank of Kentucky, the only sound local banking institution (except the two federal branches), alienated the friendship of the radical Relief Party in 1821 when it began executing its notes and mortgages. Since its immediate extinction was favored by the Relief Party, the "relief" members in the legislature proceeded to gain control of this institution by dismissing the directors, and capitalizing the prestige of the Bank of Kentucky to promote the Bank of the Commonwealth. Within the year the Commonwealth's Bank had issued $2,300,-000 in notes and had loaned $2,400,000 on mortgages. Its stocks and notes fell to a fraction of their face value, and this naturally led to financial complications. Debtors' property was seized by their creditors and sold to satisfy the outstanding debts. This course inevitably led to the courts.

A case involving the replevin laws was brought before the circuit court of Bourbon County. In this instance Williams brought suit against Blair to collect $219.67. Judge James Clark of Clark County rendered a decision in which he held that the replevin act of the legislature was unconstitutional because it violated the right of contract guaranteed in the National Constitution. He held further that this act impaired, *ex post facto,* the "right of contract clause" embodied in the state constitution. Relief partisans were embittered by the fact that a mere circuit judge questioned the acts of the state legislature, and Judge Clark was looked upon as an impertinent upstart who had far overstepped his authority. (A second case, Tapsley *vs.* Brashear, was tried before Judge Francis Preston Blair in Fayette County, who rendered a decision similar to that of Judge Clark.) When the next legislature assembled, the Clark County Judge was called before the house to explain his decision. This he did very ably in a well prepared and scholarly argument, which was followed by a full day's discussion. It was pointed out by the defense that the circuit judge's decision was in no way final, for already the case had been transferred to the Court of Appeals. Nevertheless a resolution was introduced in the legislature to "address" Judge Clark, but this act failed to receive the necessary two thirds majority.

This latter move rebounded against the legislature's position, for many who had originally favored relief were now opposed to it. A further blow was dealt legislative relief when the Court of Appeals, in 1823, upheld Judge Clark's decision. Two judges handed down decisions against the *ex post facto* aspects of the state law, while a third member of the court held the entire act unconstitutional. Composing the court were Judges John Boyle, William Owsley, and Benjamin Mills, who, although rendering three separate opinions, were in fundamental agreement.

In upholding the circuit court decision, the Court of Appeals added the final straw that broke the back of legislative patience. Kentucky's legislature stood rebuked by three men, and the whole program of relief was threatened with complete failure unless something should be done. A majority of the state's voters were so enraged that when the legislature met, petitions poured in from all sides asking that the judges be rebuked—a request which was granted. Governor John Adair was asked to reprove the judges and to reorganize the Court of Appeals, but this "address" failed to receive the two thirds majority necessary for passage. Unafraid of the legislature's threats, the court continued to declare the acts of that body unconstitutional and to warn the people that they had adopted a dangerous procedure. The Court of Appeals was positive that its decisions would be upheld by the Supreme Court of the United States. Nevertheless, sentiment in the state remained at fever pitch in favor of relief and against the court. It was generally felt that the judges were a social class apart from the rest of the people of the state. The early sins of the court were now visited upon it. In the past the judges had taken too much interest in purely political matters, and this now served as a basis for much legislative enmity.

Immediately after the meeting of the legislature, various schemes were under way for breaking up the power of the court. It was suggested that the court be divided into three units to be located in different parts of the state. Some of the more radical legislators advocated calling a constitutional convention for the purpose of revising the constitution so as to subject the court to the legislature. This latter

proposal, however, brought violent opposition from the Antirelief
Party, which shrewdly defeated the calling of a constitutional convention by holding that such a convention would doubtless lead to the
freedom of the slaves; also, that the seat of government would be removed from Frankfort; and that Transylvania University would be removed from Lexington.

While the issues of relief and antirelief were at the highest pitch, in
1825, Joseph Desha entered the race for Governor on the Relief ticket,
opposing Christopher Tompkins, the Antirelief candidate. Although
both candidates were Jeffersonian Republicans, their differing views
on the banking issue caused the campaign to be one of bitterness.
General Joseph Desha was ambitious to be Governor at all cost and
spread far and wide much information, and as much misinformation,
concerning the courts and relief. He had for his campaign slogan:
"Liberty or Slavery," and in the August elections he defeated his opponent by a majority of 16,000 votes. His election was regarded by
the Relief Party as a command from the people to the legislature to
make necessary readjustments in the state's government.

Acting on what it believed to be the dictates of the people, the Relief
Party in the legislature proceeded to adopt resolutions condemning
the courts, but a third time its activity was thwarted by the lack of the
necessary two thirds majority. The house proposed to reduce the
judges' salaries to 25 cents, while the senate wished to abolish the court
entirely. On December 9, 1824, the senate voted to abolish the court,
but on December 24, the house voted for its reorganization. Since this
bill was an ordinary legislative act it required a majority of only one
vote, but the passage involved a day and night of debating. The New
Court was made up of four judges, while the Old Court had only three.
The aggregate salaries of the Old Court amounted to $4,500, but those
of the new to $8,000. William T. Barry of the Fayette Circuit Court
was appointed chief justice, and James Haggin, John Trimble, and
W. B. Patton were made associate justices, with Francis P. Blair as
clerk.

A tug of war now ensued between the Old and New Courts because
the New Court was powerless to act without the docket and papers of
the Old Court, which refused to yield its records. Francis P. Blair and

Achilles Sneed (clerk of the Old Court) engaged in a game of hide and seek with the records. When the New Court assumed its official duties on December 12, 1825, Blair undertook to secure the records from Sneed by peaceful means, but since these failed, he smashed the door of the courtroom, thus compelling Sneed to surrender his records. Sneed was then carried before the new judicial body and fined $50 for contempt of court.

Once the New Court took its seat it immediately became deeply involved with the legislature. Defenders of the Old Court held that it was a body created by the constitution and not by the legislature, and this developed a bitter fight between these divisions of the government. The legislature assured the court that it represented the will of the people and that the court could only adjudicate law suits, because, from the legislative viewpoint, it was politically sinful for the court to maintain ideas concerning the will of the people, since it was regarded as the servant and not the master.

While the New Court was in session in the Court of Appeals headquarters, the Old Court was meeting in a Frankfort church. However, little business was conducted by the latter, since its meetings were held merely for the purpose of keeping life in the body until after the August elections.

With supporters of both sides hurling invectives, the struggle became very bitter between the two courts. A pamphlet was issued by the New Court, entitled *Liberty Saved, or the warnings of an Old Kentuckian to his fellow citizens on the danger of Electing Partisans of the Old Court of Appeals,* in which the Old Court was portrayed as a triumvirate of tyrants who wished to control the will of the people. Nevertheless in the face of this bitter criticism the election of representatives favored the Old Court. On August 9, 1826, the Old Court, or Antirelief, partisans elected fifty-six representatives and twenty-one senators, to forty-six New Court or Relief representatives and seventeen senators. With this victory in its favor, the Old Court took a new interest in life, for its reinstatement was a foregone conclusion. Governor Desha made a last desperate effort to uphold his New Court by declaring any act on the part of the Old Court a contempt subject to fine. When the original body attempted to secure the court records, it was met with guns at the door of Francis P. Blair's office, and arms were collected to chase the house of representatives from its hall.

Early in November, the house of the legislature referred the question of courts to the Committee on Courts of Justice, and the reinstatement of the Old Court was sanctioned by a vote of sixty to thirty-six. On January 1, 1827, Francis P. Blair delivered the record of the court to Achilles Sneed, the justices of the New Court resigned, and the Old Court was reinstated. In order to unravel the many tangled threads, Mills and Owsley resigned and were immediately reappointed. In the case of Hildreth's Heirs *vs.* McIntyre's Devisees the court declared all the acts and decisions of the so called New Court null and void, and, on April 15, 1829, the long chapter was closed.

In 1822 the Kentucky legislature selected the state's favorite son, Henry Clay, to succeed President Monroe, and requests were sent to the other state legislatures asking that Kentucky's choice be supported. Several states, Ohio, Illinois, Missouri, and Louisiana, responded in the affirmative. Clay, however, was not to seek unopposed the highest office in the gift of the people, for there were three other contenders. The first was William H. Crawford of Georgia, who, having adhered strictly to the rules of the Jeffersonian partisans, now offered himself as standard bearer of the Republican Party. He launched his candidacy from the vantage point of his office of Secretary of the Treasury. In New England it was felt that John Quincy Adams, also a favorite son, and Monroe's Secretary of State, was the most logical candidate for the presidency. A fourth candidate was Andrew Jackson from Tennessee, who, from the standpoint of experience, was the least well equipped of the entrants. He offered as credentials his residence in the West and his military reputation as the hero of Horseshoe Bend and New Orleans.

Despite the popularity of the other two candidiates in the West, the election of 1824 was a duel between Clay and Jackson. Rivalry between these two candidates was keen, for they had been enemies since Clay introduced resolutions in the National House of Representatives calling for an investigation of the high-handed acts of General Jackson in the Florida campaign.

In the election of 1824, Kentucky's support went to Henry Clay, but the final national vote gave Clay a total of only thirty-seven electoral votes. Jackson received ninety-nine votes, Adams eighty-four, and

Crawford forty-one. Clay, obviously, was out of the race, and Jackson, although receiving the highest number of votes, failed to secure a majority over his two nearest opponents. Thus the selection of the next President was transferred from the hands of the people to the National House of Representatives. As Speaker of the House, Clay found himself in a position to turn defeat into success by influencing the selection of one of his three opponents to succeed the venerable Monroe. Aside from a thorough dislike for Jackson, Clay did not believe him temperamentally fitted for the task of Chief Executive. Furthermore, Jackson had outraged Kentucky when he spoke disparagingly of the Kentuckians' valor at the Battle of New Orleans. Clay realized that Jackson had performed many valiant deeds but at the same time had committed some inexcusable blunders. General Jackson had irked Clay by his utter disregard for the niceties of diplomacy, and by his forthright ignorance of many principles which Clay believed important.

While Clay was weighing the merits and demerits of Jackson, he was likewise appraising John Quincy Adams. He was misled into believing that Adams would be rejected after his first term and that he, Clay, could be elected in 1828. Thus Clay in violation of the instructions sent him by the relief legislature in Kentucky supported the election of John Quincy Adams.

Kentucky was thrown into a violent indignation, and for the moment Henry Clay was branded an archtraitor, "a willful turncoat," and a defiler of public morals. In some sections the voters were so outraged that they burned the "favorite son" in effigy. Cries of "bargain and corruption" upset the entire country, and opponents of Clay and Adams were convinced that the Kentuckian had sold his influence to Adams for his appointment as Secretary of State. Clay, despite his denunciation by the Kentucky legislature, soon redeemed himself with the people by publishing a pamphlet in which he set forth his reasons for disregarding the instructions of the legislature. He answered Jackson's queries by saying that the people never intended that he should be President or they would have elected him instead of putting the responsibility upon the House of Representatives. Also, he informed Jackson that he fought much better than he reasoned.

When Clay completed his work in Washington, he returned to Ken-

The Falls of the Ohio at Louisville

The Fort at Harrodsburg, the Oldest Town in Kentucky

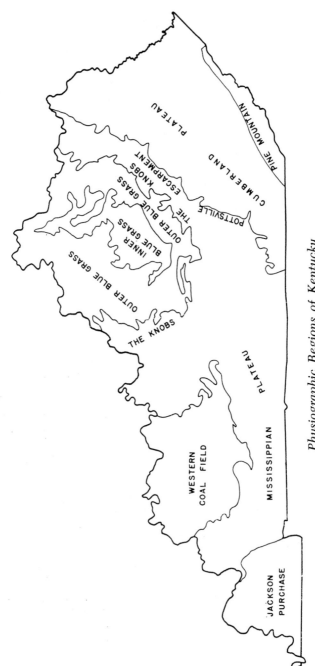

PINE MOUNTAIN

CUMBERLAND PLATEAU

POTTSVILLE

THE ESCARPMENT

KNOBS

OUTER BLUE GRASS

INNER BLUE GRASS

OUTER BLUE GRASS

THE KNOBS

WESTERN COAL FIELD

MISSISSIPPIAN PLATEAU

JACKSON PURCHASE

Physiographic Regions of Kentucky

Daniel Boone's Grave at Frankfort

Sycamore Shoals on the Holston River in Tennessee

An Early Kentucky Story-and-a-Half House

A Double Log House

tucky by way of the Cumberland Road and the Ohio River. At Maysville he was welcomed by an enthusiastic crowd of loyal partisans, and
as he proceeded to Lexington he was met by additional cheering
throngs. At Lexington, friends of the "Great Commoner" spread a
dinner in his honor, where he was toasted thus: "Our respected guest,
beloved fellow-citizen and late able representative, Henry Clay, we
rejoice in the occasion of expressing to the world, and emphatically to
his enemies, our undiminished confidence in his incorruptible integrity
and our unqualified approbation of his conduct from his first to his last
most important act, as our representative." Throughout Kentucky
Clay was feted and praised, in a way to indicate clearly that his enemies
had failed to shake the faith of his loyal constituents.

Clay's triumphant journey through Kentucky added more fuel to an
already blazing fire. Between 1824 and 1828, the Kentucky political
pot boiled furiously when partisan forces were busily engaged in the
organization of two strong political parties. One of these groups
supported the views of the Clay contingent, while the other sponsored
the cause of Jacksonian Democracy. The organization of this Democratic Party created much excitement. General and Mrs. Jackson were
invited to spend the summer of 1826 at Graham's Spring for the latter's
health, but Jackson very wisely rejected the Kentuckians' invitation
because his presence in Kentucky at this time would have fanned anew
the old hatred of his charges of cowardice. There was also grave danger that his wife, formerly Rachel Robards, would be subjected to
humiliating memories, since it was at Harrodsburg that she had lived
with her notoriously trifling husband, Lewis Robards. However, the
Jacksonians' ardor for their chieftain was not dampened by his refusal
to visit Harrodsburg, for Jackson dinners and barbecues were held in
every section of the state. On January 8, 1828, 203 delegates, under the
leadership of Robert Breckinridge, met at Frankfort to select the state's
electoral ticket. The Jackson Party was welded into a united body
when William T. Barry, formerly chief justice of the New Court, was
selected as a candidate for Governor on the Democratic ticket.

At the same time the Jackson forces were gathering their supporters
into a unified party, Clay's partisans were busily promoting their cause.
They were determined, however disappointing to the "master of Ash-

land," that John Quincy Adams should run a second time to free himself from the malodorous charges of his first election.

Tactics of the two parties were far from being open and aboveboard, for the Clay forces opened the old sore of Jackson's hotheaded charges of the Kentuckians' cowardice at New Orleans. In this charge Clay forces found a satisfying antidote for the embarrassing accusations of bargain and corruption. The Whig Party held its convention (the first of its kind) on December 17, 1827, at Frankfort, with 300 delegates, representing 60 counties, and at this meeting Adams was selected as candidate for President and Thomas Metcalfe was chosen as candidate for Governor.

In 1825–1828 Clay found himself in the midst of a political squall which a shrewd Jacksonian press made difficult to allay. He undertook to vindicate his stand in 1824 and to answer permanently the legislature's inquiry as to why he disobeyed its mandate of that year. He published a pamphlet prior to Adams' second campaign entitled: *An address of Henry Clay to the Public containing Certain Testimony in Refutation of the Charges against him made by General Andrew Jackson touching the Last Presidential Election.* When this pamphlet reached the Kentucky legislature, the Whig senate considered Clay's defense complete and adopted a set of resolutions (over the opposition of the few Jackson supporters) holding that the charges of "bargain and corruption" were clearly brought forward only to blast the reputations of certain anti-Jackson members of Congress.

In the house of the state legislature, however, Jackson supporters were anxious to add further to Clay's embarrassment by recalling his opposition to Adams in the making of the Treaty of Ghent. They cited that at the time this treaty was being made, Clay and his fellow Kentuckians suspected that Adams had attempted to trade the West's privilege of using the Mississippi to the Spanish Government in order to protect the East's commercial rights. Amos Kendall, editor of the *Argus of Western America,* and a New Court and relief partisan, conducted the Jackson campaign in Kentucky. Kendall, a school teacher, had moved to Kentucky from New England, and during his early years in the state he had often found himself dependent upon the gracious hospitality of Henry Clay's family at Lexington. Clay, as a consequence, formed an attachment for him and often confided to him his political secrets. During the negotiations of the Treaty of Ghent, Kendall published in the *Argus of Western America* a number of letters from Clay ridiculing and condemning the part played by Adams, and when Henry Clay returned to Kentucky, he unfortunately persuaded Kendall in 1822 and 1823 to republish these letters in pamphlet form. Kendall stated later to the state legislature that Clay had paid him $100 to publish this pamphlet. This testimony placed the Clay forces of the Kentucky House of Representatives in a dilemma, since a vote for or against the resolutions exonerating Clay of "bargain and corruption" would either label Clay a libeler and slanderer, or admit that Adams was willing to sell the interest of the West in order to favor the East. Hence the Jackson supporters, fully realizing their advantage, virtually forced Clay's friends in the legislature to admit that they would vote for Adams when he stood with Clay, and vote him a knave when he stood alone. Although Clay's supporters remained loyal to Adams, this dispute proved to them that Adams was a grave political responsibility. Clay and his friends worked diligently for Adams, but in vain, for Adams lost the state to Jackson by a popular vote of 39,394 to 31,460. This meant the loss of fourteen electoral votes. In the local election the Jacksonian forces also triumphed.

When Jackson was first inaugurated President of the United States, he did not forget those who had helped him to realize his ambition. He gratefully remembered his friends in his neighboring State of Kentucky when selecting members of his official family. William T. Barry was made Postmaster General, Amos Kendall was given a place in the treasury, and Francis P. Blair, a sharp-tongued New Court partisan, was made director of the administration's editorial policies.

The "Forty Thieves" or "Ali Baba's follies" were long since forgotten; the Bank of Kentucky had ceased to function, and the Bank of the Commonwealth had failed, leaving many wrecked fortunes in its wake. Branches of the United States Bank were the only banking institutions functioning in the state, and under the influence of these banks Kentucky gradually worked toward restoring its wrecked financial structure. Howls of the Relief Party were converted into praise for the United States Bank, but this influence did not reach Washington, for Kendall and Blair were whispering words of condemnation of the local branch banks into the ears of their political patron, the President. They claimed that the United States Bank was not too warmly regarded in Kentucky because it was playing politics, and made their tale of woe even more doleful when they informed the President that only a Clay supporter could borrow money from the bank. This latter assertion was wholly unfounded and is to be explained by the anxious and solicitous Blair's heavy indebtedness to the Lexington branch bank.

Time had wrought a great change, and Kentucky businessmen were frightened at the growing national disfavor of the bank, for they regarded it as the nerve center of local commerce and industry. Protests were numerous on the part of the Lexington commercial interests against presidential meddling with the national banking business, for in Jackson's first administration he and his henchmen let it be known that there was little prospect that the bank would be rechartered in 1836 when the original charter expired.

Other issues which came to the front during the Jacksonian administration were the questions of tariff readjustment and internal improvement. Need for a low tariff was keenly felt, especially in parts of the West and the South, which were the two centers of Jacksonian support. This problem was of vital importance to Kentucky; therefore the tariff of 1828 had been cleverly designed to favor the West and South, but to rest heavily upon the shoulders of New England and the East generally. Jackson was pleased with the measure of 1828, but Clay, long a friend of the idea, was provoked with the "Tariff of Abominations." He favored what he chose to call his "American System," secured the Kentucky legislature's approval of his system in 1832, and forced a reorganization of the tariff.

While dealing with the tariff question, Clay was successful in forcing the second issue into the political arena and in worrying President Jackson with it. In collusion with Nicholas Biddle, the Kentucky Congressman forced the issue of rechartering the United States Bank in 1832, although its charter did not expire until 1836.

Unfortunately for the administration, the banking situation in Kentucky had changed complexion, and the bank, which was regarded in 1820 as a monster standing ready to gulp down the wretched creditor, was now looked upon as a sound and necessary institution. For instance, the branch at Lexington was conducting an exchange business of $1,500,000 per annum and thus by opposing the bank, Jackson lost much hard-won support in Kentucky.

"Old Hickory" found himself further involved in the question of internal improvements, a matter which was also of vital importance to western commerce. A proposal was made that the National Government subsidize the construction of a national highway for military purposes which would eventually lead from Cumberland, Maryland, through the states of Pennsylvania and Ohio, to Missouri, and by way of a lateral branch through Kentucky, Tennessee, Alabama, and Mississippi to New Orleans. Unfortunately, the first bill proposing to offer a national subsidy to a public highway was labeled the "Maysville and Lexington Road Bill," a bill which proposed the construction of a highway from Maysville to Lexington. This bill was passed by the House of Representatives, but failed by a single vote in the Senate, and Senator John Rowan of Kentucky was justly accredited with its disheartening defeat. Despite this setback, however, the Kentucky Legislature, anticipating eventual federal support for the project, chartered the Maysville, Washington, Paris, and Lexington Turnpike Company, granting it the right to issue capital stock up to $820,000. A second bill proposing a national subsidy for the Maysville and Lexington Road was introduced in the National House of Representatives in 1830 and was passed by both houses (although Senator Bibb of Kentucky voted in the negative). President Jackson had announced in advance of its passage that he opposed national aid to internal improvements, and he vetoed the Maysville Road Bill on the ground that it was a local project, an unconstitutional and unjustifiable use of federal funds. This veto had its discouraging effect upon both Clay and Jackson supporters of internal improvement at national expense in Kentucky, and likewise discouraged other state proposals of a similar nature. Indignation meetings in which the President was openly accused of disregarding the interest of the people, and of recklessly using his veto power, were held throughout the state.

Clay was elected in 1831 to fill the senatorial vacancy from Kentucky, and from this point of vantage he was able to maneuver the President into several embarrassing situations. Jackson, however, met the banking question squarely by denouncing the bank as a corrupt monopoly and by declaring himself willing to assume the responsibility of destroying it. Clay, however, had the advantage of the Chief Executive when the tariff question was brought to the forefront. Clay had gone through the tariff struggle of 1824. In his "American System" he had committed himself as a protectionist. As Carl Schurz says: "He was now no longer the Kentucky farmer pleading for hemp and home-spun, nor the cautious citizen anxious to have his country make its own clothes in time of war. He had developed into the full protectionist, intent upon using the power of the government, so far as it would go, to multiply and foster manufacturers, not with commerce, but rather in preference [*sic*] of commerce." In 1831 Clay was looking forward to the presidency, and to realize this goal he attempted to embarrass President Jackson by forcing the issues of the tariff, of internal improvements, and of rechartering the United States Bank. Jackson, realizing that it would be political suicide to dodge the issue of the tariff, met the question by approving the tariff bill of 1832.

Jackson was re-elected in 1832, again defeating Clay but not without a worthy struggle with the newly organized Whig forces. This second election of the "Hero of New Orleans" led directly to the nullification controversy in South Carolina. Early in his first administration Jackson had severed friendly relations with John C. Calhoun, and the Jackson party showed little regard for the welfare of Calhoun's constituency when it came to the question of establishing tariff rates. It was said that the nullifiers of South Carolina were basing their claims upon the Virginia and Kentucky Resolutions, which ordinarily would have appealed to Clay. In this case, however, Clay was not to be duped, for he saw plainly that South Carolina's defiance in the nullification fight would result in the placement of war powers in the President's hands, and his own complete political ostracism.

In order to avoid an open outbreak in South Carolina and the combination of Jackson and Webster political forces, the compromise group in Congress prevailed upon Henry Clay to volunteer his good offices. He proceeded to secure the co-operation of Calhoun and to draw up a compromise bill which proposed to scale the tariff rate down to a twenty per cent average level by 1842, and to increase the free list.

When the provisions of the compromise measure became known, Clay was severely criticized by the country at large, but especially by the hemp growers of Kentucky. It was well known that the Kentuckian, a shrewd parliamentarian, had rushed the bill through the Senate and had stood at the elbow of another Kentuckian, Robert Letcher, while he sponsored its enactment in the House.

Unfortunately for the Whig cause, the great compromise proved a boomerang, and by Clay's own admission it was one of his most serious political blunders, for he had allowed Kentucky's influence to pave the way for relieving South Carolina of her treasonable act.

Passage of the compromise tariff bill ended the nullification controversy, but it did not solve the bank struggle. Jackson was now determined to act, and after two unsuccessful attempts he found a Secretary of the Treasury in Roger B. Taney who would withdraw the funds of the United States from the United States Bank to sustain the local "pet" banks. On September 22, 1833, Taney withdrew the United States funds from the National Bank, an act which was undoubtedly encouraged by Amos Kendall, William Taylor Barry, and Francis P. Blair, Kentuckians and intimates of the President, who had come fresh from Kentucky where they had been the chief actors as heavy debtors in the comedy of the Old and New Court struggle. At this late date, however, they did not speak for their fellow statesmen who then regarded the bank as necessary to their economic welfare.

Taney's ill-advised and rash act was in part responsible for a national financial disorganization similar to that of Kentucky during 1818–1826. Printing presses were set in motion; wildcat banks sprang up like mushrooms; and, in 1837, the nation was in the throes of an acute financial panic, caused by overspeculation which had been brought about largely by the availability of wildcat currency.

CHAPTER IX

Agricultural and Industrial Beginnings

AGRICULTURE and industry had their beginnings in Kentucky with the arrival of the first settlers. These first immigrants transferred a seasoned knowledge of backwoods agriculture from their homes in the eastern settlements to their new homes in Kentucky. From natural circumstances, the new settlers in Kentucky were forced to take up agricultural pursuits, and had it not been for the yield from their early cornfields they would have suffered starvation. Every fort had its cornfield near by, but destruction of this crop by marauding savages spelled virtual starvation during the winter months. When the Indians were driven back and the frontier had become reasonably safe from surprise raids, families moved out to individual farms in the open country to begin extensive cultivation of various adaptable field crops.

Returns from a minimum amount of work on the farms proved so satisfactory that travelers going back to the settlements east of the mountains proclaimed Kentucky a land of agricultural riches. In the communities of western Virginia and the Carolinas, the "Kentucky fever" spread so that the Wilderness Road leading from eastern Tennessee and Cumberland Gap was lined with families moving westward in the hope of becoming economically independent. At the same time numerous weary parties of immigrants survived the trying ordeal of floating southward down the Ohio River from Pittsburgh and the old Red Stone Fort on the Monongahela in order to start life anew on the frontier in Kentucky. News of Kentucky's bountiful resources was spread far and wide by travelers who were prone to exaggerate upon their stories at each telling. The effect of this land booming was soon noticeable, for Kentucky was rapidly populated. By 1800 every section of the state, except the Cherokee reservation south of the Cumberland and Tennessee Rivers, was settled. Agriculture thrived throughout the state. In the Blue Grass region, where the buffalo, elk, and deer had ranged, farmers found excellent grazing land for livestock and fertile lands for the cultivation of field crops.

Cultivation of corn dated from the beginning of settlement and was, as already noted, the most important source of food. Wheat, however, did not make its appearance in Kentucky until the year 1777, when the first crop was grown at the very doors of the fortification at Harrodsburg. This early crop was small, producing little more than enough grain for reseeding purposes, but here the start was made for one of Kentucky's major agricultural crops. Perhaps one of the main reasons wheat was not transferred to the West when the first settlements were made was that it could not be successfully ground with the awkward pestle and mortar, for it was not until 1783 that the first gristmill was established in the state.

So fertile was the land of the Kentucky Blue Grass country that grain crops planted on unfallowed land grew too rank and became subject to smut and immaturity. In order to fallow the land for suitable grain cultivation, Kentuckians early made use of hemp, a coarse plant which took from the soil a large amount of nitrogenous matter. Since 1775, the planters of Kentucky had been growing hemp, but it was not until later that they discovered a profitable use for its long stringy fibers. When the shipping industry on the western rivers developed, there was a keen demand for roping, and the hemp growers began to manufacture rope and coarse sailcloth. Very little hempen cloth of a fine texture was made, principally because of the coarseness of the raw material.

To the east and the south of Kentucky, planters were pushing out on the frontier. In 1793 Eli Whitney, an ingenious Yankee schoolmaster, accepted the challenge of his hostess, Mrs. Green of Georgia, and invented a cotton gin which rapidly developed the laggard cotton industry. With the invention of the cotton gin, the cotton belt was extended at a rapid rate, and there was an increasing demand for hempen bagging with which to wrap cotton bales. Hemp had other uses in the making of sheeting, floor covering, and, in some cases, the manufacture of paper. Another factor which made hemp highly acceptable to the Kentucky planters as a staple crop was its thorough feasibility of cultivation with slave labor.

Tobacco culture, like that of the staple grain crops, dates from the beginning of agricultural endeavor in the state, for many immigrants from east of the mountains were born in tobacco growing regions. Despite the fact that the piedmont regions of Virginia and Carolina were poor, the inhabitants met their financial obligations to the King and the coastal government with tobacco payments. Hence it was only natural that tobacco-using adventurers coming into Kentucky should bring with them tobacco seeds and begin the cultivation of this plant. Already the center of the tobacco industry was moving westward because of the depletion of the soils in the tidewater. Most of the early tobacco crops were consumed locally, since there were several difficulties to overcome in transporting this commodity to market. It was not until after James Wilkinson had made his privateering trip into the closed Spanish port of New Orleans in 1787 that tobacco became a salable product in the West. As tobacco culture was slow in gaining a headway, it was not until after 1830 that it rivaled other Kentucky agricultural crops.

Livestock Development

At the same time the early Kentuckians were busily engaged in preparing their acres for the cultivation of staple grain crops they were laying a firm foundation for the livestock industry. Nature had prepared the state for a livestock industry long before the first white man entered the region. Centuries before the European visited the eastern shores of the North American continent, large herds of buffalo, deer, elk, bear, and other game roamed through the savannah lands and cane brakes of central Kentucky to fatten on the luxuriant growth of grasses and canes. These broad expanses of grass lands, the fresh water streams, and an abundance of game afforded many hunting tales to pass on from one Indian tribe to another. Savage hunters dreamed of hunting in Kentucky second only to dreaming of the happy hunting grounds.

English settlers, crossing over into Kentucky from the piedmont country east of the mountains, recognized immediately the potentialities of its pasturelands. Thomas Walker was duly impressed in 1750 with that part of Kentucky which he saw as a land rich in livestock possibilities. He was perhaps the first white to transfer the horse to this new country of the West, but it remained for Daniel Boone and his "Long Hunting" comrades to bring the first horses into the Blue Grass. This party of hunters brought with them a number of animals which they used for packing purposes; in fact, Daniel Boone was captured the first time by the Indians while attempting to rescue his party's straying horses. These hunters were quick to note that their horses thrived in this new grazing land, and those interested in gaining material wealth returned to their homes east of the mountains to tell stories of the grazing advantages of the West.

As a result of hunters' observations, the early immigrants into Kentucky drove before them goodly numbers of domestic animals. Boone's settlers, who turned back on him in Cumberland Gap in 1773, had a large number of domestic animals with which they hoped to build an extensive grazing business on the other side of the mountains. Livestock brought by the Harrodsburg and Boonesborough settlers marked the real beginning of Kentucky's livestock history. Settlers who came to these frontier posts brought droves of hogs, sheep, and cattle. Goods were packed in by horseback, and the pack animals were kept for frontier carriers, for beasts of burden in general, and for breeding purposes. Savage onlookers interpreted the transfer of livestock to the "Dark and Bloody Ground" as an evil and unhappy omen of the whites' intention to stay, for already they knew the story of hunting grounds converted to pastures along the Atlantic coast.

Since cattle raising was typical of the westward advance of American civilization, Kentucky's meadowland formed a most important link in the chain of the westward-moving cattle industry. This was Kentucky's first major livestock undertaking, for many of the settlers who endured the hardships of the long tedious journey across the mountains into the central part of the state expected to earn a living by little more than listening to the tinkle of cow bells. Herds of range cattle supplemented the corn crop with meat, butter, and leather, and in lean years when the corn crop failed or was destroyed, the herd was the sole dependence. Professional cattlemen of the frontier were poor, lazy, indifferent individuals who devoted little or no attention to clearing the ground and to growing crops. When more industrious settlers moved too near their grazing lands, they sold their holdings and moved farther west. No frontier family was without at least one cow and calf, for the cow was regarded as a necessity. Not only did the faithful herd supply the frontier family with dairy products, but the cow was an efficient danger alarm for Indian raids. It developed that many of the raids took place near milking time, and the stampede of the cattle was a more certain warning of impending danger than was the barking of the family dog.

No emphasis was placed upon ancestral breeding as far as these first cattle were concerned. However, the pure bred cattle industry was transferred to the western grazing lands at a very early date. In 1785, the year after Kentucky began her protracted struggle to gain state independence, three sons of Matthew Patton moved from the Potomac River Valley to Kentucky, bringing with them three "grade" heifers of their father's famous stock. Thus began the blooded cattle business. Witnessing the success of his sons, Matthew Patton transferred his herd of pure bred cattle from his Potomac farm to Nicholasville, Kentucky. In his new home Patton at once began to improve an already famous herd. It was from this herd that the American strain of shorthorn cattle had its beginning.

Colonial manufacturing made the growing of sheep imperative. Since most of the manufacturing in the southern colonies was done in the home, it was only natural that each family owned its flock of sheep. When the cattle industry was being transferred to Kentucky, flocks of sheep were also driven over the Wilderness Road. To appreciate the proportions which this colonial industry has reached in Kentucky, one has only to drive through the state today to observe the well stocked pastures of sheep on almost every farm. Like the early cattle, the early flocks of sheep were without noteworthy pedigrees. It was not until sheep grazing was well established west of the mountains that the farmers became interested in improving the breeds of their herds. Most of the Kentucky flocks were improved with imported English stock. New stock was imported into Kentucky before the end of the second decade of the nineteenth century. The pioneers were dependent upon their sheep wool to substitute for the rapidly diminishing supply of native buffalo wool.

Many families migrating to Kentucky brought with them droves of hogs, and droves were brought into the state over the Wilderness Road or were floated down the Ohio River on flatboats by professional graziers. The hog proved to be one of the settlers' most valuable assets, for he not only supplied pork and lard for the frontiersman's table, but he likewise supplied lard oil for the crude lamps and grease for the soap kettles. From the beginning, pork became a valuable stock in trade outside the West, for it was discovered that the hog was an excellent traveler and could work his way to market and at the same time earn a handsome profit for his owner. Drovers built up a thriving trade between Kentucky and the eastern states. They left Kentucky in the early summer months, and by early frost they arrived in the eastern market with their hogs in excellent condition and weighing considerably more after grazing along the way. Hogs and cattle were first driven over the Wilderness Road to the Potomac Valley in Virginia, and from their graziers disposed of them in the Baltimore and Philadelphia markets.

With the cessation of hostilities in the War of 1812, and the expansion of the southern cotton belt, the livestock trade from Kentucky increased rapidly. This trade had become so extensive by 1838 that the fertile county of Bourbon, reporting a negligible production of grain and tobacco, led the list in livestock and distillery productions with 10,-000 head of cattle, 40,000 hogs, 3,000 horses and mules, $50,000 worth of bacon and lard, and $70,000 worth of Bourbon whiskey.

Travelers and toll gate keepers, as early as 1800, were impressed with the large droves of horses and mules which passed daily on their overland journey to the Cotton Kingdom. Ex-Governor Shelby was a participant in this trade, for in a letter to his wife written from Columbia, South Carolina, he complained of exhaustion from remaining up all night with one of his mules which had snatched a mouthful of skunk cabbage and suffered with the colic. He noted further that "His Excellency," the Governor of South Carolina, had generously provided him with a corral for his mules and that he had accepted the hospitality of the executive mansion for one night. This trade to the cotton state of South Carolina flourished with yearly gains. In 1828 it had reached proportions of sufficient importance to cause the South Carolinians to boycott it in an effort to force Henry Clay to reconsider his stand on the Tariff of Abominations.

Commercial Growth

Despite the fact that Kentucky showed evident signs of rapid commercial development, there was a considerable hesitancy on the part of the state to improve trade routes. As late as 1800 there existed only the two original commercial highways into the state, the Ohio River and the Wilderness Road. Travelers coming into the state over the Ohio River were favored with a southward-flowing current, but it was next to impossible to go out of the state by the same route except in a light craft. Unfortunately, the Wilderness Road, which extended from Cumberland Gap through central Kentucky to Lexington and thence to the present towns of Maysville and Cincinnati, was no more than a crude packtrail. It was not until 1795 that the state legislature was prevailed upon to forget its constitutional wrangling long enough to take cognizance of the state's internal affairs in improving routes of travel. Therefore the exportation of goods, except to New Orleans, was of necessity confined to those goods which could be transported to market under their own power. With the exception of livestock, ginseng and whiskey were the only commodities which would pay transportation costs across the mountains.

The fact that all outlets to market, except the Ohio and Mississippi Rivers, were practically closed obviously forced the Kentucky trade to assume a southern course. Since there was a lucrative demand for Kentucky goods at New Orleans, it was natural that the southern market should have a magnetic attraction for backwoods traders. When Spanish jealousies did not interfere, this trade flourished, so that Blue Grass lands increased in value by 1800 from $60 to $100 an acre. River trade in agricultural commodities dates back to 1787, when James Wilkinson, wishing to gain both political and economic prominence in the West, descended the Ohio with a cargo of tobacco and other agricultural supplies. In New Orleans he employed his suave manner to good advantage, for after making certain far-fetched promises, he was able to return to Kentucky to make a gaudy display of wealth. Not only had his trip netted him a handsome profit, but he had inveigled the suspicious Spanish Governor Miro into an agreement which permitted him to trade at will in the hitherto closed New Orleans market. On his return to Kentucky, Wilkinson advertised by handbill that he was in the market for tobacco, to be delivered at his boat landing on the Kentucky River. Wilkinson was soon repaid for his troubles, for Kentuckians turned to this trade as a profitable venture. Since tobacco, when it could be sold in Kentucky, was bringing $2.50 or less per 100 pounds, merchants experienced little difficulty in persuading local growers to take $9.50 from New Orleans. The increase which was true of tobacco prices was also true of prices paid for other commodities.

Tobacco bade fair in 1790 to become "King of the West," for during the next decade there was a trade of several thousand hogsheads per year. Unfortunately, the foreign market was fickle, and Kentucky tobacco lost its position as favorite when flour milling forged ahead. After 1800 the cotton planters of the South and the people of New Orleans were making heavy demands on the newly settled West for their bread supply. Market reports for 1802 give some interesting figures on the southern trade of Kentucky. In this year 72,000 barrels of dried pork and 2,485 barrels of salted pork were listed, and southern imports as a whole, including 85,570 barrels of flour, were valued at $626,673.

A flourishing trade with the "down river" country stimulated a healthy demand for boats in which to carry the Kentucky goods to market. Accordingly, the boat-building and shipping industry experienced a rapid expansion, and it was this trade which involved some of Kentucky's most interesting history. Kentucky's trade gave rise to some of the most romantic adventures on the western waters. Shipping interests were scattered from the forks of the Monongahela and Allegheny Rivers at Pittsburgh to New Orleans, with Kentucky as a central point. So famous was river traffic from Kentucky that the term "Kentucky boatmen" was well known, and, often, it was an opprobrious one. There were three types of Kentucky craft in general use before they were pushed aside by the more efficient steamboats. There were the "Kentucky broadhorns," or flatboats; the keelboats, long slender craft propelled by oars; and the flatboats or barges which were controlled by long sweeps on each side and aft. The "broadhorns" were most common, for, usually, they were constructed of heavy timbers and plankings which were sold to householders in New Orleans for winter fuel or for building materials. Farmers piled high these clumsy craft with products of their farms and set sail down river for Natchez and New Orleans markets. When they had disposed of their cargo and boats, they formed companies to walk the weary miles back to Kentucky over the Natchez Trace and the Louisville "Boat Road," (later the Louisville and Nashville Highway). More hardy bargemen often attempted to return home in their craft by "cordelling" them upstream. This was a task of endless days and many hardships. Keelboats could make the trip more easily, since they were light and built especially for up-river travel.

So extensive did the river trade from Kentucky become that it even created a special social class in Louisville and in other river towns. At Louisville, the river front swarmed with hardy river men and boat builders who were more at home aboard a cranky river craft than on land. A typical character of this class was Mike Fink. Floating aboard river boats created in the crusty boatmen a hearty disregard for the laws of the shores, and it was not uncommon to see peace officers battling drunken river men in an effort to make them answer in court to charges of misbehavior. Upon one occasion the roistering Fink refused to walk to court in Louisville and embarrassed the process server by requiring him to take his prisoner to court in a boat drawn up the river hill by a yoke of oxen. Not only did the "half horse, half alligator" boatmen have to confront natural and legal difficulties in their river trade, but often they were forced to fight outlaws. Even though their boats were successful in running the rapids, the boatmen never knew when a call for help from a stranded boat was a snare to deprive them of their goods. Individual planters were often forced to sell their products in the Louisville market at a severe discount rather than brave the hardships of the river journey or have their goods swindled from them by dishonest boatmen. Stories of highwaymen of Old England lose interest when compared with the atrocities committed by outlaws and robber bands along the Natchez Trace.

Despite its numerous handicaps, the boat building and river trade flourished, and Kentucky was alert to guard her privilege of trading over the western rivers, even to shedding the blood of her sons. Not only were the Kentuckians jealous of their rights to use the river, but two of her inventive sons, James Rumsey and Edward West, sought eagerly to devise self-propelled boats to increase the effectiveness of river navigation. Despite her liberal shipments to and from the South, Kentucky remained an isolated state. Most of the imported stock in trade came into the state overland from Virginia or down the Ohio River from Pittsburgh where it had been shipped overland from Philadelphia and Baltimore. All the ingenuity in the state was called upon to overcome these handicaps.

Manufacturing

From necessity, the frontier soon became a manufacturing center. A spinning wheel and a pair of wool cards were the symbols of domestic thriftiness. Women spun, wove, and knitted buffalo and sheep's wool, brittle nettles, and flax into cloth. In other ways domestic needs of the frontier household were provided for by home manufacture. Kentucky early developed a domestic system which outdid its British ancestral methods. Households were denied such luxuries as coffee, which easterners deemed indispensable, and the majority of the women of the West were seldom afforded an opportunity to gloat over eastern finery. Fathers and sons, fond of hunting, supplied an ever-decreasing amount of buffalo wool and leather, but the sheep and flax crop made up for this deficiency. Women spun and wove these coarse raw materials into equally coarse jeans, linsey woolseys, and linens, which were in turn made into family clothing. Woolens were favorites in the winter, and flaxen in the summer months. Thus the Kentucky households developed a domestic trade which has endured, for even today Kentucky woven goods bring fancy prices on the market.

As early as 1788, Kentucky's "seven hundred" linens and linseys were listed as important stocks in demand in the East. By the second decade of the nineteenth century, the southern farmers were clamoring for "Kentucky jeans," which were considered the ideal cheap clothing for their slaves.

Not only did faithful Kentucky women spin, weave, and manufacture the family's clothing, but they also provided numerous other household necessities. Soap, candles, sugar, and beeswax were products of their labors. Soap making was a major household industry, for the family saved bacon and meat scraps until a sufficient amount was collected to thicken a quantity of lye made from hardwood ashes. This household activity has long since disappeared, and the ash hopper is no longer a common structure on the farm premises. The hopper was a triangular-shaped box built of boards, the apex of which was stuck into a half section of a hollow log which served as a drain. Ashes were placed in this improvised container to be bleached free of their acid properties by water poured over them from the top. Lye and soap grease were cooked together until thick, and, after cooling, the mass was cut into handy bars, or with less cooking the soap was used in the form of a jelly.

Sugar was made from maple syrup, of which there was a limited supply, but this source of sugar was practically abandoned when Louisiana sugar came on the market. The principal early means of sweetening was sorghum, known to the pioneer as "long sweetening." Honey or treacle furnished much of the sweetening used by early families, and beeswax, a by-product, was useful in a dozen different ways, especially in waxing threads to be used by the cobbler's trade.

Crude wooden vessels for household use were made by handy men from maple and hickory staves. Most important of these vessels were the *piggins* and *noggins,* so designated by the presence and absence of a stave handle. Most every family had its own cobbler in the head of the household, and shoes and moccasins were manufactured from home tanned leathers. Harness and saddles were also made by the household cobblers. On rainy days when farmers were unable to work in their fields, they spent much of their time making spinning wheels, furniture, and looms. There was no necessity for an elaborately equipped workshop, for the average backwoodsman could accomplish much with an ax and a drawing knife. Later, the turning lathe was introduced for turning bed posts, chair legs, loom parts, and spinning wheel spokes and staffs.

Every farmer was his own miller, except in certain localities where water mills were used. On these crude mills both flour and cornmeal were ground. Some of these mills, called "chuck" mills, are seen in eastern Kentucky today. Many frontier families owned and operated whiskey stills and regarded this business in the same light as soap making, for it was a profitable method of converting corn crops into a marketable product. Men butchered, dressed, and cured the family's supply of meat, made salt, gunpowder, shot, and molded bullets as a part of their regular duties.

In the late nineties the *Kentucky Gazette* carried an advertisement from a mechanic who promised to supply textile machinery to the industrially inclined. In an earlier issue of the *Gazette* (1791) the editor boasted that the City of Lexington had for sale hempen goods, gunpowder, shoes, nails, whiskey, flour, clocks, stoves, linens, kettles, mill irons, furniture, silver ware, and many other items. At the same time, he boasted that Lexington had hemp factories a shot tower, tobacco factories, breweries, furniture factories, linen factories, and silversmiths. Trade in linen was extensive enough to justify the operation of a "rag stage," which visited the county seats on court days to exchange cloth and paper for linen rags.

At Danville in 1789 the "Kentucky Manufacturing Company" was organized for the purpose of making cloth and stockings. This society was formed as a community interest by Harry Innes, Thomas Barbee, Christopher Greenup, George Nicholas, and Samuel McDowell. Stockholders were small landholders and small investors generally. Agents were delegated to purchase a British carding machine, spinning machine, and stocking loom. Since this factory was to be established on the frontier, the promoters were faced with the difficult task of securing machinery, and experienced mechanics to operate it. Congressman John Brown was prevailed upon in the spring of 1790 to get machinery and operators and to send them on their journey westward. From Philadelphia to Pittsburgh the machinery was hauled overland, and thence it was shipped by river boat to Maysville. Unfortunately, western liquor was too plentifully available, for the chief mechanic was arrested for misbehavior. When the machinery reached Danville, no one knew how to set it up for operation. This ludicrous situation prevailed until fall, when the British mechanic was released from jail. When this plant finally began operation, it supplied a goodly amount of Kentucky's manufactured woolen and cotton goods.

Kentucky's most promising manufacture was not of woolen and cotton goods, however, for the fertile soil produced a tremendous supply of hemp. At first this crude material was used almost altogether for the manufacture of sailcloth and hempen rope, but, as the shipping and cotton industry expanded, hempen goods became more varied. Unlike the case of the woolen business, there was no machinery in existence for the manufacturing of hempen goods until 1796, when a machine for cleaning raw stock was invented by Nathan Burrows of Lexington. Public opinion favored the manufacture of hempen goods to such an extent that a lottery of $10,000 was subscribed for the purpose of establishing a factory at Georgetown.

Within an increasing demand for hempen goods in the South, Lexington manufacturers developed a thriving trade in this material, and by 1817 they were manufacturing annually 1,000,000 yards of bagging. Kentucky was accredited, by the Census of 1810, with manufacturing 450,000 yards of coarse duck cloth. As early as 1805, a Philadelphia merchant ordered from a Lexington manufacturer twenty tons of hemp yarn packed in "tight hogsheads." This same manufacturer shipped to the port of Natchez a boatload of baling rope, plow lines, and utility twists. In 1815 a Kentucky manufacturer consigned fifty-seven reels of hempen yarn to an eastern manufacturer to receive in return a large shipment of woven fabrics of foreign importation. Hence, it is not surprising that, from 1780 to 1811, the hempen industry increased fortyfold.

The early part of the nineteenth century saw the beginning of several cotton factories in Kentucky. By 1820 there were more cotton factories in Lexington and Louisville than in the whole State of Maine. Lexington alone had twelve of these factories, one of which was driven by steam. This trade reached interesting proportions in the early ante bellum days, and this can be explained only by the fact that Kentucky wished to absorb as much of the cotton trade from the South as possible.

From its beginning Kentucky's salt industry was of major importance. There was no extensive exportation of this commodity; however, the Tennessee papers, especially those of Knoxville and Nashville, were continually advertising Kentucky salt. James Wilkinson developed an extensive local trade by monopolizing the output of many of the more productive salt licks. Salt making in Kentucky dates from the arrival of the hunters who dipped and boiled the brines from the several salt springs over the state. It was at these salt wells that many of the whites were captured by the Indians; for instance, Daniel Boone and his party at the Upper Blue Licks in 1778.

During the early period of its manufacturing history, Kentucky supplied a great quantity of gunpowder. Crude niter was scraped from the floors of the many caverns in the state and boiled until the nitrate particles were separated from the foreign matter. This refined substance was then ground into a fine powder and mixed with charcoal and sulphur. In 1810, 500 pounds of saltpeter were extracted from the Big Bone Cave alone. Hyman Gratz and his associates from Philadelphia developed other sources of crude niter. It was largely through their efforts that the Mammoth Cave of Kentucky was explored and brought into prominence. Powder mills in Lexington alone were estimated to be worth $40,000, a sum which, for that date, was a large investment.

Shot for hunting purposes was also manufactured locally. Hunters using old flintlock and "cap and ball" rifles continued to cast their own bullets by hand, but those using smooth-bore firearms for hunting smaller game, or those who preferred to cover a larger area with their fire, used shot. This shot was made by the novel process of pouring molten lead from the top of a high tower or cliff into a vessel or pool of water at the base. By the fall the molten lead was broken into small particles almost perfectly round and cooled almost immediately by the water.

In Kentucky the distilling industry gained a rapid growth, for the soils of the state were conducive to the manufacture of fine liquors in two ways: first, the soil produced good yields of high grade cereals; and, second, the water used in distilling came from a limestone source. Many early settlers who moved into the West were of Irish and Scotch origin and already knew the secret of successful distilling. They had a taste for corn whiskey. Hence it was only natural that when they moved westward they should turn to distilling. Most families had their own stills, and when their fields yielded more grain than could be disposed of profitably, they converted it into whiskey which could be shipped from the state in jugs and barrels. Most of the early Kentucky whiskey was shipped by way of New Orleans, and thence up the Atlantic coast. Quite by accident the process for making Bourbon whiskey was discovered by the Craig-Parker factory at Georgetown. In 1789 these manufacturers found that whiskey distilled from sour mash could be placed in charred kegs which would remove foreign particles, change the color, and mellow the sharp taste. This discovery formed the basis for many distillers' fortunes, for it made Kentucky Bourbon whiskey internationally famous. In New Orleans this commodity was offered at a premium; in 1819 that port received over 200,000 gallons of whiskey per month from Kentucky. A single distiller in Louisville supplied more than 1,500 gallons daily to the New Orleans trade.

The founding of the *Kentucky Gazette* obviously created a demand for paper, and since it was too expensive to import a supply from over the mountains, industrious promoters manufactured their paper at home. Even the first issue of the *Gazette* carried the notice that Jacob Myers, a German immigrant, was erecting a paper mill in Lincoln County. This ingenious manufacturer addressed himself, in a none too modest note, to the public: "He flatters himself that in the execution of an undertaking which promises such advantages to the district, he will meet with the wishes to see the art of manufacturing flourish." Subscribers were solicited, and in 1793 the mill was turning out enough paper to supply the needs of the *Gazette*. On March 10 of this year the editor announced that the *Gazette* was printed on paper of Kentucky manufacture. It was made at the Georgetown plant of the Craig-Parker Company.

While energetic manufacturers were busily engaged in the production of hempen goods, shot, powder, and whiskey, George Morton established a nail factory in Lexington. He was able to produce for the first time in the West cut nails at the low price of one shilling six pence per pound for tenpenny nails. This factory was the source for nails for the territory within a 200-mile radius of Lexington. The City of Cincinnati, on the Ohio River, was forced to patronize the Lexington factory. Builders bought nails in Lexington to take to Cincinnati by pack horse.

For a long period Kentucky was the center of the furniture manufacturing business, but strangely enough this industry was accepted as such a matter of course that few records remain. Few immigrants coming into the western country brought furniture, and those who did seldom had enough to furnish a house. To import furniture from the East was impossible; hence most of the early furniture was of home manufacture. In most cases, the head of the household made the furniture during the winter months, when he was not engaged in his fields. To manufacture their furniture, the early cabinetmakers were blessed with an abundant supply of native cherry, walnut, and maple. Of necessity, the early pieces were crude, for there were few lathes and tools suitable for this work. Some of the older homes in the state still have pieces of furniture made by the early settlers. In Scott County the Suggett family possesses a secretary of home manufacture which bears the ax marks of its maker on its panelings. Much of the early furniture was made with an ax and a hunting knife.

As the West became more thickly populated, professional cabinetmakers moved into Kentucky, and the newspapers advertised their wares. Many of these craftsmen could make authentic copies of the fine English and French furniture, and this accounts for the present generous supply in the state of "period" furniture made of native woods.

A hat factory catering to members of both sexes was established on the Maysville Road. For those who were unable to pay cash the generous hatterer offered to accept sheep and cows in payment. There were other smaller industries which added to Kentucky's early commercial importance. There were fulling (the process of thickening cloth by applying moisture) mills, lard oil factories, and a number of grist and flour mills. Southern farmers regarded Kentucky as a source of supply for their plantations. Francois A. Michaux was surprised, on his journey through the state in 1802, to find such a well developed and ordered economic system. A merchant from Philadelphia considered Kentucky a flourishing commercial commonwealth. He compared favorably and generously Main Street in Lexington with the business streets of his city.

Such growth was the work of ambitious Kentuckians who were determined to overcome all the obstacles to creating a new commercial system. When families bade farewell to the East and moved to the West, they soon found themselves in the center of trade which was developing southward, a fact which insured them some permanence of trade to make the hardships of the new country more endurable. Merchandise from the East was not available except for those wares which shrewd pack peddlers traded for country produce or preferably tobacco. These peddlers sold their tobacco in New Orleans, after which they returned to the East for a new supply of gaudy merchandise with which to tickle backwoods fancies. Fortunes were made by these "foot" traders who bought their goods on credit in Philadelphia and Baltimore to sell them at a large profit in the West. Perhaps no type of person in the development of America has brought more keen enjoyment—

and often keen swindling—to isolated communities than the "Yankee" pack peddler.

Kentucky in 1810 had reached a degree of commercial importance, for in that year these industrial plants were listed: 15 cotton factories with 23,599 looms and 21 carding machines producing 4,000,000 yards of cloth valued at $2,000,000, 13 mills producing hempen bagging for cotton bales; 38 ropewalks consuming 5,755 tons of hemp annually; 33 fulling mills; 4 furnaces; 3 forges; 11 naileries making 7½ tons of nails; 267 tanneries; 9 flaxseed-oil mills; 2,000 distilleries; 6 paper mills; 63 gunpowder mills producing 115,716 pounds of powder and 201,937 pounds of saltpeter; and 36 saltworks producing 342,970 bushels of salt. Seven years later, Lexington boasted 12 cotton factories; 3 woolen mills; 3 paper mills; 3 steam gristmills; gunpowder mills capitalized at $4,-500; a lead factory; iron factories; 5 tanners and carriers; 12 hemp manufactories for making cotton bagging and hempen yarn involving a total investment of $502,000; 6 cabinetmakers; 4 soap and candle factories; 3 tobacco factories; and other manufacturing interests with a vested capital of $600,000.

The importance of manufacturing in 1809 attracted legislative aid and support, for in that year the Kentucky General Assembly adopted resolutions encouraging the consumption of home-manufactured goods. Only two negative votes were recorded against this act, and one of these was the vote of the ever-contentious Humphrey Marshall. In this same year, the editor of the *Reporter* expressed his pleasure at seeing a considerable portion of the Fourth of July crowd clothed in home-manufactured goods.

Kentucky's new sense of commercial importance prompted her approval of the embargo imposed upon the American states by Congress on December 21, 1807, in retaliation against British and French interference with American commercial rights. Complaints heard in New England were foreign to Kentucky because of the latter's self-sufficiency. However, the Nonintercourse Act of 1809 was not so cheerfully accepted, for it bore hard upon youthful manufactories of Kentucky. In that year a petition was presented to the House of Representatives of the United States setting forth Kentucky's position and requesting special consideration. Westerners pleaded independence of Europe, and they were thoroughly disgusted when foreign edicts affected American commerce. Doubtless had such foreign edicts, embargoes, and international manifestoes not interfered with American cotton shipments, the Kentuckians would have escaped most of their troubles.

Views held by the early Kentuckians are clearly set forth in their petition to Congress, for in this document they were proud to boast a local independence. Fortunately the soils of this western commonwealth were far superior to the thin, bleached, tidewater soils of the "Old Dominion." Almost every agricultural crop, with the exception of cotton and tropical fruits, could be grown successfully in Kentucky. Here, more than in any other state, the opportunity to become self-sufficient was taken advantage of to the fullest extent. Hence the independent feeling and action of the westerner have always existed in Kentuckians, because they were born of necessity and sired by a rugged ambition in virtually isolated territory.

CHAPTER X

Rivers, Highways and Railroads

Rivers

THE earliest systems of transportation in Kentucky were the primitive trails, or highways, and rivers. The early highways were little more than pack roads which followed the general course of buffalo and Indian trails. Every river was a potential channel of transportation, and Kentucky, it was thought, possessed more miles of navigable and seminavigable streams than any other state in the Union. Transportation on these two primitive avenues dates from the earliest habitation by man and beast of the "Dark and Bloody Grounds."

Early economic development in Kentucky was aided greatly by its fine system of interior and exterior rivers. Greatest of the exterior rivers is the Ohio, early known to the French as *La Belle Rivière*. It served as a channel of immigration to the state, and as a means of transportation for products from the state. For the most part the channel of the Ohio was wide and deep enough to permit the passage of the frontier crafts, but the only serious obstacle on its whole course was the fall line at Louisville which endangered the passage of crafts regardless of their draught. Deeper draught boats had to await a rise in the river to make the passage over the rocky shoals at the falls.

After Wilkinson's initial venture down the river to New Orleans, frontier trade on the Ohio and Mississippi Rivers grew by leaps and bounds. Kentucky's southward-bound commerce was fully developed within a decade. In 1789 John Rhea was advertising in the *Kentucky Gazette* that he had opened a store in Scott's warehouse on the Kentucky River and would handle "a very general assortment of Dry Goods, Hardware, and Groceries for which cash, Tobacco, Ginseng, furs, viz. Beaver, Raccoon, Foxes, Wild Cats and other skins will be taken in payment." Warehouses were established along the other rivers, and in 1792 a system of warehouse inspection was instituted. The treaty signed in 1795 between the United States and Spain further influenced the expansion of river commerce. When the port of New Orleans was opened to Kentucky trade, farm products were shipped directly to the West Indies and to Europe.

In 1804 Green Clay advertised that he had on hand 30,000 pounds of tobacco, three or four years old, and a sufficient quantity of whiskey and bacon to load a 50-foot boat. This he wished to sell at New Orleans.

By 1804 flour had become the chief commodity of export between Kentucky and New Orleans. From January to July of 1802, 85,570 barrels of flour were shipped to the South. François Michaux claimed that more than two thirds of the New Orleans commerce originated in Kentucky. Other Kentucky commodities of great importance in the New Orleans trade were hempen goods, tobacco, bacon, and lard. After the invention of the cotton gin, and after the War of 1812, there was sufficient demand for these goods by the cotton planters to absorb the Kentucky supply.

Not only was the Ohio River a vehicle by which goods were transported to the southern market, but it was also an inlet for commerce from the North. According to the French chronicler, Michaux, most of the manufactured goods sold in Kentucky in 1802 came down the river by way of Pittsburgh from Philadelphia and Baltimore. This commerce from Pittsburgh was conducted by the same boatmen who traded in New Orleans. They exchanged their goods from the East in Kentucky and loaded their boats with western supplies which they sold in New Orleans. From New Orleans these boatmen went up the coast in sailing vessels to Philadelphia and Baltimore. The trip from these eastern cities to Pittsburgh was, in turn, made by the use of pack animals traveling over the Cumberland Road to western Pennsylvania and the Ohio. There was little or no trade from Kentucky to the North because of the enormous expense and hardships involved. Ginseng was the only commodity which would pay the expense of transportation. Some of the early shippers estimated that it was as expensive to ship twenty-five pounds of produce upstream or overland from Lexington to Philadelphia as it was to ship a ton of freight downstream to New Orleans. Oftentimes it required travelers as long to make the journey by land from Lexington to Philadelphia as it did from Lexington to France by boat.

As shipping increased, the obstacle created by the Ohio Falls became more serious. In December, 1804, the legislature granted a charter incorporating the Ohio Canal Company whose purpose was the construction of a canal on the Indiana side of the river from Louisville to Portland. This canal was to aid the shipping industry to avoid the treacherous falls of the river. To insure the commerce of the river to the port of Louisville the charter was later changed to force the construction of the canal on the Kentucky side. The Governor of Kentucky was instructed to subscribe $50,000 on behalf of the state to the capital stock of the company, but unfortunately the canal was not constructed for two decades. Then this venture rested on private shoulders, since the partnership between the state and the private company had resulted in failure.

The project of constructing the falls canal was revived in 1811 when Nicholas Roosevelt piloted the *City of New Orleans* (the first successful river steamboat over the Ohio and Mississippi Rivers) southward. This trip marked the beginning of the steamboat industry, and in 1815 the *Enterprise* made the first upstream journey by a steamboat from New Orleans to Louisville, reducing the traveling time between these cities to less than half the former period. Where it had taken twenty-eight days for the broadhorns and keelboats to make the journey, steamboats required only twelve days.

A steamboat owner advertised in Lexington newspapers in 1820 that his steamer could carry from 150 to 200 tons of freight to New Orleans. The general use of the steamboat made construction of the Portland Canal imperative, and in 1825 the renewed project, unhampered by politics and joint state and national control, was placed in private hands. This private company was capitalized at $600,000, and four years later its capital stock was increased to $700,000. On December 5, 1830, the steamer *Uncas* passed through the locks of the completed canal, and the Ohio River was then opened, unimpeded from Pittsburgh to its mouth. This project was completed at a cost of $742,869 and was one of the greatest factors in facilitating the movement of western commerce. In less than a decade of the canal's existence 1,500 steamers and 500 flatboats and keelboats bearing 300,000 tons of commerce passed through the locks annually to the southern markets. So successful was this canal that Governor Desha lamented that the state had not promoted the project as originally planned.

The interior river system supplied most of the commerce to the exterior streams (Ohio and Mississippi Rivers). In eastern and central Kentucky, the Kentucky River was the major stream of commercial importance. During the ante bellum period, there were 254 miles of navigable channel on the main stem from Carrollton to Beattyville. Both forks were navigable, and, since these extensive branches of the Kentucky River drained the upper half of the state, they obviously served as excellent commercial carriers. Virginia, at a very early date, appreciated the importance of the Kentucky River, for acts were passed in the general assembly providing for the construction of ferries and commanding that all navigable streams be kept open. County courts were empowered to make necessary repairs upon the streams of the western country, and one of the first problems to face Kentucky upon its admission into the Union was that of opening the Kentucky River. Laws were enacted by the early legislatures to fine persons who blocked navigable streams with mill and fish dams. Not only did the state laws make of the river channels public property, but provisions were made to "warn out" every able-bodied man of taxable age living within five miles of navigable rivers to help improve their channels. A survey was ordered of the Kentucky River by the Constitutional Convention of 1799. On December 18, 1802, a private joint-stock corporation, The Kentucky River Company, was chartered to improve the channel of the Kentucky River, and a commission of prominent citizens was appointed to supervise the work, but this project proved too difficult and was soon abandoned. Even after an act was passed by the legislature, June 10, 1811, permitting the river company to raise $10,000 with a lottery, the project failed. No further efforts were made to improve this stream until 1818 when the demand for salt and iron had increased to considerable proportions. Despite these urgent demands, however, no efforts were made to facilitate transportation of such bulky materials over the rivers. Instead, the legislature and county courts permitted private individuals to obstruct the channel with ferry landings and fish dams.

A special committee was appointed in 1818 by the legislature to inspect the Kentucky River and to report its findings. An appropriation of $40,000 was made to improve the navigable portions of the Kentucky, Green, Barren, Cumberland, Licking, and Salt Rivers and their navigable tributaries. The amount allotted to the Kentucky River was $10,000, and three precincts were established with a board of commissioners appointed for each area. During the years 1818 and 1819, $38,-133 was spent on the navigable rivers, but so unprofitable were the results that the state sold its spades, shovels, and other equipment to prevent the undertaking from being a complete loss.

General improvements made upon the river, however, were not a complete loss, for trees, dams, and other obstructions were removed. In several instances, streambeds were choked with brick and stone dikes in order to deepen the channel and permit the passage of boats during the dry season. Buck Shoals on the Kentucky River below Frankfort was deepened in 1823 by the aid of a rock wall, and the expenditure of $3,000 in "commonwealth paper." The legislative committee on internal improvements recommended construction of twenty such dams between Frankfort and the mouth of the river at Carrollton, and between 1835 and 1845 approximately $8,000 was spent on some improvement of the Kentucky River alone. Improvements were, however, of a haphazard nature.

In 1828 the state board of internal improvements undertook its first systematic survey of the Kentucky River for the purpose of determining the best method of increasing the depth of the channel. Congress was asked for an appropriation to build a dike across the river above the mouth of Benson's Creek, but General Jackson vetoed this bill (which proposed an appropriation of $100,000) and stopped federal aid for such local projects. It was the opinion of the survey commission that at a cost of $1,950,868 the main stream of the Kentucky River could be made navigable for steamers bearing 150–250 tons of freight, and it was also estimated that the north fork could be made navigable to Goose Creek at a cost of $1,099,746. Recommendations relative to the main stream were adopted, and work was begun in 1836, but the project was abandoned in 1843 before any considerable headway had been made.

A stringent financial condition in the nation resulted in the cessation of all state supported improvements. Nevertheless Frankfort became the terminal for steamboat navigation. Five locks were constructed, and ninety-five miles of slack water were brought into use. These locks, constructed at a cost to the state of $901,932, yielded during the next twenty-four years, 1836–1860, $478,603 in tolls but incurred operating expenses amounting to $314,498. Hence the total return on this investment for the twenty-four-year period was one per cent per annum. The completion of this project proved too costly for the state, and it was turned over to the Kentucky River Navigating Company, which was no more successful than the state.

Other rivers in Kentucky received attention when, in 1835, a Board of Internal Improvements was established. This board, composed of the Governor and four members appointed by him, was created by a legislative act to coordinate the rivers, highways, and canals. An appropriation of $1,000,000 was made, to pay for beginning the work. This new plan aroused strong sentiment in the state favorable to the general plan of internal improvements, since Kentucky's need for improved routes of transportation was becoming more pressing.

In an effort to determine the extent of necessary improvements, the Board of Internal Improvements ordered a resurvey of the state's river system. This survey began with the Barren and Green Rivers, and by 1836 the state had spent $215,000 on improving its navigable streams. Before the project was completed, however, the state spent $1,000,000 on these river channels alone. A survey was likewise made of the Licking River, since this stream was of great importance to a prosperous valley. Most of the produce of the Licking territory was sent by boat to the Cincinnati market. Here the same process used on the Kentucky, Barren, and Green Rivers of removing "sawyers" and "planters" was adopted, and in places the channel was deepened by choking the main stream with dikes and dams. This project cost $375,000 and perhaps yielded the biggest return of any of the river improvements.

It was only natural that the state officials should favor those internal improvement projects for rivers alone. Any new mode of transportation was looked upon with suspicion, and state officials were unwilling to investigate a new plan for building railroads. As a result of this hesitancy, a very interesting development took place, for state officials, favoring internal improvements, lent a willing ear to the scheme of constructing internal canals to connect Kentucky with the Atlantic coast. A canal to extend from the south fork of the Kentucky River to

Goose Creek was proposed. From Goose Creek a canal was to connect with the Cumberland River and thence pass to Cumberland Gap, where a tunnel would be constructed under the gap to connect the canal with Powell River. From Powell River the canal would connect with the Clinch and Tennessee Rivers, thence pass through the mountains from Chattanooga to the Hiawassee River and to Savannah. To the present-day reader this plan sounds preposterous, but to anxious and land-locked ante bellum promoters of the eighteen twenties and thirties it seemed quite possible. Numerous enthusiastic supporters were willing to argue with the skeptics that this canal system would prove satisfactory and that it would be a profitable investment. Some of these supporters even said that the canal would cost only half as much as a railroad, but later events were to prove them inadequately informed.

Highways

Highways, next to rivers, were the most practical routes of transportation, and under certain conditions were far more satisfactory. Perhaps the only serious handicap to highway transportation was the fact that bulky goods could not be transported overland. It is interesting here to note that the course of the modern system of highways does not vary essentially from that of the earliest system of trails. Thomas H. Benton of Tennessee, and later of Missouri, made a shrewd observation on these early trails when he said that the most satisfactory routes over which to construct highways were the old buffalo trails, because buffalo traveled only over the most favorable routes. In Kentucky this fact was generally true.

In 1775 Daniel Boone and his companions blazed the Wilderness Road from Cumberland Gap to Boonesborough. The chief contribution of this party was made in trimming back limbs, removing logs, and selecting suitable fords at streams and crossings. This wilderness trail had been in existence for ages, for it had been used by the buffalo and as a war and hunting trail by Indians. When the first whites came to central Kentucky, they followed generally the route of the Wilderness Trail. Nothing more was done to improve the Wilderness Road after Boone and his companions reached their Kentucky River settlement until 1795. In this year the legislature of Kentucky passed an act providing that the road from Lexington to Crab Orchard should be

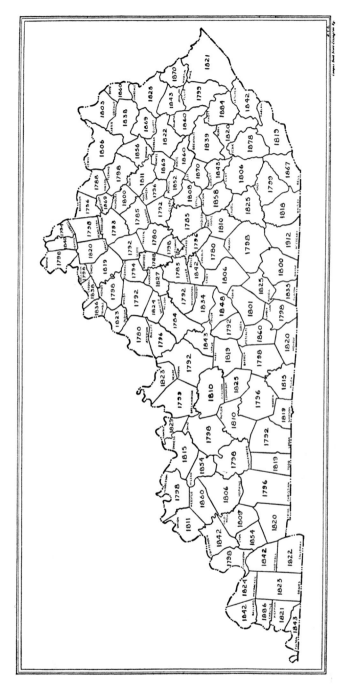

Date of the Foundation of Counties of Kentucky

The Ephriam McDowell House in Danville

A Mountain Cabin in an Isolated Spot

Morrison Chapel in Transylvania College

The Old Statehouse in Frankfort

Aylesford Place, Lexington, a Tudor Gothic House

Diamond Point, a Greek Revival Home in Harrodsburg

opened to vehicular traffic, but the fact that Kentucky was well established in the Union before this road was opened to vehicles does not lessen its importance as an early highway. Most of the immigrants coming from Virginia and North Carolina came into the state over the Wilderness Road, bringing with them their household goods and other domestic necessities on pack horses. Each year thousands of new settlers entered the state by way of the Wilderness Road, and as the state's population was multiplied, its overland trade increased. Thousands of head of livestock were driven back to Virginia and South Carolina over the Wilderness Road. Not only did traders return to the East and South by this route, but hundreds of travelers followed this route to Virginia on official business or on visits to relatives. Dozens of notices appeared in the *Kentucky Gazette* inviting parties returning to Virginia to assemble at Crab Orchard with proper arms and supplies for the journey. However, the Wilderness Road, despite the act of 1795, remained little more than a pack road until 1818, when definite legislative steps were taken to widen the roadway and to improve the fords.

In the 1817 and 1818 sessions of the legislature the state's policy toward development of roads was clearly outlined. Kentucky's legislators disregarded the highways as a public responsibility and shifted the burden of their improvement to private shoulders. Private stock companies were organized to construct and maintain public highways. Two of these companies, with a combined capital stock of $700,000, were organized to construct the roads of central Kentucky. A block of 500 shares at $100 each was to be reserved to the state, but the state neglected even this minor interest and gave the private stockholders free rein. One of these private highways extended from Louisville to Lexington, and the other from Lexington to Maysville. This latter link was most important, since it connected a national system of highways from Cumberland, Maryland, to New Orleans by connecting the Zanesville and Natchez Traces. Returning boatmen from New Orleans traveled over this road to Louisville, Lexington, Maysville, and Pittsburgh and to other Ohio River towns. Settlers moving south also used this highway. The War Department regarded this central route as important to national defense.

Kentucky asked Congress, in 1812, for an appropriation to improve the Maysville Road, but this request, under the exigency of a war, met with no response. In 1821 the state legislature appropriated a pittance of $1,000 toward opening this road, which, after all, amounted to little more than a blazed trail from Lexington to the Tennessee line. Nevertheless, the legislature's abortive activities stimulated private companies to action, and there followed a wild scramble among various companies to secure tax concessions from legislative sessions of the early twenties. An increasing number of highways was chartered in the twenties, but unfortunately the early contracting companies could conceive only of local roads. Only the Louisville and Nashville and the Louisville, Lexington, and Maysville, and the Lexington and Covington Roads were of interstate importance. Most of the other projects connected only two or three near-by towns and were wholly dependent upon local traffic for support.

The private stock companies were supported by tolls collected from the traveling public. Thus bridges, ferries, and roadbeds were maintained by only a fraction of the total income from them, and in many instances even today (1937) bridges and ferries are still maintained by tolls. The Beaver Iron Works and the Prestonsburg Highway Company were permitted by the legislature in 1822 to operate lotteries for supporting their highway projects for traffic over the roads, but this proved insufficient support. Clay, Perry, and Casey Counties were granted public lands with which to construct their highways, and when the rage for internal improvements was taking on national aspects in 1827, the Kentucky legislature granted the Lexington and Maysville Company the sum of $50,000. Later, when it was expected that the Federal Government would take over the responsibility of the Maysville Road, the state granted the project $150,000 from the public funds.

When the War between the States occurred, virtually every mile of Kentucky's highway system was under the control of private companies. Tolls were collected from every passer-by, whether afoot or mounted. Only four exceptions were made to the general rules of toll collections. Those permitted to pass free were widows, ministers, funeral processions, and, sometimes, persons going to church on Sunday.

A poor condition of the roads was often the best testimony against the toll system. During the rainy season it was a hard day's ride from Frankfort to Shelbyville, but at times the road was absolutely impassable. Many of the other roads were virtually in the same condition in the winter season, and, to make bad matters worse, these same roads became practically impassable during the summer. Mudholes turned to dust holes in dry weather, and passengers were severely jolted in attempting to travel in wheeled vehicles. Often travelers preferred to walk from Lexington to Maysville and from Frankfort to Shelbyville rather than risk injury while riding over the roads in stagecoaches. Travel was expensive, since stage companies were liable for injuries and suffered heavy losses because of wear on their equipment dragged over roads which were reduced to muddy streaks across the landscape. Transportation of goods from one place to another often cost more than the price paid for them. Many communities were left with insufficient fuel, since coal could not be hauled for any considerable distance. One of the effective arguments in favor of building the Lexington and Ohio Railroad was that of impassable highways. A case cited in the legislature during the argument over the location of the railway route was that of a party of four hacks which had left Lexington at nine o'clock in the morning bound for Frankfort. Three of the hacks reached their destination some time during the night, but not without encountering numerous perils along the way, while the fourth was stuck hard and fast in a mudhole, although a yoke of oxen attempted to pull it out. In the process of extracting this hack from the muddy clutches of the Lexington and Frankfort highway it was overturned, and a lady passenger seriously injured. In order to reach Frankfort where medical aid could be secured for the injured lady it was necessary to hire a team and wagon to complete the journey, a journey which lasted until three o'clock the next morning.

The foregoing illustration, however, is not an exact picture of the condition of all the highways at all times, since some of the local roads were slowly macadamized, and in many communities plank roads were built, while some of the other highways were corduroyed, and streams were spanned by improvised bridging. The significance of the ante bellum Kentucky roads, however, is not in the type of roads, but in the fact that here was laid the foundation for the present state highway system.

Railroads

The late twenties of the nineteenth century were years in which the railway idea was transferred to the United States from abroad. With the invention and introduction of the steamboat, western commerce showed an encouraging increase, and travel between Kentucky and the Gulf of Mexico was greatly facilitated. Many communities remained without efficient shipping facilities, for several of the important commercial centers of Kentucky were located at some distance from navigable streams.

Lexington, long the market town of the New West, found herself commercially isolated when the steamboat became a practicable carrier of passengers and freight. Unfortunately the founders of this western city subjected their community to future discrimination, when the West grew in commercial importance, by overlooking its lack of access to a navigable stream. Even today Lexington remains one of the major American cities not located on the banks of a navigable stream. When the *Enterprise* in 1815 made its maiden voyage upstream from New Orleans to Louisville, Lexington was forced to surrender the lion's share of her trade to her riparian sister, Louisville. By 1830 the "Athens of the West" was completely shorn of its commercial glory, and its merchants were casting about aimlessly in search of some means of rectifying hostile commercial discrimination. Fortunately the more progressive people decided to build a railroad to connect Lexington with the Ohio River. Already Lexington occupied a position as highway hub of the state, but if she could add another method of transportation, her businessmen felt they could restore the city's commercial status. Highways, as has been seen, were not always important assets and consequently contributed very little to the community's trading possibilities.

To win their uphill struggle, citizens of Lexington hoped to bridge the distance between Lexington and her rival markets with a railroad, but before this bridging could be done much local opposition had to be overcome. One group wanted to encourage the building of a canal from Lexington to the river-marked centers, while others wished to improve the highways. A difficult topography defeated the first plan, and President Jackson practically thwarted the second with his Maysville Road Bill veto.

By force of circumstances the citizens of Lexington were made receptive to the idea of a railroad to the West. Communities adjacent to the proposed railway route between Lexington and Louisville were fairly enthusiastic over the idea, and on January 14, 1830, a bill was introduced in the legislature asking that a railway be chartered from Lexington to the Ohio River. This charter failed to designate the road's exact terminus. After considerable argument between representatives of Fayette and Woodford Counties over the location of the road, a charter was granted on January 27, 1830, permitting the directors of the company to select the most favorable route from Lexington to the Ohio River.

On March 6, 1830, the railway company was organized at Lexington with Elisha I. Winters president, and Elisha Warfield, John W. Hunt, John Brand, Henry Payne, James Bruen, Richard Higgins, Walter Dunn, Dr. Benjamin W. Dudley, Henry Clay, Benjamin Gratz, and George Boswell directors. Professor Matthews of the mathematics department of Transylvania University was instructed to make a preliminary survey of the proposed route and report on the feasibility of building the roadbed.

Sufficient progress had been made in this survey by October 22, 1830, to begin laying track. On that day the first rail was laid and the first spike was driven by Governor Metcalfe amid elaborate ceremonies on what is now Water Street in Lexington. This ceremony was preceded by a long parade of local fraternal and social organizations which, led by General Leslie Combs and an assistant mounted on horseback, marched from the Transylvania campus. When the first rail was swung into place, a seven-gun salute was fired, and the band appropriately played *Hail Columbia* and *Yankee Doodle*.

The first problem of this infant railway venture was financial, but President Elisha I. Winters was selfish and ambitious enough to want to retain the control of the road in the hands of a selected few. He persuaded his friends to subscribe heavily to the project, and in Henry Clay's absence from the city, President Winters took the liberty to subscribe a large block of the company's stock for him. This untoward act on the part of the company's chief executive resulted in much embarrassment, for when Clay was unable to meet his payments, the directors found it necessary to sell his stock elsewhere.

Several months were required to prepare the first few miles of roadbed for operation, and during its embryonic period the company had many baffling problems to confront. Nevertheless, one and a half miles of track were ready for operation on August 15, 1832. At high noon of that day the first car left its "mooring" at the northern end of the lower market house with forty passengers aboard, one of whom was Governor Metcalfe. This first car was the marvel of the West, for one horse drew forty passengers on the rails as easily as one horse drew a single passenger in a road cart.

A year later the track was extended six miles, and the cars made regular trips with mail and passengers between Lexington and Villa Grove. In January, 1834, the road was completed to the top of the hill at Frankfort. Then there were insufficient funds to tunnel into the city, and the construction of an inclined plane by which the cars were lowered into Frankfort became necessary. The inclined plane proved a hazardous machine, for a wreck caused several deaths, and this method of reaching the town had to be abandoned. Despairing of their Ohio River goal, the railway promoters were willing to stop their work at the Kentucky River. As the *Kentucky Gazette* reported, the railroad with "a sigh of relief stopped to rest" at Frankfort so long that even its title was changed from the "Lexington and Ohio" to the "Lexington and Frankfort."

Progress at the Louisville end of the road was even slower and highly unsatisfactory; seven years were required to begin operation of the road from Portland to Louisville. Much local opposition arose because of the noise the cars made in running back and forth through the community. An injunction, issued by the Chancellor of Louisville, stayed operation between Sixth and Seventh Streets. This was a fatal blow, and the road was turned over to the Blind Asylum for operation, a fact which inevitably soon forced it out of business.

By 1842 traffic on both ends of the road was brought to a standstill, and the state was in debt for the operation of the road, with little opportunity for remedying the situation. Two bills, now found among the papers of Governor Letcher in the State Historical Society files, were presented by a wagoner who had twice hauled one of the locomotives in a road wagon from Frankfort to Lexington for repairs. Having proved an unprofitable venture in the hands of the state, the road was leased to Phillip Swigert and William R. McKee in 1843 for repair and operation. New rails were bought, the "snakeheads" of the old track were removed, and, in the hands of the private operators, who formerly had operated a stage line, the road was placed in an excellent and somewhat profitable state of operation. By 1848 the state had reclaimed the road, and a new charter was granted the Lexington and Frankfort Railroad Company.

Construction work on the Louisville end of the Louisville and Frankfort Company's railroad was resumed, until, in 1852, the two roads were connected at Frankfort by a bridge over the Kentucky River and by a tunnel under the Frankfort hill. At last, cars ran from Lexington to Louisville to bring about the realization of a long-cherished dream of the Lexington City Fathers. This dream was realized too late to preserve Lexington's commercial supremacy.

It is worthy of note that in 1842 the Lexington and Frankfort Road had the reputation of being the most poorly constructed railway in the United States, while in 1858, the Lexington, Frankfort, and Louisville Road was known to have paid the highest dividend of any road in the country, since efficient trackage had been laid from Lexington to Louisville at the remarkably low cost of $19,500 per mile.

While Louisville and Lexington were arranging rail connections, Cincinnati was busily engaged in tapping the Blue Grass region with a railway. Already much of the central Kentucky trade was inclined toward Cincinnati, and river boatmen and merchants were anxious to make this city the livestock center of the West. In 1830 when the Lexington and Ohio Railroad Company was chartered, promoters of the Ohio city were anxious to have this road extended northward to the Ohio River.

When Robert Y. Hayne and other prominent southern politicians and planters proposed in 1837 their grandiose scheme for constructing a joint system of canals and railroads from Charleston, South Carolina, to the Ohio River, Cincinnati was an enthusiastic supporter of the project, and even Lexington was much interested. Through this connection with the Atlantic coast, Lexington could deprive Louisville of much of its central Kentucky trade, and she would not be dependent upon Louisville as her only outlet to the southern market. Unfortunately this jealousy between Lexington and Louisville had much to do with the failure of the Southerners' scheme. Not only did these promoters propose to build a complementing railway and canal system, but likewise they proposed to establish a branch railway bank at Lexington. Louisville and its neighboring town were dubious of this latter proposal, for they did not wish to see any more of the state's banking business concentrated in Lexington. This opposition was largely responsible for the blighting of the Charleston project, for the legislature refused it a charter, and the panic of 1837 made financial support impossible.

Efforts to connect Cincinnati and central Kentucky were not revived until 1847 when the Kentucky legislature chartered the Licking and Lexington Railroad Company. When this road was chartered, the City of Covington responded with a subscription of $100,000, but this generous offer was an over-enthusiastic gesture, for the project never got beyond the visionary stage. Even though the first attempt was a failure, in 1849 the legislature renewed the company's charter, changing its name to the Lexington and Covington Railroad Company. A second charter, however, was more easily gained than was financial support for the road. It was not until a lapse of three years that construction work was actually begun. Officials of the company were finally successful in disposing of city and county bonds which had been subscribed to the capital stock of the company. Iron was purchased, and track laying was begun between Covington and Lexington in 1852.

While efforts were being made to construct the road, the need for such a means of transportation in this northern section became more and more apparent. Northern Kentucky counties were shipping 60,000 hogs and 22,000 head of cattle annually to the Cincinnati market, and, aside from this heavy livestock trade, there was a large local demand for coal from the Pittsburgh fields, which could be supplied only over the proposed railroad. So heavy were the demands made by the territory to be served that the promoters became ambitious enough to secure a right-of-way grant from Cincinnati to Selma, Alabama. In 1854 the Lexington and Covington Railroad connected with the Maysville and Lexington at Paris, thus completing through rail connections with Lexington.

The Maysville and Lexington Railroad was projected from Maysville and served as a "feeder" route from the Ohio River to Lexington. It was over this route that the Lexington business concerns hoped to secure the city's coal supply, but, though cars were running between the two cities in 1853, operation of the line was unsuccessful. Maysville supporters undertook to inject new life into their Lexington project by tapping eastern Kentucky with a line up the Ohio River (the Maysville and Big Sandy), but this project failed of maturity until after the War between the States.

Most of the trade of the Midwest was inclined southward, and especially was this true of Kentucky's trade. Despite the fact that the major portion of the goods sold south was produced in the Blue Grass, western Kentucky was not inactive, for the coal beds of this section promised to supply Louisville's industrial demands regardless of the low summer stages of the Ohio River. If these western coal banks were developed, Louisville's industrial plants needed no longer to fear a coal shortage. As early as 1832, the *Bardstown Herald* was actively agitating for rail connections between the coal-bearing region of western Kentucky and Louisville. However, this campaign was not given any serious consideration until 1849 when several railway conventions were held in the communities adjacent to the Louisville and Nashville turnpike. This route seemed the most logical one in the state for a railway, since Louisville rapidly became a market center for the South. Its businessmen were convinced that the city's commercial future could be measured only by its ability to form speedy connections with southern market centers. Resolutions were adopted by the city's council to subscribe $1,000,000 to the capital stock of the proposed Louisville and Nashville project.

A bill was submitted to the Kentucky legislature in 1850, asking that body to grant a charter for a railroad from Louisville to Bowling Green. On March 5 the road was chartered to extend from Louisville to the Tennessee line, with an authorized capital stock of $3,000,000. This charter made of the Louisville and Nashville railway the boldest project of internal improvement ever undertaken in Kentucky. Building this road was a stupendous task, and the obstacles encountered (Muldraugh Hills, for instance) were most difficult to surmount. On some sections of the line there were demands for high trestles, and at Nashville the company had to construct an expensive bridge over the Cumberland River before trains could run into the city.

Localities south of Louisville were enthusiastic supporters of the Louisville and Nashville project. The Lebanon community financially backed the Lebanon branch, and counties adjacent to the main line were generous in their public support. Logan County subscribed $300,000; Bowling Green subscribed $1,000,000; and Glasgow gave

$30,000. After a careful survey of the proposed route, the engineers estimated that the project would cost $5,000,000. Contracts were awarded to Morton, Seymour and Company, and construction work was begun in 1853 with the contracting company agreeing to construct the road throughout and have it in operation within two years.

Like every other southern project, the Louisville and Nashville Railroad Company soon encountered financial difficulties, and agents were sent abroad to secure loans on the European money markets. In 1852, when the foreign money market was recovering from a panic, $350,000 worth of Louisville and Nashville bonds were the first American bonds sold.

After a long uphill struggle, the road was finally placed in operation for a distance of 100 miles south of Louisville, but in 1859 the first train ran from Louisville to Nashville. Important men connected with the building of this road were Ex-Governor John Helm and Ex-Secretary of the Treasury James Guthrie. The 185 miles of trackage from Louisville to Nashville were built at a total cost of $7,221,204.91.

When this road was completed, the prophecies of the original promoters of the project were proved to be true. Freight was supplied in such quantities that the company was unable to haul all of it. Accordingly there soon grew up a spirit of rivalry between the Cincinnati and Louisville merchants. Cincinnati merchants felt that the Louisville and Nashville Company was discriminating against them in favor of Louisville, and the Louisville merchants felt that the road belonged to them. Unfortunately, the railroad company was not equipped to handle so many heavy freight shipments, and the overworking of the roadbed and equipment resulted in severe damages to both.

Before the end of the year 1860, Kentucky railway promoters and builders had placed in operation 596.93 miles of railway. This seems a rather small beginning, however, when compared with the 1,197.92 miles of railway in operation in Tennessee, and 872.30 miles in Mississippi. Nevertheless, the actual miles of railway built were not indicative of the extensive system projected. In western Kentucky the Henderson and Nashville Road was of interstate importance, and Louisville was busily engaged in promoting the construction of a road up the Ohio River to Covington. Perhaps the most important interstate railway tapping the State of Kentucky was the Mobile and Ohio, which was built from Mobile, Alabama, to Columbus, Kentucky. Unfortunately this road was not placed in operation until Fort Sumter was fired upon. Hence it really never functioned as the great planter supply route which its promoters, in its formative years, hoped it would be. From Lexington a road was projected toward Knoxville, but the war also stopped work on this line at the Kentucky River.

Kentucky's legislature favored the public land bill which was introduced in the National Congress in 1850, and Congressmen from Kentucky were given definite instructions to support the measure. Between 1840 and 1880, the state legislature acted favorably upon more than thirty railway acts, most of which permitted construction of new roads. Every community was anxious to improve its transportation system. Citizens of the state had become commercially minded because of the ever increasing demand for Kentucky products by the Southern States. Railway centers were located at Louisville and Lexington, and short rail tentacles were projected to the surrounding towns and agricultural centers.

Kentucky's struggle for improved methods of transportation mirrors rather accurately the struggles of the other Southern States. Two factors favored Kentucky's economic growth, her river system, and her fertile soils. Perhaps the geographical factors of the state played as important a part in the development of the state's internal improvements as any other single factor. Doubtless the state would have given up hope of utilizing its streams and devoted its energy and capital to the construction of improved highways and railways long before it did, had it not been for the intricate seminavigable river system. It was only natural, since Kentucky's river system pierced almost every section of the state, that its legislators should think in terms of river transportation, for the flatboat and, later, the steamboat had released Kentucky from a system of landlocked commercial bondage.

CHAPTER XI

Human Bondage

SINCE slavery was a deeply rooted institution in the United States before adventurous frontiersmen crossed the Appalachian Mountains into the Kentucky country, it was only natural that the early pioneers should transfer the institution from Virginia to their farms west of the mountains. In many accounts of raids upon the early settlements in Kentucky Negro slaves are mentioned among those killed or captured. Perhaps the only strange thing about the transfer of the institution of slavery to the West was the fact that many of the early slaves were brought into the western country by immigrating Irish, Scotch, and Germans who had settled in the piedmont regions of the adjacent eastern states. However, Virginia's economic system prevailed in the western country. Kentucky's land system was an extension of the Virginia plan, and claimants, under the land laws of 1779 and even those preceding this date, registered large tracts. Immigrants to Kentucky were endowed with good land holdings, a fact which partly accounts for an influx of settlers during the early period.

Typical of English and early American economic ideals, land was regarded as the basis of wealth in the West. Hence with ownership of large tracts of land there was an urgent demand for cheap labor. There was no source of cheap hired labor, since most of the whites were landholders and were in the market for labor themselves.

Coincidental with settlement of the Kentucky country, eastern and central Virginia planters were finding slavery unprofitable. Labor demands in the West proved an excellent safety valve for this rapidly failing system of slavery in Virginia. Many planters bought tracts of land in Kentucky and sent their slaves and overseers ahead to clear the fields and to build the homesteads. So long as pioneer conditions prevailed, slavery was a valuable asset to Kentuckians. Michaux noted, in 1802, that most of the land in central Kentucky had been placed under cultivation or pasturage, and to his surprise many farmers were cultivating fields with their own hands. However, he discovered that a majority of central Kentucky farmers were still dependent upon their slaves as laborers in the fields.

No American social group has been more sensitive to geographical and climatic surroundings than the African slaves. Fertility of Kentucky soils and their peculiar adaptation to certain types of agriculture were not conducive in the end to slavery. One of the most interesting phases of the early institution of slavery was the immigration into the state. Before 1790 there were 63,133 whites and 11,944 blacks in Kentucky, but by 1800 the whites had increased to the astounding number of 179,871, and the black population numbered 41,084. For the next two or three decades this increase continued at an astonishing rate. By 1830, slaveholding sections of Kentucky were overrun with white immigrants. Of course this rapid increase in the population greatly affected the large land holdings. Because of the absence of a primogeniture system of land tenure, estates were divided into smaller farms each time the original owner died or lost possession of his lands. Other large tracts, cut into small plots, were sold by land speculators to an ever increasing number of immigrants. The secret of this rush of immigration was the fertility of Kentucky soils and the decreasing fertility of soils in the Eastern States.

Slavery was vitally affected by a rapid change in the state's economic and social system. First of all, it thrived best on plantations where overseers could command the laborers in large groups. With the increase in Kentucky's population, the small landholders gradually broke down the so-called plantations and established small farms where owners did their own work. This system of agriculture was not conducive to involuntary servitude, for Kentucky never made any pretense at growing cotton, except on a limited scale in some of its southern counties only after 1819. In fact, the state's agricultural system was so diverse that it was not given to production of any single staple crop. A lack of transportation facilities, together with the eastern Appalachian barrier, forced early farmers to adopt a system of agriculture which could cope with these geographical handicaps. With acres of meadow grasslands and soils yielding an abundance of grain it was natural that Kentucky farmers turned to raising livestock as the most profitable agricultural undertaking. Livestock, with one or two exceptions, was Kentucky's only product which was transported profitably to the eastern markets. When by several international agreements the Mississippi River was opened to New Orleans, Kentucky's agricultural system was already established. Hence slavery became less important as a source of farm labor.

With cereals, tobacco, and hemp as Kentucky's staple crops, slavery was a failure. The growing of each of these crops required careful personal supervision, which in the end was as expensive as the labor. Where the cereal crops were grown extensively, slave owners were confronted with the vexing problem of keeping slaves profitably engaged during both growing and dormant seasons. Since it was possible, after 1810, to secure a sufficient amount of seasonal white labor to plant and gather grain crops, Kentucky farmers were relieved of the burden of caring for idle laborers during idle seasons. Conditions governing the growing of cereals also governed the cultivation of tobacco. Slaves required careful supervision throughout the process of setting tobacco plants, cultivating the crop, and of cutting and curing the matured product. Livestock breeders found slaves inefficient, and they feared that losses from slave carelessness would absorb their profits. Not a single one of Kentucky's field crops was so admirably adapted to slave labor as was the cultivation of rice, sugar cane, and cotton in the Lower South.

The decade from 1820 to 1830 marked the peak of Kentucky slavery. There are several reasons why slavery decreased after 1830. First, a legislative act prohibited importation of slaves into the state after 1833, and, second, slavery was rapidly transferred from Kentucky to the expanding cotton belt. Several new states were admitted into the Union after the War of 1812, and with their settlement cultivation of cotton increased from 2,000,000 pounds in 1791 to 457,000,000 pounds in 1834. With this increase in southern cotton production, Kentucky lost many of her planters to that industry, and they took their slaves to the cotton belt with them.

The Interstate Slave Trade

Unfortunately for the historian, the transfer of slavery from Kentucky to the Lower South was accompanied by a certain amount of social antagonism. Few writers have ventured to tell the whole truth portraying the slave trade. Accusations made by antislavery societies that Kentuckians were breeding slaves for the southern market are to be discounted. Rightfully, the slave trade was held in contempt by better elements of Kentucky society, and for this reason one phase of Kentucky's slavery history has been willfully misinterpreted. Nathaniel Southgate Shaler, a native of Campbell County, in all sincerity denied the existence of an extensive trade by citing his personal experience. Doubtless his contact with slavery was humane and generous. Slavery as Professor Shaler knew it was of a patriarchal type. Masters controlled rebellious slaves by threatening to "sell them South."

Many Kentucky historians relying upon Shaler have accepted his statements as authoritative and have not further investigated the question. However, circuit court records, contemporary newspapers, and acts of the Kentucky legislature tell a different story of this important aspect of Kentucky slavery. The account that follows is taken from sworn depositions and other reliable contemporary sources.

It would be difficult to give a specific date for the beginning of the slave trade between Kentucky and the Lower South. As early as 1818, Henry Bradshaw Fearon records having seen fourteen flatboats loaded with slaves on the lower Mississippi where they had been brought by Kentucky traders. The Reverend Dickey, a traveling divine, was horrified, in 1822, by an incident which occurred on one of his missionary journeys into the Blue Grass. While traveling from Lexington to Paris, Mr. Dickey heard strains of music and saw a flag bobbing up and down in the road ahead of him. Thinking that a patriotic procession was en route from Paris to Lexington, he drew over to the roadside to permit it to pass, but, to his sorrow, the procession was a coffle of slaves preceded by a burly African blowing a lively marching tune on a "French" harp. Slaves, chained together, were being driven to Lexington where they would be combined with a larger coffle to be shipped to the cotton belt. Upon arriving at an inn in Paris, the Reverend Dickey related his experience to his landlady. She informed him that the trader was her brother, who had an established business with New Orleans.

The *Western Luminary* of Lexington describes a coffle of slaves marching through the streets of the city in 1827:

A few weeks ago we gave an account of a company of men, women, and children; part of them manacled, passing through the streets. Last week a number of slaves were driven through the Main Street of our city, among them a number manacled together, two abreast, all connected by, and supporting a heavy iron chain which extended the whole length of the line.

The New England school teacher-novelist, J. H. Ingraham, arrived in Natchez, Mississippi, in 1834, where he was soon attracted to the slave market. He says elopements, sickness, deaths, and an expanding cotton belt created a continuous demand for slaves, and that Kentucky and Virginia marts supplied this demand. Ingraham observed that river boats landing in the ports of Natchez and New Orleans nearly always brought a cargo of slaves. During the year 1834, the New Englander estimated that more than 4,000 slaves passed through the "crossroads" market one mile out of Natchez.

The "Old Duke," Robert Wickliffe, largest slaveholder in Fayette County, shouted to the Kentucky legislature in 1840 that more than 6,000 slaves were being sold annually to the Lower South from Kentucky. Kentucky dealers were established by 1843, but many writers on the subject have concerned themselves with the decade 1850–1860, because during this period the dealers came into the open and began advertising in newspapers. In 1843, at least two established slave trading firms were driving a rich trade to the south. These traders were located in Lexington and Louisville but traded extensively throughout the slaveholding districts. The firm of Downing and Hughes entered the slave trade in 1843, and their first coffle of slaves included one from almost every central Blue Grass county. During the winter and spring of the year 1844 these traders were at the Natchez "crossroads" market disposing of their slaves to Mississippi planters. In the first coffle, Downing and Hughes had twelve slaves, which they had purchased for the total price of $8,695. During these same years, Griffin and Pullum were also engaged in the slave trade, but on a much larger scale. In his deposition given in connection with the case of Hughes *vs.* Downing, William Pullum testified that he had carried a much larger group of slaves to the Natchez market and was there at the time Downing and Hughes were trading.

The slave trade was in the process of development from 1840 to 1846. Traders plied their business as quietly as possible, so that there was little, if any, public sentiment concerning the business. The slave trade differed little from the livestock trade. When a trader was unable to drive a bargain privately, there were always public auctions which he could attend. Contemporary newspapers, carrying numerous advertisements of auctions and sales of real estate and farming implements, also mentioned slaves.

Lewis Robards was the first Kentucky trader to advertise his business in the columns of the newspapers. In 1849 his advertisement in the *Observer and Reporter* announced to the public that he could pay the highest cash prices to persons having Negro slaves for sale. Other advertisements followed Robard's in quick succession. In the same year James G. Mathers, whose jail was located on Main Street, inserted his card in the *Observer and Reporter* informing the public that he was in the market for ten or twelve likely Negro boys for whom he would pay high prices. In less than ten days John Mattingly announced that he expected to pay the "highest cash price for young and likely Negroes." His headquarters were in the Megowan Hotel, with his jail adjoining.

Slave traders were overjoyed in 1850 when the Kentucky legislature repealed the anti-importation act of 1833. With the repeal of this act, slaves from other states could be brought for sale in the Kentucky market, a fact which virtually converted Kentucky into a slave mart for the Lower South. The house of representatives of the Kentucky legislature in 1849 gave the slave traders further encouragement by adopting a resolution denouncing abolition.

By 1850 the slave trade was well established between Kentucky and the cotton belt. Traders became bolder and competition keener, for newspaper columns were filled with traders' announcements. William A. Pullum, a veteran trader, gave notice that because of ill health he was retiring to private life. In the same paper Lewis Robards advertised that he had rented the Pullum jail and that the slave trade would go on as usual. Robards seems to have been well anchored in Fayette County, for he was the only trader who remained in business continuously for the period 1850–1860. He was not only a trader but also a local farmer. As a farmer he evaded the provision made in the public sales which stated that slaves should remain in the state. Slaves purchased at the sales were transferred to the trader's farm and remained there until the sales agreement was forgotten, after which they were sent South. Many "shady" deals and evasions of the law were recorded against Robards by clerks of the Circuit Court of Fayette County, and, in fact, it appears that he felt he was becoming unpopular when his name did not appear on the court's docket. He expanded his business to such a degree that in 1849 he was in a position to lease as his jail the old Lexington Theatre on Short Street, where often in the past the best theatrical talent visiting the West had enacted popular plays of the time.

This prince of slave dealers was not without his troubles. Numerous lawsuits proved destructive to the Robards establishment, and on October 20, 1855, his jail was advertised for sale to satisfy his creditors. This jail was purchased by Bolton, Dickens and Company of Tennessee, and Robards became an agent for A. B. Caldwell, in whose employ he remained until 1857.

Difficulties of slave traders increased as competition from adjoining towns and states grew keener each month. On November 11, 1830, the *Memphis Eagle* printed a notice that a slave who had formerly belonged to Daniel McKinney of Union County, Kentucky, and was later sold South through the agency of Solomon Blue of Shawneetown, Illinois, was in jail at McClenborough, Illinois. John Mattingly's agency advertised in 1849 for 100 Negroes for the southern market and again in 1850 for 300 Negroes from twelve to thirty years of age, payments to be made in cash. This trader was located at the Megowan jail. J. M. Heady advertised that he was in the market for 200 Negroes, men, women, boys, and girls ranging in ages from twelve to thirty years. P. N. Brent advertised for likely Negroes from his offices located in the Phoenix Hotel on Main Street. Lexington dealers, after 1850, were threatened by strong competition from Louisville dealers. Mattingly maintained offices in both places, and so did the trader, William F. Talbott, who appeared at the Phoenix Hotel in 1852 and 1853, advertising for the usual lot of 200 Negroes.

The number of traders increased in Kentucky to such an extent that by 1860 there were nearly as many slave dealers as there were mule traders. More than two dozen dealers advertised in the newspapers. This list included the names of A. B. Caldwell; Joseph N. Northcutt; R. H. Thompson; P. N. Brent; Blackwell, Murphy, and Ferguson; S. Marshall; Blackwell and Ballard; W. F. White and Company; Asa

Collins; Griffin and Pullum; Lewis Robards; J. and T. Arteburn; R. H. Elam; A. H. Forrest and Company; and H. H. Haynes and Company.

Newspapers of the Lower South carried as many advertisements for slave dealers as did the Kentucky papers. On January 10, 1855, in the *Semi-Weekly Creole* of New Orleans, Thomas Foster's advertisements stated that he was in a position to serve as commission merchant for slaves and invited his Kentucky friends to visit him at his office at 157 Common Street. In the same paper, D. H. Matthews and Thomas J. Frisby were advertising slave pens located at 159 Gravier Street. In 1856, Frederick Law Olmstead, while touring the State of Louisiana, had as a traveling companion a local businessman, but to his surprise the man was a slave trader. This trader explained that his partner had a farm in Kentucky and that he went occasionally to that state to get a coffle of slaves which he held on his Louisiana plantation until they were sold. R. H. Elam of Natchez was also an importer of slaves from Kentucky and served as a local broker for small traders from the Blue Grass. Nearer the Kentucky markets were the commission merchants of H. H. Haynes and Company who accepted slaves in trade from Kentucky on a commission basis. This firm was located in Nashville, and often their yard served as a way station for Kentucky traders who drove their coffles southward overland.

Many Kentucky dealers, however, acted as their own brokers in the southern cotton belt. Blackwell, Murphy, and Ferguson advertised in the *Natchez Courier* on November 2, 1859, that they had lately received in Natchez a choice lot of Kentucky Negroes, male and female, consisting of household servants, field hands, and mechanics. This firm further stated that it expected an additional coffle of 150 slaves from Kentucky. Mississippi papers carried frequent notices of A. H. Forrest and Company, of R. H. Elam, and of W. F. White and Company.

Negro trade in the Blue Grass attracted much attention, and bidding at public sales was often keen. On January 5, 1859, the *Paris Flag* commented upon the flourishing New Year's trade. Early sales of livestock and Negroes in Paris brought a considerable amount of ready money into the town. Eight hundred mules were disposed of, and Negroes sold at peak prices. Boys eighteen years of age brought from $1,135 to $1,220; girls sixteen to seventeen years of age brought from

$435 to $695; and men twenty-four years old sold for $1,200 in cash. Twenty-five Negroes were sold at Georgetown on January 1, 1859, for a total price of $20,140. A boy of nineteen years of age brought $1,500, one twenty years old brought $1,550, and one thirty-two years old brought $1,190. Girls thirteen years of age brought $1,000, and a sixteen-year-old girl brought $1,441.

Many were the tricks resorted to by the trader in securing fresh stock in trade. The *Weekly Frankfort Yeoman* in 1854 berated the practices of the Negro thieves whose headquarters were in Maysville because of its proximity to the Ohio shore. The kidnapers had connection with the slave traders in the central part of the state, and no purchaser questioned as to where the slaves were secured. Once the slave was loaded on a southbound steamboat, he found himself without recourse to the courts. On one particular occasion, a gang of Maysville Negro thieves broke into a house in Ohio and stole a young girl. This child told passers-by in Maysville of her plight and thus aroused the suspicions of the citizens of the town. Upon investigating the child's story, Maysville police found that Lewis Allen and Henry Young of Maysville were professional kidnapers. These men threatened to burn the town if the police insisted on making further investigation. Indeed it was necessary to appoint vigilance committees to extinguish numerous fires. During this trouble a number of Maysville slaves were spirited off to the central Kentucky market and eventually to the South.

There were many interesting incidents which occurred in connection with the slave trade in the Lexington market. William M. Pratt, a Baptist minister, recorded in his diary the circumstances surrounding the sale of George Dupuy, the colored minister of Pleasant Green Baptist Church in Lexington. George was the slave and property of the late Reverend Craig, who died in 1847, but whose estate was not settled until 1856. George was permitted to preach at the Pleasant Green Church after Reverend Craig's death, but when the estate was advertised for sale, he was advertised also. Members of George's church persuaded Reverend Pratt to buy their preacher at the sale, the Negroes promising to pay for him in weekly installments. An agreement was finally made between deacons of the white and colored Baptist Churches as to conditions for the purchase of the slave-minister. The white deacons finally consented to purchase George, provided the price did not exceed $800. However, upon examination of the colored man he was found to be worth more than the $800 agreed upon. The auctioneer was interviewed on the night before the sale, when the deacons argued until nearly daybreak before they could persuade him to sacrifice the man for the stipulated price. Taylor, the auctioneer, finally came to terms, but before he could "knock" George off at $800, a Negro trader ran the price up to $830, a price which the white deacons paid. This colored minister was saved from the southern trade, and his flock made a journey every Monday to the Pratt residence to deposit the collections of the preceding Sunday. Unfortunately for his congregation, Dupuy was paid out just in time to be freed by law.

On another occasion, in 1860, Nancy Lee, a slave for life, approached Reverend Pratt in great distress because her two daughters were to be sold into the southern trade. Tony Lee, the girls' father, successful in purchasing their freedom, had turned the papers over to them just before his death. Negro traders visited Nancy and through a ruse secured possession of the papers and destroyed them. The girls were then offered for sale at public auction on county court day, February 13, 1860. Pratt bid on the first girl until the price reached $1,000. Then he stepped upon the auction block and begged the bidders to withdraw, but when the bidding was resumed and when the price was raised to $1,700, the girl was knocked off to the firm of Northcutt and Marshall. The second was sold in the same way for $1,600 to a slave trader from Covington. Pratt lamented in his diary that "such scenes are shocking to our moral natures. If God's curse does not rest on that concern (of Negro traders) then I am no prophet. Negro traders are the greatest curse to our land, and I do wish the city council would impose such a tax as to drive them from our midst."

In pronouncing a marriage ceremony, London Farrel, a Virginia-born slave preacher, united the couple in wedlock "until death or distance (did) them part," and many were the partings by distance. Traders had little regard for family ties when their pecuniary interests were jeopardized thereby.

In 1859, when there was a good deal of agitation for reopening the African slave trade, Virginia and Kentucky objected strenuously. Thomas Walton of Mississippi said in an essay appearing in *DeBow's Review* for January, 1859, that if a southern confederacy were formed,

Virginia and Kentucky would prevent the reopening of the African trade for the sake of their own traders. Immediately after the Vicksburg convention in 1859, a Kentuckian living at Lawrenceburg wrote the editor of one of the Vicksburg papers that if the African slave trade were reopened, it would ruin Kentucky, because Kentuckians were depending upon the slave trade for ready money.

It is virtually impossible to determine the volume of the slave trade from Kentucky to the South because of the clandestine manner in which the business was conducted. Much of the trade and many of the traders were kept secret because of the fear of social disgrace.

The Antislavery Movement

So long as Kentucky remained a part of Virginia, the western county was hesitant about asserting its views upon the institution of slavery. However, in the Virginia constitutional convention of 1788, the spokesmen for the West bitterly opposed leaving American ports open to the African slave trade until 1808. Although many citizens of Kentucky opposed slavery because of their personal views, there were no antislavery organizations except newly organized and struggling churches; among them, however, opposition to slavery was seriously handicapped by barriers of strict denominationalism. Perhaps the only outstanding pioneer antislavery crusader was David Rice, father of the Presbyterian Church in the West. It was he who led the majority of the opponents of slavery in the first constitutional convention in opposing the odious article IX which perpetuated slavery in Kentucky.

Numerous temperamental outbursts followed the adoption of the first Kentucky constitution, and countless sermons were preached upon the subject of "Slave Innocence." Masters were taunted with the guilt of slavery, and early preachers predicted that so long as slavery existed within Kentucky, the state could not prosper. Antislavery arguments were sown upon desert soil, for the framers of Kentucky's constitution and state laws were slaveholders. Of course, these lawmakers were disciples of the system and wholly impervious to antislavery criticism from the churches. George Nicholas, for instance, was an influential political figure and responsible for creation of a proslavery opinion.

Despite numerous difficulties, the churches remained hot on the trail of slaveholders between 1783 and 1865. Almost every religious group sponsored some type of antislavery program. The only exceptions to this general denominational opposition to slavery were the neutral Catholic, Episcopal, Cumberland Presbyterian, and Christian Churches. Militant crusaders were Baptists, Presbyterians, and Methodists. In 1789, the Baptist Church of the Salem Association declared ownership of slaves a violation of God's sacred laws. Antislavery sentiment in the Methodist Church was equally pronounced, so that in 1780 the Kentucky Methodist Conference denounced the institution in no uncertain terms. However, local Methodist conferences relaxed their discipline on slavery between 1796 and 1800. Presbyterians were stricter in their rules against slavery than were their Methodist and Baptist brethren. At its annual meeting in 1789, the Presbyterian General Assembly disapproved the ownership of slaves by the Church's members. Nevertheless this rule failed, as may be seen from the set of resolutions, adopted at the assembly in 1794, requiring that all slaves at least be taught to read and write the word of God.

Early opposition to slavery came at a time when the Negro population in the West was small, and slavery might have been peacefully abolished by gradual emancipation. Doubtless the only element lacking in religious opposition was a militant will to see the fight through to a satisfactory finish. Economically, for the country at large, this was a period when slavery had reached its most unprofitable stage. A national abolition society was formed in 1791 at Philadelphia, to which Kentucky sent delegates. Because of a lack of energy and definiteness of purpose, its Kentucky representatives soon became inactive. After this failure to rid the state of slavery, delegates to the second constitutional convention saw fit to give their stamp of approval to the institution by re-adopting article IX of the old document and making it most difficult to amend the new constitution. Preliminaries of the convention indicated that slavery would be one of the major issues, and the so-called "Aristocrats" forestalled the summons for the convention until they were certain that the slave power had the situation under control. One proslavery champion, John Breckinridge, informed Isaac Shelby that if the antislavery group succeeded in freeing the slaves, his group would in turn abolish land laws and land titles. Henry Clay was early drawn into the fight in defense of the opposition, and using the classical pseudonym "Scaevola" he addressed a series of articles to the

"Electors of Fayette County." Clay, however, wavered on the question when he suddenly found himself a popular champion of the Kentucky Resolutions.

Proslavery legislators were on constant watch for "trick" bills containing clauses endangering slavery. Lukewarm antislavery partisans were willing to concede their support to a gradual system of emancipation which promised to rid the state of the Negro. During the years 1819 and 1820 Kentucky became greatly concerned with the national attitude toward slavery, especially since it was the issue involved in the Missouri Compromise. By this time Henry Clay had regained his antislavery balance, but this did not prevent his favoring admission of Missouri as a slave state. Even the resolutions of Kentucky's legislators paid lip service to the newly admitted state, but warily side-stepped the question of committing themselves on slavery retention as a national policy.

In the meantime, the ecclesiastical storm raged, but, interesting to note, with a rapidly dying fury. Many slaveholders were brought before the associations, conferences, and synods for questioning in regard to their slavery views and activities. Many more were called before the altars of their respective churches to be rebuked for their iniquitous practices. These martyred individuals soon left the churches which opposed their holding slaves and established churches of their own, and often of the same denomination. Hence there grew up a marked degree of tolerance in the churches as a whole, so that the denominations and ministers became more and more lenient with "hardened sinners" who persisted in owning slaves.

It is only fair, however, to account for this weakening on the part of the churches by citing other substantial reasons. Where churches had battled individually in the name of "spirituality," the Kentucky Abolition Society, organized in 1808, did battle in the broader name of "humanity." This society spent the next decade in fruitless efforts to secure legislation favoring their crusade. Numerous resolutions and petitions sent to both the state legislature and the United States Congress were always ignored. It was not until 1821 that the Anti-Slavery Society, as a national organization, gained sufficient momentum to be of any influence. In that year its Kentucky chapter established at Shelbyville the short-lived, semimonthly antislavery and missionary magazine, the

Abolition Intelligencer, under the editorship of John F. Crowe. This magazine soon became a financial derelict and in 1823 ceased to exist. Since the Kentucky society had only 200 members, it was hardly possible that it could ever have become influential.

There were virtually as many abolition and emancipation plans on foot as there were individuals opposed to slavery. Overlapping the early period of the abolition societies was the movement for colonization. This organization was composed of both slaveholders and non-slaveholders, the most outstanding of whom was Robert Wickliffe, whom Cassius M. Clay had compared with McDuffie of South Carolina. Prominent slaveholders worked "hand in glove" with the state legislature to promote the welfare of the American Colonization Society, and both groups generously declared that no jealousy or opposition to this plan ought to exist. This society proposed to ship the newly freed Negroes from Kentucky to "Kentucky in Liberia" and there reinstate them on their native soil and in their native climate. Kentuckians generally regarded this as the sanest plan by which the state could rid itself of slavery and free Negroes. There were many in the state who believed the two races could not live together harmoniously. Perhaps the most outspoken of this group was Henry Clay, who repeatedly expressed his doubts on this point.

In 1833 the Reverend Richard Bibb liberated thirty-two of his slaves and provided them with $444 to supply comforts on their trip to Liberia. That same year, 106 Negroes were assembled at Louisville where they were dispatched to Liberia by way of the rivers to New Orleans and thence by sea to the African coast. This group was gaily feted prior to its departure from Louisville aboard the palatial steamer *Mediterranean*. On board the river steamer, the newly liberated passengers were given every possible comfort and service. Unfortunately, the party was soon overtaken by pestilence, so that many of the Negroes fell victims to Asiatic cholera.

In this same year the Kentucky Colonization Society succeeded in raising $1,137.67 to pay transportation fees of Negroes from the state. A fruitless attempt was made to get a legislative appropriation to send all of the free Negroes to Liberia. Actually, most of those who went from Kentucky to Africa were those living in freedom long before their deportation. It was Henry Clay who, commenting upon the pitiful plight of the free Negro, noted that he was without social caste, since he could neither secure protection of the whites, nor associate with his enslaved brothers. He was looked upon by both whites and slaves as a suspicious character, since he was isolated in his little settlement and by the laws of the state! Therefore free Negroes were anxious to escape this social discrimination by leaving the country.

Colonization soon proved a forlorn hope, since the organization undertook to carry out an expensive program but lacked necessary funds to support the venture. There were other conditions which vitally affected the scheme; the outbreak of Asiatic cholera in 1833 played havoc with several parties sent to Liberia, and those who successfully landed in Africa suffered great losses of health and life because they were not acclimated. Nevertheless, a periodic exodus of slaves and freedmen from Kentucky to Liberia continued until 1856, when this plan ceased to function.

During the year 1833, John Green proposed to Robert J. Breckinridge that a gradual emancipation society be organized to free every male slave born after July 4, 1831, when he reached the age of twenty-five and every female at the age of twenty-one. This proposal went begging, and other efforts to organize abolition societies lacked the backing of a crystallized public sentiment. At Danville, a leader came to the fore to propose organization of an outright antislavery society. This was James G. Birney, a native-born Kentuckian who had spent much of his time in Huntsville, Alabama. Birney organized the "Kentucky Society for the Relief of the State from Slavery," but it endured only two years. However, this failure was not discouraging, for he immediately organized the "Ashmunn Association." But like the first organization, it went to an early grave for lack of support. By this time Birney attracted the attention of national abolitionists and secured the co-operation of such antislavery leaders as Benjamin Lundy and William Lloyd Garrison. Soon, however, Birney outlived his welcome in Danville, but not until he had succeeded in getting Garrison to include Kentucky in the scope of his American Anti-Slavery Society. Garrison called for complete abolition and gave no heed to the plans of partial emancipation which had been proposed in Kentucky on every occasion when the existence of slavery was questioned. This scheme frightened Kentucky's proslavery forces into holding many meetings in and near

Danville for the purpose of bringing Birney and his crowd under control. A committee of thirty-three was appointed to remove from Kentucky both Birney and his newly established abolition paper, the *Philanthropist*. Birney proved obstinate and refused to leave town or desist from publication of his paper. The committee then brought out the printer who owned the press, and the postmaster refused to receive abolition literature at the postoffice.

Finally Birney was forced to leave Kentucky, but not until he had organized disciples to carry on his work. More mildly, the Presbyterian Church again condemned slavery and encouraged gradual emancipation.

Unfortunately, the American Anti-Slavery Society thwarted the purpose of more conservative movements for emancipation originating within the state, and the decade preceding 1840 saw emancipation lose ground. So long as the movement for freedom originated in the state, Kentuckians were willing to hear that the system of slavery was wrong in the sight of humanity. But once outsiders began meddling in local affairs, opposition in Kentucky became more stubborn. Even Henry Clay, who upon his arrival in Kentucky had favored emancipation, expressed himself as bitterly opposed to the methods of the abolitionists. In 1836 the legislature answered the abolitionists by adopting a resolution in which it was stated that an appeal to God alone would be made in matters of human justice. This same resolution aptly answered inevitable charges of interference with freedom of the press by saying that freedom of the press is one thing—licentiousness another. From this date until universal freedom was accomplished, Kentucky found herself overrun with abolitionists, and in constant dispute with her neighboring states across the Ohio River.

A rapidly growing controversy over abolition had definite effects upon the slaves. Slaveholders became restless and opened correspondence with the Governors of Ohio and Indiana in an effort to remove many obstacles to securing runaway slaves. Very little was accomplished, for the Governors of these states professed to see no obstacles to the enforcement of the existing agreements. The Governors of the bordering free states were not entirely at fault, for slave hunters from Kentucky were sometimes unscrupulous about the Negroes they claimed. Many of the slave-hunting raids across the border were noth-

ing short of outrageous kidnapings. As early as 1819, a case was reported where a Negro had been kidnaped in Ohio and sold in Kentucky, but later returned to his home by the Governor of Kentucky.

Free Negroes, in an ever-increasing number, crossed the Ohio River
into the free State of Ohio and into the State of Indiana. Conductors
of this traffic were often sought out and tried, but these trials resulted
in few convictions. In 1838 the Reverend John B. Mahan was tried for
stealing slaves, but as he was a citizen of Ohio, the Mason County
Court was powerless to impose its sentence. When the Kentucky Governor sent James F. Morehead and John Speed Smith to Ohio to effect
an amicable agreement on the question of returning fugitive slaves,
they secured a stricter law providing a fine and punishment for offenders. At the same time relations between Kentucky and Indiana, Kentucky's other neighboring free state, were marred by fewer incidents
of fugitive escapades. Doubtless the geographical location of the latter
state was a controlling factor.

Perhaps the most interesting case of spiriting slaves out of Kentucky
was the one involving Delia Ann Webster and Calvin Fairbanks, two
underground railway conductors from New England. Miss Webster
was engaged in teaching at a girl's school in Lexington. In 1845, this
pair of abolitionists were apprehended for smuggling slaves over the
Ohio River and were brought to trial. The court sentenced Miss Webster to two years', and Fairbanks to fifteen years' imprisonment in the
state penitentiary. However, since the Kentucky penitentiary had not
accepted women prisoners, Miss Webster was soon paroled on condition that she leave the state permanently. She failed to keep her agreement, however, for she returned to the state in 1854 and resumed operation as a conductor on the underground railway near Louisville.
Smuggling slaves from the state was a profitable business, for many of
the conductor's prices ranged from ten to fifty dollars per head. On
one day in 1852 a coffle of fifty-five slaves crossed the Ohio River from
Kentucky into the land of freedom. It was estimated that Kentucky
lost nearly 20,000 slaves annually in this way.

Unquestionably, the most interesting incident in the whole anti-
slavery movement was the publication and destruction of the *True
American,* edited and published by Cassius M. Clay. Clay, a son of
Green Clay, a prominent Kentucky pioneer, attended Yale University,

and while in New Haven came in contact with William Lloyd Garrison. So fascinated was Clay with Garrison that upon his return to Kentucky he took up the editorial cudgel for emancipation. At "number 6" Mill Street in the City of Lexington the emancipation editor prepared and published his antislavery sheet. He fortified the outside of his doors and casements with sheet iron and equipped the inside of the building with two "four pound" brass cannon, loaded with nails and Minié balls, a stand of rifles, several shotguns, and a dozen Mexican lances. Aside from this formidable array of warring instruments, Clay prepared an avenue of escape through a trapdoor in the roof. In the corner of the room he secreted several kegs of powder which he could touch off from the outside to blow up the office and its invaders.

On June 3, 1845, the *True American* made its first appearance carrying at its masthead the caption "God and Liberty." This paper soon aroused an already defiant community, and on August 14, a committee of infuriated citizens met at the courthouse to discuss plans for checking the publication of this emancipation newspaper. Clay, lying ill since July 21 with typhoid fever, got out of bed upon hearing of the meeting to go to the courthouse personally to defend himself. Lying prostrate upon a bench in the circuit courtroom he denounced, in a voice scarcely audible, the "apostate Whig," Thomas R. Marshall, who was acting as chief spokesman for the assembly. Several hours later a committee waited upon Clay at his residence on North Limestone Street to deliver an ultimatum ordering him to discontinue the publication of the *True American*. To this the editor replied, "Go tell your secret conclave of cowardly assassins that C. M. Clay knows his rights and how to defend them."

This reply further enraged the proslavery crowd, and on August 18 Judge Trotter of the Lexington Police Court issued an injunction against the *True American* and all its appurtenances. Accordingly, the city marshall presented the writ to Cassius M. Clay at his bedside, and he, with tears in his eyes, gave the official the keys to his editorial office. Later a committee of sixty men, led by James B. Clay, George W. Johnson, and William B. Kinkead appeared before the printing office door and demanded the keys of the mayor, after the latter had warned them that their proposed actions were illegal.

The committee proceeded in an orderly manner to pack up the private papers of the editor and send them to him. They then packed the printing equipment in neat packages and shipped them across the Ohio River into free territory. After the Mexican War, Cassius M. Clay was successful in securing $2,500 damages through the courts for the loss suffered by this action.

After numerous local conventions a general emancipation convention was held in Frankfort on April 25, 1849. Most prominent among the members present were the outstanding agitators of Kentucky, Robert J. Breckinridge, John G. Fee, Cassius M. Clay, Henry Clay (of Bourbon County) and United States Senator J. R. Underwood. A majority of the members at this convention were slaveholders, representing a holding of 3,000 slaves. Nearly one seventh of the convention's membership was composed of ministers from the various churches, Presbyterian, Methodist, Baptist, Unitarian, and Christian No definite action was taken in the convention, except to make arrangements for electing delegates to the next constitutional convention in the approaching campaign. The general tenor of the whole assembly indicated that slavery was an undesirable institution and that the state should adopt a program of gradual emancipation.

During this era of furious debate over the question of slavery, while Robert J. Breckinridge and Cassius M. Clay flooded the state with pamphlet literature condemning slavery, Henry Clay revealed his views on the question. In a letter to Richard Pendell he expressed a desire to see his native state rid of slavery in every form. This revelation brought down thunderous criticism on his head from every state in the South. Since Clay was more of a national figure than a local one, his letter was printed far and wide. Committees of citizens in many of the Kentucky counties asked his resignation as United States Senator. Southern newspapers generally were vehement in their criticism, and the *Richmond Inquirer* (Virginia) said, "Henry Clay's true character now stands revealed. The man is an abolitionist."

After a hard fought and bitter campaign for delegates to the constitutional convention of 1849, the proslavery partisans won unanimously. This is, perhaps, one of the more interesting of the many anomalies of Kentucky's political history. The vote for members to this convention was startling in that the return of proslavery delegates was complete even in counties which did not possess a single slave. There can be only one reasonable explanation for this peculiar turn of affairs: the voters were bitterly opposed to meddling abolitionists from other states.

In the drafting of the constitution of 1849, the slavery question bobbed up at every turn. Despite the fact that the delegation elected was unanimously proslavery, many members favored gradual emancipation and worked toward that end The Democrats were in control of the convention and elected James Guthrie president of the assembly. Every question introduced was of utmost importance, for no one knew what trick phrase or clause would be turned against slavery. For instance, the most innocent question of representation for the more populous cities of the state in the general assembly involved a question of protecting slavery, for the population of the larger towns contained many northern voters who favored abolition.

In framing the new constitution, slavery was duly guarded by the bodily adoption of the original article IX. Not only was this article re-adopted, but it was adequately safeguarded with supporting provisions. Since free Negroes, according to the constitution, menaced the institution of slavery, provision was made to send every freed slave from the state. No free Negro was permitted to enter Kentucky. If one were found there, he had to leave within thirty days or stand trial for a felony which carried a penalty of twelve months' imprisonment. Although the new constitution did not repeal the nonimportation law of 1833, the legislature did, and wholesale importation was permitted. So strong was the resentment by ministers of the gospel, particularly by the Presbyterians, of these acts favoring slavery, that the third constitution forbade any minister of the gospel the right to serve in public office or to occupy a position of public trust.

Adoption of the new constitution dealt the emancipation movement a staggering blow. It was impossible to amend the new document under a period of eight years, and before emancipationists could put on foot a movement to alter the constitution by popular demand, other problems would come to occupy the center of the stage. Nevertheless, local emancipationists such as Cassius M. Clay, John G. Fee, Robert J. Breckinridge, John G. Hanson, and James Davis, in co-operation with abolitionists from the outside, kept up a running fight against the institution of slavery until the last slave was freed after the Civil War.

Despite the bitter fight of the emancipationists and abolitionists with the slave trade, the slave population increased 6.87 per cent between 1840 and 1860. Kentuckians might have freed their slaves as early as 1849 had abolitionists from other states not interfered. Another factor which explains Kentucky's tenacious hold on slavery was the prominent place given the institution in the first three constitutions.

Despite past social and economic discriminations against them Kentucky blacks made proud contributions to a rich human chapter in state history. Earlier the famous slave ministers, Peter Vinegar and London Ferrell were highly respected as men of dignity and wisdom. In more recent years individuals like Dr. Whitney Young and his son Whitney, Jr. developed distinguished careers. Dr. Rufus Atwood and Dr. Carl Hill served the Commonwealth as highly capable educational statesmen. In Louisville Charles H. Parish, Sr. was an able president of the Louisville Municipal College. Professor Charles H. Parish, Jr. of the University of Louisville brought to his community a seasoned perspective as a sociologist. F. L. Stanley, editor and publisher of the Louisville *Defender*, maintained an outspoken public voice in racial affairs.

There have been many all but nameless blacks, among them lawyers, doctors, businessmen, bankers, and ministers who have given social and economic directions to their people. Tragically, no scholarly black historian has produced an objective history of the Negro's role in Kentucky. Until this is done this aspect of social and economic growth in the Commonwealth can not be fully described. There is an abundance of virginal historical documentary materials which awaits trustworthy and objective scholars of both races.

There are many strands indeed in the history of Kentucky, and there are many areas which need more complete treatment than space will allow. Because of the sharply defined regional division there have grown up local attachments which view localities with deep pride. Obviously every part of the state has made some kind of contribution to the total history of the Commonwealth. What is true of the sections is also true of the various social and economic groups in the state. Both major races in Kentucky have made rich contributions, and in doing so they have complemented each other. The Negro shares fully in two centuries of history. He has contributed generously to the growth of Kentucky first as a pioneer who crossed the mountains as slave, and then as a free citizen taking his place in society.

An enduring monument to the Negro pioneer is the fact that Kentucky was settled and protected more readily because of his presence. The black pioneers shared fully the trials and the triumphs of the raw frontier. Their labors and their skills were of the utmost importance. Unhappily a majority of Kentuckians did not support the early ideas of emancipation and freedom which would have spared Kentucky the stain of slavery, and especially the inhumane abuses of the interstate slave trade. Maybe beyond this moral question lies the fact that an appreciable amount of human talent and energy was wasted prior to 1865.

As freedman following the adoption of the Thirteenth Amendment, December 18, 1865, the Negro in Kentucky made even greater contributions and offered greater challenges. He struggled against almost insuperable odds to secure an education and establish an economic foundation. Kentucky in the post Civil War years was indeed parsimonious with its schools in general, and especially so with those for Negroes. It now seems almost beyond human understanding that the Kentucky General Assembly subscribed to the philosophy embodied in the Berea College or Day Law of 1904. Not even the most prejudiced Kentuckian could deny that the Negro had suffered unduly at all educational levels from 1865 to 1955. The District Court decision Johnson vs. University of Kentucky, 1949 opened the way for the beginning of desegregation of the whole Kentucky educational system. In the fall of 1954, undergraduates entered the University of Kentucky without any racial reservations. Earlier, in May, Governor Lawrence Wetherby courageously asserted that Kentucky would make every effort to conform with the ruling of the United States Supreme Court decision Brown vs. School Board.

In other areas of Kentucky life blacks have made substantial gains. Since 1945 they have served in the Kentucky General Assembly, in local political offices, and have been admitted to the practice of the various professions. They have participated in all areas of Kentucky's public life including religious and community organizations. No one can either assess with accuracy the hurt or the costly historical social mistakes and slights which have occurred in the past two centuries beyond observing they were injurious in terms of human emotions, frustrations, dignity, and thwarted ambitions.

CHAPTER XII

Educational Beginnings

WHEN the pioneers moved westward, they were slow to transfer their churches and schools as established institutions. This is a unique aspect of the development of the western country and its people, especially since the settlement of the eastern colonies was characterized by a love for religion and culture. In Kentucky, formal education, after a fashion, had its beginning in 1775 when Mrs. William Coomes, an Irish Catholic, tended school at Fort Harrod. Mrs. Coomes' school was nothing more than a dame school without significant implications of the English system of education. Here youngsters of Fort Harrod were taught to read and write from paddles with the alphabet inscribed upon them and from the Bible texts.

Despite the fact that Kentucky pioneers were slow in transferring to the western country the institutions of the eastern colonies, they brought with them the idea that to allow a man to reach maturity without being able to read was abomination in the sight of God. All the forts had crude schools taught by some literate member of the community. Glamorous accounts of these pioneer teachers' struggles on the frontier have come to the present generation. John May at McAfee's Fort, in 1779, taught the "3 R's" from memory, and, at Boonesborough, Joseph Donniphan enlightened youths on the subject. At Lexington, "Wildcat" John McKinney was teaching school while fighting wildcats and Indians. The fort schools were the immediate forebears of Kentucky's famous and notorious "old field" and "hedgerow" schools, which represented no particular educational philosophy beyond the crude teaching of the simplest principles of reading and writing.

Kentucky's first historian, John Filson, established a private academy at Lexington and depended largely upon its patronage for a livelihood. Here he succeeded in conducting a respected academy until a few months before his tragic death near Cincinnati in 1788. An interesting letter, appearing in the *Kentucky Gazette,* March, 1788, from a patron signing himself "Agricola," indicated that academies and seminaries were fairly numerous, for Agricola had no trouble finding a school in which to enroll his son. His otherwise seriously written letter twitted Filson by mockingly inquiring in response to one of Filson's public letters which type of school, country or town, was more efficient in teaching students to "hulk"!

At Georgetown, in 1788, Elijah Craig established a school for the benefit of his congregation. During the same year James Priestly took charge of Salem Academy at Bardstown, where he became one of Kentucky's most prominent early teachers.

Thus during the decades 1780 to 1800 not only did private schools appear in Kentucky, but teachers moved into the West to operate schools for profit. The Scotch, Irish, English, and German immigrants were favorably inclined toward education, but, as was typical of the people in their transatlantic background, they felt that education, like religion, was a matter of personal rather than public concern. It is interesting, in this connection, to note the arguments which appeared in the early issues of the *Kentucky Gazette.* Writing in the *Gazette* for November 15, 1787, a "Transylvanian" lamented that Kentucky schools were narrowly conducted by selfish interests. He believed it "a sad misfortune that superstition and party spirit has snatched benefits out of the hands of liberal and disinterested youth who from the cradle are enlisted in the service of some sect or interest. Every neighborhood encourages schools under different teachers according to prevailing doctrines, and who degenerate to traders of knowledge and consult more what will tell best that [*sic*] what is to the best advantage of pupils in after life. Either the state must take this up or a number of select and honorable gentlemen from the denominations must be men of large minds or else jealousies degenerate into feuds and quarrels and oppose everything for public good. Delays mean jealousy or weakness."

In 1787, citizens of Lexington, greatly concerned over their educational plight, organized the "Lexington Society for the Improvement of Knowledge." That same year, Isaac Wilson of Philadelphia College advertised that he was in Lexington to open the "Lexington Grammar School." Two students of the Reverend Doctor Robert Smith in Pennsylvania came to Lexington in the same year "to commence in the ensuing April an academy to offer advantages of a seminary where a whole circle of arts and sciences are to be taught with interest to all." In Jessamine County, in 1788, Ebenezer Brooks "expounded on cheap board [and urged the establishment of] the Jessamine Academy."

While the private academies were being established, a movement was begun to promote public schools supported by the counties. A local correspondent, signing himself "Philanthropas," advocated the establishment of schools on the Jeffersonian plan. He encouraged the division of the counties into districts four and five miles square, to be called "hundreds," at centers in which the "3 R's" would be taught. Perhaps this idea formed the background for the later founding of county academies.

Kentucky county schools, however, were unable to overcome the lead gained by the private academies. Graduates of eastern colleges and travelers from foreign countries came into Kentucky and opened private schools in which they taught numerous specialized subjects such as: western surveying, navigation, conical sections, bookkeeping, English, French, grammar, dancing, and fencing. In 1796 R. Gilbert advertised that he had opened a fencing academy on Main Street where lessons would be given nightly for the benefit of the young gentlemen of Lexington. Madame Mentelle, Peter Valentine, and P. Guerin advertised French schools where young ladies and gentlemen of central Kentucky might receive training in the French language and graces. Not only did Madame Mentelle and her husband teach French, but they also taught fancy and "decorative" dancing to students, of whom one was Mary Todd, later Mrs. Abraham Lincoln. Teachers in these private French schools were nearly all French immigrants who came to this country as exiles of the French Revolution.

As was typical of the Old South, Kentucky was overrun with private "female" academies of a literary nature, which taught young ladies the art of writing, reading, grammar, ornamental literature, poetry, painting, and fancy and practical needlework. These schools corresponded to the present finishing schools for girls, and women were considered by the patrons of these private academies as destined for maternal ornaments in the home. Boys were trained in business and in the practical affairs of life, but never women students, for feminine sensibilities were far too fine to be grated by crude everyday affairs. Girls who could go through a ballet with perfection, who could make fancy samplers, embroider their names, or mouth a little literary French were called cultured. Education fitting girls for life came from experience, for neither textbook nor teacher could tell them how to manage a husband. Their mothers taught them the secret of this art. Under such a plan of feminine education, the Kentucky girl was kept diligently at the task of cultivating herself in preparation for the coming of the inevitable romantic lover.

Surveying, arithmetic, geometry, bookkeeping, a little English grammar, and a few other practical subjects were taught to boys in private academies. If they were to become politicians, it was necessary for them to know enough Latin and Greek to impress their constituents. Classical literature, the history of England, the rise and fall of the Roman Empire, political science as embodied in Machiavelli's *Prince,* and like subjects were matters of study and interest. But many Kentucky academy masters believed that the Bible was sufficient textbook for boys. Others, with the medieval practice of Matthew Paris, used manuscripts copied from books found in Virginia. Even at present manuscript arithmetics are fairly common among early family papers.

Accordingly, education in Kentucky came to be considered a private matter and not a responsibility of the commonwealth. When the first constitution was drafted, despite the fact that it was the work of educated men, the delegates were not disposed to consider the question of public education. Nearly every delegate in the convention was a representative of a religious denomination; hence, his views of public education were no broader than the doctrines of his church. This first constitutional instrument, hailed by its framers and President Washington as the most democratic document adopted by any state, turned a deaf ear to education.

After 1787 Kentucky had two educational precedents on which to base its claim to public support of education. The Federal Government had adopted the Northwest Ordinance which reserved every "sixteenth section" of public land in each township for the support of schools, and the government of Virginia had donated public lands, in 1783, to the support of Transylvania Seminary. Each of these acts laid a basis for public support of education, but since Kentucky already had a system of private academies in the formative stage, her leaders were unwilling to accept a public plan.

In 1794, fifteen years after the establishment of the first school in the state, the Kentucky legislature passed an education act for the incorporation of the Kentucky Academy at Pisgah. This act set a precedent, and in quick succession Bethel and Franklin Academies were chartered in Jessamine and Mason Counties. Bethel Academy, however, failed under the first charter, but, on February 17, 1798, it was reincorporated. Its second charter was used as a future model for the establishment and conduct of the public academies. A second act was passed in the same year, which granted Bourbon, Winchester, Franklin, Bethel, Pisgah, and Salem Academies each 6,000 acres of land to be disposed of by a selected board of trustees.

Public lands south of the Cumberland River, the lands south of Obey's River, and any other unappropriated lands in the state were granted to public schools. Consequently twenty county academies were established and endowed with public lands, and other counties were permitted to appropriate their share of public land for schools. An act of the state legislature permitted each county to operate lotteries to raise $1,000 in order to pay preliminary expenses.

Section 3 of the act creating Transylvania Seminary provided that the state should endow county academies as "nursery schools" for the seminary. Perhaps the dominating influence responsible for this system of public education was that of Judge Caleb Wallace, who, before coming to Kentucky, had helped to found Washington College and Hampden-Sidney Seminary in Virginia. Although ideal in its basic conception, the academy system failed to function, since returns from 6,000 acres of public land yielded insufficient support. Between 1798 and 1820, county and state officials and citizens were too busily engaged in promoting their political and private welfare to be concerned with such an inconsiderable thing as education. Kentuckians took the typical backwoods attitude of "wait until we have cleared our forest, and until we have made our fortunes and we will build schools." By 1820, fifty-nine county academies were chartered and endowed with their 6,000 acres of public lands, but public interest lagged miserably. At nearly every meeting of the legislature between 1798 and 1820, bills were introduced to give the counties more time in which to locate and establish their schools. Responsibility of disposing of the public lands reposed in the hands of irresponsible trustees in many cases, and after much irregularity, the schools lost their lands. In 1815 the state turned over the entire system of public academies to their boards of trustees and washed its hands of further responsibility. This act made only one restriction, which required that funds derived from land sales be invested in the stock of the Bank of Kentucky.

In theory the academy plan was excellent, but as a practical measure it was freighted with dangerous possibilities, since early politicians had a perverted sense of what composed a well-balanced school system. By 1821 the whole plan was declared a gross failure, since a majority of the schools chartered had failed to open. Unfortunately, legislators had the notion that a state gift of 6,000 acres of unappropriated backwoods land would support a school without further public attention. By this time, too, it was discovered that public schools had other responsibilities to their communities than the preparing of students for Transylvania. It was soon discovered that the academies were more practical when developed as ends within themselves.

Since the land endowment scheme proved a miserable failure, the legislature passed an act on December 18, 1821, setting aside the net proceeds of profits derived from the Bank of Kentucky as a "literary fund." This fund was to form the basis for a permanent school fund, the income of which was to be used in the establishment of a general school system.

Part of this fund, in the hands of the state treasurer, was placed in the general state banking fund. Truly southern in its origin, the literary fund was an effort to support schools as painlessly as possible and without imposing an additional penny's worth of burden upon the taxpayers. This system never actually amounted to more than a gesture to which politicians paid eloquent lip service. Provision was made in the act of 1821 for one half of the funds from the branch banks at Lexington and Danville to be reserved for Transylvania and Center Colleges. This plan was violently opposed by representatives from outlying counties, on the ground that their county academies should be revived and converted into local colleges. One of the stock arguments used against the colleges at Lexington and Danville was that rural parents feared to send their sons into the big towns to be educated. Jesse Noland of

Estill County and Martin Hardin of Hardin County were leaders in the fight favoring the local college plan. These gentlemen introduced the argument that students educated in publicly supported institutions were public servants, and that doctors and lawyers so educated should charge less for their services. Other opponents argued that to educate a man was to ruin him for military service, citing Kentuckians in past wars. Defending educational institutions at public expense, Colonel Robert McAfee sensibly reminded opponents of public education that Kentucky would suffer an irreparable loss if she had to send her young men to other states to be educated.

Despite Governor Slaughter's plea for schools in his message to the legislature in 1816, that body refused to act. Governor Slaughter said that the state's support of the academies had been "productive of some good, but the fund had proved inadequate to meet the 'enlightened' and 'liberal' views of the legislature." County academies proved a disappointment, for they failed to achieve little permanent good. Humphrey Marshall recorded the mournful passing of Franklin Academy, observing that it had degenerated under the bad government "until it had neither acting trustees, teacher, nor student, as it is believed."

While local and state politicians squandered returns from land grants and the literary fund, the communities resorted to local resources to establish crude public schools. Teachers were employed because of their venerable ages or because of the distance from which they came; both reasons were considered evidence of wisdom. Little or no formal training was necessary to teach an "old field" or "hedgerow" school. The teacher, however, had to be a master at administering discipline with a hickory flail. These teachers were poorly paid and often not paid in money, but even so, many of them received too generous a compensation. Surveyors who had spare time usually taught school to make some extra money. Their knowledge of surveying and mathematics made them the most practical teachers. Ben Hardin cited in the third constitutional convention his experiences while attending a country school as evidence that some provision should be made to secure qualified teachers for Kentucky. He said that in a "blab" school he learned to read in a "sing-song" tone of voice, and it had taken him years to correct this shortcoming. He also told the amusing but shocking story of a country teacher who appeared before him as a witness in a case to testify that the settlement in question was made on the "39th" day of the month. Upon further questioning Hardin discerned that this teacher was unable to state how many months there were in the year.

What these early teachers lacked in knowledge they made up in harsh treatment of their students. Teachers who could whip every boy in school, make goose quill pens, and tolerate crude antics from their students on holidays and special occasions were re-elected each year. Parents judged the efficiency of the teachers by the number of hours they kept their students "in books," and by their manly capacity to use the "hickory withe."

Kentucky legislators, unwilling in 1821 to vote support for the state's public school system, appointed a committee to investigate the conditions by which the northwestern states received public land grants in an act of 1787. This committee reported that Kentucky was entitled to 1,066,665 acres of public lands, and that the United States Congress had discriminated against the older states in this act. Resolutions were adopted to the effect that "each of the United States had an equal right in its just proportion to participate in the benefit of the public lands— the common property of the Union."

Governors Metcalfe, Morehead, and Letcher expressed a desire to have Kentucky's educational institutions share in the gifts of the Federal Government. When the legislature appointed its investigating committee in 1821, it also, after gubernatorial urging, appointed a group composed of William T. Barry, D. White, David R. Murray, W. T. Ruper, John R. Witherspoon, and John Pope to study educational systems and to formulate a plan for the establishment of common schools in Kentucky. This move was noble of purpose, but public indifference toward education was deadly; hence another report was placed on a legislative shelf. In 1825, Governor Desha, in his message to the legislature, dealt education a discouraging blow when he condemned Transylvania as a hotbed of aristocracy. He advocated the state's spending less money on this institution and more on the establishment of a common school system. Desha's remarks doubtless would have been weighty had they not been ill-founded and selfish. It was self-evident that there was an urgent need for public schools, but by the most extravagant imagination, Transylvania could not be held responsible. If this institution had become, as Desha charged, a hotbed of aristocracy, it was owing to a lack of secondary school graduates in the state to supply a more democratic student body.

Had Governor Desha not lacked the necessary element of sincerity, and had the public accepted his remarks seriously, support for the common schools would have been forthcoming. However, this ill-founded remark not only materially injured Transylvania but accomplished nothing for the proposed common schools. These remarks led to an investigation of Kentucky's institution of higher learning in order to determine what should be its relationship with the public schools. In 1829 the Reverend Alva Wood (who, a president of Harvard told Henry Clay, was the most liberal Baptist available), president of Transylvania, and Benjamin O. Peers, a Transylvania professor, were appointed to study the state's educational needs and problems. It was hoped that a system of public education which would function satisfactorily in Kentucky, and at the least expense, could be devised.

Woods and Peers soon found that their problem had no background of support. Public education had been the "stepchild" of the state government, and its interests were ignored when other departments of the state government were in need of financial assistance. Funds derived from the stock of the Bank of Kentucky, as provided in the act of 1821, were juggled back and forth through the hands of irresponsible persons. To know the history of this fund and the history of the public academies is to know virtually the whole history of early public education in Kentucky. At the time the bank profits were set aside for educational purposes, the annual income for education amounted to approximately $60,000, but unfortunately this sum was never applied to educational needs. From 1821 to 1829, the accumulated funds, increasing (supposedly) at the rate of $60,000 per annum, amounted to only $150,000, and in 1833, this fund had dwindled to $141,000. So backward was the support for education that the legislature passed an act in 1825 permitting local trustees to locate and support, with community funds, as many "old field" schools as they pleased.

Governor Desha's attack upon Transylvania was prompted by the keen desire on the part of politicians to secure the accumulated literary fund to apply on the construction of turnpikes. In his message in 1826, the Governor recommended that all educational funds, proceeds from unappropriated lands, and certain other funds, be invested in the construction of turnpikes. Dividends from the turnpike investments, said the Governor, "were to be forever sacredly devoted to the interest of education." This was as false and as hypocritical a promise as any institution in the state had ever received. Nevertheless, funds for public education were prostituted to turnpike construction, and the formation of a public school system was left to the future with the hope, perhaps, that the Federal Government would give the state financial assistance.

But Woods and Peers took their instructions seriously and recommended a district system for the counties under local supervision, and supported by a poll tax of 50 cents, and a 6¼ cent tax on each assessed $100 of real property. In this report the state proposed to shift its responsibility to the shoulders of the counties, for the only semblance of a state system appeared in the general uniformity of the district schools.

In their report, Woods and Peers made intelligent observations and set forth some interesting data upon the state's educational needs. In their study of the eighty-three counties of the state, it was reported that seventy-eight of them maintained schools. They reported 140,000 children between the ages of five and fifteen years, with only 31,834 enrolled in schools, and 107,328 without educational facilities. They reported 1,131 schools maintained at an expense of $278,592. It would require an expenditure of $1,200,052 to maintain schools of a like nature for all children of school age. Distribution of schools by counties ranged from one in Russell to fifty-three in Henry County. Morgan County had nine schools, Laurel two, Harlan three, Knox four, Hickman five, Floyd six, Butler seven, Grayson eight, and Anderson nine. Many other counties had fewer than ten schools, of the poorest type. Bourbon County had the best schools in the state, in which more than fifty per cent of the children of school age were enrolled. Teachers received salaries ranging from $100 to $400 per annum. The average school had from twenty to forty pupils enrolled. This report, making known for the first time to the people of Kentucky their exact educational status, went far to create a favorable public opinion for improved public schools.

This report led directly to the calling of an educational convention in Lexington on November 7, 1833, where plans were drafted for a state-wide common school system to be at last brought into existence.

At its Frankfort meeting in January, 1834, the newly organized state "Common School Society" memorialized the legislature to organize a system of public schools, and a teacher-training normal school. The guiding spirit of this movement was Benjamin O. Peers, who, it appears, preceded Horace Mann in his ideas on what should constitute a well-organized system of public schools. Influential associates of Benjamin O. Peers were Governor John Breathitt, James T. Moorehead, Reverend John C. Young, Reverend H. B. Bascom, Thomas Marshall, and Daniel Breck.

Kentucky's representatives in Congress never abandoned the hope that the United States would come to the financial rescue of the schools of their state. On January 29, 1830, a hopeful Kentucky legislature passed an act bearing the eloquent and all inclusive title: "An act to Encourage the General Diffusion of Education in this Commonwealth by the Establishment of Uniform Schools." This act clearly anticipated federal aid, and, in order to have its house in order, the legislature recommended the adoption of the Woods and Peers report.

Federal aid for education was much delayed, for it was not until 1836, one year prior to the great panic, that the Jacksonian Government decided to distribute the surplus of the United States Treasury to the states. These funds were received by Kentucky with the general understanding that they were to be applied to educational institutions and internal improvements. By an act of February 25, 1837, the Kentucky legislature provided that $1,000,000 of the amount received from the Federal Government should be "set apart and forever dedicated to the founding and sustaining of a general system of public instruction." Unfortunately, the panic of 1837 cut short the payment of the total funds allotted Kentucky, but in 1838 the legislature dedicated $850,000 to the use of schools.

This appropriation was the actual beginning of the state's present school system, for provisions were made for the administration of the state's schools as a unit. Briefly, the provisions made were: equalized funds to the counties; establishment of a state board of education; division of the state into districts containing thirty to fifty children; districts to be permitted to levy special taxes; appointment of five commissioners of education for each county; and the appointment of five trustees for each district. This law, sponsored by Judge William F. Bullock of

Louisville, was a boon to 150,000 Kentucky children who were without educational advantages.

Benjamin O. Peer's report formed the basis for the formation of the school system. If the whole plan had been adequately financed, it would perhaps have functioned satisfactorily from the beginning. Unfortunately, provisions were made for local taxation and support instead of the concentration of these powers in the hands of the state government. Local support was slow, since taxpayers of the district felt that they were being doubly taxed to maintain both county and state governments and public schools. Not only did local taxation interfere with the efficiency of this plan of establishing schools, but local jealousies, arising from the jurisdiction of the district trustees, soon caused many schools to fail.

This predicament left the schools as they were in the beginning. Communities with sufficient initiative provided for their own schools, while those that were indifferent made no effort to remedy the situation. Such a haphazard method of establishing schools had its evil effects, since there was little uniformity or sense of co-operation on the part of the schools. Teachers, trustees, and patrons proceeded according to their private judgments and opinions; consequently the quality of education varied with the sections of the state in which the schools were located.

Following the enactment of a general state school law and the establishment of the office of Superintendent of Education there was a rapid succession of state administrators. Beginning with Joseph J. Bullock in 1838, the early superintendents were Hubbard H. Kavanaugh, 1839; Benjamin B. Smith, 1840; George W. Brush, 1842; Ryland T. Dillard, 1843; and Robert J. Breckinridge, 1847. Robert J. Breckinridge was the most influential of the early state superintendents because it fell to his good fortune to give public education its constitutional status. He got the constitutional convention of 1849 to include provisions for public schools in article XI, section I of the constitution.

In 1850, over the strong opposition of the stubborn and aristocratically inclined Governor John Helm, Superintendent Breckinridge successfully attached the financial obligations of the schools to the state debt. Breckinridge in 1851 received a just reward in his election to the state superintendency of education by a popular vote of the people. Although ungainly in appearance and possessed of a hot temper that kept him involved in one controversy after another, Robert J. Breckinridge had tenacity and foresight enough to accomplish his purpose. In 1853 he resigned the office. John D. Matthews was made his successor, who in turn was succeeded in 1859 by Robert Richardson. Through this succession of superintendents, Kentucky's public school system found itself well along in its formative years, and had the strife between the states been avoided, perhaps another decade would have seen an efficiently established system of public instruction.

When the War between the States interrupted the building of Kentucky's public schools, the state had located schools in every county and had a growing school fund of over $2,000,000. All public schools were free of tuition, and the most efficient teachers obtainable were employed. Thus Kentucky was making good her boast "that as soon as she conquered the savages, cleared her lands, built her homes, and created some wealth she would build schools." But the state did not get to this task until too late to prevent the blighting effects of the war, which almost completely wrecked the institution of public education.

Higher Education

The southern colonial gentlemen liked to think, as their English forefathers did, that institutions of higher learning gave their state and community the stamp of that intangible something called culture. They liked to think that the language of the Caesars and the political philosophy of the Greeks were being taught in their communities. While the rigors of the American Revolution were bearing most heavily upon the Colonies, Virginia was not negligent of her western daughter's educational needs. Provisions were made in her general assembly on May 1, 1780, to establish an institution of learning west of the mountains. To this seminary, the purpose of which was "promoting civilization among the pioneers," the assembly made the following grant:

Whereas it is represented to the general assembly that there are certain lands within the county of Kentucky, formerly belonging to British subjects, not yet sold under the law of escheats and forfeiture which might at a future day be a valuable fund for the maintenance and education of youth, and it being the interest of this Commonwealth always to promote and encourage every design which may tend to the improvement of the mind and the diffusion of knowledge, even among its remote citizens, whose situation a barbarous neighborhood and a savage intercourse might otherwise render unfriendly to science; Be it therefore enacted, That 8,000 acres of land within the said county of Kentucky, late the property of Robert McKenzie, Henry Collins, and Alexander McKee, be, and the same are hereby, vested in William Fleming, William Christian, John Todd, John Cowan, George Meriwether, John Cobbs, George Thompson, and Edmund Taylor, trustees, as a free donation from this Commonwealth for the purpose of a public school, or seminary of learning, to be erected within said county as soon as the circumstances of the county and the state of its funds will admit, and for no other use or purpose whatsoever.

The last signs of the Revolution had not cleared from the western horizon when the first board meeting of Transylvania Seminary was held at Crow's Station in Lincoln County. Present at this meeting were most of the pioneer Kentucky leaders including Levi Todd, Benjamin Logan, Samuel McDowell, John Bowman, Isaac Shelby, David Rice, Caleb Wallace, Walker Daniel, Robert Johnson, John Craig, James Speed, Christopher Greenup, and Willis Green. Despite the fact that this group was highly representative of the pioneering class of Kentucky, many of them were well educated. Typical of frontier conditions and times, these trustees met with the most pious intentions of starting the western seminary on its road to success and early fame. Reverend John Todd, of Louisa, Virginia, in a burst of enthusiasm, gave the board his private library, which marked the beginning of the school's famous library. Entries in the "Trustees' Book," however, tell a tragic story, for the pioneers' ardor cooled as promptly as it had been aroused. At one meeting after another the clerk made the disheartening entry, "no quorum."

At the board meeting on November 4, 1784, a resolution was adopted to erect one or more grammar schools as circumstances would permit. One of these schools was to be erected near the home of "Father" David Rice, with a tuition fee of one *pistole,* or $3.00, with a teacher employed who was versed in Latin, Greek, and the philosophies. On May 26, 1785, the board of trustees received the report that a school had been taught by the Reverend James Mitchell in David Rice's home. Mitchell fell in love with one of the Reverend Rice's daughters, married her, and "deserted his father-in-law's bed and board" for his native North Carolina. This left his backwoods school without a teacher.

Transylvania Seminary, although founded by the state, was dominated by the Presbyterians, who moved into the West imbued with a spirit to do missionary work among the pioneer immigrants. David Rice, the father of western Presbyterianism, and a Princeton graduate, was regarded by the early board of trustees as the most efficient guardian for the infant seminary. Had it not been for the nurturing by the Presbyterians, especially by David Rice, Transylvania would hardly have seen the light of day. It was solely Presbyterian interest and initiative which early created and maintained the infant school.

Before it is possible to understand the philosophy back of the actual establishment of Transylvania as a component part of Kentucky's educational system, it is necessary to comprehend the educational philosophy of the ante bellum South. Before provision was made for establishing public secondary schools, Kentuckians agitated for the founding of an institution of higher learning. Secondary schools of a public nature were unknown. Elementary education in the South had been conducted privately, and, since the Kentuckians were following in Virginia's footsteps, it was natural that they believed public maintenance should go only to the colleges. The College of William and Mary at Williamsburg and Queens College at Charlotte, North Carolina, were state supported, but the academies of these states belonged either to private individuals or to the churches. Furthermore, many of the early promoters of Transylvania Seminary were college graduates and measured education and culture in terms of college degrees. It is clear that the early Kentucky fathers attempted to build their educational structure, as their fathers had done, by laying the ridgepole first.

In 1785 the question of permanently establishing Transylvania Seminary arose. Much discussion ensued as to the most favorable location. Since some of the seminary lands were located near Lexington, which was the center of much of Kentucky's cultural activity, members of the committee decided in favor of that place. Before moving the institution from Danville, however, a definite effort was made to secure funds by popular subscription, but citizens of Danville and its vicinity were in no position to give aid. It was impossible for the Virginia Assembly to offer further assistance, because the Revolutionary War left that state stranded financially. However, an act was passed on December 13, 1787, granting Transylvania one sixth of the surveyors' fees collected in the western counties. Thus the western institution was given practically as much state aid as William and Mary's received.

After several unsuccessful attempts to raise funds in Danville, the board of trustees voted to hold its next meeting in Lexington, hoping, no doubt, to receive more encouragement there. On October 13, 1788, board members traveled from the outlying settlements to Lexington to determine definitely the location of the school. After the board had deliberated for several days, Elias Jones was appointed professor at the "munificent" salary of $333.33 with the understanding that, when conditions justified it, a grammar master and an usher were to be elected. During the first years in Lexington, Transylvania fared no better than in Danville, for the citizens of the town showed little or no interest. The school was only a plan on paper until 1789, when Isaac Wilson, master of the Lexington Academy, was employed to teach the seminary in the public schoolroom adjoining the Presbyterian meetinghouse. In all probability this move meant the consolidation of the seminary with the Lexington Academy in order to save the former's face.

Two years later the Reverend James Moore, lately of Virginia, and a Presbyterian preacher, was engaged to teach in the seminary at a salary of $75.00 per term, with special fees collected for teaching Latin and Greek classics. Lexington citizens not of the Presbyterian faith were hesitant in patronizing the seminary. It was not until John Bradford and associates organized the Transylvania Land Company that the school was assured permanent location in Lexington. On April 8, 1793, the seminary was established on land adjoining the tract owned by Peter January, in what is now Gratz Park. James Moore was re-employed as master and was authorized to engage an usher to instruct students in Greek and Latin classics. Tuition prices were raised to $13.00. The Reverend Moore's salary was increased to $333.33, and the usher received $200.00.

Unfortunately the times produced many troubles for the seminary. When it was moved to Lexington, rumors of the French Revolution were drifting into the West. In the same year, when the school was definitely established, the twenty-eight-year-old *Citoyen* Genêt arrived in Charleston to enjoy the hilarious reception of the Republicans of that place. To the West he dispatched disciples to curry American favor for his cause. Liberty poles were erected in the towns of central Kentucky, with French conspiracy under way. The French deistic philosophy found ready followers. Even the Republican helmsman, Thomas Jefferson, was accused of having a French turn of mind and of subscribing to a religion very sharply tinctured with French infidelity. With such a philosophy rampant, it was only natural that Transylvania Seminary, with a deep-dyed Presbyterian complexion, would be vitally affected. When Tarry Toulmin was elected to the presidency in 1794, upon the recommendation of Thomas Jefferson, the Presbyterians served notice that they would withdraw their support to establish a school of their own. Not only was it believed that Toulmin (later to become secretary of state in Kentucky and then founder of the University of Alabama) was impregnated with French infidelity, but he was also a Baptist.

Withdrawing their support from an institution which they had nurtured through infancy and during the trying times of post-Revolutionary days when Kentucky was holding its numerous conventions to separate from Virginia, the Presbyterians established Kentucky Academy at Pisgah, eight miles southwest of Lexington. Here they proceeded to teach school according to their own doctrines and without fear of outside interference. In organization the Pisgah institution conformed generally to the private academy plan. The law creating this school was the basic act for the whole academy system.

A committee of forty-seven members was appointed by the Transylvania Presbytery to solicit funds for its newly established school. David Rice and James Blythe attended the General Assembly of the Presbyterian Church at Philadelphia, there to succeed in securing $10,000 from interested individuals. Among the many contributors were George Washington, John Adams, and Aaron Burr.

To smooth troubled waters, Harry Toulmin resigned the presidency of the Transylvania Seminary in 1798, and, for the third time, the Reverend James Moore was recalled to head the school. Immediately upon the return of President Moore, a move was made to unify Transylvania Seminary and Kentucky Academy. An entry in the "Trustees' Book," December 22, 1798, records that the two schools were united, and that a legislative act of the same date consolidated the two institutions, and that after January 1, 1799, the schools were known as Transylvania University.

At Transylvania University, chairs of law and medicine were established. Honorable George Nicholas was appointed Professor of Law, and Samuel Brown and Frederick Ridgely were made Professors of

Surgery. It was not until 1802, however, that Transylvania conferred its first bachelor of arts degree. From 1800 to 1860, the University had on its faculty such worthy and prominent professional leaders as: George Nicholas, Henry Clay, Jessee Bledsoe, Thomas Marshall, and Madison C. Johnson (law), C. S. Rafinesque (botanist), Samuel Brown, Charles Caldwell, Benjamin W. Dudley, W. H. Richardson, James Blythe, Daniel Drake, John Esten Cooke, L. P. Yandell and Charles W. Short (medicine), Robert Peter (chemist), Horace Holley (minister), and Benjamin O. Peers and Harry Toulmin (educators).

During the first quarter of the nineteenth century Transylvania University was on the very threshold of national success. Her students, coming from most of the southern and western states, returned home as leaders of their sections. At one time the University boasted a far abler leadership than that of either William and Mary's or the University of Virginia. Lawyers trained at Transylvania were outstanding in the practice of their profession, and among its professors were national figures. Lexington was truly the "Athens of the West," and its citizens proudly boasted of "Our University." Tragedy soon converted this promising dream into a "mare's nest," for the lion and the lamb had lain down together in the dual state and denominational control of the institution.

From 1818 to 1827, Transylvania University had its most flourishing period of development. At the head of the school was Horace Holley, one of the most progressive and best informed men in the state. Since Holley's intellectual liberality had, from the beginning, a disturbing effect upon the orthodox denominationalists, the religious groups, led by the Presbyterians, declared their opposition to the president of the University.

Holley's liberal references to the Bible in Transylvania's classrooms were highly unsatisfactory and aroused so much criticism as time went on that, in 1826, he offered to resign. His resignation was refused by the board of trustees, and he was prevailed upon to remain another year. In 1827 his resignation was accepted, but his withdrawal from Lexington took away the life spark of the University. After 1827 the school showed a decided lack of intellectual energy and progress; its effectiveness was dead for many years to come.

All liberal educational development in ante bellum Kentucky can best be summed up in the Holley period at Transylvania. From November, 1818, to March, 1827, Transylvania became an outstanding institution. President Holley was a graduate of Yale College in the class of 1803. He studied law in New York, but in 1809 he was ordained a minister of the gospel under the tenets of the Unitarian Church and was made pastor of the Hollis Street Unitarian Church of Boston, Massachusetts. As a minister he proved a vivacious and stirring orator. On one occasion he delivered a sermon to the "Ancient and Honorable Artillery" of Boston, in which he provoked the staid New England audience to wild cheers.

As president of Transylvania he sponsored a liberal cultural program. With the aid of Henry Clay and Colonel James Morrison he made Transylvaina a real symbol of learning for the West. He established the medical and law schools professionally by employing able men for their respective chairs. He secured gifts for the college, most important of which was the endowment left by Colonel James Morrison on April 23, 1823. Colonel Morrison, long a friend of liberal education, willed $20,000 to endow a professorship, and a residuary fund of $50,000 to construct a building to bear his name.

Except for the dispute with the Presbyterians, which had begun before Holley reached Lexington, the growing period of the University was not marred by any unpleasantness. Other denominational colleges were attempting to get on their feet, and the various religious organizations had no time to concentrate their fire upon this "center of intellectual iniquity." However, the period of quiet soon ended, for in 1826 the hounds of denominational dispute were loosed. They drove from Kentucky to a tragic death the only man who had pointed the way to a successful system of higher public education. Since Holley took passage on a southern river steamer in departing the West, there has perhaps never been gathered together in Kentucky a more capable and more nationally outstanding faculty of college instructors.

Before President Holley was installed as head of Transylvania, the Presbyterians threatened withdrawal. The fathers of the various churches felt that a man like President Holley would undermine the very foundation on which the churches were built. When they withdrew in 1818, the Presbyterians insisted upon establishing an institution where their ministers could be trained without fear of any teachings of infidelity.

The dissenting Presbyterians appealed to the state legislature for a charter permitting them to found a college where ministers could be trained without coming in contact with a man like Horace Holley who had openly criticized certain biblical tenets before one of his classes. In 1818 the Presbyterian forces led by the Reverend S. K. Nelson sought a charter for their proposed school, but strong political forces from Transylvania intervened, and the movement failed. However, in 1819, the state officials, disgruntled at a stubborn board of self-perpetuating trustees at Transylvania, were more amenable to the proposal of the Presbyterian petitioners. In that year the legislature chartered Centre College and offered the institution a state endowment. One third of the funds derived from the branch bank of Harrodsburg was given the institution for the purpose of purchasing a library and scientific apparatus. As this arrangement was agreeable at first to the Presbyterians, they not only accepted the state's endowment, but also agreed to permit professors from other denominations to occupy chairs in the school. This arrangement, however, brought about a tremendous protest, for many could not see why the State of Kentucky should make a grant of $30,000 to the establishment of Centre College for the admitted purpose of training Presbyterian ministers. So strong was public opposition that the legislature, on publishing the school's charter, definitely stipulated that "no religious doctrine peculiar to any one sect of Christians shall be inculcated by any professor in said college." By this charter Centre College became a state rather than a denominational school, since the state did not wish to recommit the folly of uniting church and state control of a school. As the Presbyterians refused to support the school, it inherited as a state institution the property of the old Danville Academy and a share of the profits of the Harrodsburg Bank. Control of the school was placed in the hands of a board of nineteen self-perpetuating trustees. A futile attempt was made, for five years, to maintain Centre College as a state institution, but the day came when funds provided by the state failed, and the institution was financially stranded. Admitting failure, the state, on January 27, 1824, amended the charter to grant the Presbyterian Synod of Kentucky complete control of the college.

Under the guidance of the Presbyterian Church, medical and law departments were operated after 1833, the medical department being located in Louisville. Thus, after fifty years of hectic struggling, the

Presbyterians had complete control of a school in which the instructional policies could be prescribed and directed by the synod.

At the time the state chartered Centre College, the Roman Catholics secured a charter for St. Joseph's College; the Methodists established, in 1822, Cumberland College; and the Baptists founded, on January 15, 1829, Georgetown College. This latter school was established for the avowed purpose of training ministers for the Baptist Church. Like Centre College, Georgetown was the offspring of an academy. In 1798, Rittenhouse Academy was chartered and given the customary 6,000 acres of public lands, and in 1829 all property of the academy was given to Georgetown College.

These early denominational institutions bore the misleading title of "college," when in reality they were nothing more than glorified academies, where, in most cases, there were only two or three instructors. Each school had a professor of theology and a professor of Latin and Greek. These instructors spent long hours training their students to be good citizens of the land of Ur of the Chaldees or ancient Greece and Rome, but seldom, if ever, placed any emphasis upon the needs of citizenship in the land of the Mississippi Valley.

A student interested in current public affairs had to turn to local partisan newspapers, law offices, and practical politics for his training. None of these worldly arts, with the possible exception of law, which in many cases was highly tinctured with the legal and political theories of medievalism, was allowed to defile the youthful mind in the classroom. Practical arts were not considered as cultural by the ante bellum mind, for to be cultured in the sense of the time students had to be on speaking terms with the dead languages and equipped to argue incessantly on abstruse points and principles of religious dogma.

Kentucky's educational system has been hampered from its beginning by forces which the state has been unable to overcome completely. There has been no desire to discourage education; quite to the contrary, Kentuckians have loved educational advantages and have on the whole patronized the best schools in the East. At home, however, they have had an inherent fear that public education was a wolf in sheep's clothing, and the history of public education in the state until more recent years has been a series of struggles and disappointments.

Although slow in transferring their denominational organizations to the West, the Kentuckians became passionately religious when they finally succumbed to the various doctrines. Hence the period of ante bellum educational advancement was little more than a series of religious fights and denominational controversies. There were no liberalizing forces strong enough to prove the absurdity of the claim that liberal education endangered the doctrines of the various denominations.

CHAPTER XIII

The Press

IN A NEW country where transportation facilities were limited and generally inefficient and where travel was accompanied by dangers and other hardships, a medium of transmitting news became imperative. Kentucky was too far removed from any of the eastern states to communicate with them or to receive their newspapers within a reasonable length of time after they came from the press. When the early constitutional conventions met, there was not an organ by which a unanimity of feeling to separate from Virginia might be effected. Since the population of the western country was rapidly increasing, it became necessary to make a concerted move to bring about separation. To do this the western leaders determined to co-operate in the establishment of a western mouthpiece. This enterprise was the most important one at the meeting of the second convention in 1785 at Danville.

Following the precedent of some eastern states, the Kentucky representatives voted to establish an official Kentucky newspaper. A committee was appointed to organize the paper and to secure the assistance of an editor. Strangely enough, the roving habits of early printers had not caused one to migrate to the West, and the committee had some difficulty in finding a man bold enough to undertake the venture.[1] John Bradford had moved to Kentucky from Fauquier County, Virginia, in 1785 and had proved himself to be a man of unusual common sense. He had no training as a printer but was willing to undertake the publication of the *Gazette,* provided the committee would guarantee public patronage. The committee guaranteed the prospective editor that his terms would be met and instructed him to secure a press. Since the citizens of the village of Lexington were diligent in their en-

---

[1] John Parvin, a printer, had come out to Kentucky before 1787, but it seems that he was not interested in opening a print shop. Parvin, however, did assist John Bradford for a time in the publication of the *Gazette.*

couragement of the undertaking, in 1786 the town's council voted Bradford a lot free of cost on which to establish his paper.

An antiquated hand press, type, type cases, and other necessary but poor supplies were secured in the summer of 1787 at Philadelphia. This equipment was hauled overland to the Ohio River at Pittsburgh, shipped from there by flatboat to Limestone (Maysville), and then transferred by pack horse to Lexington. While drifting down the river, and while waiting for the pack horses to arrive at Limestone, Fielding Bradford, a brother and partner of the editor, set up much of the type in readiness for publication of the first issue of the paper. Unfortunately this labor was in vain, for the rough roads and numerous obstacles in the way of the horses caused the type to fall into "pi."

When the belated *Gazette* made its meek appearance on August 11, 1787, it was with the following editorial apology:

> My customers will excuse this my first publication, as I am much hurried to get an impression by the time appointed. A great part of the types fell into pi in the carriage of them from Limestone to this office, and my partner, which is the only assistant I have, through an indisposition of the body, has been incapable of rendering the smallest assistance for ten days past.
>
> John Bradford.

Unfortunately, no first issue of this paper is in existence. It is known to have been a small quarto consisting of two sheets or four printed pages. The news it carried came down the river with the press. No local news of any importance appeared in the early columns, because Lexington news was common knowledge and of no consequence to the newspaper's readers. Perhaps the readers knew more details of local occurrence than did the newspaper editor. News from France, England, and from the Mediterranean countries found space in the local paper, but, obviously, news of this sort was not published until after it was several months old and then subject to gross inaccuracies, since it had been copied time and again from different newspapers.

However, local news has been preserved to posterity in the paid notices and advertisements. These sections give the modern reader an intimate view of the developing western commonwealth. Early advertisements contained stray notices, warnings that certain food stores had been poisoned to trap Indians, and items from irate husbands stating that "I am no longer responsible for . . . my wife who has deserted my bed and board." One issue of the paper carried a notice from a subscriber asking that his watch, removed from a stump in Main Street, be returned. Occasionally, local news items would find their way into the paper, but these are highly uninformative to the present-day reader, for the editor might refer to a fire in the neighborhood or to other tragedies without saying where or what they were, because he assumed his readers already knew the facts.

Bradford's practical mechanical knowledge often stood him in good stead. When he needed crude illustrations or large capital letters, he whittled them out of dogwood with his pocket knife. Likewise he used his practical knowledge in the distribution of his papers by using riders to distribute each issue of the paper to outlying settlements, since there was no organized post by which the papers could be mailed from one town to the other.

John Bradford was one of Lexington's outstanding citizens. He served time and again on the town's board of trustees and was for a number of years a member (sometimes chairman) of the Board of Trustees of Transylvania University. At the time of his death, he was serving Fayette County as high sheriff.

Bradford not only published the *Kentucky Gazette,* but he also published pamphlets and, later, books. In 1788 he published the first Kentucky almanac and the first pamphlet in the West. Later the *Gazette* press published the first acts of the legislature and *Bradford's Laws.* These books were printed with a surprisingly attractive format, and even today, in the face of every modern printing device, they remain examples of beautiful presswork.

The *Kentucky Gazette* was not to remain long without a competitor. In 1793 Stewart's *Kentucky Herald* was established and published in Lexington by James H. Stewart. This paper, however, met an early death, and its owner was not to re-enter the printing business until 1797 when he moved the defunct *Herald* from Lexington to Paris, where he printed the first newspaper in Bourbon County. During the same year a third paper, the *Kentucky Mirror,* came into existence. It was published from the village of Washington under the editorship of William Hunter. When Hunter was elected state printer the next year, he removed the equipment of the *Mirror* from Washington to Frankfort, where he began publication of the *Palladium*.

When the state government was safely established in its new home, and the settlements of the state became more populous, newspapers and newspaper editors sprang up in every town. By the turn of the century a startling number of newspapers had come into existence, some of which remained in publication only a very short time and were of no consequence. Some of these early papers were the *Western Citizen*, Paris, the *Western Messenger*, the *Republican Auxiliary*, the *Farmer's Library*, the *Lexington Observer*, and the *Western Courier*.

The first Louisville paper, the *Farmer's Library*, was started in 1801. All that is known of its history is contained in an act of the state legislature, which, in 1807, authorized it to publish the laws of the state in its columns.

These early editors allied their papers with one or the other local and national political groups. First of all, the *Kentucky Gazette* found itself sponsoring separation from Virginia. For its columns there followed in quick succession the defeats of Harmar and St. Clair and the success of "Mad" Anthony Wayne, the Whiskey Rebellion, the French and Spanish conspiracies, the Alien and Sedition Laws, the Virginia and Kentucky Resolutions, the second constitution, the election of Jefferson, the purchase of Louisiana, the Burr conspiracy, and the War of 1812. All of these events, coupled with the less noticeable growing pains of an expanding commonwealth and nation, were sufficient food for abundant editorial thought. From the first, the newspaper editors took up their pens to do battle for the causes of the Federalist and Antifederalist groups, after which they rushed to the defense and offense of the Republican Party. For the most part, the newspapers served their communities as political weather vanes.

In 1806 the *Western World* came into existence as an organ for treason hunting with John Wood and John Street as editors. These gentlemen were out to catch all the traitors of the western country. Hardly had they finished their exposure of the Burr conspiracy, which centered about Frankfort, when news of a Spanish conspiracy leaked out. They published their paper on the press of the *Palladium,* and the appearance of each issue threw the society of Frankfort into a panic.

Many Frankfort citizens resented the thrust which the *Western World* made at Burr and were completely upset when John Street involved Benjamin Sebastian, Harry Innes, and others in the Spanish plot. An assassination of Street was attempted by George Adams, who, armed with two pistols, was repelled by his victim with a dirk. In the tussle, Street was wounded in the breast; Adams was arrested and brought to trial, but cleared. However, the trial forced the resignation of Judge Benjamin Sebastian.

Banking troubles growing out of the War of 1812 and its readjustment period separated the State of Kentucky into two sharply divided political groups. Several new papers came into existence during this middle period, but many of the old ones ceased to exist. Examples of this sporadic growth and failure are to be found in the history of the *Western Courier,* which was changed to the *Emporium and Advertiser* in 1821 only to be completely discontinued in 1832. The *Weekly Louisville Correspondent* failed to last through the panic of 1817. So it was with numerous other papers which had come into existence during the period of prosperity from 1812 to 1817.

In direct opposition to the ill-fated *Western Courier* was the formidable *Advertiser,* edited by Shadrach Penn. Penn's purpose in life was to smash his editorial and political opponents and to boost the City of Louisville through the columns of his paper. He established his paper in 1818, at a time when Louisville was still overshadowed in commercial and cultural importance by Lexington. In 1826 the *Advertiser* became the first daily paper in the West. Politically it was Democratic and was one of the most important factors in carrying the state for General Jackson in 1828.

One by one the *Advertiser* vanquished its enemies and emerged in a short time as victor in the fight between the Old and New Court Parties. As Penn had performed yeoman service for the Antirelief group, for some time it seemed that he would win his political fight permanently. He had manhandled his foes with editorial dexterity. This editorial predominance of the powerful *Advertiser* was not to last long, for, in 1830, there appeared in Kentucky journalism and politics a twenty-eight-year-old New Englander who came fresh from the successful editorship of the *New England Review.* George D. Prentice was sent by the New England Whigs to write a biography of Henry

Clay to be used in their effort to groom their candidate for the election of 1832. When he arrived in Kentucky, he found the "mighty" Penn leisurely jousting with a far weaker foe in the pseudoscientific and literary commentator, the *Focus*.

So virile was the pen of the New England youngster that his Kentucky friends supported him for the editorship of the newly organized Whig organ, the *Louisville Journal*. The Whig choice of Prentice was regarded with many misgivings and dire forebodings for the party. Despite the fact that he had already proved his ability by soundly denouncing the Democratic Party in his biography of the "Sage of Ashland," he was still an unseasoned journalist. Perhaps the only thing that tempted the Whigs to try the experiment was that they had been used badly by the Democratic press in the two preceding campaigns and had been unable to return the fire through the columns of a well conducted Whig organ.

It was with this background that young Prentice and the *Journal* set sail simultaneously upon their journalistic career in Kentucky. Circulation of the *Journal* was large from its beginning on November 24, 1830. It soon became the most widely read newspaper in the state, and certainly its editorials were the most effective. Prentice had little or no time to use his scissors in clipping news and editorials from other papers, for he spent much time in writing his own editorials. He assiduously wrote two-page and three-page commentaries which were nearly always venomous attacks upon enemies of the Whig Party. These trenchant thrusts from the New England editor were immediately accepted by the volatile editor of the *Advertiser* as a challenge to do editorial battle. As Penn had now met one who was an equal, there began a battle royal which did not slacken its fury until 1841 when Shadrach Penn discontinued the *Advertiser* to move to St. Louis.

Before Prentice had actually assumed his editorial duties on the *Journal*, his rival-to-be welcomed him with a torrid blast, accredited to the *Cincinnati Gazette*, entitled: "Prick Me a Bull Calf Till He Roar." This editorial "scalped" the young Whig, and it was partly through its influence that his Whig backers feared they were sending a shorn lamb into battle with a wily old editorial lion. When the *Journal* appeared, it was a neatly organized and well printed paper becoming Whiggish dignity. However, it soon became more than a newspaper, for it became the Kentuckians' "Whig Bible," for "every Whig to swear by and every Democrat to swear at."

Prentice attacked his well ensconced rival from all sides. Nothing pleased him more than playing practical jokes upon the dignified editor of the Democratic *Advertiser*. Perrin, in his history of the pioneer press, relates the story of one of Prentice's jokes at the expense of his rival. In looking through his files one day, Prentice discovered a copy of a New Orleans paper which was then over a year old but in perfect condition. This paper carried the story of a horrible murder in that city. While reading this article the impish young editor of the *Journal* devised a play by which he could embarrass the editor of the *Advertiser*. He sprinkled the paper and pressed it perfectly to give it the appearance of having just come from the press. Then he wrapped it carefully in white paper bearing the inscription: "With the Compliments, Clerk of the *Waucousta*, five days, seventy-eight hours out from New Orleans. Quickest trip on record. To Shadrach Penn, Editor of the *Public Advertiser*." The messenger rushed into Penn's office, threw the paper on the desk, and rushed out. When the excited Penn read the inscription, he hastily examined the contents of the paper, halted his presses, unlocked the cases, and took out two or three columns to set up the horrible New Orleans murder story. In another column he extended profuse congratulations to the mate and captain of the *Waucousta* for their record-breaking trip.

This trick embarrassed Penn considerably when he discovered that he had been duped and that the Waucousta was such a leaky old craft that its crew was afraid to leave the bank in it. Prentice, however, was in no hurry to let his rival forget this false step; when he latter published a sensational story, he would slyly ask, "Did that come by the *Waucousta?*"

Not only did Prentice cross swords with his Louisville rival with telling effect, but he likewise took all comers to task. For forty years he ran one of the most influential editorial columns in the West, rivaling the newspapers of the country for an equal. His paragraphs were pointed and pertinent, and it was said that every one of them carried an effective sting for his opponents.

Prentice remained with the *Journal* throughout his newspaper career in Kentucky. During his more than forty years as editor of the *Journal*, he had as business partners A. S. Buxton until 1833, and George W. Weissinger until 1849. Then the company became Prentice and Henderson, and, later, Prentice, Henderson, and Osborne. Despite frequent changes in partners, Prentice and the *Journal* remained the same, for Prentice was the *Journal,* and the *Journal* was Prentice. Throughout the life of the Whig Party, George Prentice fought courageously for its cause, supporting Henry Clay in every one of his campaigns for the presidency, and likewise all other Whig candidates. In the constitutional convention of 1849, the editor of the *Journal* was a leading influence. He was bitterly opposed to slavery when it threatened to tear the Union asunder; otherwise, he was indifferent to the institution. Throughout the War between the States, Prentice was one of the most straightforward Unionists in Kentucky.

When the war ended in 1865, the *Louisville Journal* became the property of the Louisville Journal Corporation. In 1868 Isham Henderson bought out Prentice's interest to sell it in turn to his successor, Henry W. Watterson.

In 1844 W. N. Haldeman established the *Louisville Courier* to succeed the unsuccessful *Daily Dime.* Haldeman became one of Kentucky's most outstanding newspaper managers, but as editor of the *Courier* he was without political leanings or strong editorial convictions. He set out to make his *Courier* a newspaper and was the first man in the West to use every facility at hand to gather news. During the constitutional convention of 1849, he established an office at Frankfort and employed H. M. McCarty as resident reporter. Haldeman went through a siege of selling and buying back interests in his paper. Throughout this period of buying and selling he had as a partner Reuben T. Durrett, who edited the paper until 1859, when he sold his interest. While Haldeman and Overton were managing and editing the *Courier* it was suppressed in 1861 by Union troops because of its rabid Southern leaning. Inside the Confederate lines, Haldeman continued to publish his paper at opportune intervals. It was called, at times, the *Louisville-Bowling Green-Nashville Courier,* and despite its migratory habits, it published much reliable information of the activities in the section. On December 4, 1865, Haldeman and the *Courier* went back home, where it was again brought from the press.

A third paper, the *Louisville Democrat,* was established in 1843 by

Phineas Kent, a native of Indiana. Kent was encouraged in his venture by the Democratic leader, James Guthrie, and this paper soon became the Democratic tocsin of Kentucky prior to the election of 1844. Its editor was unable, however, to maintain the Democratic lead in Kentucky, and the *Democrat's* financial sponsor selected as Kent's successor John H. Harney, who edited the paper until its merger with the *Courier* and *Journal* in 1868.

On November 8, 1868, after the election of Ulysses S. Grant, the *Journal, Courier,* and *Democrat* were merged into a single paper. This consolidation came at a time when the South needed a strong editorial guide to lead her through the rigors of reconstruction. In order to maintain Louisville's lead as a newspaper center, the three rival papers generously swallowed their "widely different political policies and merged into one paper, the *Courier-Journal*." This merger, under the editorship of Henry Watterson, was a most effective move in concentrating a confluent stream of public opinion upon the needs of the South.

In Lexington the *Kentucky Reporter,* established in 1807 by William Worsley and Samuel Overton, was published until 1832, when it was consolidated with Bryant and Finnel's *Lexington Observer.* During its early years the *Reporter* was a stanch Republican organ, and until the end of Monroe's second administration it remained faithful to its first love—the Jeffersonian political faith. Perhaps no newspaper in Kentucky published more local news than did the *Reporter.* Unlike its illustrious predecessor and contemporary, the *Gazette,* this paper was less concerned with foreign news and more with local events.

When the two papers were consolidated, the editorial policies regarding local news continued the same. In politics the merger favored the Whig Party, and Lexington's illustrious son, Henry Clay. The paper espoused the cause of the South. During the Civil War its offices were used alternately as headquarters for the officers of both armies. During the period of its existence, the *Lexington Observer and Reporter* had an impressive list of editors. The first editors of the consolidated paper were Edwin Bryant and N. L. Finnell, and later Robert N. Wickliffe succeeded Judge Bryant. In 1838 Wickliffe became the sole owner and editor of the paper to devote it to the support of Henry Clay and his party. Wickliffe pulled his paper through the trying storm of civil war but in 1865 sold it to the *Observer and Reporter* Printing Company.

William A. Dudley, a lawyer-politician, succeeded Wickliffe to its editorship, but in 1870 the death of the latter left the paper without an editor. The printing company than selected an ardent Confederate leader and able lawyer, W. C. P. Breckinridge, to edit the paper, until July 1868, when he was succeeded by George W. Ranck, the historian. Needless to say, the *Observer and Reporter* was a stanch Democratic organ during the reconstruction period and one of the leading editorial sheets published in Lexington.

Lexington possessed a rabid Southern paper in the *Kentucky Statesman,* which for thirteen years supported the cause of slavery and the South. This paper came into existence on October 6, 1849, to have during its life an interesting group of "fire-eaters" for editors. B. B. Taylor, a Whig lawyer-politician, wrote its editorials until 1855, when he was succeeded during the rampant "Know-Nothing" campaign by the colorful H. H. "Yuba Dam" Johnson, whose fiery pen upheld the virtues of a much diseased and degenerating Whig Party. In 1856 Major Monroe took charge of the *Statesman* to edit it until its dying moment, which occurred when Kirby Smith evacuated the City of Lexington in the fall of 1862. Ironically enough, this tempestuous southern paper was reborn in 1867 under the editorship of William Cassius and D. Owsley Goodloe. This time, however, it had changed political complexion to become the radical Republican mouthpiece for Lexington and vicinity.

In Frankfort, and at the seat of government, Colonel Albert Gallatin Hodges published the *Frankfort Daily and Weekly Commonwealth.* Hodges stands out in journalism as one of the most interesting characters who sponsored a Kentucky journal through the stormy years of early Kentucky history. Like many of the other Kentucky newspapermen, he was Virginia born. He had come as a child to Lexington, where, at the age of twelve, he started his journalistic career under the supervision of Worsley and Smith of the *Kentucky Reporter.* Six years later, this "cub" made his way to Lancaster, where he established the ill-fated *Kentuckian,* which soon proved such a complete financial failure that the young editor had to walk back to Lexington, swimming the Kentucky River because he lacked funds with which to pay ferry charges. On his return to Lexington, Hodges became foreman of the pressroom of the *Reporter.* In 1824 he and D. C. Pinkham purchased of Bullen and Hill the *Louisville Morning Post,* but when Pinkham walked off with the company's funds, collected from its debtors, Hodges took William Tanner as a partner. For the next twelve months these two young editors published a rollicking sheet, which was a house divided against itself, for two pages conveyed Tanner's arguments for the New Court Party, and two sheets proclaimed Hodges' faith in the Old Court group. Finally the editors were disgusted with their Janus-faced offspring and agreed to pitch "heads and tails" to see who should have sole possession of the paper. Hodges lost, and in 1826 he was in Frankfort where he and James G. Dana established the short-lived *Commentator.* Hodges was given the state printing contracts in 1832, and the next year he established the *Frankfort Commonwealth,* which led a hectic life under equally violent editors who included Orlando Brown, John W. Finnell, and Thomas B. Stevenson.

Until the death of the Whig Party, the *Commonwealth* was that party's mouthpiece at the state capital, and then in rapid succession it supported the Know-Nothings, the American, the Union, and the Republican Parties. After the War between the States, Colonel Hodges continued to support the Republican Party until 1872, when he refused to endorse a second inefficient and corrupt administration under Ulysses Grant. Rather than sacrifice his editorial honor or support another political party, Colonel Hodges discontinued publication of the *Commonwealth* in 1872 and moved to Louisville.

Colonel Hodges' publication of the *Commonwealth* is a typical example of much of Kentucky's journalism. Hodges was the *Commonwealth,* and the *Commonwealth* was Hodges, and since his personal views were likewise the views of his press, their failure to coincide with the trend of the party which he supported was reason enough for his newspaper to discontinue publication.

A Specialized Press

The history of Kentucky journalism is colored by many purple patches of sporadic editorial endeavor. Almost every movement for agitating a change in the state's social system brought forth a number of defending and offending journals. In 1826, when the Old Court and New Court Parties were active, two radical publications made their appearance in the *Spirit of '76* and the *Patriot*. Partisans of the Old Court were vitriolic in their denunciation through the columns of the *Spirit of '76* of the radical "judge-breakers" of the newly organized party. On the other hand, contributors to the *Patriot* diligently defended the debtor class, and the "judge-ridden" commonwealth. These papers lived a life of fury for a period of only one year, for with the first lull in the fight for control of state affairs by the two partisan groups, they died ignominious deaths.

Slavery was a subject which inspired publication of numerous short-lived journals and newspapers. As early as 1822 the emancipationists embarked upon the stormy sea of antislavery journalism by establishing in Shelbyville the monthly *Abolition Intelligencer* and *Missionary Magazine*. Its promoters had been unreasonably optimistic, for financial support was not forthcoming to sustain their publication, and it suffered an early death. Ten years later citizens of Danville were stirred to fever heat over the proposed publication of James G. Birney's *Philanthropist*. But since Birney's besetting sin was talking too much, his plan failed in the making. Before the *Philanthropist* could be established, the disturbed citizens of Boyle County and Danville prevailed upon the postmaster to refuse to accept the publication in the mails. They even bought the press and convincingly hinted to Birney that he would enjoy much better health in other and far removed parts. In 1835 this Kentuckian established the *Philanthropist* in Cincinnati, from which vantage point he supplied the abolitionists of Kentucky with much editorial encouragement. In their new home Birney and the *Philanthropist* became most influential in encouraging the antislavery crusade in the border sections of the Middle West. Birney's paper, however, was not rabid in nature; rather, it was the voice of the mildly inclined abolitionists.

Most influential of all the protesting papers was Cassius M. Clay's *True American,* published at Lexington from June 3 to August 18, 1845, under the virtuous slogan of "God and Liberty." This paper was edited and published as a mouthpiece of emancipation sentiment in Kentucky, and editorially it was bitter in its denunciation of the existing slave system. Clay was a native son who had come in close contact with slavery, at his Madison County home, from birth to maturity.

As a student at Yale College he was educated to the use of the pen and was persuaded of the belief that the institution of slavery was in direct violation of the rights of man.

Perhaps no journal in Kentucky ever created a more violent storm of protest than did the *True American*. Its editorial policy remained steadfast and fearless until the very end, when it was forcibly discontinued. Slavery in Kentucky never had a more serious threat than from this paper. Coming as it did from the heart of one of Kentucky's largest slaveholding counties, and edited by a native son, it was from its beginning a most potent factor in the formation of public opinion.

The Press of the Reconstruction Era

The Kentucky press was far better organized in the reconstruction era than it had been in the past. After the War between the States there were only two major political parties, and the Kentucky papers naturally became either Democratic or Republican. Those papers which had wavered between a Democratic and Whig leaning (1850–1860) became distinctly Democratic after the war.

One of the leading newspapers of the whole country was the consolidated *Courier, Journal, and Democrat*. The consolidation of these papers marked the beginning of a new type of newspaper democracy. Southern journalism has never contributed two more able men than Henry Watterson and Walter N. Haldeman, who edited and managed the *Louisville Courier-Journal* for thirty-four years.

Watterson, the son of a congressman from the McMinnville district in Tennessee, was born in 1840, in Washington, D. C. He knew personally every President of the United States from John Quincy Adams to Warren G. Harding. As a lad of eighteen years he began his journalistic career on *Harper's Weekly,* contributing at the same time to the *New York Times* and Horace Greeley's *New York Tribune.* In 1859 he was back in Washington reporting the activities of Congress for the *Washington States,* but with the brewing of the storm between the states he returned to his native Tennessee, where he became an associate editor of the *Nashville Banner.* During the four years following 1861, young Watterson was in the Confederate service as a scout under the commands of Nathan Bedford Forrest, Leonidas Polk, and Joseph E. Johnston. His services to the Confederate Army as chief scout were made more valuable by his publication of the *Rebel* at Chattanooga from October 1862 to September 1863.

Watterson's years immediately following the war were spent abroad in journalistic work. But the call of the South in this time of peril was strong, and he returned to Nashville to revive the *Banner* as a journalistic spur to disheartened southerners. His success on this paper attracted the attention of the aged George Prentice of the *Louisville Journal* in 1868, and Watterson was brought to Louisville as Prentice's managing editor.

Suffering personally from the pangs of the South's defeat, Henry Watterson assumed the editorship of the *Courier-Journal* on November 8, 1868, to lead the fight for political and economic rehabilitation of his beloved country. Between the years 1868 and 1918, when he retired from the editorship of the paper, the *Courier-Journal* was a foremost editorial agency in the South and in the nation. A more fearless newspaper leader did not live than "Marse Henry." He tackled high and low alike in his well written and well pointed editorials. His party knew alike stinging criticism and good counsel from one of its master spirits. All of "Marse Henry's" battles were fought through the columns of the *Courier-Journal* and within the ranks of the Democratic Party. Both Cleveland and Wilson knew what it meant to stand in favor with Watterson, or to incur his enmity. Doubtless the reputation of Henry W. Watterson as a Kentucky journalist will stand as a challenge to an aggressive state press for all time.

Three other papers stand out as influential organs of postwar public opinion and public good: The *Owensboro Messenger,* the *Lexington Leader,* and the *Lexington Herald.*

On October 1, 1881, Urey Woodson of Madisonville established the *Owensboro Messenger,* to take up the editorial cudgel in western Kentucky in behalf of that section and the Democratic Party. This paper, like many of the other Kentucky papers, soon proved a powerful organ of public opinion. It has been a powerful political indicator, following closely in the footsteps of Watterson, with its editor concentrating his attention upon the building of a new state and a new South.

In Lexington a new type of newspaper was established by Samuel J. Roberts who moved to Lexington from Canton, Ohio, after his defeat for the mayorship. On May 1, 1888, his first issue of the *Kentucky*

Leader came from the press. This paper was established mainly as a Republican sheet; however, it devoted much attention to the financial possibilities of a newspaper by boosting the community. A daily and weekly paper were published in order to reach both urban and rural subscribers. Roberts saw to it that his paper was carefully managed financially, that carriers paid for their papers before they delivered them. To make his paper more attractive, the editor sent reporters out to search the community for sensational news. This was one of the first newspapers in Kentucky to use special departments and correspondents for enhancing the reading value of the paper for all classes.

Although Roberts announced in his first issue that the paper had been established to promote the welfare of the Republican Party in the South, he did not devote much attention to writing political editorials. Robert's purpose in founding the paper was partly to promote the political fortunes of his friend William McKinley, but even this he did in the form of news.

The Lexington promoters of the *Leader* were W. O. Bradley, William Cassius Goodloe, H. K. Milward, George Denny, E. D. Warfield, J. H. Howard, W. W. Huffman, and Samuel J. Roberts. These men were likewise promoters of Republican interests in the state.

Special correspondents were hired to run columns on subjects of interest to the community. Society was given an opportunity to parade itself through the columns of the *Leader*. A special children's page was conducted, which consisted of a general make-up of nursery rhymes and of other features attracting the young reader.

The *Leader* is one of the state's pioneers in the field of a highly specialized popular type of journalism. Although it was founded as a guardian of Republican interests, it has never pursued this course steadfastly, for lack of the strong editorial policy of its more ardent sister journals.

The *Lexington Herald* is one of the last of Kentucky newspapers with a definite political editorial policy. This paper, however, has wielded its influence mainly through the editorship of an ardent disciple of the Democratic Party. In 1870 the *Herald* was founded as the *Press* by Colonel Hart Foster and Major Henry T. Duncan, as one of the first daily newspapers to be published in the city of Lexington. Since disputes over reconstruction were still raging at the time, the *Press* was predominantly Democratic. Its sympathies were entirely with the South, and many of its editorials were effective in reaching the seat of trouble between the North and the South.

The *Press* was operated as an independent paper for a very short time, after which it was consolidated with the *Lexington Transcript,* which was founded by Colonel Caldwell and later sold to James H. Mulligan and Edward P. Farrell. When these papers were consolidated, the name was changed to the *Lexington Herald,* and the editorship was placed in the hands of Desha Breckinridge in 1897, where it remained until 1935.

The *Herald* has always been politically a Democratic organ and has pursued an aggressive editorial policy. It was an influential paper in political upheavals in the late nineties and in the first part of the present century. When the state was rocked with the Goebel affair in 1900, the editorials of this paper were the products of two able writers, William C. P. and Desha Breckinridge, father and son, who made their paper the mouthpiece for Blue Grass Democracy.

Personalities of the Kentucky Press

It would be inexcusable to conclude a chapter on the history of the Kentucky Press without emphasizing the other personalities who have contributed materially to the making of this press. These personages for the most part never identified themselves with the personality or politics of their papers except for their influence upon the readers of their special columns.

Doubtless the most colorful paragrapher, aside from George D. Prentice, was Emmet Garvin Logan. Logan was born in 1849, on Bull-skin Creek in Shelby County. He obtained a meager secondary education at the community's "old field" school. Later young Logan attended Washington and Lee University at Lexington, Virginia. At this institution he tasted the sweets of editorship when he edited the *Collegian.* Returning to Kentucky, he established the *Shelby County Courant* in 1872 and later joined the *Courier-Journal* staff.

Logan specialized in Kentucky and Southern news, which he digested and passed on to his readers in the form of tabloid paragraphs. His editorials on the activities of the Kentucky State Legislature were provocative of much anger on the part of its members. He was continually pricking a sensitive legislative side by uncovering ill-managed and corrupt financial practices. On one occasion he exposed several legislators for padding their mileage reports. This threw the legislature into a panic. Many members wished to bar the prying Logan from the floors of the two houses, but it was feared that as an onlooker from the gallery he would be far more disturbing.

In 1884 Logan and E. Polk Johnston established the *Louisville Times,* and this paper soon rivaled "Marse Henry's" *Courier-Journal* as a bearer of sound and timely editorials. Logan's editorials were never lengthy, nor were they well organized essays as were Colonel Watterson's, but they were short paragraphs pointedly conveying the editor's point of view. In this respect the *Times'* lucid paragrapher was the direct successor of Prentice. Logan's editorial comments seldom filled more than a fourth of a column, but they were far more expressive than many whole-page editorials.

Other colorful personalities of the press were John Hatcher (George Washington Bricks) who, despite his youth, showed much evidence of rivaling E. G. Logan. His paragraphs were humorous in nature, and, doubtless, had he lived to middle age, his writings would stand out as the most interesting humorous comments of all Kentucky writers.

Other men who have contributed much to the making of Kentucky journalism are William Gallagher, poet-editor, "Wat" Overton, humorist, Charles D. Kirke (Ce De Kay), Charles D. Faxon, Mrs. William Geppert, Enoch Grehan, paragrapher, and George Bingham (Dink Botts), "rural correspondent."

Contemporary readers, especially in western Kentucky and Tennessee, are entertained by the witty "Dog Hill" paragraphs. The characters of Luke Methewsla, Poke Eazley, Atlas Peck, Yam Sims, the Miser of Musket Ridge, and the communities of Hog Ford, Rye Straw, Gander Creek, Hog Wallow, and Calf Ribs are familiar character and place names to many in the South. For several years, beginning with June 1, 1905, Bingham published intermittently the *Hog Wallow Kentuckian* on Saturdays from Paducah and later from Mayfield, for a reading public national in scope.

The Periodical Press

Not only did the western State of Kentucky early produce many newspapers, but it likewise produced numerous magazines which became vehicles of literary endeavor. Each of these magazines flourished only a few years before becoming bankrupt. Nevertheless, their brief existence left their imprint upon the state's literary history, for in their columns many outstanding pieces of Kentucky literature were printed. Had it not been for the willingness of these sporadic literary magazines to print them, many famous literary offerings would today be unknown.

The first magazine to make its appearance was the *Medley, or Monthly Miscellaney, for the year 1803,* edited by Daniel Bradford. This magazine was published to supply the western country with a literary messenger, but in 1804 the *Medley* gave up the ghost in financial stress. There was a distinct lack of interest in literature in the crude and growing western country. Bradford's efforts were discouraging, and it was not until 1814 that another editor dared promote a magazine. Thomas T. Skillman introduced to the religious and literary public the *Almoner,* but like its unfortunate predecessor it went begging for support within a twelvemonth.

The first worthy literary periodical to blossom upon western soil was William Gibbs Hunt's *Western Review,* which appeared in Lexington during the year 1819. For three years its struggling editor undertook to keep his venture solvent, but in 1821 the project became too burdensome, and publication was discontinued. Following the failure of the Lexington magazine came the *Literary Pamphleteer,* which an ambitious literary editor undertook to publish from Paris, but this infant did not live to celebrate its first anniversary. Thomas Skillman of Lexington, in 1826, began publication of a pseudo-religious and literary magazine in the *Western Luminary,* but like its defunct predecessors it was soon consigned to an inglorious oblivion. Even the coupling of religious and literary contributions was insufficient incentive to keep a Kentucky periodical alive. In 1824 Louisville offered a literary lamb on the altar of periodical sacrifice in the short-lived *Microscope.*

No magazine had been able to live longer than three years in Kentucky before the ambitious professor of mathematics, Thomas Johnson Matthews, of Transylvania University, established the *Transylvanian.* This magazine was initiated principally as a medium of scientific exchange, but it soon took on a literary character. The *Transylvanian* has led a life of uncertainty, flourishing at times and disappearing at others, but throughout the last one hundred years it has appeared at intervals with literary and scientific contributions from Kentucky writers.

For ten years the doctors at Transylvania supplied members of their profession with news of the latest medical findings through the columns of the *Transylvania Journal of Medicine.* This journal carried articles by the leading doctors of the West, including Benjamin Dudley, Daniel Drake, Ephraim McDowell, and numerous others.

Early literary magazines were subjected to the whims and fancies of their editors, for the periodical changed locality with the editor. J. Freeman Clark, a Unitarian minister, moved from Cincinnati to Louisville in 1836, carrying with him his already famous *Western Messenger.* For the next five years Clark and the *Messenger* remained in Kentucky, during this sojourn supplying the Kentuckians with the literary offerings of Ralph Waldo Emerson, Nathaniel Hawthorne, Oliver Wendell Holmes, William Ellery Channing, Margaret Fuller, and John Keats. However, this editor grew weary of his Kentucky stay, and in 1841 he and his *Messenger* returned to Cincinnati.

During the later years many literary magazines and periodicals bloomed to die unread and unsupported. Some of these magazines were: O'Malley's *Midland Review,* the *Kentuckian,* the *Southern Magazine,* and the *Southern Educational Journal.* Two historical magazines, the *Register of the State Historical Society* and the *Filson Club's History Quarterly* have endured the hardships of the times. These magazines have made no pretense at being literary magazines but have published only historical essays. However, local poetic offerings crept into the *Register of the Historical Society* during its early years of publication.

An examination of the indifference of the West to literature and literary magazines throws an interesting light on the life of the times. It has been only a few years since the western American came to regard a man with literary leanings as neither sentimental nor effeminate. To be effective, the early organs of public opinion had to support the readers' political taste, and a magazine of literature found itself quickly out of step with its reading public and forced to suspend publication.

The Book Press of Kentucky

Throughout its existence the Kentucky press has contributed to the art of bookmaking. Numerous books have been published on presses of the state, some of them among the rarest items of Americana today. These early books are excellent examples of the printer's art, for modern presses in the state have not improved upon the art of bookmaking.

One of the first books to come from the Kentucky press was the early *Acts of the Legislature* published in 1792, by John Bradford. In 1793 Reverend Adam Rankin had printed at the "Sign of the Buffalo," Main Street, Lexington, the first book of a literary nature published in the West. This little work was a pamphlet bearing the title, *A Process in the Transylvania Presbytery*. The following year this press published and distributed the *General Instructor, or, the office duty, and authority of justices of the peace, sheriffs, coroners, and constables, of the State of Kentucky*. In 1799 John Bradford published a pamphlet entitled *An Account of Remarkable Occurrences in His Life and Travels*.

In 1800 "Wildcat" John McKinney published at Bradford's office an account of his fight with a wildcat in his Lexington school. This little pamphlet appeared in dull binding with a yellow line running around it, but unfortunately there are no copies of it in existence. Again, in 1824, McKinney reprinted his account, but this pamphlet is now extinct, and records of it exist only in the interview between Lyman Draper and Captain John H. McKinney.

John Bradford's *Kentucky Gazette* published, in 1809, the biography of the Reverend John Gano, who, family tradition maintains, administered the rites of baptism to George Washington at Valley Forge. Seven years later the press of Worsely and Smith published Robert McAfee's *History of the Late War in the Western Country,* which remains the best account of the western aspect of this war.

Many of the school textbooks for the western country had their origin in Kentucky. In 1812 Maccoun, Tilford and Company published in Lexington the *Kentucky Preceptor, containing a number of useful lessons for reading and speaking.* It was from this same *Kentucky Preceptor* that Abraham Lincoln read as a struggling backwoods youth in Indiana and Illinois.

While the Lexington publishers were turning out books, the state printer at Frankfort was industriously plying his trade. In 1802 he published Harry Toulmin's *Report of the Kentucky Court of Appeals,* and in the next year Hughes' *Report.* Some of the early "handy medical books" for the western households were published in Frankfort. After 1802 the Frankfort printers were busily engaged in printing both their newspapers and books.

Contributions of the Frankfort printers were made to the history of their state. Humphrey Marshall's *History of Kentucky* was printed the first time in 1812, from the press of George B. Robinson. A second and enlarged edition of this work was published in 1824. From 1809 to 1819 the press of William Hunter was printing *Littell's Laws* in five volumes.

Rivaling both Lexington and Frankfort in the publishing business was Louisville. Louisville printers have produced a long list of well-known books about Kentucky. Some of the more important works published at Louisville are Spalding's *Sketches of Early Catholic Missions in Kentucky,* 1844, Deering's *History of Louisville,* 1849, Z. F. Smith's *History of Kentucky,* 1886, *The Filson Club Publications* since 1890, and other works of a like nature.

Some of the smaller presses have contributed interesting and valuable books to Kentucky literature. Perhaps one of the most important single contributions to the knowledge of Kentucky's history by a local press is Collins' *History of Kentucky,* which was published first in 1847 from the press of the *Maysville Eagle.* Later (1874) this same work was enlarged and published in two volumes from the press owned by Richard Collins at Covington.

Kentucky bookmakers have hardly been as influential as the state's newspapermen, but, notwithstanding this fact, they have contributed materially to the preservation of the state's history. The first textbooks available to the Kentucky schools came from the pioneer presses.

In every aspect of Kentucky's social growth the press has been an independent and dominant factor. Newspaper editors thrived on western soil, and they became, at an early date, the crusaders of progress.

Every paper, regardless of its politics, was first of all a booster of its community, since this was expected of the newspaper, and none could succeed without being so. The conduct of a newspaper was considered by the early Kentuckians as a personal matter. Editorial and fistic battles, growing out of vehement personal denouncements, were common. At an early editors' convention which met in Lexington in 1837 most of the editors of the state were present and voted to adopt a resolution to elevate the standards of the Kentucky newspapers. During this period local politics occupied the center of the editorial stage, and many of the editors fell into the habit of casting violent epithets at their opponents. The convention voted to refrain from the practice of casting personal epithets or from calling one another odious names and nicknames and resolved to conduct all editorial arguments with an element of common decency. Some of the epithets which were common, and used in the covention, are given by the *Kentucky Gazette* as follows: "A Little Implement of Sophistry—a little forked upstart of a whistle-toot"; A glass-eyed little skunk—a puny blow toot of a Whig Editor."

Regardless of a natural interest which Kentucky papers had in their communities, they were all vitally concerned with political issues of the time. Editor was pitted against editor, for it amounted almost to disgrace in Kentucky journalism to be outdone by a competing editor. Hence, strong personalities of the state's press were developed. Prentice was an example of an editor who reached the top of the ladder by jousting freely with his contemporaries. Thus it happens that the most important factors in the history of the Kentucky press are the editors rather than their papers. The editor became his paper so completely that, at his death or resignation, the editorial policy of his paper ceased with him.

The twentieth century Kentucky newspapers have undergone some fundamental changes in the forms of mergers, and even in editorial redirections. In Lexington the Democratic *Herald* and the Republican *Leader* are owned by a single syndicate, and are edited from the same offices but with separate staffs. In Louisville, the Louisville *Courier-Journal* and the Louisville *Times* have a common ownership, and these papers enjoy the local newspaper market alone. Throughout the Commonwealth mergers, reorganizations, and new editorships have characterized the news-

paper press. The traditional Kentucky country weekly has undergone enormous changes. Many of the local papers are now owned
by companies, and there are no longer the old style personal
editors who wrote so attractively or so furiously about rural and
small town matters. They no longer stand the fierce watchdogs
over local officials, or express such vigorous political opinions
as did the early weeklies. The Louisville *Courier-Journal* has given
generous coverage to both state and national news and politics.
Too, it has been concerned with international news. Consistently
it has won national recognition and awards for its excellence as
a newspaper. So far as a single journal covers Kentucky the
Courier-Journal does. Its news coverage is complete, and its circulation fairly wide spread. There is little doubt on the part of
friend and foe alike that this Louisville paper is influential in
pointing the course of public affairs in Kentucky.

Successors to the earlier special journalist were several popular
twentieth century columnists. Allan Trout and Joe Creason of the
Louisville *Courier-Journal* were worthy successors to that paper's
notable feature writers. Trout was master of homey and folksy
mores, superstitutions, rural customs, and earthy humor. His daily
"Greetings" was perhaps the most popular feature ever published
in a Kentucky newspaper. Too, he was an astute political observer
who revealed the constant maneuverings and strivings of politicians
with subtle insights that stripped naked many a well laid selfish
design. Joe Creason's column "Kentucky" was equally as deft in
treating humor, folkways, human drolleries, and personalities. He
was blessed with a country weekly editor's understanding of the
mental processes of both Kentucky urban and rural readers. Much
less popular indeed, but no less widely read, was Howard Henderson's independent coverage of Kentucky politics and politicians
with an inky vengeance. He spared no one, high or low, in his
stories, accusations, and shattering revelations of misdeeds. To the
miscreant he was a holy terror and to the virtuous a constant
warning. In Lexington Joe Jordan produced a popular column of
humor and folksy comment under the title "Four Bits," again capitalizing on Kentuckians' love of anecdotes and personalities. His
successor Bob Fain in "Cornered" has kept up a gentle chatter
about frustrating personal experiences, current events, and personalities.

Several Kentucky book publishers in the twentieth century have contributed materially to the state's historical literature. Earlier in the century the famous John P. Morton Company of Louisville published the Filson Club monographs which within themselves comprised a respectable outline of Kentucky history. Later the Standard Printing Company produced J. Winston Coleman's *Stage Coach Days in the Blue Grass*, James O. Nall's *The Tobacco Night Riders*, Maude Ward Lafferty's *Lure of Kentucky*, and Thomas D. Clark's *The Beginning of the L & N*. In Lexington the fledgling University of Kentucky Press sustained a desultory publishing program until 1950 when it was fully organized under the directorship of Bruce N. Denbo, a professional publisher. Within a quarter of a century it has produced a distinguished list of books relating to Kentucky, among them Charles G. Talbert's *Benjamin Logan*, J. Winston Coleman's *A Bibliography of Kentucky History* and *Kentucky a Pictorial History*, Robert Ireland's *The County Courts in Ante Bellum Kentucky*, James F. Hopkins' *History of the Hemp Industry in Kentucky*, Thomas Ford, ed., *The Southern Appalachian Region*, and the *Kentucky Bi-Centennial Bookshelf* of fifty projected titles. It undertook the ambitious task of publishing the multi-volume *Papers of Henry Clay* which at this date are approximately half completed. In 1966 this successful publishing agency became the University Press of Kentucky in 1968 in order to serve the colleges and universities and the historical societies. Its list of books has become impressive, and its scholarly authors have revealed much of Kentucky's past in dignified book form.

In solid yeoman service private printers have published a sizable volume of county histories and monographs. These have contributed much to the understanding of the background of Kentucky, if not always to its literary heritage. Sometimes the privately published books have not been subjected to scrutiny of meticulous editors in a manner which has set the titles published by the University Press of Kentucky apart as works of both historical and literary merit.

CHAPTER XIV

A Cultural Awakening

Architecture

THOUGH an isolated settlement of Virginia, Kentucky became the
pioneer cultural center of the new West. Since good roads were
unknown and rivers could be navigated only downstream, communication was slow at all times, and Kentucky's culture became provincial,
a characteristic aspect of social development in the history of the state.
Since the home has been the cultural center, much of Kentucky's history
is mirrored in its domestic architecture. When pioneers crossed the
Appalachian Mountains in search of homes in the West, they were
faced at once with the necessity of wresting territory from the Indians.
The savages saw their hunting grounds destroyed by settlers. Kentucky pioneers found no homes in the new country which could be used
even temporarily. Since driving Indians beyond the Ohio and clearing
fields in which to grow corn were of greater importance, early homes
were of temporary construction. The early Kentucky houses, dating
from the log cabin built by Thomas Walker in 1750, and on throughout
the early settlement of central Kentucky, were rude pole cabins of one
or two rooms with lean-to sheds across the rear. They were hurriedly
built sometimes in one or two days. Cracks were chinked with mud
and straw "bats." When there were windows, they were made of small
vents cut in the logs, and covered by crude hewn or rived shutters.
Chimneys were combinations of stone, sticks, straw, and mud. Floors
were of clay mud or puncheon. Furnishings consisted of built-in pole
beds, block seats, and tables, and of forked-stick hangers on which to
deposit clothing and guns.

Most of the people of the early folk-movement into Kentucky were
trappers, hunters, and adventurers, in search of political and economic
freedom, or in the process of simply following the course of free and

unexploited land westward. These people knew nothing of the more refined homes which existed in the tidewater or in the lower piedmont of Virginia and the Carolinas, for they had lived always in cabins in the stockades, or fortresses, where log cabins were grouped within puncheon walls for the purpose of concentrating white defense against murderous Indians.

After the stockade period in Kentucky, families moved to the open country where they built permanent homes. When the immigrant was finally assured that he could hold his western lands against Indian attacks, the fact was quickly indicated by a new type of house. Since there were no steam sawmills, lumber was not available, and it was necessary to use logs for home construction. These Kentucky log houses were thoughtfully planned and built. Since virgin timbers were available near house sites, only larger trees of good quality were chosen for wall construction. The logs were hewn on four sides, split in two pieces, and "finished-off" through the middle with a broad ax or foot adze. Ends of the logs were carefully notched, fitted, and pegged to form neat square corners. Large windows and doors were cut through the side walls, and cracks were carefully sealed with small riven boards and clay filler. When the walls were completed, they presented as even an appearance as those of frame houses. The interiors of the early log houses were finished with carefully dressed puncheon floors and were ceiled either with heavy plaster applied to riven boards, or with whip-sawed lumber. In the main rooms there were large fireplaces at the outer ends, surrounded by mantels of home construction. In the early houses the mantels served in the useful capacity of handy shelving for household trinkets, as smoke hoods and as ornaments to the rooms. The early log houses were of the "double," two-story type with two large front rooms, a broad hall, or "dog trot," a shed room across the back which was divided to serve as kitchen, dining room, and spare bedroom, and with a large porch across the front. The second story, in the earliest houses, was reached by peg ladders concealed behind hall doors, but later plank stairs were added. As lumber became more plentiful and houses were being weather-boarded, owners of log houses covered them with plank siding. Today many imposing old Kentucky homes, even in the towns, are of basic log construction.

When forests were cleared and the bountiful supply of timber was rapidly being depleted, Kentuckians resorted to the more conservative use of lumber, stone, and brick. When sawmills were introduced, frame houses came into common use. After wealthier settlers moved westward from tidewater and piedmont Virginia and from North Carolina, they began building brick and stone houses patterned after their homes east of the mountains. One of the first brick houses built in Kentucky was the Whitley home near Stanford. At Frankfort, John Brown built Liberty Hall, an imposing "Dominion" Georgian structure. Liberty Hall is one of the good examples of Georgian architecture in Kentucky, with its large hall, a direct, wide stairway leading up from the rear of the front hall, a large drawing room, parlor, and connecting dining room with high ceilings and panelings of native woods. At the front of the large parlor and drawing rooms are mammoth fireplaces of heavy stone construction. Each of these fireplaces is surrounded by beautiful handmade mantels. Externally the monotony of the straight Georgian walls is broken by large windows and a central door, flanked by two eight-pane side sashes and topped by an overhead sash. In most of the Georgian structures in Kentucky the doorway is capped by a Palladian window which gives balance and symmetry to the frontal appearance. Some examples of "Dominion" Georgian architecture in the state are Federal Hall, Bardstown; Liberty Hall, Frankfort; Xalapa and The Grange, Bourbon County; Clay Hill, Harrodsburg; the Vaught and Cleveland houses, at Versailles; and the Muldrow house near Tyrone. All of these homes were either designed by seaboard architects, copied from plans of seaboard homes, or made from builders' "plan books."

Many Kentucky homes built during the early period when trade with New Orleans flourished show definite influence of this commercial relationship. Farmers, boatmen, and merchants visiting New Orleans with cargoes were impressed by the iron grillwork appearing on the front of buildings in the French Quarter, and bought similar decorative work for their Kentucky homes. In nearly every town where people participated in this early trade are to be seen houses with grilled iron decorations.

In 1825 Kentuckians were rapidly recovering from the panic occasioned by economic maladjustment and by the bank failures following the War of 1812. As families prospered, they displayed their wealth by building imposing homes. When this demand for new homes increased, Kentucky architects were influenced by a new school of builders who were turning away from rigid Georgian lines to new and more pompous effects. More in keeping with this growing and expansive taste of the classical-minded Kentucky aristocracy were the imposing lines of Greek Revival architecture which was introduced into the United States by Benjamin Latrobe. As designer of the Bank of Pennsylvania, Latrobe virtually changed the whole American architectural taste. Through the influence of Latrobe, William Strickland, and Robert Mills, apprentice architects, Greek Revival buildings were popularized throughout the United States. In Kentucky, Gideon Shryock, a pupil of William Strickland, designed several buildings, including Morrison College, the Old Statehouse, the Kentucky Blind Institute, and the Jefferson County Courthouse. These buildings, with their large classic columns, present impressive and dignified external appearances. The Old Statehouse at Frankfort holds Shryock's crowning achievement, a graceful double circular stairway held together by a keystone in the upper landing.

Shryock, with his Greek Revival taste, influenced not only the pattern of public buildings, but also that of private houses. Extravagant claims are made by many home owners today that Latrobe designed their houses, or that they were designed by Shryock. It is said Latrobe designed only two houses in Kentucky, the original Ashland and the Governor Taylor house at Newport, and that Shryock designed only a limited number of private homes. There were other architects possessing either a good knowledge of architecture, or who had plan books, so that they were able to meet the demand for Greek Revival houses. Country homes designed for wealthy farmers after 1830 were nearly all of the classical type. These houses were built with broad porticoes supported by Corinthian columns, the walls were pierced by large windows, and they were equally divided by wide central doors flanked and capped with fan sashes. In the Greek Revival house the Palladian window is missing. Internally these houses are finished with hardwood floors of cherry, maple, or walnut, with window facings, copings, base boards, panelings, and mantels. Like those of the Georgian houses, the mantels which surround the cavernous fireplaces are splendid examples of Kentucky cabinetwork. The whole internal arrangement of these houses centers about a large hall which serves as a reception room and an opening for the stairway. Good examples of the Greek Revival period are the Orlando Brown house, Frankfort; Rose Hill, Lexington; Mt. Echo, Mansfield; the home of Henry Clay, Jr., and the Helm house, Fayette County; the Moberly and Stephenson houses, Harrodsburg; and the Carrothers and Browne houses, Bardstown.

In central Kentucky where land was fertile so that landowners accumulated wealth, planters became barons of large estates. It is likely that in the creation of estates these barons spent idle moments reading Sir Walter Scott's Waverley novels. As they read these, they dreamed of the "good life" so vividly portrayed by the Scottish author. To satisfy their romantic imaginations, several planters in central Kentucky built Tudor castles. Joseph Bruen sent John McMurtry, a local architect, to England to study the Tudor houses and to draw plans for Loudoun and Ingleside in Lexington.

During the forties and fifties, Kentuckians traveling abroad, impressed with the Romanesque villa, returned home to duplicate this architectural style in their homes. They added porticoes, portecocheres, towers, and domes to Georgian and Greek Revival houses to "modernize" them along Romanesque lines. Towers of Romanesque villas are to be seen throughout Kentucky, especially in the central counties. Good examples of the Romanesque villa are Maxwell Place, University of Kentucky campus; the Kincaid house, Lexington; and Hollyrood, Fayette County.

Although there are numerous fine old homes throughout Kentucky, only a small part of the state's population has occupied them. While wealthier Kentuckians were building classical structures, their less fortunate neighbors were constructing smaller and simpler homes for purely utilitarian purposes. These houses ranged from one-room frame shanties to seven-room and eight-room "plan book" brick houses common in every Kentucky community. One of the most noticeable ante bellum influences upon smaller houses is to be seen in the older towns where numerous houses were built adjoining each other. These row houses are characteristic of Maysville, Carrollton, Covington, Louisville, Frankfort, Lexington, and Paducah. These crowded homes are reminiscent of days when sidewalks were poor and streets muddy for much of the year, and when no street cars or busses transported city employees to their work.

Conflicting influences controlled postwar Kentucky architecture: an attempt to display wealth, and an effort to simplify the home. Kentucky cities during the postwar period were dotted with houses having mansard roofs, trimmings of ornate scrollwork, bay windows, and towers. However, smaller and plainer homes, the product of no particular school of architects, are characteristic of Kentucky. Efforts of the *Ladies' Home Journal* and other household magazines advocating simpler, smaller homes have had rich results throughout Kentucky.

Architects for modern public buildings in Kentucky have shown varied tastes. Courthouses have all been designed after a stereotyped pattern of a large square building crowned with a belfry or steeple. One county has copied another, and there is a monotony of design in these public buildings. Architects for the new statehouse at Frankfort designed a Federal-Romanesque building which sits on a wide, terraced base, with a central portico supported by large Corinthian columns, and is topped by a central dome. Internally this building is a labyrinth of cavernous halls, lobbies, and galleries supported by numerous Doric columns. Although of graceful design, and harmonious with its setting, the new Kentucky statehouse has proved inadequate to meet the needs of government, because of its poor arrangement. Kentucky colleges have followed no general architectural style but have constructed buildings one at a time which reflect the taste of the boards of trustees and the supervising officials. Since no plan has been followed in the construction of public school buildings, these vary from town to town. Many school buildings are the products of school board planning and show poor architectural taste, but others indicate definite appreciation of graceful lines which do not sacrifice efficiency. Churches, like schools, are the products of the planning of congregations and board members. Many Kentucky churches are distinctive for their beautiful lines. Perhaps the most graceful church houses in Kentucky are the small rural churches built during the early 1800's. Many modern church buildings show the influence of Henry Hobson Richardson, McKim, Mead and White, D. H. Burnham, and others of the modern school of design.

Silversmiths

While Kentuckians were reaping a bountiful harvest from fertile virgin soils and were planning commodious homes, they did not neglect furnishings for their homes. A source of pride with the Kentucky people has been the art of dining. Good food, beautifully served, was a cultural triumph for the ante bellum Kentucky hostess. Even the pioneers brought with them love for dining, but because of a lack of silver and tableware they were unable to make an artistic display. When the products of Kentucky's soil returned sufficient money, Kentuckians began collecting coin silverware. In order to secure this luxury, however, it was necessary to manufacture it in the West, where soon there appeared itinerant silversmiths. Perhaps the first of these artisans was Samuel Ayres. Ayres was a master craftsman and remained in business in Kentucky for many years, producing a large quantity of silverware. Advertising in the *Kentucky Gazette* on August 9, 1788, Edward West informed Kentuckians that he had opened a watch and clock shop where he expected to do not only watch and clock repairing but also silversmithing, painting, and inventing. At Paris, Robert Frazer was engaged in the manufacture of flat coin silver for subscribing patrons. In 1799 he moved from that place to Lexington, where he enjoyed a thriving trade. The next year his nephew, Alexander Frazer, opened a competing shop. These craftsmen did satisfactory and artistic work, as indicated by the Frazer pieces owned by Blue Grass families.

Master of all the early Kentucky silversmiths was Asa Blanchard. The appearance of Blanchard's name on a piece of silver is as significant in Kentucky as that of Paul Revere's is in New England. This artisan specialized in spoons, knives, forks, ladles, and julep cups, all of which were hammered from pure coin silver. Blanchard's fame spread throughout the southern country. During a long period he received from other states apprentices to learn his trade. Local tradition has it that Henry Clay, wishing to complete a silver service for his wife, ordered the pieces from the East, but the eastern silversmiths, in turn, ordered them from Blanchard.

Succeeding Asa Blanchard were Winchester and Garner, who produced more pieces of tableware than all of the other artisans combined. They remained in business from the late twenties until after the War between the States. This firm specialized in the manufacture of pitchers and cups to be given as prizes to livestock breeders at agricultural fairs. The last survivor of this firm was a mulatto son of Eli

Garner who was in business in Lexington until the early nineties. David Sayre came to Kentucky from Madison, New Jersey, to engage in the manufacture of silverware, but later went into the banking business. At Louisville, S. W. Warriner, A. Anderson, J. Werne, and John Kitts and Company produced hand-wrought tableware for wealthy Kentuckians. Throughout the state, towns of consequence supported at least one manufacturing jeweler who hammered coin silverware for local customers.

At present, manufacturing jewelers in Kentucky are making sterling and plated ware of standard design. There was no uniformity in the work of the early silversmiths except the "lips" of their spoons and their use of the same quality of materials. In order to manufacture beautiful pieces of tableware it was necessary to secure an even quality of raw materials. The best source for silver was the Spanish dollar brought into Kentucky by New Orleans traders. Of course, not all early Kentucky families owned silver sets of local manufacture. But the work of the Kentucky silversmiths represents one of the earliest aesthetic accomplishments of the Kentuckians.

Painters

Since Kentucky life centered largely about the home, it was natural that families had their portraits painted to hang on parlor walls. One of the early marks of economic well-being was a display of oil paintings of members of the family. As early as 1788, itinerant painters found their way into the rapidly growing Kentucky communities. One of the first of these painters was William West, who, although not a remarkable artist, did paint fair likenesses of his clients. He distinguished himself among his clientele by painting a life portrait of Lord Byron. As General Anthony Wayne's army advanced westward, it brought with it a scout named Beck who did beautiful paintings of still life and of landscapes of pioneer Kentucky.

Most successful of the Kentucky artists was Matthew Jouett. Like every bright ante bellum Kentucky lad, Jouett was encouraged to study law, but he had no love for legal studies, since his taste ran naturally to drawing and painting. A student who found his law books unexciting, he whiled away time with his art, and as a practicing attorney, out from under the vigilant eye of a preceptor, he became less interested in law but more absorbed in painting. The War of 1812 afforded him a chance to escape from a meager law practice, and for a short time Jouett served as a Kentucky volunteer in the Great Lakes campaign. Leaving the army, he took up painting as a profession. In his work Jouett portrayed a keen sense of symmetry and color. During the years 1816–1817 he was a student of Gilbert Stuart at Boston, and upon his return to Kentucky he painted the portraits of prominent citizens, among whom were Isaac Shelby, Robert Letcher, Horace Holley, Robert S. Todd, James Morrison, Henry Clay, Joseph Hamilton Daviess, Humphrey and Thomas Marshall, Robert and John Breckinridge, and a full-length portrait of Lafayette. Through a long period of years Jouett produced numerous paintings, many of which were remarkably well done, but it is extremely doubtful whether or not he painted all of the portraits attributed to him.

Other ante bellum painters were Joseph H. Bush, John Neagle, Louis Morgan, and Oliver Frazer. Bush gained a notable reputation as a portrait painter, ranking next to Jouett, and, through the generosity of Henry Clay, was trained by Thomas Sully at Philadelphia. Bush's better paintings are his portraits of Henry Clay, Zachary Taylor, Dr. Benjamin Dudley, George Rogers Clark, Thomas B. Monroe, Martin Hardin, and Governor John Adair. Oliver Frazer enjoyed a large patronage and succeeded as a painter. He was trained by Jouett, and in his paintings he carried on the Jouett tradition of symmetry and color. His portrait of Henry Clay is his masterpiece. Henry Clay had sufficient interest in local artists to encourage them by arranging for their training and by giving them his patronage as a prominent citizen of Kentucky.

After the War between the States a large number of Kentucky artists painted portraits and landscapes. An artist named Alexander produced creditable portraits of the prominent Confederates, John C. Breckinridge and Judge William B. Kinkead. Other artists of this period were John Grimes, Aaron H. Corwine, Neville Cain, and Thomas S. Noble. Noble's work gained national recognition, and in rapid succession he was elected to fellowships in the New York Academy of Design, the Chicago Academy of Fine Arts, and later made a director of the McMicken Academy of Design in Cincinnati. Since most of Kentucky's paintings are of the portrait type, it is an indication that patronage of local artists was prompted by home and family pride.

Paul Sawyer of Frankfort has perhaps been Kentucky's outstanding landscape painter. He had a keen affection for the Kentucky River country, and his water colors contain a warmth and feeling for the land which is exhibited by no other artist. Sawyer was highly productive. Possibly no one knows how many prints he did produce, and because of this large output his work is of an uneven quality. There is, however, a good core of his work which reaches a high state of excellence. His best work was done, 1890–1910.

Sculptors

Along with its painters, Kentucky has produced two sculptors. First of these was Joel T. Hart, born in 1810 in Clark County. He became interested in sculpturing while engraving epitaphs on tombstones in a marble yard. Through the influence of another young stonecutter, Hart was persuaded to take up sculpture as a profession. In order to cultivate a more accurate knowledge of physical form, he entered the Transylvania Medical School as a student of anatomy. Beginning as a student sculptor, Hart created busts of Cassius M. Clay, Andrew Jackson, and John Jordan Crittenden, Admirers of Henry Clay commissioned this artist to make a statue of their idol, a work which required ten years to complete. Hart studied sculpture in Italy, and on his return to Kentucky he executed pieces of statuary of prominent Kentuckians, to be placed in public buildings. His masterpiece was "Woman Triumphant." Unfortunately, this beautiful piece of marble statuary was placed in the Fayette County Courthouse where it was destroyed by fire. Frank Duveneck, born in 1848 in Covington, became internationally famous for his colored backgrounds. As a member of the Munich (Germany) Academy group, he won first honors with his paintings. A recumbent statue of his wife, created with the assistance of Clement Barnhorn, is his finest casting.

Music

Kentucky has made few original contributions to American music. Typical of the frontier attitude, male musicians were considered effeminate unless they played instruments and music of approved masculinity. Although the fiddle, guitar, banjo, and dulcimer were accepted instruments in the western country, musicians did not use them in the composition of new music. Of all the elements of eastern culture, music was easiest to transport westward, for it was carried by memory and by ear. Campfires, fortress commons, and solitary homesteads were enlivened by recitations of narrative ballads and songs transmitted from the "Old Country." This explains the existence today of the ballad in the Kentucky mountains. The mountain region is a favorite hunting ground for students of folk tunes, but this music is not indigenous to Kentucky. Although folk music is often adapted to the telling of Kentucky tales, it is based upon transatlantic ballads. Many European or English tales have been so completely warped by local adaptations that they are hardly recognizable.

Perhaps the only piece of music of any national consequence contributed by a Kentuckian is the *Arkansas Traveler.* This song was composed by Colonel Nicholas "Sandy" Falkner of Georgetown and was inspired by a visit in 1831 to the wild and mosquito-infested swamps of Arkansas. Falkner was impressed by the trifling natives of that state and told his story in an appropriately dragging semi-folk song. This piece of music appeared in 1832 and has been a favorite of "hill-billy" bands since that date.

During the early part of the twentieth century, Josephine McGill of Louisville collected and arranged folk ballads which she later published under the title *Folk Songs of the Kentucky Mountains.* She not only collected ballads, but she was also a composer. Her best-known compositions are *Duna, Sleep,* and *Gentians,* and, like her titles, her melodies are of a gentle nature. Miss McGill put into music Madison Cawein's *Road Song* and Robert Louis Stevenson's *Requiem.*

Perhaps no musical production of the nineteenth century was more characteristic of the age than that of the Negro minstrel. At Louisville, in the early 1830's, Thomas Dartmouth "Daddy" Rice, a native of the old Seventh Ward of New York, popularized Negro imitations. Rice came to Kentucky as an itinerant actor, and in 1832, while playing before a Louisville audience in Solon Robinson's *The Rifle,* he imitated a cornfield Negro. The reception of this act encouraged more entertainment of a like character. From his southern contacts Rice created his comic song character "Jim Crow." It was at Louisville, probably, that Rice learned from a crippled Negro his "heel-a-ricking" step, which soon became a familiar act to minstrel audiences throughout the country. In Kentucky "Jim Crow" was so popular that from a Louisville theater "Daddy" Rice went to Cincinnati and later to the East to enjoy success. The words of Rice's songs, like those of the Negro whom he copied, have a delightful rhythm:

> First on de heel tap, den on de toe,
> Ebery time I wheel about I jump Jim Crow.
> Wheel about and turn about and do jist so,
> And every time I wheel about I jump Jim Crow.

Literature

Kentucky and its people have furnished abundant themes for its literary sons. Not only has Kentucky inspired travelers' comments and historical writings, but novels and poetry. The hardy life of the frontier, the adventures of the pioneer, and the gentle life of the middle period have encouraged authors to adopt local themes. Poets and novelists have found in the natural beauty of the state sufficient inspiration for the production of numerous works.

One of the earliest books about Kentucky is Filson's *Discovery, Settlement and Present State of Kentucke* (1784). Filson, an adventurer-school teacher, came to the West in 1783, where he heard many tales of the pioneers. At the same time he was impressed with the possibilities for economic gain in this new and unsettled country. It was partly this motive which influenced the writing of his book. Although common usage has applied the title "history" to Filson's story, it is not a history, but rather a traveler's account of Kentucky, written specifically to entertain easterners, and to attract new settlers to the frontier. Modern readers, knowing that Daniel Boone was barely literate, are scarcely impressed when Filson attributes paragraphs to him which are creditable to an excellent linguist. It is doubtful that Boone opened his reminiscences with: "Curiosity is natural to the soul of man, and interesting objects have a powerful influence on our affections. Let these influencing powers actuate, by permission or disposal of providence, from selfish or social views, yet in time the mysterious will of heaven is unfolded . . ."! Except for its map, this book's principal worth lies in its being a literary and historical curiosity. As an historical account of Kentucky, it has no more value than any other traveler's account.

John Bradford, editor of the *Kentucky Gazette,* made a worthier contribution to Kentucky's historical literature in his *Notes on Kentucky.* These essays were based upon accounts of the leading pioneers, and since Bradford was himself a pioneer, he was able to weed out most of the frontier romances and exaggerations. Gilbert Imlay came to Kentucky from New Jersey in 1784 for the purpose of locating and surveying lands for prospective British immigrants. Like most British travelers, Imlay compiled his experiences, in a book entitled, *A Topographical Description of the Western Territory of North America.* This account of early Kentucky and the Northwest is presented in a series of letters addressed from various places in the West. Three editions of this work were published within a four-year period. The third edition, 1797, contains a reprint of Filson's work.

Through a period of political struggle public leaders continually offended one another, and many times this led to duels or "Virginia gougings." Perhaps the most irascible of all the early political leaders was Humphrey Marshall, a Virginian who moved to Kentucky in 1782, where he engaged in pioneer politics. Throughout the first ten constitutional conventions, including the Virginia ratification convention of 1788, Marshall remained a steadfast Tory. He insulted freely those Kentuckians who sought an alliance with Spain in order to open the Mississippi River. So agitated did he become over his political disputes that he resorted to the use of columns of the *Gazette* and pamphlets. These means, however, afforded the conservative Marshall only a limited opportunity to denoúnce his opponents, and in 1812 he published a *History of Kentucky* in which he assailed his enemies. In the dignified pages of history Marshall was able to present himself in a favorable light, but his book is too prejudiced to be given serious consideration. With the exception of Filson's book, it is the first history of Kentucky. Despite its highly prejudiced attitude, it does contain some valuable sidelights which are not to be found elsewhere. In 1824 Marshall revised his book and published it in two volumes, but again it was merely a personal defense. Realizing that Humphrey Marshall had failed to write a satisfactory history of Kentucky, Mann Butler, a native Virginian, published in 1834 his *History of the Commonwealth of Kentucky*. Avoiding Marshall's pitfalls, this history is a straight-forward story of Kentucky's early development.

Continuing the work of Marshall and Butler, Lewis Collins, using notes collected by his brother-in-law, H. P. Peers, published, in 1847, a *History of Kentucky,* bringing the story of Kentucky down to approximately 1845. Collins was not an interpretative historian, but, sensing the need for a general historical source for citizens and public schools, he produced such a book. The Collins history is not a connected narrative; it is in the form of a gazetteer presenting a monumental mass of undigested historical data. In 1884 Richard H. Collins expanded and reorganized much of the textbook material of his father's work and brought it to date. The new edition was published in two volumes, the second volume containing historical sketches of the counties. This work is the most fruitful source of information for Kentucky history, despite the fact that the authors were not discriminating historians and lacked access to many important sources of information. The Collins histories are remarkably free from errors and are as nearly unbiased as possible in the presentation of facts, for where two conflicting sources existed, the authors presented both viewpoints.

Other histories covering the whole period of Kentucky history are *Kentucky, A Pioneer Commonwealth,* Nathaniel Southgate Shaler, 1885; *History of Kentucky,* Z. F. Smith, 1885; *History of Kentucky,* W. H. Perrin, J. H. Battle, and G. C. Kniffen, 1888; *History of Kentucky and Kentuckians,* E. Polk Johnson, 1912; *History of Kentucky,* Charles Kerr, editor, 1922; and the *History of Kentucky,* Temple Bodley and Samuel M. Wilson, 1929. With the exception of Shaler and Smith's works, these histories of the state were written as vehicles for biographical dictionaries and were promoted by commercial biographers. Outstanding of this group are the first two volumes of Kerr's history. These volumes were written by W. E. Connelly and E. M. Coulter, both careful students of Kentucky history. Bodley's and Wilson's work presents much new material which is not to be found elsewhere, but, for the most part, it was hurriedly compiled and is not indicative of the writers' proved ability as Kentucky historians. Shaler's work is that of a Union sympathizer who placed special emphasis upon the War between the States. Johnson's work is that of a rampant

Southern newspaperman who glorified the Confederate struggle in the state. Z. F. Smith, an ex-superintendent of public instruction, made a narrative compilation of Collins' history.

Fiction and Poetry

While historians and biographers were engaged in writing Kentucky's history, novelists and poets pictured its romance and beauty. Many novelists have used the state's traditions and natural beauty as themes for their work. One of the first western novelists was Gilbert Imlay, who wrote *The Emigrants,* a novel based upon the author's western American adventures. There followed the romantic writings of John A. McClung, Robert M. Bird, and Julia Tevis. Two of the more productive of the postwar novelists were James Lane Allen and John Fox, Jr. These writers found in Kentucky's history and people numerous fascinating themes for their novels. Beginning with his first published short story, "Too Much Momentum," which appeared April, 1885, in *Harper's Magazine,* James Lane Allen produced numerous works of fiction about his native state. The novels of James Lane Allen furnish perhaps the best source for an accurate account of the mind and heart of the Blue Grass aristocracy before it underwent the changes of the reconstruction period. "The Tale of Two Gentlemen from Kentucky," *Century Magazine,* 1888, is a masterpiece presenting the economic and social changes which came over Kentucky. His best-known works are: *Flute and Violin, The Blue Grass Region of Kentucky, A Kentucky Cardinal,* and *The Reign of Law.*

James Lane Allen, born near Lexington, December 21, 1849, was, in particular, the chronicler of the Blue Grass. With a keen sense of humor and a sympathetic understanding of his subject he made the Blue Grass region of Kentucky known to a large American reading public. While Allen was writing of the Blue Grass, John Fox, Jr., was writing of the eastern mountains of Kentucky. Born December 16, 1863, at Stony Point, Bourbon County, John Fox, Jr., was educated at Transylvania and in the East to become a lawyer and newspaper reporter, but poor health forced him to return to Kentucky. Going with his family to the mountains about 1890, he immediately became interested in the mountaineer and his customs. His first work was a full-length novel, *A Mountain Europa,* published in 1892. This author was to gain recognition, however, with his short story "Hell Fer Sartain," which he wrote in a few hours and which was published in the advertising section of *Harper's Magazine*. After the publication of this story, Fox produced *The Kentuckians, A Cumberland Vendetta, The Little Shepherd of Kingdom Come, Christmas Eve on Lonesome, Heart of the Hills,* and *The Trail of the Lonesome Pine.* Perhaps there is no piece of writing in Kentucky literature which depicts the feeling which existed between the people of the Blue Grass and the mountains during the War between the States better than *The Little Shepherd of Kingdom Come.* This work is more analytical than Fox's other novels. In this story he attempts to make clear some of the points of controversy which have always existed over certain features of mountain culture. In John Fox, Jr., the mountaineers found an understanding chronicler who recorded in his novels their loves, hatreds, and philosophies.

Numerous other Kentucky novelists have attracted a national circle of readers. Among these are the members of the "Louisville Group" of women writers who include Annie Fellows Johnston, author of the Little Colonel stories, Eleanor Mercein Kelly, Alice Hegan Rice, who wrote *Mrs. Wiggs of the Cabbage Patch,* and Mrs. George Madden Martin, author of *Emmy Lou.* Other novelists are Lucy Furman, *Quare Women,* Jean Thomas, *Traipsin Woman,* Mrs. Eliza Calvert (Hall) Obenchain, *Aunt Jane of Kentucky,* Elizabeth Madox Roberts, *The Great Meadow* and *The Time of Man.* All of these writers have used Kentucky as a source, contributing greatly to the enrichment of the state's literary heritage.

Most productive of all Kentucky writers was Irvin Cobb, newspaper reporter, essayist, short story writer, novelist, and actor. Cobb, like other Kentucky authors, drew heavily upon the state's sources for his stories. His most famous creation was Judge Priest, a lovable figure in a western Kentucky community during post-Civil War years. In his Judge Priest stories, written for the *Saturday Evening Post,* Irvin Cobb caught the spirit of an old Confederate soldier living in a Confederate community, where he combined the duties of a circuit judge with those of everyday life about him. In more than fifty books, this Kentucky author established himself among the leading American humorists. Unlike many other Kentucky authors, he not only reached a large reading public but through his radio and motion picture assignments distinguished himself as an entertaining raconteur.

A small volume would be required to list by name the Kentucky poets. The natural beauty of the state, its easy life, and its political minded population have stimulated its poets to much poetic ardor. Representative poets are: Father Stephen Badin, John M. Harney, George D. Prentice, Hew Ainslie, William F. Marvin, William D. Gallagher, Theodore O'Hara, Mary E. Betts, Henry T. Stanton, Mary F. Childs, Robert Burns Wilson, James H. Mulligan, Young E. Allison, Madison Cawein, E. Carlile Litsey, Cotton Noe, Lucien V. Rule, J. Tandy Ellis, Allen Tate, Cale Young Rice, and Jesse Stuart.

In more recent years Kentucky authors have produced important novels. Among these are Robert Penn Warren, whose books, *All the King's Men, Night Rider,* and *World and Time Enough* either have a Kentucky setting or use local materials. Elizabeth Pickett Chevalier used the Kentucky scene in her novel, *Drivin' Woman,* Jesse Stuart has used native materials with marked success in *The Man with a Bull Tongue Plow, Head of W Hollow, Beyond Dark Hills, Taps for Private Tussey,* and a teacher story *The Thread that Runs So True.* A. B. Guthrie, Jr. has written of the West from a Kentucky perch in *The Big Sky* and *The Way West.* Isabel McMeekin and Dorothy Park Clark used the Kentucky scene in *Show Me a Land* and in producing their other books. Henry Hornsby utilized the mountaineer's nostalgia in *Lonesome Valley,* and Harriette Arnow has adopted the mountain theme in her *Hunter's Horn.* One of the most sympathetic treatments of the mountains is James Still's *River of Earth.*

Kentucky's writers have revealed a maturity not always evident in the activities of other citizens. For a state, where educational standards are relatively low and book reading is a minor activity, its authors have succeeded. Making less commotion and attracting less attention, Kentucky's novelists, poets, historians and newspapermen have been more numerous than its statesmen, but considerably fewer than its politicians. In a final analysis literary people have more consistently contributed to the state's good reputation abroad than have leaders in almost all other fields of human endeavor.

Some of George D. Prentice's works were compiled in 1859 under the title of *Prenticeana,* and, in 1878, John J. Piatt published all of Prentice's works in a single volume. Prentice wrote poetry and paragraphs on many and varied subjects. However, in his poetic writings he was influenced by sentimental personal themes as in *The Closing Year* and *My Mother's Grave.* Hew Ainslie wrote in a Scottish vein after the style of Robert Burns. His best contributions are *The Bourocks O' Bargeny, The Haughs O' Auld Kentucky,* and *The Hint O' Hairst.* Theodore O'Hara and Mary E. Betts glorified the Kentuckians who went away to war. O'Hara's *Bivouac of the Dead,* commemorating the death of the soldiers in the Mexican War, is a worthy contribution to American Literature. Mary E. Betts, using the statement of Colonel William Crittenden, who, when taken a prisoner in the Lopez expedition in 1850, refused to obey the orders of his captor to kneel, but said, "A Kentuckian kneels only to God and Facing His Enemy," and wrote a poetic declaration of Kentucky independence. Henry T. Stanton of Maysville became a well-known poet when in an unguarded moment he consented to oblige a traveling elocutionist by writing a poem which would provoke an audience to tears. This poem, *The Moneyless Man,* written in jest, has completely overshadowed worthier poetic works of this author. At Lexington Judge James H. Mulligan, a genial Irishman, presented the Kentuckian's love for his homeland in his poem *Over the Hill to Hustonville.*

The most finished poet of the whole Kentucky group was Madison Cawein. Cawein, born in Louisville, March 23, 1865, became one of America's best lyric poets. Born of poor parents, he was forced to leave school at an early age to secure a job in a Louisville gambling house. Having a poet's temperament, Cawein soon failed in business. In 1887 he published his first poems in a small booklet entitled *Blooms of the Berry.* With the appearance of his first publication the young Louisville poet attracted the attention of William Dean Howells and Thomas Bailey Aldrich through whose interest he began a long and productive career. Cawein's better known works are *Lyrics and Idylls, Days and Dreams, Undertones, The Vale of Temper, Kentucky Poems, So Many Ways, The Poet, The Fool and the Faeries,* and *The Cup of Comas.* Born of a father and mother who spent much time in the woods near Louisville in search of medicinal herbs, Cawein came in close contact with nature. Many critics have said of Cawein that he never got away from his genuinely natural sources.

The Kentucky Personality

Present-day travelers through most sections of Kentucky are impressed with the independence of rural Kentuckians. If, by chance, these travelers visit the state on Saturdays and Sundays, they find the highways crowded with carefree pedestrians who are oblivious to passing automobiles or other vehicles. As tax-paying citizens, they refuse to yield any of the road, believing that their rights as native citizens are inviolate, and as thorough-going optimists, they place absolute confidence in the ability of automobile drivers either to stop their machines or to drive them into the ditch. This rugged individualism is characteristic of the development of Kentucky personality. When backwoods Virginians, Carolinians, and Pennsylvanians migrated to Kentucky, they came as agrarians, and their descendants have remained close to the soil. The population of no other state in the Union is perhaps so overwhelmingly independent yet so inconsistent in its personality as that of Kentucky. From the beginning, the conquest of Kentucky's soil demanded resourceful and individual prowess. Pioneer families, living on isolated farmsteads, became self-sufficient in all things, a trait of character which has been handed down to succeeding generations. Environment created not only a sense of independence but also a light heart, a quick temper, and a keen, if sometimes grotesque, sense of humor.

Fertile lands of the western country convinced early Kentuckians that their homeland was the only place adaptable to human habitation. There is more truth than humor in the story of the old lady who reluctantly left her Bourbon County home to live in another county of the state with the odd remark that she "hated to leave her old Kentucky home." Most of Kentucky's population has always been provincially minded. François A. Michaux observed as early as 1802 that:

> The inhabitants of Kentucky, as we have before stated, are nearly all natives of Virginia, particularly the remotest part of that state; and exclusive of the gentlemen of the law, physicians and a small number of citizens who have received an education suitable to their professions in the Atlantic states they have preserved the manners of the Virginians. With them the passion for gaming and spiritous liquors are carried to excess, which frequently terminates in quarrels degrading to human nature. The public houses are always crowded, more especially during the sittings of the courts of justice. Horses and lawsuits comprise the usual topic

of their conversation. If a traveler happens to pass by, his horse is admired, if he stops, he is presented with a glass of whiskey, and then asked a thousand questions, such as: Where do you come from? Where are you going? What is your name? Where do you live? What profession? Were there fevers in the different parts of the country you passed through? These questions which are frequently repeated in the course of a journey, become tedious, but it is easy to give a check to their enquiries by a little address: their only object being the gratification of that curiosity so natural to a people isolated in the woods, and seldom sees a stranger.

Michaux might be accused of exaggerating the nature of the early Kentuckians, except that Mann Butler, the most reliable early historian of Kentucky, has left a similar description. When Mann Butler moved from Virginia to Kentucky in 1806, he was impressed with the fact that "almost every young man of his acquaintance had a horse, a gun, and a violin. Society," he said, "seemed to be viewed as if it were intended for amusement alone; that its great business was to pass off life with as little care as possible. There was a round of frolics, whenever the pressing exigencies did not forbid them, and every farmer's house was a home for all, and a temple of jollity." Timothy Flint, a New England preacher and traveler, found in 1830 that the Kentuckians had a distinct personality.

The Kentuckians, it must be admitted are a high-minded people and possess the stamina of a noble character. It cannot be said correctly, as is said in journals and geographies, that they are too recent and too various in their descent and manners, to have a distinct character as a people. They generally are of one descent, and are the scions from a noble stock—the descendants from affluent and respectable planters from Virginia and North Carolina. They are in that condition of life, which is, perhaps best calculated to develop high-mindedness, and self-respect. We aim not in these remarks at eulogy, but to pay tribute, where tribute is due. It is granted, there are ignorant, savage, and abandoned men, among the lower classes in Kentucky—where are there not such? There is a distinct and striking moral physiognomy to this people; an enthusiasm, a vivacity, and ardor of character, courage, frankness, generosity, that have been developed with peculiar circumstances under which they have been placed. . . . Possessed of such physical and moral capabilities, and from their imperfect education, their habits of idleness, extravagance and gambling, but too likely to turn their perverted and misapplied powers against themselves and their country, everything depends upon the restraining influence of right views, on the part of the parents. There is a loud call for the stern exercise of parental monition and authority. . . . They seem to feel that they have an hereditary claim to command, place and observance. This perfect repose of self-confidence is in fact their good star. I have often seen one of these young men, in the new states farther west, with no more qualifications than that ease and perfect command of all that they knew, which result from self-satisfaction, step down into the "mourning waters" before the tardy, bashful and self-criticising young man from the North had made up his mind to attempt to avail himself of the opportunity. *Sua dextra* is the constant motto, self-repose the guardian genius of the Kentuckian, which often stand him in stead of better talents and qualifications. . . .

Their enthusiasm of character is very observable, in the ardor with which all classes of the people express themselves, in respect to their favorite views and opinions. The feelings of the people naturally tend to extremes. Hear them rate their favorite preacher. He is the most pious and powerful preacher in the country. Their orators and their statesmen, in eloquence and abilities surpass all others. The village politicians have an undoubting and plenary faith, that whatever measures the Kentucky delegation espouses in Congress, not only ought to prevail, but will prevail. The long line of superlatives, the possessions of the best horse, dog, gun, wife, statesman, and country are felt to belong to them in course; and an ardent healthy race of young men, not enough travelled to have become the victims of a fastidious and self-criticising spirit, not afflicted, as in common with the untravelled, with bashfulness, yet possessing the crude rudiments and first principles of all kinds of knowledge,—such are qualified to their early habits and the impulses given them, to become the blessings or the scourge of their country. . . .

The Kentucky planters assert, that whatever article Old Kentucky turns her chief attention to raising, is sure to glut the market for that year. It would be remarked, perhaps that flour, hemp, or tobacco, were low in the market. They immediately find a solution in the fact that the Kentucky crop has arrived. In truth, the astonishing productiveness of their good lands, and the great extent of their cultivation, almost justify such conclusions.

Jacob Burnet, a traveler through the northwestern territory, wrote in his *Notes on the Early Settlement of the Northwestern Territory* that:

The patriarchal pioneers of these backwoods men were people of a peculiar and remarkable order, trained by circumstances to a character which united force, hardihood and energy in an astonishing degree. Opinion has generally invested them with a predominance of rough traits and rough habits, approximating the character of the Indians. They were in fact much distinguished by an ample basis of gentlemanly character and chivalrous notions of honor and justice as for strength, firmness and bravery.

Burnet, in his later writings, found what he considered gross inconsistencies in the Kentuckians' character, for in the forties he wrote:

Let us join the group round the old gentleman, who, with his chair in the street, his feet on the window sill, his left hand in his ruffled shirt-bosom, and his cud in his cheek, is laying down the law, pointed off with spurts of tobacco juice. These men, common as they look, are not common men; lazy as they appear, leaning against the shoulder-polished door posts, they are full of energy and ability. Such men as these won the battle of Buena Vista, and will rule the world, if they choose to. Here is one, hard featured and stern, with full veins, and a complexion like a half-tanned ox-hide, who would, like Harry Daniel, of Mount Sterling, murder the brother of his wife and see her go crazy, and yet walk his way with an easy conscience, or, at any rate, the pretense of one. Next to him sits a man who could wage war with the human race for a life time, and enjoy it; a man of the Middle Ages, with all the vices of feudalism and all of those of the money-seeking age combined. He has made his fortune by hunting up invalid titles, purchasing and prosecuting the legal claim, and turning the innocent holder to the dogs. And yet at home no one is kinder, more thoughtful, almost self-sacrificing. Send him to Mexico, and humanity is capable of no crime from which he would turn, or at which he would shudder. Take him to Boston, and his manner will be as pleasing as his conversation will be original. Search his pockets, and you will find a plan for defrauding a neighbor of his farm, a most affectionate letter to an absent daughter, a bowie knife, and *Paradise Lost*.

Beyond him, notice that face. How clear the eye, how confident the mouth, how strong and firm the chin! If he speaks you will hear a voice like the Eolian harp, pouring forth words of such sweetness that the bees might cling upon his lips. If he moves, it is the Indian's motion, quiet and strong as sunlight. In his mind the Higher Democracy is forming itself a home; and amid the low contest of politics, he will be, unconsciously, acting as the messenger of the great Friend of Man. Another comes by with a quick springy step, as if with ankle joints of India rubber; he stops, joins the discussion; words pour from his tongue more rapidly than the ear can drink them in; he looks around, his eye all seriousness and his mouth all smiles; men catch his idea, though they cannot his syllables, and their nods show that he has hit some nail on the head. That man, slight as a girl, might be safely trusted to lead any corps in any battle; and yet in his life he never struck a blow. Go for ten miles around, inquire in any household, and you will hear of him as the kind adviser, the steadiest friend, the unostentatious helper; many a son has he saved from the gambling table, the race-course, or the deadly duel, begun with rifles and finished with knives;—and he, too, is a child of the soil.

Now consider, that, while the murderer and the victim of assassination become known to you through the press, the virtues of the patriotic politician or the village philanthropist make no noise in the world. Believe us, also, that, while the towns and taverns of these western states reeking with tobacco and whiskey, are symbols of the evil Democracy of our land, and the bullies and cut-throats, the knaves and robbers, are its true children; and though you might, on first looking at such a society as you may see in almost any western town, think anarchy was close at hand, yet are the villages ever improving, the taverns themselves growing more decent, and anarchy is going farther and farther away. Remember that this Kentucky was settled by men perfectly their own masters; in government, in religions, in politics, in restraining power of any kind save the voice of God in their own breasts. . . . Kentucky began in anarchy and has risen to law;—that she was once the Alsatia of the United States, and is now in comparison quiet and peaceable,—that she once hung to the Union by but a thread, and is now bound to it by clamps of iron; and you cannot but have some faith in the workings of Democracy.

To the early Kentuckian, democracy was a throne of grace, especially from 1800 to 1860. When Lafayette toured the United States in 1825, he visited Kentucky, where he was received as the co-founder of American independence. All along the roads over which he traveled excited throngs of people cheered his coming. To be honored with the presence of the great French soldier as a guest was sufficient reason to boast of the occasion for several generations. However, there were men in Kentucky who, although they admired Lafayette, were independent in their conversations with him. Lavasseur, Lafayette's private secretary, has left an account of a meeting with an old Kentuckian near Cincinnati. This Kentuckian, said Lavasseur, was smoking his "segar" at the door of his house, but upon the approach of the travelers, he invited them into his house to have a drink of whiskey and a chew of tobacco. During the conversation the old gentleman remarked that Napoleon could have found a cheerful home in America. Lafayette replied that Napoleon might have had designs on the liberties of the American people. This latter statement did not in any way disconcert the host, who remarked:

> We should have considered such an attempt as an act of madness, but if, against all probabilities, we had submitted for the moment to his tyrannous ascendancy, his success would have been fatal to him. Look at that rifle; with that I never miss a pheasant in our woods at a hundred yards; a tyrant is larger than a pheasant, and there is not a Kentuckian who is not as patriotic and skilful as myself.

The critical English traveler, Captain Thomas Hamilton, made several comments on Kentucky character. Captain Hamilton believed:

> The Kentuckians may be called the Irish of America. They have all that levity of character, that subjection of the moral to the convivial, that buoyancy of spirit, that jocular ferocity, that ardor, both of attachment and of hatred, which distinguish the natives of the Emerald Isle. The Kentuckians are the only Americans who can understand a joke. There is a kind of native humor about them which is very pleasant; and, I must say, that several Kentucky gentlemen were among the most agreeable companions with whom I had the good fortune to become acquainted during my tour.

However much Captain Hamilton admired this keen sense of humor, he could not forego his snobbish British superiority, and he led his readers to believe that the Kentuckians were carrying pistols, knives, and instruments of torture with them at all times. He was chagrined when he lost a bet with a companion that canes carried by Kentuckians concealed daggers within their handles. Possibly these descriptions are overdrawn. Many other characterizations of Kentuckians were published by travelers during the eighteenth century, but few of them were as reasonable in their statements as those quoted. Many travelers were mistaken in believing the people who frequented the public taverns were representative of the whole community. Seldom did they come in contact with the domestic life of the people, and for this reason they lacked a well-rounded view of the Kentuckian.

Kentucky has given generously to American humor. These contributions have not always been in the form of written humor, but rather in colorful personalities. Kentuckians were travelers into all parts of the country. They carried on a tireless search for fertile land, markets, legal opportunities, and general entertainment for themselves. Wherever a Kentuckian happened to be, he felt honor-bound to make himself known and to proclaim the glories of his state. There are several choice bits of humor published by Kentuckians. In 1814, William Littell published his *Festoons of Fancy* in which he expressed humorous views of the Kentucky of that period. One of his best contributions in this volume is his poem, written in biblical style, in which he ridiculed the state legislature for its refusal to grant white women the right to divorce philandering husbands. Other humorists who have published their writings have been Charles Hatcher (George Washington Bricks), George D. Prentice, James H. Mulligan, George Bingham, J. Tandy Ellis, and Irvin Cobb. Four of these persons published their humor in newspapers. Cobb, depicting Kentuckians, has published most of his stories in book form. James H. Mulligan, lawyer, diplomat, and newspaper editor, wrote poetry as a pleasant relaxation. Most popular of his humorous productions is *In Kentucky*. This poem has been recited and reprinted more times perhaps than any other single comment upon Kentucky. Proctor Knott, lawyer, law professor, and congressman, produced somewhat accidentally an entertaining bit of American satire in his "Where Is Duluth?" speech delivered in Congress January 27, 1871. It was not the intention of the Kentucky congressman to write a humorous speech, for he was sincerely attempting to prevent the making of a congressional grant of St. Croix and Superior lands to a northwestern railway company. This speech soon proved embarrassing to its author. Although he consciously used satire in combating the St. Croix Land Bill, he had no intention of gaining for himself the reputation of being a wit. Congressman Knott in later years confided to friends that he wished he had never heard of Duluth.

It is true that not all of Kentucky's personality runs to the extreme, as some of the foregoing quotations indicate, yet these passages describe the rugged, but inconsistent, mold in which Kentucky character was cast. If, in the early days, Kentuckians startled European and eastern American travelers by their original demeanor and appearance, it must be remembered that beneath the surface they were religiously and sentimentally inclined. Nowhere in the United States did religion take such a vigorous hold as in Kentucky. In the religious revival of 1801 Barton Stone wrote:

There on the edge of a prairie in Logan County, Kentucky, the multitudes came together, and continued a number of days and nights encamped on the ground, during which time worship was carried on in some part of the encampment. The scene to me was new and passing strange. It baffled description. Many, very many, fell down, as slain in battle, and continued for hours together in an apparently breathless and motionless state—sometimes for a few moments reviving, and exhibiting symptoms of life by a deep groan, or piercing shriek, or by a prayer most fervently uttered. After lying thus for hours, they obtained deliverance. Their appeals were solemn, heart-penetrating, bold and free. Under such addresses many others were thrown into the same state from which the speakers had just been delivered.

Colonel William Stone of New York has left a colorful sketch in his *Memoirs of the Cane Ridge Meeting:*

About thirty or thirty-five years ago, there was an extensive revival of religion (so called) in Kentucky, characterized by the greatest fanaticism, accompanied by a great variety of bodily affections, and running into many painful excesses. These fanatics were reducible to various classes, some of which were affected by the *"falling* exercise"; and others by what was called the *"jerking* exercise"; others were moved by the Spirit to propose the *"running* exercise"; and others again, the *"climbing* exercise"—all of which exercises are sufficiently indicated by their names. It was a frequent occurrence for a number of people to gather round a tree, some praying, others imitating the barking of dogs, which operation was called in familiar parlance among them, "treeing the devil" (!). It was stated also concerning the same people that in their religious assemblies, or other places of worship, religious professors of zeal and standing would get out into the broad aisle, and go down upon their knees together, playing marbles, and other childish games, under the notion of obeying the sayings of the Savior—"Except ye be converted, and become as *little children,* ye cannot enter into the kingdom of heaven"; others would ride·up and down the aisle of the church on sticks.

It was farther said that the religious leaders, or at least one of them, by the name of McNamara, would affect to personate Satan: that on a certain occasion during Camp-meeting he was creeping about among the peoples' feet, exclaiming, "I am the old serpent that tempted Eve"; when approaching, in this manner, to a Scotchman, who was on the grounds as a spectator, the man lifted up his heel, and stamping on the face of the minister, replied: "The seed of the woman shall bruise the serpent's head." This man, McNamara, was regarded among them with superstitious reverence, insomuch, that it was common for them to sing in worship a hymn having for its chorus—"Glory to God and McNamara!"

A contemporary Kentuckian embodies in his personality most of the rugged influences which molded the lives of his ancestors. He is hospitable, independent, has a sense of humor, and is curious enough to get information from a stranger, yet shrewd enough not to tell a stranger too much. Among many Kentuckians whiskey drinking, horse racing, and punctual attendance at church meetings can be easily reconciled. It is not unusual in some sections of the state to see many of the same group crowding the pari-mutuel sheds on Saturday afternoon attending church on Sunday. Although the people of many other states would condemn the practices of drinking and racing, Kentuckians excuse them as "sporting." Most Kentuckians are shrewd traders, whether in buying pocket knives or farms. In many sections of the state the county court day, with its inevitable trading lot, has endured the competition of modern livestock markets. Crossroads merchants are quick to "size up" prospective customers to buy or sell.

In his own mind, the contemporary Kentuckian is convinced that no other section compares favorably with his own. When a stranger is introduced, he is asked, "Are you a native Kentuckian?" If he is a native son, he is accepted on grounds of mutual understanding, but, if not, the Kentuckian will recite Kentucky's traditions and history. History to the average Kentuckian, however, does not mean that his state was one of the first settlements in the West, that it became an important commercial link between the North and South, and that it has struggled heroically through political upheavals which have resulted in the framing of four constitutions. Instead, the history of Kentucky to the native son is a personal matter. The influence of *his* ancestry or his community upon the state and nation is the significant point. It is not uncommon for a visitor to gather from a conversation with the local historian of a remote Kentucky village a feeling that there all civilization had its real start, and that in his village events of national history had their beginning. Kentuckians search diligently the pages of state history, not only for traces of their ancestry, but likewise for bits of political strategy used by renowed Kentucky politicians. Kentuckians generally are politically minded. In their minds human relationships are of political consequence. The state's history is cluttered with political upheavals which have resulted in the election of state and county officials by bare, and sometimes questionable, majorities, but such victories were short-lived because effective minorities worked against them. At other times, elected officials have succeeded in coalition tickets only to find themselves deserted in the end by their coalition friends. Encouraging this political-mindedness is the fact that there is practically a continuous political campaign in progress in Kentucky. Wind and rain hardly banish political posters from trees, fences, and telepgraph poles before they are replaced by new ones.

A pronounced state character has lent glamour and distinction to Kentuckians. Their home state with its history and tradition is their cherished possession. It matters little whether the tradition is of polite society sheltered in Blue Grass or city mansions, or of distilling, horse racing, or bloody personal feuds. To a native son there is no more musical name in the English language than Kentucky. He uses it not only as a noun, but also as an adjective. There are Kentucky hams, beaten biscuits, mint juleps, bean soup, colonels, lambs, whiskey, horses, rifles, feuds, and innumerable other products of a peculiar value that only Kentucky can give them.

Kentucky made appreciable cultural progress in developing libraries after 1950. Three decades before the Commonwealth had fewer than a half dozen public libraries which could claim any degree of mature respectability. Most Kentuckians were without access to books in any sort of a public depository, and no matter how good schools were most citizens had poor opportunities to improve their funds of knowledge from reading. A pioneering attempt was made by the E. O. Robinson Mountain Fund to provide books to rural people in parts of Breathitt, Perry, and Knott counties. It operated the first bookmobile in the state, and one of the first in the Nation. In 1953, Mary Caperton Bingham, Georgia Blazer, and Harry Schacter began a crusade to raise by private subscription $300,000 from private sources to finance the purchase of 100 bookmobiles to be used in counties which were practically without books. Too, funds were sought to purchase books to stock the rolling libraries.

The Bookmobile Project was successful within itself, but more important it planted the idea of organizing and supporting public libraries in areas where none had existed before 1953. Already the Robinson Mountain Fund had demonstrated that there existed an intellectual hunger among Kentucky people for something to read. With the reorganization of the State Library, March 21, 1952, the availability of federal funds for library support, and the co-operative support of three or four governors after that date, Kentucky voters were encouraged to support local matching fund bond issues. The result was organization of a central library administration relatively free of traditional and petty political manipulations, development of sound book selection, purchasing, cataloguing, and organization of the rapid retrieval system called Kenclip, and the use of modern duplicating machines most Kentuckians in 1977 had made accessible to them extensive library resources.

In another area Kentucky state government finally assumed its tragically delayed responsibility for care of its neglected official records. On March 27, 1958, the General Assembly enacted a model archives law. Unfortunately irresponsible political hands later tinkered with this law in order to gain control of the Archives and Records Management agency. A state archives was organized in 1960, and by 1977 the great volume of precious public records had been gathered into a central depository. Schedules for the inventory, care, and preservation of records had been completed for most state agencies, and in the process important historical documents were discovered which had long thought to be destroyed. Despite progress in this field, Kentucky in 1976, the bi-centennial year, had still not provided secure housing for its irreplacable archival materials. To date it had spent more money on the construction of a horse park than for the preservation of the documents of its human historical heritage.

With the inclusion in academic curriculums of courses in painting, art history, and appreciation large numbers of Kentuckians have been interested in art as painters, etchers, water colorists, sculptors, and collectors. Since 1950 there has developed a lively interest in non-personal landscape, still life, impressionistic, and

bird and animal painting. Most of the universities have collections
of art of varying qualities, and so have the Kentucky State Historical Society and the Filson Club. The most distinguished collection
is in the more mature Speed Museum in Louisville. In recent years
its broad and selective collection has grown in both size and
sophistication.

CHAPTER XV

Evolution of State Politics

POLITICS, during the early years of Kentucky statehood, was not organized on a strictly partisan basis. There were differences of political opinion which dated back to the first separation convention in 1784. These differing opinions, however, did not result in the formation of political parties, except for the so-called Court and County Parties which lasted only during the election of delegates to the seventh convention. After the national constitutional convention in 1787, political principles of the Jeffersonian and Hamiltonian schools found support in Kentucky. It has been true throughout Kentucky's political history that partisan politics of the state have followed closely those of the Nation. Generally the early Kentuckians were Jeffersonian in their partisanship. In 1792, when Isaac Shelby of Mercer County, now Boyle, was nominated as the first Governor of the state, he became a stanch supporter of Jeffersonian principles in the West. Shelby's nomination was unanimous, as a reward for his active services in the protection of the southwestern frontier during the Revolutionary War. The fact that he was an active leader in the Battle of King's Mountain was sufficient to endear him to the hearts of Kentuckians. Before Governor Shelby's administration ended, however, political lines were being more sharply drawn in national affairs, and this condition was reflected in Kentucky. Humphrey Marshall and a small group of Federalists supported the Hamiltonian cause, but a majority of the Kentuckians favored western Republicanism.

When Isaac Shelby became Governor of Kentucky in May, 1792, his problems were not unlike those which faced President Washington when he assumed his duties as first President of the United States. Governor Shelby had to initiate a system of taxation, of legislation, and he had to establish courts. Within a year after his nomination, Shelby found himself involved in the French conspiracy sponsored by Genêt.

289

Besides, there still lingered sinister traces of Spanish intrigue which had marred the work of the convention. Before the end of his term, the Kentucky Governor was accused of favoring the French cause. Secretary of State Edmund Randolph intimated that Shelby had displayed indifference in dealing with traitorous French agents. What officials of the National Government failed to appreciate, however, was that the Kentucky administration kept itself well informed about the activities of the malcontents in the West, and that it believed they would fail. Of far more danger to the Kentucky government itself was the inability of the state courts to adjust themselves to the new government.

In 1796, four Republicans, Benjamin Logan, James Garrard, Thomas Todd, and John Brown, sought the nomination to succeed Governor Shelby. The legislature's vote for Governor was widely split in this election, and no one had a majority. Since Logan and Garrard received the most votes, they were selected to run off the tie, and Garrard was elected. Logan was a popular frontier figure in Kentucky. He had assumed leadership in the conventions; consequently, his friends felt that he deserved the governorship. For a time it seemed that Logan supporters would contest the election on the ground that their candidate had been elected on the first vote. Since, however, the contest threatened the government with disorganization, all protest was dropped to let Garrard serve his term.

Governor Garrard's administration inherited many of the ills which had afflicted Shelby's term. It was during his term of office that the people voted to frame a new constitution to clear up the confusion which had resulted from the vague provisions of the first. One of the outstanding demands made upon the second convention was that the people be allowed to vote directly for state officials, in order to prevent a repetition of the Logan-Garrard dispute in 1796. In 1800, when the new constitution became effective, Kentucky Republicans forgot the ill feelings of the last state election and re-elected James Garrard to a second term and supported Jefferson and Burr nationally. Politically, the West had come to hate the East because of the proposed Jay Treaty with Spain, the excise tax on distilled spirits, and the Alien and Sedition Laws of Adams' administration. More important, however, was the hope of the western Republicans that Jefferson would remove permanently the barrier to western commerce on the Mississippi River. An expansionist sentiment existed in Kentucky as early as 1800, which advocated pushing forward the westward frontier. Before Robert Livingston could complete his negotiations with France for Louisiana, the Spanish Intendant at New Orleans revoked the American right of deposit. In Kentucky, Governor Garrard appealed to the legislature, in consequence of which the general assembly adopted resolutions requesting the National Government to take immediate action to reopen the river to free trade.

In 1803, when the Louisiana Purchase was completed, the joy of Kentuckians was marred by the refusal of Spain to recognize the agreement with France. Governor Garrard called for 4,000 Kentucky volunteers to drive Spain out of Louisiana, but when the troops assembled, Spain withdrew peaceably. Kentucky Republicanism was now at flood tide. Christopher Greenup, a hardy Revolutionary War soldier, Indian fighter, and Virginian, was elected Governor in 1804. In the middle of his term Aaron Burr came West and involved many prominent citizens in his western conspiracy. Most persistent of Burr's accusers was the Federalist district attorney, Joseph Hamilton Daviess. It was he who hauled the culprit into court to try him on a charge of treason. This trial was to play an important role in local politics, for several prominent state and federal officials were involved. Many local politicians feared that under the careful scrutiny of Daviess their political futures would be ruined. Failure to convict Burr was a disappointment to the Kentucky Federalists, since they were unable to embarrass the Republicans, and they turned to other accusations of treason. At Frankfort, J. M. Street, Federalist editor of the *Western World,* started an editorial inquisition of prominent Republicans whom he linked with the Spanish conspiracy, 1795–1797.

When he published his charges, Republicans threatened to lock him in jail, and had it not been for the intercession of Humphrey Marshall and Joseph Hamilton Daviess, they would have succeeded.

Investigation of Burr's conspiracy in 1805 caused a general hunt for traitors in Kentucky. In that year John Pope and Samuel McKee introduced in the legislature a resolution to investigate the conduct of James Sebastian, a member of the Court of Appeals. Sebastian was charged with receiving a pension of $2,000 per year, from 1796 to 1806,

for negotiating commercial privileges for Spain and final separation of
Kentucky from the Union. Sebastian was entangled in the Spanish
conspiracy as early as 1795, but apparently he did not confide in other
Kentuckians until 1797. In that year he received a letter from Baron
de Carondelet of New Orleans. This letter was brought to Kentucky
by Thomas Power, a former Kentuckian, but he found Sebastian afraid
to proceed until he had consulted some of his friends. The letter was
turned over to George Nicholas, Harry Innes, and William Murray, a
Federalist. Carondelet and his Spanish agent, Colonel Gayoso, were
demanding action, but Sebastian was afraid to enter further into the
plot. Nicholas and Innes answered Carondelet's letter by refusing the
aid of Kentucky in his scheme. Instead of returning directly to Louisiana, Thomas Power, knowing the contents of the Kentuckian's letters,
went to Detroit to interview General James Wilkinson. Since, in the
meantime, news of the Spanish conspiracy had reached the national
administration, President Adams instructed Wilkinson to arrest Power
when he reached Detroit. Wilkinson knew, however, that if he arrested Power there would be an investigation in which many prominent westerners, including himself, might be implicated. When the
Spanish agent appeared at Detroit, he was sent immediately, under the
watchful eye of a captain of the United States Army, to New Madrid.
Failure of Wilkinson to arrest Power put an end, for the time being,
to the Spanish plot. When partisan politics were hottest in 1806, this
plot was again dragged out for public investigation. It was found that
even at that late date Sebastian was receiving his annual pension of
$2,000 and that he had definitely violated every oath he had taken to
Kentucky. Judge Sebastian resigned at once, but in doing so he left
several of his friends incriminated in the plot. One was Judge Innes
of the Federal District Court of Kentucky. Innes was innocent of any
complicity in the crime, but at the same time he testified to the legislative committee that he knew all of the details of the Spanish proposals
from 1797 to 1802. He informed his questioners that he would have
reported this conspiracy had it not been that John Adams was President, a fact that made him afraid of appearing to court favor with the
national administration. He said, too, that since Adams was an easterner, he was afraid that he would call out the militia, to subject the
West to militia rule.

While Judge Innes was being charged in 1806 with conspiracy and treason, Humphrey Marshall defeated the Republican candidate, John M. Scott, for the office of representative in Franklin County. As a member-elect of the general assembly, Marshall, assisted by Street's editorials, paved the way for a frontal attack upon the Republicans by publicizing the Spanish conspiracy. When the issue came before the legislature in the form of a resolution drafted by Marshall, Henry Clay, speaker of the house, surrendered the chair temporarily to introduce counter-resolutions from the floor. Marshall had condemned President Jefferson and was quick to resort to personalities. Soon he and Clay were abusing each other in strong terms. This personal abuse, plus Marshall's attack upon the Republicans generally, caused Clay to send a challenge to a duel. Marshall accepted, and the duel was fought near Evansville, Indiana. Clay was shot through the leg. Judge Innes was greatly disturbed over the charges of his connection with the conspiracy and started a personal investigation among his friends to determine their reactions. He appealed to prominent Kentuckians who replied that they believed Innes innocent. Innes now became bolder in his defense. Republicans combated the charges of Marshall and Street, and Marshall, in turn, was accused of irregular conduct in office. The general assembly dropped the Innes charge by a vote of 30 to 23, but on March 21, 1808, the resolutions were sent to the United States Congress, and the issue of Judge Innes' innocence or guilt was thus transferred to that body. After considerable examination and much debate, the lower House of Congress evaded a decision by voting 48 to 25 for commitment, and the case was never brought from the committee. This investigation had a great effect upon Kentucky Republicans. They became ultra-patriots, and within a short time completely dominated state politics. Humphrey Marshall and his Federalist cohorts did not relent, however, in their efforts to strengthen their party. When the *Western World* was bankrupted by failure of the Innes investigation, Marshall established the *American Republic,* but by 1814 federalism was a dead issue in Kentucky.

While local political irons were hot in 1808, General Charles Scott, a hardy old Virginia soldier, opposed Colonel John Allen, a member of Burr's counsel, for the governorship. General Scott was victorious.

After 1808 there was little two-party rivalry in Kentucky until the formation of the Jackson Party after 1824. Candidates, most of them Revolutionary War soldiers, opposed each other within the Republican ranks and on personal grounds. The political campaigns, 1808–1828, were almost wholly factional affairs for voters and candidates. Candidates were not supposed to engage in the undignified practice of seeking office but were to abide by the decision of the people. This seldom was the case, however, for candidates openly sought election by financing fish fries, barbecues, and public meetings at which candidates were heckled and questioned as to their stand on local issues. For those who were unable to "get at" the candidates in their public appearances, there were the newspapers. Each election year saw the publication of long lists of questions addressed to candidates for county and state offices, sometimes by their friends to give them a chance to make their views known; and sometimes by opponents in order to ask embarrassing questions.

At the polls, candidates lined up to shake hands with voters and to dispense good cheer from jugs and barrels, or to offer petty bribes. After 1799, voting was by *viva voce,* and the elections lasted three days. During the first two days, the polls were quiet, except for the activities of the candidates. On the third day, there was usually great excitement. Each candidate attempted to keep his name ahead on the voting list by supplying an abundance of free liquor. A witness to one of these elections has left a vivid description of the affair, when a native son of Mason County was opposed for the state legislature by "a New Englander by birth, a college learnt dandy schoolmaster, who carries his sheepskin in a tea cannister; an adventurer from the land of 'blue lights' and 'Hartford Conventions,' one of that race of immaculate patriots, where 'constitutional scruples' wouldn't permit them to cross the line in the late war to whip the British. Pretty Yankee notions these; but he'd peddle no more of them; and calling to all true sons of Kentucky to come to the trough and 'liquor,' he leaped down from his rostrum; the heads of liquor barrels were immediately knocked out, and amid clamorous shouts of 'huzza for Old Kentucky, Down with the Yankees,' the inspiring fluid quickly disappeared." Fortescue Cuming, a timid British traveler, was afraid to pass through Nicholasville on a third election day for fear the large crowd assembled at the courthouse would make him engage some drunken bully "rough and tumble."

Before the end of Governor Scott's administration, Kentucky was in a general state of excitement over the impending crisis with England. Two native sons, Henry Clay and Richard M. Johnson, were elected to Congress in 1810 because they demanded war with England and expansion of American territory. Even Joseph Hamilton Daviess, the Federalist district attorney who had hailed Burr into court, favored war. In fact, in 1811, he lost his life in the Indian Battle of Tippecanoe. Governor Scott was slow to act. He had grown weary in both military and civil service and was ready to retire. Since Kentucky needed a trusted soldier as Governor, General Shelby became a candidate. Shelby's name was magic to a militantly inclined constituency, for where Scott had been slow to act, Kentuckians believed Shelby would succeed. In this they were not disappointed, for the new Governor supported every demand of the people, and before the War of 1812 was over in the Northwest, he had assumed personal leadership of a division of Kentucky militia.

In 1816, when the war was at an end and the energy of Kentucky was turned toward commercial development of the state, Governor Shelby was allowed to retire to his home, Traveler's Rest. His successor was George Madison, a highly respected Revolutionary soldier from the Virginia Line. Elected with him as Lieutenant Governor was Gabriel Slaughter, Virginian, and veteran of the Battle of New Orleans. Few Kentucky Governors have been as popular as was George Madison; he had served in the Revolutionary War and in the St. Clair campaign. He had won distinction in the War of 1812 and had been taken prisoner in the Raisin River Campaign. For twenty years he had served Kentucky as secretary of state, and by every standard of measurement he promised to make a splendid Governor.

Before he could organize his government, however, he died in office, and immediately the question was raised whether Gabriel Slaughter would become "Governor" or "Acting Governor." Before this question could be settled, Slaughter had assumed duties as Governor, in fact, if not in title. Because of his strong factionalism, he made the mistake of replacing Charles Todd, secretary of state, with the unpopu-

lar John Pope. Pope, it will be remembered, was burned in effigy when
he voted against declaring war in 1812. On the other hand, Charles
Todd had made a mistake when he wrote Slaughter a "courtesy" letter
in which he agreed to step aside if the Governor so desired. He had
worded his letter, as he thought, so carefully that Slaughter could not
possibly construe it as a resignation. However, the chief executive accepted this letter as a resignation. Slaughter's second antagonizing
move was the appointment of Martin D. Hardin, former secretary of
state, to the United States Senate to fill out the unexpired term of
William T. Barry. When the general assembly met in 1817, it was influenced by pro-Slaughter editorials of the *Western Monitor* to confirm
Pope's appointment. This increased popular Republican wrath, and
again the question was raised as to the status of Slaughter; was he
"Governor" or "Acting Governor"? Led by John C. Breckinridge, a
large number of legislators opposed to Slaughter demanded a new election to select a Governor to complete the unexpired term. This move
failed, but in the election of legislators in August, 1817, candidates were
questioned as to their stand on the issue. With the popular vote favoring a called election, possibly to select a new Governor, candidates opposing the Lieutenant Governor had little difficulty in getting themselves elected. The *Kentucky Gazette,* the *Palladium,* the *Argus of
Western America,* and the *Kentucky Reporter* contained long addresses
favoring a new election, while the *Commentator* and the *Western
Monitor* favored Slaughter's cause. Prominent Republicans favoring
a new election were John C. Breckinridge, John Jordan Crittenden,
William T. Barry, Jesse Bledsoe, and Matthew Lyon. Henry Clay discreetly kept himself out of this politically dangerous dispute, even
though he entertained a bitter hatred for John Pope.

The argument over the Slaughter election led to extreme views on
the question at issue. Critics were saying before 1820 that even constitutional government was not above the control of the "people." The
election of new representatives in 1817 afforded the "people" an excellent chance to deal in extremes. "New Election" partisans elected a
majority in the house and one fourth of the members of the senate.
On August 18, 1817, the lower branch of the general assembly voted
56 to 30 to hold a new gubernatorial election, but the bill was defeated
in the more conservative senate. Public sentiment was bitter toward

the upper house for thwarting the will of the people. Slaughter remained in office, but the lower branch of the assembly insisted that his title should be "Lieutenant and Acting Governor." This affair had two definite effects on Kentucky politics: it created a strong spirit of factionalism and a popular belief that the constitutional offices were within the immediate control of the electorate.

Within a year after the decision of Slaughter's succession to the governorship was made, the general assembly was faced with the question of granting "a stay of execution" on private debts. Many people believed that Kentuckians had involved themselves so deeply in debt that the only possible solution would be a moratorium until the currency could be stabilized. Again the people were insistent upon a public hearing, even to the extent of circumventing the constitution and reorganizing the court of appeals. The election of 1820 was hotly contested by four candidates for Governor: General John Adair, Revolutionary War veteran, William Logan, Joseph Desha, and Anthony Butler. Candidates for Lieutenant Governor were William T. Barry and William B. Blackburn. The Slaughter partisans raised the election issue of 1817, but their opponents were indifferent to the question. There followed a hot contest, for some of the voters hoped to vindicate the mistreatment of Governor Slaughter. "Relief" legislation was the hue and cry generally. General John Adair won the election, largely because he was a Revolutionary veteran. He had led the Kentucky troops at New Orleans and later had defended them against General Jackson's charges of cowardice. Most important of all, however, was the fact that Adair favored relief. William T. Barry, a relief partisan, won election as Lieutenant Governor. During his four years as Governor, Adair was faced with the complete financial and political disorganization of Kentucky. As chief executive he was only moderately successful. He was unable to effect a settlement of the relief issue; instead he allowed hotheaded partisans virtually to destroy the constitution by reorganizing the court.

By 1824 Kentucky was in a state of moral, political, and financial panic. That year three candidates sought election as Governor: Joseph Desha, Christopher Tompkins, and William Russell. Candidates for Lieutenant Governor were William B. Blackburn and Robert McAfee. In the campaign Desha and Russell appealed to the mass of voters by advocating complete relief from debts. The campaign was vigorous and personal; Desha offered his hearers "Liberty or Slavery." Since economic conditions had undergone no significant changes for the better since 1820, nearly every Kentuckian was hopelessly in debt and was seeking a permanent moratorium to relieve him of his burden. Desha placed much of the blame for the conditions of Kentucky finances at the door of the state's courts and said he favored judges who would render "an honest opinion." [1] In the election Desha and McAfee won by comfortable majorities. This was the first time in Kentucky history that a Governor was not a veteran of the Revolutionary Army. Governor Desha was born in 1768, too young to participate in the war with England, but he later served with Anthony Wayne on the Ohio frontier.

Both the Governor and the legislature accepted the returns of the election in 1824 as the dictate of the people to grant relief. Thus the first two years of Desha's administration were marked by strife over the reorganization of the courts. The "Old Court" was supplanted by the "New Court," after the passage of a series of irregular acts through the general assembly.[2] At last the people were in power, but within four years they realized they had blundered, for they had created an ineffective system of courts. Before 1828 a new force was at work in state politics. Kentucky's political groups were undergoing fundamental changes. Those partisans who between 1820 and 1826 called themselves "relief" or "nonrelief" became either Jacksonian Democrats or Whigs.

Henry Clay had fast friends and bitter enemies in Kentucky. When he disobeyed the instructions of the relief legislature in 1824 to support John Quincy Adams for President, he paved the way for the formation of two parties in his home state. Between 1824 and 1828, General Andrew Jackson became increasingly popular in Kentucky. The ancient

---

[1] On February 11, 1820, the general assembly passed an act permitting debtors to endorse their notes with the words "Notes of the Bank of Kentucky or its branches will be accepted in discharge of this execution." If the plaintiff refused to accept this endorsement, the defendant could replevy for two years. In 1822 the constitutionality of the replevin act was tested in the Bourbon Circuit Court in the case, Williams *vs.* Blair, in which Judge James Clark held the act unconstitutional. In October, 1823, the court of appeals affirmed the decision in defiance of the legislature, and the court was reorganized.

[2] The original court was called the "Old Court." The reorganized court was called "The New Court."

feud between him and John Adair was forgotten by many voters, and Jackson dinners, picnics, and barbecues became frequent. At public gatherings the Jacksonian cause was nearly always pushed. A Jacksonian party was in the advanced stages of organization by 1828, and William T. Barry and John Breathitt was nominated for Governor and Lieutenant Governor on its ticket. The Clay-Adams supporters were equally active in organizing their forces and nominated Thomas (Stonehammer) Metcalfe and Joseph R. Underwood. Metcalfe, a stonemason by trade, had served in the War of 1812 and was a "man of the people" who had acquired considerable political experience. In the campaign he quietly cautioned the people against the dangers of relief legislation and advised that the Old Court be reinstated. Barry appealed to New Court partisans, but personally he was not popular with the voters. The Kentucky voters elected Metcalfe by a majority of 709 votes but defeated his running mate by a larger majority. Conflict between the two parties in the administration and in the legislature was inevitable. Upon assuming the governorship, Metcalfe appointed anti-Jacksonians to office. In the senate the Clay partisans were in the majority, a factor which gave Clay strong state support for his national policies.

In 1832 Kentucky gave its support to the presidential candidacy of its favorite son, Henry Clay. The state election was held before the general election in November, but in this test of strength the Whigs lost ground, for their candidate, Richard A. Buckner, was defeated by John Breathitt. Again party lines were broken, for Breathitt won by a majority of 1,242 votes, while James A. Morehead, Whig candidate for Lieutenant Governor, defeated his opponent by 5,582 votes. Breathitt's election was due largely to his personal popularity. In November, General Jackson lost Kentucky to Henry Clay, although he had strong support in the state and would have defeated any other opponent. Jackson became unpopular for a time because of his veto of the Maysville Road Bill, but his western origin was sufficient reason for prompt forgiveness.

In Kentucky politics the Whig Party enjoyed success from 1834 to 1850. Governor Breathitt died in office in the second year of his administration, and James Morehead succeeded to the governorship. He was the first native born son to become Governor. After his promotion to the governorship, the senate selected James Guthrie, a Democrat, as its president. After the local elections in 1835, Whig members of the legislature contended that Guthrie's term of office was for 1834 only. This dispute was bitter, because partisan politics flared up again. In 1836 James A. Clarke and Charles A. Wickliffe, Whigs, defeated Matthew Flournoy and Elijah Hise in the gubernatorial race. This was the first election since 1792 in which there was not a split partisan vote between the candidates running for Governor and Lieutenant Governor.

During the long period of Whig rule, Kentucky made definite material and cultural progress. In 1840 the state ranked high in agricultural production, especially in tobacco and hemp. The Kentucky Agricultural Society was organized in 1842, and thousands of dollars were spent improving the breeds of livestock. Kentucky's trade with the Lower South flourished. Louisville became an important southern city, and Lexington was connected with the Ohio River by rail. Paris, Harrodsburg, Russellville, Covington, Danville, Henderson, Paducah, and Bowling Green grew into towns of importance. Railroads and highways were projected in many sections of the state to open isolated communities to trade. While Kentucky was making material progress, the subject of public education was being agitated. By the early forties this movement had secured partial political support. Public support of cultural institutions, however, was slow. State administrations were extremely shortsighted, and never were election issues based upon general social improvement.

From 1792 to 1850 there were opposing political groups in Kentucky. After 1834 the Whigs were in power, but Kentucky's ante bellum politics remained largely factional. Personalities played an important part in elections. The only real political bitterness in Kentucky before 1850, however, was due to the Innes affair, the Slaughter dispute, and to the Old Court-New Court struggle. Generally, early Kentucky Governors were men of ability and were representative of the state's political talent. The same cannot be said for many members of the general assembly or the county officials of this period. Political patronage, personal relief (granting of titles to state lands or tax rebates), and personal legislation (divorces, changing of names, and granting of pardons) consumed a large part of the legislature's time. Representatives were selected in most cases for their personal popularity rather than for their legislative ability.

CHAPTER XVI

Kentucky Shares a Nation's Troubles

L ITTLE did western Americans realize, in 1803, that in their ardor to secure complete control of the Mississippi River they would complicate foreign relations of their government for years to come. When the astute French ministers, Talleyrand and Marbois, followed Napoleon's suggestion, "to create an obscurity" in the title of the Louisiana Purchase, they opened the way to future bloodshed and sectional bitterness. Had Talleyrand not slyly concealed a map of the Louisiana Purchase when American agents inquired as to the extent of their newly acquired territory, they might never have carried out his advice, "You have made a noble bargain for yourselves, and I suppose you will make the most of it."

Thus for the next forty-five years the Americans were forced to cast about in confusion in an attempt to establish their southwestern boundary. This situation left southern politicians in hot water from the Florida Treaty of 1819 to the Treaty of Guadeloupe Hidalgo of 1848. Annually there appeared in Congress some question relating to the status of the southwestern territory. Such was the importance of the Texas territory that conservative John Quincy Adams, while Secretary of State under President Monroe, tried unsuccessfully to purchase Texas immediately after concluding his Florida negotiations.

Since the whole American frontier was yearly being pushed westward, it was natural that the Sabine River should soon become the frontier line of settlement in the Southwest. So populous was the Sabine region that pioneers began to wonder about the broad expanse of unsurveyed and unclaimed lands to the west. Apparently neither the United States nor Mexico exercised any considerable control over Texas, and certainly neither showed excessive anxiety over its possession. Pioneers who were searching for new cotton lands were anxious to avail themselves of this rich territory and were quick to take advantage of the Mexican Government's offer (whether authoritative or not) of rich land bounties for bringing in settlers. So anxious were these Protestant American settlers that they even agreed to accept the doctrines of the Roman Church *in toto*. Moses Austin, a migrating soldier of fortune and cotton planter, received approximately 4,500 acres for each individual he brought to his rapidly growing colony. Thousands of acres of Texas land were promptly given away, and other thousands of fertile acres were sold by the Mexican Government at the low price of twelve and a half cents per acre.

This activity in the southwest had a very definite effect upon Kentucky. As early as 1825 there was a "Texas Emigration Society" in Lexington through whose influence many settlers were sent to the Southwest. So enthusiastic were many Kentuckians over Texas that women volunteers were collected and sent to the Southwest to become wives of adventurous single males who had moved there from Kentucky. Another explanation of the relationship between the Kentuckians and the Texas pioneers was the friendship which existed between the Hawkins and Austin families. This friendship accounts for Stephen A. Austin's attendance at Transylvania, and, later (1836), his request for Kentucky volunteers.

Kentuckians were traditionally land hungry and adventurous. Added to these motivating desires was the question of profiting from slavery expansion and cotton culture. Cotton planting was more profitable generally than grain and livestock growing, since this system of agriculture was ideally adapted to slave labor. Since Kentucky abolitionists and emancipationists were creating a sentiment of opposition to slavery, this alone was sufficient reason for Texas' popularity. Thus, by 1844, a large percentage of the 50,000 American settlers in Texas were Kentuckians. When Texas fought her war of independence against Mexico, Albert Sidney Johnston, Felix Huston, and other Kentucky officers led divisions of the rebel army.

A treaty of annexation was signed by the United States Government and the Republic of Texas in 1844, but the United States Senate refused to ratify it. Before a joint resolution to reconsider annexation could be prepared, the presidential election of 1844 was at hand. Prior to the nominating conventions of the Whig and Democratic Parties, it was generally believed that Henry Clay and Martin Van Buren would be nominated. No one was surer of this than Martin Van Buren. As a prelude to his nomination he went to Nashville to visit his aged political preceptor, Andrew Jackson. While en route, he stopped in Lexington to discuss with Clay the approaching campaign. In view of the fact that both men felt certain of their nominations, they probably proceeded to map out the course of their campaigns. Both were agreed that the Texas question should not be a factor but that if the issue were forced, they would mutually oppose annexation. With this agreement in mind, both Clay and Van Buren proceeded to commit political folly. It seems indeed strange at this date that Henry Clay should have showed so little political acumen. For more than two decades the South had grown increasingly conscious of its minority position, and its political leaders were always ready to take advantage of any opportunity to maintain a balance of sectional powers by admitting new southern states. Apparently indifferent to this fact, Henry Clay proceeded to make public his *Raleigh Letter* in the *National Intelligencer,* April 27, 1844, in which he stated his opposition to the annexation of Texas on the grounds that it would cause a needless war with Mexico. Doubtless this view was a sane one from a humane standpoint, but politically it unmasked Clay's stand on Texas prior to the Whig convention. Van Buren showed as little understanding of the political situation in the publication of his views of the Texas question the same day in the *Globe.*

Neither Clay nor Van Buren had considered sufficiently the political shrewdness of the Democrats. A year before the campaign opened, Democrats opposed to Van Buren and under the leadership of the shrewd "Yankee" politician, Robert J. Walker, of Mississippi, had frightened the aged ex-President, Andrew Jackson, into believing that the British Government was preparing to annex Texas and free its slaves. Immediately this argument struck a responsive chord in Jackson, who from childhood had hated the British. With the possibility of losing Texas haunting his thought, the ex-President was easily persuaded by the anti-Van Burenites to write a letter favoring immediate annexation of Texas by the United States.

General Jackson's letter remained a secret for almost a year, but when Van Buren made known his stand in the *Globe* in April, the Jackson letter was published. This communication was published under a current date and bore every earmark of having been inspired by Jackson's close friend and neighbor, William B. Lewis. Van Buren's chances for nomination were then blasted. Robert J. Walker of Mississippi was successful in getting James K. Polk, a Southerner and large slaveholder, nominated as the Democratic candidate for President. Polk's candidacy for nomination was not that of a "dark horse," for, doubtless, Walker had long groomed this Tennessee slaveholder for the place.[1]

Henry Clay was the choice of the Whig convention by acclamation, but, unfortunately, he was to suffer many anxious hours in the campaign. First of all, his stand on the Texas question was wholly inconsistent with his stand in 1819; for this reason he alienated much of the South's affection. Added to this disturbing factor was the support of his distant cousin and friend, Cassius Marcellus Clay. Since the latter was a known emancipationist, his relation with Henry Clay was falsely represented in the lower slave states as his being a son, a brother, an uncle. Sometimes even their own personalities were confused. In the antislavery territory Clay was accused of being a slaveholder, and in the South, of being an abolitionist. Never has a presidential candidate found himself between two hotter fires. Clay decided to restate his position. To the abolitionists Clay made it clear that their views were not his views, their cause not his cause; and to the Southerners he explained that their views on annexation did not agree with his—valid reason for the well known Clay legend, "I would rather be right than president."

When election returns came into Lexington in November, 1844, it was learned that Clay had carried Kentucky, but only by a majority of 10,000 votes, much less than that given William Henry Harrison four years before. Nationally, Clay's support was strong, but he lost New York and the election. Rejoicing over the Polk election was in evidence at every turn in Lexington. Clay supporters accused Polk's men of placing cannon where they might best be heard by the heavy-hearted Whig leader at his Ashland estate. Kentucky's support for Henry Clay in 1844 was nothing more than loyalty for a beloved son and the Whig

---

[1] The Sanders papers in the possession of Miss Annie V. Parker at Ghent, Kentucky, contain numerous references to a secret meeting held in a tailor's shop at Ghent, in February, 1844. The chief promoter of this secret conclave was George Nicholas Sanders, who wished to insure the defeat of Van Buren at the Democratic Convention. In order to do this, the Ghent Democrats pledged their support to James K. Polk. Whether or not the Sanders story is true, Jackson stood by his letter, and since Polk was acceptable to him, threw his support to his election.

Party. At heart, Kentuckians were extremely slavery-minded and favored annexation of Texas. One has only to read the voluminous *Debates* of the constitutional convention of 1849 to realize just how completely the Kentuckians favored slavery.

"Fifty-four forty or fight!" and "Annex Texas!" were as stirring battle cries as any ever used to drive voters to the polls in Kentucky. "Extend slavery in the South and push the British frontier back in the Northwest" stated ideally the sentiment of Kentucky voters. So excited did southern public sentiment and President John Tyler become that the aged Virginian anticipated what he believed to be President-elect Polk's plans to annex Texas for him. Polk, on assuming the office of President, ordered John Slidell on a special mission into Mexico to settle the southwestern boundary dispute. When Slidell was denied a reception in Mexico, the President sent a more effective messenger in General Zachary Taylor, a Kentuckian by adoption. General Taylor was instructed to invade Texas as far to the southwest as the Rio Grande. This move on the part of the United States brought war with Mexico.

While Polk was engaged in bringing about an effective settlement of the Texas question, his Secretary of State, James Buchanan, was quietly negotiating a treaty with the British Government. Subsequently the boisterous yell of "fifty-four forty or fight!" simmered down to "49 degrees and be satisfied!" Thus the northwestern boundary dispute was settled, but there was heard in Kentucky more than ever the desire to "Annex Texas—all of Texas."

When Zachary Taylor, an adopted son of Kentucky, entered Texas in 1846, the state was represented in the War with Mexico. Local military units volunteered their services, and Colonel Ormsby and his well-drilled Louisville Legion were instructed to report to General Gaines at New Orleans. Colonel William R. McKee and Humphrey Marshall, Jr., held their infantry and cavalry units in readiness. William O. Butler and the "Yale school boy-emancipationist," Cassius M. Clay, volunteered their services. A call for 2,400 Kentucky troops was answered, but when they reached Texas, Cassius M. Clay and thirty Kentucky cavalrymen were captured at Ascension and carried off to Mexico City as prisoners. William R. McKee, Humphrey Marshall, and Jefferson Davis, then of Mississippi, were under the command of

General Taylor. Thus, when the American Army faced Santa Anna's Mexican troops in the Battle of Buena Vista late in February, 1847, there were 2,000 Kentuckians among General Taylor's forces. In this battle many Kentucky volunteers were wounded and killed, one of whom was Henry Clay, Jr., the favorite son of the great Whig Commoner.

The victory in Texas deeply impressed Kentuckians. For years following the return of the volunteers it was sufficient recommendation for an office-seeker to produce evidence that he was one of "Taylor's men" at Buena Vista. So highly did Kentuckians regard the heroes of this struggle that a traditional tale still persists in Anderson County of Cassius M. Clay's emancipation speech in the courthouse at Lawrenceburg under the guardianship of his proslavery comrades in the Mexican War. "Old Zach" or "Old Rough and Ready," as General Taylor was affectionately known to fellow Kentuckians, also basked in the glory of having defeated the one-legged Santa Anna at Buena Vista and of having hoisted the American flag on the banks of the Rio Grande. In 1848, at the Whig convention in Philadelphia, he was nominated as that party's candidate for the presidency. This nomination was at Henry Clay's expense. He returned to Ashland a sadly disappointed man, for this was his last chance to satisfy a life-long ambition. Clay lamented to his political friends that they nominated him only in years when the Whigs could not elect him.

Third Constitution

Constitutional reform was uppermost in Kentucky in 1848. Ever since the framing of the first constitution, there was a periodic demand for a more liberal and satisfactory document, but each time a conservative majority prevented any variation from the established order. In 1837 a movement to call a constitutional convention was defeated by an overwhelming majority, a majority which was stimulated by the fear that a convention might cause serious damage to the state government.

Always Kentucky constitutions have borne earmarks of eccentricity, and Kentuckians have been traditionally slow to make desirable changes. For some unknown reason the commonwealth's citizens have felt that calling a constitutional convention was akin to disloyalty to established government. Especially was this true, in 1848, when the slavery question was violent enough to separate life-long friends. Slave-holders from the beginning were extremely doubtful of the outcome of a constitutional convention, for they were firmly convinced that the movement for constitutional reform had originated in abolition strong-holds outside Kentucky. This was quite easily believed, since news-papers in abolition centers showed more interest in the success of move-ments to call a constitutional convention than did many Kentucky newspapers.

Gradually, however, conditions under the old constitution became so unbearable that local sentiment grew stronger, and many conservatives inclined toward constitutional reforms. Kentucky's legislature, in 1847, voted eighty-one to seventeen in the house, and thirty to eight in the senate in favor of a bill calling for a vote on a constitutional convention. This bill had strong Democratic support despite the reformists' desires to keep the movement as nearly nonpartisan as possible. The majority of the popular vote, in 1847, favored calling a convention, but it was not until August, 1848, that a sufficient majority of 102,000 votes out of a voting strength of 141,000 clearly indicated to what extent public sentiment had shifted in favor of the convention.

Between the popular election in August, 1848, and the election of delegates to the convention in 1849, newspapers and politicians were busily engaged in a general discussion of needed reforms. Many critics of the call could find no reasonable ground whatever for a new consti-tution; they were even willing to accept Kentucky's floating debt rather than submit to change. Friends of the old constitution felt that they were cutting the anchor rope and setting Kentucky's ship of state afloat in a stormy sea headed for certain disaster. Perhaps these patriots had allowed their zeal for the stability of the National Constitution to over-shadow their views of the state document. During the heated discus-sion over the change of government two newspapers came into exist-ence: one, the *Convention,* defending the liberal stand; the other, the *Examiner,* objecting to any proposed changes. All of this discussion had a very definite effect upon the public mind. By the time the con-stitutional convention met at Frankfort on October 1, 1849, almost every man, woman, and child in Kentucky had become concerned with gov-ernmental reform.

Many of the strong constitutional-reformists busied themselves with mapping out a course of change. Slavery, doubtless, was the most fruitful source of disturbance, for no one in Kentucky, with the exception of a few abolitionists and emancipationists, wished to interfere with it in any way. However, the apprehension of the proslavery group was sufficient to cause serious difficulty. Rights of slaveholders were safeguarded in that every resolution reaching the convention was carefully scrutinized to see that it bore no obscure or implied meaning which might act as a boomerang to slavery.

Slavery, however, did not monopolize the limelight, for there were other reforms of a far-reaching nature, such as the election of local officials by popular vote under the constitution adopted in 1799. Judges of all the courts, justices of the peace, and constables secured their offices by popular election. The elections to choose local and state officers, however, were always irregular in both method and outcome. Honest Kentucky voters were never certain that they could get their will, for the polls remained open for three or four days, so that it was possible for one man, by change of name and dress, to vote several times without arousing the suspicions of "gullible" election officers. By this method of holding popular elections, strongly entrenched candidates could frequently determine the outcome. In many communities the holding of public office became virtually the monopoly of a hierarchy. Candidates could control the outcome of elections by watching the results near the close of the election day, and, by rushing in sufficient votes, whether regular or not, could insure themselves a majority. Delegates to the constitutional convention were elected with this as an issue. A majority of the citizens of Kentucky were anxious for election reform which would check the unscruplous practices which had been carried on under the second constitution.

There was a distinct need for reapportionment of representatives. For instance, Jefferson County, including the City of Louisville, was more populous than any other in the state, and justly this county deserved to be more adequately represented in the general assembly. When this question came to the front, it was unfairly linked with abolition. Since Louisville was asking for independent representation, proslavery partisans reasoned that this urban center was attempting to abolish slavery through its foreign (German) population. The old constitution had served as a guardian of slavery, and for this reason

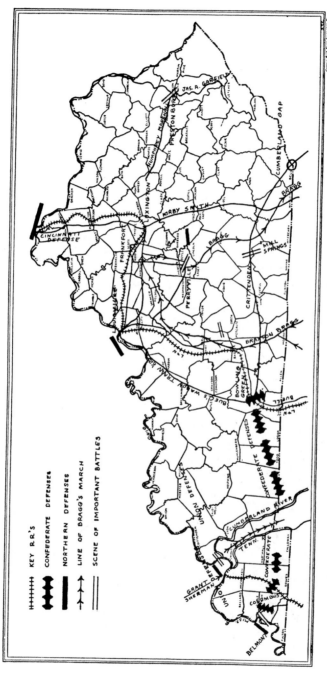

Campaigns of the Civil War in Kentucky

The Old Lexington Association Race Track in Lexington

Cumberland Falls

A One-Room School House in Anderson County

The University of Kentucky Library

Setting Tobacco on a Modern Farm

A Burley Tobacco Sales Floor

alone its framers took every precaution to prevent an easy amendment of the document.

No provision to place a check on the state's expenditures had been made in the first two constitutions. The citizens' only control over the state's financial transactions was through the legislature's prerogative of appropriating funds to various state departments. No sinking fund was provided, and the state's debt was a floating one. For this reason, Kentucky's credit was constantly fluctuating.

Taking advantage of numerous implied powers in the original constitutions, Kentucky's legislatures wandered off into a morass of petty private legislation, which seldom benefited more than two or three individuals. Often out of 500 bills introduced at a single session of the general assembly, not more than a dozen had sufficient scope to affect the state at large. For instance, divorces were freely granted by legislative acts and consumed the whole body's time. At other times the practice of granting divorces became notorious, when a number of cases were combined in a single omnibus bill and voted upon as a group. Personal names were changed by legislative acts, and as one local commentator observed, there were so many "name changing" laws, it was feared that Kentuckians would not know the names of their closest friends. Hezekiah Niles, editor of *Niles' Register,* found it an amusing sport to ridicule the purposeless state of affairs in the legislatures of Kentucky.

On Monday, October 1, 1849, the elected delegates to the constitutional convention assembled in the capitol building at Frankfort to frame Kentucky's third constitution. Prominent among the men present were James Guthrie from Jefferson County, later Secretary of the Treasury under Franklin Pierce, Robert N. Wickliffe of Fayette, Kentucky's largest slaveholder, Ben Hardin of Nelson, Garrett Davis of Bourbon, Charles Wickliffe of Nelson, and Archibald Dixon of Henderson County. However, it is significant that certain Kentucky worthies were conspicuously absent from this convention. Among these were Henry Clay, John J. Crittenden, Thomas F. Marshall, Charles Morehead, Robert J. Breckinridge, John C. Breckinridge, and Orlando Brown, all of whom would have lent dignity to the assembly.

James Guthrie was elected speaker of the convention over Archibald Dixon by a vote of fifty to forty-three. Ira Root and Archibald Dixon promptly introduced resolutions to elect the judges of all the courts by popular vote, to prohibit dueling, and to limit the state officials' powers to create debt. John Hargis of Breathitt County proposed a preamble and set of resolutions which he hoped would roughly outline the final draft of the new constitution. Thus, with immediate introduction of numerous other resolutions, the debates were begun.

They lasted from October 1 to December 21, and the published proceedings compose a volume of 1,129 pages of small legal type. Never before had so many vital questions attracted the attention of Kentucky citizens. They included representation; election of local officers, including judges of the courts; prohibition of dueling; curbing the legislature's power of enacting private legislation and creating state debt; reapportioning representation; giving constitutional sanction to public education; once again safeguarding slavery; and, lastly, voicing Kentucky's sentiment on "True Americanism."

December 21, 1849, the delegation assembled for the last time at the capitol to view its finished task. At 7 A.M. that morning the members affixed their signatures to the "engrossed" constitution (which was not regularly engrossed on parchment, and which is not now in existence).

Delegates returned to their homes with varied sentiments. Members of the general assembly were to be elected biennially by a popular vote, and the meetings of the legislature were to be called biennially instead of annually as before. All public officials (state and local) were to be elected by popular vote on the first Monday in August between the hours of 6 A.M. and 7 P.M. Louisville was granted special representation, while some of the less populous counties were forced to combine with other counties to secure representation. Representation was to be reapportioned following each decennial census, but the number of senatorial seats was fixed at thirty-eight. Judges of all the Kentucky courts were to be elected; judges of the court of appeals for a term of eight, circuit judges for six, and county judges for four years. Local officers, such as sheriffs, justices of the peace, and constables, were to be elected by a popular vote for terms of four years. Slavery was safeguarded with practically the original provisions of the first two constitutions.

Public education for the first time in Kentucky's constitutional history was given recognition. An educational fund of $1,227,168.42 was established to be held inviolate for support of schools. Special funds arising from taxation were likewise to be applied to educational purposes, and without equivocation. Each county was guaranteed an equitable amount of the accumulated fund, and a superintendent of public instruction was to be elected by popular vote for a term of four years. Thus was born Kentucky's state-supported public school system.

In spite of all of the conservatives' fears and predictions, the newly framed constitution did not make any startling innovations. Practically all the original conservative handicaps were brought over bodily from earlier documents. Provisions for amendment of the new constitution were transferred almost without change. Amendment still remained virtually an impossibility, for by the time an election was ordered to secure the will of the people so much time was consumed that the reason for amendment might become obscure. The process of amendment took from four to fifteen years. Proslavery forces prohibited ministers of the gospel from holding office as members of the Assembly or as Governor of the state.

In attempting to abolish the evil and silly practice of dueling, reformists were successful in getting delegates to the constitutional convention to make a move in the right direction. A clause was inserted in this new document requiring that every officeholder take an oath that he would not engage in a duel either as a challenger or as a second in or out of the State of Kentucky during his tenure of office. Thus the first effective check was placed upon dueling in Kentucky.

The right to vote has yielded doubtful results in Kentucky. Kentucky was second among the states to make suffrage universal, but unfortunately many corrupt practices grew out of this generosity. Suffrage under the third constitution was free to all white males meeting citizenship qualifications, and elections were to be held for one day only, when voting was to be *viva voce* (or by word of mouth). This restriction, however, was not a new one, for the second constitution had a like provision, but by careless and corrupt methods of holding elections voting was performed at times by writing candidates' names on pieces of paper.

When the new constitution was submitted to the people, Whig leaders, including Garrett Davis, John Helm, and Thomas Marshall, were bitterly opposed to its adoption. On the other hand, Democrats were thoroughly of the opinion that the document was a combination of halfway measures and Whiggish obstructions. Kentuckians, generally, were showered from all sides with speeches and pamphlets proclaiming the virtues of the constitution, while an equal amount of literature denounced it as a dangerous threat to sacred democratic liberties. Despite these bitter arguments and pronounced fears, the new constitution was adopted by a 6,000 majority.

While Kentucky's fathers wrestled with constitutional questions which arose at Frankfort in 1849, gold was discovered at Sutter's Mill in California, and there followed an unprecedented rush of adventurers and settlers across the continent. Adventurous Kentuckians were much interested in this new development, and many native sons, like their fathers before them, heeded the call of the West. Little did constitutional delegates at Frankfort, or native sons who rushed to the California gold fields, realize that this westward movement would soon reopen a national discussion of slavery and slavery extension. Hardly had the first settlers reached their new home when the problem of maintaining law and order forcibly presented itself. President Taylor and his successor, Millard Fillmore, were anxious to bring this territory into the Union as a state and to avoid a hostile outbreak there. On the other hand, to admit California was once again to raise the head of that ancient and stalking specter, slavery extension. In 1850 the Kentucky legislature had definitely committed the state to the support of slavery and had adopted a resolution denouncing abolition, but the anti-importation law of 1833 was repealed, permitting Kentuckians to bring slaves from outside the state for sale in local slave markets. Thus Kentucky became, as Henry Clay had prophesied in 1829, a breeding and market center for the Lower South.

After the introduction of the California question, national politics were in a state of violent upheaval. Uppermost in the minds of national representatives, both northern and southern, was the question of slavery extension. Perhaps at no time in national history has civil strife been more imminent than in 1850. This was a period when national political leadership was changing hands. Where there had been the "Triumvirate," Clay, Webster, and Calhoun, there was now rising into prominence a younger group of extremely ambitious leaders who were less endowed with love for the Union.

Kentucky's legislature was prompt to sense the approaching national crisis and as early as February 1, 1849, elected Henry Clay, over his protest, to the United States Senate. Clay, steeped in love for the Union which dated from his ultra-nationalism days, was willing to adopt any reasonable measure which would insure national peace. But never were Unionists faced with more conflicting political factions, most of which were so strong as to make organization of the lower House of Congress almost impossible. Neither major party, Whig nor Democrat, had a majority, but both felt that to win the organization fight was a matter of life and death.

While politicians were wrangling in Washington, California's lawlessness was rapidly increasing. The burden of maintaining order was a heavy strain upon the National Government, and President Taylor was extremely anxious to be relieved of this responsibility. However, to admit California into the Union was certain to revive dangerous arguments over the slavery issue in the territories. If California were admitted free, the North and the abolitionists would gain. If it were admitted slave, the Southern slaveholders would be the gainers. Above all, moderate conservative Union forces did not wish to see California admitted half free and half slave, for already the national side was pricked beyond endurance with other thorns.

Since a compromise was imperative, both factions turned to Henry Clay to devise some scheme by which a satisfactory solution could be reached. The Kentucky Senator was fortunate in that he could call upon a younger political leader for assistance; Stephen A. Douglas of Illinois, who had proved himself a brilliant Senate debater, was selected as chief counsel. As a manipulator of plans Douglas was even better fitted than as a debater. Through assistance of the able Senator, Henry Clay introduced an eight-point compromise program to the United States Senate on January 29, 1850. Of most importance to Kentucky in this proposal was the federal fugitive slave law, for the state suffered materially from the escape and loss of slaves across the Ohio River into neighboring free states. Perhaps the activities of the underground railroad in spiriting slaves out of the state and the refusal of peace officers in free states to assist in the restoration of this stolen property were more antagonizing than any other features of the antislavery movement. Unmistakably, Kentuckians saw in the escape of their slaves the undercover assistance of hated abolitionists.

Henry Clay's plan was regarded by Southerners, and especially by his fellow Kentuckians, with favor, because it guaranteed that their chattel property would be protected by the National Government. When Clay delivered his speeches on February 5 and 6, 1850, he performed his last public services to save the Union. Daniel Webster of Massachusetts followed with his famous "Seventh of March" speech in which he ably expressed the view of Unionists. He even went so far as to say that he would defend the Union should Massachusetts raise the standard of disunion.

By the adoption of the Compromise of 1850 both the North and South gained, but unhappily neither could enjoy its gain for coveting the powers granted the other. Doubtless the point causing most conflict was the fugitive slave law which guaranteed the Southerners the return of their slaves who had escaped across the Ohio River or to the North. President Fillmore was quick to perceive the dangerous possibilities of the act and had his Attorney General, John J. Crittenden of Kentucky, examine the document carefully before he approved it. Crittenden felt that the compromise would save the Union, or he never would have approved it, for, like Clay, his love for Kentucky and the Union was almost without limit. As Governor of Kentucky during the latter forties, he had repeatedly expressed the hope that his state would never be guilty of slackening national bonds. His message to the Kentucky legislature on December 31, 1849, expressed a belief which every Kentuckian clearly understood, that if Kentucky withdrew from the Union, she stood an excellent chance of losing her place in the trade of the Mississippi Valley. For this reason alone, said Governor Crittenden, it was imperative that Kentuckians maintain peace. Kentucky was represented at several of the southern commercial conventions which were held between 1850 and 1859, but always her delegates played the part of commercial pacificators. Southern trade was too profitable for Kentucky farmers and merchants to lose.

Both national political parties in Kentucky embraced the compromise as the safest and surest method of maintaining the Union. The Democrats voted in their state convention in January, 1851, to stand by the Union until outrages became so oppressive that the state could save herself only by secession. These same sentiments prevailed in the Whig Party.

Before the passage of another year, the "Sage of Ashland" was dead. Henry Clay died in the old National Hotel in Washington, June 29, 1852. At the time of his death he was senior Senator from Kentucky, in which capacity he devoted the last days of his life to the services of his state and his Union. Kentucky and the United States paid reverent homage at the bier of a favorite son who had been a central figure of all the Nation's struggles from the Virginia and Kentucky Resolutions in 1798 to the Compromise of 1850.

Henry Clay's death, followed within five months by that of Daniel Webster, placed the reins of national political leadership in far less experienced hands than those which had formerly directed national affairs. Kentucky's national leadership now rested on the shoulders of John J. Crittenden, John C. Breckinridge, and Archibald Dixon. The ablest of these was Crittenden, who, with all allowance for his leadership and love for both Kentucky and the Union, lacked the natural political talents which had characterized Henry Clay's public career.

Before Clay died, Harriet Beecher Stowe, of Cincinnati, set the world talking about the evils of slavery. She collected her stories which had appeared periodically in the *National Era* to publish them in March, 1852, under the attractive title of *Uncle Tom's Cabin, or Life Among the Lowly*. Material for this book was gathered from all over the South, but it was said that most of it had been gathered during the author's frequent visits to the Kennedy homestead in Garrard County, Kentucky. Thousands of copies of this work were sold, and since many of the scenes of the book were laid along the Ohio River, Kentucky and her slave system stood convicted in Northern public opinion. So bitter was Southern criticism of this book that Mrs. Stowe collected her sources to publish a supplementary text known as *A Key to Uncle Tom's Cabin*. In the North the book, despite its amateurish treatment of slavery, proved an effective organ of public opinion. It affected northern votes at the polls. Northern and northwestern communities bought large issues of the work, but in the South it was banned. Thus, Union sentiment south of the Ohio and Potomac Rivers became more and more lukewarm; Kentuckians who had been ardent Unionists found themselves more indifferent.

Following the upheaval caused by the appearance of *Uncle Tom's Cabin,* Senator Dodge of Iowa presented a bill to the United States

Senate on December 14, 1853, proposing organization of the Nebraska Territory between the western boundaries of Missouri and Iowa and the Rocky Mountains. This move of course aroused slavery forces anew, although the bill itself made no mention of slavery. Senator Douglas of Illinois attached an amendment to the Dodge Bill proposing to leave the slavery settlement to the inhabitants of the territory—or to "popular sovereignty." This application of an ancient democratic principle failed, however, to satisfy Archibald Dixon, junior Senator from Kentucky, for it was obvious that the Missouri Compromise of 1820 would keep southern slaveholders out of Nebraska during the territorial period. Dixon immediately set about making plans to repeal the Missouri Compromise, which prohibited the expansion of slavery north of the 36° 30′ parallel. This activity on the part of the Kentucky Senator resulted in Douglas' preparing and submitting a new bill (but not until he had secured the support of President Pierce and Jefferson Davis, Secretary of War) on January 23, 1854, which proposed to repeal the Missouri agreement. Thus Clay's "dove of peace" suddenly was transformed into a devouring vulture of prejudices, sectionalism, and dissension. So violently opposed were the slaveholders to the Kansas-Nebraska arrangement that the issue remained unsettled until after the Southern States seceded from the Union.

While the country was enraged over the activities of the pro- and anti-slavery groups in the National Congress, the election of 1856 occurred. The Democratic Party nominated as its standard bearers James Buchanan and John C. Breckinridge. John C. Frémont and W. L. Dayton were nominated by the newly organized Republican Party which opposed further slavery extension. Millard Fillmore and Andrew Jackson Donelson were chosen as candidates by the newly organized Native American Party, and by the remnants of the fast disintegrating Whig Party. With a native son in the race, Kentucky supported the Democratic ticket, which was elected. Results of the election of 1856 indicated the course taken by the majority of Kentucky's voters: they were favorably disposed toward slavery and its expansion.

While the Kansas-Nebraska Bill was clouding the national political horizon, local Kentucky politics were in a highly restless state over the activities of the Know Nothing Party. Generally, the Party was opposed to slavery, or at least, it was opposed to making slavery a leading issue, although it had a strong Southern following. Know Nothing leaders diverted the public mind of Kentucky from the slavery issue to the issue of foreigners and Catholics. There were few foreigners in Kentucky, except German and Irish in Louisville, in Covington, and a few other urban centers, but the Catholic population composed a large and stable block of the state's society. Nevertheless, demagogues were able to convince gullible voters that Catholics threatened their freedom. The question of temperance also was mothered under the wing of the Know Nothing Party, with the result that a large vote was captured from the "Unionist" Democratic Party. Locally, the Whiggish Know Nothings were strong. In the August election (1854) of county officials, this party won by a large majority. The next year, in the election of state officers, the Know Nothings were again victorious. This party elected six congressmen to four Democrats, sixty-one representatives to thirty-nine Democrats, also Charles S. Morehead defeated his Democratic opponent, Beverly L. Clarke, for the governorship. At Louisville the two political factions became so highly agitated that there occurred the "Bloody Monday" riot. Reports were spread throughout the wards that Roman Catholic voters were going to cause a disturbance. Twenty-two persons were killed, scores wounded, twenty houses were burned, and hundreds of dollars' worth of property destroyed. Rowdy bands paraded the streets with cannon to set foreigners' houses on fire. It took peace officers all day and night to quiet the mob and to restore order.

Morehead's election was an expression of conservatism in that temperance and salvation of the Union were the issues. Kentuckians were influenced also by the fact that foreigners might come to control local politics and society. John C. Breckinridge, before his election as Vice President of the United States, was a favorite speaker because of his vehement denunciation of Catholics, an excuse which the Know Nothings used to avoid a discussion of national political issues. This party, however, was doomed to an early death, for, in 1857, its candidates for local offices were defeated, and most of its leaders in Kentucky went over to the Democratic Party. The death knell of the local Whig Party was sounded in 1859, when Democratic nominees, Beriah Magoffin and Linn Boyd, defeated Joshua Bell and Alfred Allen for Governor and Lieutenant Governor.

National events brought to the minds of Kentuckians a stern realization that, unless some level-headed leadership could be developed, sectionalism would tear the Union apart. Especially was this true after the Supreme Court handed down the Dred Scott Decision, and the over-zealous John Brown captured the United States arsenal at Harper's Ferry.

Kentuckians watched with much interest the approaching election of 1860, for everyone believed the outcome of this election would determine the future course of the Union. Not only were Kentuckians interested in the election of 1860 from the standpoint of the Union, but a favorite son was ambitious to be the Democratic nominee. Unfortunately, when the Democrats met in convention on April 23, 1860, at Charleston, South Carolina, there was a split in the party over the adoption of the platform, so that no nominations took place. Kentucky supported the southern view, and on June 10, the Richmond Convention selected John C. Breckinridge of Kentucky as Presidential candidate, with Joseph Lane of Oregon for Vice President. A second Democratic convention was held in Baltimore on June 18, which nominated Stephen A. Douglas and Herschel V. Johnson. Meanwhile another native son was nominated for the Presidency, for the Republican convention in Chicago selected Abraham Lincoln and Hannibal Hamlin as its candidates. Another convention held on May 9, at Baltimore, nominated John Bell of Tennessee and Edward Everett as candidates to represent the Constitutional Union Party. This latter group supported the principles of Clay and hoped thereby to save the Union.

Election results in Kentucky gave John Bell and the Constitutional Union Party a vote of 67,418, Breckinridge 53,149, Douglas 25,660, and Lincoln 1,357. Lexington, Mary Todd Lincoln's home town, gave Lincoln only two votes. The election for state officers gave Leslie Combs, a Constitutional Unionist, a vote of 68,165, or a majority of almost 25,000 over his nearest opponent for the office of clerk of the court of appeals.

Thus Kentucky played an important role in national affairs during the last two decades before the war. Not only had her political leaders been foremost among the national figures, but she strove hard for the preservation of the National Union.

CHAPTER XVII

A Brother's Blood

MUCH of Kentucky's history until after the Mexican War concerns wars and fighting men. It was a distinct honor to be a soldier, and many Kentucky sons dreamed of following in their forefathers' steps. After 1847 this sentiment grew less strong. During the following peaceful years most Kentuckians, who at other times would have been fond of military affairs, became interested in business and politics. When the war clouds of 1860 and 1861 began to gather, Kentuckians were anxious to remain neutral, for peace was necessary to their business. Many of Kentucky's leaders realized that if their state chose either side it would become once again a "Dark and Bloody Ground." Hence Kentucky's refusal to declare itself for either side during 1861 to 1865.

While his native Kentucky was making a desperate effort to avoid the approaching struggle, Major Robert Anderson of Jefferson County found himself in a precarious situation in South Carolina. Anderson was commandant of Fort Moultrie in Charleston Harbor. When the South Carolinians threatened to attack his post, he had two alternatives: to burn the fortress and flee to the newly constructed Fort Sumter, or to stand his ground in Fort Moultrie and be captured. Having no desire to be taken by the Carolina militia, Anderson spiked his guns, burned Fort Moultrie, and retired, December 27, 1860, to Fort Sumter, where he found a more modern fortification and plentiful supplies. However, as commandant of Fort Sumter he was not to remain at his post in peace, for on April 12, 1861, Roger A. Pryor, Louis T. Wigfall, S. S. Lee, and Senator Chesnut disobeyed Jefferson Davis' telegram to General Beauregard and fired on Fort Sumter. Thus the war had begun with one of Kentucky's sons first to participate in the defense of the Union. Major Anderson held Fort Sumter under fire for twenty-four hours before surrendering it to the secessionary forces of South Carolina.

The firing on Fort Sumter was far distant from Kentucky, but it started activity on the whole southern front. Confederate leaders realized at the outset that one of the important areas was the lower Ohio Valley and that Kentucky was the keystone to this whole region. It became imperative that the western confederacy concentrated its forces along the southern Kentucky border. Confederate strategists believed firmly that once their forces were within the state's boundaries, Kentuckians would join them, and that the Magoffin state government would repudiate its neutral stand. While Southern leaders were planning their drive on Kentucky, Union leaders were doing likewise. While Southerners were establishing centers at Forts Donelson, Henry, and Nashville, Unionists were concentrating at Cincinnati and opposite Columbus and Hickman.

Before Southern and Northern forces met in battle, each had studded Kentucky's surrounding territory with military posts which they hoped to transfer into the state immediately following a successful invasion. General Leonidas Polk, former Bishop of the Episcopal Church of Louisiana, moved into Hickman and Columbus on September 3, 1861. Two days later, Ulysses S. Grant crossed the Ohio River into Kentucky to establish his posts at Paducah and Smithland. When Grant moved into the state, federal troops were prepared for a march southward from Cincinnati and from Camp Joe Holt opposite Louisville in Indiana.

While Polk and Grant were contesting possession of western Kentucky, General Felix K. Zollicoffer invaded the state from the east. To check this movement, Union troops were concentrated at Camp Dick Robinson. Zollicoffer represented the best of Southern generalship, but unfortunately for the Southern cause his engagement with Union troops under the command of General George H. Thomas at Mills Springs on January 19, 1862, resulted in his death at the hand of Speed Fry, a native Kentuckian. By this time Kentucky found itself in the midst of the war. Nearly 10,000 "Lincoln Guns" were judiciously distributed to "Union men" of the state by way of the rivers and the Central Railroad of Kentucky.

Citizens of Kentucky did not wait for the war to come to their doors before beginning action. Many men of military age had already left their homes to join one side or the other. Men joined the Northern or

Southern Army according to their personal convictions. Families were divided with brother fighting brother and father fighting son. The Reverend Robert J. Breckinridge had two sons in the Confederate Army and two in the Union Army. Civil officials elected on the same ticket and of the same political opinions joined opposing forces. Members of the same denominations were sharply divided in their attitudes. An outcome of this division of sentiment in eastern Kentucky was the activity of the "bushwhackers," which antedated the guerrilla warfare. Soldiers traveled in small bands and with much caution through the gaps of eastern Kentucky Mountains to join the Confederate Army because of their fear of death at the hands of these grim mountain patriots whose idea of defeating the Confederacy was to shoot volunteers before they reached the army. These "bushwhackers" were independent citizens, who, in some cases, acted under commands of Union officers. At times they were as effective as drilled troops.

General Albert Sidney Johnston invaded the neutral boundaries of his native state from Tennessee in the fall of 1861. General Johnston was convinced that if he went through Kentucky he could convert its citizens to the Southern cause. His advance followed generally the line of the Louisville and Nashville Railroad. His headquarters were at Bowling Green, and from this central base he foraged and recruited new troops. Upon his arrival at Bowling Green, Johnston found a motley army of Southern partisans reputed to have been the most unpromising troops ever assembled. They were armed with guns ranging from colonial "muzzle loaders" to modern Enfields. No manual of arms were used in drilling, but perhaps the only form of unity among these troops was a will to fight!

At Bowling Green, Johnston's ragtag army was augmented for a brief period by the well drilled and well equipped Kentucky State Guard, under the leadership of General Simon Bolivar Buckner, who had come up from Camp Boone in Tennessee. This force, with the Kentucky State Guard equipment, had deserted Frankfort earlier in the year to fight for the Confederacy. From Bowling Green, General Buckner's forces were dispatched toward Louisville to demolish the Louisville and Nashville Railroad and to destroy the locks on the Green River. Buckner's destination, however, was Louisville, but he was unable to assault this place because of the able resistance of Union troops under the command of General L. H. Rousseau. In rapid succession Buckner's men were forced back to the Tennessee line after several unsuccessful engagements. However, Buckner's command succeeded in breaking up the railroad and the locks on the Green River.

Early in January, 1862, the struggle broke out in the eastern mountains of Kentucky. Union troops under the command of Captain James A. Garfield of Ohio invaded Kentucky to attack Confederate forces under General Humphrey Marshall. A battle was fought near Prestonsburg in which the Union troops drove the Confederates from their stronghold largely because of the poor field judgment of General Marshall. Of course this battle was of no significance, except as an important factor in further creating bitter sentiment between the two contending groups in eastern Kentucky.

Every movement of Confederate troops in southern Kentucky was countered by a similar movement of Union troops. When Polk seized Columbus and Hickman in 1861, Grant moved into Paducah. Perhaps the most strategic point in Kentucky was this intersection of the four major river systems. Grant wished to secure control of the territory south of the Cumberland and Tennessee Rivers at the earliest possible moment. At this time Confederate lines were guarded by almost 60,000 men, and Southern defenses were concentrated at Columbus, Bowling Green, Fort Henry, and Fort Donelson. It was against this line that Grant moved, early in 1862. When the Union drive got under way, the Confederates in this section weakened at every point of attack to retreat southward to Fort Donelson on the Cumberland, and to Fort Henry on the Tennessee River. On February 6 Fort Henry was surrendered. On February 14 Johnston evacuated Bowling Green, and on February 16 Fort Donelson, under the joint command of Generals Floyd, Pillow, and Buckner, was surrendered. General Buckner was given the task of surrendering the post to his West Point classmate, Ulysses Grant. Grant's treatment of Buckner was considerate, even to the point of offering the surrendering Confederate officer money to be used during his detention as a prisoner of war.

Except for numerous crossroad skirmishes, the activities of the war shifted from Kentucky to the South in the spring of 1862. After the surrender of Forts Henry and Donelson, the South concentrated its troops along the Tennessee River. Grant and Buell moved southward toward Pittsburg Landing. On April 6 and 7 the Battle of Shiloh, or Pittsburg Landing, was fought. Nearly 35,000 Kentucky troops saw action in the Confederate ranks. Had it not been for the timely assistance of Don Carlos Buell's forces which resulted in defeat of the Confederate troops, Kentucky might have seen an early and furious stir of military activities within her own boundaries. Shiloh's battlefield was smeared with the blood of nearly 20,000 Confederate and Union soldiers. Of these, eight Union Kentucky regiments lost 800 men and Kentucky's Confederate companies registered a loss of 680 men.

Shiloh was the second major defeat of the Southern forces. By this time Confederate leaders were impressed with the importance of securing supplies from Kentucky. Not only did Kentucky offer an abundance of men and food supplies, but, geographically, central Kentucky was more adaptable to the South's methods of fighting than the Tennessee River frontier.

Undaunted, Southern generals once again planned to invade Kentucky in a major campaign by entering the state through Cumberland Gap. Strangely enough, it was from this quarter that the Southerners had been most successful, for from the beginning they were unable to stem the tide of Union troops in western Kentucky. The Southerners had underestimated the efficiency of the light draft gunboats used by the Northerners on the western rivers. On the other hand, Northern generals failed to appreciate the significance of Cumberland Gap as an entrance to Kentucky and the Northwest. President Lincoln was anxious to have this opening fortified, but because of the stubbornnesss of his field officers his plans were not executed. Lincoln suggested the construction of a railroad from Lexington to Cumberland Gap as a defensive measure. Later activities proved that the project would have been helpful to the Northern Army. While this plan was being discussed, however, the Southern Army, concentrated at Knoxville, began to advance toward Kentucky. Since it was impossible to pass heavy troops through the neighborhood of Nashville, the Southerners first entered Kentucky at its back door.

The first body of this command to enter the state was Morgan's Cavalry. At this time, John Hunt Morgan was under the command of General Braxton Bragg, who had succeeded General P. G. T. Beauregard in the command of the Army of the Tennessee. Morgan invaded

Kentucky at Tompkinsville in July, 1862, accompanied on this raid
into his native state by St. Leger Grenfel, an expert strategist, who had
seen service in the East Indian branch of the English Army, as well as
in the French Army in Algeria. From Tompkinsville, Morgan led his
men to Glasgow, from which place he advanced on the Green River
communities. Beyond this river, his troops were divided into two
parties which captured simultaneously Lebanon and Springfield and
reunited in the investment of Harrodsburg. Again Morgan's force was
divided, with one detachment going by way of Lawrenceburg over a
western route while the other traveled to the east. At Lawrenceburg
their paths crossed, but the attacking columns spread out again, one
branch feinting toward Frankfort while the other hurried to Midway
and the Lexington, Frankfort, and Louisville Railroad. At Midway
one of Morgan's mischievous colleagues threw all of Kentucky into a
panic over the exact location of the Confederate raider and the size of
his command. Like Shakespeare's Ariel, Ellsworth (Morgan's telegraph operator), was able to create more confusion than would have
been possible with three times as many raiders as composed Morgan's
command. When the Confederates gained control of the railway telegraph office at Midway, Ellsworth proceeded to send false orders. General John Finnell at Frankfort was instructed to send troops to Midway,
but when these troops were fairly started, Ellsworth recalled them.

Morgan's appearance in the Blue Grass country so soon after the Battle of Shiloh was startling, and his drives toward Cincinnati and Louisville were terrorizing. Really, Morgan's intention was to cut com-
munications between Lexington and Cincinnati. Nevertheless, when
Morgan appeared at Harrodsburg on Sunday morning, "Jerry" T.
Boyle, Union commandant at Louisville, succeeded in working into a
frenzy of excitement the citizens of Louisville, Indianapolis, Cincinnati,
and Lexington, and the officials of the War Department. Temporary
batteries were constructed before Cincinnati, but while Morgan was
enjoying a feast of fried chicken and hot biscuit in Harrodsburg on
Sunday morning, Cincinnatians were momentarily expecting his raiders to appear on the hill above Covington. The panic in Louisville
was a comedy, for the "Fire Eating Jerry" Boyle was performing a perfect Falstaffian act. Not only had he disturbed the peaceful Sabbath
of three or four neighboring cities and of the War Department, but he

had invaded the sanctity of the White House. Telegrams begging for help and giving ridiculous figures of Morgan's strength finally aroused President Lincoln to wire Halleck: "They are having a stampede in Kentucky. Please look to it."

While General Finnell of Frankfort was pursuing Ellsworth's "will-o'-the-wisp" with his troops, and Brigadier General William T. Ward of Lexington was undecided about the next step, Morgan rushed his troops toward Georgetown, where they arrived without creating any disturbance. On July 18 the Confederate raiders were in Cynthiana, a strategic point on the Central Railroad of Kentucky and a storehouse for federal supplies. After a brief skirmish at the bridgehead over the Licking River, the Confederate forces took the town. Morgan, however, was not to enjoy the fruits of victory at Cynthiana, nor subsequently, at Paris, for a strong Union force under the command of General Green Clay Smith and Colonel Frank Wolford advanced on Paris from Lexington. On July 22 the Southern raiders headed southward toward Cumberland Gap and Knoxville. They did not leave the state, however, until they had delivered a parting message to their old friend "Jerry" Boyle. From Somerset, Ellsworth telegraphed Boyle: "Good morning, Jerry. This telegraph is a great institution. You should destroy it as it keeps me too well posted." Perhaps no person was more relieved than Boyle when he heard that Morgan was leaving Kentucky. He gleefully and boldly telegraphed General Buell: "Morgan has left the state. General Smith ought to have taken him." To Secretary Stanton he wired: "Morgan passed through Somerset. General Smith still pursuing, I have ordered him to drive Morgan out of the state."

The War between the States produced many new military tactics. Outstanding were the cavalry raids of Sheridan, Sherman, Streight, Jackson, Forrest, Stuart, and Morgan. When Morgan left Knoxville, July 4, 1862, to make a drive into Kentucky, he started a raid in the enemy's rear which made him famous. Morgan's men were not cavalrymen at all but mounted infantrymen who traveled without stores, for Morgan, unlike Braxton Bragg, paid little attention to the accumulation of a commissary. He depended solely upon the resources of the communities through which he passed. General Morgan was a good enough judge of horse flesh to select only fine animals for his troops, but he was even wiser in the selection of subordinate officers. There was Basil Duke, a Kentuckian, Morgan's brother-in-law, and an able officer. St. Leger Grenfel was Morgan's strategist, about whom a recent biographer was pointed to the evident fact that when Grenfel planned, Morgan's raiders were always successful. Another important man was Ellsworth, the telegraph operator. Duke tells a characteristic story of him. He says Ellsworth was a misfit at everything he attempted except operating a telegraph. At this duty he was a genius, for he could dispatch such convincing messages that the Unionists were decoyed into all sorts of traps. General Duke relates that at Crab Orchard, Ellsworth decided to go after a notorious "bushwhacker" whom the best of Morgan's scouts had failed to capture.

Telling no one of his intention, he took Colonel Grenfel's horse, upon which was strapped a saddle that the owner valued very highly, and behind the saddle was a buff coat equally as much prized, and in the coat was all the gold the Colonel had brought from Richmond, when he came to join us, and thus equipped he sallied out with one companion, to take the formidable "Captain King."

He went boldly to that worthy's house, who seeing only two men coming, scorned to take to the brush. To Ellsworth's demand to surrender, he answered with volleys from shotgun and revolver, severely wounding the friend and putting Ellsworth himself to flight. King pressed the retreat, and Ellsworth, although he brought off his wounded companion, lost horse, saddle, coat and gold. St. Leger was like an excited volcano, and sought Ellsworth to slay him instantly.

Three days were required to pacify him, during which time, the great "operator" had to be carefully kept out of his sight.

But when Ellsworth was seated in the telegraph office he was always "master of the situation." When Morgan was a scout in Kentucky in the late summer of 1862 for Braxton Bragg's army, Ellsworth produced a third act to his comedy in Kentucky by wiring George D. Prentice that Morgan was on the march from Gallatin, Tennessee, with 400 Indians for the especial purpose of taking his scalp.

Morgan's early raids into Kentucky caused much confusion. He captured several towns, paroled a great number of prisoners of war, and recruited fresh troops. As usual, his expeditions were accompanied by a number of crossroad fights and skirmishes, but the main Confederate forces required several weeks to get started toward Kentucky. Late in August, Kirby Smith advanced northward from Knoxville toward Kentucky with 12,000 men. He moved directly along the Wilderness Road from Cumberland Gap toward Lexington, where he hoped to engage Union troops encamped there under the command of General William Nelson. General Nelson was a distinguished hero of the Pittsburg Landing campaign, but, unfortunately, his list of military experiences did not include sufficient precaution. Thinking his troops safe in the Blue Grass, he stationed them at Richmond and spent most of his time in Lexington. Doubtless General Nelson was wholly unacquainted with the Confederates' method of light traveling, for he was the most surprised man in Kentucky when he learned on August 30, 1862, that Kirby Smith's men had advanced ninety miles in three days. So quietly and promptly did the Confederates arrive in Kentucky that they completely surprised Manson's and Crust's troops at Richmond. The sentinels barely had time to notify their commanders before General Kirby Smith's troops were upon them. Smith found Nelson's men commanded by two inexperienced officers. Fighting began at Rogersville, which was several miles south of Richmond. The Confederates, after making a successful flanking movement, crushed through the Union ranks on their way into Richmond. Manson's line gave way so that his forces were unable to restore order, and within an hour the "Federals" had been put to rout. So violent was the Confederate attack that Richmond was soon evacuated, and the Federal forces were on the run for the bridge over the Kentucky River at Clay's Ferry. During this running fight General Nelson, in a raging temper, reached the field of battle, where he attempted to restore order by beating his soldiers over the head with the flat sides of his sword, but it was of no avail. Colonel Scott of Smith's command overtook Manson at the river bridge, but by this time the battle was over. This was indeed a day of victory for General Smith and his cavalry unit, for they were now able to march victoriously into Lexington.

While Kirby Smith was sweeping the road clear of Federal troops between Cumberland Gap and Lexington, Braxton Bragg was marching from southern Kentucky toward Lexington. Never did the Confederates have a finer opportunity to invade Kentucky with prospects of victory than when Bragg started his advance northward. Had he hastened to Louisville, he could have taken it with little difficulty, and, with the aid of Kirby Smith's 12,000 well-equipped troops, he could have captured Cincinnati. Bragg caught Buell completely off guard in Tennessee, for Buell believed that Bragg's thrust toward his position in Tennessee meant that he would attempt to regain Nashville. This move confused Buell for the moment. He concentrated his army near Nashville, where he was surprised to hear that Bragg had entered Kentucky. With the aid of his cavalry units, Bragg completely disorganized Buell's command, but with these same units he could have delayed Buell longer.

Moving through a defenseless country, Bragg allowed his desire for a well-stocked commissary to delay him. It was this desire to forage heavily upon the country which aided Buell in overtaking him. Undoubtedly the War between the States would have had at least one different chapter had Bragg marched as speedily and decisively as did Kirby Smith. Instead, he lost eight days in his movement toward Nashville, at a time when his small but effective cavalry units could have accomplished more than the complete army. His gravest error was his failure to advance on Louisville and Cincinnati. The whole Ohio Valley was his for the taking. As a further illustration of Bragg's inability to drive decisively toward his goal, he delayed his troops three days at the Green River crossing in an effort to drive General J. B. Wilder from his entrenched fortification.

Kirby Smith had not remained inactive in Lexington but had made a valuable addition to his forces by securing the aid of General Henry Heth and of a command of seasoned troops. When Heth's forces were combined with Smith's, these officers made a thrust toward Cincinnati, but they received no co-operation from the purposeless Genreal Braxton Bragg. By this time the supply trains of Bragg's army were so heavily loaded that he made extraordinarily slow progress. Buell was advancing rapidly toward Louisville with the needless fear that when he reached the banks of the Ohio there would be no point of communication or concentration open to him. He must surely have received with great relief the news that Bragg had veered around Louisville to Lexington. On September 25, Buell reached Louisville, while Bragg was on his way to Lexington. Buell's safe arrival at Louisville changed the Confederate position from one of offense to one of defense. At Louisville the Union forces were quickly reinforced with fresh troops sent by boat from Corinth, Mississippi, up the Tennessee and Ohio Rivers. Buell then reorganized his whole command to prepare to take the field.

While activity was at its height in the Union camp, the Confederate officers were losing time arranging the installation of a Confederate Government at Frankfort. Bragg, evidently believing that Buell would remain at Louisville for several days, at least, threw caution to the wind and proceeded to swear in Confederate state officials. Buell, however, a seasoned campaigner, planned an immediate flanking attack on Lexington with a feint at Frankfort. Consequently, in the midst of Governor Hawes' inaugural ceremonies General Sill's cavalrymen appeared on the hill overlooking West Frankfort. Before the Governor-elect could begin his inaugural address, he and his fellow-Confederate state officers had to desert the town by way of the railway tunnel running toward Lexington. Upon receiving news that Buell's army was flanking toward Lexington, Bragg planned a hurried retreat southward, but his decision came too late to get his army safely past the federal lines.

At Louisville, Buell definitely planned to force Bragg to evacuate Lexington in order to relieve from Confederate attack the vulnerable Union supply points of Louisville and Cincinnati. Before Buell could leave Louisville, however, orders were issued by the War Department that he relinquish his command to General George H. Thomas. It was only through the earnest persuasion of General Thomas that Buell retained his command to lead his army against the Confederates in central Kentucky. While the order proposing the removal of Buell from command was pending, Buell lost a valuable day's march and considerable prestige.

To advance on Lexington by way of the Louisville, Shelbyville, and Frankfort Turnpike would give the enemy the advantage of fighting in the rugged country surrounding Frankfort. In order to reach Lexington over the most favorable route, Buell directed the main body of his army by way of Bardstown and Lebanon. A detachment of cavalry was dispatched toward Frankfort to mislead Bragg into believing that the main army was advancing in this direction. The Lebanon branch of the Louisville and Nashville Railroad was an ideal means to transport the stores of the Union Army into the area of conflict. At Lexington, Bragg, realizing that the time had passed for capturing Louisville and Cincinnati, decided to retreat through southeastern Kentucky by way of the Kentucky and Dix River gorges. However, before the lumbering Southern Army began its retreat, Bragg wasted additional time at Frankfort. When General Sill appeared at that place, Bragg believed his troops to be the advance column of Buell's army.

General Sill's appearance at Frankfort caused Bragg to retreat rapidly toward Harrodsburg without realizing that he was pitching headlong into the main body of Buell's command. However, Buell was equally ignorant of Bragg's position. Another factor interfering with the movement of the two commands was the extreme drouth which had prevailed for several weeks. Both commanders were forced to plan troop movements along routes best supplied with water. Thus, on October 8, while Buell's thirsty soldiers were establishing themselves along the stagnant course of Doctor's Creek, they were faced unknowingly with immediate danger of attack by the Confederate Army, the main body of which was encamped only two miles away on the ridge surrounding Perryville. Since neither commander knew of the presence of the other, no definite plans of attack were made. Buell indicated that he hoped to attack on the morrow; had he sent a casual reconnoitering party forward he would have seen the feasibility of attacking at once. Bragg, on the other hand, hoped to remove his army further from the central Kentucky scene, believing that Buell was on his way to Lexington by way of Frankfort. On the afternoon of October 8, the Confederate left fell upon the Union right flank. Since the Union flank was composed for the most part of raw troops, the Confederates, under the command of Lytle, Harris, and Buckner, routed them. Before the Confederates could completely turn the right flank of the Union command, however, Sheridan's seasoned troops enfiladed the Confederate ranks, throwing into confusion what had promised to be a successful drive. This saved the day for the Union. Through four hours of bloody fighting, involving the right and center commands of the Union Army, approximately four thousand Federal and three thousand Confederate troops were killed and wounded. This battle brought victory to neither side, yet it was a stunning blow to Bragg's command.

Bragg was now completely baffled. He fell back to Harrodsburg to join Kirby Smith's forces, but this only delayed him. The Confederates then retreated southward through Bryantsville and the mountains of southeastern Kentucky. Once again the state was cleared of Confed-

erate troops, with the exception of Morgan's cavalry and a few stragglers who remained as deserters or independent soldiers of fortune.
Buell, believing that Bragg's retreat southward possibly meant that he
would attempt to regain Nashville, hastened from Kentucky to that
place. However, upon his arrival at Union headquarters, he was relieved of his command by General Rosecrans.

Fighting in Kentucky was now reduced to crossroad skirmishes and
guerrilla warfare. Bragg's ill-planned and poorly executed march into
Kentucky robbed the state of valuable supplies and hurt the Southern
cause decidedly. He might have claimed a great part of Kentucky's
support had he seized Louisville and Cincinnati, but his failure caused
many Kentuckians to desert the South. After Perryville, with the exception of John Hunt Morgan's subsequent raids, and scattered guerrilla fighting, the chapter of military activities in Kentucky was practically completed.

Morgan, late in 1862, again terrorized his home state. At the Tennessee line he executed one of his typical maneuvers; dividing his
forces, he took both Williamsburg and Waynesboro. This division
confused Rosecrans, and for a time the Union forces were drawn back
almost into Kentucky. Federal officers were nonplussed by Morgan's
ability to strike forcibly at strategic points and at the most unexpected
moments. Moving north late in December, 1862, Morgan eluded the
Union guard and captured Glasgow and Elizabethtown again. However, the Confederate raider did not travel through his native state this
time without serious interference. Since he had a strong Union force
close on his heels, his only destruction of any consequence was that of
the Louisville and Nashville Railroad to Muldraugh's Hill. His activities ceasing here when he was overtaken by superior Union troops, he
returned immediately to Tennessee.

Once again Morgan visited Kentucky. On July 6, 1863, he crossed
the Tennessee line at Burkesville and took Lebanon and Bardstown.
From there he hurried westward to cross the Ohio River at Branden-
burg into Indiana. After a threatening ride toward Indianapolis, he
sidestepped Governor Morton's state guards to move toward Cincinnati.
Unable to cross the Ohio River into Kentucky at this point, he hurried
toward Wheeling, West Virginia, but before he could cross over the
Ohio, he was captured and imprisoned in the Ohio State Penitentiary.

Why General Morgan crossed the Ohio is still a matter of speculation. Some historians of his raid believe he moved into this territory upon invitation of the Copperheads, who were anxious to make sufficient show of force to overthrow a Unionist government. It is quite plausible that the invitation of the Knights of the Golden Circle (an order formed during the war to rescue Confederate prisoners from Union prisons) and the leading Copperheads offered some hope for this Confederate cavalry officer. Doubtless Morgan must have had reason to believe that he could make political headway north of the Ohio, because it is inconceivable that he expected to make a military advance alone. Clement Laird Vallandigham of Ohio, as Copperhead leader, and since May 5 an exile, perhaps encouraged Morgan to cross the Ohio in order to give moral support to the Knights of the Golden Circle. This much is certain: General Morgan displeased his chief, General Bragg, when he crossed the river. Bragg wanted Morgan to stay in Kentucky, for the Army of the Tennessee was planning an engagement with Rosecrans.

Morgan was not detained in the Ohio Penitentiary for long. By some fantastic scheme (perhaps by Thomas H. Hines' shrewd manipulation of prison rules), which has not as yet been sufficiently explained, he escaped on November 28, 1863. In June, 1864, he was on his way from southwestern Virginia through the mountains of eastern Kentucky with 2,500 men to raid Kentucky for the fourth time. His attack at Mount Sterling was terrifying. At this place he divided his command and sent Colonel Henry Giltner into an unsuccessful engagement with General Stephen Burbridge on the Winchester Pike. Morgan, avoiding Burbridge, commanded the division which took Lexington, his home town. From Lexington, General Morgan moved on Georgetown and thence on Cynthiana, where his command was again united. At Cynthiana, Morgan captured General Edward Hobson, his foe across the Ohio, and 2,000 men. But here Morgan allowed his command to dwindle until it was unable to withstand the drive of General Burbridge. He was forced to release his prisoners and to escape through Flemingsburg and West Liberty to Abingdon, Virginia. Three months later, September, 1864, General Morgan died at Greeneville, Tennessee, shot by Union officers, but the reason for betraying

General Morgan's presence at the Williams' home yet lacks a satisfactory explanation.

Throughout the later years of the war, when Kentucky as a battleground was no longer prominent in the struggle, the state was infested with Union troops and guerrillas. Unquestionably, the guerrilla warfare became the most disturbing factor in Kentucky's Civil War history. Guerrillas, because of their hatred of the southern slaveholder's cause, had made trouble in the eastern passes at the very beginning of the war. Early attacks from these independent bands, however, differed materially from the raids of 1864. Because of the periodic invasion of the state by both Union and Confederate Armies during the early years of the war, each army left a large number of stragglers and deserters to forage and pillage at will. The eastern mountain range of Kentucky was an ideal region for guerrilla warfare. So desperate did these moving bands become, that, in 1864, commanders of the Union Army were forced to devote much attention to their dispersal. Guerrilla bands attacked Federal troops and civilians alike, respecting neither persons nor property. Their brutality caused Union officers to resort to extreme measures. Orders were issued by commanding officials that, for every loyal citizen injured or killed by these bands, five prominent "rebel" sympathizers should be taken into custody to be held as hostages until the criminals were apprehended. Citizens of the village of Caseyville, in Union County, were assessed $25,000 to pay for damages caused by guerrillas, and it was proposed that local citizens restore the station house. Governor Bramlette issued a proclamation in October, 1863, which became a law in February, 1864, stating that the aid and abettance of guerrillas would be punishable by six months' imprisonment and a fine of from $100 to $1,000. This law, however, was unjust, for it made persons injured by guerrillas guilty of high misdemeanor if they did not report the crime. Certainly this left innocent citizens in an embarrassing situation, for in reporting crimes they cleared themselves with the state but were made liable to revengeful attacks from guerrillas. General Stephen Burbridge, in 1864, ordered four guerrillas killed for every loyal Unionist murdered. This resulted in making innocent Confederate prisoners victims of unreasonable punishment. Two Confederate soldiers were hanged on the fairgrounds at Lexington, and six more were hanged in Green County to account for the death of two Union soldiers. General Sherman suggested that he be allowed to make the guerrillas run the gantlet down the Mississippi River and then exile them in a foreign colony—provided General Burbridge would capture as many as three or four hundred at a time.

Among these notorious Kentucky ruffians was a leader named Quantrill who had fled the State of Missouri as a fugitive from justice. Other border bands were the Halls, Jameses, Longs, and Pences. General John Palmer successfully dispersed many of these criminal bands and killed Quantrill in 1864. So notorious was the dispute over the guerrilla war that Governor Bramlette discontinued friendly relations with President Lincoln. Bramlette believed that the Union forces were killing innocent Kentuckians. Perhaps the reason for this was Burbridge's order, issued on July 16, 1864, that four guerrilla prisoners be killed for every loyal person killed by these gangs. Burbridge was not careful in the selection of prisoners to be killed but often carelessly confused Confederate prisoners with the outlaws. Innocent men paid a dear price for crimes of which they knew nothing. To stop the looting of Kentucky, Governor Bramlette ordered an enlistment of 10,000 "six months" volunteers to help put down the guerrilla war and to protect innocent Kentuckians.

Events of 1864 brought to the front another controversial issue in Kentucky's Civil War history. In that year, the Federal Government enlisted Negro troops—a thing which completely disgusted loyal Kentucky Unionists. Always, military service had been a Kentuckian's highest tribute to his state, for he considered it an honor to offer himself as a soldier to its cause, but no master relished the idea of having his "black Sam" in the army sharing in this Kentucky tradition. So bitter were protests from Kentucky, which had always filled its national quota with volunteers, that the War Department found itself in a quandary over the use of Negro troops. A dilatory policy was adopted in Kentucky, for Negroes were enlisted for a while, but soon enrollment was stopped. However, within a short time this embarrassing practice was revived. Finally enlistment of Negro troops degenerated into a scheme of concentrating all Kentucky Negroes in camps at or near Federal headquarters in Louisville. A curious thing about the Negro enlistments was the acceptance of men, women, and children.

In July, 1865, three months after Lee's surrender at Appomattox, there were 28,000 Kentucky Negroes enlisted in the Federal concentration camps. General J. M. Palmer supervised these Negro divisions and opened the way for his charges to cross the Ohio River as promptly as possible. Thus Louisville became a veritable haven for both free and slave Negroes, for, once inside the concentration camp, they were safe, and here a benevolent "uncle" fed, clothed, and equipped them with "Palmer's passes."

A brief chapter cannot cover all the details of Kentucky's part in the campaigns of the Civil War, for there were many minor engagements which occurred within the state. Crossroads skirmishes were numerous and indecisive. However, these raids, although not unduly destructive, did impress upon the Kentucky people the rigors of Civil War.

Kentucky's stand for neutrality probably confined to minor attacks the engagements of the war within her borders. Had its legislature made the serious error of seceding, the state would have become at the outset the battle ground of the Mississippi Valley. Kentucky would have suffered the same ravages of war as did Virginia. There is reason to believe that inevitably Kentucky would have become the keystone of the general western campaigns.

Even with only minor engagements occurring in the state, Kentucky's people were bitter toward one side or the other. Individuals hated their former friends; brothers hated brothers; and families which had been prosperous before secession were ruined by the blighting of Kentucky's trade. Even these facts become insignificant, however, when it is remembered that Kentucky was not the victim of continuous and destructive military campaigns fought on her soil. It is true that the state was invaded several times, but, with the exception of the partial destruction of Columbus and Hickman and a slight damage at Perryville, Cynthiana, Mount Sterling, Bowling Green, and Richmond, no Kentucky town suffered such destruction as Richmond, Petersburg, Vicksburg, Chattanooga, Atlanta, and Charleston. Louisville and Lexington were centers of military activities, but neither was materially harmed by the war. Kentucky's position in the sectional struggle was unique. For her, it was truly a Civil War!

It is rather difficult to say definitely what the exact results of the war were in the number of men engaged and in the amount of commerce involved. Approximately 100,000 Kentuckians took active part in the struggle. Between 30,000 and 40,000 Kentuckians enlisted in Confederate service; approximately 64,000 fought in the Union ranks; and 13,-000 were engaged in State Guard service. Perhaps there is no reliable source from which the student of Civil War history can secure the exact economic results of Kentucky's part in the war. It is possible to estimate only the general livestock and property price and quantity fluctuations. Horses decreased in number from 388,000, in 1861, to 299,000, in 1865; mules decreased from 95,000 to 58,000; cattle from 695,000 to 520,000. Property valuations decreased during this five-year period from $225,000,000 to $198,000,000. Although these decreases in values were of major proportions, they resulted from neglect rather than from destruction.

CHAPTER XVIII

Social and Political Transition

IN 1860 Kentucky's background was of a temperament which ranged from an extreme radicalism, as illustrated in Tom Paine's *Age of Reason,* in the teachings of Rousseau, and in the conspiracies of Burr, to the ultra-conservatism embodied in the slavery sections of the first three constitutions. Cradled in the American Revolution, Kentucky was from infancy a victim of plots and conspiracies which kept its citizenship in a state of political excitement. Even Isaac Shelby, stanch Kentucky patriot and patriarch, was often baffled as to the course his state should pursue; and Henry Clay, a national patriot, early found himself a victim of indecision.

However, through this long period of political upheaval Kentucky developed a conservative system of government, religion, commerce, and schools. In her maturity Kentucky had become not only mother of new states, but grandmother of many. With a maternal feeling for both the Southwest and the Northwest, Kentucky's national interest had grown annually more intense. Unlike many other states in the Union, Kentucky became a social and economic factor in a widely diversified area. Her agricultural system, for instance, differed from that of the North and that of the South; there were only 200 individual farms in 1860 which contained more than 1,000 acres, and fewer than 9,000 which contained less than 20. The majority of Kentucky farms ranged in size from 20 to 500 acres. Manufacturing establishments numbering 3,350 represented a capital investment of $20,000,000, and an annual consumption of raw material valued at $22,000,000.

Commercial relationships bound Kentucky hand and foot to both the North and the South. In many respects Kentucky was as much interested in manufactured goods from Philadelphia and New York as she was in the livestock and provisions trade to Memphis and New Orleans. This is an explanation of why "Mother" Kentucky found her brood divided both within and without her boundaries when war threatened in 1861.

Politically, Kentucky early developed into a middle ground, and under the leadership of Henry Clay the state remained steadfast in her devotion to the Whig cause in national politics. When Clay and the Whig Party were gone, however, most Kentuckians were left without a political rudder to guide them through the approaching national squall. They found themselves in the 1850's with two highly undesirable alternatives: joining the Democratic Party, or going over to the newly organized and secretive Know Nothings with their violent opposition to immigrant voters and Catholics. Many, for a time, chose the latter, and the Know Nothing movement was strengthened by the addition of nearly all the Kentucky Whig support. As early as 1854, however, "Old Line" Whig prophets rightly held that the Democratic Party, with a coalition of expatriate Whigs, would soon become the major political group in the state.

When (November, 1860) Kentucky was certain that Abraham Lincoln had been elected, mass meetings of citizens were held to plan a pacific course for the Southern Slave States. On December 9, 1860, the Democratic Governor, Beriah Magoffin, made a proposal to the Southern States which he hoped would restore the Missouri Compromise. Governor Magoffin, in fact, advocated the establishment of the thirty-seventh degree parallel as a dividing line between northern freedom and southern slavery. He also suggested a national re-endorsement and strict enforcement of the Fugitive Slave Law of 1850 to insure the return of runaway slaves to their southern owners, and restore the sectional agreement of 1850.

While Governor Magoffin was outlining his conciliatory plan to the Southern States, Senator John Jordan Crittenden was proposing his famous compromise to the United States Senate. Crittenden suggested that the Missouri Compromise line of 36° 30′ be restored as the boundary between the slave and free territories and that it should apply to all territory admitted between the western boundary of Missouri and the Pacific. Senator Crittenden's compromise effort came to naught, for it was inconsistent with policies of the incoming administration, which held to the theory that a "house divided against itself cannot stand," and absolutely opposed further extensions of slavery. Within two days after the failure of the Crittenden Compromise, South Carolina seceded.

Mississippi and Alabama were the only states to respond to Governor Magoffin's call for a meeting of the Southern States to discuss the problems before the nation. Their efforts for peace proved a forlorn hope.

An extra session of the legislature was called for January 7, 1861, to discuss Kentucky's course of action. While this body was working hopefully toward a satisfactory solution of the differences between the Southern States, John J. Crittenden, Robert J. Breckinridge, James Guthrie, Archibald Dixon, and Joseph Holt were laboring assiduously at molding a sharply divided local opinion along pacific lines. As successor to Kentucky's much beloved Clay, Crittenden was looked to for guidance in this crucial moment. In Lexington, the Reverend Robert J. Breckinridge warned against leaving the Union in an address circulated throughout the state in pamphlet form. Both political parties believed that the Union should be preserved at all cost, and few Kentuckians believed this impossible. Although Kentucky had given its native son, Abraham Lincoln, a light vote (1,366) for the Presidency, its citizens were not so thoroughly convinced as were their Southern neighbors that he was as "black" as pictured.

Not only did the major political parties under the guidance of Kentucky's highly esteemed citizens work toward a compromise of sectional differences, but the state's press was active in creating public opinion favorable to compromise. John H. Harney's *Louisville Democrat,* Albert Gallatin Hodges' *Frankfort Commonwealth,* and George D. Prentice's powerful *Louisville Journal* were outstanding in their efforts to maintain national peace.

Perhaps it was unfortunate for the whole country that Kentucky's many efforts at compromise resulted in failure. A call was issued for the meeting of a state convention to discuss Kentucky's future course. By the time this convention was ready for the question, the secessionist attitude in the state had grown, and those who wished to follow the South were desirous of prompt action. This move stirred bitter opposition of the Unionists, who wished to delay the convention. Robert J. Breckinridge was especially ardent in his efforts to prevent the calling of a convention and threatened to carry the question to the people for a vote. Thus was Kentucky torn with internal strife so that her people began to wonder and question every move made by the state government. The state's commercial interests were impressed with the geographical location of Kentucky as the keystone of the Mississippi Valley, realizing that inevitably the state would become the focal point of most sectional antagonisms.

It is well in this connection to review Kentucky's position in the Union. Wisely a native son said in 1860: "The true position of Kentucky in the present crisis is to assume the stand of pacificator. She has nothing to gain, but much to lose, by throwing herself into the arms of any new confederacy, North or South." This statement adequately sums up Kentucky's predicament and accurately expresses what came to be a prevailing sentiment.

Throughout seventy-six years of independent commercial growth Kentucky enjoyed a lucrative trade with both sections of the country. Each crop season marked the renewal of the livestock and furnishing trade with the South. Merchants and "middlemen" in Louisville, and to some extent, in Lexington, and in the smaller river towns, drove a thriving trade with the cotton states in livestock and manufactured commodities. Census reports of manufacturing in Kentucky for 1860 do not fully indicate the status of its commercial relations southward, nor do these reports portray accurately its commercial relations with the North.

Before it is possible to understand Kentucky's attitude toward her neighboring sections, or to explain her reactions in 1860, it is necessary to note that no railroad from the East tapped this rich agrarian belt. Hence, the state's economic position, so far as the South was concerned, remained at *status quo* with that of 1800. We can understand what a Kentuckian meant when he said, in 1860, that affiliation with either the North or South would bring loss to the state, in that Kentucky would suffer the loss of prosperous intersectional trade.

Doubtless another vital factor in deciding Kentucky's course was the question of slavery. One has only to cite conclusions reached by three constitutional conventions to prove that Kentuckians were slavery-minded. Many slaveholders were Unionists at heart but were afraid to undermine the status of their chattel slavery, because of severe property losses, to say nothing of burdening Kentucky society with the free Negro. As a result, many plans of procedure were suggested. Some

A Toll Gate House Across an Early Kentucky Road

A Swinging Bridge Across a Mountain Creek

Lewis C. Robards' Slave Jail in Lexington

Bybee Pottery in Madison County. It Is More than 100 Years Old

Main Street in a Small Kentucky County Seat

Court Day Crowd in a Kentucky County Seat Town

Threshing Grain on a Modern Kentucky Farm

Breaking Hemp

wanted secession and a union of border states; some wished to give up slavery rather than sacrifice peaceful Northern and Southern trade; while others, who were more radical, preferred out and out secession in the Southern sense of the word. While these dissensions were taking place, Kentucky appointed delegates to the peace conference which was to meet in Washington on February 4, 1861, hoping that the Union could be saved. Nothing came of this move, however, and Kentucky sorrowfully saw all of her pacifist plans come to naught. Accordingly, only one course remained open—neutrality!

Failure of the Washington Peace Conference thickened hopelessness all over Kentucky. The state now became an innocent victim caught geographically between two vicious neighbors, both of whom promised gross mistreatment. So desperate was the situation that the special session of the legislature adjourned *sine die* and without taking a vote on the wisdom of calling a state convention for discussing further a course of neutrality. Nathaniel Southgate Shaler has most aptly stated the situation: "All the days and nights for the dismal year that preceded the war the harrowing question of their action was upon men's minds; by every fireside and in endless meetings the conflict of opposed minds went on. Men, women and children thought and talked of nothing else. The whole life of the citizens went into the matter as never before among any people. In all the other stages of our race conflicts there has been a lower portion of the populace which gave little thought to political questions. They have acted, when the time came, in the way their leaders led them; but in 1860 no white man's cabin in Kentucky was so remote in the wilderness that grave care did not sit by its fireside during all the year."

Such leaders as James Guthrie of Louisville were convinced that the great mass of the American people would hold out for peace at almost any price. Archibald Dixon said on April 19, 1861, that Kentuckians were always ready for a fight when Kentucky's soil was stained with blood, but that he believed that the state would keep out of the War between the States. However, this same political leader denied vehemently the right of a "black" Republican to invade his state. Other Kentuckians hotly expressed the sentiment that they would not stand by to see their Southern neighbors coerced by an armed force of the National Government.

Unlike Kentucky, the Confederate Government acted promptly. While Kentuckians debated their position in the approaching struggle, the Confederates were active in devising schemes to bring about Kentucky's secession. If Kentucky seceded, reasoned the Confederate leaders, it was almost a foregone conclusion that the South would win its fight against the Union. With Kentucky in the Confederacy the Southern frontier would be extended to the Ohio River. Furthermore, a fairly certain supply of food and livestock could be secured in Kentucky. Two factors, however, explain Kentucky's failure to respond promptly to the Confederacy's efforts. First, there was a total lack of unanimity in the legislature, which met for a month beginning May 6, 1861. This legislative session finally resulted in the adoption of a set of resolutions which, for the first time, defined Kentucky's course on paper—that the state was to remain neutral. However, few Kentuckians believed that this stand for neutrality could be sustained. Interestingly enough, Kentucky's native son, Abraham Lincoln, doubted that its neutrality would endure. At Richmond, Kentucky's other native son, Jefferson Davis, was of like opinion. Neither President respected Kentucky's neutrality, for the United States War Department asked for four regiments of Kentucky volunteers on April 15, 1861. On April 22, 1861, L. P. Walker, Secretary of War in Davis' cabinet, followed the precedent of Secretary of War, Simon Cameron, and requisitioned Governor Magoffin "to furnish one regiment of infantry without delay." Governor Magoffin emphatically refused to heed either call, once again asserting Kentucky's neutrality. Dissatisfied with Magoffin's answer and most desirous of securing the support of Kentucky, the Southerners became impatient. Unfortunately for the Southern cause a chance remark, attributed to Howell Cobb of Georgia, greatly antagonized many pro-Southern Kentuckians. It was reported that Cobb had said that Southerners of the lower states would only "have to go home and raise cotton, and make money" while the border states fought and won the war.

Southern newspapers were likewise indiscreet in their anxiety to drag Kentucky into the conflict. They were continually hurting Kentuckians' sensitive pride with cutting remarks about their neutrality and by veiled suggestions of using Kentucky as a "buffer." In order to coerce Kentucky, they advocated trade restrictions, which the Confederate

Government imposed in the spring of 1861. The first year of sectional strife placed a hardship upon Kentucky, for trade restrictions were placed upon Mississippi River steamers. Kentucky merchants then found themselves in a situation similar to the one which confronted their fathers when Governor General Morales removed the right of deposit at New Orleans in 1800.

Southern impatience failed to achieve an advantage for the Confederacy; instead it played directly into President Lincoln's hands. Paying strict attention to the Confederacy's activities in his native state, Lincoln was able to avoid much of the South's folly. He did not commit the dangerous act of openly pushing the Union cause in Kentucky but waited for an opportune moment when he could move into the state without creating undue disturbance to either Kentucky or the secessionary powers.

A military board of five members was created by the Kentucky legislature on May 21, 1861, to supplant the board of control, composed of pro-Southern Governor Magoffin and Adjutant General Simon Bolivar Buckner. The legislature feared that at any moment these officials would hand over Kentucky's State Guard to the Confederacy. The new board was given an appropriation of $1,000,000 with which to equip a new home guard. This organization was to be a loosely organized body of troops entrusted with the protection of Kentucky, but, more specifically, to offset the influence of the State Guard under the command of General Buckner.

Early in 1861, Kentucky, despite her neutrality, became a center of military activity. Muskets and bayonets were shipped into the state from Cincinnati by the Federal Government. While hundreds of young men in many communities deserted their state to go South and join the Confederate Army, Camp Dick Robinson became a Union training center, and Camp Joe Holt grew into an important army post. Governor Magoffin was now convinced that neutrality was a will-o'-the-wisp, for his state was being invaded from all sides. Both Union and Confederate troops swarmed over southern and western Kentucky. Simon Bolivar Buckner and John Hunt Morgan led the State Guards and the Lexington Rifles away to join the Army of the South. The former were equipped and drilled at considerable expense by the State of Kentucky.

One year before his term was up (1862), Governor Magoffin, reaching the conclusion that Kentucky's course was hopeless, resigned his governorship. Thus ended Kentucky's claim of neutrality. Kentucky had innocently drifted into a state of fratricidal strife which perhaps has had few equals for bloody consequences. Division of sentiment in Kentucky was marked by individual personalities rather than by sections and communities. Father was set against son, brother against brother, and friend against friend. Most significant of all, the state suffered vandalism at the hands of its native sons. Many of them directed their attacks at their home counties in efforts to coerce Kentucky into joining forces with one side or the other.

Political Developments During the War

When the Confederates from Tennessee posts invaded southern Kentucky at the beginning of the war, it was their desire to establish the Confederate Government within the state. It was planned that this government would declare the immediate secession of Kentucky. A "Sovereignty Convention" was called on November 18, 1862, to meet at Russellville to discuss procedure. Sixty-five counties were represented in this convention by two hundred and ten delegates. A committee under the chairmanship of John C. Breckinridge was appointed to draft plans for setting up a Confederate state government. These counties declared their right of independence and proceeded to elect a Governor, a legislature, or council composed of ten members, and minor state officials. Kentucky's third constitution was adopted, G. W. Johnson chosen Governor, and Bowling Green selected as legislative headquarters. Upon receiving word that the Kentuckians had acted, Jefferson Davis immediately recommended to the Confederate Congress that Kentucky be admitted into the United Confederate States. On December 10, 1862, the state was granted permission to send ten congressmen to Richmond.

After all, the sovereignty convention accomplished nothing definite, for it was never able to fill its quota of men for the Confederate Army nor to raise its share of Confederate taxes. Since the Confederates were driven out of southern Kentucky, the Confederate Kentucky State Government became a negligible factor. Governor Johnson, a private in the army, was killed while fighting in the campaign at Shiloh, and in

October he was succeeded by the exceedingly brief administration of Robert Hawes. Governor Hawes was inaugurated at Frankfort in October, the only time the Confederates had complete control of the state capital, but, unhappily for the new Governor, he was unable to finish his inaugural address before having to evacuate the city. While the inaugural ceremonies were in progress, General Sill with a detachment of troops from Buell's army appeared on the hill above the town to force the Confederate Governor and his party to depart through the railroad tunnel. The secessionary government in Kentucky was no stronger than Bragg's army and logically ceased to exist when Bragg left the state. Nevertheless, the Richmond Government continued to receive representatives from the "Confederate State of Kentucky," but this was pure fiction, for these representatives had little sanction at home.

Although partial to the Confederate cause, Governor Magoffin was bitterly opposed to that government's high-handedness, and he encouraged legislation which would curb its interference with Kentucky's neutrality. However, all of Kentucky's troubles did not originate in the South, for while Magoffin was upset over the activities of the Confederate Government, the United States Government in June, 1862, appointed General Jeremiah T. Boyle as Commander of the Department of Kentucky. Boyle, facing his position with undue seriousness and authority, arrested many of Kentucky's private citizens. Among these outraged citizens were James B. Clay, son of Henry Clay, Reuben T. Durrett, an outstanding newspaper editor, and Charles S. Morehead, a beloved citizen and former Governor. Boyle charged these men with disloyalty and was quite abusive in his treatment of Morehead. Charges of disloyalty issued against scores of others for expressing private opinions were sufficient reasons to incur the enmity of the federal "war dogs" of the officious Boyle at Louisville. Hence relations between civil and military authorities became strained, as Governor Magoffin pointed out in his address to the legislature on August 15, 1862. The legislature passed laws declaring Confederate agents guilty of felony, and any person who sided with the Confederacy was automatically expatriated. In the same year federal officials required strict oaths of fidelity from all public servants such as representatives to the legislature, lawyers, preachers, doctors, and teachers. For the most part, rabid

Unionists in the state legislature subscribed to the stringent federal measures, but the laws passed were sufficiently irritable to cause the pro-Southern Governor to resign a year before the end of his regular term. James F. Robinson, who, by political maneuvering, was substituted for John Fish as speaker of the house in the legislature, was duly sworn in as Magoffin's successor.

Arresting Kentuckians on trumped-up charges of treachery proved one of the sorest points of contention between Kentucky and the Union. General Sherman quickly perceived the dangers of these arrests, and he ordered political prisoners to be retained in the state until their cases were heard before a duly constituted state court. With a multitude of provost marshalls in Kentucky there was no uniformity of authority, and certainly little centralization of control. Hence many Union arrests bore every evidence of personal spite. Besides, Senator Powell's resolution in the United States Senate, asking for an investigation of the Kentucky arrests, was defeated, and this defeat added additional fuel to the fire. Kentuckians were further enraged when federal military officials began arresting women and children. To the Kentuckians, who, in 1845, refused to send Delia Anne Webster, an underground railway conductor, to the penitentiary for a prolonged stay, the arrest of women was regarded as an unforgivable outrage.

Throughout Governor Robinson's brief administration, federal military authorities increased their disregard for Kentucky's civil agencies. Even Robert J. Breckinridge, one of President Lincoln's most faithful friends in Kentucky, advocated recalling Kentucky troops from the army to drive the "Yankees" from the state. Further insult was offered citizens of Kentucky when military officers began meddling with the courts. This act made the Unionist Governor Robinson defiant, and he threatened state military opposition to the federal interference with the institutions of justice.

A second point of contention was the total disregard by Union officers of Kentucky's slaveholding rights. Despite the fact that President Lincoln's Emancipation Proclamation, effective January 1, 1863, did not apply to Kentucky, Union military officers wished to encourage the desertion of slaves so that they could use them for laborers in camps or in building fortifications and military highways. This abuse brought forth violent protests. A delegation composed of Garret Davis, Charles

Wickliffe, and John J. Crittenden presented Kentucky's complaint to President Lincoln. Lincoln promised the delegation that he would pay $300 per head for slaves taken from their masters illegally, a proposition which the Kentucky delegates denounced immediately, for they believed Congress would not appropriate the money.

"Bounty Scalpers" found Kentucky a fertile field in which to practice their nefarious trade. Many slaves were enticed across the Ohio River to the North and freed, only to be hired as substitutes in the army at $800 to $900 each. The Negroes received only about $100, the remainder going to their abductors. However, Kentuckians were active in the protection of their slaves, for they carefully watched the Ohio River frontier. Not only did they halt and capture their own slaves, but they also took into custody those from the Lower South who attempted to cross the Ohio.

Widely differing views between the Kentuckians and the Unionists who had invaded Kentucky led to a badly disorganized and vicious political system. There were in 1864 two major political parties: the Union Democrats and the regular Democrats. Meeting in Louisville on March 18, 1863, the Union Democrats nominated Joshua Bell, an old-line Whig, for Governor, over the ambitious Jerry Boyle, and Richard Jacobs was nominated Lieutenant Governor. Bell, however, was not enthusiastic over the future relations of Kentucky with the Union, and on May 2, he withdrew his name from the campaign. The Union Democratic Central Committee then nominated Thomas E. Bramlette, a former Union officer, to lead the ticket. Charles A. Wickliffe, a regular Democrat, was selected by his party as nominee for Governor. Leading the regular Democrats was far from an easy task, however. Despite the fact that the approaching election had placed a quietus on federal activities in Kentucky, it did not check federal intimidation of Democrats. When election day arrived, the Democrats were in a serious position, for most of their supporters were in jail, exiled, or afraid to brave threats of violence at the polls. Bramlette received a vote of 68,000 to Wickliffe's 18,000. At the polls, fraud and corruption were rampant, and it takes little political insight to realize that the election of 1863 was far from being a frank expression of the Kentucky electorate.

The state election further complicated matters for the approaching national election in November of 1864. It took much faithful fanning to revive the spark of Republicanism for President Lincoln. Perhaps the most ardent Kentuckians supporting Lincoln were Robert J. Breckinridge, Cassius M. Clay, and Joshua Speed. It was the untiring labor and influence of Breckinridge which sent a fairly strong Kentucky delegation to Baltimore in June to nominate Lincoln and Johnson on the Republican ticket. Leaders of the Democratic Party in Kentucky were Charles A. Wickliffe, John G. Carlisle, Senator Lazarus W. Powell, John H. Harney, Joshua Bullitt, John Y. Brown, George Baber, Asa P. Graves, and R. R. Houston representing one wing, and George D. Prentice and James Guthrie and others representing the other. When these two groups reached Chicago in August for the Democratic convention, the difference in their views was so slight that both delegations were seated.

Before the election of 1864 President Lincoln issued his proclamation (on July 5) suspending the writ of habeas corpus in Kentucky, with specific instructions that this order should not affect the approaching elections. Three days before the election for members of the state court of appeals, General Burbridge ordered that Alvin Duvall's (a member of the court of appeals since 1856) name be taken off the ballot. This forced Judge Duvall to leave the state.

Out of a possible 45,000 Unionist votes only 11,000 were cast, and these went to the exiled Duvall's opponent, George Robertson. In the general election in the fall Lincoln received 26,592 civilian votes, and McClellan received 61,478. Lincoln received 1,205 soldiers' votes, and McClellan received 3,608.

Kentucky's relations were strained with both sides throughout the war because of their respective recruiting tactics. Faithful to her colorful military history and despite much hostility, Kentucky kept her Union quota filled for the first months of the war. However, it was soon found that the state was being abused, and Kentucky's promptness in answering requests for volunteers grew less enthusiastic. President Lincoln's call for 30,000 volunteers in 1862 was answered in full, but by 1864 the state's patience was exhausted by continual requests for large numbers of troops. Orders for recruits in 1864 were almost ignored, for the response of volunteers to two calls for a total of 26,000 troops was only about 4,000. When the draft was instituted, the Kentuckians avoided it. Doubtless Governor Bramlette shared the feelings of his constituents on the subject of the draft, for in May, 1864, he offered to lead a state guard of 10,000 "six months" troops to rid the state of guerrillas. Furthermore, he emphatically stated to the War Department that he was bitterly opposed to having Kentucky troops leave the state to fight in Union ranks. Lincoln's plan to use Negro troops (which is discussed more fully in another chapter) brought forth a bitter attack from Kentuckians and from Frank Wolford, a Union cavalry commander. Wolford's attack came as a surprise, for the occasion on which he addressed citizens of Lexington in Melodeon Hall at the corner of Upper and Main Streets was to pay tribute to Lincoln. Robert J. Breckinridge presided and was much chagrined to hear Wolford speak so disrespectfully of his commander in chief. Wolford was immediately removed from the service, but not before he had adequately voiced the sentiment of many Kentuckians in regard to the vacillating policy of the Federal Government at Washington. Altogether, Kentucky politics remained in a state of flux until reconstruction politicians gave them a second stirring after the end of the war in 1865.

Commercial Relations During the War

Perhaps the most plausible reason for Kentucky's attempt to remain neutral is found in her commercial relations with the South and East. There is every reason to think that Kentucky's political and commercial leaders believed their state would be able to trade with other states without regard to their position in the Union. Another factor to be considered seriously was the influence which routes of travel to the South had upon the Union military strategists. There were the Louisville and Nashville, the Mobile and Ohio, and the Mississippi Central Railroads, and the Mississippi, Ohio, Cumberland, Tennessee, and Kentucky Rivers, flowing southward and capable of floating a tremendous amount of commerce. Thus is explained the act of Congress on July 13, 1861, which restricted trade from Kentucky to the Southern States. Captains on southbound river steamers were required to secure special licenses for their vessels. It is laughable to recall that the "Yankee" could not resist his temptation to trade, so greatly interested was he in the possibilities of profit offered in the South.

Rules in the Federal Army were made stricter with the passage of time. After April 15, 1862, all river vessels had to show their manifests at every port. Aids from the United States Treasury Department traveled with the vessels to see that freight was not loaded at way landings. On¹y persons known for their loyalty to the Union were permitted to engage in trade, a thing which led to much bickering between the War and Treasury Departments. Petty trading and grafting in the direct line of fighting by various attachés of the Government virtually converted the war into a farce of many acts. For instance, railway cars and army wagon trains were so busily engaged in transportation of cotton to market that army stores spoiled in freight stations. So prevalent was this practice that troops often could not be sustained at a post for lack of food and munition supplies. Sherman and Grant were bitterly opposed to the practice of trading with Southerners. General Sherman said the use of Treasury aids to guard against trade infractions in the Southern area was comparable to "setting a rat to watch the cheese to see that the mice don't get it." He argued with much wisdom against the ill-advised contention that the United States Government needed cotton, for, he said, money was as much a contraband of war as gunpowder.

One of the arguments used at the outbreak of the war by George W. Johnson for pushing Confederate lines into Kentucky was the extension of the trading area of the Confederacy. While the Union was forcing traders to the South to secure special licenses, and while southern trade was being restricted, the South likewise attempted to hinder trade northward. The Confederate Government passed restrictive acts August 2, 1861, to keep the Southern States, including Kentucky, from trading with the Union. At first the Confederacy tried to coerce Kentucky to secede by restricting her commerce to those sections not under Confederate control. By so restricting Kentucky's commerce, the Confederate Government hoped to win the friendship of the populace of the important distributing center, Louisville and its adjacent territory.

Kentucky, in attempting to steer a neutral course, naturally did not pledge fidelity to the Union cause in the Mississippi Valley, for, surely, commercially minded Kentuckians hoped this stand would guarantee commercial independence. Quite contrary to popular hopes, Kentucky early became a center of dispute between the North and the South. Like her civil government, her commercial activities were soon dictated by military powers. Grant ordered complete restriction of trade in southwestern Kentucky and southern Illinois, for traders in these sections had resorted to trickery in shipping goods under false labels to Jonesborough, Illinois, and thence southward. For instance, large shipments of whiskey in barrels were made, but the contents of these barrels, like Lot's wife, mysteriously turned to salt on reaching southern destinations. Shipments labeled "whiskey" became not only salt, but likewise gunpowder and pork. So corrupt was this trade between the North and South that the Paducah branch of the Union League of America protested that the "Rebels are doing all the business, and they are reaping all the advantages of trade." As a result of slack river control, the commander at Cairo issued an order on April 2, 1862, forbidding vessels to land between Paducah and Memphis. However, this was a doubtful remedy, for it was said that Southerners had little desire to disturb commerce at Memphis by attacking the city, since it was a valuable supply post. Certainly a restraining order issued at Cairo was hardly an effective check upon trade between southern Kentucky and the Southern States, since all of Kentucky's intersectional railroads and rivers tapped this region. It is a fact that this proved a poor foraging area when Johnston's and Polk's forces were encamped there, yet suddenly it became an important exporting center for supplies from elsewhere, the Blue Grass. Evidence of this is found in Grant's attitude when in disgust he ordered his officers to leave the regulations of trade in southern Kentucky to the treasury officials. A communication to Sherman noted that the Confederate officers halted river vessels only when they wished to cross the river. The historian, Collins, calls attention to the resources for trade in Kentucky in the fact that Braxton Bragg's commissary department purchased 7,000 barrels of pork and $90,000 worth of clothing in the fall of 1862.

The southern Kentucky counties of Union, Crittenden, Graves, Marshall, Calloway, Trigg, Lyon, and Caldwell shipped vast quantities of salt, sugar, and leather to the South. Few, if any, of these supplies were produced in these counties. Livestock drovers had little trouble making their customary trips into the cotton belt.

Besides trading extensively with the South, Kentucky was supplying quantities of foodstuffs to the Union Army. In some cases this trade was used to enforce loyalty to the Union, for only loyal persons could cash their trade vouchers. Not only was there an extensive independent trade with the Union, but much more was enforced by federal officials. This practice of commandeering supplies enraged the Kentuckians. George D. Prentice said that the United States Government was depriving innocent Kentuckians annually of hundreds of droves of hogs, horses, and cattle. Moreover, long wagon trains loaded with supplies were hauled from Kentucky to feed the Federal Army.

One of the most dastardly tricks imposed upon Kentucky during the war was the so-called Burbridge "hog swindle." On October 28, 1864, Major General Burbridge ordered, in an apparently innocent dispatch, that all Kentucky hog raisers sell their surplus hogs to the United States Government. No one suspected a swindle in this dignified order. General Burbridge became so solicitous as to assure his Kentucky friends that there would be no chance of losing their pork in Confederate raids. Major H. C. Symonds was in charge of the hog trade, and General Burbridge obliged him by closing both the Cincinnati market and the Ohio River to the trade. Louisville buyers were politely ordered to hold off and "patriotically" give the government buyers a chance to stock the federal larder. However, Governor Bramlette, suspecting duplicity in these activities, prevailed upon President Lincoln to revoke Burbridge's order. Lincoln reopened the pork markets on November 27, when it was learned that Kentuckians had been swindled of $5.00 per head for every hog they had sold for a total of over $60,000.

During much of the war, trade was unnecessarily placed under petty restrictions because of intermittent raids into the state. Morgan's frequent invasions caused suspension of trade. Business to the South was checked temporarily. Because of periodic destruction of the Louisville and Nashville Railroad, Kentuckians were often without a satisfactory means of transportation. It was estimated by the Louisville and Nashville Company's board of investigation that the war caused over a quarter of a million dollars loss in railway property.

By the latter months of 1862, however, contemporary observers noted that Louisville had assumed her ante bellum commercial appearance. Trade with many areas in the South was unrestricted. Cotton, which was selling for eight cents per pound, was arriving daily at the port of Louisville, and some of this even passed with the approval of General Grant. Direct commerce between Louisville and New Orleans was restored on September 23, 1863, and other branches of trade in the South were rapidly reopened. With the exception of certain restrictions imposed by Congress on July 2, 1864, Kentucky's Southern trade prospered. Not only did this trade flourish, but local packers did a rushing business, in 1864, when they easily filled a government contract for 100,000 hogs. All restrictions upon Kentucky's trade were removed on April 29, 1865, and her merchants were the first to gain a new foothold in the war-ridden Southern States.

The story of much interference in Kentucky's trade by both sections of the country during the whole period of the war would be monotonous if it were not for the importance of the tremendous commercial interchange between the two sections. When the Kentucky war trade is considered, it is difficult to believe that the Southern States were always as short of foodstuffs as reputed. Of course, the frontier of the War between the States was a long one, extending through several diverse areas, but even this considered, the great amount of traveling and trading between the opposing sections is surprising.

General Robert E. Lee, on April 8, 1865, surrendered the Army of Northern Virginia at Appomattox Courthouse, making the war officially over. No Southern State was more pleased than Kentucky, for peace would restore commercial order in the state. Hardly had word of Lee's surrender reached Kentucky before news came that Lincoln had been assassinated by the fanatical actor, John Wilkes Booth. Upon word of Lincoln's death, Kentucky was truly sorrowful; Governor Bramlette ordered fitting ceremonies for the passing of the President; and James Guthrie and the Governor were generous and kind in their memorial addresses.

Despite the fact that Kentucky did not suffer the severe material losses through the heartless ravages of war which Mississippi, Alabama, Georgia, and South Carolina experienced, it was in a turmoil over the control of civil and commercial institutions. From the beginning, federal officials had been important in the control of Kentucky affairs. Kentucky had always guarded its institution of slavery with jealousy and was quite hostile to the Proclamation of Emancipation in 1863.

With the end of the war and the call upon the states to ratify the new federal legislation, Kentucky could not amend her constitution to meet these new demands for at least five years. Unlike the other slave states, Kentucky did not revise her constitution at the end of the war. As a consequence, the constitution of 1849 stood as a protecting bulwark of slavery not only by its special slavery section, but also by its amending clause. To abolish slavery, in 1865, in the face of the constitution, was impossible. To amend the constitution required that a majority of all the members of each house of the legislature vote for an amending convention in the first twenty days of the session. The sheriffs of each county were then to hold a vote on the specific constitutional issue at the next general election and to report the results to the Secretary of State. At the next session of the legislature, which, after 1850, met biennially, the Secretary of State reported the result of the election, and the legislature again voted upon the measure. If a majority still favored the issue, the assembly instructed that a second poll be taken at the next general session; and if a majority of the voters favored the amendment, the next general assembly was to call for an election of delegates at the next general election; and these delegates were to meet within three months after the election. A majority of the qualified voters, and not a majority of those voting, was necessary to keep the issue alive. If at any time the issue failed to receive a majority of qualified votes, it was killed. Hence, slavery in Kentucky constitutionally was guaranteed this additional period of life.

Slaveholders refused to yield chattel slaves to freedom without compensation. Kentucky representatives in Congress voted steadfastly against the submission of the Thirteenth Amendment, but the Federal Government was asked to appropriate $34,000,000 to pay their constituents for slaves. Public opinion was aroused, and the freeing of slaves became the subject of discussion in every household in central Kentucky. In the meantime, Kentuckians raised their estimate of the total value of their slaves, and a second request went to Congress asking for $100,000,000 to compensate them for their property losses.

Most Kentuckians, as was typical of Southerners, were thoroughly convinced that freeing Negroes would have ill effects in destroying the source of labor and in encouraging vandalism and general disorder. So definite was this fear that the Kentucky legislature voted 57 to 28 in the house, and 22 to 11 in the Senate, to cast aside the federal proposal of compensated freedom of slaves. A few days later the Thirteenth Amendment was defeated unconditionally, and no pressure national officials could bring to bear upon the Kentuckians was successful in securing a ratification of the amendment.

While Kentucky was wrangling with the National Government over the ratification of the Thirteenth Amendment, slave prices dropped to a fractional figure of their former value. For instance, slaves which had sold for $1,500 now brought only $300. It is natural that this should happen in the face of "Palmer's passes," so-called from General J. M. Palmer's plan of granting Negroes the right to travel where they pleased on passes. Palmer's military forces concentrated the Negroes in Louisville, a move which proved effective in breaking down Kentucky's slave system. This method of ridding Kentucky of slavery caused a hue and cry during the year following the war, for it concentrated more than 28,000 Negroes in the Louisville camp. Embittered Kentuckians asked for an immediate demobilization of this threatening army. Numerous attempts were made to defeat Palmer's plan by passing laws in the legislature denying Negroes free right to travel on stages, boats, and trains, and by preventing their being hired as laborers. Unfortunately this system of regulation led to further misunderstanding, for federal officials immediately required slaveholders to pay their slaves wages from the date of the ratification of the Thirteenth Amendment until they were freed. All this wrangling led nowhere, for, finally, the constitution-loving Kentuckians were forced to bow to the rule of the Thirteenth Amendment and to recognize the end of slavery.

When Kentucky finally recognized the Thirteenth Amendment, it would have been well for both parties if the radicals had abandoned their plans to reconstruct the state. Here it is fitting to recall that Kentucky never seceded, in the true sense of the word, from the Union. It failed to ratify the Thirteenth Amendment, but this was far from an act of secession. Therefore, the radicals were wrong when they looked upon the State of Kentucky as they did upon the secessionary states of the Lower South. Radical politicians, however, were reluctant to let such a productive political hunting ground go untouched. Ambitious scalawags and carpetbaggers saw an excellent opportunity for graft and personal gain. This is the secret of the extreme sectional bitterness which still exists in Kentucky. Had the federal forces been removed from Kentucky immediately after the war, and had this proud state not been submitted to the cheap trickery and deception of reconstruction politics, little of the strong sectional feeling would still exist. The radicals misjudged the attitude of the citizens of this southern commonwealth. Quite contrary to popular belief north of the Ohio, the Federal and Confederate soldiers returned to Kentucky to agree at least on one matter, a steadfast admiration for their state.

Kentucky's first relief from the wartime disruption came on October 12, 1865, when President Johnson revoked the rule of martial law. In November following, the President restored the writ of habeas corpus and returned Kentucky to the roster of loyal states. However, there still remained many national and domestic barriers to prevent harmony in Kentucky. There was the Freedmen's Bureau supplying national protection to both free and enslaved Negroes. Originally this institution had undertaken rehabilitation of the freed slaves, but under the direction of radical Republicans it became an agent of partisan politics and exploitation. It was first established by an act of Congress on March 3, 1865, but it did not become effective on any extensive scale until after July 16, 1866, when an act to continue it for two more years was passed over the President's veto.

Bureau posts were established in Kentucky at Louisville, Lexington, Maysville, Covington, and other towns. Where the centers were small, special traveling officials were provided. Had this organization carried out its humane purpose it would have been a boon to Kentucky. Undoubtedly, the Freedmen's Bureau could have eliminated much of the fear of the free Negro if it had not entered politics, and had it received the co-operation of the best citizens of the state. As it was, efforts were made by many of the farmers of the state to stabilize labor at a uniform wage scale of $100 to $150 per year for males, and $50 to $100 for females. These efforts were fruitless, however, for both groups lacked a willingness to co-operate. White employers were dubious always of the Freedmen's Bureau, and the Bureau doubted the sincerity of these whites.

Kentucky's labor problem became acute. Farmers rented their lands to tenants who had been encouraged to move into the state from other parts of the country. Several Kentucky commercial interests undertook a widespread campaign to encourage foreign laborers, including Chinese coolies, to settle in Kentucky. This plan, however, failed, for only about 3,500 foreigners moved to Kentucky, most of whom were concentrated in Louisville. Tenancy resulted from several causes. The source of Negro labor for the time being was exhausted, and, in order to secure new laborers, whites were encouraged to immigrate to the more fertile sections of the state. Not only was there a shifting of the white population in Kentucky, but there was an influx of landless whites from neighboring states to the North. Postwar dislike for the Negro forced him to settle in villages which had their beginnings as "free towns," away from the white communities. Negroes also migrated away from the farms to the towns and the cities to become public laborers. During this movement of the Negro from the farm, the tobacco industry was growing, and the white tenant soon got the reputation of being the more trustworthy "hand" with tobacco. This belief still prevails in most of the tobacco growing area. White tenancy in postwar years showed a rapid increase, and the term "tobacco tenant" became more indicative of social and economic degradation.

Efforts to secure cheap labor from elsewhere had a wholesome effect upon Kentucky Negroes' attitude toward their former masters. It resulted in the organization of a mutually approved Intelligence Office which directed the re-employment of the Negro and set about systematically to restore good feeling between the races.

Whereas the Intelligence Office brought harmony, the Freedmen's Bureau had antagonized the two races. For instance, the Bureau delayed the recognition of the Negro's right to testify in Kentucky courts. It was not until the Bureau was disbanded in 1872 that the state legislature of Kentucky voted to accept Negro testimony.

Another conflict between the races in Kentucky was the question of the Negro's newly acquired right of franchise. For the first time in Kentucky's history, the Negro was permitted to vote. The Civil Rights Act, 1872, gave the Negro this privilege, and it was around this problem that much of the organized violence revolved. General Palmer informed the Louisville Negroes that they were equal to the whites and urged them to make good use of this advantage. In Lexington, C. B. Fisk and Cassius M. Goodloe exhorted Negro listeners on the subject of voting and on the wickedness of rebels and Democrats. J. B. Brisbin advised Negroes of Winchester to read their Bibles and trust God, and never to vote for a rebel or a Democrat. These same radicals were influential in organizing most of the 52,000 black voters into secret societies such as the "Union Benevolent Society," "United Brothers of Friendship," and the "Loyal League." Perhaps the radicals could not have invented a more successful appeal than these secret societies, for the ex-slave had an inherent weakness for mysterious proceedings.

Organization of the Negro by the Freedmen's Bureau led to violence on the part of the whites. Perhaps much of Kentucky's organized raiding was simply a spark from the dying embers of guerrilla warfare. One historian of Kentucky has explained the feuds on the basis of this period of strife. He says that grudges between self-respecting citizens of the Kentucky mountains and the outlaw bands led to subsequent fighting which endured many years. Whether or not this is true is highly debatable; at any rate there existed in the state bands known as "The Regulators," "Sue Munday's Men," "Rowzee's Band," and "Skagg's Men." These bands terrorized the counties of Marion, Madison, Mercer, Boyle, and Lincoln. Not only did they frighten organizations of the colored, but they robbed and murdered self-respecting whites. Lynch law ruled in certain sections of Kentucky between 1866 and 1871, and the whole social system was in a needless turmoil. The Ku Klux Klan was not so successful on Kentucky soil as elsewhere, but there were chapters, or klans, in Kentucky, for even Governor Bramlette was accused of being the local Grand Cyclops.

With the election of a new legislature in 1871, comparative peace and order were restored. Since that time the state government has been in the control of Kentuckians, elected by Kentuckians. Through the influence of the press, the dean of which was "Marse" Henry Watterson, Confederates became local and state leaders in most sections. The Democratic ticket for local and state offices was elected in 1871, for the whites soon learned the art of manipulating Negro voters. Preston H. Leslie was the Democratic Governor; Thomas B. McCreary and Garret Davis were United States Senators. The Democrats had a majority of the congressional delegation. Kentucky lived through the aftermath of the War between the States soon to accept, not only the Thirteenth Amendment, but also the Fourteenth and Fifteenth.

CHAPTER XIX

Educational Advances

N O KENTUCKY institution suffered more than the public schools did during the trying years of the Civil War. When war broke out, educational leaders had just succeeded in arousing the people of the more progressive communities to a sense of educational need. Since politics and commerce were dearer to the hearts of Kentucky's leaders in the struggle from 1860 to 1865, the movement for free public schools was the first one halted when the Southern States seceded.

Groups of leaders who had labored steadfastly and harmoniously for the establishment of equal educational opportunities in this democratic commonwealth during the forties and fifties soon found themselves at odds over political differences regarding the struggle in the South. Unfortunately, when these leaders ceased to push the issue, public opinion became indifferent, and funds for the support of schools in these trying years were seriously limited. A war-torn legislature at Frankfort found time only to enact a financial bill awarding the schools fines, money confiscated in gambling games, and a $1.00 tax per dog for each one over two owned by residents of the state.

Besides, Kentucky's public school movement did not begin long enough before the war to be thoroughly fastened in the public mind. Her people became hopelessly divided over the issue involved in the war, and communities which ordinarily would have been interested in promoting public schools became either too poor or too indifferent to make the much needed effort.

Historians have said with a great deal of truth that the years 1861 to 1867 saw little or no social development in Kentucky. Z. F. Smith, superintendent of public instruction, found the school system, with a few exceptions, at the point where Robert J. Breckinridge had left it. Superintendent Smith possessed the foresight and determination necessary to force the idea of public schools upon an indifferent legislature.

He was successful in convincing his constituents that his ideas of education were in perfect harmony with those of democracy and secured a
majority of the voting strength of Kentucky. Whereas a war-minded
legislature had begrudgingly appropriated 5 cents per $100 of assessable
property, the fines from the gamblers, and the dog tax to a groveling
school system, Professor Smith demanded a levy of 20 cents on assessable property. He also asked that the counties be redistricted and that
each district be given $97 to $237 for the support of public schools over
a period of five months. He worked on the sound assumption that, in
a majority of the districts, the state would have to take the lead if
public schools were to be established.

To establish a school system in Kentucky, following the war, was an
enormous task. Obtaining financial support was the first major problem confronting educational leaders. Equally baffling were questions
of administration, for there were no trained commissioners, few trained
teachers, and fewer facilities for training them. Persons with professional preparations were lawyers, doctors, and preachers. The first two
of these professions were far more lucrative than teaching school. The
few partially trained teachers available used their jobs as school teachers
for stepping stones to something better. There were no high schools
(with the exception of a few inferior private academies in the more
populous centers) where teachers might secure even a rudimentary
knowledge of the subject matter to be taught. Lack of textbooks, to
say nothing of an abominable lack of uniformity, was a serious handicap.

Many were the stirring addresses delivered by Z. F. Smith in order to
awaken his constituents to the importance of education to the state.
He used the effective argument that, because of her state of ignorance,
Kentucky was losing many of her finest citizens by emigration to other
states. Perseverance won for the state superintendent the attention of
the legislature, for on February 20, 1869, a law was passed by that body
permitting Louisville to elect a commissioner of education. This law
led to the election of other city commissioners and to the present useful
administrative official, the city superintendent.

A forward step was taken on January 23, 1869, when the legislature
passed a bill permitting the people of the state to vote in the August
elections on the question of raising the school tax on property from

5 to 20 cents per $100. This date stands as a red-letter day in Kentucky's educational progress.

At the same time the legislature provided for an increase in school tax, it also enacted a bill for popular election of county commissioners, county selection of textbooks, and the establishment of teacher-training institutions. Selecting textbooks to fit the curriculum was complicated (as will be described) because of a lack of books. The course of study followed steadfastly the proverbial 3 R's, with history and geography thrown in for good measure. A third bill was proposed by the state superintendent, but unfortunately the legislature had grown weary of granting public school privileges and refused to pass it. Had the bill of 1869 proposing additional revenue become a law, it would have permitted liberalization of the school system and, in the end, would have laid the foundation for a school system equal to those of the Northwestern States.

The job of organizing the postwar Kentucky school system was one of many trials and tested the patience of more than one conscientious state superintendent. Every report between 1865 and 1890 stressed the imperative need for better trained teachers and expressed dissatisfaction with county commissioners, boards of trustees, textbooks, location of schoolhouses, and public support. Under the pressure of these vital problems Kentucky's school development has of necessity followed a zigzag course.

After Superintendent Stevenson's administration, Superintendent H. A. M. Henderson expressed a desire to build a system of public education, though he realized, of course, that it would have an unstable foundation. Before a school system could be constructed, the state department of education itself needed organization. From 1838 on, the state board of education was composed of the Superintendent of Public Instruction, the Secretary of State, and the Attorney General, ex officio members. The latter two could give little attention to the needs of the department of education, and, besides, the partisan nature of these offices made meddling with education a ticklish job. Hence the superintendent's duties were for many years nothing more than clerical. He supplied blanks, forms, and textbooks, and collected reports from the counties. However, the postwar superintendents were diligent almost to a man in stimulating a demand for schools. Superintendent Henderson made headway when he compared the costs of private and public schools. He found that citizens of Frankfort were paying $38 per student to profit-making private academies, while public schools were training more students at $14 per capita.

An increasing demand for teachers and the total lack of well-trained ones made it imperative that arrangements be made to supply them. A system of county normal schools was organized to offer teacher-training courses of from two to six weeks at county seats. These normal schools were taught by lawyers, preachers, and school teachers and were for the most part inefficient. Few of the short summer sessions did more than publicize a list of state department rules, such as: "No pupil under the age of six or over the age of twenty shall be received or continued in common school," or "The hours for instruction shall be from 8 o'clock A.M. to 4 o'clock P.M. Such intermissions or recesses may be had as the Board of Trustees or the teacher may direct." At this time the state department issued a list of eighteen "do's" and "don'ts." Another function of the normal schools was to instruct prospective teachers in the mere mechanics of conducting their schools. Examples of discipline other than administering a sound thrashing with a hickory limb were demonstrated. The best methods of assembling a school in the morning, "taking up" at recess periods, and dismissing in the afternoon were demonstrated by model teachers. Perhaps, after all, the most useful function of the normal schools was the opportunity given county teachers to develop a sense of co-operation.

Rural schools were inefficiently taught and as poorly disciplined. So careless were many of the early teachers that one superintendent recalled having visited a rural school where he listened outside the door to the teacher quarreling with his students because they bothered him while he was hulling black walnuts. Another state official reported having visited an early school where he found pupils playing on the grounds, but no teacher. He was informed that the teacher had been absent for three days because he did not want to walk to school on the damp ground. Unhappily for local education the state department at Frankfort was so overburdened with establishing an institution for teacher training and school organization that it was forced to leave the responsibility of local schools to county commissioners and local district trustees.

County commissioners were seldom qualified for their jobs and were never paid enough to justify their giving much time to their official duties. They frequently used their office as a clearinghouse for local politics. Although teaching was not remunerative, it offered a fair subsidy to ambitious citizens who wished to spend lean winter months with profit to themselves. The reactions of the commissioners present an interesting study in local educational philosophy, as many of their letters which have been preserved in the state superintendent's reports indicate.

It is worthwhile to examine some of these comments from local administrators. One commissioner expressed the belief that, "The people, as a general rule, are not willing to tax themselves for the payment of teachers, and only the large districts get the best teachers." Another believed, "The system has accomplished more good since 1869 than it did in thirty-five or forty years previous," said a commissioner from Caldwell County in 1881. "There is a want of more money to secure a higher grade of teachers. The wages of the average teacher is [sic] not more than $22 per month. The people are opposed to taxation! Consequently no immediate relief is seen." A Blue Grass commissioner reported, "The school fund is insufficient—local or district taxation impracticable. The people [of Fayette County] will not listen to the discussion of the question." In 1887 the commissioner from Woodford County said he was faced with the embarrassing situation of getting his people to understand "that a Woodford County child is worth as much as a race horse, and is entitled to as good a house in which to study." This commissioner found his trustees as honest and efficient as the system would permit, but wholly inadequate. He expressed the view that trustees should be paid, because he felt that "no pay, no work" was an adage especially adaptable to Kentuckians. Letter after letter from county commissioners to the state superintendent expressed the idea that the trustees were at the root of the school system's multitudinous troubles. These local officials were entrusted with the duties of locating schoolhouses, examining, certifying, and electing teachers, and selecting textbooks. Locating schoolhouses proved a thorn in the sides of many communities, for patrons protested that schoolhouses were located for selfish reasons. These protests were not always without just reason.

A sentiment still prevailing in Kentucky among parents is that certain textbooks are more satisfactory than others. Local sentiment has always been a determining factor in the selection of textbooks. For instance, the "Kentucky" edition of "Little" Alexander H. Stephens' *History of the United States* was popular in certain communities after the war, while the versatile S. G. Goodrich's numerous editions of histories of the world, England, and the United States were popular in others. The methods of selecting textbooks provide one of the most fascinating chapters in the development of Kentucky schools. Immediately after the war the superintendent attempted to plan a curriculum with enough freedom to please all communities; at the same time he attempted to select a number of suitable textbooks for each subject. The curriculum consisted of reading from readers graded from the first to the eighth grade, writing, arithmetic, geography, and the history of the United States. Textbooks selected for these courses were Butler's or Harvey's grammars, Goodrich's or McGuffey's readers and spellers, Stephens', Goodrich's, Barnes', or Venable's histories of the United States, and J. P. Morton and Company's *School Records*. As well as selecting textbooks for the pupils, the superintendent prescribed aids for the teachers. In most cases, teachers knew no more of the subjects which they taught than was contained in their handbooks. It was once a favorite pastime for bright students to catch their teachers working arithmetic problems from their handbooks.

To trace the history of textbook selection it is necessary to begin before 1853, when parents selected books they wanted their children to study, selections which were as varied as trinkets in a curiosity shop. Textbook selection in Kentucky has run the whole course from selection by individuals from recommended state lists, by county boards of examiners, by district trustees, to selection by a textbook commission, and by the board of education in the more populous cities and counties. Some light on this particular phase of educational history in Kentucky is given by one county superintendent who reported that he virtually had to threaten to call the state militia in order to get rid of Webster's *Blue Back Spelling Book*. Trustees were given to thinking in terms of their experiences. This is best illustrated in the report of the superintendent of the Butler County schools. He records the argument among his board members over the question of providing new seats for county schools. One member remarked, "We sot on a split log and our children are no better than us." It is unfortunately too true that some Kentucky schools have used textbooks which were not only antiquated but of many different philosophies, and woefully testifying to their long service as texts for earlier generations.

Special Legislation

When Z. F. Smith left the office of State Superintendent of Education in 1871, Kentucky schools possessed a state bond worth $1,327,000, and $73,500 worth of the Bank of Kentucky stock. The legislature had appropriated a 20-cent tax on income from assessable property, gambler's fines, and the dog tax. With these provisions the schools received meager aid from the state. Public support, however, did show an increase from $352,587 in 1868 to $968,176 in 1872, but the number of schools increased.

On account of numerous experiments there was practically no stability to report in the whole history of Kentucky education between 1860 and 1900. There has always been a conscious desire on the part of educational forces to create a popular demand for free public education. It is with this matter that the remainder of the chapter will be concerned.

A forward step in public education was made in 1882, when an additional tax of two cents was levied on public property for the schools. A slight change was made in the local administrative unit, in 1884, when the county commissioners became known as county superintendents. The legislature, however, failed to restore the county boards, which were abolished in 1856. Creating the office of county superintendent was a wise move, but the state superintendent was still faced with the difficulty of operating a school system under the control of local district trustees. These local districts were established according to the traditions of the old English hundreds. Trustees theoretically divided their districts to include 100 children of school age. It was not until 1909 that the county board system was restored and the whole scheme reorganized. Whereas taxes had been collected and controlled by districts, they were now collected by counties. By this action the school board became a county unit.

Changes made in 1908 formed the nucleus for the law of 1912, which increased funds available for the county schools and permitted a combination of state and county funds to be equitably distributed by the county boards. The county board was given additional freedom by an act of the legislature (1909) which placed the responsibility of the election of the county board in the hands of the people. However, this law was changed in 1920 and the office of county superintendent was made appointive, an act which removed this important officer from control by local politics.

Generally, county superintendents have varied in qualifications. Like early state superintendents, many of them were ministers of the gospel serving charges, or men of other professions devoting most of their time to private business. Salaries for this office have ranged from $100 per year in 1856 to a minimum of $2,200 per year in 1950. Until the last twenty years no county superintendents were trained for their positions, and few were even experienced teachers. When the office was an elective one, the man with the most political influence was chosen.

Outstanding legislative progress in Kentucky's educational development since the war was the adoption of the 20-cent tax levy in 1881, plus the additional 2 cents in 1882, the provision for a local property levy of 25 cents, and the collection of the "rate bill" or "patrons' tax" of $2.00 for each child enrolled in school. Provisions also were made to have public health taught in the public schools.

Subsequent school legislation has come because of popular demand and not from legislative initiative. On four different occasions, 1849, 1855, 1869, and 1885, Kentucky voters approved measures to levy school taxes. Successive legislatures, however, turned a deaf ear to these demands, and it was not until thirteen years after the fourth constitution was adopted that the general assembly responded to the wishes of the people. The fourth constitution guaranteed state support of public education and a permanent place to it in the organization of the state government.

Epochal years in Kentucky's school system were 1908–1909 and 1933–1934; 1948–1950. Superintendent John Grant Crabbe conducted what he called the "whirlwind campaign of 1908," or a "biennium of publicity." During this campaign the famous "Educational Legislature of 1908" met in November in the parlors of the Galt House at Louisville. It was in this assembly that educational forces of the state agreed to a number of necessary reforms to reorganize the whole school system from the lowest district trustee to the State College at Lexington. Superintendent Crabbe secured the assistance of able speakers from business circles, from the Kentucky Confederation of Women's Clubs, from the Kentucky Commission for Improvement of Education, and from the teachers' associations to visit every community of the state. Newspapermen were willing supporters of the movement. One editorial writer said, "The real problem of Kentucky is the improvement of her citizenship, and we are taking relatively too little interest in matters of home concern." He cited Thomas Jefferson's observation that "it is of more vital concern to the people to know who is elected bailiff than president."

Definite gains were made in the "Educational Legislature of 1908." When the state legislature met, it enacted a county school district law, provided for the establishment of a high school in every county, changed the name of Kentucky State College to Kentucky State University, restored the title Transylvania College, increased collegiate appropriations for the University and state normal schools, established a state educational commission to make a thorough investigation of the school system, instituted a compulsory school law applying to cities from the first to fourth classes, and passed a child labor law.

Several useful surveys of the Kentucky educational system have been made in the last fifteen years. In 1921 the General Education Board of New York published the *Kentucky Educational Commission Report*. A second report of this same commission was published in Frankfort in 1933, and Jesse E. Adams published, in 1928, through the University, *A Study in the Equalization of Educational Opportunities in Kentucky*. Perhaps the most important of all of the educational reports was made in 1933 by the special educational commission appointed by Governor Laffoon. This committee, composed of able men selected from several professions, was provided with an abundance of qualified research men who made a thorough inquiry into the state's educational needs. Under the direction of the state superintendent, James H. Richmond, a second "whirlwind campaign" was conducted. Public school debating teams and oratorical contestants discussed Kentucky's needs for educational reform and for additional and more stable public support of education. Able speakers were provided for every community, and state officials at Frankfort used the facilities of radio station WHAS, of the *Louisville Times* and the *Louisville Courier-Journal* to discuss the needs of public schools. Kentucky's newspapers gave ample space to a discussion of the problem, and the Kentucky Educational Association exerted considerable influence in creating a distinct and favorable popular sentiment for public schools. By midsummer of 1934 the Kentucky legislature, in extraordinary session, made additional financial provisions for its schools. In 1945–1946 Griffenhagen and Associates made another survey of the Kentucky school system. At times, it appears that a manifestation of weakness is the appeal to outside survey agencies to say what is wrong with the schools. Unfortunately vitally needed funds have been expended on these surveys which often have been ignored in their major parts or as a whole. In 1950 the Legislative Research Council sought an answer to the various national surveys which have listed Kentucky's school as being near the bottom. Perhaps the only true answer lies in the simple statement that educational accomplishment is at best a relative matter. The emergency teachers, though thoroughly patriotic and helped to keep the Kentucky schools open during World War II, were not adequately equipped to prevent doing the Kentucky school system irreparable harm. No survey ever shows either the human virtues or failures. Nor do the surveys show the local failures due to inadequate tax support, personal politics, official philandering by school boards and personal inadequacies of teachers. All of these things must be considered when assessing the real achievements of Kentucky schools.

Kentucky's public school system has climbed steadily from 1865 to 1950. For instance, the per capita support, with inadequate county and district aid, has advanced from less than $2.00 in 1865 to $28.60 in 1949 plus a generous special district and county aid. At the same time the enrollment has increased from a little more than 400,000 to more than 676,383 pupils. In 1948 a general process of reorganization and consolidation has been going on since 1908. Many counties have reduced the total number of schools in order to increase the efficiency of teaching. High schools have been conveniently located in nearly every county to permit the transportation of students from one community to another. Graded schools have been consolidated, and the counties have provided transportation for their pupils.

Along with the movement for consolidation, compulsory education, and a complete recodification of school laws, the curriculum has undergone considerable change, so that now it includes a wide range of subjects from reading to manual arts. To appreciate changes which have taken place it is only necessary to contrast present curriculum-making with the efforts of H. A. M. Henderson in 1870. With Superintendent Henderson the problem of the curriculum was not one of offering the best possible arrangement of courses to meet the social and educational needs of the pupil, but it was one of finding textbooks that would please teachers, parents, and pupils.

Negro Education

Before the Civil War, the education of the Negro in Kentucky was the responsibility, to a large degree, of the slaveowners. If the free Negro wished to secure an education, the responsibility rested directly upon his own shoulders. However, the end of the war completely changed this situation. Through the influence of the Freedmen's Bureau a bill passed the Kentucky legislature on February 16, 1866, appropriating a small percentage of funds derived from taxation of Negro property and taxes levied on Negroes' dogs to the support of schools for the colored. These schools were placed under the supervision of the state superintendent and the county commissioners. However, while school laws were being studied by Z. F. Smith, schools for the colored suffered a setback, for the legislature passed an act requiring that colored paupers be cared for from the school fund first.

During the administration of Superintendent Henderson, the Negro leaders brought considerable pressure to bear upon the state administration and asked that educational opportunities be equalized between whites and blacks. There were 375,000 white children costing $2.35 each for their education, while 100,000 Negro children were receiving less than $1.00 each. Had the number of Negro children been added to the number of white children, the state's per capita school tax would have been reduced to $1.85 per capita. Henderson bitterly opposed equalizing the general funds between the races but suggested the impossible solution that the white people of the colored communities contribute funds to the support of the Negro schools.

The legislature passed a special act regulating Negro schools, in February, 1875. As was hoped, this legislation increased interest in

Negro education so that additional financial support was provided. A levy of 45 cents on each $100 worth of property belonging to colored persons was appropriated. Each colored male over twenty-one years of age was required to pay a poll tax, and every colored dog-owner was taxed for support of schools for the colored. County institutes for the benefit of Negro teachers were organized under the supervision of colored trustees. This division of labor in the school system was short-lived, however, for on May 12, 1881, under the superintendency of Elder J. D. Pickett, the entire school system was consolidated.

Special efforts have been made by the outside philanthropies to create educational opportunities for colored children equal to those of white children. A portion of the Julius Rosenwald fund was assigned to Kentucky for the purpose of building schoolhouses for the colored population. Kentucky Negroes have also received grants from the Slater fund. In some of the central Blue Grass counties, racing interests have provided special schools for their young colored employees.

Educational Associations

One of the most important auxiliaries of the organized educational system has been the Kentucky Educational Association. This organization had its beginning under the superintendency of the Reverend Daniel Stevenson, when his department received an appropriation of $300 to promote a teachers' association. The first teachers' auxiliary was known as the "Teachers' Association." Through the assistance of the county institutes, local teachers were made to appreciate the value of organization. Several years after the beginning of this preliminary organization, Nathaniel Southgate Shaler and State Superintendent Henderson organized (July 15, 1874) the "Society for the Advancement of Education in Kentucky." At the same time, the teachers of the Louisville city schools organized an independent teachers' association. The Kentucky Educational Association has developed into the guardian of the public school system. Not only has this society grown in size and influence, but it now publishes a respectable professional journal. In the "whirlwind educational legislatures" of 1908 and 1909, the teachers' organization actively engaged in publicizing the need for school reform. Again, in 1933, the Kentucky Educational Association was a vital factor in securing a revision and consolidation of school laws for generous support of public schools. Other societies playing a leading role in the creation and maintenance of the schools are the Kentucky Federation of Womens Clubs and the Parent Teachers Association.

Special Schools

Not all of the postwar schools have been state supported, for philanthropic organizations have maintained an excellent system of schools. The Catholic Church has a well organized system of parochial schools in many sections of Kentucky. Churches and religious organizations have established schools in the eastern Kentucky mountain counties. The Protestant churches maintain schools at Stinnett's Creek, Ebenezer, Morehead, McKee, London, Stanton, Jackson, Beverly, Red Bird, Salyersville, and Buck Horn. A school was established at Hindman, in 1892, by the Woman's Christian Temperance Union. Mrs. Cora Wilson Stewart distinguished herself in 1911, when she introduced the "moonlight" schools for the purpose of teaching adults to read and write. This move led to the appointment of Governor McCreary's "Illiteracy Commission" in 1920.[1]

Higher Education

At the top of Kentucky's educational ladder is the State University. This institution typifies Kentucky's postwar educational growth, for it was made possible by the Morrill Act passed by Congress, in 1862. This act, passed during the absence of the southern Senators and Congressmen, granted each state 30,000 acres of public lands for each congressional district in the state. This land was donated for the purpose of establishing in the states agriculutral and mechanical colleges. Of course, Kentucky was in no position in 1862 to use her grant. It was not until 1865 that Colonel John B. Bowman wisely proposed moving Kentucky University (Bacon's College) from Harrodsburg to Lexington and consolidating it with Transylvania to form Kentucky University. It was proposed that the consolidated schools receive the federal grant to enable them to grow into a powerful state university. This seemed ideal, and Colonel Bowman worked valiantly to realize his

---

[1] Kentucky now ranks thirty-fifth in illiteracy, with a rate of 6.6 per cent. Kentucky ranks lowest in illiteracy of the Southern States.

dream, but, true to Kentucky's tradition, a split occurred. The lion and lamb were not to lie down together in peace; the state and the church could not agree on the educational policies for Kentucky University.

Kentucky's share of the public lands was poorly managed. Out of a grant of 300,000 acres of public land the state received only $165,000, but this was combined with the $110,000 raised by citizens of Lexington and Fayette County to open an agricultural and mechanical college on the Henry Clay farm. This college was begun as a division of Kentucky University, but this arrangement did not succeed, for in ten years the two departments were wrangling over their respective administration. The agricultural and mechanical unit withdrew, and in 1880 the present "University of Kentucky," then called "State College," was located in the Lexington City Park and received a gift of $50,000 from Lexington and Fayette County. In its new location the Kentucky State College proceeded to broaden its curriculum and to multiply its functions. Not only did it continue to offer technical courses and public laboratory services in agriculture and engineering, but it trained teachers for the public schools. Many of these prospective teachers were received in their elementary preparatory years but were given an opportunity to remain in school at moderate costs until they had finished their college course.

Delegates to the "Educational Legislature" in 1908 voted to change the name of the Kentucky State College to Kentucky State University and to restore to the so-called State University its original name of Transylvania. In 1916 the state legislature increased the support of the university and changed its name from State University to the University of Kentucky.

The University of Kentucky has expanded its functions, until now it is possible for every home in the state, no matter how remote, to receive its assistance. Through its agricultural extension service, county and home demonstration agents have been sent into every county in the state to assist farmers and their wives to learn new methods of farming and housekeeping.

An educational extension department was organized in 1919 which now sends trained university teachers into the communities of the state to offer instruction to persons who are not able to attend the University.

Not only does this department offer cheap instruction to communities, but it also supervises school contests, supplies materials for school discussions and debates, and helps to create a sense of cooperation among the county schools.

Beginning with the pioneering of John B. Bowman, the University of Kentucky grew from an agricultural and mechanical college into a university. There are eleven colleges: the College of Arts and Sciences, of Agriculture, Commerce, Law, Engineering, Education, the Graduate School, Pharmacy, Medicine, Nursing, and dentistry. Within these colleges are almost a hundred instructional and service departments which offer several hundred courses of instruction. The Library has become a mature research institution, housing more than 1,000,000 volumes of books, documents and manuscripts.

The staff of the University has grown from 17 to over 2,383, which includes the agricultural and maintenance personnel. The resident student body numbers over 8,000. In its century of existence, the University has become an important socializing agency in Kentucky. Beginning with the administration of James Kennedy Patterson and continuing to date in the present administration, the curriculum of the institution has been steadily expanded and adapted to the needs of the state's social system. Special courses have been planned and taught to meet the needs of the state. Public servants from school teachers to highly trained professional men have been made available, and through its Graduate School the University offers Kentucky students advanced training at a minimum cost. By the action of the Council on Higher Education (1936), most graduate work of the state schools has been concentrated at the University. Throughout its history the University of Kentucky has made remarkable progress with limited public support. Since 1917 the University has grown from a state college into a university of good quality. Under the liberal direction of President Frank L. McVey, a trained economist, the University began to realize many of the ideals of Colonel John Bowman and its pioneer supporters. President McVey proved an able leader in the important post World War I years. In subsequent years Dr. Herman Lee Donovan and Dr. Frank Graves Dickey have served as presidents of the University in the important period since 1940. World War II had a tremendous impact on all Kentucky institutions of higher learning. The University was called upon to supply a tremendous amount of technical training. After the war the veterans swelled the ranks of the student body. This time there was a need for special student housing, and special administrative organization to care for the new demands. The Library has grown to nearly a half million volumes, the Graduate School has a large enrollment, and the institution, through its special services, has become more a factor in the life of the state.

One of the most important functions of the University of Kentucky has been its encouragement of better libraries in the state. Although late in starting this particular phase of social and intellectual development, it is now making headway. To meet the demands of the in-structional departments, the University Library is rapidly building a collection of books and manuscripts to supplement libraries owned by other state and municipal institutions.

Since the development of Kentucky's public schools outran the state's facilities for supplying trained teachers, in 1906 two normal schools were created. One of these was located at Bowling Green and the other at Richmond, named Western and Eastern State Normal Schools respectively. Both schools have grown rapidly, and under progressive presidents expanded their curricula. The Western State College at Bowling Green has performed yeoman service for the public schools of western Kentucky. This school, under the leadership of H. H. Cherry and Paul Garrett, has laid the foundation for a good library collection and has special arrangements for housing its collection of Kentuckiana. At Richmond, the Eastern State College, built upon the basis of Central University, founded in 1873, has developed a well-trained teaching staff and is building a sound library collection. Enrollment in both of these schools has more than doubled in the past twelve years.

Morehead State College was founded in 1887 by Mrs. Phoebe Button and her son as the Morehead Normal School. For many years it received its support from the Kentucky Christian Missionary Society and the Christian Women's Board of Missions. This school was taken over by Kentucky in 1922 and converted into a state teachers college for the purpose of supplementing the work of Eastern State College, at Richmond, in training teachers for eastern Kentucky. That same year the state opened another teachers college at Murray in western Kentucky for the purpose of training additional teachers in the "Purchase" area. Thus Kentucky has provided for the training of her teachers by making available facilities for teacher training in every section of the commonwealth.

When the Kentucky General Assembly passed a law in 1873 establishing a common school system for colored children, provisions had to be made for the training of colored teachers. Superintendent H. A. M. Henderson called a special meeting of the colored teachers' association. The next year this organization held a meeting in Danville, at which time the president, J. H. Jackson of Lexington, and a Berea College graduate, advocated the establishment of a normal school for colored persons. Repeated appeals were made for the establishment of a normal school for training colored teachers, and on May 18, 1889, Governor Proctor Knott affixed his signature to a bill creating the "Kentucky Normal School for Colored Persons." The following year, on October 11, the school opened its doors to colored students at Frankfort. Since that time, this school has secured much favorable legislation and has experienced a steady improvement. The state legislature changed its name in 1902 from the "Kentucky Normal School for Colored Persons" to the "Kentucky Normal and Industrial Institute."

The Kentucky Normal and Industrial Institute has expanded its curriculum to include most of the liberal and manual arts. Students attending this school are afforded opportunities of studying under a curriculum which closely parallels that of the state teachers colleges and of the Arts and Science College of the University of Kentucky. They likewise have an opportunity to learn one of the manual arts to fit them for a practical trade when they have graduated. A second school, a junior college, has been established at Paducah for training colored students.

In April, 1949, the Federal District Court at Lexington ruled, in the case of *Johnson vs. Univ. of Ky.*, that Negro graduate and professional students should be admitted to state schools along with whites. This was a major decision which opened the doors of state white schools to Negroes, but it did not invalidate the Day Law which contains the added issue of segregation. Negroes entered the summer session of the

University of Kentucky in 1949 without incident. To date no legislation has been passed changing the Day Law to accommodate this new arrangement.

Berea is a unique postwar educational institution. This school was founded through the influence of James G. Fee, minister of the gospel and an abolitionist. He was graduated from Lane Seminary in Cincinnati and endowed with the self-sacrificing spirit of the missionary. Through the influence of Cassius M. Clay, Fee established a school and church at Berea in Madison County. For many years Fee's Kentucky venture received its sole support from the American Missionary Association. This association likewise encouraged the foundation of a school in 1855 for the purpose of encouraging antislavery education. Instructors were imported to Berea from Oberlin College, at Oberlin, Ohio. Because of the excessive turbulence of the times, there was a constant changing of faculty members until 1858, when the college board was organized. Four of the newly appointed trustees purchased, at their own financial risk, a 100-acre tract of land, but before they could build a house on it, John Brown committed his act of folly at Harper's Ferry. When news of this raid reached Kentucky, the Berea professors were notified, December 23, 1859, to leave the state.

When the war ended, however, friends of Berea returned and secured from the legislature in 1865 a charter for their college. That year Berea's doors were opened to seventy-five white students and three Negroes.[2] When the school authorities accepted the Negro students, two thirds of the white applicants withdrew. By 1869 temporary buildings were constructed, and the school began a period of growth.

---

[2] The act of March 22, 1904, prohibiting the education of Negroes at Berea College was tested before the Kentucky Court of Appeals in the famous Berea *vs.* Commonwealth case. This decision attracted widespread attention and was the source of strong feelings of racial animosity in Kentucky. The major portions of the decision are given here:

"(1) Constitutional Law—Police Power—Schools for White and Colored Persons—Act, March 22, 1904, p. 181, c. 85, in that as it prohibits and imposes a punishment for maintaining and operating an institution of learning in which white and colored persons may be taught at the same time and in the same place, is within the police power and valid.

"(2) Same—Act, March 22, 1904, p. 181, c. 85, in so far as it prohibits maintenance by an institution of learning separate and distinct branches for white and colored persons less than 25 miles distant from each other is unreasonable, and not within the police power."

The court likewise held that the Negro had not been deprived of equal protection of the law, or by due process of the law. Also, that the right to teach white and colored students in the same school was not a property right. *Reports of Civil and Criminal Cases decided by the Court of Appeals of Kentucky,* 123, pp. 209–229 (Frankfort, 1906).

Through private contributions from northern and eastern philanthropists, Berea has become well endowed and well established. It now offers a wide range of courses in the liberal arts, sciences, mechanics, and agriculture.

Perhaps no other educational institution in the country performs exactly the same services as Berea. It is maintained, at present, for boys and girls from the Appalachian Mountains, with a possible exception of ten per cent of the student body. A system of labor is maintained which affords every student an opportunity to work his way through college. Its students are admitted on a selective basis, and its waiting lists have been large for several years.

Professor Clarence Nixon of Tulane University has expressed the belief in "Colleges and Universities," in *Culture in the South,* that Berea has outlived its usefulness as a mountain school, but it has a brilliant future as an institution for educational and social readjustment and experimentation. Perhaps these views are somewhat extreme. Berea does occupy a unique and important position in Kentucky's social-educational system and stands as a monument to social planning and direction. Its contribution to Kentucky's social development has been invaluable, for not only has it offered education to Kentuckians of the eastern counties at a low minimum cost, but it has relieved state schools of overcrowding.

Kentucky has numerous colleges endowed by various religious denominations. Each of these has played a part in Kentucky's educational history and has occupied an important place in the social development of the state. There are about twenty-three active senior and junior colleges at present, most of which came into existence between 1850 and 1900. Some of these are: Centre, Transylvania, Kentucky Wesleyan, University of Louisville, Presbyterian Seminary, Nazareth, Union, Pikeville Junior College, St. Joseph's, Southern Baptist Seminary, Cumberland, Paducah Junior College, and Villa Madonna College.

Practical public education is largely a product of postwar Kentucky. With an expanding population and a development of its natural resources, Kentucky's citizenry felt education to be imperative. However, there are yet sections of Kentucky which have not felt too strongly the influence of public schools. In many backward centers private institutions such as the churches and philanthropic societies are maintaining schools.

Now that her system of education is fairly well co-ordinated, the educational leaders of Kentucky have almost realized the dreams of the promoters of the 1830's. It is now possible for students to receive efficient training from the kindergarten time to the final years of highly specialized professions. The schools of medicine, agriculture, law, theology, dentistry, engineering, pharmacy, and education are now able to supply much of the state's demands for trained political and professional leadership.

End of World War II began a new era in Kentucky higher education. Verterans flocked to classrooms demanding broad areas of instruction. This necessitated expansion of offerings, of academic departments, and even of new fields. Enrollments in all public universities and colleges increased overnight, and most private institutions shared in this influx of students. Between 1945 and 1960 the University of Kentucky, for instance, underwent major revisions of both instruction and offerings. The four teachers colleges outgrew the chrysallis stage of their founding, evolved into colleges, and then universities. In 1970 the University of Louisville became a part of the state system of higher education, and in 1970 Kentucky State College became a university. The Northern Kentucky Community College became a full-fledged four-year institution, and in 1976 was designated a university.

A sense of the evolution of higher education in Kentucky since 1918 is to be gained in the mushrooming number of institutions. In that year there were four semi-private normal institutes which employed 129 instructors, and enrolled in some kind of a course 2,130 students. Predominantly these were women teachers who took only one or two courses. At the same time there were only 1,969 students enrolled in public colleges and universities, and there were only 64 graduates that year. By contrast in 1946 there were thirty-four Kentucky institutions of collegiate rank which enrolled 22,000 students, of whom 13,289 were veterans. By 1973 there were thirty-six colleges and universities which enrolled 110,700 students. Collegiate properties were valued at $757,000,000.

During the latter decades enrollments in professional, graduate, and technological areas had increased phenomenally. Prior to 1920 no Kentucky institution offered work of truly graduate caliber. It was not until after 1930 that the doctorate in selected fields was awarded by the University of Kentucky, and much of the work leading to the masters degree was on a level with undergraduate studies. By 1945, however, demand for graduate work had increased, a fact which necessitated the collection of libraries, organizing laboratories, and the employment of higher caliber staff members. Even as late as 1977 the offering of advanced graduate work involved some confusion if not rivalry and controversy among the universities.

A modern Kentucky university student would have difficulty imagining the paucity of materials available in the University of Kentucky Library a half century ago. Even as late as 1930 that institution hardly deserved the library designation. Nowhere in Kentucky was there either a significant collection of books and manuscripts of sufficient content to sustain mature studies in any field of learning. It is difficult to discover dependable library statistics, but it can be assumed that the University of Kentucky Library in 1977 with more than a million books, a decent rare book and manuscript collection, an excellent assembly of public documents, and other materials has grown almost miraculously strong. This can also be said within limitations for the other university libraries. The Kentucky State Historical Society, the Filson Club, and the various special university regional holdings of manuscripts and other original materials have provided substantial scholarly foundation under higher education.

Kentuckians in the latter half of the twentieth century have come to appreciate the importance of the training and maturing of the state's precious human and intellectual resource. Persistently Kentucky has fallen under national averages in expenditures for higher education, the quality of work, and it has not always compared favorably with its neighbors, especially those north of the Ohio. Nevertheless, it has made tremendous advances over its relative position in 1920. This has been true to a large extent in the fields of engineering, law, medicine, dentistry, agriculture, and pharmacy. There has been in large measure a realization of that timid dream of 1780 when the Virginia General Assembly chartered Transsylvania Seminary to light the torch of learning in its western country.

CHAPTER XX

Economic Readjustment

WHEN the War between the States ended, maladjustment was the most evident fact in Kentucky's economic system. Preceding chapters have explained in detail the intimate relation of Kentucky's trade to the ever-expanding southern cotton belt. It had been a matter of natural expectation that as the cotton belt expanded so would Kentucky's trade enlarge. Cotton planters in the South were dependent upon the border sections, and in particular upon Kentucky, for their plantation supplies, ranging from pork to slaves. The economic system of Kentucky dovetailed with that of the Lower South. Commercially minded Kentuckians had watched the beginning of changes in transportation and other movements which bore upon the southern market, with keen interest. When plans were formulated in the early fifties to supplant the rivers with railroads, the rivers were carrying to market goods valued at more than $10,000,000 per annum. As the southern market expanded, and as the foreign demand for American cotton increased, the exportation of that product rose to sixty per cent of the entire American exports. The southern cotton planters became more exacting in their demands. Since prompt and sure delivery of freight became a matter of the utmost importance, the building of the Louisville and Nashville, the Mobile and Ohio, and the various southern short lines which now compose the Illinois Central Railroad to New Orleans resulted.

It is significant to note that the fifties saw the construction of three important trunk rail lines from Kentucky to the South, while not one mile of railroad was built to the East or the North. It is also significant that the New Orleans and the Mobile and Ohio Railroads were engaged in a construction race to a point on the Mississippi, just south of the Ohio's mouth, to secure for their respective cities the trade of the border states.

380

During the years of the war, Kentucky's trade with the South was badly disrupted, principally for lack of transportation facilities. Trade restrictions were imposed upon the local dealers by military authorities. Had these restrictions not been imposed upon the Kentucky merchants, they would have experienced other difficulties, however, for the southern purchasers lacked the necessary purchasing capital. When the war ended, the South, its properties either destroyed or at least greatly reduced in value, was virtually bankrupt. Perhaps the principal economic assets remaining to the South were the three semisouthern distributing centers in the Mississippi Valley: Louisville, Cincinnati, and St. Louis. But even in these cities merchants enjoyed only a dubious advantage, for they were faced with the problem of supplying goods to bankrupt southern planters whose credit was questionable at best.

Too much emphasis cannot be placed upon the statement that the war left the South a changed section. Before the war, the Louisville merchants enjoyed what, in a sense, was a unique trade. They sold their goods to the large plantation holders, who, as middlemen, in turn distributed the goods through their plantation stores. Ravages of the conflict, however, destroyed the plantation store, and it was replaced with the crossroads community store. Thus a new system of merchandising sprang from the wreck of the old. This change in local merchandising necessitated a distinct change in methods of distributing. No longer could the wholesale grocery or supply merchant sit comfortably in his office to await the coming of the planter to buy his year's supply of goods. Goods were now distributed by the small independent merchant who did not earn sufficient capital from his trade to call on the wholesaler in the larger towns. Instead, the local dealer now awaited the coming of the wholesaler's representative, the commercial traveler, or drummer.

Louisville dealers were among the first to realize this change. Since, historically, the South had been their territory, they made immediate plans to continue this southern trade. Traveling salesmen, or drummers, were sent South in great numbers. The Louisville drummer's two-horse rig was a familiar sight at the hitching rack of every crossroads store from Columbia, South Carolina, to Shreveport, Louisiana. These representatives were sent out to secure southern trade at any cost. It was with a great degree of subtlety that the Louisville wholesalers selected Confederate veterans to represent them. They shrewdly realized that nothing would sell a bill of goods to an indifferent southern merchant like a good story by a veteran of the Chickamauga or Vicksburg campaigns. Southern merchants were cordially invited to the four commercial conventions which were held in Louisville prior to 1869. Southerners came without reluctance, for like their Louisville neighbors, they had a profound interest in the development of the Mississippi Valley, in that they wished to maintain the commercial importance of New Orleans.

Unfortunately for Louisville, the southerners who were most active in their fight to maintain New Orleans were shortsighted as to the method. They wished to continue the use of the Mississippi River as the main channel of trade, for they regarded railways as feeble auxiliaries. They were backward in realizing that the slow and uncertain method of shipping by river boat was antiquated. Few, if any, of the southerners were cognizant of the fact that the railroad was becoming the most important factor in the economic life of the Mississippi Valley.

Fortunately for Louisville, Mother Nature had placed her in the mouth of the funnel of trade down the Ohio Valley to the South. Louisville was located strategically to control the livestock and supply trade southward, and she showed the advantages of this ideal location by growing from a village of 4,000, in 1820, to a city of 100,000, in 1870, and 307,745, in 1930. Although the victim of martial control during the years of war, Louisville showed a surprising increase in trade from $37,000,000, in 1860, to $51,000,000, in 1865.

Since the Louisville trade was already inclined southward, it had only to encourage better transportation and distributing facilities. The Louisville and Nashville Railroad was a start toward better rail connections, but competition from the rest of the valley became a serious menace. Louisville had shared with Cincinnati the vainglorious title of "Porkopolis," but the production of cheap corn in the Northwest was threatening this advantage. Suffering less by the ravages of war, Cincinnati stood ready to snatch the prize of southern trade from her sister city's hand. In Cincinnati, Louisville had a real and dangerous rival, for nature had smiled as kindly (if not more so) upon Cincinnati. As Cincinnati had long enjoyed a prosperous southern trade, naturally merchants of that city had many connections in the South. Consequently, there grew up such a tense spirit of rivalry between Cincinnati and Louisville that the next twenty years of the economic history of the lower Ohio River Valley revolved around this struggle.

At the beginning of the struggle, Louisville merchants had the advantage, for as early as 1851 the city council was prevailed upon to invest $1,000,000 in the building of the Louisville and Nashville Railroad. Another advantage enjoyed by Louisville was control of the falls canal through which most of the southward-flowing commerce had to pass.

Throughout the war, the Louisville and Nashville Railroad was subjected to heavy losses from military raids. As a matter of fact, this road was the *centre pointe* of most of the attacks on southern Kentucky. The original track and roadbed were torn up several times. When peace was resumed, restoration of the line called for heavy expenditure, of which Louisville contributed $1,000,000 in 1867. Branches were built into central Kentucky, and under the able direction of Albert Fink the Louisville and Nashville formed connections with the Lower South. Fink perhaps had more imagination than any other railway superintendent of his time. It was he who broke down the unfriendly rivalry between Louisville and Nashville to make satisfactory arrangements for through rail traffic from Louisville to the South. Perhaps no other individual in Louisville did more to expand the influence of his city than did Albert Fink. He foresaw that, if Louisville and her railroad were to prosper, a southern territory must be developed. It was this belief which led him to defeat the plans of northern capitalists who proposed to haul iron ore from the Birmingham district to Chattanooga for smelting. Fink encouraged the building of towns in the South to increase the purchasing power of Louisville's territory. He formed connections with Memphis, Tennessee, over the southwestern branch of the Louisville and Nashville from Guthrie. Connections were made with New Orleans over the present southern lines of the Illinois Central; with Mobile, over the Mobile and Ohio; and with Atlanta and Savannah over the Central of Georgia. At home, the Louisville businessmen, anxious to expand their market to the Blue Grass, contributed to the construction of branch lines into the central Kentucky counties.

At the same time, "Marse" Henry Watterson, through the editorial columns of the Courier-Journal, was advocating an extension of Louisville's railway system west of the Ohio to tap the grain-growing Northwest. He argued that Louisville could expand her trade and retain her pork industry by importation of cheap corn.

Behind this movement to build efficient rail connections to the South was a life and death struggle to strangle Cincinnati's southern trade. A point of contention was that trade from central Kentucky went to the southern market largely through Cincinnati. This is explained by the fact that the Licking River was, at an early date, an artery of trade to Cincinnati, and that later central Kentucky was connected to Cincinnati by the Central Kentucky Railroad. For this central region there was likewise an advantage in shipping through Cincinnati, since its market prices were often higher than those at Louisville. It is quite true that the Lexington, Frankfort, and Louisville Railroad hauled large quantities of central Kentucky freight, but never giving Louisville a preponderance of this trade. Thus there developed a rivalry between Louisville and Nashville railroad officials to discriminate against freight originating in central Kentucky. Instances are recorded to show that it cost as much to ship a carload of freight from Frankfort to Louisville as from Louisville to New Orleans. It was said that tobacco, whiskey, livestock, and other supplies shipped southward little more than paid transportation costs. Further discriminations were made against merchants and shippers from these rival sections by a delaying of freight cars in Louisville until the purchaser's patience was worn threadbare. Purchasers in Chattanooga asserted that it took from thirty to sixty days to get a carload of freight from Cincinnati. Many times, cars loaded with perishable freight were held over until their contents were spoiled, or until irate purchasers canceled their orders.

In conventions and mercantile gatherings Louisville revived the question of sectional allegiance during the war, very much to Cincinnati's embarrassment. Louisville pleaded loyalty to the South and appeared solicitous for southern welfare. When Atlanta was still in a state of panic in 1866, partly because of Sherman's "drive to the sea," Louisville merchants rushed to its relief with funds. In other sections of the South sufferers from local disasters knew what it was to secure liberal aid from Louisville mercantile interests. Drummers who represented the Louisville houses were loyal not only to their employers, but likewise to the collective business of their city. If a hardware drummer found his prospective customer well stocked with hardware but short on dry goods, he immediately turned his talk to dry goods to secure the order for a Louisville dry goods merchant. At home Louisville merchants were alert to see that no prospective purchaser got through their city to Cincinnati. Many were the sarcastic jibes which passed back and forth through the press. The *Cincinnati Commercial* stood a watchful guardian of local trade and oftentimes resorted to making fun of Louisville's efforts to outdo its neighbor. This paper frequently remarked that Louisville businessmen consumed their profits in celebrating their success at snatching a bit of trade from Cincinnati.

At the Commercial Congress in 1869 Louisville spent a large sum of money to impress its southern visitors with the importance of the city as a southern mercantile center. Visitors were given free run of the city, and many of its accommodations were likewise free. Never before had Kentucky merchants gone so far out of their way to encourage trade with the cotton belt; ten years had wrought a miraculous change in the relations of the two sections.

This "cutthroat" competition between Cincinnati and Louisville could not endure. Nature had seemingly decreed that Cincinnati should become a powerful market center, for since she was located with such a geographical advantage, unlike Louisville, she did not have to carry all her eggs in one basket. She could trade profitably both with the South and with the rapidly expanding grain belt of the Northwest. However, the Ohio city did not wish to slacken its efforts to maintain its trade to the cotton belt.

In order to revive southern trade, Cincinnati started cultivating the friendship of central Kentucky. Prizes donated by Cincinnati businessmen were sent to the Blue Grass county fairs. At these fairs Blue Grass stock was praised by livestock dealers from the Ohio city, and, at the same time, Kentucky growers were given enticing information of the Cincinnati stockyards.

A delegation of Cincinnati businessmen went to the Lower South in 1870 to visit with the Southerners and to study, firsthand, southern conditions. While in the South, the Cincinnati delegates invited southern merchants to send representatives to a commercial congress to be held in their city. When the time came to entertain their southern guests, the Cincinnatians were greatly perturbed as to how they could get the Southerners through Louisville without embarrassment. They sent an honorary guard, called a welcoming committee, to Louisville to see that the southern delegates were not deterred. Once in Cincinnati, the delegates were treated to every courtesy which an ingenious group of merchants could contrive. To outdo Louisville's generosity, Southerners were extended free use of street cars, telegraph lines, and other conveniences which the city offered.

Louisville made the mistake of doubting Cincinnati's ability to stem the tide of competition against her. Unfortunately for Louisville her merchants overlooked the advantages of the business of the state in their anxiety to secure the trade of the Lower South. The Falls City had grown haughty in its attitude toward the rest of the state without realizing the dangerous political possibilities.

Cincinnati was a dangerous competitor which demanded an outlet, and there was little chance (1865–1875) that it could be stifled by Louisville. As early as 1836, southerners had suggested, through John C. Calhoun of South Carolina, that rail connections be formed with Cincinnati, Lexington, and Louisville by a railroad constructed from some place in South Carolina to the Ohio River. This project, however, was premature, for the panic of 1837 completely defeated the idea. Nevertheless, the possibility of such an undertaking had been suggested, and progressive businessmen of Kentucky and Ohio believed the project possible.

When the whole country, in the fifties, accepted the railway idea as a satisfactory solution of transportation problems, citizens of Cincinnati and Lexington put a project on foot to connect the South with Cincinnati over the route proposed by Calhoun. Unfortunately, the War between the States checked the building of the Lexington and Danville Railroad at the Kentucky River. Between 1865 and 1870, when Louisville wished to monopolize use of the Louisville and Nashville Railroad, businessmen of Cincinnati and central Kentucky again suggested building a railroad southward to connect with the East Tennessee and Virginia and the Central of Georgia at a point near Knoxville or Chattanooga. By this route Cincinnati would be in touch by rail with both the Atlantic coast and the Mississippi River basin.

While the possibility of connecting Cincinnati with the South by way of a direct southern railway was being considered, a proposal was made that the 132 miles by river from Cincinnati to Louisville be reduced to 110 miles by rail. A "short line" railway was proposed to join these market centers, but its construction failed to end the rivalry between the two towns. Louisville politicians used their influence to require the "Short Line" to adopt the standard gauge of 4 feet 8½ inches, since the Louisville and Nashville operated its cars on a gauge of 5 feet. This difference of gauges insured Louisville drayage and its warehousemen continuous and prosperous business, for it was necessary to transfer every pound of freight shipped over the Short Line. Louisville had a distinct advantage over Cincinnati in cheaper freight rates on goods shipped to the South. Thus Louisville merchants hoped to entice southern merchants to buy supplies in the Falls City.

Louisville had an advantage over Cincinnati not only by rail but also by river. A bridge which limited the height of vessels passing under it was constructed over the Ohio Falls Canal. This bridge immediately proved a menace to boats going southward from Cincinnati. The Federal Government returned the control of the Portland Canal to private hands. This canal was allowed to deteriorate immediately, for all of Louisville's freight was loaded south of its mouth and below the falls. The canal soon fell into such a poor state of repair that only small vessels could pass through it. Accordingly, Cincinnati boats were forced to unload to dray their freight around the falls, a fact which added considerably to the cost and delay of shipping goods from Cincinnati to New Orleans. A delegation from Cincinnati was sent before the United States Congress to present its grievances against Louisville. A waggish *Chicago Tribune* reporter said that the appearance of the Cincinnati delegation before Congress begging protection from Louisville was as comical a performance as he had ever witnessed; certainly the Cincinnatians had ample grounds for complaint. When their freight shipments were delayed in Louisville yards for an unreasonable period, they appointed special freight directors to see that cars from Cincinnati were not shunted indefinitely onto sidings. The Louisville City Council was not to overlook this encroachment but levied a $20 annual tax upon each agent.

This discrimination brought into the open the fight to send freight from Cincinnati to the South. Cincinnati promoters went to work in earnest to build a railroad southward through central Kentucky. A survey showed that this road would be 272 miles in length and would connect in east Tennessee with several thousand miles of southern railway. Unlike the case of financing such a railroad before the war, local subscribers were so few as to make it necessary for Cincinnati practically to finance building of the road. Before promoters, however, concerned themselves to any extent with financial aid, they had to secure a charter from the Kentucky legislature.

Cincinnati proposed to the Kentucky General Assembly that it wished to take over the Kentucky Central as far as Nicholasville, Kentucky, to build it to Knoxville, Tennessee; its rival city, Louisville, tried to thwart this plan. Representatives of the Louisville districts and special lobbyists bitterly opposed the propositions in the legislature, and the two cities carried on a comic tug-of-war over the Kentucky legislature. Each city resorted to petty bribery through lavish entertainments for the Kentucky representatives. Louisville's press was outspoken against the Cincinnati-Southern project, while the press of the Blue Grass was just as vehement in its plea for a charter. Louisville merchants suggested a subscription of $2,000,000 to build a competing line to Chattanooga. This proposal was doubtless stimulated by a revival of the Louisville and Nashville, and the Nashville and Chattanooga Railway rivalry which made it difficult to ship Louisville goods through Nashville.

The first Cincinnati-Southern bill was called before the Kentucky legislature in January, 1870, to be passed in the house by a vote of 46 to 45. On February 12, however, the senate defeated this bill 25 to 12. Since it seemed impossible to secure a charter for a railway from the Kentucky legislature, Cincinnati promoters transferred their activities to Congress. It was believed that matters could be greatly facilitated by an appeal to the national body for aid. Kentucky supporters, with Colonial Albert Gallatin Hodges' *Frankfort Commonwealth*, demanded immediate congressional action. After failure to find a congressman from a local district to sponsor their bill, the Ohio promoters turned to Senator John Sherman for assistance. Senator Sherman introduced the railway bill on March 15, 1870, explaining in precise terms that the road would greatly improve the transportation of mails and naval and military supplies shipped from Cincinnati to Chattanooga. As proposed by Senator Sherman, the bill soon caused uneasiness among its supporters, for it proposed to make of Cincinnati a profit-earning corporation responsible for operating the railroad. Cincinnati friends of the project were hardly in a position, or of a mind, to assume such a liability. Hence the original bill was recalled and another substituted. On February 9, 1871, Senator Sherman introduced the second bill, and Congressman J. E. Stephenson of Cincinnati presented the measure to the House. Kentucky opponents, led by Senator Garrett Davis, made unreasonable and bitter attacks upon the Ohio congressional delegation. Throughout the territory of the proposed railroad in Kentucky, Tennessee, and Georgia petitions were circulated, and mass meetings were held to encourage Congress to charter the Cincinnati-Southern.

Louisville had failed to evaluate correctly the influence and power of the central Kentucky counties in Congress. The ensuing fight between the two sections of Kentucky in the National Congress presented a sorry spectacle, yet the struggle was not without its humorous aspects. So wrought up were the central Kentucky counties that James N. Beck, representing the Ashland District, was placed in quite a quandary. His constituency was demanding that he support the bill, yet the Kentucky legislature instructed him to oppose it. In order to clear his conscience of any misgiving, he offered to resign to allow his district to elect a man with the Cincinnati-Southern bill as an issue. When his resignation was refused, he consented to support the wishes of his constituents. Not until this question was forced upon the floor of Congress did the Kentucky legislators realize that a Kentucky political tradition had been violated. If Kentucky Congressmen voted for the bill, they immediately prostituted the state legislature's rights to charter a local enterprise to the Federal Government. Beck, although in favor of the road from a personal standpoint, was bitterly opposed to this method of chartering the company. When the Sherman bill was in final form, he proposed an amendment to read that the corporate powers of Cincinnati be extended over Kentucky and Tennessee. Such an amendment, of course, was preposterous, for Congress lacked power to extend the corporate limits of Cincinnati beyond the Ohio boundary.

After a vehement struggle among the Ohio, Georgia, Tennessee, and Kentucky Congressmen over the question of granting the railroad a charter, the Kentucky legislature again considered the project. A test vote held in the Kentucky House of Representatives indicated that the bill would pass that body by a vote of 59 to 38. Few doubted that it would pass the senate, for this branch of the legislature was presided over by John G. Carlisle of Covington. When the bill was voted upon by this body, the vote stood 19 to 19, but the presidential vote broke the tie in favor of the charter. With this action on the part of the Kentucky legislature, Congress dismissed the matter.

Work was begun on the road immediately. Promoters believed that it could be completed at a total cost of a little over $9,000,000. It was a much wiser group of trustees, however, who accepted the finished road on March 8, 1880, at a total cost of more than $28,000,000. The road was built under the direct supervision of the trustees in short lengths by private contractors. Had this fact been known in 1871, the Kentucky opponents might have been far more successful in their fight against the charter. True to the promoters' predictions, however, southern freight was plentiful, and the road yielded a profit from the start.

The completion of the Cincinnati-Southern Railroad was a powerful factor in allaying the stormy rivalry between Louisville and Cincinnati. When the fight was ended, the central Kentucky towns proceeded to re-establish their southern trade on a sounder basis. Southern trade was not relinquished by local merchants, so that an investigation near the close of the nineteenth century would have revealed a majority of southern merchants displaying goods purchased of Kentucky wholesalers. Few persons today, not connected with the wholesale distributing business, have an appreciation of the valuable interstate trade which is carried on between Kentucky and the cotton belt.

It is difficult to treat the industrial growth and the expansion of Kentucky without citing tedious statistics. Although Kentucky decreased its number of manufacturing establishments from 3,160, in 1860, to 2,246, in 1932, it has expanded its capital return from $36,330,-000 to $502,638,722. It is not difficult to account for the decrease in number of manufacturing plants, for at the present time the factories are larger, and output is far greater in a single factory than the entire output of manufacturing communities in 1860. At present all manufacturing is on an industrial scale, while, before the War between the States, it was largely domestic. The last decennial census report lists approximately eighty lines of industrial endeavor. These range from the manufacture of sporting goods, tobacco and tobacco by-products, and distilled spirits to fine pipe organs. Most of these eighty manufacturing interests are of interstate importance, making Kentucky a significant factor in the national industrial system.

One of the major developments in the industrial readjustment of Kentucky was the building of adequate railway lines. The Railroad Commissioners' report in 1931 listed forty-one steam, and five electric railroads, operating over a total of 5,006 miles of road, as compared with 571 miles projected in 1860. Before the establishment of the Interstate Commerce Commission on February 4, 1887, Kentucky railroads were of varying gauges, a fact which made rate and service discriminations against towns and sections possible. Happily, most of the Kentucky railroads were interstate and were forced to adopt a uniform gauge.

Most of the track in the modern Kentucky railway system was constructed at an enormous expenditure both of money and energy. Roads piercing the eastern coal fields taxed to the maximum the finest railway engineering skill. It is virtually impossible to appraise the cost of these eastern Kentucky railroads, for, during the period 1920 to 1930 alone, one railway company spent more than $160,000,000 to improve and extend its system. To date, rail transportation has been the salvation of Kentucky industry, for many of Kentucky's latent resources have been developed only through the building of railroads.

Complementing the railroads of Kentucky are the improved highways. In an earlier chapter the historical development of the Kentucky highway system was given careful consideration. In efforts to improve rivers, and later, to build railroads, little attention was given by the state to highways. Perhaps this was only natural, for vehicles of highway transportation were limited to the drawing power and speed of the horse. Hence, limited improvements were made upon the system of highways in Kentucky from 1830 to 1912. President Andrew Jackson's veto of the Maysville Road Bill virtually thwarted the ambition of Kentucky to build better roads, until the coming of the automobile.

Before 1912, responsibility for the building and maintenance of most of the highways in the state was entrusted to private toll companies and local communities. No move had been made to create a centralized department of public highways. When the legislature met in 1912, public agitation had reached a stage where it demanded a hearing; a highway department of supervision was created; and $25,000 of the funds collected from automobile licenses was appropriated to pay supervisors. This move was merely a gesture in the right direction, for actually no definite plans were at hand. Perhaps the highway act did little more than anticipate the possibility of building a system of arterial highways to connect county seats. By 1914 the plan to improve arterial highways had become fairly popular, and a special road fund was created by the state legislature from the automobile license fund and 5 cents on each $100 of assessed property. Counties were given special permission to issue bonds for a reasonable amount in order to secure funds to construct highways connecting with the general state system. Counties which constructed their highways on standard specifications prescribed by the highway department were promised state aid to fifty per cent of the total cost, provided no county received more than two per cent of the entire state highway fund in any one year. These early acts were important in that they marked the beginning of a centralized system, but the counties were slow in responding to the state's offer of funds. It was believed that the building of highways should be encouraged by supplying public labor. In 1916, while labor was scarce because of the increased demands of industry and the World War, the Kentucky legislature passed an act authorizing use of convict labor on the roads. This plan, however, did not succeed, for after six years of unsuccessful experimentation the plan was abandoned.

From 1912 to 1920, the state highway department did a prodigious amount of experimenting without definite accomplishments. Profiting by such experience, the state legislature passed the Kentucky Road Law which authorized the state department to accept federal aid for state roads. This law likewise established the originally projected system of primary highways guaranteeing connections between county seats.

Many improvements were made in highway construction during the decade from 1920 to 1950. Toward the end of this period more than $98,000,000 was spent biennially in building and improving the state highways. A primary system of more than 12,000 miles was constructed and in operation. In 1950 there were approximately 8,600 miles of hard surfaced roads, with a considerable amount of mileage under preparation for surfacing. Arterial highways have been surfaced and widened, and most local connecting highways have been improved.

Perhaps Kentucky's highway building program is little past a secondary stage, for its transportation problems are constantly changing. Main arterial highways which were considered ample to take care of traffic at the time of their construction less than ten years ago are already antiquated. Many main highways are too narrow and have high crowns which make traveling at a high rate of speed and in wet weather exceedingly dangerous.

Freight transportation methods have undergone such rapid changes that after a period of 100 years, freight and passenger service is again being divided between the highways and railroads. Improved highways are rapidly changing the state's social condition. The fact that no section or county in 1950 is without an improved hard surfaced road is causing a complete readjustment of the state's industrial system. Resources which have hitherto been too limited to justify construction of a railroad to isolated communities are now being developed, and their products are being hauled to market by motor truck. Not only have improved highways and the gasoline motor car aided in the development of natural resources, but they have also created new markets.

Kentucky coal miners were producing, in 1860, approximately 280,-000 tons of coal per annum, but the Civil War caused a serious slump in this industry. Interference from the war did not completely check coal mining, but the lagging development of transportation facilities almost spelled doom for the coal mining industry. As was pointed out in connection with the building of new railroads, the development of transportation lines into the coal regions was an expensive undertaking. Especially was this true of the eastern coal mining region, for it was here that the eastern mountains formed an almost impenetrable barrier. Once these problems of transportation were solved, the coal mining area was materially expanded, and the annual output of the mines jumped to an unprecedented mark.

In 1879 the 1,000,000 ton mark was passed for the first time. Improved methods of drilling, blasting, lighting the mines, loading, and hauling were introduced. It would be difficult to say which improvement did most to speed up the process of bringing coal to the surface, but the introduction of the safety lamp perhaps occupies first place. Through the use of the safety lamp, coal mining was made reasonably safe from unexpected and disastrous explosions.

The first significant coal mining activity in Kentucky began in the Western Coalfield. During the first half of the nineteenth century the industrial town of Louisville had depended upon the upper Ohio River beds for its coal supply. This coal was transported down the Ohio River, but, unhappily for Louisville, the river reached such a low stage during the dry seasons that the city was often without coal with which to fire its furnaces. The city's demand for fuel increased annually, a factor which made the possibility of failure in river transportation a greater hazard than ever before. As the coal supply from Pennsylvania became more uncertain, the Kentuckians directed attention to local beds. When the western beds were finally opened, they served as the main supply for the industrial centers of the state until the eighties, when expansion of the railway system and growth of industry enforced a shifting of the coal mining industry to the eastern counties. During the years 1886 and 1887 there were forty-three mines operating in western Kentucky, eight in northeastern, and twenty-four in southeastern Kentucky. The total number of mines had increased by 1934 to 1,749, with a majority of them located in the eastern fields. During 1885 the western fields made a cash return of $790,000, while the eastern area returned $745,000 worth of products. In 1947, the combined mining industry of Kentucky produced more than $354,782,108 worth of coal and coal by-products. In the meantime, the center of the industry shifted from western to eastern Kentucky, with Pike County leading in 1919 with an output of 4,784,899 tons, worth $11,916,261. Production for the whole state in 1947 was 88,695,527 tons. Not only has the coal industry become a major industry from the standpoint of raw fuel, but the manufacturing of coal by-products has been profitable.

Kentucky's market for its coal is as varied as the uses of the fuel. Most of the coal produced within the state is shipped to the large industrial centers of the North and Northwest. The iron smelting and automotive industries of the Great Lakes area have purchased large supplies of Kentucky coal. For instance, the Ford Motor Company of Detroit, Michigan, owns and exploits large holdings of Kentucky coal lands, and the same is true of the steel corporations.

There is little doubt, however, that the industrial historian of Kentucky will view the industrial development of the state from an entirely new perspective because of the recent utilization of the state's electrical power resources. Electric power was first used commercially in Kentucky from 1876 to 1882, and two years later Mayor Charles D. Jacob of Louisville issued a contract for lighting the water-front district from First to Fifth Street. In 1913 a contract was issued for the complete electrification of Louisville's streets. Other cities throughout the state followed this example.

Since this electric industry is yet to be developed, a historian can do little more than make a prophecy. There are ten power sites in the state with plants erected upon them which are capable of developing at least 50,000 kilowatts. This industry has grown rapidly within the last decade. Approximately seventy per cent of the state's industrial machinery is driven by electric energy. During 1929 more than two hundred Kentucky towns were connected with high tension power lines. Three hydroelectric plants, which produce from 2,500 to 50,000 horsepower, were constructed between 1926 and 1929.

With the Federal Government experimenting with the social and industrial possibility of electrical power, Kentucky will perhaps become one of the foremost states in the production and distribution of cheap power. It is not unreasonable to expect that the production of electrical power will become the most important single factor in local industry.

After the War between the States the American tobacco users underwent a change of taste. Before the war, use of tobacco was confined to the conventional forms of cigar, pipe, snuff, and chewing tobacco. For the most part, the habitual user of tobacco of the ante bellum period preferred a strong product. However, taste soon changed, for northern soldiers coming southward in the Union Army cultivated a taste for mild tobaccos. Ingenious manufacturers in the South began to supply this demand, for example, George Washington Duke of North Carolina. This was the beginning of a large American industry. From this taste for mild tobacco came the cigarette, which today is the most widely used form of tobacco. Once the cigarette manufacturers broke down moral prejudice against smoking tobacco wrapped in paper, the market grew rapidly. Since 1925, when the use of tobacco has been publicly indulged in by women, the smoking tobacco industry has reached major proportions in American manufacturing. The cultivation and preparation of tobacco for the market comprise one of the mainstays of staple agricultural crops in Kentucky.

Since the earliest settlement of Kentucky, cultivation of tobacco has been a matter of importance. Immigrating Virginians and Carolinians were thoroughly acquainted with the culture of tobacco along the Atlantic seaboard. As a matter of fact, the standard by which these early western pioneers judged the fertility of Kentucky soil was the issue of whether or not it would produce tobacco. Farmers immigrating to Kentucky were not disappointed in the adaptability of their soil to tobacco, for at an early date this commodity was listed prominently in trade with New Orleans. Throughout the ante bellum years tobacco held its own in spite of strong competition from other commodities offered for sale in the Cotton Kingdom.

After the war the volume of the tobacco trade in Kentucky increased rapidly. In 1865 Kentucky found herself in the lead in the production of tobacco, a position which the state still enjoys. Tradition has it that, in 1868, a man named George Walsh of Brown County, Ohio, accidentally discovered burley tobacco. It is said that this planter ordered a packet of seed from the United States Department of Agriculture. When his plants matured, he was surprised to find that they had large green leaves with lighter colored stems and stalks. He also discovered that these leaves cured nicely and that the tobacco was much milder in taste. This new variety of tobacco was transferred across the Ohio River to the northern counties of Kentucky. From this accidental beginning the burley industry has developed so rapidly that forty-eight of the central Kentucky counties produce annual crops of more than 200,000,000 pounds.

Tobacco was first offered for sale by the planters directly to the manufacturer or exporter. Under this system the planter had to pack his crop in hogsheads ready for shipment. Investigation of prices current before 1860, and even after, shows tobacco listed according to the number of hogsheads sold. After the war, Louisville became the chief tobacco market of Kentucky; in fact, it was virtually the only market. A centralized system of selling tobacco was not formed until 1890, when the American and other tobacco companies began buying tobacco from planters in an established market center. This practice of purchasing the annual production of cured tobacco was satisfactory in theory, but within a few years the planters realized that the centralized market placed them at a disadvantage with the buyer, for the tobacco companies controlled the whole marketing process. During the market year 1895, tobacco prices began to decline, and much dissatisfaction arose over the method of selling.

Before the trouble which beset the next twelve years of tobacco marketing can be explained, however, it is necessary to show what had taken place in the sale of tobacco. Under the old system of selling tobacco, the price was settled between the buyer and the purchaser. Then came the auction system in which samples of tobacco crated in hogsheads were presented to the buyer for bidding. While this system prevailed, the tobacco companies pooled their interests in a trust. The American Tobacco Company purchased much of its tobacco at private sales in county purchasing depots. In the "Dark Tobacco" area, the marketing centers were located at certain key towns conveniently situated for trust operation. Foreign buyers were charged with forcing prices down, especially the Regie agents, representing English manufacturers, and who were suspected of being in collusion with the American Trust to secure lower prices. Since the trust purchased about 400,-000,000 pounds of southern leaf, and the foreign tobacco combination purchased the remainder of the crop, planters were almost defenseless against low prices. The buying power of the American Trust and Tobacco Combination rested in few hands, and price control was easy. This system of controlled markets proved to be a source of agrarian revolution in Kentucky.

Planters in the "dark" and "burley" belts began to form organizations to check the power of the combine. These planter organizations composed the Equity Society which was active in the dark and burley belts of Tennessee and Kentucky. Local chapters of the Equity Society were influential in pooling the farmers' interests in raising prices and reducing the annual production. On December 7, 1907, five hundred night-riding tobacco farmers, masked and armed, entered the village of Hopkinsville and destroyed property valued at $200,000. This outbreak had come as a result of unfair market practices and reduced prices. Resorting to the practice of the Ku Klux Klan, farmers undertook to break the tobacco trust by scraping tobacco beds, burning warehouses, and destroying tobacco in storage. This practice led to uncontrolled violence, so that masked night riders, representing a group of ruffians, became a terror to the western Kentucky communities. Since

Governor Beckham refused to send troops to the scene of the trouble, it was not until Governor Willson took office that a move was made to use state troops to end the disturbance. So violent was this uprising to regulate the process of marketing and prices in the dark-tobacco district that the United States became involved in an international dispute over the destruction of the property of Italian farmers near Hopkinsville. These were years of revolution which resulted in much useless bloodshed and in a complete upsetting of the morale of the state. Nevertheless, the farmers' revolution accomplished several distinct results. During this struggle, the first burley pool was formed, and a vast improvement was made in the quality of burley tobacco offered for sale. This new type of tobacco yielded a lighter pound return per acre, but it proved to be a choicer commodity.

Charles Bohmer of Virginia organized the first loose-leaf sales houses in Kentucky. This early warehouse was established in 1906 at Lexington. Then was begun the highly organized system of selling tobacco which resulted in the burley pool of 1922. In 1933 the Agricultural Adjustment Act of the Federal Government marked the beginning of a new method of production and market control—an act which was declared unconstitutional in 1936, and supplanted by the soil conservation plan.

The tobacco industry increased to such an extent during and immediately following the World War that the 1919–1920 crop sold for $80,-000,000. This crop, however, brought the downfall of the tobacco planter. Tobacco tenants bought farms, and planters, both large and small, made every effort to expand their tobacco acreage. A large crop was planted in the spring of 1920, but because of unfavorable weather conditions the yield was light and inferior. Added to Kentucky's misfortune of a crop failure was the fact that Virginia, Georgia, and Carolina planters had likewise over-planted their tobacco lands, glutting the market before the Kentucky sales floors were opened. When the Kentucky market was finally opened after a month's delay, prices were so ridiculously low that it was found judicious to close the warehouses at once in order to avoid serious trouble from rebellious planters. Planters who had received $325 as their share for crops of 1920 received only $2.75 in 1921.

Realizing that something had to be done immediately to save the burley industry, Robert Worth Bingham, editor and owner of the *Louisville Courier-Journal* and the *Louisville Times,* encouraged the restoration of the old Burley Association. A committee composed of Bernard Baruch, of New York, and former chairman of the War Industries Board; Ralph Barker, Carrolton; Samuel H. Halley, Lexington; John W. Newman of Woodford County, and president of the Burley Association; Arthur Krock, editor of the *Louisville Times;* and Congressman J. C. Cantrill met in New York to discuss the situation. All discussions pointed to a co-operative system of marketing. Judge Bingham and Bernard Baruch suggested the California plan, and Aaron Sapiro, counsel for a number of western fruit co-operative associations, was brought East to help plan a burley pool. At the suggestion of the original committee and Sapiro, Judge Bingham appointed an executive committee composed of James C. Stone, Lexington; Ralph M. Barker, Carrolton; William F. Simms of Spring Station; and John T. Collins of Paris. Later J. N. Kehoe was appointed to fill the place left vacant by John T. Collins' death. Joseph Possaneau of Spokane, Washington, was brought East at the suggestion of Aaron Sapiro, to lay the groundwork for the organization of the burley planters.

A goal of seventy-five per cent of the Kentucky planters who would sign a pledge was set for November 15, 1921. This plan included Kentucky, Ohio, Indiana, and West Virginia and proposed to have pledged to the burley pool all tobacco grown for the next five years. There followed a long campaign of discussion, with Possaneau speaking at key towns throughout the tobacco belt, and with special agents voluntarily assisting in convincing burley farmers that it was to their interest to organize. Finally, seventy-five per cent of the farmers expressed their confidence in the program, and by November 15, 1921, plans of the association had advanced far enough to permit organization. The association had a membership of more than 57,000 planters, producing a crop valued at $50,000,000 or more.

Immediately, the banks of Kentucky and Cincinnati came to the aid of the association. James B. Brown, president of the National Bank of Kentucky, pledged his bank's limit of $500,000; Judge Bingham pledged $1,000,000 personally; Monte Goble, of the Fifth-Third National Bank of Cincinnati, pledged $1,500,000; and other banks in Kentucky pledged more than $1,500,000. The War Finance Corporation pledged a loan of $10,000,000 after the tobacco was placed in the warehouse. Thus the Burley Association was formed, with favorable results within the first year of its existence. Methods of marketing tobacco in Kentucky were almost completely revolutionized. In 1934 and 1935, Kentucky farmers sold their crops through the control of the National Agricultural Adjustment Administration, with satisfactory returns from the average price received for their tobacco.

The Kentucky tobacco growing and marketing problems have undergone a marked change with the advent of farm legislation passed in the early 1930's. Tobacco acreage and poundage were limited first by the Agricultural Adjustment Act of May, 1933, and subsequently by the Soil Conservation and Domestic Allotment Act, 1936, and the Agricultural Adjustment Act of 1938. These federal acts struck at the basic complaints of the Kentucky tobacco farmers. Some of the ills which they attempted to cure were the same ones which had brought about the Tobacco War and the collapse of the tobacco market in 1921.

Postwar Kentucky has proved itself a state of many resources to produce numerous finished materials. Despite the fact that the state has increased the output of its strictly industrial products, it has maintained its rank in agricultural commodities. The state is still noted for its livestock, which ranges from high standard bred horses to good quality poultry. It is interesting to show, briefly, the growth of agriculture since 1860. At the end of the market year 1860, 7,644,217 acres of improved land yielded a cash return of $291,496,955, but in 1947 the Kentucky farmers made a cash return of approximately $588,000,000. The farm census of 1945 indicated there were 238,501 farms with a total of 10,-399,886 acres under cultivation.

The story of Kentucky's industrial reorganization has really been one of expansion rather than change. Especially is this true of the vast livestock-growing industry which has been an integral part of the state's history from the time of the first pioneers. Another industry, which will receive treatment in the chapter on social changes, is the growth, disintegration, and reorganization of the distilling interests. Kentucky's natural resources have blessed her by making of the state an important link in the industrial system of both the North and South.

CHAPTER XXI

New Social Responsibilities

PROFOUND changes in social conditions characterized the period of postwar readjustment in Kentucky. This postwar era of social readjustment has attracted the attention of other states, and Kentucky has been placed in the floodlight. Kentuckians have always proudly boasted of their home state; they have always been land lovers, often paying far more for land than it is actually worth, for the satisfaction of owning it. Even as early as the beginning of the nineteenth century, Timothy Flint found Kentuckians closely rivaling the British in pride of their homeland. True enough, this pride is of long standing, but the years following the War between the States witnessed the creation and cultivation of even more local pride. Homesick Kentucky sons and daughters in other parts of the country referred to their native state in exaggerated and endearing terms.

It is worth a social historian's time to analyze several factors which have contributed to the social development of Kentucky. Hardly anyone in the United States has failed to hear at some time or other the stereotyped expression that Kentucky is a land of "beautiful women, fine horses, and good liquor." This boast has spread far and wide, so that strangers, without proper regard for the sectional nature of the state, expect Kentuckians to be courtly colonels, julep drinkers, Lord Chesterfields, and excellent judges of horseflesh. One may hear Kentuckians questioned in Boston drawing rooms as to their particular part in family feuds. Such ideas of Kentuckians as social beings, however false they may be, are not without a reasonable basis.

After the war, Kentucky made a desperate struggle not only to maintain itself commercially, but to develop its latent resources. Naturally, as this developing process went on, the state's wealth was increased accordingly. Even in the face of the acute national financial panic of 1873 there was no noticeable halting of the general upward trend. As

Kentucky, along with the United States as a whole, grew commercially independent, more attention was given to sports and pleasing pastimes. At an early period Kentuckians began playing baseball with enthusiasm. The *Cincinnati Commercial,* in 1867, gives accounts of games played between Cincinnati and Louisville. As a matter of fact, it was here in the Middle West that this sport was first commercialized.

At the time that Kentucky athletes were learning to play baseball, travelers into Kentucky, and especially one writing in the *Cincinnati Commercial,* were led to believe that fully one half of the populace was continually riding the trains to and from dances. Strangers were much impressed with the Kentuckians' lightheartedness and enthusiasm for sports and entertainment. It was during this period of readjustment that the age-old sport of horse racing was revived, to become the characteristic sport of the Blue Grass. It became economically profitable for owners of Blue Grass farms to breed and train the thoroughbred horse. Soon after Harvard, Yale, and Princeton introduced intercollegiate football, Centre, Transylvania, "State," and Georgetown Colleges likewise introduced this sport, to the delight of their alumni and friends.

However, there was a more serious aspect of the development of the state. The years immediately following the war marked the observance of numerous memorial exercises commemorating the Civil War dead. Ladies' memorial societies were organized, and monuments were erected (by both Northern and Southern sympathizers) throughout many sections of Kentucky to the honored dead. Bodies were exhumed from foreign graves and returned to their native Kentucky soil for burial in family lots. Southern military and naval leaders, among whom were John C. Breckinridge, W. C. P. Breckinridge, Joshua Bullitt, and Raphael Symmes, were welcome speakers. Thus it was that a southern sentiment was developed into a strong love for southern traditions. On the other hand, there were those who had remained faithful to the Union throughout the years of the crisis. To these ardent and loyal Unionists the National leaders were as worthy of praise as were the Southerners. Grant and Sherman were as highly esteemed in many sections of Kentucky as were Lee, Breckinridge, and Johnston. Even yet, seventy years after the war, embers of the Southern cause glow bright. But sentiment still divides Kentuckians two ways, with the same independence which typified Kentucky loyalty to both causes during the war. This has been so true that in many cases wartime Unionists have become peacetime Confederates, and peacetime Confederates ardent Unionists.

Although there existed pronounced differences of opinion in Kentucky by reason of sectional and sentimental variations, economic developments of postwar years have bound Kentuckians together in a common interest. The panic of 1873 was a powerful factor in helping Kentucky's people to reach a common ground of mutual understanding. This panic affected Kentucky in a rather unique manner, for it bore heavily upon individuals, but did not materially affect the welfare of the state's institutions.

Coming from the grain-growing Northwest, the Patrons of Husbandry, a farmers' protective society, spread to Kentucky, where it caused dissension within the ranks of the Democratic Party. Two democratic leaders, W. B. Machen and John W. Stevenson, wished to write the grangers' doctrines into the Democratic platform. The granger movement, however, did not become so general in Kentucky as in the Northwest; nor did its leaders become ambitious to establish cooperative manufacturing plants to supply Kentucky farmers with clothing and farm implements. Nevertheless, the Patrons of Husbandry materially increased prices of farm products.

Temperance

While Kentucky was attempting to recover socially and economically after 1865, she became involved in the nationwide temperance movement. The country as a whole was suffering from an era of intemperance, an era of which Henry Adams said, "No period so thoroughly ordinary had been known in American politics since Christopher Columbus first disturbed the balance of American Society." Certainly it was an age of industrial growth accompanied by a loosening of morals, especially recognized in intemperance.

The spirit of the times was accurately mirrored in the industrial growth of Kentucky. Before 1865, 166 Kentucky distillers were producing 3,348,083 gallons of whiskey valued at $959,651. A majority of these distilling plants were small, and much of their output was consumed locally and in moderation. After the war, national fondness for whiskey increased fourfold, and the output from Kentucky distilleries for 1910 yielded $11,204,649. From 1914 to 1919, the value of the liquor annually distilled in Kentucky increased from $44,360,104 to $48,862,-526. Liquor manufacturing led all other Kentucky industries in cash returns. Distilling interests, however, had to contend with a steadily growing prohibition movement.

Prohibition received its first legislative hearing in Kentucky within a year after the government was founded. Taverns were required, in 1793, to procure licenses in order to retail spirits, and it was from this beginning that the temperance movement gained momentum. Legislative acts were passed in rapid succession to regulate tippling houses, especially during the years of social reform 1832 and 1833. Two years before, the churches of Augusta organized a temperance society which proposed to regulate drunkenness by voting for temperance candidates at the polls. Four years later, the Augusta movement resulted in the organization of the Kentucky Legislative Temperance Society, of which Governor Breathitt became the first president. After the organization of this society, the temperance movement in Kentucky lagged until the advent of the Washington Society, founded in Baltimore in 1840 by a group of newly reformed drunkards. That same year, two of these reformed Washingtonian drunkards came to Kentucky to install a chapter of their society. Within a year, 30,000 Kentucky "dram drinkers" took the "vow" and displayed a chaste white ribbon to proclaim openly their stand against the demon rum.

The influence of the Washington Society was temporary, however, for the 40's and 50's periodically burst out with many temperance revivals. There appeared in Kentucky a multitude of beribboned "Knights of Temperance," many of whom reverted to dram drinkers within an unreasonably short time. Temperance was forgotten when the War between the States began.

When the war was over and its accompanying confusion was cleared up, the temperance movement again appeared on the scene as a measure of moral reform. At Covington a celebration was held in February, 1869, to honor the pledging to total abstinence of 1,000 veteran dram drinkers. Pressure was brought to bear on the general assembly, to make it take active steps to control the sale of liquor within the state. Numerous petitions proposed that retailers of spirits be held personally responsible for the misdeeds of their inebriated customers. Others—more successfully—demanded the right of local option, and, within a short time twenty-three counties prohibited the sale of intoxicants within their borders. At the same time, Governor Leslie made a friendly temperance gesture by prohibiting the use of whiskey at official functions. Faculties and boards of trustees of private and public schools forbade the sale of liquor within a certain prescribed distance from schoolhouses. Numerous acts of the general assembly permitted the restriction of liquor sales in certain specified areas.

Liquor dealers were restricted by a legislative act of 1871 from selling whiskey to minors and inebriates. After this date, specific local option legislation frequently interspersed the pages of the legislature's proceedings. Most of this legislation was ineffective. However, a specific act was passed in April, 1878, to prohibit the sale of liquor within two miles of the High Bridge meeting grounds. But this act was ridiculous in that it did not make it a misdemeanor to drink whiskey on the campmeeting ground. Nevertheless, the pattern was set, and nearly every campmeeting in Kentucky petitioned the legislature to pass restrictive acts for its protection.

Early Kentuckians, like all pioneering western people, regarded crimes of drunken persons as inexcusable, but, at the same time, heartily condoned the use of whiskey as a "medical" stimulant. As a consequence, every restrictive legislative act contained the "medical" loophole. Nearly every Kentuckian looked upon liquor as a thing which he could control. He saw no harm in dram drinking. But in the hands of some men whiskey became immediately dangerous. However, with all the laws passed in fifty-five years calling for restrictive legislation, it becomes obvious that temperance leaders wished only for temperance and not for total prohibition.

While Kentucky's legislature was busily engaged in devising and passing prohibition laws, various temperance organizations whose work had been checked by the war were once again renewing their bitter fight. One of the first societies to resume this work was the Order of the Good Templars. This order organized the Arlington Lodge in Lexington, November 22, 1867. From this parent chapter Good Templar lodges were established throughout the state. Colonel George Bain of Lexington took the stump to fight the liquor evil in his famous speech, "The Defeat of the Nation's Dragon." From 1870 to 1873, Colonel Bain edited the *Good Templar's Advocate* as the official organ of all temperance groups. An honorary lodge known as the Royal Templars of Temperance was organized to promote sobriety by a program of education. At one time, this order was successful in enlisting 20,000 members.

At Hillsboro, Ohio, December 24, 1873, the Woman's Crusade had its beginning. This movement was promoted by Dr. D. Lewis, partly, it was said, by his impressive recitation of the story of his mother's successful fight against a saloon which was wrecking her community. This was the beginning of the Woman's Christian Temperance Union, which spread to Kentucky at first as a branch of the Women's Missionary Union. Throughout the 80's, this society went through a successful stage of organizing. Behind its motto "For God and Home and Native Land" it promoted an intensive program of reform.

Kentucky, through leaders like Colonel George Bain, General Green Clay, Mrs. Frances Beauchamp, a militant woman reformer, and a large and faithful following of laymen and lay women, prevailed against the political influence of strongly entrenched distillers. Before the Eighteenth Amendment became a part of the National Constitution on January 16, 1919, Kentucky, an important distilling center, had virtually become a dry state through enforcement of the universal local option law of 1912.

Practically, prohibition proved a failure in Kentucky. From 1919 to 1934, the problem of enforcing provisions of the Eighteenth Amendment proved impossible of solution. Instead of checking completely the manufacture of liquor, the amendment encouraged moonshining and bootlegging. Consequently, temperance suffered an unhappy setback similar to that which it suffered during the war (1860–1865). When the voters of the United States repealed the Eighteenth Amendment in 1933, Kentucky was numbered among the wet states by a large majority of votes. However, the State of Kentucky was left a dry state by constitutional restriction. The legislature of 1934 provided for the sale of liquor in the state by repealing the enforcement clause of the Rash-Gullion Act of 1912, and in the general election of November, 1935, the prohibition amendment to the constitution was repealed.

Nevertheless the plan of local option prevailed, and immediately the dry forces under the leadership of the Anti-Saloon League began a campaign to close the liquor trade in local areas. By 1950 more than ninety of the one hundred and twenty counties were dry. Somewhat more confusing is the fact that communities within counties have voted either wet or dry and created islands of resistance. During and following World War II whiskey distilling and the brewing of beer have become big business. The state itself depends upon a big backlog of liquor tax to support its bi-annual budgets.

As Kentucky became increasingly industrial, larger centers of population came into existence. Population of towns such as Louisville, Covington, Paducah, Owensboro, Bowling Green, Ashland, and Lexington increased at a rapid rate. Louisville's population grew from 68,033 in 1860 to 161,129 in 1890, and to 307,745 in 1930. Lexington has grown from a town of 9,231, in 1860, to a small city of more than 50,000, within the borough limits, in 1950. While urban centers were showing a startling increase, the population of Kentucky as a whole was growing rapidly. At the time of the outbreak of the war in 1861, Kentucky's population numbered 1,155,684; in 1890 it was 1,858,635; and in 1950 it was 2,931,588. This increasing population presents some interesting problems in the state's social development. There were in the state in 1940, 609,450 families, 503,468 of native parents, 10,470 of foreign-born parents, and a miscellaneous mixture of 35,000 native American families. This analysis tells a complete story within itself; Kentucky is populated predominantly by native, white, Kentucky-born Americans; a fact to indicate an independent and self-sufficient social population. Unfortunately, however, Kentucky has shown a rapid slump in social independence within the last seventy years, for it has changed from a state with an independent rural class of home owners to a state with a large class of rural tenants. The last decennial census shows clearly that the birthrate of the farm tenant class of Kentucky is increasing more rapidly than is that of the home owning rural group. There were, in 1940, 290,379 tenant families and 306,284 owner families. In these figures lies one of the secrets of Kentucky's social condition and a reasonable explanation of why the state's social responsibility is rapidly increasing. Tenancy is one of the offsprings of the War between the States; although it existed before 1860, it did not reach proportions of vital social significance. Of such little importance, in fact, was this social condition in the country as a whole, prior to 1860, that the United States Census Bureau devoted only a limited amount of space to the subject. Dr. Edward N. Clopper, in his report to the Consolidated Charities of Kentucky in 1919, called attention to living conditions of farm tenants, particularly since their dependence added additional burdens to already inadequate charitable agencies of the state.

Although lagging far behind in social welfare and social readjustment, Kentucky has not been altogether neglectful of these obligations. One of the first steps towards the establishment of a system of state welfare was taken in 1874, when the legislature passed a law requiring the counties to keep vital statistics. This act paved the way for other legislation of a similar nature. Following examples of Louisiana and Massachusetts, Kentucky established, in 1878, a state board of public health. Powers of this original board, however, were limited, until the new constitution was adopted in 1891. There followed the adoption of the new constitution a series of acts consolidating and expanding the health department's functions. One of the most important functions of the State Board of Health has been its continuance of the fight, started by the United States Public Service, against trachoma, which prevails in the eastern mountain area. As a result of the findings of the federal health service, a trachoma hospital was established in 1927 at Richmond. This disease has been a frightful menace, threatening the eyesight of thousands of Kentuckians.

Since 1911 a vigorous fight has been made against tuberculosis. Through the assistance of the general assembly and private charities much headway has been made in the prevention and cure of this disease.

Tuberculosis has taken a heavy toll of life in Kentucky. In 1910 it was causing the deaths of 224 persons out of each 100,000 of the state's population. In 1943 sixty-four persons per 100,000 were still dying from the disease. To combat this plague the legislature, in 1944, passed an act appropriating a half million dollars to build five hospitals for the treatment of tuberculosis. For more than a century people who have been aware of the heavy toll of life from tuberculosis have fought against it. These five hospitals are located at Paris, London, Madisonville, Glasgow, and Ashland. In the campaign, in 1949, to revise the salary limitation section of the Constitution it was said Kentucky could not employ trained personnel to staff these hospitals. As this is being written in 1950 the new hospitals are still not in operation. The Kentucky Medical Association has been active in its efforts to study the diseases which are most prevalent in the state. This association has co-operated with the Department of Public Health, at the University of Kentucky, in acquainting county health officers with the latest findings in public health service. Through this department a valuable brief survey was made, in 1931, of Kentucky's medical needs, revealing many interesting facts about the demand for trained medical personnel in many sections of the state. At present, the State Board of Public Health is a most important department of Kentucky's government. Its services, with state supervision, are available to every county within the state.

Despite efforts of Kentucky's health department, it has been impossible to supply medical aid to many of the underdeveloped and more inaccessible sections of the state. Efforts to supplement the work of the public health officers and private physicians have been made by private charities. In 1925 Mrs. Mary Breckinridge of Lexington organized the Frontier Nursing Service, which now supplies trained midwives and nurses to Perry, Leslie, and Clay Counties. This service has been offered in districts where private medical care is unobtainable for lack of money and of medically trained men.

Only recently has Kentucky undertaken a definite program of corrections and charities. There have been penitentiaries in Kentucky since an early date, and public institutions to care for the deaf, dumb, and blind. But unfortunately these institutions were established and maintained primarily as places of detention rather than of correction. Dorothea Dix's fight for the humane care of social dependents and insane in public institutions only indirectly affected Kentucky. Thus, after a long period of badly managed penal and socially corrective institutions, and after the carrying out of a badly disjointed program, during which public charities were entrusted to many inefficient partisan hands, a systematic plan was finally adopted. Kentucky's charities were in the hands of the Board of Trustees of Houses of Reform to 1896, the State Board of Penitentiary Commissioners to 1898, the State Board of Control of Charitable Institutions to 1906, and in the hands of the State Board of Control established in 1918 and reorganized on a "nonpartisan" basis in 1920. In reviewing this bit of history, it is easy to understand how unmethodically Kentucky has cared for her socially indigent population. Perhaps the most urgent need for reform is to be found in the penal institutions, both local and state. Throughout the *post bellum* period, Kentucky's county jails have been notorious for lack of ordinary sanitation and care of prisoners.

During the administration of Governor W. J. Fields, 1923–1927, a definite effort was made to reform Kentucky's charitable and penal institutions. A bond issue of $75,000,000 was proposed in 1926, but was defeated at the polls. Governor Fields wished to remedy the notorious crowding and idleness in the state penal institutions. His efforts, however, bore little or no fruit, for his successors have been sorely troubled with this problem, a fact which partly accounts for the much criticized abuse of the pardoning power by the governors. Governor Laffoon (1935) suggested that an investigation be made to select the 300 most worthy prisoners to be pardoned in order to relieve overcrowding. Before the end of his administration, he issued hundreds of pardons. Lack of prison reform in Kentucky was brought forcibly to public attention in the flood of 1937. The Kentucky River exceeded the highest flood stage on record, and the muddy waters poured into the cell blocks of the state penitentiary at Frankfort, causing a state of panic to exist among the 2,900 prisoners incarcerated within its walls. For several days care for these prisoners presented a most serious problem to the state administration.

Under the Chandler administration, and stimulated by the scare of the flood, a new state penitentiary was built near LaGrange in Oldham County, and the old Stockade in Frankfort was demolished. Except for one unfortunate bit of mismanagement and defective record keeping, the new reformatory has been far superior to the old one. Old traditions, defective old buildings, and an unsatisfactory sanitary condition, because of location, were destroyed.

Large urban centers in the state have maintained private charitable institutions. Louisville, Covington, Paducah, Bowling Green, Lexington, and other towns have supported charitable institutions through use of both public and private funds. In recent years, private support for many public charities has come through community chests.

Perhaps the most outstanding social and economic liability which has arisen in the state is the frequent labor disputes which occur in the coal mining areas. As Kentucky's coal fields have become of national industrial importance, they have created ever-recurring labor uprisings. Typical of the industrial development throughout the United States, Kentucky's coal industry soon outgrew the domestic stage of labor. Where early miners operated as unorganized domestic laborers, the increasing demands of industry have created a detached type of labor. One of the first strikes to occur in connection with the coal mining industry took place in 1886–1887, in the western coal fields. Here the miners questioned the honesty of operators in weighing their daily loadings. This led to the appointment of "labor-paid" weighers who protected the miners' right to honest weight. Two years later a strike occurred in the Jellico field in eastern Kentucky which vitally affected the coal output for that year. There have followed serious strikes in 1897, 1920, 1921, 1932, 1934, 1935 and in the years since 1945. An especially bitter strike was the one in the winter months of 1950. This latter conflict grew out of disagreement over the miners' contracts. A federal court instructed the miners to return to the mines, but they refused to do so in large numbers because of the absence of a contract specifying the conditions under which they would work. These strikes have reached dangerous proportions so far as the peace of their areas was concerned. It has often been necessary for the Governor to order the State Guard to quell disturbances. In 1921 President Harding was forced to send a detachment of the United States Infantry into Kentucky. Nearly every one of these outbreaks has prompted serious consideration from the state legislature, and much remedial legislation has resulted therefrom.

These labor disputes, however, have placed the state in an unfavorable light in the eyes of the nation. For instance, the Associated Press reports of 1932, prompted by Theodore Dreiser's trial for interference in labor troubles, and by the refusal of several eastern Kentucky county officials to admit interfering "radical" college students from Columbia University in New York and Commonwealth College of Mena, Arkansas, to the Pineville area, received a wide publicity none too good for the state.

Labor uprisings have been stimulated greatly by periodic recurrence of economic depressions since 1893. Especially has this been true since

1920, when outside industry consumed less and less fuel from the Kentucky mines. During years of prosperity and brisk demand for Kentucky coal, eastern counties were so greatly over-populated by birth and immigration as to place an unbearable strain upon their resources during panic years. During years of depression it is almost impossible to prevent a horrible social disaster in the Kentucky coal fields. This is a frontier for social readjustment; inevitably the State of Kentucky will have to face this problem as a reality.

When humanitarian activities of the war ceased, social leaders were not satisfied to become idle. Women's rights had been a matter of minor national concern for many years before the war, but, before 1865, the movement had gained little headway. Few Kentucky politicians believed the dissatisfied "Yankee Girls" who appeared on the political scene after the war would have sufficient influence on the Kentucky women to cause them to sue for their rights. Mrs. Blackwell of New York argued before the Kentucky legislature that the women's vote would offset the Negro vote. It was also argued that if Kentucky had been so kind, under the several reconstruction constitutional amendments, as to enfranchise the Negro, it should place as much confidence in its women. This struggle for women's rights aroused nearly all of the newspapers in the state to humorous comments. Workers for the women's franchise were dubbed "Jerushas" to be laughed at on all sides. The editor of the *Georgetown Weekly Times,* February 28, 1872, said that members of the Kentucky legislature should marry the "fussy old Yankee girls, and convert them into sensible women." The Reverend Stuart Robinson of Louisville condemned the suffragettes as "notorious as the leaders of a fiery partisan infidel assault upon, not only our common Christianity, but our social order." Despite these many attacks, however, the women's rights movement survived, and in 1920 the state ratified the woman suffrage amendment to the National Constitution. This movement has succeeded in Kentucky under the ardent and militant leadership of Miss Laura Clay and Miss Madeleine Clay Breckinridge.

Few aspects of Kentucky's history have given it more notoriety outside of the state than its mountain feuds between 1865 and 1910. These feuds throw an interesting light on the make-up of Kentucky's population. In 1890 there were 1,858,635 persons in Kentucky, of which number 1,799,279 were native born. This homogeneous population, together with the great influence of environment, gives the explanation of the Kentucky mountain feud. Perhaps few questions have caused more arguments than the ancestral composition of the people of the eastern area of Kentucky. Sociology and history scholars have developed many and differing theories about the composition of the mountain race and theories as to why it settled in the eastern highlands. Contrary to popular belief, there has never been any such thing as a pure Anglo-Saxon race in the Kentucky mountains. This term has been used to imply that the racial composition of the highlands of Kentucky is of the original European and English stock. The people represent an original colonial mixture of native English, Scotch, Irish, German, and Swiss, who have combined certain Old World characteristics to create a unique class in American society. The blending of these bloods created a volatile race of English-speaking, "western" American mountaineers. These groups settled in the Appalachian highlands largely because of a love for the hills of their transatlantic homelands. Many learned discussions have taken place to explain the mountaineer. These have ranged all the way from a theory of his feeling of social inferiority to an explanation in the natural expansion of Kentucky's population. The first of these explanations is without foundation. The settlement of the mountains can be explained simply by the fact that, in a natural westward migration from Pennsylvania, Virginia, and the Carolinas, immigrants selected lands on which they wished to live and then remained there. Natural increase by birth, together with their immunity from certain deadly diseases, has caused the mountain areas of Kentucky to become thickly populated.

Without dealing further with the highly controversial subject of the origin of the mountaineer, it is enough to say he has developed a distinct and unique personality. The mountaineer, like his other agrarian brothers of the United States, has made his living solely from the soil. Since his natural environment has landlocked him, he has been denied constant contact with the outside world. The interior sections have been denied a sufficient amount of legal knowledge and protection until the past few years. If a crime was committed in an isolated eastern county, it proved an expensive and trying ordeal to transport prisoner and witnesses to the "outside" for trial. The eastern counties were in a similar situation to that of Kentucky during her colonial period, when major cases were transferred to Virginia for trial. Therefore it was only natural that the mountaineer developed his own code of ethics and law. In the absence of an application of statute law in the mountains, there was developed a common law, which was not unlike time-honored English common law. The common law of the mountains was simple in its structure. It provided a strict code of honor which forbade abuse of women and helpless individuals. Thievery was and still is the basest of crimes in the mountain area. Houses and cribs of some sections are left unlocked and are seldom broke into. If a thief was caught in the act, he was tried, condemned, and executed on the spot, if the owner of the property had a gun. When such a thing occurred, the neighborhood accepted it as the normal course of the common law. It is interesting to note the regard for this common law, as illustrated in an old warrant issued by a magistrate in Breathitt County, in which the constable was instructed to take the accused man "on the level or on the hill, dead or alive," to be brought in and tried by the law of that particular creek.

When one neighbor killed another, it upset the whole community, and, especially, all the blood kin of the unfortunate victim. Such crimes weighed heavily upon the minds of the solitary, landlocked, agrarian highlander, for there was nothing to distract his line of thought. The more he considered the crime perpetrated against his kinsman, and the more he felt his helplessness in bringing the offender to trial in a regularly constituted court, the more determined he was to bring revenge with his own hands. Thus a feud, such as the Hargis-Cockrill dispute in Breathitt County, was started. These mountain outbreaks made exciting copy for the daily press, and the newspapermen did not neglect their opportunity. Unfortunately, persons in and out of Kentucky were impressed with the armed disturbances in the state, but few people in Louisville or Lexington realized that there occurred more homicides within their own city boundaries during any single five-year period than have occurred throughout the mountains for all times. A killing in a rural community of the mountains naturally created more comment than one in the more populous centers of the state.

It is indeed an interesting social study to observe the influence which improved highways are exerting upon Kentucky society. Especially is this true of the eastern counties, for they are rapidly ceasing to be isolated communities. It is no longer true that circuit judges go to many county seats with any anticipation of serious trouble. So rapidly is improved highway transportation changing the status of social intercourse that the present organization of counties is faced with inevitable consolidations. As a matter of fact, the state auditor has already advised in his reports that certain counties be discontinued. It is no longer necessary to establish a county courthouse within mule-back ride of every community in the state.

Not only has improved highway transportation vitally affected the social status of the more isolated sections, but the introduction of high-speed automobiles has enforced a continual improvement of highways which shortened distances in driving time to a fraction of that required in former days. This factor has tended to unify all parts of the state into a compact social, economic, and political unit. Sectional lines are daily becoming less pronounced than they were in the days when a large part of the state's population was more or less permanently attached to the community of its birth. Social intercourse has changed. Once, traveling was done by boat, horseback, or on public stagecoaches, and travelers lodged at the numerous taverns which dotted the landscape. Today, traveling is done by train, by motor bus, or by private automobile. The livery stables and spacious taverns have made way for hundreds of filling stations, quick lunch stands, and less spacious tourist homes, which line Kentucky highways. Life in Kentucky has been set to a much quicker tempo, and the average Kentuckian is not so provincial as he was in former years.

CHAPTER XXII

A New Political Order

KENTUCKY'S postwar politics were unique in the Southern States. Despite the fact that Kentucky failed to secede, it presented from 1865 to 1876 perhaps the most solid Confederate-Democrat front of any state south of the Ohio. Kentucky's postwar political system was built largely upon the basis of political upheaval from 1850 to 1860. The Whig Party, ineffective by 1853, was succeeded in turn by the Know Nothing and National Republican organizations. Since the Republican faith, however, was too closely linked with the antislavery issue, it lost a large portion of Kentucky Whig support to the Constitutional Union Party in 1860. Republican sentiment gradually became a major factor in Kentucky politics, but it was not until 1895 that the party was able to gain control of the state.

Five years of war had a rather peculiar effect upon the local political condition. In 1865 the Democrats were definitely opposed to the radical influence of the National Republican Party. The new Republican opposition was regarded as a revolt against native white rule, and it was a source of real annoyance until 1868, when the Democrats were easily victorious. Since there were many influential conservatives left stranded on a middle ground, each political group sought their votes. Democrats made a strong bid for such votes by effecting compromises between Union and secession partisans. These compromises secured for the Democrats the votes of Colonel Frank Wolford and other Union Army officers. The Republican, or radical, Party likewise possessed native leadership in John M. Harlan, James Speed, W. H. Wadsworth, and C. P. Burnham. In 1868, when a whole slate of candidates from presidential electors to constables was to be chosen, Kentucky experienced a real test of partisan strength. Supporting a colorless campaigner in John W. Stevenson, candidate for Governor, Democrats triumphantly polled 115,000 votes to 39,000 for the opposition. For the next eight years the Democrats and radical Republicans carried on a political tug of war, with the balance of voting strength overwhelmingly in favor of the native democracy. The newly formed Democratic *Courier-Journal* and its young rampant Confederate editor, Henry Watterson, courageously bore the brunt of editorial fusillading between campaigns. Watterson early reached the editorial zenith in excoriating what he regarded as a whining and hopelessly defeated radical contingent. Behind much political braggadocio, however, was the fear that Kentucky radicals (Republicans) would create a situation which might lead to the establishment in the state of a miltary government. Fortunately for Kentucky's democracy, the radicals failed to realize that the state bore a different relationship to the Union than the Southern States, which had seceded, for Kentucky had not joined the Confederacy.

National ratification of the Thirteenth, Fourteenth, and Fifteenth Amendments of the United States Constitution stirred anew the bipartisan issues which had existed in ante bellum Kentucky. Democrats declared "we are not sunk so low as to be governed by Negroes," but radicals hoped to equalize their opponents' advantage with the Negro vote.

The radicals were jubilant over their prospects of using Negro votes, and over ousting from office Democrats who were disqualified by the Fourteenth Amendment, but they feared the effects of the Negro vote upon white mountaineers. Braving a possible loss of eastern Kentucky support, the radicals attempted to oust several "illegally" elected state officials. Before any headway could be made in dismissing Democrats, however, Congress, in 1871, removed the disabilities of sixty of the cases in question.

To both political parties the Negro vote was a vital but minor factor. Democrats feared that the Negro would help to overcome white leadership, and radicals feared that Democrats would pull over a large block of colored support. This fear prevailed throughout Kentucky, especially in the larger municipalities where the Negro population was concentrated. Here the issue had to be solved first, since municipal elections preceded state elections. City fathers in Democratic strongholds were thoroughly aroused, and the legislature was requested to permit changes of city charters to make "satisfactory adjustments" of municipal registration laws. Danville allowed white citizens of Boyle County to vote in its municipal elections, provided they owned property within the corporate limits. "Property rights," however, could not be loosely interpreted, said the Court of Appeals, to mean grave lots and bank stock. Undaunted by these restrictions, ninety-three "unterrified" Democrats purchased twenty-three front feet of a weed-covered vacant lot and divided it into four-inch democratic "bands of white supremacy and property rights."

Kentucky's congressional election was delayed on the flimsy excuse that the new census report was not available and that there might be a fundamental change in the proportionment of representatives. Delay as they might, in 1870, Democrats realized that the test of the Negro vote had to come. If the congressional election were delayed until August, Kentucky would be without representation in Congress for a period of six months, for it was not until 1872 that all congressional elections (with the exception of Maine) were required to be held in November. Kentucky's electorate soon realized that Negro suffrage was inevitable and wisely ignored the issue. With few exceptions, the election was quiet and well conducted. In some precincts white Democrats hindered timid Negro voters by asking them hundreds of irrelevant questions, with the result that the polls were closed before any considerable number of colored voters had cast their ballots. If the Democrats entertained doubts as to their party strength in the face of the Negro vote, these were dissipated when returns from the election gave them 88,000 votes to 57,000 for the Republicans. Doubtless the Democratic lead was increased by an addition of several thousand colored votes. Sensible Negroes, appreciating their economic position and the influence of their votes upon its future, supported their white neighbor's party. After 1871 the radical wing of the Republican Party was rapidly dissolved, and the carpetbaggers and scalawags gave up control completely to native leadership. When this occurred, white Democrats ceased to fear the bugaboo of radical usurpation of leadership in state politics.

The year 1871 stands out in bold relief in Kentucky's political history. No longer did consolidated white Democracy entertain real fear of radical and Negro votes. Favorable results at the polls were conclusive evidence that Democrats could indulge with safety in some internal warring over Kentucky's domestic situation. Ante bellum and "war" laws cluttered the statute books; education sought public sanction and support; and Kentucky's industry needed both legislative coaxing and prodding. All these demands were urgent, for, in defying radical opposition, loyal Democrats spent entirely too much time in legislative halls on Southern glory and sentimentality, to the neglect of Kentucky's real needs. Jousting with radicals had been so heated that Democrats were startled, in a moment of meditation, to learn, for the first time, that their party was cut in twain. Two philosophies were self-evident —"Bourbon" and "New South." Believing radicalism forever banished from the state, young Henry Watterson admonished Democrats to accept Negro suffrage, to adjudge a candidate's fitness for public office by standards other than service in the Confederate Army, to accept the Fourteenth and Fifteenth Amendments, to develop the state's resources, and to subsidize railroads. This was a departure from historical Democratic philosophy, a "new departure" in fact. Since Watterson had willfully drawn the party rip cord, he was at once set upon by "loyalists" or "Bourbons," led by J. Stoddard Johnston's *Kentucky Yeoman* (Frankfort). Johnston's "Bourbon" editorials were echoed throughout Kentucky by his local and conservative editorial brethren who looked upon Henry Watterson's "new departure" program as shameless sacrilege. Undaunted by "Bourbon" heel-nibbling, Watterson was soon to leave his opponents groping hopelessly among the decayed ruins of a sentimental political past. Coming too late to figure in the election of 1871, "new departure" support was in time to give Preston H. Leslie a 39,000-vote majority over his able Republican rival, John M. Harlan. Since Harlan polled a large vote (89,000), it was clear that, with native support and leadership Republicans could look forward hopefully to success. Despite the fact that Democrats rushed to Leslie's aid in 1871, Kentucky had gained a position which, with the exception of Tennessee, was unique in the South, for it had not only two factions of the Democratic Party, but also two parties.

The Third Party Movement

National third party movements have always found support in Kentucky. Those third party movements which have succeeded, however, have promised solution to agrarian and labor problems. A main cause of party bolting in Kentucky was the generosity shown corporations, especially railroads, by the state legislature during the latter sixties and early seventies. In 1869 there was a proposal before the legislature advocating a bond issue of $10,000,000, the proceeds to be used as a subsidy to encourage an expansion of industry, and to build railroads. Among the railroads under construction at the time were additions to the Louisville and Nashville system, the Lexington and Big Sandy, the Chesapeake, Ohio, and Southwestern, the Kentucky Union, the Cincinnati-Southern, and numerous local connecting branches. Henry Watterson and his "new departure" Democrats were diligent in the behalf of new industry. In Louisville, Watterson took the lead in pointing out new and profitable industrial opportunities. Boards of commerce distributed thousands of circulars at home and abroad describing Kentucky's resources and proclaiming Kentucky a land of unlimited business promise. Using the state's credit to encourage corporations was too unusual, however, for conservative agrarian legislators, and enthusiastic "new departure" partisans had to content themselves with granting generous tax exemption and special privileges. This encouragement to capital was soon noticeable, for railway mileage increased from 567 miles built and projected in 1860, to more than 1,500 miles in operation, in 1880. These roads represented a stated capital investment of $100,000,000. Along with the expansion of the Kentucky railway system, eastern capital poured into the state to develop timber and coal resources, and to build distilleries and tobacco warehouses.

By their ardent courtship of capital and industry "new departure" Democrats created the basis for a third party movement in Kentucky. In adjusting itself to the new industrial order, Kentucky early found its ante bellum agricultural staples of hemp, grain, and livestock pushed into the background by tobacco. After 1865, tobacco became the major "money" crop. Thus in adopting a single major cash crop, Kentucky acquired many of the economic and social ills of the cotton South. Just when Kentucky farmers believed they had successfully outlived the demoralizing effects of war, the panic of 1873 came as a sickening blow. It was disappointing to Kentuckians, who, as a contemporary writer said, were ready "to enjoy their jowls and greens," to find themselves in a bewildering financial panic. Tobacco prices fell to ruinously low levels, banks closed, and business houses were bankrupt. The depression of 1873 was acute and lasted six years. Nationally, the surge of economic expansion was too strong for the country to flounder for a long period under the wreckage of the crisis. But the Kentucky farmers saw tobacco prices fall from 10 cents in 1872 to 6 cents in 1878, with consequent ruination to a large number of one-crop farmers who had to mortgage their property to prevent starvation. Land values declined sharply, and farm mortgages were foreclosed by the hundreds. Kentucky farmers were left sadly deflated, with little tangible reason to hope for better times. Naturally their unhappy predicament caused these farmers to hunt for a solution of their problems. Farm leaders were impressed with the prosperous operation of Kentucky railroads, which, between 1870 and 1880, had earned annual dividends of more than 9 per cent. These earnings were augmented materially by the state in grants of tax exemption and special privileges.

If the panic of '73 was insufficient reason for agricultural grievances, the "crime of '73" amply made up for its shortcomings. The change in the monetary system caused by demonetizing silver, and the resumption of the payment of greenbacks in gold by 1879 were believed to work a hardship upon farmer-debtors. On January 12, 1875, Congress passed the Resumption Act, which instructed the Secretary of the Treasury to accumulate an amount of gold sufficient to resume specie payment on January 1, 1879. By 1879, greenbacks were on a par value with specie. Kentucky farmers agreed with the editor of the Paris *Western Citizen*, April 15, 1875, when he said that resumption was "a plot upon the part of the international money powers to control the world's exchange and obtain control of the world's wealth." Debtor farmers wanted more and cheaper money to raise prices. In Congress, Kentuckians voted unanimously against the Resumption Bill. John G. Carlisle, later to become Secretary of the Treasury, distinguished himself in Kentucky as a diligent foe of the bill. To combat the money evil by advocating inflation, Kentucky farmers followed the example of the other southern farmers and organized chapters of the Order of Patrons of Husbandry. By 1876 this order had 1,135 chapters, which resolved themselves into local political clubs to fight resumption and special concessions from the Kentucky General Assembly to private industry.

It was not the purpose of Kentucky "grangers" to form a new political party, but to exert a major influence upon the election of candidates from the existing parties who would favor agrarian interests in the Governor's chair and in the legislature. The farmer had neglected his political influence during the years after the war. During this period of prosperity, the farmer vote was blinded to the true political situation, and public officials had become industrially minded. Kentucky had always been predominantly agricultural, with the central counties assuming the lead, but, in 1875, new agrarian political leadership came from the western counties. These counties were in the dark tobacco belt, and their product was the first to feel the blighting effects of the panic. When the Kentucky Assembly met, in 1876, its membership was composed largely of the agrarian-Democrats. Captain W. J. Stone of Lyon County was elected speaker of the house, and James B. Beck of Lexington was elected to the United States Senate. Beck's election was the first legislative victory of the agrarians, for they defeated a "special interest" man in ex-Governor Preston H. Leslie. Leslie had the reputation of being a powerful lobbyist, or "third house member," in behalf of the railroads. Unfortunately for agrarian interests legislators whom the grangers sent to Frankfort, although sincere enough of purpose, were inexperienced in law making. Proof is lacking, but it is highly probable that a few "special interests" and experienced members kept the farmer-legislators so badly confused that they were unable to accomplish anything. It is likely also that inexperienced and apprehensive legislators watched every move made by the general assembly, with the result that they did nothing themselves. After the whole legislative session was wasted in arguments over rules of procedure, only one piece of legislation, reducing interest rates from ten to eight per cent, was passed.

While "granger-legislators" were bickering over a hodge-podge program, "new departure" Democrats were re-emphasizing the need for a low tariff, partly as a device to detract attention from local to national issues. Watterson believed "the grangers may tinker as much as they please, but they will never get relief until they vote the radicals out of Congress, and get a Democratic free trade majority in." The editor of the *Courier-Journal* was a shrewd political leader, for he promoted harmony in his party's ranks. By the end of 1876, grangers had their fill of lawmaking and were safely back in the Democratic fold. But they did not submit until they had accused "Marse Henry," keynoter of the St. Louis Democratic convention, 1876, of subservience to banker interests. Early attacks upon Watterson are reflected in the gesture made to greenback Democrats in the Democratic platform of 1876. The platform declared that the Democratic Party was ready to reform the whole fiscal system of the United States Government. It stood pledged, in 1876, against creating "an artificial scarcity of currency, and at no time alarming the public mind into a withdrawal of that vaster machinery of credit by which 95 per cent of all business transactions are performed." The Democrats denounced the Republicans for twelve years of failure. Since such a statement on the part of the national party pacified Kentucky's agricultural voters, little interest was manifested in the greenback convention held at Indianapolis. B. L. D. Duffy, Warren County, and Colonel Pollock Barbour, Louisville, attended this convention and in turn called a state convention to meet in Louisville, July 4. Agricultural distress was greatest in the Third Congressional District, and this was the only district to nominate a separate congressional candidate. In November the Hayes-Tilden vote swamped the third party, with Tilden carrying Kentucky by a plurality of 159,690 to 97,156 for Hayes. Again in 1878 the Greenback Party was active in eight of the ten congressional districts. In the Seventh, or Ashland District, Joseph S. C. Blackburn was almost defeated by the Greenback candidate, L. B. Woolfolk.[1] Oscar Turner, a Democrat who failed to secure his party's nomination, broke the Democratic slate as an independent in the First District.

Despite the fact that grangers and Greenbackers made little independent headway in Kentucky, they wielded a powerful influence in major party ranks. In its state convention in 1879 the Democratic Party adopted resolutions favoring third party demands. Democrats loudly denounced resumption and advocated free silver and a state board of equalization to adjust equitably the tax burden. Dr. Luke P. Blackburn, a hero of the southern yellow fever epidemic, was nominated as gubernatorial candidate to oppose Walter Evans, a Louisville Republican, and the Greenbackers nominated C. W. Cooke of Owensboro. Doctor Blackburn carried the state by a plurality of 43,917, while Cooke

[1] L. B. Woolfolk, minister of the gospel, created a dissension in his flock by his candidacy. He withdrew, to re-enter the campaign twice, but withdrew finally just before the election. Had he remained in the campaign there is good reason to believe that he might have been elected.

increased his party's strength from 8,000 to 18,954 votes. Again, the Greenbackers were a strong factor in the congressional election—in which they shared honors with Labor. A visit from General J. B. Weaver, national nominee for President, increased the Kentucky third party's prestige. Kentucky Democracy became genuinely apprehensive, for it feared Republican duplicity. A stirring campaign followed, in which issues appealing to the farmer-voters were stressed, with the result that the Greenback-Labor vote was reduced to 11,500. There was some reason, perhaps, for Democrats to believe the Greenbackers were innocently serving as tools of the Republican Party, for the two groups merged their voting strength in the election of legislators. But the movement met with slight success, for the Democrats lost only eleven seats in the lower house of the Kentucky General Assembly. Its failure in the election of 1881 was a death blow to the Greenback Party. Its supporters returned to the ranks of the two major political groups, and in 1884 Grover Cleveland carried Kentucky by more than 30,000 votes. Returning prosperity, especially in higher agricultural prices, caused the dissolution of the third party. The end of the first period of political insurgency in Kentucky did not come, however, until it had effected some major accomplishments for the farmer. A Bureau of Agriculture was created in 1876; the Agricultural and Mechanical College was established; and the way was paved for the creation of a railroad commission.

Returning prosperity, after 1884, proved unstable for Kentucky farmers. A sane analysis of the agricultural situation at this date indicates that, fundamentally, Kentucky's basic economic situation had changed so radically since 1860 that its citizens, in 1885, misunderstood their predicament. Farm lands had decreased in value, and large farms were rapidly being divided into smaller holdings with small collateral values. Where ante bellum farmers had bountiful virgin land resources to produce abundant field crops or to be used as collateral in securing credit, postwar Kentuckians had neither advantage. A slight national panic, in which farm credits were affected, resulted in near revolution for debt-ridden farmers. This was especially true in western Kentucky counties where dark tobacco was the staple crop. Besides a generally unstable system of land tenure, credit, and marketing conditions, local taxes were almost high enough to be confiscatory. In their anxiety to secure outside rail connections, officials in many of these western counties had granted generous subsidies to railroads. By the latter eighties the Kentucky farmers were convinced that they had nurtured an unsympathetic organization in the railroads, whose rates were so high that all farm profits were consumed in freight payments. With a general downward trend in tobacco prices and with increasing abuses in marketing, a Kentucky agricultural revolt was imminent by the late eighties.

In 1885 Kentucky Knights of Labor nominated George Thobe of Covington to oppose the strongly entrenched congressional incumbent John G. Carlisle. Thobe secured a considerable Republican vote and was almost successful in defeating his distinguished opponent. The next year the Laborites nominated A. H. Cragin of Crittenden County to oppose Simon Bolivar Buckner, Democrat, and W. O. Bradley, Republican, as nominees for Governor. When the ballots were counted, it was found that Cragin had polled 4,434 votes, 3,800 of which came from the semiurban counties of Kenton and Campbell. The Labor Party was not completely routed, however, for it returned several representatives to the legislature.

While the Knights of Labor were battling Democrats and Republicans in northern Kentucky, the farmers were again aroused to action. Old agricultural troubles had recurred, and a new agrarian party was in the making. This new party resulted from deflated farm values, low prices, and uncontrolled railroad companies. Furthermore, since the functions of state government were increasing, more demands were made upon the state treasury. As Kentucky's government was called upon to meet new demands, it had to levy new and higher taxes, which increased the private burdens of the state's citizens. The bane of agricultural sections is high taxes and mounting public debts, and the Kentucky farmers of the eighties reacted promptly to such a situation. In order to make itself felt in the legislature, the agricultural vote organized in 1885 the Wheel (an agricultural lodge or society), and presently the whole state was once again organized into a series of local clubs. To secure united action against an entrenched opposition, these local units were combined into a state organization known as the Farmers' Alliance.

In 1889 the state organization of the Alliance was created in the

Paducah convention, and John G. Blair of Carlisle was elected president. There was unanimous support for the platform, which demanded free coinage of silver on a basis of sixteen to one; abolition of national bank currency; that the national debt not be paid in gold; popular election of United States Senators; a graduated federal income tax; popular election of all state officials; reduction in salaries, state and federal; enactment of antitrust legislation; state control of railway rates; taxation of all property at uniform rates; elimination of all "special privilege" legislation; a national tariff for revenue only; abolition of the school book trust; and an increased appropriation for the State Agricultural and Mechanical College. As a political organization, the Farmers' Alliance placed few independent candidates in the field. It had learned a valuable lesson from the grangers, to concentrate its influence behind picked Democratic and Republican candidates. Alliance support, in 1887, was given largely to the Democratic Party and to its gubernatorial nominee, General Simon Bolivar Buckner. In his first executive message, Governor Buckner urged the passage of much of the proposed Alliance legislation. This message received the endorsement of Alliance clubs throughout Kentucky, with the result that the legislative program for 1890 was progressively an Alliance program. The Railroad Commission was to be empowered to proceed against offenders upon its own motion and to inflict fines for extortion; all combinations and understandings which restrained trade were forbidden; capitalistic control of politics was outlawed; bank property was to be assessed at the same rate as real estate; financial institutions were to be inspected; turnpikes and bridges were freed of tolls; textbooks for public schools were to be uniform; and collection of fees charged by tobacco warehousemen was to be regulated.

With the proposal of this legislation, it was clear that the Alliance had made material headway. Although agrarian leaders were happy over their prospective victory, the "new departure" Democrats' patron saint, Henry Watterson, was angry. Editorial columns of the *Courier-Journal* contained daily tirades against the activities of the "misguided" legislature. Since 1868 Henry Watterson had preached industrialization of Kentucky, and to this end he had lent gallant efforts. Thousands of dollars had been spent to attract outside capital to Kentucky, and conservative editors felt that the legislature of 1890 had set about deliberately and systematically to drive capital from the state. Delegations descended upon Frankfort, and the "third house" was a scene of nervous activity. Alliance bills were lobbied against. Ignoring outside pressure, both houses were determined to pass remedial legislation. Two bills, the McCain antitrust measure and the Richardson Bill, which proposed to tax railroads for public school support, were passed. Other powerful Alliance bills would have been passed likewise had there not arisen a misunderstanding between the legislature and the Governor. Groundwork for further Alliance influence was laid, however, and the farmers had only to complete their task in framing the new constitution.

Election of delegates to the constitutional convention of 1890 gave the Alliance an opportunity to exert its influence at the polls. In western Kentucky, where there was doubt regarding Democratic nominees, independent Alliance delegates were chosen. When the constitutional convention met in Frankfort in the spring of 1890, it was fully conscious of Alliance demands. The experiment of tempering Democratic and Republican opposition with Alliance support was a success. Occasionally it failed, as in the case of the endorsement of the Republican congressional nominee, Alexander Bruce. Bruce was defeated by Thomas H. Paynter, a professed free-silver Democrat. John G. Blair, state president of the Alliance, likewise suffered defeat at the hands of Thomas H. Gardiner. These setbacks, together with declining agricultural commodity prices, and with an attempted railway monopoly on the part of the Louisville and Nashville Company, spurred the farmer voters on to new efforts, and to the eventual formation of an independent third party. When Senator John G. Carlisle and Congressman W. C. P. Breckinridge, stanch Kentucky Democrats, declared for hard money, Kentucky populists endorsed the free silver plank of the Ocala, Florida, Alliance platform. The national economic situation had a vital effect upon the Kentucky farmer. Delegates were selected to attend the national Alliance convention held in Cincinnati in 1891, but the election of a Kentucky Governor was of greater importance. Candidates for this post were John Young Brown, Democrat, and A. T. Wood, Republican. President Thomas H. Gardiner promised Alliance support for Democratic endorsement of the Farmer-Labor program. This left the Populist wing of the Democratic Party in a paradoxical situation, for it had endorsed not only the Farmer-Labor program in Kentucky, but likewise the candidacy of Grover Cleveland for President and John G. Carlisle for United States Senator, both of whom were hard-money disciples. Unwilling to trust the Democratic stand, many Alliance voters believed the hastily prepared planks of the Democratic platform promising further demands of the Alliance to be weak-kneed vote-catching gestures. Gardiner had pledged the Democratic Party Populist support, and no amount of persuasion at the Cincinnati convention caused him to change his stand. As a result of Gardiner's refusal to support the Populist ticket, many local groups put independent candidates in the field. S. B. Erwin of Warren County was nominated as the Populist candidate for Governor. Democratic editors, led by Henry Watterson, thundered and roared editorially in criticism of the Populists. They called them "men of gab," "addled pates," "half-cracked," and "windy theorists." Leaders of the two major parties hated their third party rival. Nevertheless, the Democrats were forced to take a positive stand against the proposed Louisville and Nashville monopoly and endorse the new constitution and free silver. John Young Brown was elected by a majority of 88,000 over A. T. Wood, but the People's Party had polled 25,631, electing one senator and twelve representatives.

The Farmers' Alliance vote, since the Democratic Party polled much Alliance strength, was a real threat to major political party control. Governor Brown was thoroughly cognizant of this influence when he sent his first message to the legislature. He requested that body to have the Kentucky statutes rewritten to harmonize with the constitution, to consider legislation governing corporations, and to pass honest and efficient corporation laws. He appointed a railroad commission of men opposed to the wildcat practices of the past, and with authority to fix rates. As a candidate soliciting votes, John Young Brown went the whole way with the Alliance, but as Governor, his attacks lacked force. On the surface, it seemed that his first message was an answer to agrarian demands, but the closing sentence, "Beware of legislation which will discriminate against the legitimate interests of corporations and property; they have done much toward economic upbuilding of the commonwealth," did not sound genuine to farmer voters. After a continuous session of one year, the "Long Parliament," as the Alliance legislature was called, adjourned. It had accomplished only a part of the Populist program. There remained the "school book trust" to be regulated, and the railroads were left with a free hand. Had it not been for an injunction granted by the court of appeals, the Louisville and Nashville Railroad would have succeeded in annexing the Chesapeake, Ohio, and Southwestern, to form a powerful corporation. John Young Brown's administration was largely the undoing of the Populist Party in Kentucky, for just enough of its program was adopted to cause Democratic bolters to return to their party. In 1892 the Kentucky delegation, with William C. Owen of Georgetown as keynoter, was committed solidly to Cleveland. A Kentucky delegation also attended the People's Party convention in Omaha, and several candidates were nominated for the state legislature. The Populist Party had lost ground, however, as the votes of the general election showed. Grover Cleveland carried Kentucky by a majority of 40,020 votes instead of the 30,000 which he received in 1884. The congressional campaign of 1894 likewise saw the Populist group lose ground. Democrats adopted a free-silver stand and absorbed most of the Alliance vote. This virtually ended third party influence in Kentucky, except for a peculiar minor influence in the gubernatorial elections of 1895 and 1899.

In 1893, panic conditions and labor outbreaks caused President Cleveland to lose favor in Kentucky. Political affiliation proved more fickle than ever in the state's history, for Cleveland's majority melted into a minority in two years. P. Watt Hardin, Confederate soldier, a professed silverite, a member of an old family, closely identified with the Blackburn machine and the Louisville and Nashville Railroad, was nominated by the Democrats. Realizing the handicaps of the Democratic candidate, the Republican Party put forth its strongest representative in W. O. Bradley. Bradley advocated a stable currency, sane and practical government, and was opposed to "hare-brained" radicalism. Dubious of Hardin's sincerity in free-silver promises, the Farmers' Alliance nominated an able candidate for Governor in Thomas Pettit of Owensboro. Pettit sought election on the platform of the free coinage of silver and a denunciation of President Cleveland's administration; he demanded an income tax and the free issuance of currency in sufficient amount to supply a circulating medium of $50 per capita. Since the Democrats had absorbed a large number of Alliance votes,

that party split on the silver issue. Joseph S. C. Blackburn straddled
the issue by preaching free silver on one hand and supporting Hardin
and special interests on the other. Hardin remained silent until he
advocated free silver at Louisville in a joint debate with W. O. Bradley.
Conservative Democrats believed party recognition of free silver only
a gesture. Hardin's stand widened the breach in Democratic ranks.
With Bradley hammering at him on one side and Pettit on the other,
the campaign became extremely embarrassing to Hardin. Bradley
carried the state, the first Republican to be elected to the governorship,
by a majority of 8,912 votes, 4,000 of which were Jefferson County "gold
bug" Democratic bolters who left their party because they favored
sound money. Pettit secured a vote of 16,911, a number sufficient to
deny Hardin the election. Once again, the Farmers' Alliance had
raised an enfeebled hand to wreak vengeance upon a recalcitrant Kentucky Democracy. Then the third party movement ceased to be a factor
in Kentucky elections.

The New Constitution

When Kentucky was in a position to survey her political and economic situation after the war, she found her most obvious need a new
constitution. Shortsighted proslavery delegates to the constitutional
convention in 1849 had considered themselves the appointed guardians
of slavery. As a result, they framed an extremely biased constitutional
document. When slavery was abolished in Kentucky by adoption of
the national constitutional amendments, the state constitution was
almost wrecked, for it had been built around the protection of slavery.
To secure a new constitution at a time when Democrats, Republicans,
and granger partisans were engaged in a life and death struggle to
secure political control was a difficult task. Another handicap was
the traditional respect which the Kentucky people had for the state's
fundamental document. Of more importance, however, was the fact
that farmers of the third constitution made it difficult to amend it or
to make a new constitution. On December 18, 1873, a vote was taken
to determine the opinion of the people regarding the calling of a constitutional convention. This election failed to receive the sanction of a
majority of the "registered" voters who were qualified to vote for
representatives to the legislature. Every two years the question of a

convention was placed before the people with the same results, until 1887. Before the constitution could be changed, it was evident that some definite number of qualified voters had to be established, for there was a discrepancy between votes "cast" and votes "registered." The issue was clearly one of how many registered voters Kentucky had. Were there as many males in the state as the assessors claimed there were registered voters? To settle this important issue, the legislature enacted a law, January 8, 1886, requiring county assessors to determine specifically the number of qualified voters. This resulted in the registration of 300,339 names, and 175,362 voted in 1887 for a constitutional convention. Again, in 1889, out of 296,700 voters, 180,280 signified a desire to call a constitutional convention. When the second election favored a change, the legislature issued a call, May 3, for a constitutional convention to meet in Frankfort on September 8, 1890.

Since there were 100 legislative seats, 100 delegates were chosen to draft a new constitution. This fourth convention was composed of as motley a delegation of constitutionalists as had ever been seen in a convention hall. Kentucky would have been well served had at least fifty of these delegates remained at home. True to historic form, this convention came in a year when there were strong partisan issues before the people, issues which were to disappear within a decade. One of the first battles fought on the convention floor after that body was called to order by General Simon Bolivar Buckner was that over the selection of a permanent president. The choice rested with Bennett H. Young, an avowed railroad partisan, Proctor Knott, an ex-Governor, and Cassius M. Clay, a wealthy Bourbon County farmer. Clay was elected permanent president, but his selection was not to end the struggle, for there was some doubt as to the specific task before the convention. Twenty-seven delegates were of the opinion that a revision of the old constitution was sufficient. They believed that removal of the slavery sections and insertion of a section requiring the Australian ballot would complete their task. Never before were delegates more anxious to speak at length on all issues. Farmer members opposed the sinister influence of corporations; and corporation lawyers, lobbyists, and self-styled constitutionalists opposed Alliance leadership. Practical politicians who delayed staff appointments by introducing many useless arguments concerning the selection of stenographers and the recording of official proceedings were present in the convention in a large number. The convention was in session from September 8, 1890, to September 28, 1891, and four large volumes containing 6,480 quarto pages of eight point print were required to publish the proceedings. Discussion of the Bill of Rights alone consumed over a month and required eight hundred pages to report the debates. With a few minor changes and substitutions, the present Bill of Rights of twenty-six sections is a copy of the original of 1792. Word changes were made to adapt the original provisions to modern conditions. For instance, the original constitution was not specific in the matter of changing venue, but the new one corrects this fault.

Kentucky's fourth constitution is not so much a fundamental rule of government as a piece of omnibus legislation. Apparently the new document is the handiwork of delegates who worked diligently in behalf of an embattled constituency. Implied powers were eliminated wherever possible; nothing was left to interpretation or to changing conditions of the future. Delegates to the convention attempted to anticipate future needs of the government and provide for them in specific sections of the constitution. Under the heading "Local and Special Legislation," the new constitution gave complete control over local government to the legislature. Sections relating to railroads, commerce, and corporations placed these matters directly in legislative hands. Likewise, taxing and revenue sections attempted to seal all loopholes and to discourage judicial or legislative juggling. It was the aim of a majority of the delegates to prevent the accumulation of a large bonded indebtedness to save the state from bankruptcy. The tax burden was equalized; the constitution providing that taxes "shall be uniform upon all property subject to taxation within the territorial limits of the authority levying the tax." This section has caused much political dispute and almost prevented the formation of an efficient tax commission. Internal improvements to a majority of the delegates were matters of local and private concern, a point of view which left Kentucky without a system of public highways until 1912. The submission of the completed constitution to the people led to much discussion, but it was adopted in 1891, by a popular vote of 213,432 to 74,017.

Practical application of the fourth constitution soon exposed several fundamental weaknesses. First, it was difficult to adapt the Kentucky statutes to its provisions, a fundamental weakness which still exists. In the last thirty-three years, nine amendments have been adopted, but these have failed to correct many weaknesses. The constitution provides that only two amendments may be voted upon at a time. This has handicapped adequate changes of the constitution. Often amendments have been submitted to the people for adoption, but they have been defeated at the polls for lack of interest on the part of the electorate. Despite the fact that most Kentuckians realize that the constitution is a source of maladjustment in state government, and that it frequently prevents constructive legislation, a majority opposed the calling of a new constitutional convention in the election of 1931. This proposal to change the constitution created much editorial excitement, but a majority of the local editors opposed calling a convention. One of these editors, in a moment of passion, proclaimed the constitution of Kentucky "the most perfect document ever drawn by the hand of man."

In 1945 the Kentucky Legislature again passed an act calling for a revision of the state's constitution. This act was passed, according to constitutional provision, a second time in 1947. Once again the issue of constitutional revision was before the people. Both sides of the issue were represented by groups supporting separate views. Paul G. Blazer of Ashland was chairman of the Committee for Revision of the Constitution and Edward C. O'Rear of Woodford County presided over the opposing Committee of One Thousand. In the general election in November, 1947, the question of revision by convention was defeated by a percentage vote of 57.01 against and 42.09 in favor of change. The significance of this vote lies more in the general apathy of the people. In the gubernatorial contest 677,479 votes were cast as contrasted with the small total of 336,568 on the constitutional issue.

In the general election in 1949 the Kentucky electorate voted to revise upward Section 246 which contained the 1891, $5000 salary limitation, and to revise the equalization amendment so as to permit the distribution of twenty-five per cent of the school funds to equalize educational opportunities in the state. Fourteen amendments have been added to the Kentucky Constitution, and many more have been rejected. There is evidence that the modern Kentucky voter is much

less apt to vote for a change in government than was his pioneer fore-
father. Correcting some of the handicaps to government is an almost
impossible undertaking, largely because of public indifference to the
changing needs of constitutional government.

The Goebel Affair

No other single incident affected the course of modern Kentucky
politics so much as did the assassination of William Goebel. This
gruesome tragedy came as a climax to three decades of triple-sided
political warfare. Free-silver-Alliance bolting defeated the Democratic
gubernatorial candidate, P. Watt Hardin, in 1895, elected the Republican William O. Bradley, and reopened the bitter Democrat-Republi-
can feud. For the first time in its history, the Republican Party had
elected a Governor, but, unhappily for Governor Bradley, he was really
elected by a large block of protesting Democrats. Democratic legislators raised the first partisan issue in the election of a United States
Senator. Two candidates, Joseph S. C. Blackburn, a perennial office-
seeker, and W. Godfrey Hunter, a western Kentucky Republican, were
brought forward. The legislature was equally divided on the senatorial
election, although a majority of the senators were Democrats. But
fifteen "gold plank" Democrats refused to support Blackburn, and
after fifty-two ballots the deadlock appeared hopeless. Friction reached
a dangerous point when the house of representatives sought to break
the tie by unseating a "Blackburn Democrat." The seats of three
Republicans were challenged, and this threw the legislature into
pandemonium. After a lapse of the constitutional "sixty days" allotted
the legislature for its session, it was still deadlocked and had accomplished nothing. Sentiment was such that enraged partisans threatened
the statehouse with a mob, and Governor Bradley called out the militia
to protect the government offices. Immediately Democrats accused the
Governor of using the militia to influence the election of a Republican
United States Senator.

Before the senatorial election squabble could be settled, the presidential election was at hand. By this time, there were three distinct
groups in Kentucky, free-silverites endorsing William Jennings Bryan,
gold Democrats supporting John M. Palmer, and Republicans enthusiastically favoring William McKinley. The split in Democratic

ranks placed such strong party leaders as Henry Watterson, W. C. P. Breckinridge, Simon Bolivar Buckner, John M. Atherton, and W. N. Haldeman in the gold wing supporting Carlisle and Cleveland's principles. The campaign of '96 was hotly contested in Kentucky. Free-silver voters established a newspaper, *The Louisville Dispatch,* which virtually destroyed "Marse" Henry Watterson's *Weekly Courier-Journal.* With the exception of two congressional districts, Populists voted the straight free-silver ticket. McKinley, however, carried Kentucky by a majority of 281 popular votes, but received 12 of its 13 electoral votes (since reduced to 9). Because the Kentucky electorate had used the Australian ballot only a few times, it was said that Democrats were confused, and that they marked the first name on the electoral list instead of the circle under the party symbol. This may have caused Bryan the loss of Kentucky. If the Democrats did make this mistake, it was a sad commentary on Democratic intelligence as compared with general Republican understanding of the new ballot. This election added fuel to partisan flames, for to Democrats the defeat of Bryan was a "great steal."

Bryan's failure to carry Kentucky was one of the causes which led to Goebel's assassination. When McKinley carried the state, Governor Bradley called a special session of the legislature in the hope that a United States Senator might be elected. Again silver Democrats were adamant in their support of Blackburn, and gold Democrats were obstinate in their opposition. W. Godfrey Hunter was again nominated by the Republicans but failed repeatedly of election. Realizing that they could not elect Hunter, the Republicans nominated William J. DeBoe. DeBoe was elected upon the sixtieth ballot. This contest, together with the loss of Kentucky to McKinley, set the Goebel stage. Joe Blackburn was defeated, and Goebel's hour to assume party leadership had arrived.

William Goebel was a son of a German immigrant who settled in Pennsylvania. Moving from his home in Pennsylvania, William Goebel came to Covington in Kenton County, Kentucky. Early in life he began the practice of law in John G. Carlisle's office. He was elected to the state senate in 1886 and was re-elected each time until 1900. Not only did Goebel serve as state senator, but also as a member of the constitutional convention of 1890–1891. He was an active leader in the

local politics of northern Kentucky.   This led to his unfortunate duel
with John Sanford, a Confederate veteran, about whom, it was said,
Goebel published a scurrilous news article in which he gave Sanford an
obscene title.   In 1895, Goebel killed Sanford in a gun battle on the
steps of the First National Bank in Covington.   From this date, Goebel
was a "marked" man in Kentucky politics.   He made hundreds of
fast friends by his cold-blooded courage and determination, but with
the same traits he made scores of bitter enemies.

Three years after the Sanford duel, Goebel could not forget the
defeat of William Jennings Bryan.   He believed the Republicans had
stolen Kentucky's vote, and, with the support of the "silver" Democrats,
he was determined this should not happen again.   On February 1,
1898, he introduced a bill in the senate bearing the title "To Further
Regulate Elections."   On March 11, 1898, over Governor Bradley's
veto, this bill became a law.   It provided that a state returning board,
or commission, of three members should be appointed to canvass
election returns.   The state commission was to appoint three commissioners from each county, who were to select canvassers for the precincts.   Provisions were made for a distribution of party members, but
it was impossible to equalize party strength in a committee of three,
with the result that the committees were controlled by Democrats.
This law was so unusual that many Democrats and all Republicans
were outspoken in their condemnation of it.   It was one of the shrewd-
est political maneuvers which had been made by a Kentucky legislature
in many years.   Henry Watterson declared the law to be "a monstrous
usurpation of power by a few unscrupulous men."   *The Lexington
Herald,* another Democratic paper, vigorously denounced it as a piece
of Goebel machination.

Senator Goebel virtually had the Kentucky electorate in his power,
since he was entrusted, as a reward for his activities, with the selection
of the first state election board.   He appointed Judge William S. Pryor,
a former chief justice of the court of appeals, William T. Ellis, an ex-
congressman, and Charles B. Poyntz, an ex-railroad commissioner.
The election of 1898, the first to be held under the new law, was without incident, but it was known that the gubernatorial election of 1899
would test the fairness of the new act.

The stage was set for Goebel's candidacy for the governorship.   Three

Democrats sought their party's nomination: General P. Watt Hardin of Mercer County, and the "martyr" of '95; Captain William H. Stone of Lyon County; and William Goebel of Covington. Hardin claimed to be one of the first "sixteen-to-one" Democrats in Kentucky, and he had the support of the Louisville and Nashville Railroad and its influential president, Milton H. Smith. It mattered little to General Hardin that he favored "sixteen-to-one" on the one hand and special privilege on the other; his special claim was that he was an honest martyr. Captain Stone was a rock-ribbed, First District, loyal Confederate Democrat. Goebel was a northern Kentucky machine Democrat and centered his attack on the Louisville and Nashville Railroad. He said, "The Louisville and Nashville Railroad (must) become the servant rather than the master of the people." Goebel likewise advocated the McChord Railroad Bill, and the Chinn Bill to regulate the selection of school textbooks, and the passage of an antitrust law. In national politics Goebel proclaimed himself a "Chicago Platform" free-silverite.

Prior to the meeting of the state convention, the three candidates made a speaking tour of the state. Each speaker accused his opponents of being the tools of corporations. Before the meeting of the convention, Hardin had the support of the powerful Louisville district and a majority of the local state conventions. Stone claimed at least 350 delegates, but Goebel could be sure of not more than 300. Goebel's only hope of nomination was to organize the Music Hall Convention beginning at Louisville, June 21. As a third party factor, he held a position of power, for he could join forces with either of his opponents to weaken the opposition. Goebel combined his strength with that of Stone to defeat the strongly entrenched Hardin by organizing the convention under Goebel rules. Judge D. B. Redwine, a Goebel partisan, was made temporary chairman, and the business of throwing out Hardin votes by disqualifying Hardin delegates was begun. After provoking a state of near insurrection, the convention endorsed the Chicago Platform, William Jennings Bryan, and the Goebel Election Law. By this time, the convention was safely in Goebel's hands, and Stone was forced out of the race, with the result that Goebel was nominated over Hardin on the twenty-sixth ballot by a vote of 561 to 529. The northern Kentuckian had proved too facile in convention strategy to be defeated by his less ambitious opponents. Goebel had gone to the Music Hall Convention a weak third candidate supported by an unstable group of protesting Democrats but, by clever manipulation, had secured the nomination.

When the Music Hall Convention, June 21–30, 1899, had completed its task, many Democrats charged trickery and deceit. They declared they would not support such an unscrupulous politician as William Goebel. These disgruntled partisans held local mass meetings to chart a course of action. On August 2, 1899, a general anti-Goebel meeting was held in Lexington. Ex-Governor John Young Brown and Pelham J. Johnston were nominated to oppose Goebel and Beckham. Their platform denounced the Goebel Election Law, the Chinn Bill, and the Music Hall Convention and invited "freedom-loving" Democrats "to join the battle to preserve our beloved Commonwealth from domination of these ruthless cutthroats and assassins."

The Republican Party kept an eye upon the course of events within Democratic ranks and planned to take advantage of its opponents' division of strength. William S. Taylor, a western Kentucky Republican, and Attorney General, had built a powerful personal machine to support his nomination for Governor. It was thought at first that he would be as good a sacrifice as any other member of his party, but when victory appeared possible, it was with regret that the Republican Party nominated him. As Attorney General, Taylor had a record of efficiency, but he was far from being the ablest Kentucky Republican. Rather than cause a split within party ranks, Taylor was unanimously nominated on August 2, by the Lexington Convention. This convention likewise denounced the whole legislative scheme of Senator Goebel.

The rapidly decaying People's Party was to make one more effort to gain a foothold in Kentucky. This party nominated as its candidate for the governorship, John G. Blair of Carlisle. Thus the campaign of 1899 became a four-cornered affair, with most of the fighting occurring within the ranks of the Democratic Party. Bolting Democrats charged Goebel with being a "gold-plank" supporter in '96, but he answered with charges that John Young Brown was a hand-picked tool of Milton H. Smith and August Belmont, and of the Louisville and Nashville Railroad. At the peak of the campaign, the Goebel Democrats persuaded William Jennings Bryan to come to Kentucky on a speaking tour. Bryan declared "a victory for Goebel will be a sure way of bringing about a Democratic victory in 1900." The campaign grew bitter; Taylor worked diligently in Democratic territory in western Kentucky; and Goebel spent much time in eastern Republican counties. Epithets too vicious to be published were hurled by all four candidates. Goebel declared at Harrodsburg, "I am not entitled to the vote of any man who does not favor the Goebel election law." At London, Taylor replied, "I will be as liberal as Mr. Goebel. I do not want the vote of any man who is in favor of his election law." In Louisville, where the campaign centered, a state of near civil war existed. Goebel, in his attack upon Basil Duke and his lobbying activities in behalf of the Louisville and Nashville, called him a "professional corruptionist." The Louisville and Nashville employees were drawn into politics, and the Honest Election League, said by Goebel to be a Louisville and Nashville tool, was used against him. The Republicans, led by Taylor and Governor Bradley, concentrated their attack upon Goebel's legislative record and ignored his national politics. Blair refused to allow Goebel to forget the charges of "gold" support, and the bolting party made numerous other embarrassing accusations.

Except for the normal number of election day quarrels, the election of 1899 was quiet and orderly. Such bad feelings existed in Louisville that Governor Bradley called out the militia to patrol the polls. Here the Louisville and Nashville had its greatest influence, and Goebel said it used both money and intimidation to control the election. When the ballots were cast, the people waited calmly for the announcement of the results. First unofficial returns indicated that Goebel and Taylor were in a neck-and-neck race for election. The final official count gave Taylor a majority, and this was the signal for Democrats to start challenging votes. It was claimed that Governor Bradley's troops had prevented an honest election in Louisville. Most outrageous of all, however, was the fact that by political chicanery or "oversight," votes of many eastern Republican counties were registered upon "tissue paper" ballots, which, it was claimed, were not printed on legal weight paper. This charge, a fine piece of Kentucky political chicanery, was trumped up to throw out the election. Since a controversy had arisen, Goebel Democrats demanded that the state election board examine the returns. Immediately the question arose whether or not the Goebel Election Law authorized the commissioners to go behind the returns. This dispute unfortunately led to much careless talk by both sides. Goebel Democrats threatened to file a protest with the overwhelmingly Democratic assembly, while Republicans, it was said, declared that Goebel would never live to be inaugurated. The most threatening aspect of the whole affair was the trickery of the "tissue paper" ballots. When Democrats suggested that these be thrown out, it aroused the high-tempered citizens of the mountain counties, who felt they had been tricked by scheming Democrats. Not only eastern Kentucky voters but also voters of Louisville were faced with repudiation. Wrangling over election returns consumed almost a month and a half, and the inauguration date was approaching. Kentucky was now in a dangerous turmoil. Its electorate was vigorously aligned behind the two candidates, with each group threatening violence if it lost. One week before inauguration day, the returning board declared, by a two-to-one vote (this vote resulted despite the fact that Goebel was supposed to have absolute control of the election boards), that Taylor had received 193,-714; Goebel, 191,331; Brown, 12,140; and Blair, 3,038. A majority of 3,000 votes in Louisville and a generous support of Taylor in western Kentucky had decided the election. Goebel was defeated, not by a large Republican vote, but by anti-Goebel Democrats, Populists, and united Republican strength.

To all outward appearances, the report of the election board was final and made the election of 1899 a closed chapter. Senator Goebel indicated that he was going West on a visit. On December 12, Taylor was inaugurated. Even though Goebel had given up the fight, his friends had not. Joseph S. C. Blackburn, leading the Goebel Democrats, threatened, after holding a conference in Frankfort on December 12, to file a protest with the legislature. A charge was filed, and both parties prepared their forces for battle. The Democrats accused the Louisville and Nashville Railroad and the American Book Company of corrupt use of funds to get Taylor elected. Before it could proceed, the legislature had to choose a joint committee to pass upon the election of all state officials. The law required that this committee be selected by placing names of all legislators in a box and by drawing the requisite number of slips. Only fate could have defeated the Democrats in this drawing, since they dominated the legislature. One Republican and one Populist were chosen. The other members were Democrats.

At this stage, the Democrats seemed assured of victory, but the

Republicans were determined not to be removed from the state offices which they had assumed on December 12. A division of the government at Frankfort over the validity of the general state election in 1899 created strong sentiment throughout the state, and hundreds of voters flocked to the capital. Among these enraged visitors were at least a thousand mountaineer Republicans armed with pistols and rifles, who, it was said, had been brought to Frankfort by the Louisville and Nashville Railroad. Caleb Powers, Secretary of State, and a Knox County Republican, assumed leadership of this mob when his election was threatened with annulment. Bryan came back to Kentucky to plead for Goebel, but he only increased the fury at the capital. So tense had feelings become that the slightest mishap was apt to throw Kentucky into violence.

On January 30, 1900, while the legislature and the special committee were discussing the possibility of unseating the Republicans, William Goebel, while approaching the capitol, was shot through the abdomen by a rifleman concealed somewhere in the capitol office building. Senator Goebel was rushed to the Capitol Hotel, and Governor Taylor retired to the statehouse behind heavy militia guard. He declared Kentucky in a state of insurrection and instructed the legislature to meet in London. The Democrats refused to do this, but when they were forbidden by the militia to assemble in the statehouse, they met at the Capitol Hotel. The contest committee declared Goebel and Beckham elected, and Goebel was administered the oath of office, but he died on February 3. The Democrats retired to Louisville, and Kentucky had two state governments. Beckham, who succeeded Goebel, instructed General John B. Castleman to assemble a militia company, while at Frankfort, Taylor was virtually a prisoner of his own militia. Taylor recalled the legislature to formulate an agreement to submit the question to the courts. On its return to Frankfort, the legislature became a farce, with two presiding officers trying to keep order at the same time. The case of Taylor *vs.* Beckham was decided in favor of the Democrats by Circuit Judge Fields of Louisville, a decision upheld by the court of appeals, and by the federal courts.

Taylor left Kentucky for Indiana. Caleb Powers, attempting to pass through Lexington on a Chespeake and Ohio passenger train, was arrested on a charge of being accessory to the fact in the assassination of Goebel. He was tried four times before the Scott County Petit Jury. Three times he was sentenced to life imprisonment, and once to be hanged. Powers was finally pardoned by Governor Augustus E. Willson. Henry Youtsey of Covington, a clerk in Powers' office, was sentenced to life imprisonment but was pardoned by Governor A. O. Stanley. There reposes in the Scott County courthouse a large mass of records labeled "The Goebel Trial." These and the published proceedings are, of course, silent on the question of who fired the fatal shot. J. C. W. Beckham, a young man thirty-one years of age, became Governor after Goebel's death and was re-elected in 1903.

The "Goebel Affair" was the most disturbing episode in Kentucky's political history. It left the state's electorate in a highly embittered frame of mind. The Republicans said, "They stole the election," and the Democrats answered, "They killed our Governor." It matters little to posterity who fired the shot that killed Senator Goebel; the important fact is that it forced Kentucky into a long period of partisan and factional war which prevented passage of much-needed progressive legislation.

In 1900 Goveror Beckham called a special session of the legislature to modify the Goebel Election Law. It changed the unfair plan of selecting committee members, the source of most of the bitter partisan struggle. Beckham's administration was without special incident, except for the outbreak of the tobacco war in western Kentucky, which involved the immediate political future of the Democratic Party. The farmers were dissatisfied with conditions affecting the marketing of tobacco, but Governor Beckham hesitated to become involved in the struggle. He was anxious to prevent the accumulation of public debt, but equally concerned to handle Kentucky's income with frugality. To engage in the tobacco struggle would threaten his policy with failure.

From 1907 to 1936, the Kentucky Democrats and Republicans have, with regularity, alternated in the holding of office. In 1907, Augustus E. Willson won the election from the Democratic nominee, W. S. Hager. The popular support of the Republican candidate was the result of several causes: Beckham's defeat by W. O. Bradley in his effort to be nominated United States Senator, the tobacco war, and the general loss of popularity of the Democratic Party in the Nation. Governor Willson called out the state militia to end the reign of the night riders in the dark tobacco sections. In 1909 the system of education was expanded through the efforts of the "Educational Congress." In 1911, Governor Willson was succeeded by former Governor J. B. McCreary, a Democrat who had been in state politics for nearly forty years. Outstanding among the accomplishments of his administration was the organization of the State Highway Department in 1912. This was the first organized effort to improve transportation by eliminating poor roads. Seeking election in 1915, A. O. Stanley and Edwin Morrow conducted a rollicking campaign of personal mudslinging. Morrow sought election partly on the platform of freeing "Old Dog Ring" by removing the tax from the mountaineer's dog. Stanley countered with charges of Morrow's inability to conduct the affairs of the state. Election returns gave Stanley a bare majority over his opponent.

Governor Stanley proved an able executive who advocated a liberal legislative program. It was during the Stanley administration that the State Tax Commission was organized for equitably administering Kentucky's fiscal affairs. Governor Stanley appointed Attorney General Mills M. Logan of Edmonson County, chairman of this commission. Other legislation passed during the Stanley administration was a corrupt practices act, abolition of railroad passes, and an anti-lobbying law. If World War I had not disturbed Kentucky conditions, Stanley's tenure of office might have produced other needed legislative reforms. When Senator Ollie James died in 1918, Stanley became a candidate to succeed him and won the election. His resignation as Governor in May, 1919, left that office to Lieutenant Governor J. D. Black. In the state election, Black was nominated to succeed himself, but Edwin Morrow, a gallant campaigner and popular Republican, defeated him at the polls. Morrow was popular with both Republicans and Democrats, and yet Kentuckians recall with merriment his joint campaign with Stanley and his administration. He freed "Old Dog Ring" and gave Kentucky four years of peaceful government, except for the coal strike, the Lexington lynching, and the tobacco panic of 1921. Under Morrow the highway system was expanded, educational facilities improved, penal and charitable institutions reformed, and the anti-evolution law defeated. His administration was the last connecting link between the systems of state politics which prevailed from 1865 to 1908 and 1908 to 1920.

In 1923 there appeared on the political scene in Kentucky an issue which blasted the hopes of many politicians and aroused a militant public opinion. The racing interests in Kentucky persisted in legalizing pari-mutuel betting at the state's race tracks. The Democratic Party was split into two factions over the moral issue involved. Alben Barkley of McCracken County was the choice of the Haly-Bingham faction, while J. Campbell Cantrill of Scott County had the support of the racing interests. Barkley also proposed to relieve Kentucky farmers of their heavy tax burdens by levying a tonnage severance tax on coal and other minerals at the mines in the eastern and western Kentucky areas. Cantrill was supported by the race-horse and coal interests, and Barkley had the support of farmers and church leaders. Cantrill was an astute politician with a long campaign experience. He organized a powerful machine in opposition to Barkley to defeat him in the state Democratic primary. The nominee died, however, before the general election, and William Jason Fields, Carter County, was substituted as the party's nominee. In the general election Fields defeated the Republican nominee, Charles I. Dawson of Louisville. Fields' administration was marked by internal party bickering and failure of his proposed $75,000,-000 bond issue to improve conditions of the schools, roads, and charitable institutions. This administration seemed to be especially victimized by "special interests," and by the infidelity of many of the Governor's professed supporters.

Flem D. Sampson of Knox County was nominated for the governorship by the Republican Party, in 1927, to oppose former Governor J. C. W. Beckham. Sampson defeated Beckham by a plurality of 32,131 votes. This election came just prior to the Hoover-Smith presidential campaign of 1928, and at a time when party lines were less significant than usual in the history of Kentucky. The election of a Republican Governor was due largely to the influence of a "bipartisan combine" which was controlled by leaders from both parties. It was said that this combine constituted a powerful lobby which was certain of success, regardless of which party was in power. Governor Sampson entered office with a definite program to improve the Kentucky highways, to free toll bridges, to supply free textbooks to public-school children, and to create a progress commission to advertise the state. The legislature was Democratic, but during his first year in office it supported the Governor's program. In 1929, however, conditions changed, and the Governor was attacked by the machine which had supported him. By the passage of "ripper" [2] legislation, he was left politically stranded. Governor Sampson also became implicated with the textbook companies, and a new selection of textbooks became necessary. The Governor proposed to supply free textbooks. He proposed a printing of several public-school books by the state, in omnibus volumes.

The unpopularity of the Republican Governor caused Kentuckians, in 1931, to support the Democratic nominee, Ruby Laffoon of Hopkins County, in preference to William Harrison, Republican mayor of Louisville. The Laffoon administration, in many respects, was one of the most turbulent the state has had for many decades. Governor Laffoon came into office as the state was rapidly sinking into the depression. He secured the passage of the governmental reorganization bill, the adoption of a new school code, the sales tax, and the Democratic dual primary bill. Like that of his Republican predecessor, Governor Laffoon's program was largely a product of a coalition support, but before his administration was two years old, it was torn asunder by depression and party defection. Governor Laffoon undertook to weaken his opposition by securing the passage of a "reorganization" bill which proposed a housecleaning in the government. Unfortunately, this legislation bore the earmarks of controlled politics. Opposing Governor Laffoon in his legislative program was Lieutenant Governor A. B. Chandler, Woodford County, who, during one of the numerous extraordinary sessions of the assembly, was relieved of his powers as president of the senate. By clever political strategy, in 1934, Lieutenant Governor Chandler placed the Laffoon partisans in an embarrassing situation when he insisted on calling the general assembly into extraordinary session during an absence from the state of Governor Laffoon. He proposed that the legislature undo the work of the nominating convention and submit the question of selecting a Demo-

[2] The term "ripper" is applied to any legislation which attempts to strip one department of government of its political privileges in favor of another. This may be accomplished by a transfer of functions, creation of a special committee of officials to control budgets, and by making appointments for partisan purposes.

cratic candidate directly to the people. In this special session, the Laffoon-Rhea forces insisted upon two primaries instead of one—a factor which resulted in the election of Albert Benjamin Chandler as Governor. Chandler was elected Governor in November, 1935, largely by a popular endorsement of his militant stand against the three per cent sales tax. In the second primary election, Chandler defeated Thomas Rhea (the convention nominee) of Logan County by an effective plurality. In November he had little difficulty in defeating Circuit Judge King Swope, Republican nominee, to win the gubernatorial nomination.

The general trend of Kentucky politics since 1900 has been toward factional control. For the first eighteen years after 1900, the dead hand of William Goebel was a powerful factor. Since 1918, party lines have been less significant; for the years 1920–1931, the "bipartisan combine" bossed state politics. The Kentucky Jockey Club, with other special interests, matched strength with the Kentucky electorate to see which would control the state. An outstanding characteristic of state administrations since 1900 has been factional use of "ripper" legislation, passed under the guise of "reform." This device has been used freely by the special interests which have sought power. Passage of ripper bills has kept the Kentucky government in a general state of confusion. On two occasions, an inventory of Kentucky's government was necessary to perfect a legislative program. In 1922–1924, the Kentucky Efficiency Commission, employing Griffenhagen and Associates, of Chicago, made a thorough investigation of governmental needs and published its recommendations in two large volumes. These recommendations were ignored. Again in 1933 Griffenhagen and Associates were employed to make a second detailed study of the state's government. Governor Laffoon's administration adopted the new educational code which was recommended by a special educational survey. Under Governor Chandler's administration much of the two efficiency reports has been adopted. In some respects, when the Griffenhagen reports have not been practicable, the legislature has followed the advice of state agencies in providing for governmental reorganization.

Since 1930 Kentucky has undergone some major changes. The great depression of that decade took a heavy toll of the state's productive resources. Manpower was left stranded in many instances because of unemployment, and it was forced to rely upon employment by federal agencies such as the WPA and the PWA. As demands for coal dropped off, the coal mines were unable to offer either extensive or continuous employment. There were relatively few factories in the state which employed any considerable number of laborers. On top of the devitalizing forces of depression, the great flood of 1937 displaced hundreds of families and businesses, and the property damage was appalling. Cities like Frankfort, Carrollton, New Port, Covington, Louisville, Henderson and Paducah were badly injured.

By 1939 the worst of the depression was ended, and the impending World War II was already having some economic effect on Kentucky. When the German Army marched into Poland in September of that year, employment in the state was to receive a boost. For the next five years Kentucky social life and economy were to feel the surging impulse of the great war. After the Pearl Harbor Attack on December 7, 1941, Kentucky troops were dispersed over the entire area of conflict. There were finally 323,798 men and women in uniform. Of these 4,064 were killed in action, and 6,802 died in service. National guardsmen to the approximate number of 5,300 became a part of the 38th Infantry Division. Some, such as the tank company from Harrodsburg, saw service with the 197th Tank Battalion. It was this company which was captured by the Japanese on Bataan; and, near the end of the war, this capture was to be avenged by the 38th Infantry, or the so-called "Avengers of Bataan" Division.

When the war ended in 1945 and the Kentucky veterans returned home they swelled the ranks of students in schools and colleges and of labor. The immediate post-war years made heavy demands for Kentucky coal and other raw materials. Manufacturing expanded rather rapidly. Many small Kentucky towns which had depended upon agricultural income since their foundings became semi-industrial communities with small factories paying out a steady flow of wages.

In the field of politics, the governorship was held by two Democrats and one Republican. In the general election of 1943, Judge Simeon S. Willis, a Republican from Ashland, defeated his Democratic opponent, Lyter Donaldson, of Carrollton, and in 1947 Earle C. Clements, Democrat, from Morganfield, defeated Eldon Dummitt, Republican, from Lexington. A constitutional provision prevents the governor from succeeding himself, and this usually causes a marked break in the administrative affairs of the state. As for politics, the governor is the titular head of his party, and because of this position he has to pay strict heed to partisan political fence mending in order to keep his party in power. Because he has two regular legislative sessions in a four-year term, the governor faces a real problem in devising a program which will receive legislative support at each of the two sessions. There has been a tendency for the second session of the legislature to become obstreperous and to interfere seriously with administrative plans.

Any interpretation of Kentucky politics is a difficult undertaking. It has of necessity to deal with personalities as well as intricate and badly involved and obscured incidents. One is impressed often in hearing Kentucky political leaders discuss problems of government by the fact that they give clever dissertations on the techniques and maneuvers of politics rather than on the fundamental concepts of the responsible democratic process of government. Politics in Kentucky is essentially a game at which politicians have ever played with vigor and relish. Its rich vein of political folk lore tells abundantly of manipulations, maneuverings and personal triumphs.

The old political pattern has been somewhat reshaped by modern demands upon the state. Education, eleemosynary institutions, penal institutions, state hospitals, public health service, world wars I and II veterans, old age pensions, highway construction and maintenance all make heavy demands on the state for funds. The legislative session of 1950 faced these problems with more funds at its disposal than any other legislature has perhaps ever had, but the demands were greater. There was much dissatisfaction on the part of many state agencies, and the legislature itself became stalemated by its inability to stretch limited funds to meet almost unlimited demands. A special session of the legislature in the spring of 1949 enacted much needed legislation to revise assessment rates over the state. In this way the counties were enabled to come nearer collecting the taxes due on a fair appraisal of property and increasing the funds at their disposal for support of schools and other county services. The big stumbling block, of course, is the unwillingness of local officials to carry out the intent of the law. But in a final analysis most of Kentucky's fiscal worries simmer down to a rather simple point: there is insufficient industrial exploitation of many of the state's resources to properly balance its agricultural system. Too, the entire prevailing tax structure needs a complete overhauling with the enlarged areas of state services clearly in mind.

Outside the political pale, private Kentucky citizens did much to stir the state out of its lethargy. The Committee for Kentucky worked in the face of some considerable local opposition, to point out the needs of the state, the means by which these needs could be served, and a goal for which Kentuckians should strive. It published a series of graphic pamphlets touching most phases of Kentucky life, and on two occasions its guiding spirit, Harry Shacter, took blueprints for the future to the legislature. In 1949 he published a book, *Kentucky on the March,* which made an optimistic approach to the future. Perhaps the most concrete fact in Kentucky history at mid-twentieth century was that a large body of thinking citizens had become aroused to the ever-expanding demand for public services.

A popular misconception in Kentucky history has been the notion that all citizens of the state have concerned themselves with political matters. Consistently an important segment of the Kentucky population has concerned itself in the electoral process, in local and state races, and with office holding. An astonishingly large segment, however, has ignored this process. Since 1891 Kentuckians have been subjected to a continuous process of electioneering and elections. Repeatedly efforts to reform this process have failed. In like manner the ballot has grown in length and complexity, and the special session of the General Assembly in 1976 provided for an even more involved one in carrying out the constitutional mandate to re-structure the court system.

Partisan voter behavior in the twentieth century has been erratic. In the presidential election in 1920, for instance, 452,480 Kentuckians supported Warren G. Harding, and 456,497 favored James M. Cox, an almost even division between the two major parties. This was an unusually large turn-out of voters as compared with later years. In 1974 Kentucky had a potential voting population above eighteen years of age of 2,450,000, racially it was divided 2,296,000 whites and 154,000 blacks. Only 64.2 per cent of this voting age population was registered, and only 32.5 per cent voted. In most state and general elections Democratic candidates have received majorities. In the general election of 1972 the balance between the parties was 529,000 to 494,000, in the General Assembly there were 73 Democrats and 27 Republicans in the House of Representatives, and in the Senate the division was 27 Democrats and 11 Republicans.

Two cardinal facts seemed to be pronounced in Kentucky politics: both state and national officials where chosen by a minority of the voters, and, except under extraordinary circumstances, the Democratic Party has been the dominant force in elections. This fact, however, was not always reflected in voter behavior when intra-party factionalism has developed, especially in the choice of governors.

Significant modifications have been made in the governing process in Kentucky largely by adaptive usage. Beginning with the creation of the Railroad Commission. March 19, 1880, down to 1974 various broad administrative functions have been performed by special departments, including the sprawling Department of Human Resources which grew by accretionary processes, and was organized into a single body in 1974. Through these various administrative arms the executive powers of Kentucky have been greatly expanded. By 1974 it was evident the Governor's office overshadowed the powers of the General Assembly to such an extent that it seemed to be firmly subjected to executive guidance, and jokingly the Governor was referred to as the "third house." The Fourth Constitution from the outset was never sufficiently adaptable to the demands of an emerging modern commonwealth to permit a classical balancing of powers between the executive and legislative branches in the classical eighteenth century sense. More recent legislative actions have been more reflective of the executive will than that of the legislature.

The pressures of change were exerted in many areas, but nowhere did they reveal greater needs than in the field of constitutional adequacy. In the campaigning for revision of the Fourth Constitution in 1947 some opponents to the calling of a convention contended that revision could be accomplished more effectively by amendment. As indicated earlier an immediate attempt was made to revise articles restricting official salaries, and to liberalize the amount of money the state should distribute to equalize educational opportunities. It was clear in practice that so long as only two amendments could be submitted at a time to voters, it would be almost impossible to adjust the Constitution to the demands of changing times. Voters in 1950 were asked to approve an amendment which would permit the submission of an unlimited number of proposals for revision. This was defeated, with opponents of the amendment saying this was a sly method of redrafting the Constitution without calling a convention.

Three years later the people were asked to consider shortening the ballot for state officers by appointing the State Treasurer, Clerk of the Court of Appeals, Commissioner of Agriculture, and the Superintendent of Public Instruction for extended terms. This proposal failed. In 1956, after intensive campaigning, voters approved an amendement to allow the Commonwealth to sell $100,000,000 worth of highway bonds to finance its share of the cost of building the four interstate highways crossing the state. Constitutional amendments were again placed on the ballot in 1959. This time it was proposed that Kentucky would pay a bonus to veterans of the Spanish-American War, World Wars I and II, and the Korean War, this to be financed by levying a sales tax. The second amendment proposed that sheriffs could succeed themselves in office. Again eastern Kentucky voters supplied the necessary majority to adopt the bonus amendment, but defeated the one pertaining to sheriffs.

In the submission of these amendments it became rather clear that an informal policy had evolved by which a popular amendment was coupled with a less popular one with the hope voters would approve both. The amendment procedure was too slow and too uncertain to meet the pressing needs for reforms in state government. In 1964 Governor Edward Breathitt suggested that an extra-legal delegation meet in Frankfort and draft a new Constitution embodying the changes and modernizations which it deemed necessary. A good model constitution was drafted after sober consideration of all its articles, but the voters defeated this proposal. In 1975 the voters adopted an amendment permitting a complete revision of the judicial system of the state, and in December of that year the General Assembly enacted the necessary legislation to activate its mandate. In many respects this was a revolutionary change becaue it cut one of the major historical ties with both English and Virginia legal tradition.

CHAPTER XXIII

An Enduring Commonwealth

K ENTUCKY during the early and middle decades of the twentieth century was caught in the turmoil of constant social and economic change. Hardly an aspect of life in the Commonwealth escaped the institutional and human revolutions which bore upon national life. Use of the term "change" in modern terminology has almost reduced it to a cliche, nevertheless the revolution which occurred in Kentucky cannot be otherwise described. Too, only by a generous appeal to statistics can an objective sense of progress, or lack of it in Kentucky be conveyed.

The Shifting Sands of Population

In no area of Kentucky life and economy did more important changes occur than those relating to Kentuckians themselves. Thousands of Kentuckians, trained and untrained, drifted away during most of the twentieth century to search for professional opportunities and industrial employment. Kentucky since the 1830's has been traditionally a "breeder" state pouring out thousands of its natives into an expanding Nation. The twentieth century saw an inordinate number of its sons and daughters depart their homeland. No one can reckon accurately the social and economic loss in the migration of so potentially a productive human resource. Out-migration in 1940 was 148,735, and that year 946,669 Kentuckians lived in other states, or 27.2 per cent of the current population. A quarter of a century later, 1960-1970, there was a loss of 153,000 persons. Despite losses Kentucky's residual population increased by 181,000 in this decade.

Internally there was an impressive amount of shifting and relocation of Kentucky's people. By 1975 the Bureau of the Census listed five standard population centers, either inside or straddling state borders, with Louisville and Lexington constituting major internal concentrations. In the latter census report Kentucky's

452

population center had moved outward to a point ten miles northeast of Springfield in Washington County.

The latter fact clearly indicates that Kentucky's population was moving in two general directions, north and southwest along the Ohio River frontier. It was being drawn by the magnet of industrial and urban expansion. Of greater importance, the changing location of population indicated a significant movement away from traditional residual rural areas where much of the Kentucky folk mores were formed. By 1970, more than 50 per cent of Kentucky's people lived in urban communities, and the Commonwealth had outgrown its predominantly rural classification. More impressive was the fact that the entire social tone of Kentucky society had undergone phenomenal change.

If the social tone had changed, so had the nature and age of the population, two thirds of it in 1970 was in the category under five to forty-four years of age, and only 17,000 of the total 3,328,000 were foreign born. This meant that more than 97 per cent of the population was born of native American stock. There were 230,800 blacks, or 7.2 per cent of the population in 1973. Since 1790 this ratio between the races has deviated little if any.

Throughout its history Kentucky's people have been its most precious resource, and they have had the potential to be creative and productive. From the outset the Commonwealth's central challenge has been the refinement of its human resource, a task it was slow to undertake. So long as Kentucky remained predominantly rural and agricultural the majority of its people were engaged in subsistence agrarian pursuits, and education and vocational training had limited meaning in the gaining of a mere livelihood. This condition changed radically after the depression of the 1930's dispossessed so many people from the land. By 1970 there were only 425,000 Kentuckians left on the land and classed technically as farmers; in the decade 1960-1970 there was a population reduction in this area of 26.8 per cent. As the farm population was reduced in numbers farm production, paradoxically increased, returning a worth of $1,587,000,000 in 1974, and $1,259,218,000 from crops above in 1976. The fact that sales and value of livestock comprised two fifths of the 1974 income was within itself an indication of change.

In sharp contrast with its economic past, Kentucky's 3,167 manufacturing plants added a cash value of $5,682,000,000 in 1972. This plus wages paid more than a quarter of a million employes exceeded agricultural income more than ten-to-one.

A Changing Way of Life

The basic quality of most areas of Kentucky life after 1940 experienced significant improvement. With the expansion of the Tennessee Valley Authority and private utility electrical generating systems even the most isolated rural Kentucky homes were brought within reach of power lines. The construction and expansion of Rural Electric Administration lines after 1945 carried electrical energy in to homes of hundreds of thousands of Kentuckians. Because of this the tenor of their lives underwent radical modifications. Their daily tasks were lightened with machines performing labors which historically had strained and exhausted human muscles. Though Kentuckians long boasted that their state had more miles of navigable streams than any in the Union, this resource was at once an asset and a menace. Ironically an overwhelming majority of rural and marginal urban homes prior to 1930 were without running water. Despite the fact Kentucky's landscape was indented by creek and river valleys, and hillsides were lined with fresh water springs, most homesteads were dependent upon uncertain supplies of water. Certainly the eternal task of making water available the year-round was an arduous and frustrating one for large numbers of Kentuckians.

Availability of abundant and cheap electrical current reduced dramatically the amount of human energy necessary to perform the chores of daily living in Kentucky. In the public areas of health, hospitalization, medicine, diet, and physical comforts there occurred a complete revolution. No Kentuckian living anywhere in the Commonwealth, even buried amongst the remotest dales and hollows of Appalachia, could excuse himself for not being informed about the course of happenings in the world about him. With the coming of radio and television Kentucky families, rural and urban, were exposed to programs of genuine cultural worth and even to ephemeral trash that was worthless. The specific impact of broadcasts of public social and political issues on Kentuckians is unknown. It is certain, however, that during the bi-centennial years of the mid 1970's they were able to view almost first-hand the political turmoils of their state and nation on an intimate television screen. They were permitted to sit at the hearing table with United States Senators unfolding the intricacies and misdeeds of a presidential administration in the Watergate debacle. Then they were able to listen in on one of the most remarkable constitutional debates in American history when the special committee of the United States House of Representatives decided whether or not to bring impeachment charges against the President of the Republic. They viewed the presidential candidates campaigning, heard them answer reporters' questions, saw Richard M. Nixon turn pale under questioning from John F. Kennedy, and Gerald Ford stumble in answering questions about Russia's influence in Middle Europe. Almost constantly they had a view of the seat of decision and decision-making in the Governor's office.

Just as electric current and motors emancipated modern Kentuckians from the labors which had worn and aged their forbears, use of the gasoline tractor, improved plow attachments, mechanical harvesters, and the pick-up truck placed in the hands of individual farmers tremendous instruments of production. It was a poor submarginal Kentucky farm in 1975 which did not have a tractor and the necessary accessories for its use on the land. Even the production of the traditional man-mule crop of tobacco had by the latter date given way to a large degree of mechanization. Or just as great importance as mechanization, farming in Kentucky by 1950 had become almost as much a capital business enterprise as operating a store or factory. Heavy out-migration had robbed the land of an abundance of human labor, and machines had filled the gap, and these were costly and demanding of constant and experienced up-keep.

Mechanization and capital management were only two-thirds of the Kentucky farm revolution after 1940. Plant scientists and breeders produced improved types of field crops which increased yields and quality many fold. Introduction of hybird corn, for instance, greatly increased production of this traditional food and feed grain. Kentucky in 1937 produced on 2,504,000 acres 70,219,000 bushels of corn, and averaged 28.2 bushels per acre. In 1974 on less than half the acreage farmers harvested 95,000,000 bushels, or an average of 85 bushels per acre. In 1976 the corn

crop was estimated to be worth $325,992,000. This increased pro-
duction on decreased acreage applied to other crops. If plant
scientists had not introduced disease-resistent strains of tobacco
this cash field crop would have been severely curtailed if not destroyed. In the late 1930's when the Tennessee Valley Authority
made available to Kentucky farmers fertilizers of high and adapted
chemical analyses for use specifically on Kentucky soils, agricultural production entered a new era.

Whatever may have been reservations in public discussions of
the subject, most Kentuckians in 1977 lived in far superior houses
as compared with those they occupied in the 1920's. In 1974 the
state's contractors and builders received $1,522,000,000 for all con-
struction, and $570,000,000 of this was for new homes. Four years
earlier there were 1,060,000 year-round housing units in Kentucky,
and 81 per cent of them had plumbing facilities, and virtually all
of them were wired for electricity. These are the raw statistical
facts, their social significance lay in far more complex data interpretation. Every Kentucky town of appreciable size in 1977 was
surrounded by mushrooming subdivisions, shopping centers, and
service facilities. On the outskirts of many of them were small
manufacturing plants and warehouses. Larger metropolitan centers like Covington, Ashland, Bowling Green, Lexington, Louisville, and Paducah had expanded well beyond their earlier boundaries. In this era of "urban sprawl" the Kentucky surburban community became a residential center. Shopping malls and centers
supplanted main streets as market places, and plantation-sized
parking areas became as prime pieces of real estate as were building sites.

Older Kentucky urban communities in the 1970's suffered from
"inner city blight." Famous old commercial streets in Louisville
and Lexington grew tawdry in fact and appearances. Once profitable business properties were now reduced to accepting tenants,
the nature of whose business symbolized further blight. In many
Kentucky towns, as in the Nation, where main streets survived
they had grown shabby, and their businesses underwent personality changes.

Rising to the surface in the modern era of "urban renewal" and
high rise public housing for low-income families was the bold fact
of social change. As Kentucky's urban communities expanded real

estate became more expensive and difficult to attain. Even though housing might be cheap, which it was not, the ground on which to build traditional family homes cost almost as much as the house itself. In out-moded inter city areas bulldozers and wrecking cranes ground thousands of ancient building landmarks into rubble, and almost overnight the space they occupied became sites for new buildings and parking lots. Nowhere in Kentucky was this process of destruction and restoration more evident than in the heartland of old Louisville. Here efforts were made to capitalize on the river front by facing new buildings and businesses on a broad concourse. A shopper's mall was built along much of lower Fourth Street and traffic was directed around it. In Lexington the downtown area was seriously blighted and, except for banking and professional services, there was a commercial flight to the shopping malls. This change in the urban Kentucky community created significant new social and political responsibilities, many of which could not be met within the context of traditional procedures. After 1945 there was instant need for a sprawling network of wider streets, lighting, services, and police protection. Disposal of sewage and solid waste tested the capabilities of city planners and engineers to adapt to the demands of an exceedingly fluid new age. No one in 1976 dared make more than a generalized estimate of the time and planning energy expended on adjusting Kentuckians to their new urban civilization.

Violence and Crime

Reflective of rising social problems, economic inflation, human displacement, and a largely undefined condition of public and parental permissiveness, was the dramatic rise in the commission of crimes. Between 1970 and 1972 Kentucky ranked in the higher brackets of states in the commission of robbery, rape, and other capital crimes. The location of branch businesses in shopping malls and even lone surburban locations made them vulnerable to robberies, and parking lots became lairs for rapists. Branch banks, filling stations, restaurants, and liquor stores especially were victims of robbers. The introduction of new types of merchandising encouraged shop-lifting and pilfering, and the burglarizing of private homes, and the theft of automobiles increased. The rate of vandalism rose phenomenally after 1950. Businesses, schools, and private property were plagued by this type of wanton destruction. Fair game was the contracting and building industry which suffered such heavy losses at the hands of both vandals and thieves that it created a vigilance organization to protect machines, materials, and unfinished buildings.

An increased rate of drug addiction accounted for much of Kentucky's crime after 1950. There were constant needs for increasing police forces, enlargements of jails and penal institutions, and the courts were burdened in the trial of criminals. There were incarcerated in Kentucky and federal prisons in 1950 for extended terms 3,259 prisoners; by 1974 this number had been reduced, because of a more lenient parole policy. A constant challenge to the state was the discovery of some means of rehabilitating many of its prisoners. Since the great flood of 1937 and the abandonment of the old Penitentiary in Frankfort, Kentucky has been much less medieval in the management of its prison population.

The Rise of Suburbia

Almost every social problem in Kentucky has been aggravated by the rise of suburbia. In the larger communities the population movement to outer subdivisional circles has created racial imbalances, and the maintenance of desegregated institutions and schools has required extraordinary, and, sometimes, what has seemed to some communities, bizarre methods of maintaining racial balances. An overwhelming preponderance of Kentucky's school age population in 1972 was white. Out of a school population of 722,000 there were 62,600 blacks, and there were sharp variations in the distribution of these, depending upon community locations, enrolled in integrated schools. As a comparison with a national average of all minority enrollment in all schools of 11.2 per cent, Kentucky had 7.4 per cent, and these schools were located in the larger urban communities. In Louisville, 1970-1976, the shifting of population created an especially difficult problem of attaining a racial balance. Ironically this city had planned so thoroughly for desegregating its schools in the late 1950's only to have its plans nullified in 1975 by internal population changes. Too, the consolidation of the Louisville and Jefferson County school systems created new and more complex problems, one of them the broader geographical distribution of schools. The School Board was put under mandate in 1975 by the Federal District Court to achieve a racial balance in the public schools by busing children across district borders, and frequently away from neighborhood classrooms. This provoked protests because many children were hauled long distances from their homes and parents contended they were needlessly exposed to traffic hazards and other threats to their safety. There occurred demonstrations, mass marches, personal abuse of Judge James Gordon, some violence and vandalism, and the stimulation of general community unrest. Perhaps the racial factor involved in the social turbulence was less disturbing than the community dislocation of children and their exposure to safety hazards.

City and county governments in Lexington and Fayette County were merged into a metropolitan government in 1969. Here both racial and geographical factors were less sensitive and complicated than in the larger urban center of Jefferson County. So it was in other Kentucky cities and towns. Kentucky experienced only one incident worthy of consideration following the United States Supreme Court decision of Brown *vs*. Board of Education, May 17, 1954. This was threatened disruption of school openings in the rural western Kentucky villages of Sturgis and Clay in Union and Webster counties in 1958. This incident was provoked by members of the segregationist Citizens Council, and apparently by outsiders at that. Governor A. B. Chandler acted promptly to halt the disturbance by threatening to order out the National Guard to disperse the protestors; Kentucky's public schools opened in 1959 without racial incidents.

Agriculture and Natural Resources

A multitude of forces were at work in Kentucky after 1930 to bring about a redirection of traditional and historical approaches to the changing processes of life in the Commonwealth. In Lexington the Agricultural Experiment Station and the Agricultural Extension Service had sought since the turn of the twentieth century to modernize Kentucky's agricultural procedures. The Great Depression in the 1930's, the New Deal Administration with it various fresh programs, and, to a lesser extent, the Farm Security Administration, revealed how archaic and inefficient many of Kentucky's farming practices had remained over one and three quarters centuries. Approximately half of the state's 120 counties did not produce enough food and capital support to sustain themselves. Farm prices were ruinously low, and many practices, or rather lack of conservative land policies, fell materially short of preserving the state's basic natural resource for use by future generations. Land erosion was a serious threat to soil preservation in most areas of Kentucky, and so was the exhaustion of soil nutrients. Three new federal policies helped to begin a revision of Kentucky land use practices and policies. These were the Civilian Conservation Corps with its reforestation, terracing and control of erosion, and the building of rural farm access roads. Subsequently the Soil Conservation Administration with its modernized land classifications and controls, and the Tennessee Valley Authority conservation program began a major revolution in the protection of Kentucky's basic land resource. The latter federal agency introduced and popularized modern methods of reforestation and the reclamation of submarginal lands. By 1945 it made available new chemical fertilizers of higher and more dependable analyses and adaptations for use on Kentucky soils.

The Farm Security Administration's survey of Kentucky landholds revealed that in a disproportionate number of counties there was grave danger of both ruinous sub-division of family farms and of soil exhaustion. In 1910 the average Kentucky family farm contained 85.6 acres, and in 1925, 70.8 acres. By 1940 the acreage had decreased even more, but in 1969 it had crept up phenomenally to 128 acres, and out of Kentucky's total 25,852,000 acres, 17,031,000 were classified as farmed. The Federal Government by 1977 had acquired 531,000 acres of sub-marginal lands in eastern Kentucky as part of its national forest system. In the Jackson Purchase area the Tennessee Valley Authority began in 1964 the acquisition of approximately 115,000 acres of privately owned land to be added to 58,000 acres owned by the Kentucky Woodlands National Wildlife Refuge. This picturesque area of natural lands between the Cumberland and Tennessee river was opened to the public in 1968 as a recreational area. Thus it was in the decades, 1930-1970 that the Kentucky landed area underwent considerable changes in both ownership and policies of use.

Closely interrelated with changing surface policies was the problem of management of Kentucky's expanding water resources and surface. From the pre-historic age to the most recent rainy season Kentucky has been a region of seasonal floods as is documented in the configurations of its topography, rocks, and fossil remains. In recent Kentucky history loggers, land developers, highway builders, miners, and industrialists have changed much of the surface of the land. This in turn has contributed heavily to more severe flooding and damaging of the countryside. This has been especially true in areas where heavy coal strip mining has taken place. In 1937 the great flood in the Ohio Valley threatened the futures of the river towns of Louisville, Frankfort, Carrollton, Henderson, Owensboro, and Paducah. Lasting damages from this disaster approximated perhaps a half billion dollars. In Paducah alone 22,000 of the city's 33,000 persons were driven out of their homes by flood waters, and immediate damages were estimated to be $26,000,000. Between the devastating flood of 1884 and that of 1937, estimated damages may have amounted to as much as a billion dollars in their lasting consequences.

In 1937 there were practically no head-stream controls existing in the Kentucky valleys, and flood waters roared rampant down the creeks and rivers in what eastern Kentuckians called "tides." Historically the worst offending inland stream has been the Cumberland River. Hardly a year has elapsed in the twentieth century in which this arterial stream has not wrought some kind of damage on homes and farms. In 1957 unusually damaging flash floods laid waste the bottoms along the Kentucky, Cumberland, and Big Sandy rivers. Twelve persons drowned, and 10,000 families were driven from their homes. Damages from this deluge were estimated to be $50,000,000. After 1937 flood control became a major concern in Kentucky, and in the next two decades flood walls and levies were constructed around such towns as Barbourville, Carrollton, Louisville, Henderson, Owensboro, and Paducah. Three major high rise dams were built, one at Wolfe Creek on the Cumberland on the Russell-Clinton county boundary, Barkley Dam in Lyon County near the mouth of the Cumberland, and the big Kentucky Dam on the Tennessee in Marshall and Livingston counties. Besides these there were ten impoundments along headstreams.

Few public issues in Kentucky history stirred so much controversy as the damming of streams and the creation of sizable water impoundments. This has involved running argument among farmers, town and city officials, the United States Corps of Engineers, and environmentalists. Farmers fought to keep their bottom lands from being flooded, towns sought flood prevention and stabilized water supplies, and the environmentalists contended for the preservation of the ecology and natural beauty of the valleys. Two of the most bitterly contested projects was the construction of a dam across the Licking River near Falmouth, and one across the Red River below the beautiful Gorge and Natural Bridge State Park.

The question of flood control, maintenance of fresh water supplies, and of navigable channels on the rivers raise issues which perhaps are beyond completely satisfactory solution. In 1920 Kentucky's river trade was stagnant. Eight years later the Ohio bore 20,938,000 tons of freight, and the lateral streams bore comparatively a neglible amount of freight. Tonnage passing over the Ohio in 1976 was estimated at 140,000,000 tons and river-related industries returned more than a third of Kentucky's industrial wages, profits, and added values. The Ohio flows 660 miles through the state's boundary, and between Greenup and Cairo, Illinois, there are ten locks and dams which equalize stream flow and insure a nine-foot navigational channel. Since 1945 the United States Corps of Engineer has engaged in a billion dollar undertaking to enlarge dams and locks. The larger ones within Kentucky are Greenup, Anthony Meldahl, Markland, and McAlpine. The Barkley and Kentucky dams have helped increase many fold commercial traffic on the Tennessee and Cumberland rivers. The Tennessee Valley Authority estimated in 1974 that the Tennessee River bore 27,100,000 tons of freight, much of which moved through Kentucky.

As the twentieth century advanced into its closing quarter water resources became most vital to Kentucky welfare. With the expansion of urban communities, the rise of new industries, and the generation of vast amounts of electrical power, water became an indispensable part of modern life. In 1972 Kentuckians withdrew from underground and surface sources 4,500,000 gallons of water daily or 1,400 gallons per capita. Reflective of the rapidity which change had come to Kentucky homes, 81.2 per cent of them depended upon a public water supply. In the 1970's an increasing number of rural homes were served by rural water districts and their spreading pipe ganglia, and the ancient well and hillside spring were forced into the backshed of history along with the spinning wheel and the hand plow.

Although this increasing consumption of water reflected an almost phenomenal rise in the Kentucky standard of living, it also magnified problems of waste disposal and stream and ground water pollution. As late as the 1940's the Ohio River was a virtual interstate sewer bearing urban wastes from Pittsburgh to Paducah. Nevertheless it was lined with public water intakes, and the difficulties of purifying domestic water supplies were and still remain monumental. In 1977 the Ohio River Valley Sanitation Commission represented eight states in the maintenance of water standards, and the prevention of dumping chemical wastes and sewerage into the stream. The reports of this organization made less than flattering announcements about the river's purity. The Commission in 1976-1977, declared the famous Ohio River catfish unfit for human consumption. Their bodies had developed cancerous lesions caused by the presence of polychlorinated bipthenyls and other industrial chemicals in the stream. Since 1968, said the Commission, the fish had declined in numbers and weight. Other Kentucky streams were polluted in varying degrees with quantities of industrial waste and sewerage.

In a far more palatable fashion Kentucky's rivers after 1945 became primary sources of sport and recreation. Though fishing along the Ohio and some of its laterals was practically tabooed by pollution, elsewhere boating and fishing enjoyed a rising crescendo of popularity. The spreading lake impoundments and the huge dams turned Kentucky into an important fishing area. While an increasing number of powerful towboats roiled the waters of Kentucky streams hauling everything from sand to automobiles, the waters in season were lined with light pleasure crafts. No material symbol so vividly reflected an affluent standard of middle class living as did possession of a luxury cabin crusier, galley, bar, and couch. Each passing season saw more boats nudge family automobiles out of front drive-way garages of surburban ranch and split-level houses.

Just as family garages became boat anchorages, every sizable stream and lake in Kentucky was bordered with boat docks and marinas, and boat clubs vied with country clubs as prestigous social affiliations. Louisville, Lexington, and the riverside and lake towns and cities played host to boat shows and sales, and boat agencies were slightly less prosperous than those selling automobiles. For thousands of Kentuckians with new found leisure time the state's 745 square miles of watered surface opened a new frontier of escape from the realities of everyday industrial employment and urban life. Further, the modern era of leisure and the frantic search for recreation signalled in large measure a renunciation of the ancient puritan ethic of work.

Steadily increasing numbers of electrical generating and industrial plants along the Ohio and its lateral streams presaged the rise of new Kentucky economy. In many respects state history in the field of transportation and power generation had come full circle, and Kentucky's rivers again became vital arteries of transportation, sources of power, and increasing amounts of water withdrawal. There were in 1977 either in operation or projected eight river ports and a booming river trade, much of which neither originated nor terminated in the state. Nevertheless it had a vital bearing on Kentucky's economy. In many areas the rural agrarian image of Kentucky was being transformed as industry and population puddled along the Ohio River frontier.

There was abundant indication that Kentucky was undergoing a rather fundamental revolutionary revision of many phases of life in mid-twentieth century. This revolution was evoked by both internal and external forces. Kentucky responded to strong national impulses of change; at the same time it thrust against the eternal barrier of an improving national economic and institutional level. Internally there occurred radical departures from the past. None stimulated change more fundamentally than a revamping of archaic revenue policies.

New Fiscal Policies

Desperately in need of revenue in the bitter depression years, the Kentucky General Assembly, following the example of other southern states, enacted a gross retail sales tax law under the politically palliative title, "Gross Receipts Tax Law of 1934," on June 15, 1934. Sensitive of public resistance to the tax, the law contained the provision that it would automatically expire June 30, 1936. Immediately on its enactment a demagogic hue and cry went up that the tax robbed the widow and starved the orphan.

It became a veritable political football for ambitious politicans to kick about. On January 15, 1936, the law was repealed with legislators stating the people opposed it. In the meantime other sources of revenue had to be found in order to maintain any sort of level of state function.

In March 1958 the Governor and legislators were again faced with the sales tax issue. Veterans of the Spanish-American, two world wars, and the Korean War campaigned for bonuses ranging from $300.00 to $500.00, for a total payment of $300,000,000 to $500,000,000. This huge payment was to be secured by a thirty-year bond issue. To finance this obligation, approved by the voters in a constitutional amendment, the General Assembly enacted the "Veterans' Bonus Sales and Use Tax," February 5, 1960. An added percentage of this tax went to finance other state agencies; later the rate was raised from three to five per cent.

Some sense of the urgency of Kentucky's need to generate more revenue was reflected in the fact that in 1927 it had an assessed general property tax base of $2,999,000,000 from which it collected $30,720,000, or $12.14 per capita. At the same time the Commonwealth operated on a general budget of $18,500,000, including some federal funds spent on war-time and continuing New Deal commitments. By 1945 tax collections had risen to $119,729,000, and a quarter of a century later they were $1,106,000,000. The latter sum included increased collections from personal incomes, and $334,000,000 from the 5 per cent gross sales tax, this despite the fact the General Assembly had freed food purchases from the tax.

After 1950 the Kentucky Finance Commission initiated a program to revise real property assessments. Land values, rural and urban, were increased to a more realistic relationship to current market values. Income from this source increased to $60,000,000 in 1974. Tax collections in the 1970's revealed dramatic improvements in employment and income in Kentucky. For 1,070,000 Kentuckians employed in 1974 their incomes per capita averaged $4,470 as compared with a national average of $5,434. Kentucky ranked 41st in the Nation in this category, but by 1975 it sank to 44th position with a wage differential of $1,031.

As tedious as the foregoing statistical facts may seem they constitute the kernel of Kentucky's eternal challenge in attempts to modernize its way of life. Buried in statistical columns is the leaven of change which has stimulated the Commonwealth's efforts to evolve from a struggling provincial agrarian society to an urbanized-industrial one with entirely different social and economic dimensions. Every Kentuckian after 1940 felt in some fashion the impact of improvement in his financial condition. At one extreme were indigents dependent upon public assistance, and at the other capitalists and industrialists who prospered greatly. There was a staggering expansion of the dependent group by 1976 when 400,000 persons depended upon food stamps or other forms of welfare assistance. Foodstamp recipients alone comprised 11.9 per cent of the state's population. Kentucky received from the Federal Government in 1974, $819,000,000 in public grants, or $248.23 per capita, and it ranked 14th in the Nation. In January 1977 the Department of Commerce reported that Kentucky had become even more dependent upon the central government, and it then ranked third in the distribution of food stamps to 11.86 per cent of its population. Even so the state's improved fiscal condition internally marked an important transformation of its traditional image.

The Highway Revolution and the Automobile

Beginning in 1912 the "good roads movement" in America was no more than a nebulous dream. In Kentucky the General Assembly began a cautious move for the state to begin the construction and maintenance of its roads. For the next half century the Commonwealth struggled to break the social and economic strangulation of geographical isolation. It had at the end of World War I, except in its more populous and prosperous parts, only a faint tracery of improved roads. A highway map for that period revealed remarkably little improvement over one for 1860. Nevertheless the Bureau of the Census reported 57,916 miles of road in 1918, and only 13,900 of this had the semblance of a surface. Only 214 miles were classed as state highway. Half a century later, 1973, there were still, city streets and rural roads included, 69,791 miles, and of this 58,528 miles were hard surfaced. Three years later Kentucky had completed 737 miles of four-lane limited access interstate highways, three of the four completed roads were intersectional arteries bearing a continuous stream of domestic and commercial traffic. The four roads connected Louisville and Cincinnati. There was under construction I-24 which connected north and south across the Jackson purchase. These modern high speed roads supplanted winding and archaic throughfares which had become deathtraps. In addition to the federal aid super highways there were either in use or under construction six state toll parkways which gave all sections of Kentucky limited access connection to the outside.

It is beyond the capability of a historian to assess with factual certainty the social and economic impact of the automobile and motor truck on Kentucky life. It is apparent that with their advent the Commonwealth has experienced revolutionary changes. Obviously they destroyed most of Kentucky's land-bound provincialism. After 1930 thousands of Kentuckians traveled well beyond state boundaries, and for the first time viewed the larger world beyond. Essentially the automobile proved a siphon which transported thousands of Kentucky natives beyond state boundaries to seek employment. First, it was a vehicle of passage carrying emigrants to new homes, then its manufacture created jobs for workers fleeing Kentucky mines and farms. Like all Americans, Kentuckians following the 1920's became restless and mobile people crowding their roads with high speed traffic.

As the tempo of human movement on the highways was stepped up the automobile became a fiercer threat to human life during almost any month after 1945 than were all the Indian raiders who menaced the pioneer settlements prior to 1782. In 1973 2,091,000 cars, buses, and trucks bearing Kentucky registry traveled the roads, and that year 1,155 persons died in highway accidents. Paradoxically the motor vehicle was an active factor in preservation of life as ambulances, conveyors of emergency care, as police and fire fighting equipment, and as a transporter of all sorts of materials vital to human welfare. As an all but cruel jest of ultimate triumph it also bore its accident victims to their graves in a sort of funereal dignity.

No area in Kentucky life or tradition remained untouched in 1977 by automobile and truck. The nostalgic institution, the railway passenger train, lost its patronage for the family car, and the local freight train was robbed of its burden by the motor truck. Ancient social mores which long had been the very ribs of Kentucky conservatism withered quickly in blasts of gasoline fumes, or they were changed almost beyond recognition. Even such an ephemeral thing as individual social images and status were intimately related to the automobile. Modern Kentucky homes were designed so as to shelter the car as a fixture of family life. Where once an affluent agrarian society had adorned its dwellings with pompous Greek and Roman revival facades, and set off grounds with carriage houses and mounting blocks, the modern inside garage and hard surfaced driveway became the new symbols of domestic life.

There may have been no populated area in Kentucky in 1976 which was not beset by some kind of automobile parking problem. Trading towns and cities had on one hand become stylized by the automobile, and stifled on the other by its insatiable demand for space. Historical landmarks were shamelessly smashed under wheel by bulldozers opening down-town vistas for more automobiles. Merchants became almost as much concerned about their nearby parking facilities as with their store equipment and stocks of goods. Entire blocks in Louisville, Paducah, Owensboro, Lexington, and Covington were cleared of buildings and their former sites sealed over with acres of asphalt. Paradoxically the flight from Kentucky's inner cities was stimulated by this rapaciousness. Twentieth century Kentuckians had virtually become legless when it came to walking any distance; in 1977 they did much of their banking, eating, postal chores, and scores of other missions from the seats of their automobiles. Even in worship they struggled to park their cars as close to the altar as possible.

In less easily defined areas the automobile had other and profound effect on Kentucky society. Family life became more fluid if not actually disrupted, a kind of separateness blighted, and even the conjugality of man and wife was threatened. There seems to be no objective criteria by which changing standards of Kentucky's historic moral code can be appraised, or attributed to the automobile. In a material sense the motor car created a chronic drain on family budgeting and financing. As a measure of Kentucky's credit structure, banks in 1974 held various kinds of commercial paper for domestic loans and federal accounts in the amount of $6,316,000,000; a portion of this represented home purchases, debts for household appliance, and a major sum for automobile financing. A more precise documentation of the latter fact were the official records of liens and mortgages lodged in the offices of county clerks. It is possible that a considerable number of Kentuckians after 1940 were never free of debt. As soon as their automobile went through two model changes they bought a new one on installment and continued a form of twentieth century serfdom to the dukedoms of automobile dealers and finance companies. Officially Kentucky profited from the ever-increasing number of automobiles on its road and streets. It collected purchase taxes, gasoline levies, advalorum assessments, and annual registration fees. In 1974 the latter tax yielded $40,000,000.

The economic and social fate of Kentucky came to depend upon car and truck. An untold number of Kentuckians commuted daily to jobs, some of them as much as hundred fifty miles round trips daily. As mentioned above the construction of modern four-lane roads with their spiraling access circles removed permanently from conventional use a large acreage of both rural and urban lands. In the meantime the Kentucky environment suffered damage from exhaust emissions and the deposits of rubber residue. Even Kentucky's picturesque countryside was cluttered with abandoned and derelict automobiles. Governor Bert T. Combs prevailed upon the General Assembly to enact legislation requiring spare parts and junk automobile dealers to conceal their ghastly vehicular "graveyards" behind walls of prescribed heights. The walls, however, were almost as unsightly as the vehicular corpses they were supposed to conceal, and in time the law was indifferently executed. The state also began a public campaign to collect and crush the rusting carcasses of abandoned vehicles to be sold as scrap metal. So dependent had every aspect of Kentucky society become on the automobile and motor truck by 1975 that a shortage of gasoline, and threat of a general truckers' strike against reduction of the speed limit, the state was threatened with economic paralysis.

In one other area the era of the "good road" and the automobile had a distinct impact. The general appearance of the Kentucky countryside was marred by the erection of thousands of commercial signs. The building and servicing of signboards along Kentucky highways following 1920 became a capital industry. Kentucky's law prohibiting erection of signs within a prescribed distance from the new interstate roads and parkways only forced sign builders to seek out strategic ridgetop perspectives and enlarge the size and lighting facilities of their garish displays of motels, pecan rolls, fast food restaurants, gasoline stations, scenic rides, and natural wonders. Towering pylons over gasoline stations exceeded in height, if not in beauty, anything ancient Egyptians created in their more durable monuments. The hand of commercialism came to rest heavily upon the bosom of Kentucky outdoors nature in the advancing decades of the twentieth century.

The Environment

Between 1930 and 1976 there crept into Kentucky consciousness an awareness that both resources and environment were being threatened by wasteful and careless exploitation. No natural resource was more sorely abused and threatened than the forest cover. The Great Depression and the advent of the New Deal with its broad social legislation stimulated some concern in these areas. Since the settlement of the first families west of the Appalachians, Kentucky farmers cleared and cultivated their lands with too little concern for their potential exhaustibility, there was, they said, always more available. Erosion, aggravated by wasteful methods of cultivation, failure to rotate crops, and the clearing of ground unsuited to purposes of row farming, contributed annually to the impoverishment of Kentucky. Even in the fertile Inner Bluegrass, on the rich Ohio Flood Plain, and in broad stretches of rich lands in western Kentucky, soil exhaustion by 1935 had become serious enough to necessitate radical changes in land uses and management.

During the half century, 1870-1920, logmen slashed through Kentucky's magnificent stand of virgin timber with almost drunken abandon. World War I and the western allied nations made ruinous demands on the Commonwealth's woodlands, and it is indeed a sad memory that literally hundreds of thousands of premium quality ship timbers and lumber went to rest in the North Atlantic during the submarine war. Historically there came first the hard-handed Kentucky mountain raftsmen who annually drifted millions of feet of prime logs out of river headstreams to be sold for pittances at lowland sawmills. Later the sawmills migrated up stream all the way from the Ohio to the watershed of the Appalachians, and into the Mississippi bottom cypress brakes of the Jackson Purchase. By 1930 Kentucky had been stripped of most of its proud wooded heritage, and left behind were stumpy remains of rapacious butchery and a wasted resource from which the state derived so little permanent profit. Except for a few private fortunes like those accumulated by J. C. C. Mayo and E. O. Robinson, most Kentucky lumbermen were left worse off than they were in the beginning. There were established no enduring fine furniture-making industry, no real tradition of expert craftsmanship, and no developed sense of forest preservation. For many counties the exhaustion of timber resources in the 1920's began a social and economic decline. All was not disaster, however, because Kentucky has no vital resource which is more readily renewable than its timber. Beginning in the distressed 1930's the state attempted to disseminate information about modern reforestation and wood-land management. With the organization of the Tennessee Valley Authority with its modern forestry and land use programs Ken-tuckians began to sense the lasting significance of their timber-lands and became more amenable to the concept of treating their forest trees as a valuable renewable crop.

Purchase by the Federal Government of the large block of sub-marginal Appalachian land in the old Cumberland National Forest, now the Daniel Boone Forest, was of enormous importance in improving so broad an area of Kentucky's timberlands. Inter-spersed in the federal domain are numerous tracts of private lands, and the owners have profited from fairly good demonstration of management. Kentucky in 1970 had 11,969,000 acres which were considered to be potentially productive timber lands. Approxi-mately half of this was in small farm woodlots which could be made highly productive. That year the annual growth of all ages and types of trees was estimated to be 1,198,000,000 board feet, and the annual cut was 728,000,000. In financial terms this dif-ferential would have seemed a conservative balance, but not so in reckoning the status of Kentucky's dependable timber resource in any given year. There remained two sobering facts, young and growing timber stock was still being destroyed by marginal loggers and greedy sawmill operators. In 1975 one had only to make a casual examination of logs piled about "peckerwood" sawmills to understand that despite the solid work of the Kentucky De-partment of Forestry, and the various examples of good forest management, Kentucky woods were still being raped by rapacious timbermen. Too, parts of the natural forested area in both the eastern and western coalfields were threatened with destruction by the spreading areas of strip mines.

Strip Mining, the Land, and the Environment

In the decades between 1945 and 1977 no single economic and environmental issue generated so much controversy as augur and surface strip coal mining. These processes made readily available marginal seams of surface coal which could not be exploited by shaft mine operation. No one in Kentucky during these decades seemed able to answer with objective certainty what long-range effects this drastic assault on Kentucky's natural environment and physical topography would have on the land or future generations of Kentuckians. Strip miners, when they discussed the subject publicly, contended they could restore the land's contour to approximately its original conformity. They even contended they could improve on nature, and some efforts were made to create a vision of grassy meadows, contented cows, and blissful men. Opponents contended with equal certainty that strip mining destroyed the land by burying top soils, which had required millions of years to form under heavy layers of chemical-ladened and sterile earth, poisonous chemicals were released to kill land, vegetation, and streams. Perhaps most important of all, it disrupted the rhythm of nature itself. Highly visible was the fact that mining procedures left behind ghastly deserts which belied Kentucky's boast of sylvan beauty. Far more central was the unanswered question of what effects such radical land disturbances would have on future generations of human beings. No one could answer this question in 1977 with convincing scientific assurance, nor could anyone be absolutely positive what quality timber harvest might result in an indeterminate number of years in the future from this reforested coal lands. In 1976 the official Kentucky environmental agency issued certificates permitting the stripping of 180,000 acres of land, and there was constant political pressure on officials to speed up the process of certification. In ten years 1,800,000 acres, even at the 1976 rate of certification, would either create a vast wasteland or a tremendous improvement over nature itself. No one could say with assurance in 1977 which it would be.

Kentuckians in 1970 faced legal problems of state creation. In the latter decades of the nineteenth and the first one of this century there was created a legal monster in the so-called "broad" or "long form" deed which assured owners of sub-surface rights that they could extract minerals even at the surface owner's destruction. The negotiating and registry of these deeds took place in an era when ignorant land owners were oblivious to the rich mineral resources underfoot. On at least two occasions this deed form was sustained in court decision. This legal device has in many cases, given strip miners access to lands, even when it meant certain destruction of the surface owner's property and way of life. Almost annually Kentucky newspapers have carried stories involving deep human emotions stirred by miners slashing through fields and pastures, hurling debris onto schools and homes, and even disturbing the peace of rural cemeteries.

Repeatedly the Kentucky General Assembly has dealt with issues of strip mining, but never with the full provision of statutory force which would amply protect Kentucky's resources and environment. Pressures exerted by mine operators and related special interests have so far proved impressive. Even the most dedicated legislators and state officials were caught in a socio-economic whirlpool between the Scylla and Charybdis of miner employment, urgent need for energy from coal, capital income from the coal industry, and the destruction and pollution of considerable areas of Kentucky's picturesque streams and sylvan lands, and the displacement of an untold number of families. These bothersome issues, plus the more traditional ones associated with the coal mining industry in the western and eastern fields, involve the broader one of continuing to provide generous amounts of human welfare support in areas where some of Kentucky's hardiest pioneers settled. Finally there was the unanswered one of whether a considerable scope of the Kentucky surface would become a coal-stained wasteland comparable to that revealed by the two Viking space crafts on Mars in the summer and fall of 1976, or would there actually be lush meadows and forests?

History and Continuity

Always there have been multiple strands and contrasts in Kentucky history. There has almost seemed to pulsate in the individual Kentuckian the rhythms of a folk past in which particular values have been more cherished than others. How vitally the individual

Kentuckian may have been concerned with some of the major problems confronting his Commonwealth has remained a vague if not unanswered question, and especially since 1930. He read periodically in newspapers or heard discussed on radio and television the fact that his state lagged behind in national categories of education, personal income and per capita wealth, but ranked high in the area of receiving public assistance. He was able to do this without expressing publicly any anger or revelation of gripping concern. Throughout history Kentuckians opened avenues of escape from the realities which confronted them. Pioneers faced with an Indian menace and the hardships born of nature were on the whole cheerful people who handed down traditional songs, playparty games, and competitive sports. The twentieth century native was true to his heritage. He developed an all but insatiable love for high school and college athletics. Both basketball and football were sources of vicarious satisfactions and escape. An enormous amount of energy and emotion was spent on organized athletic competition, and literally hundreds of thousands of youth were encouraged almost from the cradle up to participate in some kind of sport. Backyards, garage gables, and vacant lots sported basketball hoops, and passing and punting of footballs became almost as much a part of autumn as falling leaves. Many a young girl learned to twirl a baton with the dream that a day might come when she would strut before a cheering crowd demonstrating her style. Athletic events in Kentucky after 1920, became in essence a folk pageantry, as much so as the great festivals of Europe and England. Daily newspapers devoted almost entire sections after 1930 to athletic news, and a brigade of sports writers kept the public abreast of individual athlete's capabilities and school game statistics. So did radio and television programs.

Ironically the athletic accomplishments of many of Kentucky's schools and colleges were brighter than their educational achievements. In fact it seemed at times that athletic achievements blurred a lack of academic attainments. High schools and colleges built stadiums and halls of basketball, organized regional and state divisions, and maintained rather elaborate administrations to control conduct of games and player recruitment. University talent scouts attended high school tournaments with the same zeal that livestock raisers attended cattle breeder sales. Kentucky's universities and colleges built and maintained more elaborate stadiums and gymnasiums than classrooms. Sometimes they transparently shielded these under euphimistic titles, it seemed to ease a sense of guilt. Often formal academic ceremonies were held in these structures and in physical surroundings far more suggestive of athletic emphases than scholarship.

Contrasts were sharply drawn by size and nature of crowds assembled for even the most inconsequential athletic contests, than those gathered for academic lectures, sophisticated musical programs, and dramatic productions. In like vein there was an impressive discrepancy between sums of money spent on athletics and those spent on libraries, art collections, and auditoriums. Extrovert interests in individual physical prowress during two centuries of state history have been central facts in the human continuity of Kentucky history.

Since the era when long-hunters crossed the eastern mountain range to spy out the land the horse has been an integral part of Kentucky history. This faithful animal enjoyed its master's affection, stimulated his ego, and boosted his pride. He was at once a beast of burden and a pawn of sport. Horse racing in Kentucky began with the settlements, and early in the nineteenth century breeding and training of the animal became big business which exerted an appreciable economic and political influence on the state. Kentucky race tracks have drawn ever-increasing crowds, bluegrass farms have attracted untold numbers of tourists, and the Kentucky Derby and Churchill Downs became known as an internationally famous sporting event and arena. The finely bred horse comprised a colorful part of Kentucky's symbolical trinity. Again, there was marked discrepancy between Kentucky's national standing in the statistical comparisons in social and economic fields and the brilliant reputation of its horses and racing. The two actually seemed to exist almost worlds apart.

In year-to-year existence Kentucky like the Nation experienced the social and political unrest and turbulence of the late 1960's, and underwent some fundamental changes. Although far removed geographically, the Viet Nam War was very much an emotional and factual reality. Youthful Kentuckians gave their services and lives in their country's service, or they protested and resisted a needless war. These years of revolt and defiance made in-roads on many phases of human relationships. The Kentucky home and family were effected. Parent-child relationships were set upon a new social and moral course. Revered puritanical codes, so faithfully observed by earlier generations, were altered after World War II. Marriages became more fragile, and divorce and the illegitimacy of children less stigmatized. The old spirit of neighborliness which Kentuckians had cherished since the days of pioneer common-workings and Indian fighting was being stifled by the rise of the new urbanism. Quite evident in the less wholesale enthusiastic celebration of the state and national bi-centennial anniversary was the fact that the beloved old patriotic orators had vanished from the scene, and people were satiated with excitement. By modern standards the old ways and values had become too archaic to serve a complex urban people. Nevertheless they did linger on in those precious elements of human nostalgia and escape, and even more, they represented the advances of two centuries of constantly maturing experiences.

In the broad transitions from a rural agrarian past to an industrial-urban future, fundamental changes were mandated in the fields of education, cultural relationships, humanitarianism, public health, and communication. Perhaps a majority of Kentuckians surrendered to the beat of a new age with the stubborn reluctance of a people bound to the land by stout historical and ancestral ties, but were being separated from it by an impenetrable wall of progress and future uncertainty.

Two impressive forces stirred modern Kentucky; first, was a desire to maintain a distinct state and regional personality in the face of levelling and standardizing social processes. Second, was an abiding desire to soften the realities of revolutionary change itself. Two areas of Kentucky life after 1945 revealed the import of this fact. Kentuckians had not arrived at a clear conclusion as to what they expected of their educational systems. Since the great public educational crusades of 1908 and 1910 the state made repeated surveys to determine its educational needs, and still in 1977, they were again seeking definitions of purposes, directions, a revision of institutional structures, and means of meeting the educational needs of a constantly changing society. In the latter year education in Kentucky was caught up in a conflict of purposes, intellectual and vocational. The schools were asked to assume many of the traditional responsibilities of the home, church, and community. Nevertheless the brightest hope for maintaining vital continuity in Kentucky civilization was in the vitality of its educational efforts.

Kentucky's historical shame was the fact in its first century and a half of its existence it permitted so much of its brightest human potential and trained talent to slip away from it. Too, in the middle decades of this century too many untrained Kentuckians were stranded on islands of blighted promise and were largely ignored by the state except as a statistical cipher in the field of public assistance. Both they and their children were handicapped in trying to take their places in a rising urban-technological society because they were functionally illiterate and incapable of performing with intelligent human efficiency. This went far to explain why the state and Federal Government in 1974 contributed $111,200,000 in food stamps to 391,000 recipients, and why the press in January 1977, shouted from capital headlines that Kentucky stood near the bottom of the scale of states in several categories of attainments.

By 1974 there were indications that the tide of Kentucky emigration was ebbing if not actually receding. The population increased 5.9 per cent, and it was relatively young, 2,328,000 individuals were under forty-five years of age. Women exceeded men 1,636,000 to 1,576,000. There were registered in elementary and secondary schools 740,000 pupils, the largest number to maintain an average daily attendance in Kentucky history. There were 113,000 college registrants, and the illiteracy rate had dropped to 1.6 per cent. Also in a positive vein, 413,000 Kentuckians had finished high school, and 124,000 had completed four years of college training. In abstract human terms even this brief statistical profile revealed a qualitative contrast with Kentucky's past.

After 1920 Kentuckians like all Americans fell victims to a monotonous standardization of their lives. They were served by chain stores, big oil company filling stations, national or branch businesses, standardized educational procedures, bureaucratic rules and regulations of the Federal Government, and the drumming frenzy of a national media of communication. No longer was the uninhibited Kentucky country bumpkin easily identifiable among a bewhiskered generation of youth. Feuding and moonshining were relics of the past. Even the affable "Colonel" figure now emitted an incongruous aroma of fried chicken instead of mint and bourbon. In almost every conceivable manner Kentucky's historical past was placed on sale in parcels of scenery, sports, and recreational facilities to a lucrative tourist trade. Historic spots like Shakertown, Farmington, Ashland, Locust Grove, South Union, the pioneer forts, Lincoln and Davis shrines, and Revolutionary and Civil War battle sites have been included in the deal.

Late twentieth century Kentucky faced a continuing challenge of modernizing its political system. During the past half century the Constitution became outmoded, and repeated attempts to modernize it failed at the hands of the voters. It was revised in part by adoption of a patchwork of amendments, but the essential structure of general government needed sharp revision. In the general election in 1975 voters approved a constitutional amendment permitting a complete overhauling of the court system, and an extra-ordinary session of the General Assembly in December 1976 enacted laws providing for a somewhat major revision of the judicial structure, but not without some serious misgivings at changing a traditional system. The Executive branch of the government grew progressively stronger during the latter decades. The creation of boards and commissions to administer and ever-broadening public service concentrated major powers in the hands of the Governor. He and his cabinet composed of commission and department heads exercised most of the functional and administrative powers of state government. The General Assembly lost momentum really to strong-minded governors who controlled much of the process of legislation from their position of dispensers of administrative and patronage power.

The Kentucky of the bi-centennial year of 1976 had progressed tremendously as compared with its social and economic conditions of 1930. Statistically it had made miraculous gains in every field. This, however, was not the gauge by which Kentuckians were permitted to measure their progress. As their state progressed so did all the others, and it was against the harsh and objective barrier of national averages that they battled. Thus the eternal conflict between a Kentucky of the future, and an abiding desire to maintain a vital continuity with the past, stirred emotions and human determinations. The twentieth century was no less a pioneering period than was the latter quarter of the eighteenth century.

Bibliography

CHAPTER I—GEOGRAPHICAL DIVISIONS

Sources for this chapter:

J. Winston Coleman, Jr., *A Bibliography of Kentucky History* (Lexington, 1949); this work is indispensable in the study of Kentucky history. It contains a classified and annotated listing of all the books that seem to be pertinent to the study of Kentucky history. Arthur C. McFarlan, *Geology of Kentucky* (Lexington, 1943); this is the most modern and most complete single work on Kentucky geology. Arthur M. Miller, *Geology of Kentucky* (Frankfort, 1919); this study is older than McFarlan's, but it contains some useful social material along with its scientific treatment of the subject. An abstract of this rare work appears in W. E. Connelley and E. M. Coulter, *History of Kentucky*, Vol. II, pp. 1016-1030. W. H. Twenhofel, *The Building of Kentucky* (Frankfort, 1931); a series of papers relating to the historical geology of Kentucky. W. C. Phalen, *Clay Resources of Northwestern Kentucky*, United States Geological Survey, bulletin 385; a study of ceramic materials. Henry Ries, *The Clay Deposits of Kentucky* (Frankfort, 1922). Darrell Haugh Davis, *The Geography of the Blue Grass Region of Kentucky* and *The Geography of the Jackson Purchase* (Frankfort, 1927); these studies are significant because they take into consideration two significant geological regions of the state. Too, they mark a significant bit of pioneering in the consideration of geology in its cultural and social relationships to the people. W. H. Perrin, *History of Fayette County, Kentucky* (Chicago, 1882); the introductory chapter of this work was written by Dr. Robert Peter, a chemist, and treats the geology of the Blue Grass and its influence upon the development of the section. David Dale Owen, *Kentucky Geological Survey* (Frankfort, 1857); the earliest survey of the state. Willard Rouse Jillson, *Kentucky's Mineral Resources* (Frankfort, 1927); a summary of the state's resources. Willard Rouse Jillson, *The Topography of Kentucky* (Frankfort, 1927); this is a volume of papers dealing with the principal physiographic aspects of Kentucky. G. W. Farster, *Land Prices and Land Speculation in the Blue Grass Region of Kentucky* (Lexington, 1922); Kentucky Agricultural Station, bulletin 240.

General sources:

A. P. Brigham, *Geographic Influences in American History* (Boston, 1903). Ellen Churchill Semple, *American History and Its Geographic Conditions* (Boston, 1903).

CHAPTER II—ENGLAND MOVES WEST

Sources for this chapter:

Clarence W. Alvord and Lee Bidgood, *The First Explorations of the Trans-Allegheny Region by the Virginians, 1650-1674* (Cleveland, 1912); this is a most satisfactory study of this period. This work not only contains a complete narrative of the early explorations, but many pages of journals and pamphlets are reproduced in facsimile. Philip Alexander Bruce, *Economic History of Virginia in the Seventeenth Century,* 2 vols., and, *Institutional History of Virginia in the Seventeenth Century,* 2 vols. (New York, 1895, 1910), constitute the best available background study of the westward movement. J. Stoddard Johnston, *First Explorations of Kentucky* (Louisville, 1898) is a combination of Walker's and Gist's journals with editorial notes added. W. M. Darlington, *Christopher Gist's Journal* (Pittsburgh, 1893); journal is supplemented with valuable notes and biographical matter. Thomas Pownall, *A Topographical Description of the Dominions of the United States of America* (Pittsburgh, 1949); this is a new edition of a major contemporary account of early exploration. Thomas Perkins Abernathy, *Three Virginia Frontiers* (Baton Rouge, 1940); an excellent brief account of Virginia expansion westward. W. W. Hening, *Statutes at Large of Virginia* (Richmond, 1819-1823) gives the legal background of westward expansion. Frederick Jackson Turner, *The Frontier in American History* (Baltimore, 1920) is a broad general study. Ellen Churchill Semple, *American History and Its Geographic Influences* (Boston, 1903) is a good general source for early frontier activities. Of value for the period of settlement are: Edna Kenton, *Simon Kenton* (New York, 1930); Robert S. Cotterill, *History of Pioneer Kentucky* (Cincinnati, 1917); William Stewart Lester, *The Transylvania Colony* (Spencer, Indiana, 1935); Archibald Henderson, *The Conquest of the Old Southwest* (New York, 1920). Consult also: Mann Butler, *History of the Commonwealth of Kentucky* (Cincinnati, 1836); W. E. Connelley and E. M. Coulter, *History of Kentucky,* 2 vols. (Chicago, 1922); John Filson, *History of Kentucke* (Wilmington, 1784); Daniel Bryan, *Mountain Muse, Comprising the Adventures of Daniel Boone* (Harrisonburg, 1813); Timothy Flint, *Biographical Memoir of Daniel Boone* (Cincinnati, 1844). James G. M. Ramsay, *Annals of Tennessee* (Charleston, 1853) is a good study of folk movements through East Tennessee. Francis Parkman, *The Jesuits in North America* (Boston, 1906) is an account of the French (La Salle) in the West; Justin Winsor, *Cartier to Frontenac* (Boston, 1895), a study of French movements in the West; and Otis Rice, *Frontier Kentucky,* (Lexington, 1975).

General sources:

Z. F. Smith, *History of Kentucky* (Louisville, 1885). Richard H. Collins, *History of Kentucky* (Covington, 1874). C. W. Ambler, *History of West Virginia* (New York, 1933). Oliver P. Chitwood, *Colonial America* (New York, 1931). Constance Lindsay Skinner, *Pioneers of the Old Southwest* (New Haven, 1921). William Allen Pusey, *The Wilderness Road to Ken-

tucky (New York, 1921). C. W. Alvord, *The Mississippi Valley in British Politics,* 2 vols. (Cleveland, 1917). Theodore Roosevelt, *The Winning of the West,* 6 vols. (New York, 1889). Robert M. McElroy, *Kentucky in the Nation's History* (New York, 1909).

CHAPTER III—STORM CLOUDS OF REVOLUTION

Sources for this chapter:

John Filson, *The Discovery, Settlement and Present State of Kentucke* (Wilmington, Delaware, 1784), reprinted by W. R. Jillson (Louisville, 1929), is a contemporary account of pioneer Kentucky. John Bradford, "Notes on Kentucky," *Kentucky Gazette* (August 25, 1826 to January 9, 1829), reprinted by the Grab Horn Press as *John Bradford's Historical Notes on Kentucky* (San Francisco, 1932), constitute an invaluable contemporary source of information. William Stewart Lester, *The Transylvania Colony* (Spencer, Indiana, 1935); Robert S. Cotterill, *History of Pioneer Kentucky* (Cincinnati, 1917); and Archibald Henderson, *The Conquest of the Old Southwest* (New York, 1920) constitute a trilogy presenting three distinct views of the highly controversial subject of the Transylvania Company. Archibald Henderson: "A Pre-Revolutionary Revolt in the Old Southwest," and "Richard Henderson and the Occupation of Kentucky," *The Mississippi Valley Historical Review* (October and December, 1914); also, "The Creative Forces in Westward Expansion: Henderson and Boone," *American Historical Review* (October, 1914); "The Authorship of the Cumberland Compact and the Founding of Nashville," *Tennessee Historical Magazine* (1916); and, *The Transylvania Company and the Founding of Henderson, Kentucky* (Henderson, 1929). Clarence W. Alvord, "The Daniel Boone Myth," *Journal, Illinois State Historical Society* (April and July, 1926); "Genesis of the Proclamation of 1763," *Michigan Pioneer Historical Collection* (XXXVI); "Virginia and the West, an Interpretation," *The Mississippi Valley Historical Review* (June, 1916); and, *The Mississippi Valley in British Politics,* 2 vols. (Cleveland, 1916); an authoritative work on the Mississippi Valley of the Revolutionary period. Lucien Beckner, "John Findlay: The First Pathfinder of Kentucky," *The Filson Club History Quarterly* (April, 1927); and, "Captain James Harrod's Company," *The Register of the Kentucky Historical Society* (XX, 1922), two critical articles by a careful student of pioneer Kentucky. Temple Bodley, *George Rogers Clark* (Boston, 1926) is a complete biography written from primary source material. James A. James, *Life of George Rogers Clark* (Chicago, 1928) is a satisfactory biography of this frontier leader. J. Stoddard Johnston, *First Explorations of Kentucky* (Louisville, 1898) serves as a background for the early settlement of Kentucky. Its contents deal mainly with Walker's and Gist's explorations. William Allen Pusey, *The Wilderness Road to Kentucky* (New York, 1921) contains a useful series of maps.

Robert L. Kincaid, *The Wilderness Road* (Indianapolis, 1947); a fresh and full treatment of the history of this important road to Kentucky. John Bakeless, *Daniel Boone, Master of the Wilderness* (New York, 1939); by far the best life of Daniel Boone. Edna Kenton, *Simon Kenton, His Life and Period, 1755-1836* (New York, 1930). Thomas Speed, *The Wilderness Road* (Louisville, 1886) is another account of this historic highway to Kentucky. See also: Archer Butler Hulburt, "Boone's Wilderness Road," *Historic Highways of America,* Vol. VI (Cleveland, 1903). Lewis Kilpatrick, "William Calk's Journal," *The Mississippi Valley Historical Review* (March, 1921), is a colorful journal of the journey made by Richard Henderson's party to Kentucky, written in the picturesque language of a North Carolina backwoodsman. William Rouse Jillson, *Tales of the Dark and Bloody Ground* (Louisville, 1930); and, *Pioneer Kentucky* (Louisville, 1934) locate most of the frontier fortresses. George W. Ranck, *Boonesborough* (Louisville, 1901) is perhaps the best account of this important frontier settlement. Edna Kenton, *Simon Kenton* (New York, 1930) is a biography of a colorful frontier figure. Constance Lindsay Skinner, *Pioneers of the Old Southwest* (New Haven, 1921) is a highly readable modern study of the whole westward movement. Theodore Roosevelt, *The Winning of the West,* 6 vols. (New York, 1889), is a study of the whole westward movement. A major portion of this work is devoted to Kentucky. See also: Robert McAfee, "The Life and Times of Robert B. McAfee and His Family Connections," *The Register of the Kentucky Historical Society* (January, 1927). John A. M'Clung, *Sketches of Western Adventure* (Dayton, Ohio, 1847) is a dubious but interesting source. The author was more interested in romance than historical facts. James H. Perkins, *Annals of the West* (Cincinnati, 1846) contains a useful chronology with a brief narrative. Joseph Doddridge, *Notes on the Settlement and Indian Wars of Virginia* (Wellsburg, Virginia, 1824) is a valuable contemporary account. A. S. Withers, *Chronicles of Border Warfare* (Clarksburg, 1831) is another useful contemporary account. Daniel Drake, *Pioneer Life in Kentucky* (Cincinnati, 1870) is useful for its description of pioneer social life. Samuel M. Wilson, *Battle of the Blue Licks, August 19, 1782* (Lexington, 1927) is a complete history of the post-Revolutionary struggle which ended with the Battle of the Blue Licks. W. H. Bogart, *Daniel Boone and the Hunters of Kentucky* (Buffalo, 1854) is a biography of limited value. Reuben Gold Thwaites, *Daniel Boone* (New York, 1902) is a brief biography.

General sources:

Humphrey Marshall, *History of Kentucky,* 2 vols. (Frankfort, 1812, 1824). Mann Butler, *A History of the Commonwealth of Kentucky* (Louisville, 1834). William Ayres, *Historical Sketches* (Pineville, 1925). John Spencer Bassett, "The Regulators of North Carolina," *Annual Report of the American Historical Association* (1894). William K. Boyd, "Early Relations of North Carolina and the West," *The North Carolina Booklet* (July, 1907). Richard H. Collins, *History of Kentucky* (Covington, 1874). James Hall, *Romance of the West* (Cincinnati, 1857). John W. Monette, *The Valley of the Mississippi,* 2 vols. (New York, 1846). J. G. M. Ramsay, *Annals of Tennessee* (Kingsport, reprint, 1926). M. J. Spalding, *Sketches of the Early Catholic Missions in Kentucky* (Louisville, 1844). Edmund L. Starling, *History of Henderson and*

Henderson County, Kentucky (Henderson, 1887). Stephen B. Weeks, "General Joseph Martin and the War of the Revolution in the West," *Annual Report, American Historical Association* (1893). Justin Winsor, *The Westward Movement* (Boston, 1899). Temple Bodley, *History of Kentucky* (Chicago, 1930).

CHAPTER IV—THE FOUNDATIONS OF KENTUCKY SOCIETY

Sources for this chapter:

William Ayres, "Land Titles in Kentucky," *Proceedings, Kentucky State Bar Association* (Louisville, 1909), gives a brief statement of the confusion which has existed in the Kentucky land system. See also, Francois A. Michaux, *Travels to the West of Allegheny Mountains* (London, 1805). W. W. Hening, *Statutes at Large of Virginia, 1619-1792*, 13 vols. (Richmond, 1819); contains the early land laws of Virginia and Kentucky. James R. Robertson, *Petitions of the Early Inhabitants of Kentucky* (Louisville, 1914) refers to land disputes which were back of many of these petitions. See also: Frederick Jackson Turner, "Western State Making in the Revolutionary Era," *American Historical Review*, Vol. I (October, 1895); and Robert S. Cotterill, *History of Pioneer Kentucky* (Cincinnati, 1917), a good secondary source of information on the formation period. A. B. Hindsdale, "The Western Land Policy of the British Government from 1763-1785," *Ohio Archeological and Historical Publications*, Vol. I (December, 1887), gives a brief study of the early land laws. W. R. Jillson, *Kentucky Land Grants* (Louisville, 1925) is a compilation of early land grants. Daniel Drake, *Pioneer Life in Kentucky* (Cincinnati, 1870) contains information on social life. James Albach, *Annals of the West* (Pittsburgh, 1851) has a chronological table and a fair description of early life. *Francis Asbury's Journal*, 3 vols. (New York, 1821), is the account of a Methodist preacher who perhaps came in contact with the pioneers in a more understanding way than any other western traveler of that date. L. Garrett, *Recollections of the West* (Nashville, 1834) is the romantic reminiscences of a pioneer. A. B. Faust, *The German Element in the United States*, 2 vols. (Boston, 1909), has several chapters on the German population of the pioneer West. James A. Perkins, *Annals of the West* (Cincinnati, 1846) is similar to Albach's *Annals*. John M. Peck, *Annals of the West* (St. Louis, 1850) is a new edition of Perkins' *Annals*. John A. M'Clung, *Western Adventures* (Dayton, 1847) is responsible for many of the controversies which have existed in Kentucky. M'Clung was too much of a romanticist. Elizabeth Ellet, *Pioneer Women of the West* (Philadelphia, 1873) provides a fair description of pioneer social life. Reuben T. Durrett, *Bryan's Station* (Louisville, 1877) contains an account of the frontier fortress at Bryan's Station. Jacob Burnet, "Notes on the Northwest," *The American Review* (Cincinnati, October, 1847), reveals a keen appreciation of frontier character and life. John Bradford's *Notes on Kentucky* (Lexington, 1829, printed first in the *Kentucky Gazette,* and later published as *Stipp's Miscellany*) is one of the most reliable contemporary sources on the pioneer

West. A. S. Withers, *Chronicles of Boarder Warfare* (Clarksburg, Virginia, 1831) is a splendid contemporary source on the early society of the West. George W. Ranck, *Boonesborough* (Louisville, 1901) is a reliable account of life at this frontier post. Archibald Henderson, *The Conquest of the Old Southwest* (New York, 1920) is a personal defense of Richard Henderson. This work, however, contains a vast amount of valuable material on this period.

Everett Dick, *The Dixie Frontier* (New York, 1948); a general social history of the southern frontier from the first westward settlements to the Civil War. Harry Toulmin, *The Western Country in 1793: Reports on Kentucky and Virginia* (San Marino, Calif., 1948) edited by Marion Tinling and Godfrey Davies; new materials on early Kentucky. Thomas D. Clark, *The Rampaging Frontier* (Indianapolis, 1939); a study of frontier humor and customs. Harry Toulmin, *A Description of Kentucky* (Lexington, 1945); a reprint of the original 1792. John P. Hale, *Trans-Alleghaney Pioneers* (Cincinnati, 1886) is a popular account. Alexander Fitzroy, *The Discovery, Purchase and Settlement of Kentucky* (London, 1786) is a narrative of early western adventure. See also: S. H. Ford, "History of Kentucky Baptists," *Christian Repository* (1856-1858); William H. Milburn, *Pioneer Preachers of the Mississippi Valley* (New York, 1860); and M. J. Spalding, *The Rt. Rev. Benedict Joseph Flaget* (Louisville, 1852), the biography of an early Catholic Bishop. Sister Ramona Mattingly, *The Catholic Church on the Kentucky Frontier* (Washington, 1936) is a scholarly study of the early Catholic Church in Kentucky. M. J. Spalding, *Sketches of the Early Catholic Missions in Kentucky* (Louisville, 1844) contains an interesting account of the early religious revivals. Richard McNemar, *The Kentucky Revival, or a Short History of the Late Extraordinary-Outpourings of the Spirit of God* (Cincinnati, 1808) is the story of a participant in the early revivals. Benjamin Cassedy, *History of Louisville* (Louisville, 1852) treats of pioneer Louisville. Also valuable are: E. G. Swem, *Letters on the Condition of Kentucky in 1825* (New York, 1916); William Fleming, "Colonel William Fleming's Journal of Travels, 1779-1780, and 1783" in N. D. Mereness, *Travels in the American Colonies* (N. Y., 1916); and George W. Ranck, *The History of Lexington, Kentucky* (Cincinnati, 1872), a good municipal history. A. H. Redford, *The History of Methodism in Kentucky*, 3 vols. (Nashville, 1868); Benjamin J. Webb, *The Centenary of Catholicity in Kentucky* (Louisville, 1884). Timothy Flint, *Memories of Daniel Boone* (Cincinnati, 1837) is a fairly reliable biographical sketch of Daniel Boone, and J. G. M. Ramsay, *Annals of Tennessee* (Charleston, 1853) is a good source for the population movement in eastern Tennessee. Joseph Smith, *Old Redstone* (Philadelphia, 1854); Redstone was important on the route from the East by way of the Ohio River. "Diary of Major Erkuries," *Magazine of American History* (New York, 1877), is the reminiscences of an army officer stationed near Louisville. James A. James, *Life of George Rogers Clark* (Chicago, 1928). Gilbert Imlay, *A Topographical Description of the Western Territory of North America* (London, 1797), the letters of an observant traveler. Charles G. Talbert,

Benjamin Logan Kentucky Frontiersman, (Lexington, 1962). Lawrence Elliott, *The Long Hunter, a New Life of Daniel Boone,* (New York, 1976).

Newspaper sources:

The Kentucky Gazette, 1787-1825. *The Lexington Reporter,* 1811-1825. *The Palladium,* 1804-1806.

General sources:

Fortescue Cuming, *Sketches of a Tour to the Western Country in the years 1809-1810 and 1811* (Pittsburgh, 1823). James Hall, *Sketches of the History, Life and Manners in the West* (Philadelphia, 1835). John Taylor, *History of Ten Baptist Churches in Kentucky* (Bloomfield, 1826); Henry Ker, *Travels Through the Western Interior of the United States from the years 1808 up to the year 1816* (Elizabethtown, New Jersey, 1816). Henry Bradshaw Fearon, *Sketches of America* (London, 1819). John Melish, *Travels Through the United States of America in the years 1806, 1807 and 1809, 1810 and 1811,* 2 vols. (Philadelphia, 1815). W. Winterbotham, *A Historical, Geographical, Commercial and Philosophical View of the United States of America* (New York, 1796). F. L. Paxson, *History of the American Frontier* (Boston, 1924). Constance Lindsay Skinner, *Pioneers of the Old Southwest* (New Haven, 1921). John Bradbury, *Travels in the Interior of America in the Years 1809, 1810, and 1811* (London, 1817). W. R. Jillson, *Index to the Kentucky Land Grants* (Louisville, 1925).

CHAPTER V—A STRUGGLE FOR INDEPENDENCE

Sourches for this chapter:

William Littell, *Political Transactions in and Concerning Kentucky* (Frankfort, 1806) was republished with copious footnotes by Temple Bodley (Louisville, 1926); Littell has left the best contemporary accounts of the political situation existing in Kentucky from 1783 to 1792. Not only is Littell's narrative of historical value, but likewise the documents included as an appendix. James R. Robertson, *Petitions of the Inhabitants of Kentucky* (Louisville, 1914) constitutes a documentary source book for the period of the conventions. Temple Bodley, *Our First Great West* (Louisville, 1938); this is a study of the Revolutionary War and the long period of diplomacy which followed. Thomas Robson Hay and M. R. Werner, *The Admirable Trumpeter* (New York, 1941); a biography of James Wilkinson. J. M. Brown, *Political Beginnings of Kentucky* (Louisville, 1889); although written partly in defense of John Brown, first United States Senator from Kentucky, it is a valuable source of information on the conventions. W. W. Hening, *The Statutes at Large of Virginia, 1619-1792* (Richmond, 1819), remains the chief source for official acts relating to Kentucky under the Virginia government. James Wilkinson, *Memoirs of My Own Times,* 3 vols. (Philadelphia, 1816), reflects the cautious nature of the author, although there are some unintentional hints of the Spanish conspiracy. Humphrey

Marshall, *History of Kentucky,* 2 vols. (Frankfort, 1824), is a history written
for the purpose of personal defense, and exposition of the author's enemies.
This work gives a highly prejudiced view of the conventions. A copy of
the first constitution is appended to Volume II. Thomas M. Green, *The
Spanish Conspiracy* (Cincinnati, 1891) is another defense of individuals who
participate in the constitutional conventions prior to 1792. Tom Paine, *The
Public Good* (1780) is an attack upon Virginia's treatment of Kentucky.
Thomas Speed, *The Political Club of Danville, Kentucky* (Louisville, 1894)
is a sudy of early political discussion in Kentucky. James D. Richardson,
Messages and Papers of the Presidents, Vol. I (Washington, 1896), contains
some comments on Kentucky. William Littell, *Statute Law of Kentucky,*
5 vols. (Frankfort, 1809-1819) is a splendid compilation of early Kentucky
laws. See also: Ethelbert Dudley, "The Constitutional Aspect of Kentucky's
Struggle for Autonomy, 1784-1792," *American Historical Association Papers,*
Vol. IV (New York, 1890). Patricia Watlington, *The Partisan Spirit. Kentucky Politics, 1779-1792,* (New York, 1972). Sylvia Wrobel and George
Grider, *Issac Shelby Kentucky's First Governor & Hero of Three Wars,*
(Danville, 1973). John D. Barnhart, John D., *Valley of Democracy,* (Bloom-
ington, 1953).

Newspaper sources:

    The Kentucky Gazette, 1787-1792.

General sources:

    Mann Butler, *History of the Commonwealth of Kentucky* (Cincinnati,
1834, 1836). W. E. Connelley and E. Merton Coulter, *History of Kentucky,*
Vol. I (Chicago, 1922). Robert M. McElroy, *Kentucky in the Nation's His-
tory* (New York, 1909). Robert S. Cotterill, *History of Pioneer Kentucky*
(Cincinnati, 1917). Lewis and Richard H. Collins, *History of Kentucky*
(Covington, 1882).

CHAPTER VI—STATEHOOD AND ITS PROBLEMS

Sources for this chapter:

    Mann Butler, *History of the Commonwealth of Kentucky* (Cincinnati,
1836) goes into detail with the border campaigns. Humphrey Marshall,
History of Kentucky, 2 vols. (Louisville, 1824), is the account of a contemporary, 1785-1800. Justin Winsor, *Westward Movement* (Boston, 1897)
presents a national view of the struggle. His *A Narrative and Critical History,* Vol. VII (Boston, 1897), likewise treats the western wars from a national viewpoint. Samuel L. Metcalf, *A Collection of Narratives of Indian
Warfare* (Lexington, 1821) is a local and contemporary view of the western
war. Jacob Burnet, "Notes on the Northwestern Territory," *North American Review,* Vol. LXV (October, 1847), written from a traveler's point of
view, gives a general view of western expansion. John Bach McMaster,

History of the People of the United States (New York, 1884-1913) affords a splendid background study for westward expansion. J. D. Richardson, *Messages and Papers of the Presidents* (Washington, 1896), contains many of Washington's official papers. Thomas M. Green, *The Spanish Conspiracy* (Cincinnati, 1891) is a defensive history of the times. James Wilkinson, *Memoirs of My Own Times,* 3 vols. plus atlas (Philadelphia, 1816), is a prejudiced account, by one of the leading military figures. James A. James, *Life of George Rogers Clark* (Chicago, 1928) contains Clark's memoirs and other materials bearing upon this early period. Samuel Flag Bemis, *Jay's Treaty; a Study in Commerce and Diplomacy* (New York, 1924) is a scholarly study of early diplomacy. William Littell, *Statute Law of Kentucky,* Vol. I (Frankfort, 1809); contains copies of the first two constitutions. Temple Bodley, *Littell's Political Transactions* (Louisville, 1926) provides a worthwhile background study. Frederick A. Ogg, *The Opening of the Mississippi* (New York, 1904), covers the commercial and diplomatic activities of the Mississippi Valley during the early years of American control. George Tucker, *The Life of Thomas Jefferson* (Philadelphia, 1837), contains Jefferson's views of the West, and Virginia and Kentucky Resolutions. Ethelbert Dudley Warfield, *The Kentucky Resolutions* (New York, 1887) gives a full statement of the political situation in Kentucky. Robert M. McElroy, *Kentucky in the Nation's History* (New York, 1909) has several reproductions of the original drafts of the Kentucky Resolutions. See also: *American State Papers,* "Indian Affairs," Vol. I. Thomas Speed, *The Political Club of Danvillle* (Louisville, 1894). Theodore Roosevelt, *The Winning of the West,* Vol. III (New York, 1889). James Hall, *Sketches of the West,* Vol. II (Cincinnati, 1835). Albert J. Beveridge, *Life of John Marshall,* Vol. III (Boston, 1916). *History of the Expedition under the Command of Captains Lewis and Clark,* Vol. I (New York, 1804). Jonathan Elliott, *The Virginia and Kentucky Resolutions of 1798 and 1799* (Washington, 1832).

Newspaper sources:

The Kentucky Gazette, 1787-1810.

General sources:

W. E. Connelley and E. Merton Coulter, *History of Kentucky,* 2 vols. (Chicago, 1922). Robert Cotterill, *History of Pioneer Kentucky* (Cincinnati, 1917). Temple Bodley, *History of Kentucky* (Chicago, 1929).

CHAPTER VII—KENTUCKY IN THE STRUGGLES OF THE WEST, 1800-1815

Sources for this chapter:

James Parton, *Life and Times of Aaron Burr* (New York, 1864) relates much of the Burr conspiracy. W. F. McCaleb, *The Aaron Burr Conspiracy* (New York, 1903) relates the story of Burr's western adventure. Samuel M. Wilson, "The Court Proceedings of 1806 against Aaron Burr," *The Filson*

Club History Quarterly (January, 1936), is a documentary treatment of Burr's trials. Mann Butler, *History of the Commonwealth of Kentucky* (Cincinnati, 1834) presents an especially valuable contemporary account of conditions in Kentucky during the war. Humphrey Marshall, *History of Kentucky*, 2 vols. (Frankfort, 1824) contains an account of the war, but is flavored with Marshall's strong personal views. Robert McNutt McElroy, *Kentucky in the Nation's History* (New York, 1909) contains a good chapter on the war of 1812. John Bakeless, *Lewis and Clark, Partners in Discovery* (New York, 1947); an excellent narration of the material contained in the original journals. Bernard Mayo, *Henry Clay* (New York, 1937); an excellent biographical study of Clay up to the War of 1812. Glyndon Van Deusen, *The Life of Henry Clay* (Boston, 1937); the best single volume life of Clay. Carl Schurz, *Life of Henry Clay*, 2 vols. (Boston, 1887). L. W. Meyer, *Life and Times of Colonel Richard M. Johnson of Kentucky* (New York, 1932) is a good biography of Clay's fellow Kentucky War Hawk. J. D. Richardson, *Messages and Papers of the Presidents*, Vols. I and II (Washington, 1896), reprints most of the important executive papers. Julius W. Pratt, *Expansionists of 1812* (New York, 1825) is an able study of the expansionist philosophy which pervaded the West in the early nineteenth century. L. M. Hacker, "Western Land Hunger and the War of 1812: A Conjecture," *Mississippi Valley Historical Review* (Madison, Wisconsin, March, 1924), suggests the same viewpoint. Robert B. McAfee, *History of the Late War in the Western Country* (Lexington, 1816) is the best contemporary account of Kentucky's part in the war. Milo Quaife, "Governor Shelby's Army in the River Thames Campaign," *The Filson Club History Quarterly* (Louisville, July, 1936), contains much of Shelby's unpublished correspondence. See also: "Correspondence between Governor Shelby and General William Henry Harrison, During the War of 1812," *The Register of the Kentucky Historical Society* (Frankfort, May, 1922); and Anderson Shenault Quisenberry, "Kentucky Regulars in the War of 1812," *The Register of the Kentucky Historical Society* (Frankfort, January, 1914). *Acts*, Kentucky General Assembly (Frankfort, 1808-1815), are valuable because appended to the published acts are the legislative resolutions pertaining to the war, giving the viewpoints of the legislators. Lorenzo Sabine, *Notes on Duels and Dueling* (Boston, 1855) contains a brief notice of the Clay-Marshall duel. Carl Wittke, *A History of Canada* (New York, 1928) in chapters VII and IX discusses the war as it affected Canada. Bennett Young, *Battle of the Thames* (Louisville, 1903) is a satisfactory secondary account of this struggle. Z. F. Smith, *The Battle of New Orleans* (Louisville, 1904) is a good secondary account of this battle from the Kentuckian point of view. H. M. Brackenridge, *History of the Late War* (Pittsburgh, 1839) is a fair account of the war. Marquis James, *Andrew Jackson, the Border Captain* (New York, 1933) is a popular biography of General Jackson which throws some human sidelights on his treatment of the Kentuckians at New Orleans. John K. Mahlon, *The War of 1812*, (Gainesville, 1972). G. Glenn Clift, *Remember the Raisin Kentucky and Kentuckians in the Battles and Massacre at Frenchtown, Michigan Territory in the War* of 1812, (Frankfort 1961.) W. Clement Eaton, *Henry Clay and the Art of American Politics* (Boston, 1957). Lowell H. Harrison, *John Breckinridge Jeffersonian Republican,* (Louisville, 1969). James F. Hopkins, ed., *The Papers of Henry Clay,* Vol. I, 1797-1814, (Lexington, 1959). James W. Hammack, Jr., *Kentucky and the Second American Revolution: The War of 1812,* (Lexington, 1976).

Newspaper sources:

The Kentucky Gazette, 1787-1830. Frankfort Palladium, 1807-1811. Niles' Register, 1812-1830. The American Republic, 1810-1812. The Argus of Western America, 1808-1816. The Western Citizen, 1808-1820.

General sources:

Edward Channing, *History of the United States,* Vol. IV (New York, 1905). William H. Townsend, *Lincoln and His Wife's Home Town* (Indianapolis, 1929). Z. F. Smith, *History of Kentucky* (Louisville, 1885). Theodore Roosevelt, *The Naval War of 1812* (New York, 1882). *W. E. Connelley and* E. Merton Coulter, *History of Kentucky,* 5 vols. (Chicago, 1922). Frederick L. Paxson, *History of the American Frontier* (Boston, 1924). Henry E. Chambers, *Mississippi Valley Beginnings* (New York, 1922).

CHAPTER VIII—AN EPISODE IN FINANCE AND POLITICS

Sources for this chapter:

William Littell, *Statute Law of Kentucky* (Frankfort, 1809-1819) contains some of the earliest banking laws. *Acts,* Kentucky General Assembly (Frankfort, 1812-1830), is the most satisfactory source for the legal aspects of the bank controversy. Victor S. Clark, *History of Manufactures in the United States, 1607-1860* (Washington, D. C., 1916), contains frequent references to Kentucky. Arndt M. Stickles, *The Critical Court Struggle in Kentucky, 1819-1829* (Bloomington, Ind., 1929), is the most complete study of this specific aspect of Kentucky history. Basil Duke, *History of the Bank of Kentucky* (Louisville, 1895) includes the history of the early bank struggle. *Journals* of the Kentucky House of Representatives and the Senate (Frankfort, 1812-1830); contain the daily proceedings of the legislature. Carl Schurz, *Life of Henry Clay* (Boston, 1887) presents a good study of Clay's activities during the critical period. See also: Calvin Colton, *Works of Henry Clay,* 10 vols. (New York, 1904), which contains many useful letters and documents. This work, however, has the abominable fault of having been carefully edited so as to remove derogatory passages. Samuel M. Wilson, "Old Court and New Court Controversy," *Proceedings of Kentucky Bar Association* (Louisville, 1915), gives a good legal view of the bank struggle. See also: John C. Doolan, "The Old Court-New Court Controversy," *The Green Bag,* Vol. XII (Boston, 1900). John Spencer Bassett, *Life of Andrew Jackson,* 2 vols. (New York, 1911), affords a good account of Jackson's political activities. Claude G. Bowers, *Party Battles of the Jackson Period*

(New York, 1928) gives an account of the political maneuvers of the thirties. See also: George Baber, "The Blairs of Kentucky," *The Register of the Kentucky State Historical Society*, Vol. XIV; and Amos Kendall, *Autobiography* (Boston, 1872), for the life story of an active figure in Kentucky politics, 1818-1832. Thomas B. Monroe, *Reports*, Kentucky Court of Appeals, II (Frankfort, 1826), gives the decisions of the New Court.

Newspaper sources:

The Kentucky Gazette, 1800-1836. The Argus of Western America, 1824-1842. The Spirit of '76 (Frankfort, March 10, 1826 to August 4, 1826). The Patriot (Frankfort, April to July, 1826). The Lexington Reporter, 1808-1831. The Louisville Advertiser, 1818-1842. The Louisville Journal, 1830-1840. Niles' Register (Baltimore, 1812-1836).

General sources:

John Bach McMaster, *History of the People of the United States*, 8 vols. (New York, 1914). R. M. McElroy, *Kentucky in the Nation's History* (New York, 1909). Lewis and Richard Collins, *History of Kentucky*, 2 vols. (Covington, 1847, 1874, 1882). H. Von Holst, *Life of John C. Calhoun* (Boston, 1889). Francois A. Michaux, *Travels to the West of the Alleghany Mountains* (London, 1805). John Bradbury, *Travels into the Interior of America in the Years 1809, 1810, 1811*, reprinted in Vol. V, Reuben Gold Thwaites, *Early Western Travels*, 32 vols. (Cleveland, 1904).

CHAPTER IX—AGRICULTURE AND INDUSTRIAL BEGINNINGS

Sources for this chapter:

Gilbert Imlay, *A Topographical Description of the Western Territory of North America* (London, 1793, 1797); although a traveler's accounts written to attract settlers to Kentucky, it contains some splendid notes on pioneer agriculture. William Stewart Lester, *The Transylvania Colony* (Spencer, Indiana, 1935) contains many comments on early agriculture. Robert S. Cotterill, *History of Pioneer Kentucky* (Cincinnati, 1917) is similar to Lester's study. Francois A. Michaux, *Travels to the West of the Alleghany Mountains* (London, 1805) reveals agriculture through the eyes of a scientist. William Allen Pusey, *The Wilderness Road to Kentucky* (New York, 1921) is an excellent study of this important channel of commerce. Henry Bradshaw Fearon, *Sketches of America* (London, 1818) is a valuable traveler's account. Mann Butler, *History of the Commonwealth of Kentucky* (Louisville, Cincinnati, 1834, 1836) is the best early history of the state. James Franklin Hopkins, *The Hemp Industry in Kentucky* (Lexington, 1950); the best study of a Kentucky crop. Victor S. Clark, *History of Manufactures in the United States, 1607-1860*, 2 vols. (Washington, 1916, 1926), is a good general study of manufacturing especially on the frontier. Philip Alexander Bruce, *Economic History of Virginia in the Seventeenth Century*, 2 vols. (New York, 1895); although not devoted to Kentucky agriculture and industry directly, it is a valuable background study. Guy Steven Callender, *Selected Readings in the Economic History of the United States, 1765-1869* (New York, 1909), contains many extracts relating directly to Kentucky industry and agriculture. J. B. DeBow, *Industrial Resources of the Southern and Western States*, 3 vols. (New Orleans, 1852-1853), is a compendium of DeBow's *Commercial Review*, with many references to Kentucky. Ivan E. McDougle, *Slavery in Kentucky, 1792-1865* (Lancaster, Pa., 1918) is a good study of part of Kentucky's labor system. See also: Theodore G. Gronert, "Trade in the Blue Grass Region, 1810-1820," *The Mississippi Valley Historical* Review (December, 1918). Adam Beatty, *Essays on Practical Agriculture* (Maysville, 1844) is a collection of essays written by Kentucky farmers and is especially valuable as a source for the study of animal husbandry. Brent Moore's study of the hemp industry in Kentucky (Lexington, 1905) provides a thorough study of this early Kentucky industry. I. Lippincott, *Manufactures in the Central Mississippi Valley* (published in part as *The History of Manufactures in the Ohio Valley up to 1860*) (Chicago, 1914) treats early Kentucky manufactures. Adelaide R. Hasse, *Index of Economic Materials Concerning the State of Kentucky* (Washington, 1915) is an indispensable aid to the use of Kentucky's state documents. Consult also E. G. Swem, editor, *Letters on the Condition of Kentucky in 1825* (New York, 1916). Elizabeth L. Parr, "Kentucky's Overland Trade with the Ante Bellum South," *The Filson Club History Quarterly* (Louisville, January, 1928); and *Patent Office Reports* (Washington, 1840-1852), containing many letters from progressive Kentucky farmers. William H. Perrin, *History of Bourbon, Scott, Harrison, and Nicholas Counties* (Chicago, 1882) contains several chapters which deal specifically with agriculture and industry. L. C. Gray, *History of Agriculture in the United States to 1860* (Washington, 1930) is a detailed study of American agriculture. See also: T. D. Clark, "Livestock Trade between Kentucky and the South." *The Register of the Kentucky Historical Society* (Frankfort, September, 1929). Benjamin Cassedy, *History of Louisville* (Louisville, 1852) contains useful statistics. George Ranck, *History of Lexington* (Cincinnati, 1872) is valuable because Lexington was the earliest market center. "Introduction of Imported Cattle in Kentucky," *The Register of the Kentucky Historical Society*, Vol. XXIX, Nos. 89, 90 (1931), is a publication of a part of the herd book of the Northern Kentucky Cattle Importing Company, and the diary of its agent, Charles Garrard. Paul C. Henlein, *Cattle Kingdom in the Ohio Valley 1783-1860*, (Lexington, 1959). Anna Virginia Parker, *The Sanders Family of Grass Hills*, (Madison, Indiana, 1966). Frances L. S. Dugan and Jacqueline Bull, *Bluegrass Crafts, Being the Reminiscences of Ebernezer Hiram Stedman Papermaker 1808-1885*, (Lexington, 1959).

Newspaper and periodical sources:

The Kentucky Farmer (Franklin Farmer), 1837-1842. *The Western Farm Journal* (Louisville, 1856-1857). *Southern Quarterly Review* (New Orleans, 1842-1850. *Kentucky Gazette*, 1787-1841. *Louisville Advertiser*, 1818-1842.

Louisville Journal, 1830-1860. DeBow's *Commercial Review* (New Orleans, 1846-1860). *Cincinnati Price Current,* 1844-1860. *Louisville Commercial Review,* 1855-1857. *Louisville Farmers' Library,* 1801-1807. *The Dollar Farmer* (Louisville, 1842-1845).

General sources:

W. Winterbotham, *An Historical, Geographical, Commercial and Philosophical View of the United States of America,* 4 vols. (New York, 1796). U. B. Phillips, *Life and Labor in the Old South* (Boston, 1929). John Bristed, *The Resources of the United States of America* (New York, 1818). William E. Dodd, *The Cotton Kingdom* (New Haven, 1921). *Review of the Trade and Commerce and Manufactures for 1850* (Cincinnati, 1850). Katherine Coman, *Industrial History of the United States* (New York, 1910). William H. Perrin, *History of Fayette County* (Chicago, 1882). Theodore Roosevelt, *The Winning of the West* (New York, 1889, 1896). *The B. O. Gaines History of Scott County,* 2 vols. (Georgetown, 1905).

CHAPTER X—RIVERS, HIGHWAYS, AND RAILROADS

Sources for this chapter:

William Littell, *The Statute Law of Kentucky,* 5 vols. (Frankfort, 1809-1819), contains all of the early Kentucky transportation legislation. F. A. Ogg. *The Openings of the Mississippi* (New York, 1904) is a useful study on the early restrictions placed upon American use of the Mississippi River. Consult also: Zadoc Cramer, *The Ohio and Mississippi Navigator* (Pittsburgh, 1803, 1806, 1814, and 1818). Archie Butler Hulburt, *The Ohio River, A Course of Empire* (New York, 1906); and Hulburt's *Boone's Wilderness Road* (Cleveland, 1903); splendid treatment of early Kentucky travel. Ben. Cassedy, *History of Louisville* (Louisville, 1852) gives a good account of early river traffic along the Louisville riverfront. William Calk's Journal, owned by the Calk family, Mount Sterling, is an interesting pioneer document which gives an account of Henderson's journey over the Wilderness Road behind Boone's men in 1775. Thomas Speed, *The Wilderness Road* (Louisville, 1886) is a history of the development of the Wilderness Road, and the trials of the pioneers who used it during the latter part of the nineteenth century. William Allen Pusey, *The Wilderness Road to Kentucky* (New York, 1921) is a detailed study of the route and is especially good for its maps. C. H. Ambler, *History of Transportation in the Ohio Valley* (Glendale, California, 1932) is a study of the development of transportation from pioneer days and is useful in connection with the immigration to Kentucky and the state's Ohio Valley trade. J. Winston Coleman, Jr., *Stage-Coach Days in the Bluegrass* (Louisville, 1935) provides a highly readable study of early Kentucky transportation facilities. The author makes a careful study not only of stage travel, but also of roads, taverns and drovers. Charles Muncey, "The First Railroad in the West," *Engineering Record* (University of Kentucky Department of Engineering, 1909) presents a brief but satisfactory story of the Lexington and Ohio Railroad. T. D. Clark, "The Lexington and Ohio Railroad, A Pioneer Venture," *The Register of the Kentucky State Historical Society* (Frankfort, January, 1933), recounts the complete story (1830-1860) of the building of the Lexington and Ohio Railroad, later the Lexington, Frankfort, and Louisville Railroad. Maude Ward Lafferty, *A Pioneer Railroad of the West* (Lexington, 1916) is a brief pamphlet. T. D. Clark, *The Beginning of the L. & N.* (Louisville, 1933) is a narrative history of the building of this trunk line. See also: *A Pioneer Southern Railroad, New Orleans to Cairo* (Chapel Hill, 1936); the story of the southern branches of the Illinois Central. Mary Verhoeff, *The Kentucky River Navigation* (Louisville, 1917) is a thorough study of the Kentucky rivers. Joseph G. Kerr, *Historical Development of the Louisville and Nashville Railroad System,* (Louisville, 1926). John Leeds Kerr, *The Story of a Southern Carrier, the Louisville and Nashville: An Outline History,* (New York, 1933). American Guide Series, *Louisville,* (New York, 1940).

General sources:

Bathasar Meyer (Caroline MaGill) *History of Transportation in the United States before 1860* (Carnegie study, Washington, 1917) has frequent references to the development of western highways and railways. John G. Starr, *One Hundred Years of American Railroading* (New York, 1929) contains references to Kentucky Railroads; and Z. F. Smith, *History of Kentucky* (Louisville, 1886), general references to travel. Also: Connelley and Coulter, *History of Kentucky,* 5 vols. (Chicago, 1922), for general references. Gilbert Imlay, *A Topographical Decription of the Western Territory of North America* (London, 1793) is a series of letters on the West, principally Kentucky. Walter Blair and Franklin Meine, *Mike Fink, King of Mississippi Keelboatmen* (New York, 1933) provides a splendid study of personalities engaged in the early river trade. Otto A. Rothert, *The Outlaws of Cave-in Rock* (Cleveland, 1924) is a study of southern outlaws who were menaces to down-river trade. Robert M. Coates, *The Outlaw Years* (New York, 1930) covers almost exactly the same materials contained in Rothert's study. Francois A. Michaux, *Travels to the West of the Alleghany Mountains* (London, 1805) is one of the best travel accounts. Frances M. Trollope, *Domestic Manners of the Americans* (London, 1832) is interesting but prejudiced. Henry Bradshaw Fearon, *Sketches of America* (London, 1818) contains good accounts of early Kentucky taverns; and Fortescue Cuming, *Sketches of a Tour to the Western Country* (Pittsburgh, 1810) is a general traveler's account.

CHAPTER XI—HUMAN BONDAGE

Sources for this chapter:

J. Winston Coleman, Jr., *Slavery Times in Kentucky* (Chapel Hill, 1940); by far the best study of the Kentucky slave system. Asa Earl Martin, *The Anti-Slavery Movement in Kentucky Prior to 1850* (Louisville, 1918) is the most complete study to date on this subject. Although this work does not cover the whole period, it treats many of the fundamental issues underlying opposition to slavery in Kentucky. Robert Davidson, *History of the Presbyterian Church in Kentucky* (New York, 1847) is a valuable study, since the earliest opposition to slavery in Kentucky came from this particular denomination. William Henry Townsend, *Lincoln and His Wife's Home Town* (Indianapolis, 1929); although dealing mainly with Lincoln's contacts with Lexington, treats of the slavery question and perhaps is the only study which accounts for many of Lincoln's views concerning the institution. Several chapters are devoted to the slavery issue in Kentucky and its influence upon Lincoln. Cassius M. Clay, *Cassius Marcellus Clay, Life and Memoirs, Writing and Speeches* (Cincinnati, 1886) is a defense of his stand on the emancipation question and supplies many sidelights on the fight which went on in Kentucky during the middle period. Ivan E. McDougle, *Slavery in Kentucky, 1792-1865* (Lancaster, Pa., 1918), supplements the Martin study and perhaps treats the subject of slavery more thoroughly from the standpoint of its economic and social significance. David Rice, *A Kentucky Protest Against Slavery* (N. Y., 1862) is one of the earliest protests against Kentucky slavery. William C. Watts, *Chronicles of a Kentucky Settlement* (New York, 1897) contains an account of slavery in western Kentucky. Mann Butler, *A History of the Commonwealth of Kentucky* (Louisville, 1834) is a good source for the discussion of slavery in the two constitutional conventions. Robert H. Bishop, *Outline of the History of the Church in Kentucky* (Lexington, 1824) is a contemporary account of the early churches and slavery. Nathaniel Southgate Shaler, *Kentucky: A Pioneer Commonwealth* (Boston, 1885), written by a native of Campbell County who saw slavery as it existed under the patriarchal system, is outspoken in its views of the institution. W. H. Collings, *Domestic Slave Trade of the Southern States* (New York, 1904) contains some material on the Kentucky slave trade. See also: Harriet Beecher Stowe, *A Key to Uncle Tom's Cabin* (Boston, 1853). Theodore D. Weld, *American Slavery As It Is: Testimony of a Thousand Witnesses* (New York, 1839) contains numerous bits of information on Kentucky slavery. See also: T. D. Clark, "Slave Trade between Kentucky and the Cotton Kingdom," *Mississippi Valley Historical Review* (Cleveland, September, 1934). *Report of the Debates and of the Convention for the Revision of the Constitution of the State of Kentucky* (Frankfort, 1849); a collection of many views on slavery. David L. Smiley, *Lion of White Hall. The Life of Cassius M. Clay,* (Madison, Wis., 1962). H. Edward Richardson, *Cassius Marcellus Clay, Firebrand of Freedom,* (Lexington, 1976). Boynton Merrill, Jr., *Jefferson's Nephews, a Frontier Tragedy,* (Princeton, 1976.)

Newspaper sources:

Louisville Journal, 1830-1868. *Kentucky Gazette,* 1787-1865. *Lexington Kentucky Statesman,* 1849-1862. *Louisville Daily Courier,* 1844-1860. *The True American* (Lexington, 1845). *The Western Luminary* (Lexington, 1826-1828).

General sources:

James Lane Allen, *The Blue-Grass Region of Kentucky* (New York, 1911). Robert S. Cotterill, *History of Pioneer Kentucky* (Cincinnati, 1917). William Stewart Lester, *The Transylvania Colony* (Spencer, Indiana, 1935). J. H. Ingraham, *The Southwest* (New York, 1835). Nathaniel Southgate Shaler, *Autobiography* (Boston, 1909). James L. Albach, *Annals of the West* (Pittsburgh, 1857). J. B. DeBow, *Statistical View of the United States* (Washington, 1854). Hinton Rowan Helper, *The Impending Crisis of the South* (New York, 1860).

CHAPTER XII—EDUCATIONAL BEGINNINGS

Sources for this chapter:

Frank L. McVey, *The Gates Open Slowly* (Lexington, 1950); an excellent general treatment of Kentucky educational history. Moses Ligon, *A History of Public Education in Kentucky* (Lexington, 1942); a brief but complete history of eductation. Niels Sonne, *Liberal Kentucky, 1780-1828* (New York, 1939); a good study in the field of dogma and intellectual conflict in early Kentucky. J. S. Champeers, *The Conquest of Cholera* (New York, 1938); a vivid account of a perilous year in Kentucky History.

M. J. Spalding, *Sketches of the Early Catholic Missions of Kentucky* (Louisville, 1844) gives a good account of certain aspects of cultural beginnings in Kentucky by a well-educated archbishop of the Bardstown Diocese of the Catholic Church. Humphrey Marshall, *History of Kentucky* (Frankfort, 1812) is a highly prejudiced work in its treatment of contemporary politics but rather able in its treatment of social institutions and pioneer life. Alvin Fayette Lewis, *History of Higher Education in Kentucky* (Washington, 1899) is the most accurate secondary source for educational history in Kentucky. The introductory chapters are especially good for the ante bellum period. William Littell, *Statute Law of Kentucky,* 5 vols. (Frankfort, 1809-1819) contains all of the early seminary and academy legislation. "Littell's Laws" are made more usable with William T. Smith's *Index to Littell's Laws* (Lexington, 1931). Another valuable source is Littell's *Political Transactions in and Concerning Kentucky* (Frankfort, 1806), edited later by Temple Bodley with many enlightening footnotes and other materials (Louisville, 1926). William H. Perrin, *History of Fayette County, Kentucky* (Chicago, 1882) discusses educational beginnings in central Kentucky. John H. Spencer, *A History of Kentucky Baptists from 1769-1885,* 2 vols. (Cincinnati, 1886), mentions beginnings of church schools. See also: A. H. Redford, *History of Methodism in Kentucky,* 3 vols. (Nashville, 1868). R. Davidson, *History of the Presbyterian Church in the State of Kentucky* (New York, 1847). Robert H. Bishop, *An Outline of the History of the Church in the State of Kentucky* (Lexington, 1824) treats educational as well as church beginnings. Consult also: Harriet W. Warner, editor, *Autobiography of Charles Caldwell, M.D.* (Philadelphia, 1855), an early professor of the Transylvania Medical School. E. D. Mansfield, *Memoirs of the Life and Services of Daniel Drake* (Cincinnati, 1855) likewise deals with a Transylvania Medical School professor: Robert and Johanna Peter, *The History of the Medical Department of Transylvania University* (Louisville, 1905) and *Transylvania University* (Louisville, 1896) are spendid secondary sources for the struggles of Transylvania. *Reports* (Frankfort, 1836-1860) of the various state departments combined and issued in a single volume contains all of the early superintendents' reports. Barksdale Hamlett, *History of Education in Kentucky* (Frankfort, 1914) contains the reports of the early superintendents of public instruction, 1837-1869. In *Report of the Proceedings of the Convention for the Revision of the Constitution* (Frankfort, 1849) the sections containing the debates on whether or not the new constitution should contain an educational clause are an excellent source for the understanding of public indifference toward the public school idea.

Newspaper sources:

Kentucky Gazette, 1787-1850. *Louisville Journal,* 1830-1860. *Louisville Advertiser,* 1818-1841.

General sources:

Alonzo Willard Fortune, *The Disciples in Kentucky* (St. Louis, 1932). Gilbert Imlay, *A Topographical Description of the Western Territory of North America* (London, 1792, 1793, 1797). Julia A. Tevis, *Sixty Years in a School-Room* (Cincinnati, 1878).

CHAPTER XIII—THE PRESS

Sources for this chapter:

William Henry Perrin, *The Pioneer Press of Kentucky* (Louisville, 1888) is a good study of the early press, especially the *Kentucky Gazette* and the two important Louisville papers, the *Public Advertiser* and the *Louisville Journal.* Ludie J. Kinkead and T. D. Clark, *Checklist of Kentucky Newspapers contained in Kentucky Libraries* (Lexington, 1935) contains a brief history of most of the papers listed. J. M. Brown, *Political Beginnings of Kentucky* (Louisville, 1889) mentions the conditions surrounding the founding of the *Kentucky Gazette.* John Wilson Townsend, *Kentucky in American Letters,* 2 vols. (Cedar Rapids, 1913) is the most satisfactory source for the literary history of Kentucky. This is a monumental work. Ralph Leslie Rusk, *The Literature of the Middle Western Frontier* (New York, 1926) contains frequent useful references to the Kentucky press. William Littell, *Statute Law of Kentucky,* 5 vols. (Frankfort, 1808-1819) contains much press legislation. *Acts,* Kentucky General Assembly, 1792-1936, contains all of the legislation regulating the press. See also: Reuben Gold Thwaites, "The Ohio Valley Press before the War of 1812-1815," *Proceedings of the American Antiquarian Society* (new series, Vol. 19). Clarence S. Brigham, "Bibliography of American Newspapers, 1690-1820," *Proceedings of the American Antiquarian Society* (new series, Vol. 24). W. H. Venable, *Beginnings* of *Literary Culture in the Ohio Valley* (Cincinnati, 1891). Willard Rouse Jillson, *Early Kentucky Literature, 1750-1840* (Louisville, 1932). J. Stoddard Johnston, *Memorial History of Louisville,* 2 vols. (Louisville, 1896). "Henry Watterson," *The Register of the Kentucky Historical Society* (May, 1922). Morton M. Cassedy, "Henry Watterson," *The Mid-Continent Magazine* (Louisville, May, 1895). John J. Piatt, *Prenticeana* (Cincinnati, 1878).

Newspaper sources:

The Kentucky Gazette (Lexington, 1842). *The Western Citizen* (Paris, 1808-1886). *The Kentuckian-Citizen* (Paris, 1886-1950). *The Kentucky Statesman* (Lexington, 1849-1862). *The Lexington Reporter* (1808-1873); changed to *Lexington Observer and Reporter,* 1833. *The True American* (Lexington, 1845). *Louisville Commercial* (1855-1857). *Louisville Public Advertiser* (1818-1841). *The Louisville Journal* (1830-1868). *The Louisville Courier* (1844-1868). *The Louisville Daily Democrat* (1843-1868). *The Louisville Daily Dime* (1843-1844). *The Louisville Daily Times* (1853-1857; 1884-1936). *The Clarion* (Danville, 1841). *The Advertiser* (Danville, 1825-1826). *The Argus of Western America* (Frankfort, 1808-1840). *The Commonwealth* (Frankfort, 1833-1872). *The Palladium* (Frankfort, 1798-1816). *The Western World* (Frankfort, 1806-1810). *The Kentucky Yeoman* (Frankfort, 1840-1862). *The Hopkinsville Kentuckian* (1879-1920). *The Lexington Leader* (1888-1936). *The Lexington Herald* (1895-1950). *The Courier-Journal* (Louisville, 1868-1936). *The Owensboro Daily Messenger* (1877-1936). *The News Democrat* (Paducah, 1905-1929). *The Evening Sun* (Paducah, 1905-1929). *The Sun-Democrat* (Paducah, 1929-1950). West T. Hill, Jr., *The Theatre in Early Kentucky, 1790-1820,* (Lexington, 1971). Clark L. Keating, *Audubon: The Kentucky Years,* (Lexington, 1976). J. Winston Coleman, Jr., *Three Kentucky Artists,* (Lexington, 1974). Earl H. Rovit, *Herald to Chaos, the Novels of Elizabeth Madox Roberts,* (Lexington, 1960). John Walton, *John Filson of Kentucky,* (Lexington, 1956). Sister Mary Carmel, *Kentucky Authors,* (Evansville, Indiana, 1968). Issac F. Marcosson, *"Marse Henry" a Biography of Watterson,* (New York, 1951). Joseph Frazier Wall, *Henry Watterson, Reconstruction Rebel,* (New York, 1956). *Antiques in Kentucky,* (New York, 1974. Helen Bartter Crocker, *The Green River of Kentucky,* (Lexington, 1976).

General sources:

George W. Ranck, *History of Lexington, Kentucky* (Cincinnati, 1972). Charles M. Mecham, *A History of Christian County, Kentucky, from Oxcart to Airplane* (Nashville, 1930). W. E. Connelley and E. M. Coulter, *History of Kentucky* (Chicago, 1922). E. Polk Johnson, *History of Kentucky and Kentuckians,* 3 vols. (Chicago, 1912).

CHAPTER XIV—A CULTURAL AWAKENING

Sources for this chapter:

Elizabeth Patterson Thomas, *Old Kentucky Homes and Gardens* (Louisville, 1939). Rexford Newcomb, *Old Kentucky Architecture* (New York, 1920); a scholarly history of Kentucky architecture.

Rexford Newcomb, "The Architecture of Old Kentucky," *Register of the Kentucky Historical Society* (July, 1933), is a splendid article by a careful scholar of domestic architecture. This article has a footnote appended to it (without the author's consent) saying that Thomas Jefferson designed Liberty Hall. See also: "Gideon Shryock—Pioneer Greek Revivalist of the West," *The Architect,* Vol. II. Thomas W. Bullitt, *My Life at Oxmoor* (Louisville, 1911) giving an account of life on an ante-bellum Kentucky plantation. Elizabeth Simpson, *Blue Grass Houses and Their Traditions* (Lexington, 1932) is a study of a romantic nature. Robert S. Cotterill, *History of Pioneer Kentucky* (Cincinnati, 1917); contains much material on the early homes of the pioneers. Lewis Kilpatrick, "William Calk's Journal," *Mississippi Valley Historical Review* (March, 1921); refers to William Calk who came with Richard Henderson to Boonesborough. William Stewart Lester, *The Transylvania Colony* (Spencer, Indiana, 1935); contains some information on early social life. George W. Ranck, *History of Lexington, Kentucky* (Cincinnati, 1872); contains many references to early western craftsmen. Anne W. Callahan, *Early Silversmiths* (manuscript, University of Kentucky); contains much material gathered from family papers and court records. Benjamin Cassedy, *History of Louisville* (Louisville, 1852); contains a list of early craftsmen. Samuel R. Brown, *The Western Gazetteer; or Emigrants' Directory* (Auburn, N. Y., 1817); contains a sketch of Kentucky. Daniel Drake, *Pioneer Life in Kentucky* (Cincinnati, 1870) is a series of reminiscent letters to his children on pioneer Kentucky. Also valuable is Fortescue Cuming, *Sketches of a Tour to the Western Country in the Years 1809, 1811 and 1812* (Pittsburgh, 1818). Francois A. Michaux, *Travels to the West of the Alleghany Mountains* (London, 1805) is one of the best of the travelers' accounts. Michaux was a keen observer, especially of the population in the West. Samuel W. Price, *The Old Masters of the Blue Grass* (Louisville, 1902) is a sketch of Kentucky artists. "Jouett's Portrait of Lafayette," *Register of the Kentucky Historical Society* (January, 1922), is a series of official letters concerning this portrait. Richard Collins, *History of Kentucy,* 2 vols. (Covington, 1874), has a section on artists. M. J. Spalding, *Sketches of Early Catholic Missions in Kentucky from Their Commencement in 1787 to the Jubilee of 1826-1827* (Louisville, 1844) quotes some interesting material on the early revivals. Elder Levi Purviance, *The Biography of David Purviance* (Dayton, Ohio, 1848) is the life story of a crusading backwoods preacher. See also: Henry Hamilton, *Men and Manners of America* (Philadelphia, 1833). James Rogers, *The Cane Ridge Meeting House* (Cincinnati, 1910); describes the beginning of the great western religious awakening. W. P. Strickland, editor, *Autobiography of Peter*

Cartwright (Cincinnati, 1856) is another account of a vigorous western preacher. William Warren Sweet, *The Story of Religions in America* (New York, 1930) is a scholarly treatment of the spread of religious groups in America. John Wilson Townsend, *Kentucky in American Letters,* 2 vols. (Cedar Rapids, 1913) is a thorough study of this subject and constitutes an encyclopedia of Kentucky literature. John Shaw, *A Narrative of the Life and Travels of John Robert Shaw, the Well Digger* (Lexington, 1807; reprinted, Louisville, 1830). Grant C. Knight, *James Lane Allen and the Genteel Tradition* (Chapel Hill, 1935). Fred G. Neuman, *Irvin S. Cobb, His Life and Achievements* (Paducah, 1934). John Wilson Townsend, "In Kentucky" and Its Author, "Jim Mulligan" (Lexington, 1935). Samuel M. Wilson, *History of Kentucky* (Chicago, 1922); contains a good chapter on Kentucky literature. Timothy Flint, *Recollection of the Last Ten Years* (Boston, 1826) presents a Yankee's view of the uncouth West. Irvin Cobb, *Kentucky* (New York, 1924) is a booklet on Kentucky pride. Charles Dickens, *American Notes* (London, 1842) contains valuable observations. Frances Trollope, *Domestic Manners of the Americans* (London, 1839) is the writing of a highly prejudiced English observer. Consult also: Ralph Leslie Rush, *The Literature of the Middle Western Frontier* (New York, 1926). W. H. Venable, *Beginnings of Literary Culture in the Ohio Valley* (Cincinnati, 1891). Willard Rouse Jillson, *Early Kentucky Literature 1750-1840* (Louisville, 1932). Garvin F. Davenport, *Ante Bellum Kentucky, a Social History, 1800-1860,* (Oxford, Ohio, 1843). Harriette Arnow, *Seedtime on the Cumberland and Flowering of the Cumberland,* (New York, 1960, 1963). John B. Boles, *The Great Revival, 1787-1805, the Origin of the Southern Evangelical Mind.* (Lexington, 1975). Arthur F. Jones, *The Art of Paul Sawyier* (Lexington, 1976).

Newspaper sources:

The Western Luminary, 1826-1829. *Kentucky Gazette,* 1787-1842. *Louisville Public Advertiser,* 1818-1841. *Louisville Journal,* 1830-1868. *Courier-Journal,* 1868-1936. *Lexington Leader,* 1888-1936. *Lexington Herald,* 1895-1936. *Kentucky Progress Magazine,* 1927-1936.

General sources:

E. Polk Johnson, *History of Kentucky and Kentuckians* (Chicago, 1912). William B. Allen, *History of Kentucky* (Louisville, 1872). Robert M. McElroy, *Kentucky in the Nation's History* (New York, 1909); *The South in the Building of the Nation,* 12 vols. (Richmond, 1909). Ulrich Bonnell Phillips, *Life and Labor in the Old South* (Boston, 1929). *Autobiography of Dr. J. J. Polk* (Louisville, 1867). J. F. Cook, *Old Kentucky* (New York, 1908). Otto A. Rothert, *History of Muhlenberg County* (Louisville, 1913).

CHAPTER XV—EVOLUTION OF STATE POLITICS

Sources for this chapter:

Richard H. Collins, *History of Kentucky,* 2 vols. (Covington, 1874), contains a splendid chronology of early Kentucky politics and brief biographical sketches of the early Governors. Good background studies of political beginnings are: William Littell, *Political Transactions in and Concerning Kentucky* (Frankfort, 1806), Thomas M. Green, *The Spanish Conspiracy* (Cincinnati, 1891), John Mason Brown, *The Political Beginnings of Kentucky* (Louisville, 1889), and Mann Butler, *History of the Commonwealth of Kentucky* (Cincinnati, 1836). William Whitsitt, *Life and Times of Judge Caleb Wallace* (Louisville, 1888), Amos Kendall, *Autobiography of Amos Kendall* (Boston, 1872), Mrs. Chapman Coleman, *Life of John J. Crittenden,* 2 vols. (Philadelphia,1871), and George Robertson, *Scrap Book on Law and Politics* (Lexington, 1855) contains much worthwhile material bearing directly upon early Kentucky politics. The best source for the study of current issues facing the administrations for 1792 to 1840 are the *Journals* and *Acts* of the Kentucky General Assembly. For the text of the first three constitutions see Bennett H. Young, *History and Text of the Three Constitutions of Kentucky* (Louisville, 1890). William H. Perrin, *Pioneer Press of Kentucky* (Louisville, 1888) and Benjamin Drake, *Tales and Sketches from the Queen City* (Cincinnati, 1838) contain interesting accounts of the three-day elections.

Newspaper sources:

Kentucky Gazette (1787-1845). *American Republic* (1810 to 1812). *The Argus of Western America* (1824-1830). *Kentucky Reporter* (1818-1832). *Observer and Reporter* (1832-1845). *The Patriot* (1826). *The Spirit of '76* (1826). *The Louisville Public Advertiser* (1824-1840), and *The Louisville Journal* (1831-1845).

General sources:

There are three general sources worthy of investigation: Humphrey Marshall, *History of Kentucky* (Frankfort, 1824), Robert M. McElroy, *Kentucky in the Nation's History* (New York, 1909), and W. E. Connelley and E. M. Coulter, *History of Kentucky,* 2 vols. (Chicago, 1922).

CHAPTER XVI—KENTUCKY SHARES
A NATION'S TROUBLES

Sources for this chapter:

William H. Townsend, *Lincoln and His Wife's Home Town* (Indianapolis, 1929) given an excellent treatment of the "middle period" of Kentucky history. Calvin Colton, *The Life and Times of Henry Clay,* 2 vols. (New York, 1846), contains a chronological sketch of Clay's earlier life; and *The Private Correspondence of Henry Clay* (Cincinnati, 1856) is a fairly good source for Clay's activities of this period. Carl Schurz, *Life of Henry Clay*

(Boston, 1896). Lucius P. Little, *Ben Hardin: His Times and Contemporaries* (Louisville, 1887) is the biography of an influential Kentucky politician of the "middle period." Justin H. Smith, *Annexation of Texas* (New York, 1919) is a thorough and scholarly study of the Texas question. Arthur C. Cole, *The Whig Party in the South* (Washington, 1913) deals with Kentucky's part in the Whig struggle. George R. Poage, *Henry Clay and the Whig Party* (Chapel Hill, 1936) concentrates especially on the campaign of 1844. William E. Dodd, *The Cotton Kingdom* (New Haven, 1921); *Expansion and Conflict* (Boston, 1915); and, *Statesmen of the Old South* (New York, 1929) are splendid background studies. Cassius M. Clay, *Life of Cassius Marcellus Clay, Memoirs, Writings and Speeches* (Cincinnati, 1886) is an autobiography of a colorful Kentuckian who actively participated in the struggles of 1840 to 1860. W. Clement Eaton, *A History of the Old South* (New York, 1949); a good general work on the South which contains a generous amount of Kentucky materials which relate the state to the rest of the southern region. Same author, *Freedom of Thought in the Old South* (Durham, 1940); a thoroughly mature study of the intellectual life of the Old South in which Kentuckians receive much attention. Asa Earl Martin, *The Anti-Slavery Movement in Kentucky Prior to 1850* (Louisville, 1918) is a careful study which deals with the antislavery activities prior to the constitutional convention in 1849. *Report of the Proceedings of the Convention for the Revision of the Constitution* (Frankfort, 1849) gives the speeches of the convention, a splendid index to the politics of Kentucky. Stephen F. Austin, *An Address delivered by Stephen F. Austin of Texas to a very large audience of Ladies and Gentlemen in the Second Presbyterian Church, Louisville, Kentucky, on the 7th of March, 1836* (Lexington, 1836) is an appeal to Kentuckians in behalf of Texas. George Robertson, *Scrap Book on Law and Politics, Men and Times* (Lexington, 1855) is a collection of speeches and papers. Mrs. Chapman Coleman, *The Life of John J. Crittenden* (Philadelphia, 1871) is a biographical sketch of a leading Kentucky politician, 1840-1860. George Fort Milton, *The Eve of Conflict* (Boston, 1934) is a thorough study of the period 1830 to 1860. J. Stoddard Johnston, *Memorial History of Louisville, Kentucky, from Its First Settlement to the Year 1896* (Louisville, 1896) contains an account of the Know Nothing disturbances. Albert D. Kirwan, *John Jordan Crittenden, the Struggle for the Union.* (Lexington, 1962).

Newspaper sources:

Kentucky Gazette (1830-1842). *Lexington Observer and Reporter* (1830-1860). *Louisville Journal* (1830-1860). *Louisville Advertiser* (1830-1841). *Frankfort Commonwealth* (1833-1860). *Louisville Democrat* (1843-1860). *The True American* (Lexington, 1845).

General sources:

W. E. Connelley and E. M. Coulter, *History of Kentucky* (Chicago, 1922). Richard H. Collins, *History of Kentucky* (Covington, 1874). Z. F. Smith, *History of Kentucky* (Louisville, 1882). James Ford Rhodes, *History of the*

United States from the Compromise of 1850, Vols. I and II (Boston, 1916). Albert J. Beveridge, *Abraham Lincoln, 1809-1858,* 2 vols. (New York, 1893). Levi Coffin, *Reminiscences of Levi Coffin* (Cincinnati, 1876). George W. Ranck, *History of Lexington, Kentucky* (Cincinnati, 1872). *Report of the Kentucky Commissioners to the Late Peace Conference Held at Washington City* (Washington, 1861).

CHAPTER XVII—A BROTHER'S BLOOD

Sources for this chapter:

E. Merton Coulter, *The Civil War and Readjustment in Kentucky* (Chapel Hill, 1926) is a complete and scholarly treatment. The author has brought together a mass of detailed information relating both to the conduct of the war and the reconstruction which followed. Thomas Speed, *The Union Cause in Kentucky* (New York, 1907), a highly prejudiced story of a Kentucky Unionist, contains much useful detail. Nathaniel Southgate Shaler, *Kentucky: A Pioneer Commonwealth* (Boston, 1888) is another Unionist account of the war, but not as prejudiced as Speed's book. Ed. Porter Thompson, *History of the First Kentucky Brigade* (Cincinnati, 1868) is the product of the author's active participation in the war. *American Annual Cyclopedia and Register of Important Events* (New York, 1861-1873) gives a splendid daily account of the war, with much attention to the struggle in Kentucky. Basil Duke, *Morgan's Cavalry* (Cincinnati, 1867) is a colored, but good account by Morgan's brother-in-law. *Reminiscences of General Basil W. Duke* (Garden City, 1911) deals largely with the war. John G. Nicolay and John Hay, editors, *Complete Works of Abraham Lincoln,* 12 vols. (New York, 1905) contains an account of Lincoln's attitude toward Kentucky. Howard Swigett, *The Rebel Raider* (Indianapolis, 1934) is a recent biography of General Morgan. Cecil Holland, *Morgan and His Raiders* (New York, 1942); the best study of General Morgan and his spirited command. A. M. Stickles, *Simon Bolivar Buckner* (Chapel Hill, 1940); an able military biography. Don Carlos Seitz, *Braxton Bragg, General of the Confederacy* (Columbia, South Carolina, 1924) is useful. Hambleton Tapp, "Battle of Perryville, 1862," *The Filson Club History Quarterly* (Louisville, July, 1935), is the best account of this conflict. See also, John B. Castleman, *Active Service* (Louisville, 1917).

Newspaper sources:

Cincinnati Commercial, 1860-1872. *The Crisis* (Columbus, Ohio), 1861-1863. *Frankfort Commonwealth,* 1861-1871. *Kentucky Yeoman,* 1861-1872. *Louisville Journal,* 1861-1868. *Lexington Observer and Reporter,* 1861-1865.

General sources:

Edward Pollard, *The Lost Cause: A Southern History of the War of the Confederacy* (New York, 1867). E. C. Smith, *The Borderland in the Civil War* (New York, 1927). Lowell Harrison, *The Civil War in Kentucky,* (Lexington, 1975). Robert E. McDowell, *City of Conflict, Louisville in the Civil War, 1861-1865*, (Louisville, 1962). William C. Davis, *Breckinrdige Statesman Soldier Symbol*, (Baton Rouge, 1974). Frank H. Heck, *Proud Kentuckian: John C. Breckinridge, 1821-1875*, (Lexington, 1976).

CHAPTER XVIII—SOCIAL AND POLITICAL TRANSITION

Sources for this chapter:

E. M. Coulter, *The Civil War and Readjustment in Kentucky* (Chapel Hill, 1926) is a thorough study of the political and economic aspects of the Civil War period. This book contains several useful chart maps which illustrate specifically the influence of the war in Kentucky. *Acts, Journals, Documents*, Kentucky General Assembly (1855-1876), constitute a reflection of the state of the Kentucky mind. *An Address by the Hon. Joseph Holt to the People of Kentucky* (New York, 1861) is a plea for peace. *Report of the Excursion made by the Executives and Legislatures of the States of Kentucky and Tennessee to the State of Ohio, January, 1860* (Cincinnati, 1860) describes a political junket of good will, which had in view a closer co-operation of the borderland. William Cassius Goodloe, *Kentucky Unionists of 1861* (Cincinnati, 1884) is a brief pamphlet written by a Lexington Unionist and newspaper editor. *Autobiography of Dr. J. J. Polk* (Louisville, 1867) is the life history of a Kentuckian who was active as a preacher, storekeeper, farmer, and newspaperman during the critical period. E. Merton Coulter, *The Cincinnati Southern Railroad and the Struggle for Southern Commerce, 1861-1872* (Chicago, 1922) is an excellent study of economic struggle in Kentucky. Nathaniel Southgate Shaler, *Kentucky, A Pioneer Commonwealth* (New York, 1888) emphasizes the period of the Civil War, a period through which Shaler lived. Thomas Speed, *The Union Cause in Kentucky, 1860-1865* (New York, 1907) is a highly prejudiced account of the war. Mary Scrugham, *Peaceable Americans of 1860-1861* (New York, 1921) is an account of the efforts of the Kentucky pacifists. *Reminiscences of General Basil W. Duke, C. S. A.* (New York, 1911), is a genuinely interesting series of stories and reminiscences from which the author deleted much pertinent material. *American Annual Cyclopedia and Register of Important Events, 1861-1872* (New York) is one of the most fruitful sources for contemporary information. Ross A. Webb, *Benjamin Helm Bristow Border State Politician*, (Lexington, 1969). Leonard P. Curry, *Rail Routes South, Louisville's Fight for the Southern Market, 1865-1872*, (Lexington, 1969). Joseph C. Robert, *The Story of Tobacco in America*, (Chapel Hill, 1949). Paul E. Fuller, *Laura Clay and the Woman's Rights Movement*, (Lexington, 1975).

Newspaper and periodical sources:

Cincinnati Commercial, 1860-1872. *Frankfort Commonwealth*, 1860-1872. *Cynthiana News*, 1873. *Lexington Observer and Reporter*, 1861-1878. *Louisville Journal*, 1861-1868. *Louisville Courier-Journal*, 1868-1876. *Kentucky Yeoman* (Frankfort), 1861-1872. *Louisville Commercial*, 1870. *Georgetown*

Weekly Times, 1870-1872. *Kentucky Statesman*, 1860, 1872, 1873. *DeBow's Review* (New Orleans, 1860-1870). *Hunt's Merchant's Magazine* (New York, 1860-1870).

General sources:

W. E. Connelley and E. M. Coulter, *History of Kentucky*, 5 vols. (Chicago, 1922). Z. F. Smith, *History of Kentucky* (Louisville, 1886). J. H. Battle and W. H. Kniffen, *Counties of Todd and Christian, Kentucky* (Chicago, 1884). Edward A. Pollard, *The Lost Cause: A Southern History of the War of the Confederacy* (New York, 1867). R. M. McElroy, *Kentucky in the Nation's History* (New York, 1909). Petroleum V. Nasby (David Ross Locke) *Ekkoes from Old Kentucky* (Boston, 1868). E. P. Oberholtzer, *A History of the United States since the Civil War*, Vols. I and II (New York, 1917). *The South in the Building of the Nation*, 12 vols. (Richmond, 1909). Otto A. Rothert, *History of Muhlenberg County* (Louisville, 1913). J. C. Schwab, *The Confederate States of America, 1861-1865. A Financial and Industrial History of the South during the Civil War* (New Haven, 1913).

CHAPTER XIX—EDUCATIONAL ADVANCES

Sources for this chapter:

Alvin Fayette Lewis, *History of Higher Education in Kentucky* (Washington, 1899) is the best story of higher education in Kentucky, especially the sections which deal with the postwar school system. Barksdale Hamlett, *History of Education in Kentucky* (Frankfort, 1914), is a compilation of superintendents' reports and reports from county commissioners. This book constitutes a valuable collection of sources, but it is not a history. *Kentucky School Laws* (Frankfort, 1870, 1873, 1882, 1888, 1900, 1909, 1920, 1936), plus the annual reports of the superintendents, constitutes the principal official source for the history of public education in Kentucky. *Report of the Debates in the Constitutional Convention, 1890*, 4 vols. (Frankfort, 1890), contains debates on constitutional provisions for public education in Kentucky. Like the reports of the debates for 1849 these debates are enlightening as to the sentiment of the communities of the state toward the organization of public schools. *Public Education in Kentucky* (New York, 1922) is a report prepared by the General Education Board. This survey is thorough and presents a scientific but startling analysis of Kentucky's educational needs. Jesse E. Adams, *A Study in the Equalization of Educational Opportunities in Kentucky* (Lexington, 1928) is a detailed comparative study of educational opportunities. *Report of the Kentucky Educational Commission* (Frankfort, 1933) is the special report of a commission appointed to make a study of the educational system for the purpose of proposing definite reforms. This report formed the basis for the educational bill passed by the general assembly in 1935. William Walter Jennings, *Transylvania Pioneer University of the West*, (New York, 1955). John Wright, *Transylvania, Tudor to the West*, Elisabeth S. Peck, *Berea's First Century, 1855-1955*, (Lexington, 1955).

Charles G. Talbert, *The University of Kentucky, the Maturing Years*, (Lexington, 1965). Herman Lee Donovan, *Keeping the University Free and Growing*, (Lexington, 1959). Frank L. McVey, *The Gates Open Slowly, a History of Education in Kentucky*, (Lexington, 1949). Ellis Ford Hartford, *The Little White Schoolhouse*, (Lexington, 1977).

Newspaper sources:

Louisville Courier-Journal, 1868-1950. *Owensboro Messenger*, 1877-1950. *Kentucky Advocate*, 1865-1950. *The State Journal*, 1919-1950. *Lexington Leader*, 1888-1950. *Lexington Herald*, 1895-1950. *Paducah Sun*, 1905-1929. *Paducah Sun-Democrat*, 1929-1950.

General sources:

Z. F. Smith, *History of Kentucky* (Louisville, 1886; written by an ex-superintendent of public instruction. Richard H. Collins, *History of Kentucky* (Covington, 1874). E. Merton Coulter, *Civil War and Readjustment in Kentucky* (Chapel Hill, 1926). Samuel M. Wilson, *History of Kentucky* (Chicago, 1929). W. E. Connelley and E. M. Coulter, *History of Kentucky*, 2 vols. (Chicago, 1922). Mabel P. Daggett, "Kentucky's Fight for an Education," *The Delineator*, Vol. 74 (New York, November, 1909). William F. DeMoss, "Wiping Out Illiteracy in Kentucky," *The Illustrated World*, Vol. 24 (New York, 1916). "Education in Kentucky," *Journal of Education*, Vol. 82 (1915). William Lindsay, "Social Conditions in Kentucky," *International Monthly*, Vol. 1 (New York, 1900).

CHAPTER XX—ECONOMIC READJUSTMENT

Sources for this chapter:

E. Merton Coulter, *Civil War and Readjustment in Kentucky* (Chapel Hill, 1926); in the later chapters of this study, Coulter introduces the reconstruction of Kentucky's commercial system. Likewise this author's book, *The Cincinnati Southern Railroad and the Struggle for Southern Commerce, 1865-1872* (Chicago, 1922), is an excellent introduction to economic reorganization in Kentucky. Nathaniel Southgate Shaler, *Kentucky, A Pioneer Commonwealth* (Boston, 1888) gives numerous details on postwar Kentucky. General Duke and J. Stoddard Johnston, *Kentucky Resources, Transportation Systems, together with a Review of Transportation Problems and Opportunities to be Developed* (Louisville, 1887) gives an excellent summary of Kentucky's economic possibilities. The decennial *Census* of the Federal Government furnishes useful statistical information. *Charters, Acts and Ordinances of Louisville, 1780-1869* (Louisville, 1869), contains municipal ordinances governing local industry. Joseph G. Kerr, *Historical Development of the Louisville and Nashville Railroad System* (Louisville, 1926) presents a series of special documents arranged chronologically. *Report of the State Planning Board* (Louisville, 1930) is a good statistical source for economic facts concerning the resources of Kentucky. See also: *Acts*, Kentucky Gen-

506 BIBLIOGRAPHY

eral Assembly, 1865-1936. W. R. Jillson, *Kentucky's Mineral Resources* (Frankfort, 1927) presents a general summary for mineral developments to date. *Kentucky Natural Resources, Industrial Statistics, Industrial Directory by Counties* (Frankfort, 1929) contains special sections on highways, forest resources, mineral resources, electrification in Kentucky, city growth, and a classified directory of industries. John Sherman's *Recollections of Forty Years in the House, Senate, and Cabinet*, Vol. I (New York, 1895), contains some information on the Cincinnati-Southern Railroad. J. H. Hollander, *The Cincinnati-Southern Railway, A Study in Municipal Activity* (Baltimore, 1894) contains much legal material regarding the construction of this railroad. *The South in the Building of the Nation,* 12 vols. (Richmond 1909) is a co-operative study which contains several essays on postwar Kentucky economics. Martha McCullough-Williams, "The Tobacco War in Kentucky," *American Review of Reviews*, Vol. 38 (New York, 1908) is a contemporary account. Samuel H. Halley, "The Growth and Culture of Tobacco in Kentucky," in Connelley and Coulter, *History of Kentucky,* Vol. II (Chicago, 1922), is a splendid account of the organization of tobacco growers written by a Lexington warehouseman who took an active part in the burley pool. J. P. Killibrew, *Tobacco Districts and Types* (Washington, 1909) presents results of a government survey; also, Killibrew's *Tobacco Report* (Washington, July 11, 1911), a statistical report. "General and Special Orders of Governor J. C. W. Beckham" (1908) are in *Governors' Papers,* State Historical Society, Frankfort. See also: General and Special Orders of Governor Augustus E. Willson. Elmer James Kilpatrick, "The Changes in Market Demand for Dark Tobacco" (Thesis, University of Kentucky, Lexington, 1929). Marie Taylor, "Night Riders in the Black Patch" (Thesis, University of Kentucky, Lexington, 1934). There is a large volume of popular magazine material which was printed during the years 1908 and 1909 which presents a good contemporary view, John G. Miller, *The Black Patch War* (Chapel Hill, 1936). This book was written by the lawyer who finally discovered the legal loophole through which the western Kentucky marauders were brought to justice. James O. Nall, *The Tobacco Night Riders of Kentucky and Tennessee, 1905-1909* (Louisville, 1940); the best account of the tobacco war. Thomas D. Clark, *Pills, Petticoats and Plows* (Indianapolis, 1944); contains some material on expansion of Louisville's trade Southward. W. F. Axton, *Tobacco and Kentucky,* (Lexington, 1975). Gerald Carson, *The Social History of Bourbon, an Unhurried Account of Our Star-American Drink,* (New York, 1963). Henry Crowgey, *Kentucky Bourbon the Early Years of Whiskey Making,* (Lexington, 1971).

Newspaper sources:

The Courier-Journal, 1868-1950; the best newspaper source on the growth of the whole state. *Louisville Commercial,* 1870. *Cincinnati Commercial,* 1860-1872. *Frankfort Commonwealth,* 1861-1872. *Lexington Herald,* 1895-1950; the *Herald* is a splendid source for the tobacco war. Other papers which carefully reported this struggle were: the *Bowling Green Messenger,*

1908; the *Clarksville Journal* (Tennessee); *Crittenden Record Press,* 1906-1909; *Louisville Evening Post; Louisville Times; Paducah Evening Sun; Princeton Twice-a-Week Leader; Hopkinsville Era;* and the *Henderson Journal.*

General sources:

Samuel M. Wilson, *History of Kentucky* (Chicago, 1929). William H. Perrin, J. H. Battle, and G. C. Kniffen, *History of Kentucky* (Louisville, 1886). Z. F. Smith, *History of Kentucky* (Louisville, 1886).

CHAPTER XXI—NEW SOCIAL RESPONSIBILITIES

Sources for this chapter:

Acts, Journals, Kentucky General Assembly (1830-1935) contains the most complete record of the temperance movement in Kentucky. The legislature was the starting point for regulation of the liquor traffic. E. Merton Coulter, *The Civil War and Readjustment in Kentucky* (Chapel Hill, 1926); in the later chapters of this book there is a discussion of the beginnings of the period of social readjustment. See also: *American Annual Cyclopedia* (New York, 1861-1900). Arthur Krock, *The Editorials of Henry Watterson* (New York, 1923) presents "Marse Henry" as a militant opponent of woman suffrage. Basil Duke, *Reminiscences* (Garden City, 1911) is especially good for its accounts of politics and society. Nathaniel Southgate Shaler, *Kentucky, A Pioneer Commonwealth* (Boston, 1888) in its later chapters is useful for the postwar period. J. G. Trimble, *Recollections of Breathitt* (Jackson, *n.d.*) affords an interesting biographical sketch of a Kentucky mountaineer. Ernest Poole, *Nurses on Horseback* (New York, 1933) is a study of the services rendered by the Frontier Nursing Service. John S. Chambers, *Medical Service in Kentucky* (Lexington, 1931) is brief but useful. William T. Wright, *Devil John Wright of the Cumberlands* (Pound, Virginia, 1932) is the biography of a colorful old mountain character. Charles Mutzenberg, *Kentucky's Famous Feuds and Tragedies* (New York, 1917) gives the best account of the mountain feuds. L. F. Johnson, *Famous Kentucky Tragedies and Trials* (Cleveland, 1922) is a study of all of Kentucky's fights. Consult also: S. S. McClintock, "The Kentucky Mountains and their Feuds," *American Journal of Sociology* (New York, 1901). J. Stoddard Johnston, "Romance and Tragedy of Kentucky Feuds," *Cosmopolitan,* Vol. XXVII (1899), is a popular article. W. D. Frost, "The Southern Mountaineer," *American Review of Reviews,* Vol. XXI (1900), is another popular treatment. J. W. Raine, *The Land of Saddle Bags* (New York, 1924) is the result of intimate associations with the southern mountaineer. John F. Day, *Bloody Ground* (New York, 1941); a penetrating study of eastern Kentucky. Molly Clowes, *One-Fourth Kentucky* (Louisville, 1941); a series of articles on the moutainous area. Dreiser and others, *Harlan Miners Speak* (New York, 1932); a chapter in the troubled coal fields of eastern Kentucky. Malcolm Ross, *Machine Age in the Hills* (New York, 1933); another chapter in industrial conflict and re-adjustment. Mary B. Willeford, *Income and Health in Remote Rural*

Areas (New York, 1932); a study of 400 families in Leslie County. W. R. Thomas, *Life Among the Hills and Mountains of Kentucky* (Louisville, 1930) is useful on Eastern Kentucky. J. W. Haney, *The Mountain People of Kentucky* (Cincinnati, 1906) is written by a mountaineer. Although sketchy, it is written from an interesting viewpoint. *Majority and Minority Reports, and Testimony* taken by the Rowan County investigating committee (made to the Kentucky General Assembly, Frankfort, March 16, 1888) is a complete examination into the Tolliver-Martin "War." *Kentucky Natural Resources, Industrial Statistics, Industrial Directory by Counties* (Frankfort, 1829) contains special sections on economics and transportation.

Newspaper sources:

   Louisville Courier-Journal, 1868-1950. *Lexington Leader*, 1888-1950. *Lexington Herald*, 1898-1950. *Georgetown Weekly Times*, 1870-1872. *Cincinnati Commercial*, 1860-1872. *New York Times*, 1870-1950.

General sources:

   W. E. Connelley and E. M. Coulter, *History of Kentucky*, 5 vols. (Chicago, 1922). John Fox, Jr., *The Little Shepherd of Kingdom Come* (New York, 1903). H. G. Miller, *The Black Patch War* (Chapel Hill, 1936).

CHAPTER XXII—A NEW POLITICAL ORDER

Sources for this chapter:

   E. M. Coulter, *The Civil War and Readjustment in Kentucky* (Chapel Hill, 1926) contains a splendid account of early postwar politics. *American Annual Cyclopedia and Register of Important Events* (New York, 1863-1899) gives a good chronological account of important political events. Arthur Krock, *The Editorials of Henry Watterson* (New York, 1923) is a highly selected list of editorials, but it indicates Watterson's political philosophy. Solon Justus Buck, *The Agrarian Crusade* (New Haven, 1921) gives a brief account of postwar agricultural upheaval, with some reference to Kentucky. James A. Barnes, *John G. Carlisle* (New York, 1931) is a useful biography of an important Kentucky politician. The best source of information for economic and political development in Kentucky is the *Acts, Journals,* Governors' *Messages,* and departmental *Reports,* 1865 to 1937, published by the legislature. The best source of information concerning the making of the present constitution is the *Proceedings and Reports in the Convention,* 4 vols. (Frankfort, 1890). Basil Duke, *Reminiscences of General Basil W. Duke* (Garden City, 1911) is a general autobiography in which much pertinent information has been discreetly left out, but much of the text is useful. George L. Willis, *Kentucky Democracy,* 3 vols. (Louisville, 1935) is an especially valuable source of information for Kentucky politics since 1890, as the author recounts many things which he saw as a newspaper reporter. See also: Samuel Hopkins Adams, "The State *vs.* Caleb Powers," *McClure's Magazine,* Vol. XXII (1904), and Caleb Powers, *My Own Story* (Indianapolis, 1905), an autobiography written while the author was confined in jail. It contains much valuable information. The best source concerning the Goebel case is R. E. Hughes, T. W. Schaefer, and L. E. Williams, *That Kentucky Campaign; or the Law, the Ballot and the People in the Goebel-Taylor Contest* (Cincinnati, 1900). Three sources relating to the status of modern Kentucky government are: *The Reports of the Efficiency Commission* (1924), *The Griffenhagen Reports* (1934), and the *Progress Report of the State Planning Board* (Louisville, 1935). Two good studies of the present tax system in Kentucky are Simeon E. Leland, *Taxation in Kentucky* (Lexington, 1920) and Nollie Olin Taff, *History of State Revenue and Taxation in Kentucky* (Nashville, Tennessee, 1931). James W. Martin has either published or directed the study of numerous scholarly articles in *The Tax Magazine*, 1933 to 1950. These studies make a scholarly analysis of the modern tax situation in Kentucky. Howard W. Beers, ed., *Kentucky, Designs for her Future* (Lexington, 1945); a social inventory of Kentucky. Irvin S. Cobb, *Exit Laughing* (Indianapolis, 1941); the chapter on the Goebel affair is a vivid one.

Newspaper sources:

The *Louisville Journal*, 1865-1868. The *Louisville Courier-Journal*, 1868-1950. The latter, although Democratic in politics, is an invaluable storehouse of information. *The Lexington Herald*, 1895-1950, like *The Louisville Courier-Journal*, is valuable, especially for the period from 1899-1908. *The Lexington Leader*, 1888-1950, is a good Republican source. See also the Paducah *Sun-Democrat*, 1929-1950. *The Owensboro Daily Messenger*, 1877-1950, edited by Urey Woodson, a prominent western Kentucky Democrat, is the best source on western Kentucky politics. *The Frankfort Commonwealth*, 1865-1872, was a Republican paper, but not radical in its attitude. *The Kentucky Yeoman*, 1861-1872, was a "Bourbon" paper. See also: *The Western Citizen* (Paris), 1865-1886.

CHAPTER XXIII—AN ENDURING COMMONWEALTH

Very few books discuss modern Kentucky. Historians have not had an opportunity to sift through the enormous collections of public and private records which would reveal parts of this story. No doubt the best sources of a narrative nature are the newspapers. So far as Kentucky has a state paper, the Louisville *Courier-Journal* covers the Kentucky story since the end of World War II. This is also true of such papers as the Paducah *Sun-Democrat*, the Lexington *Leader* and *Herald*, the Kentucky *Post*, Ashland *Independent*, and the Louisville *Times*.

Kentucky's Resources, Lexington, revised edition, 1958, Thomas P. Crawford, *Compilation of Coal and Petroleum Production Data for Kentucky*, Lexington, 1958, *Kentucky Agricultural Statistics*, Frankfort, 1952, and *Action Program for Eastern Kentucky; Flood Rehabilitation Study*, Frankfort, 1957 are semi-official publications dealing with both resources and conservation in present day Kentucky. The most trustworthy satistical source for the state are the annual volumes of the *Statistical Abstract,* United States Census, Washington, 1945-1960. An important book on the desegregation of the Louisville schools is Omer Carmichael and Weldon James, *The Louisville Story,* New York, 1957.

The best record of public actions and proposed changes is to be found in the numerous publications of the Legislative Research Commission. All of these were published in Frankfort, and are listed here in chronological order and by title. Kentucky's *Rank in Education,* 2; *Child Welfare Laws,* 4; *Strip Mining,* 5; *Social Security and a Kentucky Retirement Plan,* 6; *School Census and Attendance,* 9; *Classification of Teachers,* 10; *School Finance,* 11; *Taxation, the Over-all Picture,* 15; *Flood Insurance and Flood Plain Zoning,* 17; *Metropolitan Government,* 25; *Public Higher Education,* 25; *Sales-Gross Receipts,* 26; *County Health Program,* 27; *Pupil Transportation,* 28; *State Highway System,* 29; *Vocational Educational,* 32; *Youth Problems,* 33; *Government Financing,* 40; *School Entrance Age,* 54; *Municipal Government,* 53; *Rural Secondary Roads,* 55; *Teacher Retirement System,* 56; *Public Utilities,* 61; and *Public Library Facilities,* 65.

Mary Jean Bowman and W. Warren Haynes, *Resources and People in East Kentucky: Problems of a Lagging Economy,* (Baltimore, 1963). John L. Johnson, *Income in Kentucky County Distribution by Amount, by Type, by Size,* (Lexington, 1955). Robert M. Ireland, *The County Courts in Antebellum Kentucky,* (Lexington, 1972), Joseph L. Massie, *Blazer and Ashland Oil a Study in Management,* (Lexington, 1960). Bryan Woolley and Ford Reid, *We Be Here when the Morning Comes,* (Lexington, 1974). Malcolm M. Jewell and Everett W. Cunningham, *Kentucky Politics,* (Lexington, 1968). Jesse Stuart, *The Thread that Runs so True,* Harry M. Caudill, *Night comes to the Cumberland,* (Boston, 1962). *My Land is Dying,* (Lexington, 1976), *The Watches of the Night,* (Boston, 1976). Henry P. Scalf, *Kentucky's Last Frontier,* (Prestonburgh, 1966). Thomas Ford, Ed., *Southern Appalachian Regions, a Survey,* (Lexington, 1962). John Fetterman, *Stinking Creek, the Portrait of a Small Mountain Community in Appalachia,* (New York, 1967). Shelby S. Elam, *Kentucky Thru Thick and Thin,* (Lexington, 1955). Frank E. Smith, *Land Between the Lakes Experiment in Recreation,* (Lexington, 1971). Thomas R. Ford, Health and Demography in Kentucky, (Lexington, 1964). Wendell Berry, *The Unforseen Wilderness: An Essay on Kentucky's Red River Gorge,* (Lexington, 1971).

Appendix

THE GOVERNORS OF KENTUCKY

THE GOVERNORS OF KENTUCKY

Name	Born	Term	Party
Isaac Shelby	Maryland, 1750	1792–1796	Jeffersonian Republican
James Garrard	Virginia, 1749	1796–1804	"
Christopher Greenup	Virginia, 1749	1804–1808	"
Charles Scott	Virginia, 1749	1808–1812	"
Isaac Shelby	Maryland, 1750	1812–1816	"
George Madison	Virginia, 1763	1816	"
Gabriel Slaughter	Virginia, 1767	1816–1820	"
John Adair	South Carolina, 1757	1820–1824	"
Joseph Desha	Pennsylvania, 1768	1824–1828	"
Thomas Metcalfe	Virginia, 1780	1828–1832	"
John Breathitt	Virginia, 1786	1832–1834	Democrat
James T. Morehead	Bullitt, 1797	1834–1836	"
James Clark	Virginia, 1779	1836–1839	Whig
Charles A. Wickliffe	Washington, 1788	1839–1840	"
Robert P. Letcher	Garrard, 1790	1840–1844	"
William Owsley	Virginia, 1782	1844–1848	"
John J. Crittenden	Woodford, 1786	1848–1850	"
John L. Helm	Hardin, 1802	1850–1851	Democrat
Lazarus Powell	Henderson, 1812	1851–1855	"
Charles S. Morehead	Nelson, 1802	1855–1859	American
Beriah Magoffin	Mercer, 1815	1859–1862	Democrat
James F. Robinson	Scott, 1800	1862–1863	Union Democrat
Thomas Bramlette	Cumberland, 1817	1863–1867	Democrat

THE GOVERNORS OF KENTUCKY

Name	Born	Name	Party
John L. Helm	Hardin, 1802	1867	Democrat
John W. Stevenson	Virginia, 1812	1867–1871	"
Preston H. Leslie	Clinton, 1819	1871–1875	"
James B. McCreary	Madison, 1838	1875–1879	"
Luke P. Brackburn	Woodford, 1818	1879–1883	"
J. Proctor Knott	Marion, 1830	1883–1887	"
Simon Bolivar Buckner	Hart, 1823	1887–1891	"
John Young Brown	Hardin, 1835	1891–1895	"
William O. Bradley	Garrard, 1847	1895–1899	Republican
William S. Taylor	Butler, 1853	1899–1900	"
William Goebel	Pennsylvania, 1845	1900	Democrat
J. C. W. Beckham	Nelson, 1869	1900–1907	"
Augustus E. Willson	Mason, 1846	1907–1911	Republican
James B. McCreary	Madison, 1838	1911–1915	Democrat
Augustus O. Stanley	Shelby, 1867	1915–1919	"
James D. Black	Knox, 1849	1919	"
Edwin P. Morrow	Pulaski, 1878	1919–1923	Republican
William J. Fields	Carter, 1874	1923–1926	Democrat
Flem D. Sampson	Laurel, 1875	1926–1931	Republican
Ruby Laffoon	Hopkins, 1869	1931–1935	Democrat
Albert Benjamin Chandler	Henderson, 1898	1935–1939	"
Keen Johnson	Lyon, 1896	1939–1943	"
Simeon S. Willis	Lawrence, 1879	1943–1947	Republican

513

THE GOVERNORS OF KENTUCKY

Name	Born	Term	Party
Earle C. Clements	Union, 1896	1947-1951	Democrat
Lawrence Wetherby	Middletown, 1908	1951-1955	"
Albert Benjamin Chandler	Henderson, 1898	1955-1959	"
Bert T. Combs	Clay, 1911	1959-1963	"
Edward T. Breathitt	Christian, 1924	1963-1967	"
Louis B. Nunn	Barren, 1924	1967-1971	Republican
Wendell H. Ford	Daviess, 1924	1971-1974	Democrat
Julian M. Carroll	McCracken, 1931	1974-1979	"
John Y. Brown, Jr.	Fayette, 1933	1979-1983	"
Martha Layne (Hall) Collins	Shelby, 1936	1983-1987	"
Wallace G. Wilkinson	Casey, 1941	1987-1991	"
Brereton C. Jones	Ohio, 1939	1991-	"

514

Index

515